ALSO BY GREGORY CROUCH

Enduring Patagonia

China's Wings

THE
BONANZA
KING

**John Mackay and the Battle Over
the Greatest Riches in the American West**

GREGORY CROUCH

SCRIBNER

New York   London   Toronto   Sydney   New Delhi

Scribner
An Imprint of Simon & Schuster, Inc.
1230 Avenue of the Americas
New York, NY 10020

First Scribner hardcover edition June 2018

For information about special discounts for bulk purchases,
please contact Simon & Schuster Special Sales at 1-866-506-1949
or business@simonandschuster.com.

The Simon & Schuster Speakers Bureau can bring authors to your live event.
For more information or to book an event, contact the Simon & Schuster Speakers Bureau
at 1-866-248-3049 or visit our website at www.simonspeakers.com.

Manufactured in the United States of America

1   3   5   7   9   10   8   6   4   2

Library of Congress Cataloging-in-Publication Data is available.

ISBN 978-1-5011-0819-8
ISBN 978-1-5011-0821-1 (ebook)

For my wife,
Tina Rath

Seest thou a man diligent in his business? He shall stand before kings.

—Proverbs 22:29

Contents

Prologue: The New Camp   1

1. A Rough Irish Lad   5
2. Gilded Dreams—and the Hard Fist of California Reality   21
3. The Lure of the Washoe Diggings   45
4. The Rush to Washoe—and an Indian War   81
5. Surrounded by Riches—and Unable to Get Them Out   105
6. Revving Up the Boom   131
7. The First Boom, Frenzied and Exuberant   151
8. A Tiny Sliver of a Mine   173
9. The Rise of the Bank Ring   199
10. The Irish Coup   223
11. The Lode's Worst Day   247
12. Jones's Sick Child   269
13. The Consolidated Virginia Mine   281
14. The Strike   301
15. The Big Bonanza   319
16. The Bonanza King   359
17. The Cable War   393
18. Twilight   415

Acknowledgments   433
A Note on Sources   437
Photograph Credits   439
Index   441

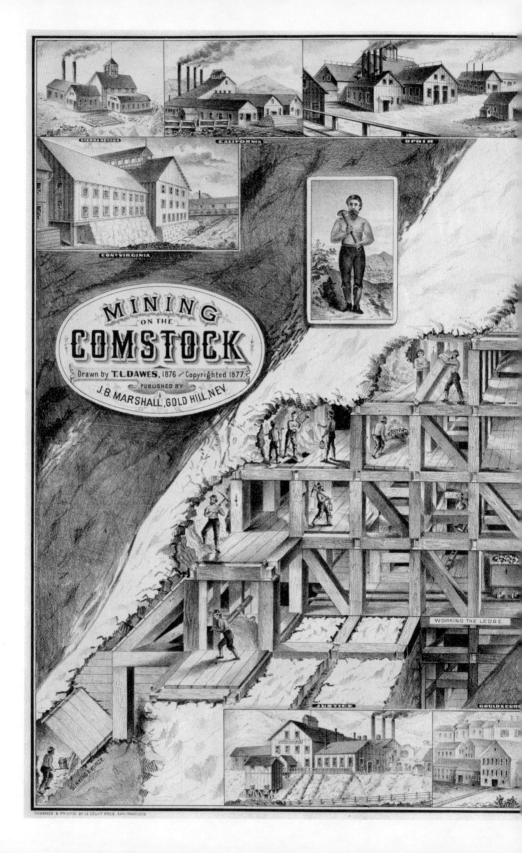

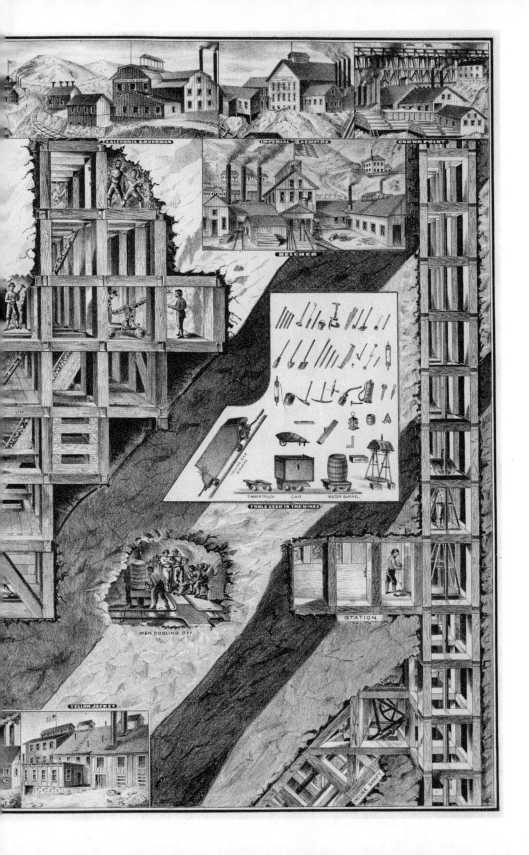

CALEDONIA & OVERMAN

IMPERIAL & EMPIRE

CROWN POINT

BELCHER

TOOLS USED IN THE MINES

TIMBER TRUCK   CAR   WATER BARREL

MEN COOLING OFF

STATION

YELLOW JACKET

INCLINE SHAFT

The New Camp

"Gold is where I ain't." A restless miner,
unsatisfied with the prospects of his claim,
prowls the hills for new diggings.

———

**California drew to her golden shores the pick of the world,
Nevada drew to herself the pick of California.**
—C. C. Goodwin, *As I Remember Them*

John Mackay (pronounced *Mackie*) and his partner Jack O'Brien bent
beneath their loads and slogged to the top of a high ridge at the crest
of what would become known as the Virginia Range. They'd climbed

more than twenty-three hundred feet from the valley beneath. It was sometime in July or August of 1859, and a hard sun shone down from the pale sky. A fierce, dry wind blew across the ridge. The rocky soil beneath their boots didn't support much besides scrappy piñon pines and waist-high sagebrush. Behind them, westward, on the opposite side of the valley out of which they'd just climbed, rose the high peaks of the Sierras. On the far side of those mountains lay the California goldfields from whence they'd come. Eastward stretched a landscape of lonely, sorrowful magnificence, chain on chain of brown desert mountains fading into the uttermost limit of vision.

Too poor to afford a horse or a mule, they'd walked more than a hundred miles, lured by rumors of a rich new strike of gold and silver in what was then the western Utah Territory. Only a few more miles remained. Mackay shouldered everything he owned: a bedroll, several cooking implements, maybe a change of clothes, and the basic tools of mining—a pick and a shovel and perhaps a sledge and a heavy, handheld drill. The flush of effort had put dewdrops of sweat under his hairline and ruddy Irish color up in his cheeks, a complement to the reddish-brown of his hair and the luxuriant mustache that stretched an inch or two beyond the corners of his mouth. Mackay stood a touch above average height and looked on the world with clear blue eyes. He was nearly twenty-eight years old, and his tight-knit frame didn't carry an ounce of loose flesh. Mackay had coarse, callused hands and a grip like iron. Seven years with a pick and shovel will do that to a man. He moved with easy, athletic grace and an air of contained violence. He also seemed to be enjoying himself. Mackay found the pleasure in hardship. He didn't say much, and when he did, he spoke slowly, fighting a childhood stutter. Mackay was proud, touchy, and quick with his fists. He would share his last morsel of food with a friend, but nobody ever took anything from John Mackay without a fight.

Work was all he knew. He'd been laboring to support his mother and sister since his father died when he was eleven years old. He'd managed to remit small sums home to New York City since he'd come to California at age twenty-one, but despite seven years of excruciating toil in the goldfields, Mackay's existence was every bit as hand-to-mouth as it had been when he stepped off the boat in San Francisco. Few recognized that his reticent demeanor hid a burning desire to make something of himself.

Mackay and O'Brien adjusted their loads and traversed the last few miles down and across the eastern slope of Sun Mountain. Skirting the base of Cedar Hill, they passed stakes and rock piles marking the claims of hopeful men. Scattered miners hacked at chunks of outcropping quartz, eager to reveal an ore lead. From test pits farther up the slopes of Sun Mountain, men threw up piles of brownish-yellow dirt that from a distance resembled gopher mounds. Soon, Mackay and O'Brien looked across a shallow ravine to a nexus of activity around the base of a little knoll, the site of the original strike. Mackay saw at a glance that the mining in front of him was of an entirely different kind than what he'd known in California. In an open pit, a handful of men worked with picks and shovels to expose a vein of bluish-black ore. A few others loaded black rock into sacks. A string of pack mules waited near a handful of canvas tents. Other draft animals plodded in circles, harnessed to the sweeps that pulled the dragstones that pulverized chunks of ore to dust in circular, rock-paved patios sunk twelve or eighteen inches into the ground called "arastras" that resembled the rings of a small circus. Several men nearby used trickles of available water to wash the resultant crushings through miners' rockers—cheap, easily cobbled together rectangular wooden boxes that relied on a small stream of water and a gentle side-to-side rocking motion to trap precious, and dense, gold flakes behind one-inch-high "riffle bars" while the water carried off the lighter worthless material in which the gold had been embedded. Mackay had heard that ore dug from this barren mountain held gold and silver twinned together. He knew gold, having served a long, hard apprenticeship in the gold-bearing streamway sediments and ancient riverbeds of California. He knew nothing about silver and itched to hold a chunk of the veinstone in his hands, to feel the ore's weight, to learn how the royal metals had been locked up inside—and more important, how to get them out.

Before they walked the last few yards into the new camp, O'Brien asked Mackay if he had any money about his clothes.

Mackay said that he didn't have a cent.

Thinking they ought to walk into the new camp penniless, "like gentlemen," O'Brien fished his last fifty-cent piece from a pocket and heaved it down the hillside into the sagebrush.

Asked about the incident years later, Mackay acknowledged that it did happen, then grimaced. "That's what Jack did with his money all his life," he said.

Mackay turned his attention back to the bleak landscape and the mines. The bustle put his blood up. He didn't know it, not yet—and neither did anyone else—but the men hacking at the ore lead before him were scratching at the tip of the most concentrated storehouse of gold and silver ever discovered in the United States and one of the richest ever discovered anywhere on earth. The work of understanding, find-ing, extracting, and controlling the vast treasure vaults beneath their feet would mobilize the energies of thousands, raise a city from the bleak desert wilderness, play a vital role in helping stabilize the Union economy through the Civil War, give birth to a state and an entirely new industry, transform San Francisco from a trading port into the innovative financial powerhouse it still is today, precipitate some of the great corporate struggles of the nineteenth century, and create one of the biggest fortunes in the world.

That work would shape John Mackay's life—as would his fight to seize some portion of the riches beneath his feet.

CHAPTER 1

A Rough Irish Lad

Tens of thousands of destitute Irish immigrants lived packed
into the rickety tenements of Five Points in lower Manhattan.
It was the most notorious slum in the world.

**The poorest and most wretched population that can be
found in the world—the scattered debris of the Irish nation.**
—Archbishop John Hughes, 1849

Few great men ever started further down the ladder of success than
John William Mackay. He was born into dire poverty near Dublin, Ireland, on November 28, 1831. Mackay, his younger sister, and his mother

and father shared a crude cottage with the family pig. That was in no way unique, for grinding need wore at the foundations of nineteenth-century Ireland. Walls of loose-stacked stone slathered in mud enclosed the one-room shelters that housed fully half the Irish population. Most didn't have windows. A roof of tree branches, sod, and leaky thatch protected them from the worst of the Atlantic rains; an open peat fire warmed them through the dark winter months. Beds and blankets were rare luxuries. Most Irish families slept on bare dirt floors alongside their domestic animals. A British government official reporting on the living conditions of the Irish peasantry noted that "in many districts their only food is the potato, their only beverage water. . . . Pigs and manure constitute their only property." Like many Irish families, the Mackays didn't always get enough to eat.

They were Catholic, and in the eyes of Ireland's Gaelic Catholic majority, theirs was a conquered country, subjugated to the foreign English crown since the mid-seventeenth century. Although Catholics constituted more than three-quarters of Ireland's population, by 1800, 95 percent of the country's land had passed into the hands of English or Anglo-Irish Protestant aristocrats. Interested only in extracting rents and raising grain and cattle for cash sale in England, those absentee owners typically spent the bounty of the Irish countryside supporting lavish lifestyles in England while the laborers and tenants who worked their estates endured desperate poverty.

Irish tenants exchanged their labor for the lease on the small plots of dirt they needed to feed themselves. On such meager acreages, only the potato yielded sufficiently to feed a family. Poor Irish men and women ate them at almost every meal. Chronically indigent, often underfed, unable to purchase land, deprived of political power, and ferociously discriminated against for the sin of being Catholic, more than a million people left Ireland in the first four decades of the nineteenth century.

The Mackays held firm until 1840, but when young John reached the age of nine, the family immigrated to America. In 1800, some 35,000 Irish men and women lived in the United States. When the Mackay family arrived forty years later, that number had bloated to 663,000, the overwhelming majority of them poor and barely educated. Unskilled laborers nailed to the cross of extreme poverty, most Irish male immigrants did casual day labor, taking whatever employment they could find. Ten to twelve hours a day, six days a week, they performed the brutal, back-breaking toil nobody else would do, for paltry wages, digging sewers and canals, excavating foundations, loading ships and wagons, carrying hods of bricks and mortar for skilled masons, paving streets, and building railroad beds. Irish women worked as washerwomen and domestic servants, or sewed piecework in the needle trades. Widows took in boarders and collected rags they recycled into "shoddy," a cheap cloth made from shredded scraps of wool. In New York City, Irish peddlers lugged merchandise to every neighborhood, hawking sweet corn, oranges, root beer, bread, charcoal, clams, oysters, buttons, thread, fiddle strings, cigars, suspenders, and a host of other inexpensive items. Rag-clad Irish children scavenged wood, coal, scrap metal, and glass, swept street crossings for tips, shined shoes, dealt apples and individual matches, and sold newspapers.

Rather than be grateful for their inexpensive labor and service, established Yankee Protestants despised the Irish immigrants, scorning them as "superstitious papists" and "illiterate ditch diggers." The huge numbers of Irish-born Catholics enfranchised by the universal white male suffrage of Jacksonian democracy terrified native-born Americans. Many Protestants judged Catholicism—with its devotion to an imagined papal dictatorship—to be philosophically incompatible with the ideals of American democracy. Established, respectable Americans discriminated ferociously against the filthy Irish suddenly infesting the slums of eastern cities and manning the work camps of railroad- and canal-building concerns. Help wanted advertisements often carried the qualifier "any color will answer except Irish." The twin millstones of being Irish and Catholic kept most Irish immigrants firmly anchored to the bottom of the American social spectrum.

In 1840, the year the Mackay family crossed the Atlantic, nearly half of the eighty-four thousand immigrants received in the United States came from tiny Ireland, and like thousands of their countrymen, the Mackays settled in New York City. The opening of the Erie Canal in 1825 had transformed the city into the most important port in the Western Hemisphere. Dense forests of masts and spars sprouted from ships docked against the piers, wharfs, quays, and slips cramming the southern shores of Manhattan Island. Banking, insurance, and manufacturing industries developed alongside the trade. New York's population grew from 123,700 in 1820, five years before the canal opening, to 202,000 in 1830 and roughly 313,000 in 1840, making New York three times the size of Baltimore, America's second largest urban concentration.

The Mackay family took quarters on Frankfort Street in the heart of the Fourth Ward. In their earliest days, the city's Fourth, Fifth, and Sixth wards running from the East River to the Hudson River between City

Hall Park and Canal Street had housed a mixed community of free blacks and French, German, Polish, and Spanish immigrants, but as more and more people abandoned Ireland for the United States, those neighborhoods acquired a distinctly Irish flavor, an influence that spread north into the Fourteenth Ward and east to permeate the Seventh. When the Mackays arrived in 1840, the Irish presence filled much of lower Manhattan,* and it centered on the Five Points intersection, just a few hundred yards from the Mackay family's front door. At that time, Five Points was the most notorious slum in the United States.

Originally, Five Points had been an attractive marshy pond, the Collect. As the city expanded, tanneries and slaughterhouses set up on its banks and dumped their effluents into the pond. The Collect grew so disgusting that it depressed local real estate values. The municipality dug a canal to drain it (and gave a name to Canal Street), and when that didn't improve conditions, filled in the pond. Without bedrock beneath it, the landfill proved too unstable to support major construction. Speculators bought the land and erected cheap one- to two-and-a-half-story wooden houses among the businesses of the neighborhood.

Property owners originally designed the houses for artisans, their families, and their workshops, but as budding manufacturing industries undercut the prosperity of individual craftsmen, landlords discovered that they made much larger profits by partitioning the buildings into tiny rooms rented to immigrants. Originally known as "tenant houses," the term morphed into the word "tenements." The rickety wooden fabrications were damp and frigid in winter, sticky and sweltering in summer, and always choked with foul, smoky air from the fires of cooking and warming. Inside, entire families crammed into single rooms entered from dim, lightless corridors. Unceasing din harried the inhabitants. Street noise reverberated in the front rooms. Rooms in the rear filled with the sounds of neighbors facing the backyards and alleys—spouses argued, babies screamed, siblings fought. Occupants shared filthy, overflowing outhouses with dozens of neighbors and drew water from common hydrants outside. The horses, mules, and oxen used everywhere for drayage defecated in the streets. The municipal government sponsored no garbage collection. Foot, animal, and wheeled traffic churned the improperly drained streets and alleys into fetid quagmires choked with an-

---

* Described in terms of modern New York City neighborhoods, the Irish concentration comprised most of Chinatown and Tribeca as well as the southern portions of SoHo, the Bowery, Little Italy, and the Lower East Side.

imal corpses, human and animal waste, kitchen slops, and ashes. The stench was overwhelming.

Mice, rats, roaches, fleas, lice, maggots, and flies thrived in the squalor. Thousands of feral pigs roamed the streets. Despite the pigs' grotesque snouts, coarse hair, and black-splotched skin, New York residents tolerated them because the pigs were far and away the city's most effective street cleaners, even as they waged pitched battles with wild dogs for choice morsels of food. Among their own kind, the pigs rutted with loud, gleeful abandon. Refined Knickerbocker ladies sent up howls of protest, complaining that exposure to such indiscriminate sexual behavior undermined their respectability and lowered the moral tone of the whole city. For Irish women, most of whom had been raised in a rural countryside, fornicating domestic animals barely seemed worth a raised eyebrow. Besides, the pigs supplied valuable meat.

The outrageous quantities of animal and human feculence contaminated local wells. Dysentery, typhoid fever, diarrhea, and other waterborne diseases wreaked far more havoc in the immigrant wards than they did in the rest of the city, as did tuberculosis, diphtheria, smallpox, measles, mental disorders, and alcoholism. Crime and prostitution were ubiquitous, murder commonplace. Astronomical mortality rates haunted New York's immigrant neighborhoods.

America's new penny newspapers thrilled readers with lurid descriptions of the violence, dirt, mayhem, poverty, and moral depravity of Five Points. Visiting journalists could seldom resist characterizing the Irish neighborhoods as nests of vipers and sinks of filth and iniquity, unable or unwilling to do justice to the poor, working-class families who lived there. Most scribes, making brief forays into the slums, had eyes only for the dark side of the Irish wards. They failed to credit the immigrants' ferocious struggle, or to perceive the community strength building in their churches, saloons, benevolent societies, fraternal orders, and fire companies. Immigrant families bent on improving their lot in the new country fought a constant battle to maintain any semblance of dignity in the face of such filth, squalor, and anarchic ruckus. The vast majority of Irish immigrants worked as hard as humanly possible to better their lives and the lives of their children as they fought to claw their way up from circumstances so desperate they were difficult for established Yankees to comprehend.

Among the thousands of immigrant families in New York City, the Mackays struggled forward in anonymity, and for their first two years in the United States, the family did reasonably well. Mr. and Mrs. Mackay scraped together enough money to send their ten-year-old son to school. In that, John Mackay was lucky. Only about half the school-age Irish children then living in New York City received any education at all.

Disaster struck the family in 1842. John Mackay's father died of a cause lost to history. The catastrophe forced eleven-year-old John Mackay to quit school and work to support his mother and sister. Mackay could read, write, and figure, but he would never receive another day of classroom schooling. A taciturn lad who spoke slowly and awkwardly, fighting a stutter, he'd regret his lack of formal education for the rest of his life.

In an age devoid of social safety nets, when circumstances forced Irish boys not yet old enough to apprentice to earn money to help their family survive, most of them started selling newspapers or shining shoes. No resident of Frankfort Street would have been surprised that John Mackay fell into the world of the New York newsboys after his father's death—most of the city's newspapers had their headquarters on Park Row a few blocks west of the Mackay family lodgings.

For a job so near the bottom of the capitalist ladder, selling newspapers forced the young boys to accept a whopping ton of risk. Most New York dailies sold for two cents, and newsboys made a half-cent profit on every sale. However, wholesalers forced the newsboys to purchase their supply outright, for 1.5 cents per paper, and the newsboys couldn't return unsold stock. Any newspapers they didn't sell therefore cut a significant chunk from their earnings. The newsboys called it "getting stuck," and they hated it. The more fortunate ones, like John Mackay, knew how to read, since basic literacy conveyed a major selling advantage. A literate newsboy could scan the leading stories and make a snap judgment about how many papers he'd sell. Ones who couldn't read had to find a trusted ally to perform the service.

Newsboys bought their stock of morning papers before sunrise and immediately hit the streets crying the headlines, their clear, young voices among the all-pervasive sounds of the New York streets. Astute newsboys tailored their cries to their intended marks, touting commercial news at the approach of a Wall Street sharp or social happenings to a fashionable lady, and they all led a rough-and-tumble territorial existence. Newsboys staked claims to the best street corners and selling locales and fiercely defended their fiefdoms against interlopers. Fistfights were common, and John Mackay both received and administered his fair share of thrashings.

Midmorning, newsboys who had exhausted their stock grabbed a bite to eat and then hustled odd jobs—perhaps sweeping street crossings or carrying packages for tips at a ferry terminal—until the late papers dropped in the afternoon. They'd repeat their selling routine into the evening. An average newsboy, on an average day, earned twenty-five to fifty cents. A good salesman, on a good day, hustling hard until he'd sold his last paper, took home between sixty cents and a dollar. A day with incendiary headlines might earn a newsboy as much as two dollars.

Selling newspapers was an endless grind, but the newsboys reveled in their self-sufficient autonomy and liberty. Each boy worked on his own account, suffering no boss. Off-duty, they crowded the rowdy galleries of the Bowery and Chatham theaters, notorious aficionados of low entertainments and equally ardent spectators at prizefights and cockfights. A love of musical and dramatic productions and sporting entertainments, engrained as welcome relief from his sharp-elbowed New York upbringing, would persist for the rest of John Mackay's life. The man he thought the greatest in the world was innovative newsman James Gordon Bennett, founder and owner of the *New York Herald*, a Scottish immigrant whom Mackay often watched hustle through City Hall Square with a bundle of newspapers tucked under his arm. Unnoticed, Mackay peddled Bennett's newspaper on New York's dirty streets.

John Mackay sold newspapers and scrounged odd jobs for four or five years. The Mackays eked out a living with John's earnings and whatever money his sister and mother made in the needle trades or domestic service, but poor Irish immigrants struggling to scratch together a living was hardly a unique story in Manhattan in the middle 1840s. And street-level competition was about to get a whole lot more ferocious, because on the other side of the Atlantic, disaster had hit Ireland.

The nutrition of Irish tenant farmers and their families depended almost entirely on potatoes. Over the course of just a few days in the late summer of 1845, Ireland's millions of subsistence farmers watched in horror as the leaves of previously healthy potato plants blackened, curled, and withered. Dug potatoes emerged from the ground full and healthy, but quickly shriveled to repulsive, inedible slime. The disease ravaged about half of the island's potato crop in 1845. The next year, the blight destroyed nearly every potato in Ireland. *An Gorta Mór*, The Great Hunger, gripped the land.

Potato yields didn't recover for five long years. The population of Ireland collapsed. Starvation and disease killed a million and a half Irish men, women, and children out of a prefamine population of about eight million. Another million fled the country, most to the United States, where they inundated the port cities of the eastern seaboard.* Fully 650,000 wretched Irish men, women, and children settled in New York City during the famine years.

Predictably, the influx provoked a backlash among native-born Americans. Anti-Catholic Yankees regarded the newest wave of destitute, starving refugees as "Saint Patrick's vermin." Many businesses—and some entire industries—refused to hire Irishmen. Conditions could hardly have been more difficult for a young Irish immigrant struggling to gain a toehold on an American adulthood. The first waves of famine immigrants arrived just as John Mackay reached the age at which he was old enough to apprentice. Without means or a secondary education, he needed a trade to carry him into adulthood, and the surge in anti-Irish sentiment made it harder to find a suitable apprenticeship. At the time, shipbuilding was one of New York's most lucrative industries. An almost unbroken string of shipyards extended along the East River shoreline from just below Corlear's Hook at the bend in the East River to the end of Twelfth Street. All were within reasonable walking distance of the family lodgings on Frankfort Street. Somehow, Mackay caught on as an apprentice ship's carpenter at the William H. Webb shipyard, located on the East River between the ends of Fifth and Seventh streets. In that, he'd already accomplished something unusual—shipbuilders generally refused to employ Irishmen.

How Mackay overcame that obstacle isn't clear. Whatever the reason, Webb provided an excellent opportunity. As Mackay advanced through the four or five years of his apprenticeship, his earnings would swell from fifty to seventy-eight cents per day. Although that didn't greatly exceed newsboy earnings, an apprentice pulled in a guaranteed daily wage, and when Mackay had finished his term of service, as a qualified ship's carpenter in an industry that seemed to promise lifetime employment, he could expect to earn two dollars per day, twice the amount earned by a common adult laborer. And of all of New York's shipyards, Webb might have been the best place to learn the trade. Mariners considered William H. Webb the world's best naval architect. Webb's merchant packets, tea clippers, and sidewheel steamships brought new standards of engineering precision to a profession previously considered more art than science.

---

* Ireland's population fell by nearly 50 percent between 1841 and 1926, from 8.18 million to 4.23 million. Ireland still hasn't recovered—its population today is about 2 million less than it was before the potato famine.

Out in the world beyond the shipyard, the United States had been fighting a war against Mexico since the spring of 1846. Major hostilities ground to a halt in the fall of 1847. U.S. forces had defeated and scattered Mexico's armies and controlled most major Mexican cities. The Treaty of Guadalupe Hidalgo formally concluded the war on February 2, 1848. Its provisions gave the United States uncontested control of Texas, recognized the Rio Grande as the international border, and, in exchange for $15 million, ceded to the United States Mexico's two northernmost provinces—Alta California and Santa Fe de Nuevo Mexico. The "Mexican Cession" added 1.2 million square miles to the United States—a landmass roughly equivalent to the size of western Europe—that included parts of the modern states of Texas, New Mexico, Arizona, Colorado, and Wyoming, and the entireties of Utah, Nevada, and California.

Unbeknownst to both the Mexican and United States governments, nine days before they inked the treaty, an event of monumental import had occurred in California, in the obscure valley of Coloma in the foothills of the Sierra Nevada Mountains on the South Fork of the American River. At Coloma, millwright James Marshall supervised construction of a sawmill intended to serve the appetites of "Sutter's Fort," the hub of an agrarian colony managed by Swiss immigrant John Sutter centered at the confluence of the Sacramento and American rivers (at the site of the modern city of Sacramento). In the morning of January 24, 1848, a glimmer in the gravel of the mill's tailrace caught Marshall's eye. He pinched up a pebble of yellow metallic substance about half the size of a pea, then picked out a second piece. Marshall's heart thumped; he was certain he'd found gold. Biting, hammering, boiling in lye, dousing with vinegar and nitric acid, and a specific gravity test proved the substance. Nothing in North America would ever be the same.

Within days, Marshall's employees were using their free time to hunt gold flakes in the riverbed. Good, hardworking Mormons, they finished constructing the mill before quitting. John Sutter's agrarian dream evaporated like fog as more and more of his employees abandoned wage labor in favor of gold mining. On March 2, several veterans of the Mormon Battalion—a volunteer unit that had marched to California from Iowa during the Mexican War—who had been working for Sutter since their discharge, struck a fabulously rich gold deposit at what became known as "Mormon Diggings" or "Mormon Island," a bar of sand and gravel at a bend in the South Fork of the American River about fifteen miles below the sawmill. In the best pockets, the men scooped out gold dust by the glittering handful. Somehow, the Sierra foothills had kept their treasure hidden through seventy years of Spanish and Mexican administration.

Rumors of the gold strike reached the small outpost of San Francisco soon thereafter. A sleepy village sited at the northeastern tip of a long peninsula that divided the waters of the wild Pacific from the deep bay into which drained the Sacramento River, San Francisco had about eight hundred residents in early 1848, and it boasted two weekly newspapers, the *Californian* and the *Star*. The first public mention of the discovery appeared on the back page of the *Californian* on March 15, in a paragraph titled "GOLD MINE FOUND." Wild stories circulated thereafter. The *Star*'s editor went to Coloma to investigate in April, but returned unimpressed, his exploratory party having traveled in company with John Sutter and unearthed only a few flakes of the desired metal. Attempting to check the story's momentum, the *Star*'s May 6 issue declared "the gold fever . . . all sham."

As of mid-May, skepticism held much of the population in check—until a Mormon named Sam Brannan took matters into his own hands. Brannan had arrived in San Francisco two years before, leading a group of 245 Mormon exiles who had made the long voyage around Cape Horn from New York. Brannan's eye for business opportunity exceeded his religious ardor, however, and by May 1848, Brannan knew the gold excitement was no "humbug," as went the then common term for fraud, trick, or sham. Miners down from the Sierra foothills paid for provisions at the store he'd opened at Sutter's Fort with gold dust, and he'd personally visited Mormon Island. Brannan had decided to make money outfitting and provisioning miners, and he wanted more of them in the goldfields. On May 12, 1848, Brannan strode up San Francisco's Montgomery Street, swinging his hat with one hand. In the other, he held aloft a quinine bottle filled with gold flakes, and he yelled, over and over, "Gold! Gold! Gold from the American River!"

Brannan held the proof in his hands. In California, the rush was on.

Sam Brannan had already bought every pick, shovel, and pan he could find. He became California's first millionaire. Church elders expelled him from Mormon fellowship three years later.

The crucial detail was that nobody owned *anything* in the California interior, not the land, timber, or water, and certainly not the gold. (Everybody took it for granted that the native tribes inhabiting the area could be muscled aside.) Historically, kings, queens, and governments had reserved gold mines for themselves; California possessed no such entities. No laws regulated mining—or much of anything else—in California, and considering the recently expelled Mexican administration and the light hand of U.S. control, no entity possessed a shred of enforcement capability. For practical purposes, California had no government at all. California was a tabula rasa salted with gold, and gold mining required no capital investment except the effort to pick it up. On May 29, the *Californian* said, "The whole country, from Los Angeles to San Francisco and from the seashore to the base of the Sierra Nevadas, resounds with the sordid cry of '*gold*, Gold, GOLD!' while the field is left half planted, the house half built, and everything neglected but the manufacture of shovels and pickaxes." That was the *Californian*'s last issue. The newspaper's employees vanished into the goldfields. The *Star* survived another fortnight, until June 14. The gold excitement carried off its staff, too.*

California's social order collapsed. Virtually the entire male population of California's coastal strip bolted for the goldfields. Deserted ships swung at anchor in San Francisco Bay. Tied to the pace of sail, steam, and steed, news of the gold discovery spread like disease, at the speed of human contact, reaching the Oregon Territory, the Sandwich Islands (Hawaii), Mexico, Peru, Chile, and Australia. Everywhere it touched, adventurous and avaricious souls contracted "the yellow fever," dropped their business, and made haste for California.

On the other side of the continent, John Mackay and everyone else had no inkling of the momentous upheaval convulsing the Pacific Coast. The biggest event in the spring of 1848 for those whose lives orbited the Webb shipyard was a fire that swept the yard on April 8. The blaze started in a nearby stable and quickly spread, torching an office and storage loft. A pile of ship's timbers caught fire. On the stocks nearby, ready for launch, stood the magnificent sidewheel steamships *Panama* and *California*, sister ships intended to inaugurate passenger, mail, and freight service between the Isthmus of Panama and the newly acquired territories on the Pacific Coast. Only the prodigious efforts of firemen and police saved the ships.

News of the gold discovery broke slowly in New York. Not until August 19, 1848, would careful readers of a two-column article describing "Affairs in Our New Territory" on the front page of the *New York Herald* be able to linger over a few surprising sentences, printed far down the second column, that mentioned a "gold mine discovered in December

---

* Sam Brannan owned the *Star*. A few months later, the remnants of the *Californian* and the *Star* consolidated into a new newspaper—the *Daily Alta California*.

last . . . in a range of low hills forming the base of the Sierra Nevada"—
assuming their perusal had survived dull tidbits touting California's resources of quicksilver, silver, coal, copper, saltpeter, sulfur, asphaltum,
limestone, soda springs, and salt.

Such an arid story didn't provoke excitement. A much more incendiary article appeared a month later, on Monday, September 19, 1848,
when the *Herald* published a letter from the Pacific Coast that described
"gold for the gathering" and said that "he that can wield a spade and
shake a dish can fill his pockets," and admitted "only one serious appre-
hension, that we are in danger of having more gold than food."

The rival *Tribune* printed a more official item the next day—a letter written from Monterey, California, on July 1 by former U.S. Consul
Thomas O. Larkin and endorsed by Commodore Thomas Jones of the
U.S. Navy. According to the letter, gold mining had stopped virtually all
other work in California. "Three-fourths of the houses in the town of
San Francisco are shut up," Larkin wrote. On an inspection tour, Larkin
had found more than a thousand people "digging and washing" for gold
on the north and south forks of the American River. Larkin had also
spent several consecutive days with eight miners working a branch of the
Feather River. They operated two crude rockers, and every day he was
with the eight men, Larkin witnessed each of their two rockers produce
twelve to sixteen ounces of gold.

Considering gold's value of $18 an ounce, each rocker was clearing
$216 to $288 per day. Those were astronomical sums. Each man on the
crew earned between $54 and $72 every day—fifty to seventy times the
daily wage of the average unskilled laborer then working in New York.*

Through September, October, and November, a steady stream of California stories captured public attention, but didn't provoke wholesale migration: California was too far away, and the details seemed too farfetched
to credit; nor could anyone discount the risk of hoax, error, or fraud—
nineteenth-century newspapers regularly bent facts to boost sales, and
prudent citizens kept an ever-skeptical eye on the nation's army of shady
promoters relentlessly touting the latest and greatest in land and stock
sales, patent medicines, and newly created mechanical devices ripe for investment.

---

* Calculating based on the 2017 gold value of about $1,250 per ounce, each one of
those rockers was earning between $15,000 and $20,000 *per day*—or between $3,750 and
$5,000 per man, per day, sums for which many of us would walk across a continent and
risk death.

Popular skepticism changed on December 5, 1848, when President James K. Polk delivered his State of the Union address. The outgoing president's accounting began with a self-congratulatory discourse on the "peace, plenty, and contentment" that "reign throughout our borders" and the "sublime moral spectacle . . . our beloved country" presented to the rest of the world. Polk, who had contended with rabid domestic opposition to the recently completed war with Mexico and faced a Congress bitterly divided over how to handle the admission of the new territories, whether as slave or free-soil, then segued into an extended justification of the benefits the conquests accrued to the United States. One of which was California. "The accounts of the abundance of gold in that territory are of such an extraordinary character as would scarcely command belief were they not corroborated by the authentic reports of officials in the public service who have visited the mineral district and derived the facts which they detail from personal observation."

In other words, everything about gold in California was true. Newspapers carried transcripts of the president's twenty-one-thousand-word address in its entirety. Simultaneously, the whole nation caught gold fever. "The gold of California . . . may strengthen and benefit, or it may deprave and destroy," opined the *Tribune*.

To men and women, the gold would do all four. The rush of people hungry to cross a continent and make their fortunes would visit apocalyptic devastation on the Edenic landscapes of California—and give rise to a whole new civilization on the Pacific Coast.

John Mackay had these questions and others to ponder after the "Mechanics' Bell" tolled the end of the ten-hour workday on December 6, 1848. (Shipyard employees erected the bell on a street corner near the shipyards in the 1830s after strikes won them the right to a ten-hour workday—few working-class men owned pocket watches; fewer trusted owners' timekeeping.) Aided by the yellow glow of the city's gas lamps, Mackay navigated home through what that day's issue of the *Tribune* described as a "wilderness of filth"—the "uncovered sewers" and "putrid pollution" of the New York streets.

Such filth had suddenly become an object of serious concern. On December 1, the packet ship *New York* reached New York Harbor from France with seventeen or eighteen of its more than three hundred passengers infected with a disease that had already killed seven of those afflicted. The Board of Health quarantined the arrivals at Staten Island. The disease "resemble[d] Asiatic Cholera in all its symptoms."

Although the dreaded scourge had been blessedly absent from North America for the preceding fourteen years, few words provoked as much terror as "cholera." The sickness's 1832–34 visitation had killed more than thirty-five hundred in New York City. Nationwide, tens of thousands had died. From one stride to the next, an apparently healthy person could be felled by explosive, uncontrollable diarrhea, vomiting, and agonizing cramps. Half of the stricken died, many within a day. Some died within hours. Since few people possessed the courage to minister to the afflicted, and most of those who did contracted the disease themselves, the majority of cholera victims died a horrid death, alone and caked in excrement. The plague had ravaged Europe through the summer and fall of 1848, seemingly shackled to the violent popular uprisings shaking the despotic governments of the continent, until it jumped to England in October. Few doubted its power to vault the Atlantic.

Among the quarantined passengers of the *New York*, four new cases— and three deaths—occurred the day the president's address appeared in the *Tribune*. From the Battery to Murray Hill and from West Street to Kips Bay, "the three C's"—Congress, cholera, and California—dominated conversation.

A letter from California's military governor, Colonel Richard Barnes Mason, ran in the *Tribune* on December 8. Colonel Mason told of the goldfield tour he'd made in company with an obscure army lieutenant named William Tecumseh Sherman. They'd found the vanished population of California's coastal strip in the Sierra foothills, where Colonel Mason estimated that four thousand people were digging and washing gold from the beds of the Feather, Yuba, Bear, American Fork, and Cosumnes rivers, averaging one to three ounces of gold per person, per day. He mentioned one spot where two men had raised $17,000 in two days, another location that had produced $12,500, and a third where $2,000 came out in three weeks. "I might tell of hundreds of similar occurrences," he added. One man showed him fourteen *pounds* of clean-washed gold. Another returned to Monterey with thirty-seven *pounds*—the fruit of seven weeks of labor. A soldier on twenty-day furlough from the Monterey garrison earned $1,500, even though he'd spent half his time traveling. The value of the gold that that soldier mined exceeded the total of the rations, pay, and clothing he'd receive during his entire five-year enlistment.

The gold was on land belonging to the United States government.

Colonel Mason mused about trying to extract a tax, but "considering the large extent of country, the character of the people engaged, and the small scattered force at my command, I resolved not to interfere, but to permit all to work freely.

"No capital is required to obtain this gold," he added. "The laboring man wants nothing but his pick and shovel and tin pan with which to dig and wash the gold, and many frequently pick gold out of the crevices of rocks with their butcher knives, in pieces from 1 to 6 ounces."

The courier who brought the initial dispatches from California had also arrived with a tea caddy filled with gold—233 ounces of it. A Mr. David Carter, apparently a private citizen who had traveled with the courier, brought 1,980 ounces, a whopping 123.75 *pounds* of gold. Both samples went to the U.S. Mint in Philadelphia for assay.

The Mint silenced the "sneers of the unbelievers" when it telegraphed the War Department a summary of its findings: "Genuine."

Suddenly, there was a place to go. No longer the slow, plodding creep of a rough frontier edging away from the settled eastern states, the West had taken an almighty bound, overstepping a continent, to a land of glittering promise lining the shores of a distant ocean where a man might pick up more wealth in a morning than he could earn in a lifetime of eastern drudgery.

A flood of California-themed advertisements filled the newspapers. More ominously, another advertisement touted an "Infallible Remedy for the Asiatic Cholera." Many passengers sequestered at Staten Island had fled quarantine, and the cholera already had a foothold in the city, at a German boardinghouse at the corner of Cedar and Greenwich. The disease seemed unlikely to confine itself to the location.

By December 14, just eight days after the publication of the president's address, in New York Harbor alone, forty-five vessels were outfitting for Panama or California direct, through the Straits of Magellan or around Cape Horn. The gold mania built through the Christmas season, the New Year, and the first months of 1849. Names of men departing for California filled column after column of the New York newspapers. Reporters made much of teary-eyed departures on the city's docks and piers. Men unwilling to chance the storms of Cape Horn or the pestilential jungles of Panama—or unable to pay the passage fees—headed to the frontier towns of the Missouri River from which they could undertake the two-thousand-mile overland crossing to California.

"The spirit of emigration, which is carrying off thousands to California, so far from dying away increases and expands every day," said the *Herald* on January 11, 1849. "All classes of our citizens seem to be under the influence of this extraordinary mania."

The rush to California was the biggest event in the history of the young Republic. John Mackay stayed at the shipyard through all of it. His time was yet to come.

CHAPTER 2

Gilded Dreams—and the Hard Fist of California Reality

Booming San Francisco in 1851, with elaborate multistory buildings crammed against the downtown waterfront, tall ships crowded into the anchorage, and Yerba Buena Island in the background.

The civilized world is now half mad about California. Like children with a new plaything, they cannot take their attention from it.

—*New York Herald*, March 19, 1849

The California gold discovery put spurs to the entire world. In the eastern states, most men earned a living, nothing more. For farmers, laborers, clerks, and others in the emerging middle classes, it took years of drudgery to gain a yard of advantage. Poor Americans couldn't ever seem to win an inch. California promised more. California offered a man the opportunity to enlarge himself, to escape the pigeonhole of his eastern existence, to aim for heights beyond his previous imaginings.

Mothers, fathers, wives, and newspaper editors railed against the "unhallowed crusade for gold," but no shrill warning could suppress the pull of the Sierra foothills. Churchmen extolled the virtues of home and family and honest toil and deplored the depravity of "Mammon," warning against the moral quicksand sure to collect around the pursuit of instant wealth. To no avail. California emptied their congregations of young men. Most saw California as, quite literally, the chance of a lifetime, and although it took courage to leave everything behind, the United States had no shortage of restless, energetic, industrious men unsatisfied with their lives. Tens of thousands bolted for the new El Dorado. The pull of California proved equally powerful in Central and South America, Australia, China, and Europe. In the late spring of 1849, a *New York Tribune* writer claimed gold fever raged "worse than the cholera"—strong commentary considering the terrors of the disease.

Only a few cholera cases appeared in New York City during the cold months, but ships from Europe lodged the disease in warmer New Orleans that winter. River traffic spread the sickness up the Mississippi River Valley. Cholera decimated the populations of New Orleans, St. Louis, the South, and the trans-Appalachian West. On the Missouri frontier, the sickness ravaged wagon trains of California-bound '49ers. In New York, the cholera blossomed with the spring weather and raged through the hot summer. The president, Zachary Taylor, declared Friday, August 3, a national day of "fasting, humiliation, and prayer" in the hopes the Almighty would remove cholera's ravages. He did not. Affluent citizens fled New York City en masse. Among those left behind, the disease killed five thousand before fading in the autumn. Forty percent of the dead had been born in Ireland—stark commentary on the grotesque sanitary conditions of New York's immigrant neighborhoods.

John Mackay survived the cholera epidemic, as did his mother and sister, but 1849 can't have been an easy year for him. The prospect of adventurous experience tugs hard on many young men, and stories of what a man could make of himself on the Pacific Coast propelled the largest voluntary migration in world history. Mackay must have wanted to test himself in the new country, but responsible for helping support his mother and sister, just barely of age, obligated to the employer sponsoring his apprenticeship, and not having the means to finance the expensive trip, he remained rooted in New York for the next two and a half years, while day after day, thrilling California stories filled the newspapers.

He did benefit—the California excitement created a huge boom in shipbuilding. Demand for vessels to transport men and materials to the West Coast and to enter the California coastal trade kept Yankee shipwrights furiously busy. During Mackay's time at the shipyard, William H. Webb completed ten packet ships, eight sidewheel steamships, and six spectacular sailing vessels—the clipper ships *Celestial, Gazelle, Challenge, Comet, Invincible,* and *Swordfish.* Although the work surely felt dull in comparison to the wonders of California, the shipyard provided steady, if unspectacular pay, an important consideration for a man trying to claw his way out of immigrant poverty. However, if he stuck with shipbuilding, he'd do so for the rest of his life. John Mackay wasn't quite ready to surrender to that existence.

What combination of factors gave Mackay the final shove remains unknown. He finished his apprenticeship in the latter half of 1851, quit Webb, took ship for the Pacific Coast, and joined the gold rush.

Just nineteen, Mackay might not have appreciated the plethora of useful skills he'd acquired at the shipyard, even as a low man on the totem pole. He'd learned carpentry and how to handle tools both large and small. He'd gained an appreciation for the logistical management of large physical projects, and he'd internalized the importance of doing tasks the right way. He'd experienced good and bad leadership firsthand, and he knew what it felt like to be a cog in a complex operation that required the contributions of men of varied skills and experience. He'd learned how to rig a derrick and gain a mechanical advantage to ease the work of hoisting heavy timbers. He knew how to stay vigilant and safe around large-scale, dangerous constructions, and he'd learned to value the efficiencies gained by adopting new techniques and technologies. Every one of those abilities and attitudes would prove valuable in the decades ahead.

Reliable sources don't record whether Mackay went to California around South America or crossed to the Pacific through Central America, although by 1851, most passengers opted for the routes across Panama or Nicaragua, since those took six predictable weeks in lieu of the four to six months doubling Cape Horn sometimes required. (About half of the gold rushers went to California by sea; the other great mass of immigrants made an epic two-thousand-mile overland crossing, westering from the Missouri frontier across the waist of the continent on the Oregon and California trail network.) Considering the number of Webb-built vessels plying both sea routes, Mackay may have voyaged in a ship he'd helped construct.

In either case, Mackay made the journey in the light of full knowledge—California news had been constant fodder in East Coast newspapers for nearly three years, and many thousands of people had already returned from the Sierra foothills. Some came home loaded with gold. Many more returned bearing modest sums, disillusioned by California difficulties and eager to return to the lives they'd left behind. And quite a significant number weren't coming home at all—as many as one gold rusher in five died of disease, hardship, violence, or accident.

Nobody heading for the Pacific Coast in the last half of 1851 held illusions about the easy wealth they'd find in California. The first arrivals had skimmed the best pickings in 1848 and 1849, and although California still offered broad economic opportunities and high earnings, the difficulties and dangers, as well as astronomical cost of living, also afforded a man a gigantic opportunity to fail.

By the time John Mackay debarked from the ship that brought him to California in late 1851, the sleepy eight-hundred-person bayside village had vanished, replaced by the roaring city of San Francisco, the newest and most exciting town in the world. No city in history had ever experienced such explosive growth. On June 25, 1849, the city had been "composed chiefly of tents." Two years later, San Francisco had acquired almost thirty-five thousand inhabitants, making it the only urban place on the American frontier and one of the twenty-five biggest cities in the country. A journalist on scene remarked that San Francisco "accomplished in a day the growth of half a century." Even so, San Francisco presented an improvised appearance. Slap-dash shacks, shanties, and crudely rigged canvas tents sprawled across the hills, dunes, and flats that ringed the wooden and brick structures of the city's core, which crowded against the commercial waterfront. Ramshackle wharves stretched across tidal mudflats to reach deep water through the hulls of hundreds of abandoned ships, deserted since the frantic early days of the gold rush. Bay water seeped into the bilges of the derelicts. Many listed at obscene angles, their masts, spars, and rotting rigging tangled overhead. As the gold rushers said, "Nothing is strange in California," because, of course, everything was.

Opportunistic businessmen had winched dozens of hulks to firm high-tide groundings, connected them to the wharves with planks and piers, sawed openings in their hulls, and pressed them into service as warehouses, restaurants, stores, saloons, and hotels, even banks. As fixed points, the hulks served to solidify the landfills extending the city's business district into the bay.

Ashore, amidst the mud, the ooze, the garbage, and the hustling crowds, San Francisco's shocking dearth of women and the near total absence of children struck newcomers as the city's most instantly noticeable characteristics. The population was more than 80 percent male, a figure that represented a doubling of distaff representation in the past twelve months—the year before, women composed just 10 percent of the California population. No place in the world was more male.*

San Francisco amalgamated all the world's cultures. Persons abroad in the streets commonly heard English, Spanish, French, German, Chinese, Malay, and Hawaiian spoken on the same city block. A grasping mania infected the populace, everyone obsessed with making money as fast as possible. Everybody came from somewhere else; hardly anyone wanted to stay. A man's past meant nothing in San Francisco. The city simply had no past. A man's worth depended on who he was today, and what he might do tomorrow.

The city's extraordinary extended even unto the weather. San Francisco's could be both the best and the worst most people had ever experienced. Sunshine predominated, but cold northwest winds blowing in from the Pacific drove thick blankets of fog over the hills and dunes and through the Golden Gate—the narrow strait connecting San Francisco Bay to the open ocean—named in 1846 by "The Pathfinder," western explorer and Army officer John C. Frémont, who had led several expeditions to Alta California when it belonged to Mexico. (Frémont's naming had nothing to do with the mineral for which California would soon become famous. He'd originally named the strait "Chrysopylae," the "Golden Gate" in loose translation from the Greek, after the Golden Horn of the Bosporus, another renowned harbor, because the beautiful opening onto the Pacific suggested a golden gate to the trade of the Orient.)

Just as suddenly, the sun could shove the fog seaward and reveal glorious views of the headlands north of the bay, the sparkling harbor, the hills above the small settlement in an oak grove on the bay's eastern shore not yet incorporated as "Oakland," and the distant summit of Mount Diablo. Summer tended to be foggy and gray, but during fall and win-

---

* California's population wouldn't achieve a natural balance between men and women for a hundred years, not until 1950.

ter, spells of crystalline sunshine could run for weeks, astonishing those who originated in New England or in the upper Mississippi and Ohio River Valleys. Days of steely rain broke the winter sunshine and rendered the hodgepodge town into a quagmire. Miserable mules, horses, and oxen hauled the hacks, carts, drays, and carriages of commerce through slimy, muddy streets. Wooden planks paved the best streets, an expensive proposition considering the price of lumber often exceeded fifty cents per linear foot, but business boomed along paved streets, and San Franciscans cared about business more than anything else. San Francisco had many two-, three-, and a few four-story brick buildings lining the narrow streets of its downtown core, and many still built of wood. New arrivals couldn't help but fixate on the city's wealth. Gold glittered everywhere, in astonishing quantities, the likes of which easterners never saw. Immense sums changed hands. Gold dust passed for currency, weighed on scales kept in every store, restaurant, and saloon, as did privately made gold slugs and octagonal $50 ingots struck by the recently established U.S. Assay Office, foreign coins in denominations both large and small, and what few of the $10 eagles and new $20 gold double eagles of legitimate United States coinage had managed to make it to the coast. In California, all of it was good, as long as it was gold. Californians believed only in gold. The state's 1850 constitution forbade the use of paper banknotes.*

Ironically, considering the quantity of gold coming out of the ground, lack of genuine United States coinage dragged on the young state's economy. Gold dust and privately coined slugs circulated at a discount due to inconvenience and fears of lesser-than-advertised weights and purity. Residents incessantly petitioned the federal government to establish a branch mint in San Francisco, which it finally did in 1854. Banking houses and commercial establishments took deposits of gold dust, slugs, and ingots, stored the metal in heavy iron safes, and made cash loans on good security at usurious interest due to the shortage of coin and the high probability that the supported ventures would fail.

Confirming the warnings of the hometown clergy, much of the gold in San Francisco flowed toward businesses with shaky moral underpinnings. Gambling, theatrical productions, whoring, and drinking thrived like nowhere else in America. Drunks staggered through the San Francisco streets at all hours. Nearly every mercantile establishment sold intoxicating liquors, and the city's most impressive buildings housed the

---

* Silver and copper passed for sums under one dollar.

gambling "hells" around Portsmouth Square. For life on the coast, a pile of wagered gold gleaming on a gaming table surrounded by hard-eyed men couldn't have been a more perfect metaphor.

Wild speculation drove San Francisco business, on cargoes just landed or expected to arrive, and in real estate, despite uncertain ownership. People won and lost fortunes every day, and the roulette wheel of San Francisco existence created a unique dynamic between rich and poor. As the city's first historian observed, "The sand-shoveler and the millionaire may change places tomorrow, and they know it; so the former does not usually cringe nor the other strut when they meet."

For all the excitement of San Francisco, John Mackay hadn't come to California for city work. He'd come west to mine gold. He decided to try his luck in "the northern mines," or "the wet diggings," the gold country north of the American River, where water, the one essential ingredient of gold mining, was more abundant. Mackay lugged his outfit to the rich mines around Downieville, a remote, booming mining community tucked into the steep canyons lining the North Fork of the Yuba River about one hundred miles north of Sacramento. A population of around three thousand made Downieville one of California's largest interior towns,* and a dastardly act perpetrated by the town's own people the previous summer had gained Downieville a fair measure of "infamous notoriety." Late on the night of July 4, 1851, a successful, popular, and almost certainly drunk American miner smashed into the house of a married woman, Josefa Segovia. She stabbed him to death during or after the assault, or for threatening one, which, had she been Caucasian, would have almost certainly excused the killing. Segovia, however, was of Mexican extraction and not entitled to the same considerations. A vigilante court convicted Josefa Segovia of murder the next morning and hanged her from a Yuba River bridge. She remains the one and only pregnant woman ever lynched in California. The act haunts Downieville to this day.

Thanks to "good diggings" nearby, the town survived the disgrace. Those gold-rich diggings had formed through passing eons as water eroded dirt and rocks from higher in the hills. Among that eroded material were small yellow flecks of "the precious needful," "the circulating medium," or "the necessary" stripped from gold-bearing quartz veins or the beds of ancient rivers, relics of a distant geological time when the California landscape differed from its modern form. As the water flowed downhill, the gold particles and the other eroded material settled out of

---

* In the 2010 census, Downieville had 282 inhabitants.

suspension and accumulated as gold-impregnated sediments deposited in the gulches, ravines, streamways, and riverbeds of the Sierra foothills. Miners called those deposits "placers" (pronounced *plassers*), a term adopted from Spanish that described small concentrations of a heavy and valuable mineral—like gold—mixed with much larger quantities of lighter dirt, gravel, or sand. The quality of any given diggings varied with the concentrations of gold the local placers contained and the ease with which the gold was separated from the worthless material around it. "Placer mining" was the labor-intensive art of making that happen.

All placer gold-mining techniques hinged on gold's extraordinary density, nineteen times denser than water and almost twice as dense as lead. To pan for gold, the most basic mining method, a miner swirled water around the inside of a pan full of promising dirt and allowed the moving water to slosh the lighter sediments over the pan's lip, leaving denser material behind—some of which would, ideally, be gold. Rockers (also called "cradles") allowed miners to wash a greater volume of dirt—and therefore recover a greater volume of gold. Abundant water made possible the use of "long toms," narrow rectangular U-shaped troughs made of wood about one foot wide and one foot high and usually between six and twenty feet long, and "sluice boxes"—up-sized long toms that processed more dirt but required even more water. At the end of a long day of digging and washing, the men "cleaned up" the captured gold. To capture the smallest particles of "fine gold," miners often deposited mercury above the riffle bars. The mercury formed an amalgam with the gold. Later, they separated the substance to constituent ingredients in a "retort," a distilling apparatus that allowed heat applied to the amalgam to boil off the mercury, condense and collect the mercury vapor for reuse, and leave behind the gold. (Miners commonly called mercury "quicksilver.")

Since one of the first great needs in California after the gold discovery was some political framework to arrest the devolution into brute-force anarchy, the men in each geographically logical area banded together, formed a local "mining district," and codified rules to govern their one important interest: gold mining. The specifics varied between districts, but in general, the men designed the rules to give each person a fair chance at the gold so long as he didn't infringe on the rights of his fellows. First and foremost, mining district rules allowed an individual to "claim" a specific location for mining purposes. A mining claim conveyed no permanent ownership— nobody wanted to own the land for fear of one day being forced to pay taxes on it—but a claim did give its holder the exclusive right to extract precious metal from within its confines, provided he complied with the district rules.

The claims were small, no larger than one man could reasonably work—on rich placers, sometimes as small as ten-foot by ten-foot squares, although larger on lesser quality diggings. Claims had to be visibly marked by stakes, cairns, or tools left in sight—a shovel or pick struck in the ground usually sufficed—and they had to be worked at least one day a week. If not, the owner forfeited his right to mine the claim, leaving it subject to "relocation" by someone more industrious. Claims could be bought and sold, but district rules typically didn't allow a person to hold more than two claims at the same time—one by purchase and one by location. The rules usually allowed the man who discovered a new placer—"the original locator," a universally honored man—a double-sized claim as reward for his exploratory zeal. Claim holders could hire helpers for fair wages, but rules usually banned slave, peon, indentured, or tricked labor (that last rule created to stop men hiring Indians and paying them with beads, glass baubles, and trinkets), and they initially banned corporations. The miners elected a district "recorder" to enter the claims in a local record book upon receipt of a fee, and arranged for juries of miners to adjudicate disputes.

A miner prospected for "good diggings" by removing the overburden of worthless dirt atop promising sediments and testing the deepest gravels with a gold pan. If the sediments "panned out" an acceptable return (five to eight grains of gold dust per pan would "pay"), the man staked a claim, or "located," dug down to bedrock, since crevices directly atop the bedrock—"the ledge," as the men named it—almost always held the richest gold deposits, and washed the sediments through a rocker, long tom, or sluice box, always hoping for the flash of a big strike. Mackay learned to mine gold watching the doings of other men.

As the miners exhausted the streambed placers, they explored farther afield and found paying placers in nearby flats, gulches, and ravines. Additional searching revealed significant quantities of gold in the beds of extinct rivers whose courses wound their way through bluffs, ridges, flats, and hillsides without connection to the modern drainages.

Gold mining was hard, dirty, and repetitive, like digging an endless ditch. Miners quickly learned to appreciate the search for gold as Mother Nature's grand lottery scheme. A man could easily dig an entire season, carry and wash hundreds—even thousands—of buckets of gravel, and finish poorer than when he started, while the men working mere feet away on adjacent ground hacked open a "glory hole" and carried off more wealth in a morning than a man could earn in a decade working for wages. That ugly truth stood at odds with the old Puritan notion that honest toil earned a just reward. Gold mining was like gambling, it *was* gambling, and the hope of making a "raise" kept the men at the hard labor, gouging and crevicing along the bedrock or up to their knees and thighs in the cold streams, not knowing what the next stroke of the pick or shovelful of gravel might reveal. That trying to grub color from the ground could be simultaneously incredibly exciting and stupefyingly dull was one of California's many ironies. Nobody knew a sure way to judge a claim other than to dig it down to bedrock and find out. Miners considered locations that returned an ounce of gold per day extremely valuable, and such "ounce diggings" changed hands for many hundreds of dollars, even when stacked against the risk that the claim would "play out" before one recovered the investment. California's more fortunate men raised enough gold to cover the price of their food with a decent sum left over, but the state's speculative mania often convinced miners to plow one season's "clean up" into a larger-scale venture the next year— often a "river-turning" operation done in company with other miners that required the pooled investment of capital. To turn a river, a group constructed a wing dam, which would divert the river's entire flow into an expensive lumber flume or ditch. The current in the by-pass channel turned pumps that drained the water remaining in the river's deepest holes, and with the riverbed finally exposed, the men set to work washing the sediments at the bottom of the deepest pools, the ones in which they expected to find the richest deposits. Such endeavors required months of industrious, intelligent labor to bring to fruition.

Sometimes the investments paid handsome dividends, but in making what was essentially a double-or-nothing gamble, the miners exposed themselves to the vagaries of gold's uneven distribution and California's misunderstood climate. Some river-turning schemes didn't find enough gold to cover their expenses. In other instances, sudden floods from early autumn rains overwhelmed the wing dams, ditches, and flumes. The rivers raged back into their natural channels just as the consortiums hustled to expose the deepest and most valuable sediments, the ones needed to make the river-turning operations profitable. Such failures drove the invested miners back to square zero and ruined the merchants who had been extending them credit in anticipation of a late-season payoff.

The new state teemed with business opportunities ancillary to the mining boom. Men seized on all manner of schemes: They opened stores; ordered steam engines shipped through San Francisco from the East Coast to power sawmills or run hoists and pumps; imported seed or fruit stock for agricultural endeavors; built ferries and roads and charged tolls; opened saloons and grog shops; and fronted gambling operations.

Some businesses thrived, many busted. As the *Marysville Express* told it at the end of the decade, "There are but few persons who have lived long in California whose experience cannot recall at least one instance of the sudden failure of what they considered a 'dead thing.'"

Fortunately, in California, failure carried no special stigma. A bankrupt man rolled up his sleeves and went back to work, that was all. Pacific Coast society expected a man to have the sand to go "all in" in pursuit of the main chance—that was the whole point of being there. The entire California project was a speculative endeavor. In the rest of the nation, a bankruptcy dogged a man for his entire career. In California, many of the richest men had been busted several times, and all of them knew they might well be broke again tomorrow.

Aside from gold by the shovelful, miners next desired news from home. The manifold shortcomings of the U.S. Postal Office—described by Sacramento City's *Placer Times* in December 1849 as "a shadow of an apology for the transmission of letters and newspapers"—opened a business opportunity. Miners in the remote camps would pay generous sums to have letters carried to and from the post offices in San Francisco and Sacramento. From one man and a mule string carrying letters and high-value provisions to the camps, "express" operations evolved to fill another great hole in the mining economy—the need to send money home. Trustworthy operations that could handle the difficult logistical and security considerations grew into stagecoach lines that transported passengers and high-value freight. They bought gold dust at a discount (typically 5, 8, or 10 percent of its value), stored the dust in iron safes, transported it to San Francisco, shipped the gold to the Philadelphia Mint—which struck it into coin—and credited the corresponding sum into a hometown bank account. Attracted by the enormous volume of gold and the correspondingly large value of the trade, New York banking houses established California affiliates that bought out smaller express companies and took over their operations. Adams & Company and Gregory & Company dominated until Adams & Company failed in 1855, after which Wells, Fargo & Company rose to prominence.

Although in aggregate, tens of millions of dollars of gold emerged from the dirt of California, on the individual level, intense physical misery constituted gold mining's only certain return. In summertime, the sun pushed down through a hot, pale sky, and the miners sweated through scorching afternoons. The rivers dwindled. The streams vanished. The season turned and the men shivered through cold weather, standing in swollen, icy streams, soaked to the skin. They suffered heat exhaustion and hypothermia, hernias, and strained backs. Minor wounds became tetanized or gangrenous. Diarrhea, dysentery, and cholera tore at their intestines. They fell sick with diphtheria, pneumonia, smallpox, typhoid, tetanus, and typhus and scratched at the bites of fleas, ticks, and lice. Detritus, garbage, and excrement fouled the crude camps. Enormous rats thrived. Cave-ins of poorly shored shafts or "coyote holes" buried inattentive or unlucky men. Undermined boulders shifted, crushing fingers, toes, and limbs, sometimes whole persons. Provisions were scarce, simple, and extortionately expensive. Those who didn't invest in fresh food developed scurvy, which, despite centuries of seafaring, still wasn't properly understood as a vitamin deficiency. Miners cooked rough meals in greasy pots over open fires. Few troubled to make leavened bread. They wore sturdy boots, coarse, durable canvas trousers, wide belts, slouch hats, gloves, and blue or red flannel shirts until they rotted from their bodies. Before the Gold Rush, most men in the United States kept clean-shaven faces. In California, many wore beards. Wild, unkempt whiskers symbolized independence and freedom and whiffed of rebellion, and as California captured the American imagination, the gold rushers' bristly custom caught on nationwide—the West Coast's first contribution to American fashion. Absent the rudiments of civil society, minor disputes erupted into violence. Stabbings, shootings, and murders roiled the camps, as did "jumping," meaning claim jumping. Absent difficult-to-organize miners' courts—nobody wanted to lose valuable mining time suffering through kangaroo legal proceedings—a man had to be willing to fight to hold his ground against an interloping thug. For better and often for worse, "Judge Lynch" handled most of what passed for justice in the early California mining camps. A fair fight excused most transgressions, but a man caught thieving another's dust could expect no mercy. "When caught in the act, up they go, and that's the end of it," one man wrote his family.

For many of the new Californians, alcohol offered the only relief. Ardent spirits, so scandalous in Puritan society, were everywhere at hand. In the fall of 1851, a rare string-straight woman at a remote camp in the northern mines not far from where Mackay had gone to work noted that little could be accomplished in California without "the sanctifying influence of the spirit." As one miner reported, "The thoughts of the people are entirely preoccupied with drinking, gambling, or getting gold out of the earth."

The men lived under canvas or in bricolage cabins constructed of scrounged materials. They buried their dust in bags, jars, and tins, often under flat stones hidden beneath the ashes of their cook fires. Dogs yowled. A rough plank laid across the tops of empty barrels or two tree stumps often served as a camp's first saloon. Before long, canvas snugged in the walls and roof to make a room, it acquired a rough floor, and a plank door swung on leather hinges.

In many camps, prostitutes offered the only "female society" available. Absent female companionship, men gambled strictly for the pleasure of sitting in the presence of a woman—having one deal a game practically guaranteed its success, and crafty gambling houses imported women for that express purpose. As one chronicler noted, "Mining camps always wear their worst side out."

To those attempting to cleave to their hometown morality, California seemed like the devil's playground. The Sabbath, considered a cornerstone of healthy religious observance in the eastern states, died a quick death in the mining camps. Come Sundays, men working outlying claims flocked to the larger camps to settle debts and buy provisions. Merchants presented miners with "villainous looking paper[s] charged with figures." Miners returned "long, greasy bag[s] charged with gold." Accounts resolved, mining camp Sundays devolved into massive community ventings of accumulated steam heated by rotgut whisky, cut-rate wine, and stovetop brandy. Groggeries went full blast in perfect pandemonium, selling booze by the gold-dust "pinch." (Successful saloon-tenders had notoriously fat fingers.) "Cat-gut scrapers" sawed out music on battered fiddles that had somehow survived the journey "the plains across." Touts staged bear, dog, or cock fights, horse races, boxing contests, and coarse, makeshift theatricals. Bewhiskered miners roamed the streets, pistols and bowie knives dangling from their belts. Gentleman sports in spotless boiled shirts and broadcloth suits manned the faro tables. Clouds of flies rose above garbage and offal in the dirt streets. Fights erupted. Pack mules staggered under preposterous loads. A tattered stars and stripes fluttered from a makeshift liberty pole. As one gold rusher wrote, "Drinking has become very prevalent, swearing a habitual custom, and gambling has no equal in the annals of history."

The thing was, amid the California welter, a man got to choose, absent the tyranny of moralizers who had ever plagued the American nation. As one Gold Rush trader described it, "We come and we go and nobody wonders and no Mrs. Grundy talks about it." A man did as he pleased. If he chose to cleave to his religious traditions and keep the Sabbath, that was his business and that was fine, nobody much cared. Conversely, a man could gamble, smoke, blaspheme, buy the services of a prostitute, and paralyze himself with ardent spirits and nobody much cared about that, either. Mining camp philosophy held that "every man has the right to go to hell in the manner of his own choosing."

That had a downside, too. California was a heartless place. Nobody much bothered when things went wrong. Test pits in the camps filled with water. Drunks fell in and drowned and nobody raised an eyebrow. The fool shouldn't have drunk so much. Men fell ill and died thousands of miles from the hand of the closest person who loved them. The person who scraped his shallow grave might not trouble to learn his name. Men found California's anonymity depressing and lonely, sentiments that may have catalyzed much Gold Rush debauchery.

The shoddy social fabric held nobody in place. People came and went unnoticed. Men disappeared into the camps, swallowed whole by the dangers and dissipation of life on the mining frontier. Many were never heard from again. Camps thrived while the local placers produced good returns. Men drifted away from faltering diggings and wandered the Sierra foothills in an endless, restless search for the next big thing, hoping to be first to skim the cream from a new strike. Few miners were content with what they had. The merest whisper stampeded frustrated miners to some new flat or gulch, a steady, unspectacular claim having nothing on the hope of "new diggings." For many, for most, California's promised fortune proved as elusive as every other. The frustrated restlessness worsened as the years passed.

In California, immigrants discovered a geography swollen to immense size. Stands of enormous trees covered hills and mountains and ran off beyond the limits of vision. At lower elevations, the emerald grasses of winter glowed like Irish vistas, then sprouted spring carpets of wildflowers that tinted the landscape impossible yellows and oranges. As each year aged, the verdure seared into the tans and duns of summer and fall, which somehow managed to glow vibrant gold in the lingering Pacific sunsets. Abundant wildlife patrolled the hills and valleys. Hawks, vultures, eagles, and enormous condors pinwheeled overhead. Oaks, pines, and coarse chaparral climbed the hills and canyons of the Sierra foothills and away eastward, the gray white peaks of the high Sierra towered into a cobalt sky. Coastward, the immigrants marveled along shores pounded by the swells of a different ocean. No one could gaze on San Francisco Bay without sensing the power it held to unlock the Pacific slope of the continent. Nothing previously known rivaled the majestic grandeur of California. The state excelled even in monotony. California's Central Valley was simply the flattest place anybody had ever seen.

But for all of California's heart-stopping beauty, the gold rushers felt no obligation to care for that which the vagaries of history had dropped in their laps. Since no one planned to stay in California longer than it took to make his "pile," nobody bothered to take care of the land. The gold rushers attacked California with the fury of an invading army, elbowing aside the native cultures that had thrived in California for thousands of years. Although Spanish and Mexican soldiers, missionaries, and ranchers had done their fair share of harm to California's coastal Indian cultures during the preceding eighty years, California's native population collapsed during the 1850s, hounded unto death by the horsemen of the white man's apocalypse—disease, murder, and the wanton annihilation of the natural resources on which the Indians depended. In-flooding Americans claimed the best natural resources on a first-come, first-served basis, "posting" mining ground, timber, and water and calling them their own. In a decade of unrestrained pillage, the mining frenzy turned the Sierra foothills into a wasteland, a grubbed-over landscape of caved hillsides, barren holes, heaped tailings, garbage, tree stumps, and polluted rivers. Worst damage of all came with the invention of "hydraulic mining." Miners learned to direct high-pressure water cannons at gold-bearing sediments and wash entire hillsides through enormous sluice boxes. "Hydraulicking" produced large returns, but also choked streams and rivers with mining debris, called "tailings," causing floods that buried some of California's most fertile bottom lands under sterile gravel.*

The Mexican Californianos fared nearly as badly as the native Indians. The United States had promised to uphold the sanctity of their land grants in the treaty that ceded California to the United States, but they quickly found themselves overrun by an army of gringo ruffians, huge tracts of their lands occupied by squatters claiming "rights," and their fates gripped by a legal system that seemed rigged to dispossess them of land their families may have owned for generations

California changed a man. It broke him of his illusions. A Gold Rush axiom held that "a man in California either grows better or worse." The

---

* The battle waged in the courts between California's agricultural and hydraulic mining interests culminated in a landmark 1884 legal decision that identified and defined a "public interest" and banned hydraulic mining as "a public and private nuisance"—one of the first and most important environmental decisions in United States history.

state either sent him home in tatters, ruined him in place, leaving a shell of the former man, or he rose to meet its challenges. In that case, even if California never made him rich, the state filled him with sure, steady confidence and a good measure of pride—if a man could handle California, he could handle anything.

John Mackay lived in that world for seven years, mining gold in the gulches and bars around Downieville at camps and locales with names like Cut-Throat Bar, Allegheny, Forest City, Cut Eye Foster's Bar, The City of Six, Secret Diggings, Poker Flat, Deadwood, Pardner's Pint, the Hardscrabble District, Hell's Half Acre, Shenanigan Flat, Whisky Diggings, Fair Play, Portwine, Potosi, Brandy City, Puppytown, and Poverty Hill. Whether ironic, playful, personal, or realistic, the place names conveyed much of gold mining's essential truths, and as the decade wore on, the mining life grew increasingly precarious. According to Joseph T. Goodman, then a thick-bearded typesetter working for the *Golden Era*, San Francisco's most prestigious literary magazine, by 1858, "the palmy days of placer mining were past."

News from the Pacific Northwest that told of major gold strikes on the Fraser and Thompson rivers in Canada, 950 miles north of San Francisco (east and northeast of modern Vancouver) triggered California anxieties in the spring of 1858. San Francisco headlines howled about "Miners Making $8 to $50 per day!" On April 4, the *Daily Alta California* quoted "a gentleman of reliability" with Fraser River experience. "Tell your friends to come soon," he said.

And come they did. The "Fraser fever" raged with "unabated ardor" and "wild, ungovernable excitement" through May and June 1858, with "every steamer fit to send to sea" and "innumerable" sailing vessels pressed into service to carry passengers and freight to the new goldfield. The value of mining claims in the Sierra foothills plummeted as men sold out, wanting just enough money to make the trip north. Some went by sea; others made the hard and dangerous overland journey. The exodus shriveled the populations of the interior mining districts, injured the commerce of Stockton, Sacramento, and Marysville, towns that survived by supplying the miners' needs, and panicked San Francisco, where property owners rushed to sell "while there was yet a chance to save something from the general wreck." In early July, the *Daily Alta California* estimated that twenty-five thousand men had stampeded north. "For sale" placards swung from hundreds of San Francisco buildings. The *Stockton Independent* described California as "a cholera patient in the collapsed state, when stimulants and narcotics are of immediate necessity to check the exhausting disease."

The disappearance of so many men crushed commerce and trade throughout the state. The assessed value of San Francisco real estate dropped nearly 15 percent. As Joseph T. Goodman wrote more than thirty years later, "The extent to which San Francisco suffered from this disaster would not be credible to those who have known the city only in later and more prosperous years. It is within bounds to say that a quarter of the houses stood tenantless. Confidence was gone, trade was killed, and San Francisco sat in sack-cloth and bewailed her hopeless fate."

Disaster hit the men who'd gone north, too. Up north, the rivers refused to lower in the late summer and autumn, the best placer deposits remained submerged, and the men mined little gold. Immense water volumes prevented use of the river-turning techniques developed in California. Of the thousands who rushed north, few made grub. Measurable quantities of gold did exist in the Fraser River drainage—most of it submerged beneath large, swift-flowing rivers from which profitable extraction proved impossible. By early October, the gold dust received at the San Francisco Mint from the Fraser River totaled a mere 3,532 ounces, a fraction of an ounce per man, and the *California Farmer and Journal of Useful Sciences* said, "The Fraser swindle overtops all other[s] in its gigantic proportions, and puts to the blush all humbugs that have preceded it."

The majority of men who rushed to the Fraser River went broke. Hundreds, then thousands of disappointed miners straggled back into California. They'd lost all the money they'd invested in the trip, which in most cases was all the money they'd made in California. Only the shipping lines had flourished, which gave rise to the persistent rumor that most of the gold exhibited in San Francisco that had supposedly been mined on the Fraser River had made a round trip from California.

With the bitter sectional tensions over the future of slavery and a painful economic depression harrying the eastern part of the nation and the Fraser River rush walloping California, among the few pieces of good news loose in the summer of 1858 was the announcement that Cyrus Field and his Atlantic Telegraph Company had successfully laid a submarine telegraph cable from England to Ireland and another across the floor of the Atlantic Ocean nearly two thousand miles to Newfoundland. A third leg of submarine cable connected Newfoundland into the land telegraph network of Nova Scotia. Transmission rates limited messages to a few words per hour, but that speed seemed miraculous compared to the weeks-long duration of the sea voyage. The first official message started westward from England on August 16: "Europe and America are united by telegraphy. Glory to God in the highest; on earth, peace and good will toward men." Queen Victoria followed with a telegram of congratulations to President Buchanan, a ninety-eight-word missive that took eighteen hours to transmit. Through the much faster overland telegraph network, news of the transatlantic telegraph communication flashed around the United States. The joyful peel of church bells and the scream of steam whistles heralded the achievement to an awe-struck populace. In an era of wonders, the Atlantic cable seemed "the event of the age."

Since no tendril of the telegraph network touched California, rumors of the successful intercontinental connection didn't begin trickling into San Francisco until late August. California's fastest communications with "the States" arrived and departed on the dusty, bumpy stagecoaches of the overland mail, either via South Pass (in modern Wyoming) and Salt Lake City, or on the recently opened southern, snow-free route between San Francisco and the railheads on the Mississippi River at Memphis or St. Louis that traveled via 139 relay stations in Southern California, the New Mexico Territory, Texas, and Arkansas. Dangers, difficulties, and delays plagued both routes. Not until mid-September could the San Francisco newspapers confirm the transatlantic telegraph triumph and describe the enormous celebrations with which virtually every town and city in the Union had greeted the world-changing innovation. The *Daily Alta California* opined that beside the "magnitude and importance of this re-sult . . . all former human accomplishments fade into Lilliputian dimen-sions." California businessmen worried that lack of integration with the newly connected world would marginalize the Pacific Slope economy.

To demonstrate to the people of the Atlantic states that California pos-sessed "a full sense of the importance of the work," California scheduled celebrations for Monday, September 27, 1858. Sacramento, Stockton, Marysville, and Placerville all manifested great civic rejoicings, but none of their efforts matched that put forth by San Francisco to gin up cheer—and business—in that dark autumn of 1858.

San Franciscans festooned their city with flags, banners, and "acres of many-hued bunting," and launched a parade so enormous that it took ninety minutes to pass any fixed location. After sunset, the warm glow of gaslights, candles burning in nearly every one of the city's windows, and bonfires blazing in the public squares gradually replaced the gloaming. To an observer in the harbor, San Francisco appeared "one vast crystal palace." The festivities climaxed with a fireworks display above Portsmouth Square. To everyone's great relief, nowhere in the city had the thousands of naked flames leaped to a wooden structure and touched off a conflagration. Die-hard revelers carried intemperate festivities into the wee hours of the morning.

The *Daily Alta California* missed its issue the next morning, the staff having spent the previous night in "unrestrained rejoicing." When the newspaper returned to print on Wednesday, it hailed the celebration as "the most magnificent affair that has ever taken place upon the Pacific coast." Unbeknownst to the thousands of San Franciscans recovering from the revelries, the transatlantic cable had ceased functioning ten days before, for reasons its engineers didn't yet understand. News of the failure hadn't yet reached California. Service wouldn't resume for another *eight years*.

John Mackay stayed rooted in the Sierra foothills around Downieville through all of it. He resisted the temptations of the Fraser River rush and an earlier "duffers rush" to the Kern River and, so far as is known, didn't attend the cable rejoicing in San Francisco. Although he'd never made a big strike, with hard work and diligence, he'd earned enough to support himself with money left over to remit to his mother and sister. (At some point, his sister took religious vows and joined a convent.) Mackay loved the outdoor, physical life, the camaraderie, and the chaotic excitement and menace of the camps. Nobody worked harder than he did, and he often cooked for himself and his partners, a universally despised chore. A man who knew him in those days claimed with a wink that Mackay could "throw a slap jack up a chimney and catch it at the door."

For the rest of his life, John Mackay looked back on those years of hard labor in the narrow, pine- and oak-clad canyons echoing with the rush of cold Sierra waters as his best times, when he was free to enjoy his friendships without the complications and responsibilities of later years. Mackay was popular with his peers, and Robert Gracey, a friend of his during his Downieville years and for many years thereafter, remembered Mackay as "lighter hearted in those days than ever afterward." In 1858, while so many "old Californians"—who were almost exclusively very young men—rushed to the Fraser River, the Masonic Lodge at Forrest City, a mining camp in the hills south of Downieville, admitted John Mackay to its membership. (The Independent Order of the Odd Fellows, the Freemasons, and other benevolent societies and fraternal orders played important roles in Gold Rush society. They organized social events, gave members a sense of belonging somewhere on the chaotic, anonymous California frontier, served a crucial role as mutual aid societies to help sick or injured members in an age devoid of government social safety nets, and in the event of a member's death, typically funded and held a funeral and passed the hat for his widow, if he left one.)

Mining's grueling toil toned hard muscle onto Mackay's middleweight frame. Mackay had keen, noticing eyes beneath brows that tended to knit together over the bridge of his nose, and although he wasn't prone to the alcoholic binges that plagued so many of his countrymen, his cheeks often flushed red. He'd grown into a ruddy, powerful, healthy-looking man, and despite the fashion of the much-bewhiskered mining frontier, he kept his cheeks clean-shaven. He was handy with tools, and the carpentry skills he'd learned in the Webb shipyard made him a good man to have in a mining camp. By the winter of 1858–59, John Mackay had "seen the elephant" from the tip of its trunk to the very end of its tail, and he would have stayed mining around Downieville forever but for the problem of declining returns. The average miner's daily earnings had dropped from $20 in 1848 to $16 the next year and then steadily down to about $5 per day in 1855. By 1858, a miner was exceeding the norm if he gleaned more than $3 worth of gold from a long, hard day of digging and washing. Mackay, his great friend Jack O'Brien, with whom he'd been partnered for years, and four other men spent the 1858 mining season working a claim on Durgan's Flat, a few hundred yards below the confluence of the Downie River and the North Fork of the Yuba. The six men shared a log cabin nearby. Dozens of miners had worked Durgan's Flat in 1850, to great profit. Other men reworked the ground a few times through the middle 1850s, for lesser returns. Mackay and his mates worked like rented mules on Durgan's Flat in 1858, but no amount of labor could find gold where little remained.

Years later, one of his fellow miners remembered Mackay throwing down his tools in frustration and announcing, "All I want is $25,000. That's enough for any man. With that I can make my old mother comfortable," adding that if he "ever got hold of $25,000," he'd "spend his life loafing."

The coming decades would prove the lie of that. But Durgan's Flat was played out. Mackay's group couldn't make grub. The partnership dissolved. O'Brien and Mackay walked over the ridge south of town and hired themselves out for wages felling trees and shaping framing timbers for somebody else's mine. Reminiscing as an old man, Baruch Pride, who had worked alongside Mackay felling trees, recalled, "Mackay worked like the devil and made me work the same way."

They'd probably worked for wages before, since it was common for miners in the middle and late 1850s to spend part of the year hiring out for wages, and to prospect and mine on their own account with the remainder of their time, but the failure of the Durgan's Flat venture forced Mackay and O'Brien to assess their prospects. Honestly, they weren't good. Earning wages working for someone else removed the risk of hunger, but only at the sacrifice of their chance of making a raise. In either case, mining or making wages, Mackay couldn't set aside much money to help his mother, and although he'd helped support her for more than fifteen years, he wasn't doing anything to build a secure future.

For years, mining in the Downieville area had grown increasingly corporate—as it had elsewhere in the goldfields, the original rules banning corporations having been relaxed through the years as corporations proved to be the only entities willing to buy claims from men who wanted out. Well-capitalized consortiums could afford to finance the "dead work" of unproductive digging required to reach the more valuable sediments at the bottom of the ancient riverbeds, where the best deposits collected on the bedrock. Mackay had done plenty of underground mining—"drift mining," "drifting," or "coyoting" as it was often called—and he'd built a reputation for hard work and competence, but he'd always done it on somebody else's account, for somebody who could pay the wages and buy the timber and tools opening an underground mine required. The burgeoning technique of hydraulic mining likewise required immense quantities of start-up capital. Mackay and his partners couldn't finance such endeavors. Downieville itself had shriveled from its halcyon days in the early 1850s. By the end of 1858, Mackay was twenty-seven years old, and despite more than seven years of backbreaking toil in the California goldfields, his existence was every bit as hand-to-mouth as it had been fifteen years before when he was selling newspapers on the streets of New York.

Thus primed, in the spring of 1859, John Mackay and Jack O'Brien lent their ears to rumors of a strike made more than one hundred miles to the east, in the rugged desert mountains of the western Utah Territory on the other side of the Sierra Nevada, at a new locality with the pompous name of "Gold Hill"—in reality a low mound tucked into the upper reaches of steeply descending Gold Cañon—in a place called the Washoe Diggings (pronounced *Wash-o*, as in "Tahoe").

When the handful of Gold Hill miners had started washing the mound's top dirt through their rockers, likely in early April 1859, they made about five dollars a day—in line with the steady, unspectacular returns the Washoe Diggings had produced through most of the 1850s. Dwindling supplies of food and drink on the eastern slope of the Sierras likely held more of their attention. Snow clogging the high passes prevented resupply. Mining returns from tiny Gold Hill took a huge upswing through the middle of April. On April 21, a pair of independent reports from the Carson Valley claimed Gold Hill miners were cleaning up as much as $40 per day, per man, and that only meager supplies of water stopped them from earning $50 to $100 per day. A week later, a four-month-old Carson Valley newspaper called the *Territorial Enterprise* reported the Gold Hill miners doing "remarkably well," and "as an evidence of their prosperity hold their claims at from $4,000 to $5,000." By the standards of placer miners on either side of the Sierras in 1859, all those figures represented fortunes. Spring weather opened the Sierra passes, and pack trains hurried over the mountains to resupply the suddenly flush Washoe miners. Many California newspapers carried stories about Gold Hill in May. A letter published in the *Territorial Enterprise* on May 21 and reprinted in the *Sacramento Daily Union* on May 30 specifically mentioned the success of a group of Gold Hill miners referred to as "Comstock & Co"—likely the first newspaper mention of a name that would soon be famous the world over.

The intensity of the rumors jumped another notch in late June and early July when stories shot through the California goldfields of the discovery of a vein of gold and silver ore in Washoe worth more than $3,000 per ton. Silver was something entirely new. A dispatch to the *San Francisco Bulletin* reported "considerable of a stir" in a cadre of mining men in Nevada City and Grass Valley, two important camps about halfway between Sacramento and Downieville, and "men leaving hourly" for the new strike.

Conflicting opinions formed. The El Dorado County clerk returned to Placerville from Washoe in the middle of July and told the *Placerville Observer* that "the diggings are unquestionably the richest ever known on the continent." Tempering the enthusiasm, among many similar articles, one in the *California Farmer and Journal of Useful Sciences* thought it unlikely that anyone would obtain "large quantities of gold" in Washoe, water being scarce and the diggings "not extensive." Miners began trickling toward Washoe, but the rumors didn't provoke a general stampede. According to the *Sacramento Daily Union*, "remembrance of Fraser River exert[ed] a salutary influence."

Mackay and O'Brien talked over their options. The stories of extraordinary wealth in a place with such an arid reputation sounded fantastical, but any fool could see that Downieville's glory had passed. In the end, the decision wasn't difficult. There wasn't much upside in working for wages in a dying district, and quite frankly, they didn't have a lot to lose. Without money to afford a mule or a donkey to aid with the 110-mile journey, there was only one way to make it happen. In late July or early August, Mackay and O'Brien packed their worldly goods into blanket rolls, shouldered their loads, and started walking. They trudged over the Sierras via Henness Pass and descended the eastern slope of the range into the Truckee Meadows, headed south beyond the Truckee River crossing toward Steamboat Springs, then climbed a twenty-three-hundred-foot grade on a trail blazed over the chain of mountains that would come to be known as the Virginia Range. The long trek took them about a week.

Silver! Mackay knew nothing about mining silver. What if the stories were true?

CHAPTER 3

The Lure of
the Washoe Diggings

Underground miners "drifting" for a living,
always hoping for a rich strike.

———

The country looks something like a singed cat, owing to the
scarcity of shrubbery, and also resembles that animal in the
respect that it has more merits than its personal appearance
would seem to indicate.
> —Mark Twain, "Washoe: Information Wanted,"
> *Golden Era*

When Mackay and O'Brien reached Washoe, they looked across a shallow ravine to a small hive of mining activity at the base of a knoll. The knoll sat on the north end of an out-sloping bench that stretched about a mile and a half across the eastern base of Sun Mountain. To their right front, the rugged upper slopes of the mountain rose sharply above the bench to its 7,864-foot summit. The left side of the bench angled down to the east, into the upper reaches of what was known as Six Mile Cañon (pronounced just like the English "canyon"). Mackay and O'Brien examined their immediate environs, learning what they could about the local geography. They surely explored the angled terrace, weaving through sagebrush and protruding rocks as they passed along the base of Sun Mountain, pausing to examine whatever haphazard mining activity they encountered. After rambling a little over a mile down the bench, a small rise took them up to "the Divide" between the Six Mile Cañon and Gold Cañon drainages. Beyond the Divide, Gold Cañon dropped steeply. Contained within its walls, not far from where they stood on the Divide, was the long, low mound of Gold Hill—fifty or sixty feet high, four or five hundred feet long, and about one hundred feet wide—and it was another anthill of activity, striped across from end to end with narrow mining claims. Several dozen men—both claim owners and hired hands—worked on the hill, hacking out masses of crumbly red-tinted quartz from the bottom of open pits and crushing the gold-impregnated material in mortars or arastras, a few of which worked nearby. A long, narrow flume built of rough lumber conveyed water to the claims from a small spring higher up the cañon. Miners used the water to wash gold out of the crushed quartz with rockers.

Below Gold Hill, Gold Cañon sloped south into the Carson River Valley for about two and a half miles to where the drainage passed through a narrow rocky defile called Devil's Gate. Beneath Devil's Gate, the cañon bent to the southeast, and several ravines joined the cañon at a place called the Forks. Downhill from the Forks, the cañon ran southeast for another two or three miles to meet the Carson River, named for renowned frontiersman Kit Carson. The Carson River drainage, all of the Washoe region, and the entire eastern slope of the Sierras lay within another piece of monumental western geography named by John C. Frémont—the Great Basin, that enormous two-hundred-thousand-square-mile desert bowl formed from parts of the modern states of Utah, Idaho, Oregon, California, and nearly the entirety of Nevada, from which no rivers escape to the sea. From perches around the Divide, Mackay and O'Brien could see the first few of the succession of north-south mountain ranges that striated the basin. Between the ranges lay desolate lowlands.

Down where Gold Cañon met the Carson River and the great immigrant road that ran alongside it—the California Trail—gold had been discovered in 1849 and 1850. Perhaps as many as 60,000 gold-crazed men, and a handful of women, stormed down the California Trail in those years. Many of them paused at Gold Cañon to practice the gold-mining skills they'd need in California. Flecks of color generally rewarded their efforts, but in their haste to reach the greater wealth surely waiting on the other side of the Sierras, most simply hurried on. None of them paused to ponder the monumental significance of a gold-bearing cañon in a region geologically unrelated to the western slope of California's Sierra Nevada Mountains. In any event, the rocky, wind-blasted desert topography north of the Carson River held little appeal compared to the Elysian descriptions they'd heard of California. They didn't know it, but in their fevered haste, they were rushing past a concentration of mineral wealth greater than anything that would ever be found in California.

Only one immigrant seems to have decided that Gold Cañon merited permanent settlement in 1850—James Fenimore, more commonly known as "Finney," or "Old Virginia," in homage to his home state. The clearest early memory of Fenimore comes from John Reese, who led a wagon train west from Salt Lake City in the spring of 1851 and reestablished a store and cattle ranch called Mormon Station at the foot of the Sierras, near where the overland trail began the final climb into California.* According to Reese's memory, Fenimore ran a trading post until he'd sold his stock to the overland immigrants, then took up mining and "drinking whisky" in Gold Cañon. Reese described Fenimore living in a small dugout about a mile above the overland road, half underground, tented over with "rags or any old stuff" he could scavenge, and having built a reservoir to help wash his paydirt. Discovering that he lived under Mormon administration in the recently organized Utah Territory probably didn't please James Fenimore—miners were notoriously hostile to Mormons. Although it hardly mattered, because for all practical purposes, Fenimore lived beyond reach of *any* law. John Reese knew of "no other white man . . . settled within 50 or 100 miles," the closest likely being on the western slope of the Sierras on the way to Placerville, in California. In the opposite direction, the nearest settled Caucasian lived more than 500 miles away, near Salt Lake City. Around Fenimore lived members of the nomadic Washoe Indian tribe, the native people whose domain

---

* Mormon Station had operated in 1850 but wasn't permanently occupied until 1851. The settlement changed its name to Genoa (locally pronounced *Ge-noa*, with the accent on the second syllable) in 1855; it's the oldest immigrant settlement in modern Nevada.

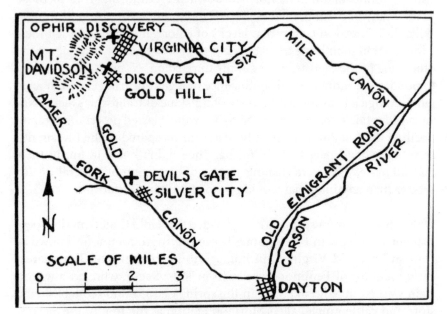

A rough map of the Washoe Diggings.

encompassed the enormous mountain lake they knew as "Tahoe" some eighteen miles to the west and the rugged mountains above Gold Cañon. (Caucasian immigrants called it Lake Bigler in honor of California governor John Bigler until the Civil War, when Bigler's objectionable secessionist sympathies motivated a switch to the native name.) Paiute bands roamed the country to the north and south.

Thirty-three or thirty-four years old in 1851, Fenimore had been born in Parkersburg, Virginia. As with one-fourth to one-fifth of Americans in the middle nineteenth century, Fenimore couldn't read, and he never learned to sign his name. According to persistent rumor, he'd fled to the remote canyons of the western Utah Territory because he'd killed a man in California.

Assuming John Reese's memory was accurate, James "Old Virginia" Fenimore must have done reasonably well in Gold Cañon through the winter of 1850–51, because Reese recalled "a good many" miners trickling back across the Sierra to join Fenimore and work through the following year. In a rare gesture of deference to the local Washoe Indian tribe, miners came to know the locale as the Washoe Diggings. John Reese's cattle thrived in the tall Carson Valley grass, and in exchange for little pouches of gold dust, he and the scattering of other ranchers trying to start cattle stations on the eastern slope sold beef to the Gold Cañon miners at thirty cents per pound. Other settlers, many with ties to Salt Lake City, claimed land in the Carson, Washoe, and Eagle valleys. In late 1854, the *Sacramento Daily Union* reported about fifty men working Gold Cañon "with good prospects, the dirt paying from the surface to six inches below in some instances fifteen cents to the pan" and counted seven or eight hundred other settlers living in Carson Valley, with "three saw and grist mills, either built or in the process of erection, and forty thousand head of stock."

Through the middle 1850s, miners worked Gold Cañon when sufficient water flowed to slosh worthless silts from their rockers. Most returned to California to find jobs or work other claims when the cañon waters failed. Despite the isolation, aridity, and primitive living conditions, the miners suffered the harsh desert climate—almost always either too hot, too cold, or too windy—because the Washoe Diggings paid steady returns. When the miners had sufficient water, the best Gold Cañon claims often yielded an ounce of gold per working day, but average returns held steady at about five dollars per day. Several dozen Chinese built a camp at the mouth of Gold Cañon (originally—and unimaginatively—called "Chinatown," at least by others, Caucasian immigrants changed the locality's name to "Dayton" in 1861) and reworked abandoned placers in the lower cañon. The established Gold Cañon crew left them mostly unmolested.

In warmer weather, most of the men lived near their claims, either outside, beneath the stars, counting on the tight wrap of a wool blanket to fend off the overnight cold, or in canvas tents or shallow dugouts with canvas stretched over crude walls of brush and stacked stones. During the coldest months, those who stayed in Washoe collected in Johntown, a rough mining camp centrally located in lower Gold Cañon, a mile or so below Devil's Gate, where they wintered over in smoky, mud-plastered stone or brush huts, and subsisted on a monotonous diet of beans, bacon, and bread, broken occasionally by beef driven over on the hoof by Carson Valley ranchers or by game hunted nearby. One man who worked the Washoe Diggings in those years described it as a life of "Arcadian" simplicity that provided a "precarious livelihood" to those willing to subject themselves to the backbreaking labor. Among the positives, the men existed in wild freedom, beyond reach of governmental, legal, or ecclesiastical authority. In season, if so inclined, they worked six days a week, gleaning what color they could from the cañon's sediments, their most complicated logistical requirements being "a reasonable stock of whisky and tobacco," without the latter, the miners' existence "would have been intolerable." As for the former, a gallon of whisky that cost thirty-seven and a half cents one hundred miles away in Placerville sold for four dollars in Gold Cañon.

Their Arcadian existence was exclusively an immigrant experience. For the natives of the Washoe and Northern Paiute tribes who had inhabited the region for generations, the white-skinned invasion was an unmitigated disaster. The concept that a man could own land to the exclusion of all others just by making squiggles on a piece of paper tucked into empty cans or whisky bottles and affixed to a post or placed atop a stone cairn eluded them entirely. White settlers fenced the best grazing lands, displacing game animals not decimated by indiscriminate hunting; scorned the Washoe and Northern Paiute as savage "diggers" because part of their diet consisted of roots scratched from the earth, apparently finding some moral distinction between roots eaten by Indians and the potatoes, onions, and garlic common to the diet of the eastern states; and reveled in "progress," unconcerned by the consequences their colonization imposed on the native bands.

As in placer mining regions everywhere, the best locations in Gold Cañon were found, cleaned up to bedrock, and then reworked until the gold-bearing sediments played out. As time passed, Gold Cañon returns declined, just as they had in California. Many Washoe pioneers suspected the mountainous deserts of the eastern slope and the Great Basin harbored vast mineral wealth, and they launched regular expeditions to search for it. They prospected many locations without discovering anything better than what they had in Gold Cañon, where they continued to work without any inkling that they were within a few miles of underground wealth the likes of which the world hadn't found since the heydays of the Spanish empire. Ignorance or sloth didn't delay discovery of the great lode, however. Most of the men mining Gold Cañon had served an apprenticeship in the goldfields of California. They all knew that gold filling a drainage with profitable placer diggings had washed down from somewhere above, and even if they lacked the equipment and capital needed to advantageously work the quartz veins that held the original gold, canny placer miners knew that the most profitable deposits tended to concentrate directly beneath a gold-bearing vein. That knowledge drove them to search for the local mother veins.

Miners soon recognized that although people washing dirt in Gold

Cañon above Devil's Gate continued to find gold, they didn't find enough to "make grub." Experienced miners took that as prima facie evidence that the quartz veins above Devil's Gate didn't contain much of "the necessary"—a perfectly reasonable conclusion. They concentrated their efforts in the more profitable placers in the ravines that converged below Devil's Gate. A thousand feet of elevation higher up Gold and Six Mile cañons, eons of erosion had worn the surface rocks and sediments close to two large ore bodies lurking just beneath the surface in a monster vein hiding in the mountain above, but hadn't actually exposed either one. Without any surface cues to distinguish it from the other quartz croppings running through the Gold and Six Mile cañons' watersheds, only striking one of the ore bodies directly would reveal the great lode.

By the summer of 1857, only the Chinese community and three or four dozen other miners remained in Gold Cañon. Among them were "Old Virginny" James Fenimore, the Irish partners Peter O'Reilly and Patrick McLaughlin, Emanuel "Manny" Penrod, and a man named Henry Tompkins Paige Comstock. The Washoe Diggings wouldn't survive without fresh discoveries.

In a letter Comstock wrote to the *Saint Louis Republican* many years later, he claimed to have trapped in Canada, Michigan, Indiana, and the Rocky Mountains for the American Fur Company, played a part in the Black Hawk War and the Mexican War, and "roved" all over California and Mexico. Comstock's self-descriptions merited caution, however, as many men who knew him would have warned. Long after Comstock's death, a man who had Comstock's acquaintance in the early days described him as "a singular genius, unburdened with virtues," and "a hell of a liar." Manny Penrod, his friend and partner, remembered him more fairly, as a "wild and visionary man who would buy anything that was for sale," paying cash if he had the money or taking possession on credit if he could get it extended.*

The remaining Washoe miners considered Old Virginny the best prospector among them. Dan de Quille, the pen name of William Wright, one of the region's leading journalists in later years, described Fenimore as "fond of the bottle," but "by no means a loafer." Seasons of "great activity" followed his sprees. Finney hiked up Gold Cañon on one of his hunts in the late spring or early summer of 1857. Near the head of the cañon, he huffed up a rise onto "the Divide" between the Gold Cañon and Six Mile

---

* Comstock's few surviving contemporary communications make him sound like Penrod's assessment—enthusiastic, visionary, and a bit self-important.

Cañon drainages, then descended slightly onto the out-sloping bench that ran across the eastern base of Sun Mountain. Old Virginny wandered along the angled terrace, across two shallow washes, to the vicinity of a gulch near its far end.

Downhill, in one of the shallow ravines feeding the top of Six Mile Cañon, Fenimore noticed yellowish dirt similar in color to that which yielded decent dry diggings near the Forks of Gold Cañon. The surface dirt proved to contain profitable quantities of gold. Finney, Manny Penrod, and a handful of others marked out placer claims and systematically worked the ravine's stubborn, arid ground through the summer of 1857, finding color mixed into a heavy clay that needed to be "puddled"—soaked with water in a box or hole and mashed into a loose, muddy pudding before it could be worked through rockers. Despite the additional hassle and the paucity of water, the diggings yielded about five dollars to the hand per day.

About the time Old Virginny and others began puddling their first shovelfuls of Six Mile Cañon's paying clay, two brothers, Allen and Hosea Grosh, came over the mountains from California with a novel idea—to mine silver in the Washoe Diggings. They'd mined there twice before, and their hopes resided in some dark, crumbly rocks they'd picked out of a quartz vein near the Forks of Gold Cañon that they thought contained silver. The Grosh brothers spent the summer of 1857 trying to discover how to get the rock to release the metal. Finally, in a letter to their father, Allen Grosh claimed to have "mastered the rock," possibly having produced small metallic buttons from a few ore samples—which he and his brother hoped would prove to be silver. Then struck a trio of disasters. Desperados murdered the man who had promised to back their silver-mining venture. Forced to work furiously at placer mining to earn enough to lay in winter provisions before the close of the mining season, Hosea Grosh tore a "frightful gash" in his foot with a pick and died of blood poisoning. Trying to get back to California via a late-season crossing of the Sierras, Allen Grosh frostbit his feet and died of gangrene. With him went whatever knowledge of silver in the Washoe Diggings he and his brother had managed to amass.

The Grosh brothers were probably the first persons to attempt to wring silver from hard rock ore veins in the Great Basin, a seminal event in the history of American mining, and although they were ultimately unsuccessful, their tragedy marked a rising interest in the possibilities of quartz mining. Nineteenth-century miners didn't fully comprehend the complex geological and chemical processes that formed quartz veins, but that didn't change the fact of their existence. Tens of thousands of them striated the mountains and canyons of California and the Great Basin. In broad terms, the veins had formed when hot, high-pressure groundwater carrying dissolved silicon dioxide—quartz, one of the most common mineral compounds—circulated up from deep underground into faults and fissures in the earth's crust. As the pressure relaxed and the water cooled, the silicon dioxide precipitated out of solution, filling the cracks and crevices with masses of milky quartz. (Although called quartz "veins," they more closely resembled "sheets" hanging underground, surrounded on both sides by the worthless "country rock"; they presented a visible linear vein only on the surface.) In some instances, other dissolved substances such as sulfur and calcium traveled in the hot water solutions along with the silicon dioxide and, sometimes, so did such common metallic elements as copper, iron, and lead. As they fell out of solution, those dissolved materials formed minerals, most of which weren't valuable. But sometimes, on rare occasions, the solutions of hot, circulating groundwater forced up from below managed to dissolve, transport, and deposit gold and silver and other elements into complex mineral compounds. If the concentrations of precious metals rose high enough, *those* quartz veins could be valuable, and in the rarest of instances, they could be *extremely* valuable. Complicating matters, silver ores, even in spectacularly high concentrations, didn't at all resemble the "native" metal they contained.

The Washoe miners of the 1850s had little idea how to recognize mineral ores, let alone exploit them. They knew placer gold, and through years of bitter labor, they'd come to know it well. They also knew that quartz veins in California and Washoe held tiny particles of gold—inside the quartz, gold specks were sometimes visible to the naked eye. The problem of mining quartz was profitably separating the precious metal from the "gangue," the valueless surrounding matter, either by developing a vein with a sufficiently high gold concentration or by efficient, low-cost extraction of the metal from a lower-grade vein. Either alternative compounded mining's many risks. Extracting gold from quartz demanded much more investment of time and money than placer mining, and no matter how fabulous the quartz samples that motivated a man to invest in a vein, or "lode," there was no guarantee that quality ore existed at greater depth. And unlike placer mining, quartz mining paid no immediate return. "Opening" or "developing" a vein required weeks, and sometimes months, of nonpaying dead work. Mining the ore required even more time and money, as did the "milling" or "reducing," the mechanical and chemical process or processes that extracted metal from the ore. Only when the full reduction process was complete did the true value of an ore reveal itself, and a man had to support himself that entire time. California's various quartz crazes had bankrupted many miners and investors.

Undeterred, and inspired by the show of fine gold, plain to the naked eye, mineralized into a milky quartz vein near Devil's Gate, a group of Washoe miners banded together in 1858 and formed the "Pioneer Quartz Company." Since the risks and difficulties of quartz mining differed greatly from those of placer mining, they wrote a set of by-laws to cover quartz claims, the first codification of quartz-mining law east of the Sierra Nevada—another watershed moment in American mining history. Unlike a gold placer, in which the metal was diffused—or potentially diffused—through an entire area of sediments, in quartz mining, only the material of the vein or "lode" held any expectation of value. A quartz vein showed just a line at the surface, known as the "croppings." Quartz claims therefore divided that line—"the line of the lode"—into distinct slices. To offset the much heavier initial expenses of quartz mining, the rules the Pioneer Quartz Company wrote allowed each man to claim and hold six hundred linear feet of ground "on the line of the lode." (That number was later reduced to three hundred feet and then to two hundred feet per man to spread the wealth—or potential wealth—more democratically.) And since nobody knew a surefire way of telling how a lode might angle—or change angles—beneath the surface of the earth, between the two end lines of a quartz claim, owners had the right to follow the "dips, spurs, and angles" of the lode, or "lead," wherever it went underground.*

The Pioneer Quartz Company built an arastra to crush what they hoped would prove to be ore. (By mining definition, it's not "ore" if it won't pay.) They dug a circular hole in the ground about ten feet in diameter and eighteen inches deep, and paved the floor and walls with flat stones. They sank a round post in the center, steadied the post with framing timbers anchored to the arastra's rim that allowed the post to rotate, and mortised timber arms into the center post below the anchor frame so the arms could rotate within the sunken circle. They tied heavy drag rocks to the timber arms with strong ropes or rawhide cords and attached a long sweep to the top of the center post, the end of which extended well beyond the rim of the circle. The company "charged"— meaning filled—the arastra with quartz from their promising vein,

---

* In mining law, those are termed "extralateral rights."

added thirty or forty pounds of quicksilver and a dose of salt, hitched a mule and a horse to the long sweep, and started marching the animals in circles. As the animals turned the sweep, the center post and the timber arms rotated, and the drag rocks following behind crushed the quartz against the paving stones. They marched the animals in circles for *three weeks* to pulverize the quartz and stir the mixture, then rocked out the amalgam with a cradle. Down in Johntown, the company heated the amalgam in a frying pan, taking care not to inhale the fumes as the mercury cooked away. The mass shriveled. The resulting bullion weighed a mere six ounces and assayed at forty-four dollars, a minuscule return for a month's labor of eight men, and a "cold bath" for the Pioneer Quartz Company. The company dissolved and the men returned to placer mining.

Although he hadn't belonged to the Pioneer Quartz Company, Old Virginia took some interest in the local quartz that season. Fenimore claimed a plainly visible quartz "lead" running across the eastern face of Sun Mountain, at the upper edge of the out-sloping bench. When he refused to name the lead, another man named it "the Virginia Lead" in his honor. Fenimore did nothing to develop it, but none of the other miners disputed his claim. (Old Virginia's quartz lead wouldn't ever become a profitable mining claim, but in the hands of other men, it would prove to be a perfectly positioned "fighting claim" from which to dispute the ownership of other leads that would soon be located nearby.)

Many more miners abandoned the Washoe Diggings that year. Only a stubborn handful remained to sweat subsistence wages from the pale, lightweight gold found in Six Mile Cañon through the spring, summer, and fall of 1858. As a mining region, the Washoe Diggings teetered toward extinction.

Late in the year, a hard freeze stopped the water flowing in Gold and Six Mile cañons and ended the mining season. The men retreated from the cold, high bench to their warmer, less windy, lower elevation accommodations in Johntown. Not until late January did a spell of mild weather start water running in the gulches and ravines of Gold and Six Mile cañons. Fenimore used the improved weather to prospect for new diggings. Exploring the spur east of Gold Cañon with John Bishop and two other men, Fenimore pointed to a low, flat-topped hillock lying inside upper Gold Cañon like a sandbag. Fenimore knew it from previous hunting expeditions. "Boys, I believe there are some good diggings over there," he said. "In a few days, we will go over and try it."

The others deferred to Fenimore's experience, and on Friday, January

28, 1859, the four men made the three-mile uphill slog from Johntown to examine the hillock. Fenimore took note of the mound's yellowish dirt, similar to other modestly profitable spots he'd worked in the region. John Bishop kicked dirt into a pan with his boot and carried the full pan to a rivulet trickling from an "Indian spring" in a stand of willows on a nearby hillside. Swirled down to paydirt, Bishop found about fifteen cents worth of flourlike fine gold in the bottom of the pan. Fenimore got good color from dirt scooped from a nearby gopher hole. Other pans the men tested yielded between eight and fifteen cents worth of gold, a "fair prospect" by any local measure. Fenimore rambled up the main drainage and discovered a small spring from which water could be flumed to the little mound. Returning to the others, Fenimore pronounced it a good location. The group staked four adjoining placer claims along the line of the little hill, each one fifty feet wide and four hundred feet long. After measuring the ground, the foursome wondered what to name their new location. Since it was "decidedly not Gold Cañon," in the opinion of John Bishop, the new ground being a little hill, they settled on "Gold Hill."

On Sunday, most of the male residents of Johntown hiked up Gold Cañon to "pass upon" the new location. Nothing about the sagebrush-covered mound impressed them. So-called Gold Hill didn't seem likely to out-earn the claims they had in the lower canyon. However, a few days later, Henry Comstock, a lapsed Mormon named James Rogers, Joseph Plato, Alexander "Sandy" Bowers, and William Knight added one last fifty-by-four-hundred-foot claim to the Gold Hill mound, assigning ten feet to each man—the group "Comstock & Co." referred to in the published May 20 letter that probably contributed to Mackay and O'Brien's rising interest in Washoe.

More freezing weather delayed the start of the mining campaign. The original locators constructed a crude lumber flume to convey water to their new claims. At the first thaw, likely in early April, they began washing Gold Hill's top dirt through their rockers and found themselves making about five dollars a day—a decent return, but nothing spectacular. However, returns improved as the miners dug deeper into the yellowish dirt. Within a fortnight, the men were cleaning up $20 to $40 per working day. Those quantities of "the needful" converted the "Johntown unbelievers." Almost to a man, Johntown's thirty or forty residents moved three miles up-cañon to Gold Hill, where they took up residence in hastily erected tents, huts, and shanties or simply cast their blankets on the ground and slept under the stars. Some went to work for the original claim holders; some prospected nearby gulches, ravines, and hillsides hoping to make similar strikes; others opened businesses catering to the needs of the new camp. A few feet below the surface of the flat-topped mound, the miners began encountering crumbly quartz masses shot through with gold flecks. Blows from their hammers and picks easily crushed the quartz. Running the resulting grains through their rockers doubled their earnings again.

The Gold Hill miners soon made a most unwelcome discovery. About ten feet below the surface, the gold-bearing quartz chunks interspersed in their yellowish paydirt coalesced into a single reddish quartz mass, still friable, but nevertheless a dismaying discovery for the original locators. Suddenly finding themselves owning quartz mines instead of the rich placer ground they'd been rooting through for several weeks, they faced the same difficulties that had dogged the Pioneer Quartz Company, whose failure the previous year loomed fresh. The unwelcome revelation put many of them in a mind to sell and touched off a confused frenzy of interest in claiming the nearby quartz croppings in the hopes that some of them might prove valuable—or, better yet, sellable.

Among the dozens of vague location notices tagged to the surrounding croppings, three men drove a stake downhill from the Gold Hill mound and scribbled out a crude note: "We the undersigned claim Twelve hundred (1200) feet of this Quartz Vain including all of its depths & Spurs commencing at Houseworth claim and running north including twenty-five of surface on each Side of the Vain." While examining the ground, one of the men bumbled into a yellow jacket nest. The ferocious little insects inspired their naming: They called their "Vain" the Yellow Jacket.

The miners didn't create a formal Gold Hill Mining District until June 1, and the Yellow Jacket's location notice didn't make it into the record book for another three weeks after that. The record book, filled out in pencil and stored behind a crude camp bar, was soon so full of erasures as to render parts of it indecipherable. The barkeep, a friend to many of the miners, could easily be encouraged to wipe his whisky glasses while one of his many associates enjoyed private time with the record book. Miners had enormous incentive to keep their claim boundaries loose. No man could see into the earth, and every one of them feared cutting themselves off from a hidden bonanza. Much better the potentialities contained within fungible boundary lines. The vagaries of the Yellow Jacket's location notice and of the many smudgy claims suddenly clogging the record book gave them a propensity to "float." As a Comstock historian working under the auspices of the United States Geological Survey wrote in 1883, "every man naturally wished to cut off the richest slice of the prospective bonanza and was not disposed to cut the loaf until he knew its contents." In the years ahead, only protracted, expensive, and often corrupt legal warfare proved capable of pinning down their boundary lines.

The madcap excitement boiled to an evil head on May 28. William Sides stabbed John Jessup to death with a Bowie knife over a dispute at cards. Jessup was a popular man, the first person buried in Gold Hill. Most of the local miners traveled the fifteen miles to attend and serve in the "People's Trial" of Sides that convened in Carson City on May 31. The "mustang" court summoned 48 jurors, of whom 12 cast votes—8 for conviction, 4 for acquittal—and although Sides eluded the noose, the vigilantes still held him in custody a week later, perhaps to shield him from the reprisals of Jessup's friends.

Two of the few miners who remained behind in Washoe were Patrick McLaughlin and Peter O'Reilly. Left out of the Gold Hill claims and fed up with their prospects, they only wanted to raise sufficient means to finance a journey to diggings on the East Walker River, one hundred miles to the south. With most of the other miners decamped to the trial for several days, McLaughlin thought it a good opportunity to try his suspicion that decent placer deposits lurked beneath the thick bed of clay that James Fenimore, Manny Penrod, and a few others had worked atop the previous year on the bench at the head of Six Mile Cañon. McLaughlin and O'Reilly didn't own the ground in question, although the various claims could perhaps have been considered abandoned for neglect. In any case, nobody was around to say them nay, so the two Irishmen hefted their tools and hiked up the Divide and across the natural out-sloping bench to the diggings near the top of Six Mile Cañon.

To test McLaughlin's theory, the two Irishmen hacked a trench through the clay bed near the head of the flat. With only a trickle of water "scarcely an inch and a half" wide available, they got poor results from their labors, only $1.50 to $2 per working day. To improve earnings, McLaughlin and O'Reilly needed to wash more dirt, and to wash more dirt, they needed more water. In an effort to maximize their supply, they decided to shovel out a reservoir in the little rivulet some yards above their cut. On the chosen site, they heaved out spadefuls of yellowish sand mixed with lumps of crumbly quartz. About four feet down, they struck a bluish-black layer of frangible rock about six inches thick. Although the crumbly substance was substantially heavier than the surrounding strata, it was barely hard enough to qualify as "rock." They could crumble it with their fingers.

They'd never seen anything like it. On a whim, they crushed some of the strange substance and ran the debris through their rocker. They gawked as the lighter sediments rinsed away. Thick lines of gold dust shimmered behind the riffle bars. Flabbergasted, they attacked the crumbly black stuff in earnest. Once crushed, each successive bucketful yielded a similar flush of color. The residue, they tossed aside. Working the trench, they'd been cleaning up about an eighth of an ounce of gold per day—now, they had whole ounces of the stuff piled behind the riffle bars. The gold seemed lighter and paler than that normally found in Six Mile Cañon, which was itself lighter in color and weight than California gold, and the two Irishmen worried that they'd uncovered some bogus variety, hitherto unknown, but pale or not, if they were fingering the genuine article, they'd picked out a season's worth of dust in just a few hours. By evening, they'd gleaned nearly $300, with one last cleanup yet to make.*

The overjoyed Irishmen had just paced off the boundaries of a placer claim when Henry Comstock rode up on a pony. He hadn't attended the trial, either. Comstock's buzzard eyes caught sight of the yellow harvest glittering on the apron of the Irishmen's rocker. "You have struck it, boys!" he exclaimed, leaping from his horse. The gaunt miner fell to his knees and inspected the blackish streak. Although the yield of his Gold Hill claim had put Comstock into money the likes of which he'd never touched in his life, that didn't stop him from wanting a piece of any other action that might develop elsewhere in the Washoe Diggings. Comstock hoisted himself up and gave the Irishmen a trifecta of bad news— that James Fenimore, Joe Kirby, James White, and William Hart[†] had a prior placer claim to the location, that he and his friend Manny Penrod owned nine-tenths of the water from the spring they were using (Old Virginny owned the last tenth), and that he, Henry Comstock, claimed the surrounding 160 acres for "ranching purposes." They were therefore trespassing on his land and using his water. To make things right, he demanded the two Irishmen take him and Manny Penrod into their location as equal partners.

Although O'Reilly and McLaughlin recognized that Comstock's land claim had just sprung full grown from his imagination, proving otherwise was difficult, especially to the satisfaction of a jury in a miner's court packed with his longtime friends. After a brief consultation, the two Irishmen quieted Comstock's demands by admitting him and Penrod to

* They probably made the strike between June 8 and June 12, 1859.
† In some sources, he is called James Hart.

their claim. As compensation, having two additional men in the group meant they could stake off more ground, which, if the strike proved extensive, would increase the value of their holding.

"Clearing title" to the claim was the next order of business. The new partners camouflaged the strike and called Penrod into consultation. If the four previous claimants got any inkling that $300 had been washed from their formerly modest placer ground in a single day, they'd manifest renewed interest in a property they were currently neglecting. Given Penrod's reputation for "honesty and good sense," O'Reilly and McLaughlin wanted him to approach the others and acquire their interests. Penrod suggested otherwise. His straightforward, businesslike demeanor might tip the others to the fact that the ground held "something good." Considering Comstock's well-known propensity to buy most anything put up for sale, and to pay with cash if he had it, Penrod thought Comstock better suited to getting signatures or the marks of illiterate men on bills of sale and quitclaim deeds without raising the other men's suspicions. Hoary mining legend says that Comstock traded a "superannuated," "bob-tail horse" and "divers [sic] bottles of exhilarating fluids" to Fenimore for his share of the spring—"a fact which no one having any acquaintance with the convivial habits and commercial usages of those Washoe Pioneers [would] feel inclined to call into question," Henry de Groot wrote many years after he had worked alongside them in the diggings. No matter the exact particulars, Old Virginny, Joe Kirby, and James White made themselves the butt of what is perhaps the worst deal in American mining history when, for either thirty-five or fifty dollars in coin (supplied by Manny Penrod), and with or without the bob-tail horse and the ardent spirits, Comstock secured all three of their signatures on a quitclaim and bill of sale for the water and the claim. Comstock was unable to locate William Hart, who had left the area.

Despite that point of remaining vulnerability, with the grimy, smudged documents in hand, Comstock, Penrod, O'Reilly, and McLaughlin resumed mining, stripping the overburden from the pay streak as they worked uphill. According to Penrod, they all thought they were mining "a continuation of the placers that had been worked lower down on the flat." Crushing the bluish, blackish substance, and washing the results through three rockers, the cleanup continued to be spectacular, about $300 per rocker, per day, even as the dark, auriferous streak thickened and solidified. Their only real complaint was the difficulty the heavy, bruise-colored substance gave their quicksilver. "The troublesome black stuff," as they termed it, clung to the mercury and hindered its ability to amalgamate with the gold. But however annoying, it was hard to take such an objection seriously when some single pans filled with the crushed substance yielded multiple ounces of gold.

About June 12, their pay streak "dipped," as miners say, meaning that it suddenly changed directions and angled down into the ground at about forty-five degrees. The blackish substance had continued to harden, and Penrod became convinced they were working a quartz lead and should claim it as such, since that would allow them to reserve much more ground. The others scoffed, saying it was "only a crevice washed out by a current of water." They were on to the richest placer ground they'd ever imagined. They didn't want to mine quartz. The character of the rock hadn't changed, washing the pay streak continued as rich as ever, and if they staked off a much larger quartz claim and it eventually proved to be placer ground, they would be rendered vulnerable to "jumpers." Penrod harangued his partners until Comstock agreed to help him stake and measure the ground as a quartz claim, which allowed them to reserve three hundred feet per man, plus an additional three hundred feet for discovering the lode. In total, the four partners claimed fifteen hundred feet "on the line of the lode."

In such a small mining district, with such a tight-knit group of men, most of whom had known each other for several seasons, containing news of such magnitude proved impossible. Comstock's disappearing over the Divide to Six Mile Cañon for a few days running when he held excellent ground right in front of the camp at Gold Hill would have been remarked upon, as would their fat dust pouches. Nothing prevented other men from wandering over to have a look, and within a few days, the Gold Hill and Gold Cañon miners cottoned to the fact that O'Reilly, McLaughlin, Comstock, and Penrod were harvesting gold by the pound. (Penrod claimed they were making $300 per day, per rocker, which means, if calculated from the $12.50-per-ounce value of the local gold, they were rocking out roughly four and a half *pounds* of gold per day.) With the ground staked off, title apparently cleared, and Comstock running his fingers through dozens of ounces of gold, nothing could stop him from crowing about the mine, "his mine," as he told it. Word of the strike spread to townsfolk and ranchers in and around Carson City, Genoa, Washoe and Eagle valleys, and the Truckee Meadows. Men flocked to the site like condors drawn to an ox carcass, and all comers raced to stake claims as close as possible to the strikes, just as had happened at Gold Hill.

When local miner and rancher Joseph Winters learned that William

Hart's signature wasn't on the bill of sale and quitclaim, he found the man and got his signature for "a horse and $20 in coin." Winters returned to Six Mile Cañon with the bill of sale. McLaughlin, O'Reilly, Comstock, and Penrod bowed to the inevitable and admitted him to their partnership.

Although the pay continued superb, the sooty, bruise-like streak solidified into what was definitely a rock, in places obligating the little company to crush it with axes and hammers and to further pulverize its harder nodules in a mortar. Then, about a week after its discovery, the streak merged into a quartz lead about four feet wide. In gratitude, the three other members of the company awarded Comstock and Penrod one hundred feet of the claim in compensation for the one day of work they'd sacrificed to measure out the ground as a quartz claim and for the nine-tenths of the small spring Comstock said they owned. Penrod and Comstock took their segregated section two hundred feet from the south end of the claim, a nice little hundred-foot slice just the two of them owned.

The unwelcome quartz discovery obligated the company to invest in arastras. On June 22, they drew up a contract with J. A. Osborne, a Kentucky native known locally as "Kentuck," admitting him to the company as equal partner in exchange for building two arastras and providing horses or mules to power them. Jolts of whisky probably cemented the deal, "a drink all 'round" being, for the Washoe pioneers, "not only a pledge of friendship but a token with which they sealed all bargains." The agreement brought to six the total number of people in what, in the record book, was officially termed "Penrod, Comstock & Co." (which wasn't the same Comstock & Co. that owned a slice of Gold Hill).

Miners wouldn't understand the exact nature of what the two Irishmen had found for another several years, but they'd struck the top of a truly gigantic "fissure vein" that came to the surface along the out-sloping bench running across the eastern slopes of Sun Mountain. The flurry of claiming activity kept the recorder of the local mining districts furiously busy— one for Gold Hill and another for the area of the new diggings at the top of Six Mile Cañon. Amid the claiming frenzy, fourteen men banded together into the Sierra Nevada Mining Company and "located" thirty-six hundred feet immediately north of the Union mine, which had already claimed ground adjacent to Penrod, Comstock & Company's north line. Two members of the Sierra Nevada group were B. Augustus Harrison, who ran cattle on the Truckee Meadows,* and J. F. Stone, keeper of Stone & Gates' crossing on the Truckee River. Stone had formerly mined quartz in California, and the "blasted black stuff" being crushed and cast aside on the Comstock claim piqued his interest. The rock's weight made him suspect a high metallic content. Stone scavenged a few chunks and gave them to Harrison, who took them over the Sierras to Judge James Walsh, another veteran quartz miner. Like everybody else who had thus far encountered the odd blackish material, Walsh had never seen its like before. Walsh gave specimens to two professional assayers: J. J. Ott in Nevada City and Grass Valley's Melville Atwood. The assayers tested the material on June 27, 1859. Ott's investigation returned a value of $840 per ton in gold. That was itself a fortune, but Atwood's results were so astounding that he felt compelled to repeat his examinations. The second test confirmed the first. Besides the gold, the "black stuff" contained *three thousand dollars* per ton in silver. Over in Washoe, Comstock and his companions had been crushing it and washing out the gold for two weeks, but just casting aside the bluish-black tailings.

Atwood and Walsh showed the substance to an Irish metallurgist named Richard Killaha and several German assayers with experience in the silver mines of Saxony. All of them identified the black rock as a rich "sulphuret of silver," as nineteenth-century miners termed the many varieties of silver ore formed around silver-sulfur combinations, none of which looked anything like "native" silver.[†]

Walsh asked the others what they thought he should do.

Go to Washoe, they said.

Nobody who came into contact with the ore proved capable of keeping their lips sealed. Judge Walsh and his partner, Joseph Woodworth, headed for Washoe on Wednesday, June 29, 1859. Among the first in the know was Almarin B. Paul, who owned a quartz mill in Nevada City. Paul told his friend George Hearst, a Missourian who owned a moderately profitable quartz mine and mill nearby. Reared on the harsh Missouri frontier, Hearst had managed crude iron mines and a small farm manned by a few slaves before coming west to California in 1850, where he had

---

* The modern city of Reno, Nevada, is built on what were then called the Truckee Meadows.

† Acanthite (Ag_2S) predominated among Comstock ores, but argentite, stephanite, and polybasite were also common.

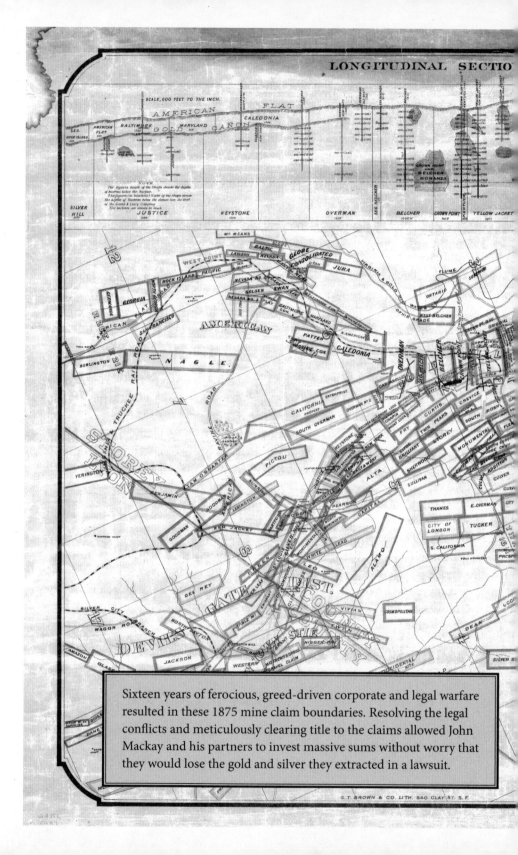

Sixteen years of ferocious, greed-driven corporate and legal warfare resulted in these 1875 mine claim boundaries. Resolving the legal conflicts and meticulously clearing title to the claims allowed John Mackay and his partners to invest massive sums without worry that they would lose the gold and silver they extracted in a lawsuit.

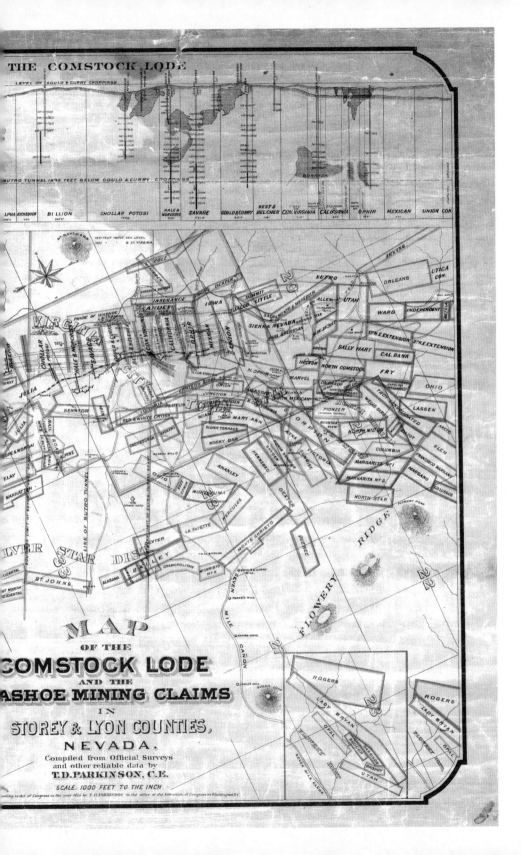

THE COMSTOCK LODE

MAP
OF THE
COMSTOCK LODE
AND THE
WASHOE MINING CLAIMS
IN
STOREY & LYON COUNTIES,
NEVADA.
Compiled from Official Surveys
and other reliable data by
T.D. PARKINSON, C.E.

SCALE. 1000 FEET TO THE INCH.

mined placers, kept a store, farmed, raised cattle, and worked quartz, all without much distinction. He was one of the first to dog Judge Walsh's tracks into the mountains.*

Judge Walsh and his cohorts needed several days to cross the spine of the Sierras and reach Washoe. According to an article written five months later, when Walsh arrived as the first man bearing the fantastic secret of the soft bluish-black rock, he found Comstock, Penrod, Winters, O'Reilly, and McLaughlin casually working their claim, content to turn themselves out long after sunrise, set mules to work turning the sweeps of their arastras, and then spend a few hours either hacking gold-bearing quartz and the soft black rock out of their lead or washing the previous day's arastra crushings through rockers with the scarce midsummer water. They laid off every afternoon, content to clean up a hundred dollars from half a day of halfhearted labor without doing much to explore or test the diggings, while a mile and a half to the south, over the Divide on Gold Hill, the miners, according to the article, "united the usual vice and recklessness of mining with indolence," and used "the rocker mainly to pay their gambling debts." Old Virginny James Fenimore excepted—according to the story, he was using his rocker to wash out "whisky money."

The article's author cast Judge Walsh as the first of the "intelligent gentlemen" to push Washoe mining development, but his scorn did a grave injustice to the original locators in both Gold and Six Mile cañons. Although none of them possessed the black stuff's secret, they were placer miners with many years of experience who knew they'd made an incredible strike. They suspected the presence of silver, but considered it a bad indication. Silver ores were notoriously "stubborn," "refractory," or "rebellious," meaning difficult to reduce, and everyone knew the famous Spanish mining aphorism that went, "To work a mine of silver, one needs a mine of gold." The owners of the claim just south of Comstock, Penrod & Company had struck the vein and found a one-ounce chunk of native silver. They showed it to Manny Penrod and swore him to secrecy, not wanting the silver discovery to "injure the sale of their mine as a gold mine." Worse, if the black stuff and the quartz continued to solidify, they'd soon have a hard time crushing it without industrial-scale investments for which they had neither the capital, the know-how, nor the inclination. With notions of selling out, absolutely the last thing in the world they wanted to do was expose the bottom of the vein. They had no way of knowing whether they were ingesting the best portion of a rich quartz

* William Randolph Hearst of yellow journalism fame would be George Hearst's son.

vein that pinched off thirty feet below the surface or nibbling at the top of a massive underground bonanza. Given the unhappy history of quartz mining, the former seemed by far the more likely alternative. That being the case, it served the best interests of the original locators to chip at the rich ore without working overhard to plumb the mine's dimensions.

The strategic intelligence of the original locators lounging under the shade trees was therefore on perfect display when Judge Walsh rode onto the diggings and found that the only one of the original company's assets doing a full day's work was Henry Comstock's mouth. From the minute the trail-weary judge and his companion dismounted, Comstock extolled the wonders of the mine. To them and to everybody else drawn to the site in the coming days, Comstock lauded the strike from the moment he shook loose from his bedroll until long after the sun dropped behind Sun Mountain, and people soon found themselves referring to the location as "Comstock's ground," "Comstock's mine," "Comstock's lead," or "Comstock's vein," where, as Henry Comstock never tired of telling, he and his mates had hacked open the apex of the biggest, richest, deepest, most wonderful mine ever revealed in North America. And since, in the real world of sweat, dirt, toil, and quartz beneath the unblinking sun, neither Henry Comstock nor anyone else could see farther into the ground than the point of the next pick stroke, Comstock's relentless "puffery," which would both affix his name to the greatest lode of precious metals ever discovered in the United States and cut him from its ownership, was nothing more than the diligent endeavor of a hardworking salesman. As he was the mouthpiece of a company of original locators interested in selling for a high price, Comstock's braggadocio made perfect sense. Quite simply, he was "kiting" the mine.

Judge Walsh, George Hearst, and a few other Grass Valley and Nevada City miners remained in Washoe for a week, and although they probably didn't communicate the full extent of what they knew about the ore to the men of the original company, that knowledge coupled to what they saw inclined them toward buying the ground. They went back to California to secure financing.

In truth, buying into the mine would be an enormous gamble. Even the men with knowledge of the Grass Valley assays didn't have total confidence in the results, since the assays had tested only small ore fragments. The only way to know if bulk quantities were as rich as the assays claimed was to reduce the ore in large quantities, and nobody had anything except guesses as to how much that might cost.

James Walsh returned to Washoe toward the end of July, his financial resources augmented by those of his partner, Joseph Woodworth. The two men camped with Comstock near the claim, which the original locators had started calling "the Ophir mine" or "Ophir Diggings" in honor of the mythical gold mines of the Old Testament. Henry Comstock sang its praises at every opportunity, declaring with complete conviction that the mine he was considering selling would "turn out to be one of the biggest in the world" and that the barren site where they sat would blossom into a great city.

To be induced to sell, Comstock wanted monies sufficient to set himself up in business and free him from the rigors of mining. Walsh wouldn't pay over any cash without the opportunity to test a bulk quantity of ore. Negotiations between Comstock and Penrod and Judge Walsh dragged on for more than a week before the parties agreed to contingent sales on August 12. Provided a large-scale test of the "blue stuff" in San Francisco satisfied Walsh's expectations, Walsh would pay $11,000 for Comstock's one-sixth of the original locators' claim and the half-interest in two hundred feet of ground in a nearby claim Comstock had somehow managed to acquire, Comstock's interest in the spring water, and his mysterious "ranche on the aforementioned village of Ophir" on which so much had hinged, and $5,500 for Penrod's one-sixth portion of the original claim. (Penrod may have accepted the smaller sum because he didn't own an interest in Comstock's "ranche" and held none of the nearby ground.) Walsh gave Comstock ten dollars in coin to secure the deal and began stowing ore into sacks for mules to freight over the mountains to the Fulsom railhead, by train to Sacramento,* and thence downriver to San Francisco on a steamship. The arrangement delighted Henry Comstock. He expected it to fix him for life, and he still retained one-half interest in the hundred-foot section segregated to him and Penrod for staking off the claim. To the miners who'd been working the Washoe Diggings for years, $11,000 seemed a fantastic amount of cash money to pay for a one-sixth interest in an unproven mine. Beyond Walsh's hearing, Comstock and his Washoe cronies called Walsh "the California Rock Sharp," with disparaging irony.

Despite the plethora of activity spread across the eastern and southeastern flanks of Sun Mountain, the only profitable locations remained those in the rich quartz at Gold Hill and those near the site where Patrick McLaughlin and Peter O'Reilly had cut the ore lead three months before.

---

*The twenty-two-mile stretch of track was the only railroad on the Pacific Slope in 1859.

Nobody knew whether the region's mineral wealth concentrated into a narrowly defined lode or diffused throughout the dozens, even hundreds, of quartz croppings that laced the local mountainsides. The perceived value of the mining claims rose and fell as the picks and shovels uncovered new evidence.

Over the summer, Alva Gould and Abram Curry* had acquired what they thought was twelve hundred feet of ground on the direct line between the Ophir strike and Gold Hill. Alva Gould couldn't believe his good fortune when he found a newcomer willing to pay $450 in gold coin for his share of what had become known as "Gould & Curry's ground." None of the Washoe miners thought him a dunce when he got boiled on rotgut whisky the night he closed the deal and rode a horse down Gold Cañon yelling, "I've fooled the Californian!"

Not a trace of ore had turned up on the claim he'd just sold.

Carrying some three thousand pounds of the blue-black ore, Judge Walsh's mule train started the 125-mile plod over the mountains on August 14, 1859. Walsh's departure precipitated a cascade of deals as, one after another, the original locators succumbed to the temptation of a sure thing and sold out. Perhaps fearing the failure of Walsh's large-scale test, Patrick McLaughlin granted George Hearst a $3,500 option to buy his one-sixth interest in the Ophir mine. Hearst raced back to Nevada City to hunt up coin.

James Walsh returned to Washoe from San Francisco on September 9 and closed his deals with Comstock and Penrod. On the three thousand pounds of ore Walsh had taken "below" and smelted at Mosheimer & Kustel's Smelting Works in San Francisco, he'd profited $4,871 *after* deducting the costs of transportation and smelting. Hearst completed his purchase of McLaughlin's interest on September 23, 1859, the first example of his uncanny ability to acquire profitable mining property at bedrock prices.[†]

John "Kentuck" Osborne and V. A. Houseworth,[‡] another old Washoeite who'd located ground adjacent to the Yellow Jacket near Gold Hill and had managed to gain a fractional slice of the original Ophir company, sold soon thereafter, for modest four-figure sums. Patrick O'Reilly held out for another month and did much better, selling his one-sixth interest for $40,000 on October 20. O'Reilly's compatriots ridiculed the "wild

---

* Variously "Alvah" and "Abraham."

† George Hearst would develop some of the best mines in the West, among them the Ontario and Bingham Canyon mines in Utah; the Anaconda Mine in Butte, Montana; and the Homestake Mine in South Dakota. (Hearst is "the heavy" who arrives in camp in the second season of the serial drama *Deadwood*.)

‡ Also "Housworth."

enthusiast" who paid such a fantastic sum. Of the original company, only the Winters brothers refused to sell. They joined Walsh, Hearst, and several other California purchasers and incorporated what they called the Ophir Mining Company.

Comstock and Penrod also sold the segregated hundred feet they owned independent of the original company that season. That ground ended up in the possession of Gabriel Maldonado and Thomas J. Hughes.* Maldonado, a Sonoran with experience in Mexican silver mines, set the mine to work in the fashion of his homeland, and Washoe miners began calling the location "the Spanish Mine," or "the Mexican." To capitalize on his certainty that the mines would birth a great city, Henry Comstock invested the proceeds of his sales in mercantile supplies. In the grand tradition of Sam Brannan, crier of the Gold Rush, Comstock intended to open a store.

Similar sell-outs and consolidations occurred in the surrounding ground and over the divide in Gold Hill. Old Virginny parted with his remaining Gold Hill interests for $2,000, likely the largest sum of money he'd ever held in his life. The confusing array of joining and dividing transactions left the Gold Hill mound striped with many small claims. The end of October saw most of the original sales completed.

Among those in the know in Washoe, the new mines provoked wild excitement. However, on the other side of the Sierras, the California mining community took the reports at a substantial discount, and although the state's newspapers teemed with articles extolling the rich discovery through August, September, and October, they provoked no general rush over the mountains. The Washoe population grew from a few dozen to several hundred.

John Mackay probably arrived at "Comstock's Lode" and the Ophir mine around the time Henry Comstock, Manny Penrod, and Judge Walsh settled on the terms of their contingent sales. Those three fortunate men and others of the old Washoe miners, such as James Fenimore and J. A. "Kentuck" Osborne, controlled either thousands of dollars' worth of coin or valuable mining property. John Mackay didn't own an inch of ground and he didn't have so much as a dime.

Flat broke, and with other men already holding the most promising ground, Mackay didn't bother locating a claim, and he didn't try to horn his way into one already existing, as so many others had done. Nor did

---

* Sometimes Francis J. Hughes.

he join the herd of prospectors grubbing over the surrounding mountainsides in hopes of finding their own rich location—or one with "indications" they could "puff" and sell to an unsuspecting "flat," as "sharps" called overeager mine investors. Instead, John Mackay did what he'd done all his life, what he did best. He went to work. With the sleeves of his flannel shirt pushed up his arms, Mackay hefted a pick and shovel and hacked at the ore lead, a common miner in one of the surface pits on or around Ophir Diggings, sweating in the late-summer sun and earning four dollars a day. He came to know the local lore and all the significant local characters, at least by sight, and he participated in and observed all mining developments firsthand as a core member of the local mining community.

With the mines developing nicely, the camp at the site of the strike in upper Six Mile Cañon needed a name. The Washoeites proposed various options. Ophir, Ophir Diggings, Ophirtown, Pleasant Hill, Mount Pleasant Hill, and Win-e-moca, for the esteemed chief of the Paiute Indians, all received consideration. On September 24, the *Territorial Enterprise* reported, "The miners at Ophir Diggings have changed the name of their locality to Virginia City, in honor of Mr. Berry" (a misprint of "Finney").* A letter to the *Sacramento Daily Union* explained that the name hadn't been bestowed as "indicative of his immaculate virtue," but to honor the man most responsible for Washoe development.

"Virginia City," "Virginiatown," or just plain "Virginia" wasn't an immediate success. Through the fall, Washoe residents continued to roll the various options off their tongues and write them into their correspondence. Ophir variants lost adherents once someone recollected the mines of the biblical Ophir as famous only for gold. Silver differentiated the new mines. Henry Comstock advocated for "Silver City" in a letter to the *Sacramento Daily Union* published on October 31, 1859, but with Comstock's name perhaps already too prominent about the lode, his suggestion didn't catch. However, by early November, the naming of the camp in honor of Fenimore had been settled upon. "Virginia City is the absurd name the miners have given to the little settlement of thirty or forty houses and tents a hundred yards or so below the excavations in the silver lead," wrote a *Sacramento Daily Union* correspondent. That same week, a reporter for the *North San Juan Press* called it a "savage and dirty" mining camp.

---

* An oft-told tale of Old Virginny, drunk, falling over, shattering a full whisky bottle, and using the disaster as occasion to christen the camp in honor of his home state is almost certainly apocryphal.

The men lived in rough circumstances. At night, some sheltered in the makeshift constructions and canvas tents erected in a haphazard line along what would become A Street. Dusty "Washoe zephyrs," the savage winds that scoured the east side of Sun Mountain, "often blew the shelters apart." Other men scraped aside the surface rocks and slept under the stars, nestled in blankets beside clumps of sagebrush. The most comfortable slept in the hay piles hauled up the cañons to feed the mules that turned the dragstones in the fifteen arastras working below the open cuts. Wells, Fargo & Company transacted banking and express business from a location nearby. Loftily named Virginia City didn't yet have a hotel, although several were under construction, and it possessed only one restaurant, an establishment more tent than building "at which six persons on a watch may partake of poor quality of victuals, at seventy-five cents per head." As a correspondent of the *Daily Alta California* noted, "Rum mills are becoming numerous, as also gamblers, the usual concomitants of a new and rich mineral country." Most groggeries hosted gambling tables under canvas and sold whisky over a board by the gill, pint, quart, or gallon. None had yet graduated to selling individual drinks, although one had gone to the trouble to have teamsters freight in a billiards table.

Conditions a mile and a half away in Gold Hill mirrored those of Virginia City, albeit on a smaller scale. The camp boasted one store, three or four drinking and gambling establishments, and a population of about one hundred. The effects of the strike began to reverberate into the surrounding economies. Recrossing the Sierras after making an inspection of the new mines, the mayor of Placerville met more than seventy-five freight wagons heading for Washoe laden with merchandise, comestibles, and mining supplies. Around Carson City's thirty buildings, the value of vacant lots boomed from $5 to $600. A communications company hurried to extend a telegraph line to Virginia City, a step in an ambitious endeavor to link California to Salt Lake City and the rest of the nation with a transcontinental telegraph line. "Below," in San Francisco, at the behest of leading Comstock mining interests, several of the city's iron foundries tooled up to manufacture steam engines and stamp batteries for crushing quartz, and the deepwater steamship *Uncle Sam* had just left for Central America, carrying four tons of high-grade Washoe ore bound for Le Havre, France, via New York, one among several shipments of Washoe ore to European smelters.

On Gold Hill, the miners worked through open surface pits and a few small tunnels to extract paying dirt and decomposed gold-bearing quartz. Mules plodding endless circles around several arastras crushed the richest quartz. The Gold Hill mines reaped a phenomenal "yellow harvest," but it was all gold. They dug no silver, and yet it was silver at the center of everybody's obsession over the Divide in the ragtag camp at Virginia City. The legendary silver mines of Mexico, Bolivia, and Saxony had disgorged metal for centuries. One man who claimed Spanish American mining experience described the Washoe ore as "far richer than any he had ever handled." The thought that they were onto such a discovery overvaulted the excitement of the large daily earnings. As a correspondent of the *Marysville Express* reported, "It is the universal opinion among miners here that silver leads never give out."

By the end of October, the ore lead around the original strike in the Ophir mine had been exposed on four adjacent claims over a linear distance of five or six hundred feet. From north to south they were the Mexican, the Ophir, the Central, and the California mines. In total, they employed about forty or fifty miners, among them John Mackay and Jack O'Brien. Ophir miners delved into the ore seam in two separate open cuts about forty feet apart. The north and south ends of both twenty-foot excavations exposed the cross-section of the lode—yellowish surface dirt covered a broken and seamy ledge of whitish, gold-bearing quartz that varied in width from nine to twenty feet and angled down into the heart of Sun Mountain on a westward dip of forty-eight degrees. The silver-laden treasure vein of bluish-black ore ran through the center of the quartz mass, four to fifteen inches wide and soft enough for a man to crumble in his fingers. Miners sacked the dense, dark sulphuret for shipment to San Francisco. With ten men hacking at the lode and wheelbarrowing ore and waste out of the pits on inclined ramps cut through the downhill sides of the excavations, the Ophir extracted about one ton of the sulphurets and eight tons of the whiteish quartz per day. Immediately south of the Ophir, the Central Company's six owners supervised a similar operation. The two companies had mined about fifty-five tons of the blue-black sulphurets and about one thousand tons of gold-bearing, lower-grade quartz. On the hundred-foot Mexican claim, miners had recently exposed the blue vein in a surface cut, and it promised to be just as rich as the Ophir.

John Mackay worked as hard as any miner in camp. In the three months since he'd come to Washoe, he'd helped dig tens of thousands of dollars' worth of royal metals from what was now universally known as the Comstock Lode, the Comstock Lead, or the Comstock Ledge, more wealth than he'd ever touched in California. Unfortunately, Mackay owned none of it. All that wealth belonged to the mine owners. Mackay did receive something in addition to his wages, however, something that would serve him well over the course of the next twenty years. With his eyes a foot or two from the rock, he received an education in the new mining conditions from the face of the lead itself. Like every other man in Washoe, Mackay tried to cast his imagination into the rock, looking for clues that would lead him to a greater understanding of what wealth lay underground. He also looked for an opportunity to gain some ownership of a potentially productive mine.

While the Ophir, the Mexican, and the Central mines worked through open cuts, the California Company, south of the Central, tried a different approach. They chose to dig a horizontal tunnel back toward the ledge from a point on the hillside farther down the slope. (To facilitate drainage, it was driven on a slight upraise, making it an "adit" in technical mining parlance.) Once they hit the quartz ledge, they intended to take advantage of gravity and extract the wealth by opening an underground chamber in the ore body—a "gallery" or a "stope"—and extract the ore body *above* the level of the adit, mining uphill, with the aid of gravity, which required less effort, although the technique would force them to figure out how to support the gallery, not always an easy undertaking.

Indeed, if the owners of the productive mines had a problem, it was the sheer volume of ore they were extracting from the vein. The arastras couldn't crush it fast enough, and no known mechanical and chemical milling process had any hope of keeping pace. Smelting worked only for small volumes, required large amounts of expensive fuel, and was only economically viable for the highest-grade ores. The Mexican patio process "saved" a high percentage of precious metal, but it needed from ten days to three months to reduce a few tons of ore, and it only worked in warm weather. The productive claims had already stockpiled more than one hundred tons of ore, and their miners were disgorging tons more every day. An optimist writing for the *Sacramento Daily Union* thought the Comstock lead "probably surpasses in richness anything recorded in the history of mining." Such astounding reports reached the *Placerville Observer* that the editor lost faith in his correspondents and refused to publish their dispatches. No matter the local excitement, over the mountains in California, the Washoe silver discovery still "commanded little faith."

That was about to change. James Walsh and his Ophir co-owners had been sending regular ore shipments to San Francisco since September. Apart from the raw ore they'd sold for overseas shipment, they'd managed to accumulate thirty-eight tons of their highest-grade stuff in the city by the end of October. After passing through San Francisco smelters, that ore yielded $114,000 worth of precious metal. Deducting transport and milling costs of $512 per ton netted them a profit of nearly $95,000. Knowing exactly how to provoke a mining excitement, the Ophir owners piled the bars of resultant bullion in the windows of the Alsop & Company banking house on California Street—which probably had about the same emotional impact as a bullion stack worth $36 million would today. San Franciscans gathered outside and gawked at the gleaming ingots. Even the most hardened skeptics found it hard to squawk against such a tangible display. Californians struggling to recover from the Fraser River–related recession needed no great leap of insight to realize that such wealth cracked open would stimulate a world of industrial, agricultural, and transportation-related opportunities supplying California-dependent mines and new towns sure to spring into existence on the eastern slope of the Sierras. "Washoe [was] all the talk," all over San Francisco—and all over the state. Only snow clogging the Sierra passes kept the would-be Washoe stampede pent in California.

At Virginia City and Gold Hill, snow fell "without intermission" for much of the last week of November until five feet lay atop the camp. Working with Jack O'Brien, Kinney Said, and Alec Kennedy, John Mackay excavated a dugout into the hillside below the open cuts, built walls with stacked stones slathered with mud, roughed together a door and a stone chimney, and roofed the makeshift structure with poles, brush, and dirt over which they stretched a sheet of canvas. Snug and dry inside, they wintered in reasonable comfort, as they'd done in similar winter quarters through the Gold Rush years. The foursome cobbled together bunk beds, a table, and three-legged stools from limbs of piñon pine and cedar. Later in the winter, they took in two other men, who slept on the dirt floor, wrapped in blankets. Elsewhere in Virginia City, men with coin or gold dust paid a dollar per night to pack like tinned oysters into the few public houses, where they hoped the fierce winds careening down the mountain above the camp (recently renamed "Mount Davidson") wouldn't blast apart the flimsy canvas walls they sheltered behind.

Temperatures bottomed at eleven degrees below zero in mid-December. All the arastras in Virginia City and Gold Hill froze solid. There seemed little hope they'd thaw until spring. Precipitation choked the surface cuts with snow and ice or water and mud and paralyzed mining activity in anything but subterranean tunnels.

A *Sacramento Daily Union* correspondent estimated that of the several hundred men (and a handful of women) in and around Virginia City after the first snowfalls, only about one-sixth composed the camp's "real mining population." The majority consisted of speculators, mercantile operators, teamsters, hotel, saloon, and boardinghouse proprietors, loafers, aspiring politicians, horse thieves, cut-throats, gamblers, and members of the "prospecting gentry."

For serious miners pushing to develop paying claims, the foul winter weather left digging an adit from farther down the slope aimed to intersect the lode in depth as the only viable strategy. After six weeks of digging, the California Company struck the main silver lead sixty feet below the surface, deeper than any other mine had yet explored. The ore vein crosscut by the California Company adit equaled that found in the open cuts of the Central, Ophir, and Mexican mines, and although of the other three only the Ophir had gotten as deep as thirty feet, all had discerned a tendency of the quartz vein to widen with increased depth. The value of claims thought to be on the line of the lode vaulted five hundred percent.

Other mine owners wanted to emulate the California Company's success, but not all of them possessed the large quantities of coin required to finance such construction projects as adits. However, without such major development endeavors, their mines would never pay dividends, either. Some owners became willing to trade "feet" in their claim—meaning a share of its ownership—for the construction of an adit that might reveal ore in their mine. That was exactly the opportunity John Mackay had been awaiting. Although Mackay hadn't managed to save enough money to *buy* his way into ownership, his demonstrable competence, leadership ability, and initiative gave him the opportunity to *work* his way into ownership. He contracted with the owners of the Union mine, a mine on the line of the Comstock Lode between the Ophir and the Sierra Nevada, to run an adit from lower down Cedar Ravine designed to intersect the lode at depth in exchange for "feet" in the claim.

Each "foot" represented one share in the mine, with the number of shares determined by the length of the claim on the line of the lode. Thus, a four-hundred-foot mine would have four hundred "feet," or shares. One "foot" in a four-hundred-foot mine didn't pertain to one specific geographical foot, but rather to a one four-hundredth share in the mine's ownership.

Without any capital except his native human qualities, earning sweat equity was Mackay's best avenue to mine ownership, and for the Union owners, also without capital, trading "feet" for work was the fastest method to develop their claim. Everyone's fortunes would be made if the tunnel struck ore. Since Mackay and his cabin mates could dig an adit regardless of surface weather conditions, they probably labored at it through most of the winter. The drawback to the arrangement was that with all their remuneration paid in "feet," they earned no cash money, and with the winter continuing severe and but scanty supplies crossing the Sierras, prices rose to what one commenter called "forty-nine prices . . . with slim prospects of a reduction this side of the spring months." Little coin circulated, an irony considering the tens of thousands of dollars of mining wealth within a hundred yards of camp. Like many others, Mackay and his companions ran low on coin. Mackay had the cabin's last thirty dollars. He spent it buying a sack of flour and bacon and shared it among his mates. After that, they ran out of both money and food. Fresh meat was the only inexpensive provision, ranchers in the Carson and Eagle valleys being happy to unload stock at the mercy of the keen weather. One day, the butcher they'd patronized stopped Mackay and asked why he and his cabin mates weren't buying meat. Embarrassed, Mackay stuttered out an explanation. The butcher heard him out, then said, "You boys come and get what you want and pay me when you can." The butcher's extension of credit carried the foursome through the winter.

Despite the increasing bitterness of the pro- and anti-slavery sectional disputes in the eastern nation, winter isolation seemed to diminish the importance of news from elsewhere in the nation. Local developments held more significance: improvements in the overland mail network, efforts to construct a transcontinental telegraph line, men freezing their feet trying to cross the Sierras, George Hearst's sale of half his Ophir interest (likely one-twenty-fourth of the total) to Henry Meredith for $10,000, Hearst's purchase of a more substantial share of the Gould & Curry claim 1,534 feet to the south, and on the day of the leap year, February 29, 1860, "a very heavy wind" that blasted apart several buildings and unroofed the newest hotel.

Tangible evidence kept the silver strike before California eyes. One Placerville jeweler displayed "a lump [of silver] about the size of a frying pan" in his shop window. The San Francisco Mint had accepted fifty-eight thousand ounces of Washoe silver in January 1860—nearly two and a half tons—and everyone was "stark, raving mad" about Washoe and silver. The fever infected all classes of inhabitants alike, from merchants, businessmen, and lawyers to mechanics, teamsters, and "hard fisted men of muscle and rude industry," as the *San Francisco Weekly Bulletin* described common laborers. As a city journalist wrote during the winter of 1860, "Go where you will, in the street, in the counting-house, in the saloon, at home—and we had almost said at church—and the topic is Washoe. It is all Washoe. People think, talk and dream of Washoe." In Marysville, "Are you going to Washoe?" was the question on everybody's lips, and Washoe was the talk in all the saloons. "For the Washoe Country!" "Washoe!" "For the Silver Country!" "Washoe Express!" "Bound for Washoe!" "Washoe Mines!" "Washoe Mining Stocks!" "Go it, Washoe!" blared from the advertising columns of the newspapers, and all over California, would-be silver nabobs requisitioned that celebrated forerunner of migration—"the Ho!"—into service for their proposed trans-Sierran rush. No one doubted that the first blush of spring would unleash a torrent of immigration on the new mining localities of the western Utah Territory.

Only the severe winter contained the hegira. Ice formed on the Truckee and Carson rivers thick enough to support loaded freight wagons. Three to five feet of snow mantled the mountainsides around Virginia City. For sixty days, snow more than a foot thick covered the Carson, Eagle, and Washoe valley bottoms. Ranchers ran out of feed, and no resupplies came over the Sierras. Incapable of truffling through snow to reach nourishment, horses and cattle starved. When not drowned by the wind, the valleys sounded with the "heartrending" lowing of dying cattle. Nothing relieved the polar monotony of the landscape "save an occasional flock of carrion birds hovering over the carcass of some starved victim." As many as fifteen thousand horses, oxen, cows, and swine died in the Carson, Eagle, and Washoe valleys—livestock worth a quarter of a million dollars.

With their traditional hunting grounds in the valley bottoms of the eastern slope now "owned" by white ranchers, the winter of 1859–60 visited intense suffering on the Washoe and Paiute tribes. A government official on an inspection described Indians on the Truckee Meadows "freezing and starving to death by scores." In one Washoe hut, he found three children dead and dying. A few whites tried to alleviate the native misery, offering to share their own scant supplies of bread and provisions. Many Indians refused assistance, fearing poisoned food. They blamed the severe weather on the white immigrants.

A *Sacramento Daily Union* correspondent in Virginia City worried that both the quantity and quality of persons in the mining rush certain to flood over the Sierras from California would further worsen relations with the Indians. "The recent discoveries in this region will bring across the mountains some of our Digger [Indian] killing, squaw embracing

Californians, who will be sure to indulge their sportive propensities . . . and bring about a serious Indian War."

That was a prescient concern. The coming rush would also touch off the long chain of tragic events that led, many years later, to John Mackay's meeting the lovely young widow who would become the love of his life.

CHAPTER 4

The Rush to Washoe—
and an Indian War

Fanciful view of Virginia City in the spring of 1860, when the "city" had only a handful of substantial buildings—and dozens of tents, dugouts, and shanties.

———

> Of one thing you can be assured; these mines are no humbug; they are richer than any I ever saw, and I would not give the little hill on the east slope of which Virginia is situated for a fee simple title to the whole of Fraser River.
>
> —"Letter from Virginia City," *Marysville Express*,
> November 26, 1859, reprinted in *Daily Alta
> California*, December 28, 1859

If the Gold Rush had proven one thing, it was that Californians were a gambling people, willing to risk a bitter fizzle for a chance at sudden fortune. In spite of all the editorial croaking, to many Californians it seemed foolish not to try to grab an early piece of the next big thing. A spell of mild weather in late March 1860 unleashed the rush.

Moneyed San Francisco speculators bolted out of Placerville astride horses or sure-footed mules, climbing the long ridge east of town. Traders led strings of loaded pack mules, and it being "an article of faith with California teamsters that where a horse can go a wagon can follow," stage and freight drivers *hee-yawed* their mule or ox teams after the hindquarters of the mounted vanguard. Affluent prospectors led mules or donkeys burdened with equipment and provisions. Men unable to afford draft animals slogged uphill on foot, straining forward under heavy packs. A few mud-splattered immigrants shoved wheelbarrows toward Virginia City, one hundred miles away, beyond the spine of the Sierras. Men who'd been born in France, England, Ireland, Germany, Mexico, and a dozen other countries plodded alongside Pike's County Missourians, Connecticut Yankees, hotheaded southern-rights secessionists, New Yorkers, free-soil New Englanders, Ohioans, and men from all other corners of the thirty-three united states. A few women struggled along with the general migration, many wearing men's clothes.

From atop Junction Hill, which in clear spring weather provided a commanding view of the Sacramento Valley that stretched all the way to Mount Diablo and the Coast Ranges, more than a hundred miles away, the Washoe-bound multitudes descended a heavy grade into a canyon toward Brockliss's Bridge over the South Fork of the American River. The bridge keeper extracted a one-dollar toll for the right to make a safe, dry crossing of the snow-melt-swollen torrent and served "execrable brandy, warrented [sic] to kill at twenty paces" from a log hut. Beyond the bridge, on the north side of the river, an "exceedingly bad" road continued up canyon. Water running out from under banks of melting snow flooded the footprints and wheel ruts. Hundreds of hooves, boots, and wheels churned the track into a quagmire. Some days, it rained. Wagons, horses, mules, and oxen bogged down in the muck. Teamsters whipped and cursed exhausted, straining animals. Overloaded wagons capsized, dumping crates of merchandise into the muddy road margins. Trains of draft animals struggled past the wreckage, those of the many whisky peddlers "stopping now and then to quench the thirst of the toiling multitude."

The Washoe migration labored toward the spine of the Sierras at Johnson's Pass "like a great snake dragging its slow length along." Descending beyond the pass into Lake Valley, the trail turned south, away from the massive mountain lake called Lake Bigler (now Tahoe), to meet the West Fork of the Carson River. The Washoe rushers followed the Carson down a narrow canyon and continued the long descent north to Genoa, in the Carson Valley.* Although they had the worst seventy miles of the journey behind them, thirty miles yet remained to reach the new mines.

A strong storm hit the Sierras on April 4 and temporarily shut down the migration. That day, Adolph Sutro, a Prussian Jew who had been in Virginia City inspecting the new mines for the *Daily Alta California* and would spend much of the next twenty years bidding to control the Comstock Lode, was trying to make it back to California. Sutro and his traveling companions reached the summit of Johnson's Pass in the early afternoon, pressing toward Placerville, and were stunned to see a lone rider galloping toward them out of the driving snow. They couldn't imagine what could spur a man to travel so fast through such an awful gale. Only as the rider thundered past did they realize that it was the Pony Express making its inaugural run.

The first rider had departed San Francisco a few minutes before four o'clock the previous afternoon, taken a steamboat upriver to Sacramento, and galloped off the boat at 2:45 a.m. He made the 45 miles to Placerville in less than four hours and passed the mail off to the next rider—a young man named Warren Epson—12 miles out of town. Epson had done 40 mostly uphill miles when he raced past Sutro in Johnson's Pass, and he did 47 more before he passed the mail to the next rider in Carson City at 8:36 p.m., having ridden hard for thirteen consecutive hours. From Sacramento to Carson City, the two Pony Express riders had managed 144 miles in just eighteen hours. Newspapers all over California lauded the riders' astonishing velocity—they'd *averaged* eight miles per hour over the mighty Sierras.

The eastward stampede from California to Washoe resumed when the storm spent its fury. Dozens of bedraggled rushers reached the Com-

---

* Loosely, the rush to Washoe over the Sierras on the Placerville Route followed modern Highway 50 east from Placerville to Strawberry, over Echo Summit (Johnson's Pass) into Lake Valley, then south on Highway 89 through Luther Pass to Highway 88, down Highway 88 past Hope Valley Resort through Woodford's Canyon to Woodford's, continued down Highway 88 into the Carson Valley, passed through Genoa and Carson City and then went east on U.S. Highway 50 to Nevada Route 342 and climbed to Silver City, Gold Hill, and Virginia City. All told, it was about 110 miles, Placerville to Virginia City. The author, a rock climber for more than thirty years, has spent many happy days on the crags that line this route—Sugarloaf, the Phantom Spires, Lover's Leap above Strawberry Station, Woodford's Canyon, and others.

stock every day, either afoot, ahorse, or a-mule, heaped into freight wagons, or in stagecoaches making round trips from Carson City. The rough camps at Virginia City and Gold Hill teemed with new arrivals, most appalled to find themselves perched on a desert mountainside in the middle of what one of them described as "a primitive wilderness so scorified, saline, and sulphurous that it would seem to have been rained upon with fire and brimstone, and afterwards sown with salt."

Despite the bleak scenery visible from Virginia City's few rough streets running parallel along the out-sloping bench, unimaginatively named A, B, C, and D streets from highest to lowest (nobody had yet bothered to lay out cross streets), none of the newly arrived Washoeites could fail to notice the tons of ore, worth tens of thousands of dollars, piled up below the Ophir, Central, and California mines. Every man wanted a chance at such riches. They took that chance by buying and selling feet in the mines.

The heavy expenses of quartz mining forced mining companies or claims without a cash flow to sell feet to raise capital. People bought feet for two reasons: the speculative hope of capital gain—that they could sell the feet at an increase in value sometime in the future—and the hope that the mine would develop a rich strike and find itself with such strong earnings that it paid dividends to its stockholders, the people who owned feet in the mine.

The camp's manic speculative energy concentrated along A Street, the uppermost street, called "the Exchange," directly below the active mine cuts. Wearing red or blue flannel shirts, canvas trousers, and sturdy boots under heavy overcoats, and in a state of great "mental tension" to make hasty wealth, miners, prospectors, speculators, sharps, flats, greenhorns, veteran "yon-siders" (as old California pioneers often referred to themselves), and most everyone else gathered on the Exchange to buy, sell, bull, bear, or trade "feet" in the mines. Men sensed they might never again have such a clear chance to make a speedy fortune, and they acted with "the concentrated energy of those having issues of life and death before them."

Walking along A Street on his way to and from the mines, John Mackay watched wildly bewhiskered men peer at mineral specimens through the magnifying glasses or jeweler's loupes everyone kept tucked in their vest pockets and hash over the dips, spurs, quartz, clay, free gold, assays, croppings, overburdens, clorides, and sulphurets that constituted the quality of a given location's "indications." People jangling pockets full of rocks demeaned themselves in their berserk frenzy to get rich.

Someone quipped that the Comstock had "corralled" all of the world's "insane geologists." A few credulous prospectors desperate for "good tidings from any imaginary Ophir" made locations based on the advice of one Mr. Peck, who boasted the ability to locate underground ore deposits with the aid of a one-hundred-year-old "electro-magnetic" mineral rod, a wand that encased two or three ounces of quicksilver. Mr. Winn, who owned a restaurant on B Street one block below the Exchange, cut a streak of silver ore while excavating the foundation for an oven. He and several friends immediately located a claim, thinking their fortunes made. A correspondent counted about one man in fifty actually at work mining. The rest bought, sold, and talked. The sharps kept on the qui vive, buttonholing each other and whispering mysteriously in corners as they puffed claims and eyed one another for speculative indications. The fact that most couldn't tell a chloride from a sulphuret or a pick from an adze and had never spent a minute underground surely had John Mackay shaking his head. "Endless chaffering" over the value of feet made the Exchange "a perfect Babel" for eighteen of the day's twenty-four hours. Female members of the "sporting fraternity" plying their trade openly along the street "made good use of the remaining six."

The thickening ore vein in the Ophir and Mexican mines, good indications on the Gould & Curry claim on the line of the lode 1,534 feet south of the Ophir, and the large returns expected once miners opened to sufficient depth the numerous parallel quartz croppings that had been claimed both above and below the Comstock vein all contributed to a euphoric communal confidence in the region's mining wealth.

The recently completed telegraph line to Virginia City extended the speculative ruckus to all classes of San Francisco society.* Morse code buy and sell instructions and daily mining news flashing over the Sierras created an "under-current" of speculative energy in San Francisco that proved capable of washing "large amounts of coin from one man's pocket into that of another," and created a panoply of opportunity for unscrupulous operators to fob dubious mining schemes on a public obsessed with easy-made wealth.

One observer lauded the salesmanship of a man who parlayed a cheap pocket watch into stock certificates for thirty feet of an obscure—and almost certainly worthless—Washoe silver mine he subsequently traded for a vacant lot in San Francisco worth $1,000. Back on the Exchange in

---

* The telegraph reached Virginia City on March 19, 1860 ("Telegraph to Washoe," *Daily Alta California*, March 20, 1860).

Washoe, a man watched two or three chunks of ore pass from hand to hand as specimens from the Pine Nut claim. Later, he watched the same pieces circulate as examples from the Gould & Curry, then the Ophir, the Mexican, and finally as morsels of the Rogers claim, a well-regarded mine in the Flowery District five miles east of the Comstock, down Six Mile Cañon. He cautioned those buying into the Rogers to inquire whether they were getting feet in the James F. Rogers or the Uncle Billy Rogers. "It makes a difference," he said. "The former is a silver lode, five miles east of Virginia City; the latter is a copper claim, at the head of Hope Valley, fifty miles the other way."

Nor had mining sharps cornered the market on nefarious business practices. Placerville teamsters fleeced merchants desperate to get supplies over the Sierras. Through the foul weather of winter and spring, the packers promised to haul supplies to Washoe at twenty-five cents a pound. Instead, they dumped the loads forty or fifty miles out of town, returned to Placerville claiming they couldn't get through the mountains, and made another contract at twenty-five cents per pound with another person and repeated the process. Once rates dropped to five cents per pound, the normal summer charge, they hired additional help to haul the supplies the rest of the way. The practice ruined several businessmen whose wares spent months in transit.

Virginia City had finished March 1860 with ten stone and thirty-one wooden structures in various stages of construction, ninety canvas tents, and an uncounted number of improvised shelters like the one occupied by John Mackay and his companions. In the first two weeks of April, the camp added more than a hundred tents. It added two hundred more in the last fortnight of the month and still didn't have sufficient bed space to accommodate its booming population—although the Washoe "beds" didn't amount to anything more than straw-stuffed sacks, even in the canvas-walled structures their proprietors styled as hotels and boardinghouses. Those filled with men happy to pay a premium for comfort. People left over either paid a dollar per night to the owners of tents, shanties, and saloons for the privilege of sleeping on the floor or slept outside, huddled together like sheep through the cold spring nights.

With little firewood in camp, the population packed the public houses in the evenings and with, as one writer observed, "a view toward maintaining their animal heat, draw largely on the resources of the bar." Fortunately, whisky remained plentiful, the only abundant item in a camp that in the first week of April was "entirely out of flour, and nearly every other staple of food" besides tough, stringy beef cut from cattle butchered to save them from starvation. The few hardy freighters who had driven mules through the winter passes had imbibed too much '49er lore. They arrived leading "laboring, panting, staggering" animals with "a cask of whiskey on each side of the pack-saddle, with never a sack of flour for companion." Frank Soule, correspondent of the *Daily Alta California*, estimated that mules brought in "ten kegs of whisky to every half sack of flour." Periodic resupply coupled to the ability of the local whisky casks to emulate Old Testament oil jars gradually converted the Washoe ardent into a "Dashaway beverage,"* devoid of intoxicating properties. So, while hunger abraded the camp's innards in March and early April and the cost of edible commodities advanced "from one hundred to one thousand percent," there remained a "superabundance of whisky," and its price remained standard—"two bits a glass."

Mule trains arriving in mid-April brought gastronomic relief. Dark, scudding clouds spitting a wintry mix of rain and snow began alternating with warm, clear, windless days. Far to eastward, dust devil whirlwinds three thousand feet tall sped across the arid flats of the Carson Sink. By far the month's most glorious achievement occurred on April 12, when the first westbound Pony Express rider galloped past the mouths of Six Mile and Gold cañons on his way up the Carson Valley. The mail pouches reached Carson City, fifteen miles southwest of Virginia City, at 3:30 p.m., eight and a half days after leaving St. Joseph, Missouri. They included a news summary that the local telegraph operator relayed to a California population amazed to be reading news *less than ten days old*.

The *Daily Alta California* spoke for many yon-siders when it contextualized the Pony Express's accomplishment: "Only those who have toiled wearily over the great deserts between California and the Missouri River will be able to fully estimate what has been accomplished." For most of them, the journey had taken four or five months.

National news was interesting, but it didn't capture and hold the Washoe interest like developments pertaining to the local mines, where the mining properties belonged to one of three classes. "Outside claims," also known as "wildcats," those locations off the line of the main lode, occupied the third and lowest tier. Based on the strength of their indications,

---

* The Dashaway Association was a temperance pledge society founded in San Francisco in 1859 by a group of volunteer firemen.

wildcats commanded between 50 cents and $50 per foot, with much con-
centration at the low end, most of which would prove overvalued. Claims
on what men *supposed* was the line of the Comstock Lode that had not
yet produced pay ore constituted the second class. Depending on their
distance from the exposed lead and the quality of their indications, speculators valued their stock as high as $500 or $600 per foot. The fact that
mining men didn't yet understand the dimensions and boundaries of the
lode complicated matters for many claims, but people recognized the difference between those locations that *might* own a slice of the Comstock
and those that definitely did not. First-class claims had exposed the treasure vein, either in a surface cut or via an adit that had struck the lode at
depth. Despite all the wild excitement, there were still just the California,
the Central, the Ophir, and the Mexican mines of this class above Virginia City and the many small ones that striped Gold Hill. Speculators
fancied them worth from $800 to $5,000 per foot, but most of the owners
wouldn't sell an inch, at any price. The *Marysville Daily Appeal* reported
that well-known lawyer Henry Meredith, who had bought one-twelfth of
the Ophir from George Hearst for $10,000 the previous November, re-
fused an offer of $150,000.

Much of the speculative excitement centered on claims of the second
class, those thought to be on the main lode but without proven ore—
and therefore without a cash flow. In Virginia City, where $50,000 lo-
cations were "plenty as blackberries," there were also "many very rich
men who cannot pay for breakfast." The perceived future value of the
mines they owned represented most of their wealth, and the need to finance mine development—or pay basic living expenses—forced many
of them to sell or trade "feet" of their claims. Owners making deals
of this nature had several dozen adits under construction in the district, including the one Mackay and his companions had contracted
to dig for the Union mine. The adits advanced a few feet per day, and
speculators carefully tracked their progress. As an adit approached its
anticipated intersection with the vein, excitement grew surrounding
its parent mine. Sharps started nosing around the adit's mouth, ingra-
tiating themselves with members of the work crew, or bribing them
outright, in the hopes of being favored with whiffs of news. The speculative fever peaked as the miners chipped into the quartz vein. If the adit
struck ore—or even indications—the mine's price vaulted. If it didn't,
values collapsed. As was the habit of most miners, Mackay likely followed the fluctuating values of the mines, looking for opportunities to

capitalize on his underground knowledge if he thought he perceived under- or overvalued ground.

Sources don't reveal the exact nature of the arrangements Mackay had with Union ownership or with his workmates. Nor do they reveal on what date Mackay acquired his first feet of the Union mine, likely in exchange for passing a milestone in adit construction, or on what date the tunnel struck the vein, but county mining records do show him transacting feet in the Union mine on four separate occasions in the first half of 1860—the first of which was him deeding feet to another man. Mackay and his cabin mates may have been acting in partnership, with their gains pooled and the recorded transactions reflecting their taking advantage of speculative opportunities, or Mackay may have been bossing the job, receiving and parceling out slices of the mine as members of the crew met various benchmarks.*

With the Union only five hundred feet north of the treasure vein exposed in the Mexican, speculators held sanguine opinions of the Union's prospects, especially after a report circulated that the Sierra Nevada Company immediately north of the Union had struck "ore of rich prospect." Mackay's adit approaching the lead must have touched off a frenzy. Depending on the nature of his contract with the Union ownership, that may have provided him with excellent opportunities to trade into other mines and diversify his holdings, or to extract some cash as reward for the months of hard work. Alternatively, he perhaps held all his stock in the hopes of a rich strike. Mackay and his mates must have hit the vein in a lather of anticipation. If the recorded transactions represent all of their acquired feet, their sweat equity had earned a roughly 20 percent share in the mine. "Podgers," the nom de plume of Richard L. Ogden, a very well-informed California correspondent of the *New York Times*, may have referred to Mackay's Union adit on April 20, 1860, when he wrote that "a company owning a claim beyond the Ophir claim, that is to say, 1,400 feet from the first shaft, have struck the vein, and $400 per foot is offered and refused; two weeks ago it was selling at $50 per foot, the vein not then having been struck." If the adit developed rich ore, their fortunes were made. Unfortunately, Mackay's

---

* Conspicuously absent from the transactions is Jack O'Brien's name, which other historians have taken as evidence of his disdain for hard work. The author thinks it also possible that O'Brien and Mackay were still acting in partnership. Sealed with a handshake, as were most mining partnerships, the agreement would have left no written record.

adit crosscut the Comstock Lode through a great mass of low-grade quartz, none of it profitable. Nowhere did Mackay encounter the dense bluish-black ore that yielded such riches to the claim owners a few hundred feet farther south. Its conspicuous absence must have been a major disappointment.

If so, the letdown did nothing to diminish Mackay's appetite for hard work—or his budding ambition. Although a socially reticent man embarrassed by his struggles to overcome his stutter, Mackay showed no reluctance to push himself forward through sustained physical effort. In mid-March, almost certainly before completing the Union project, he contracted with the Buck Ledge, a claim between Virginia City and Gold Hill just above the Chollar mine, to run "a prospecting tunnel . . . until he strikes the ledge or pay dirt." As part of the agreement, Mackay promised to work on the adit "five days in every week till his contract is completed." Only a man with a work ethic like John Mackay's could have cleaved to the terms of the contract, because he also took a full-time job, six days a week, working for wages in the Mexican mine. Before completing his Union contract, Mackay might well have worked all three jobs at the same time.

In Virginia City, Gold Hill, and throughout the booming region, miners seemed poised for a season of steady development. That changed on the evening of May 7, when a Pony Express rider urged a lathered horse up Six Mile Cañon, reined up in camp, and gasped out news of an Indian massacre at Williams Station, a none-too-reputable trading post and grog shop on the immigrant road thirty-six miles to the east. The rider said that Indian raiders had killed two of the three Williams brothers and five other white men. He'd heard it from the surviving Williams brother, who had escaped, spurring and whipping one of his two mounts until it collapsed from exhaustion, then outdistanced Indian pursuit on his fresher second horse. Twelve miles west of the bloodshed, he'd reached safety at Buckland's Pony Express Station and told his tale: He'd returned from hunting a lost mule to find the station burned, one of his brothers dead, and the other dying, but able to gasp out the story of Indian treachery and murder. The Pony Express man carried the story to the nearest sizable white settlement—Virginia City.

The surviving Williams brother had neglected a crucial aspect of the story. Sometime before, he and his brothers had abducted two Indian sisters who were about twelve years old, tied them up, stuffed rags in their mouths, and held them captive beneath a trap door in the floor of their station house. They'd almost certainly raped the two children. The fathers of the missing girls tracked them to Williams Station, gathered a warrior band, and retaliated in a fashion that most people in the West, of any culture, would have condoned had they understood the full story. Unfortunately, those ugly facts didn't surface until events had slipped far beyond containment.

Among the native tribes of the Great Basin, anti-immigrant resentment had been mounting ever since the California gold discovery. Herds of privately owned livestock ravaged ecosystems that had formerly supported abundant game. Whites decimated nut-bearing pine forests for lumber and fuel. White ranchers around Honey Lake, eighty miles northwest of Virginia City, reneged on grazing agreements. Then came the Comstock discovery. For the natives of the region—Paiute, Washoe, Bannock, Goshute, Western Shoshone—the rush to Washoe was the biggest catastrophe since the Gold Rush. Their ire surged. With their grasp on their way of life loosening, tribal leaders gathered at Pyramid Lake in the spring of 1860 to discuss alternatives.

Sarah Winnemucca, daughter of the great Paiute chief Winnemucca, had lived in Carson City with prominent settler William Ormsby and his wife for more than two years. She would grow into one of the most fascinating women of the nineteenth century, her lectures and book, *Life Among the Paiutes*, drawing much attention to the injustices visited upon Native American peoples. Although in it she described the Paiutes as "not fond of going to war," the ferocious winter recently endured and the endless white incursions made many Paiutes fear their alternatives had been reduced to fighting or starvation. Militants advocated a war to scourge the invaders from their homelands. Only the much-respected Paiute chief Numaga, who had toured California and understood the overwhelming preponderance of white power, counseled accommodation. Chief Winnemucca held himself aloof. Into the volatile debate came news of the outrage and punishment meted out at Williams Station. "There is no longer any use for counsel," Numaga said. "We must prepare for war, for the soldiers will now come here to fight us."

Numaga was correct. The Pony Express rider's account of "the Williams Station massacre" had thrown Virginia City into an uproar. "That sovereign cure—a public meeting" appointed Henry Meredith and four other men to a "committee of arrangements." The committee called for a volunteer force to "chastise the savages," telegraphed Carson City, and dispatched riders to warn other settlements and parties of prospecting miners, and solicited monetary contributions to support a militia force. According to Frank Soule, who represented the *Daily Alta California* in Virginia City, the camp passed Tuesday, May 8, in "a vast deal of talk, noise, and confusion, collection of rifles, muskets, revolvers, and knives, and an immense punishment of whiskey. Could the Indians be as effectually consumed, peace would soon be restored."

Saloon soldiers worked themselves into a patriotic, anti-Indian delirium, made rousing speeches, appointed themselves militia captains, and declared their right to press into service any horse in camp. Rumors swept the camp: that the initial report was exaggerated, that Brigham Young and his Mormons were behind the whole business, that five hundred heavily armed Indians were within raiding distance of camp, that thieves had concocted the excitement to steal mules and horses under the guise of patriotism and valor, that gamblers had murdered the Williams brothers, torched their station, and blamed Indians.

All over the eastern slope, reports of the massacre had the white citizenry in a furor. Towns posted guards, alarms were raised—all of them false—and wild opinions circulated. Wiser people argued that if the Paiutes intended a general campaign to "clean out the whites," they wouldn't have confined their aggression to an insignificant trading post. Over in Genoa, a *San Francisco Herald* correspondent found "truly amusing" the plight of "three females of tender nerves," who, fearing Indian outrage, locked themselves in the stone cellar of a merchant's house. In his estimate, they were in no more Indian danger in Genoa than they would have been in San Francisco. He held a dim impression of the men who ran "the little grog shops called trading posts along the great immigrant road," and he ventured his guess regarding the Indian difficulty: "It originated in the gross outrages of the whites themselves."

Nothing pacified the hotheaded whites. Hallooing slogans like, "an Indian for breakfast and a pony to ride," a group of Virginia City volunteers trotted out of camp dragoon style at 2:00 p.m. on Wednesday, May 9, spurs jangling, shotguns and ropes tied to their saddles, brandishing knives and pistols. Prominent among the Virginians was Henry Meredith, the black-haired, goateed lawyer from Nevada City who'd purchased a share of the Ophir from George Hearst. Looking ahead to what many expected would be the creation of a new territory and state from the western portion of the Utah Territory, Meredith reportedly nurtured political ambitions. Prominent citizens would fill the governorship and the senatorial seats of a new state, and Indian-fighting heroes did well in American politics. Whatever his ambitions and those of other "toughs" in the volunteer force, a rigorous military inspection would have found them much more liberally supplied with whisky than with provisions, ammunition, and long-range, muzzle-loading Minié rifles, riding mules and horses of middling quality, and lacking discipline. The vigilantes reached Williams Station in the middle of the following morning. John Mackay was not among them. Raised in the Irish slums of New York City and having mined for eight years, he might not have been an accomplished horseman. He might not have owned any guns, and he might not have approved of the "tone" of what passed for soldiers. Mackay stayed in Virginia City.

Amid the charred remains of the outpost, the vigilantes found three bodies, blood and brains staining the blade of an axe, the tracks of Indian ponies, and a wounded dog with an arrow protruding from its side. The men extracted the arrow from the dog and buried the bodies. Late in the evening, William Ormsby trotted into camp at the head of a force from the Carson and Eagle valleys. Ormsby was a controversial figure on the eastern slope. His influence had waned since the arrival of more legitimate authority in the person of U.S. District Judge John Cradlebaugh, seated in Genoa since August 1859, and although Ormsby had always maintained good relations with the Paiutes, he may have also been hoping for the political benefits of a successful anti-Indian expedition. Most vigilantes agreed to serve under Ormsby, and they voted on what they ought to do. Unanimously, they chose to pursue the Indians. They rolled up in their blankets and passed an uneventful night.

Behind them in Virginia City, two thousand feet higher on the slopes of Mount Davidson, a furious gust of wind awakened the camp about midnight. Tent canvas flapped in sudden anger; new, hastily constructed buildings creaked; and a wave of dust tore through camp. Then other blasts, "hollow and threatening," boomed down Mount Davidson. A pregnant silence dropped after each impact, the air calm as death, until the sound of the next bludgeoning gust built on the mountain seconds before it struck the camp. Each successive blow seemed stronger. Flapping tents strained at their moorings. The angry winds flung piles of kindling down the mountainside. A fierce gust whipped away the canvas sheltering two "women of light character" and left them together in bed, clinging to flapping blankets. Hundreds, half clad, turned out to save the camp. About one o'clock in the morning, Rassett's Hotel blasted apart. Flying debris carried away four tents. The stronger gusts that followed collapsed other buildings. Boards, shingles, scantling, and sheets of gritty dust flew through the camp. Loaded clotheslines took wing. A man named Ned Batturs clung to a tent rope in the hopes of keeping his habitation grounded. A gust shot his thirty-two-dollar Peruvian hat into the desert.

At daybreak, Virginia City looked like an Arkansas saloon the morning after a midnight brawl. The windstorm had destroyed fifty-seven houses and tents. Many of the latter had vanished entirely. Residents laughed at their misfortunes and heaped maledictions on the Washoe climate. Soon after, it started snowing.

While residents of Gold Hill and Virginia City searched for their scattered possessions and rebuilt their shelters, the volunteer force rode north from the wreck of Williams Station in "high glee," through heavy wind and snow, easily following the trail left by the Indian ponies driving fifty head of stock they'd liberated. The vigilantes pounded twenty-two miles north. About half an hour past noon, they reached the Big Bend of the Truckee River, where the river swerved from its eastward course and curled north toward Pyramid Lake—the Great Basin "sink" of the Truckee. They elected to camp and allow their animals to recruit strength from the abundant grass.* A few late arrivals raised their numbers to 105 or 106.

After sunrise on Saturday, May 12, 1860, the white force shook free of damp wool blankets to find three inches of snow on the ground. They dawdled through most of the morning, waiting for sun and wind to remove the snow and reveal the Indian trail. Not until eleven o'clock did they saddle up and continue pursuit.

Following the Indian trail, the vigilantes stayed on the Truckee's right bank and advanced a few miles down the valley to where the river squeezed between two ranges of brown hills. A natural terrace cutting around the foot of the hills above the river provided the only reasonable avenue of advance. The Indian trail went straight down it. Ormsby ordered scouts to check the terrace for trouble.

The scouts probed along the terrace for two miles without incident. At the end of the terrace, the hills backed away from the river. A commanding view stretched north to the shore of Pyramid Lake, about three and a half miles distant. A little over halfway to the lake, the trail dropped sixty to eighty feet into a shallow, flat valley at the river level, bounded on its east side by the edge of an ancient floodplain. Some distance ahead and below, the scouts spotted two Indians. They reported back to the main body of the force.

* They camped on the site of modern Wadsworth, Nevada, a few hundred yards north of I-80, thirty-two miles east of Reno.

Ormsby ordered them to return and capture the two Indians, if possible, while he continued bringing up the rest of the vigilantes.

The scouts trotted out front again, dropped into the shallow valley, and moved forward, searching for the two Indians. A mile or more down the valley, they found them—along with a significant group of their fellows. The Indians charged, and the scouts fled back to the main body of the volunteers, who by then had reached the top of the slope into the lower valley. The time was about 4:00 p.m.

Suddenly, about a mile and a half to their front, a line of mounted Indians roughly equal to their numbers appeared along the edge of a rise. Four or five war chiefs galloped back and forth in front of the Indian line, displaying remarkable skill in handling their horses. The Indians' shrill war whoops echoed over the intervening distance.

They presented just the sort of force the whites hoped to punish. The vigilantes advanced about three-quarters of a mile. Stands of cottonwoods and underbrush lined the banks of the snowmelt-swollen Truckee about two hundred yards to the whites' left. A steep rise to the edge of the ancient floodplain overlooked their right flank. The Indian force before them stayed in sight the whole time.

One of the Indian chiefs stunted a gorgeous black charger. Oddly, he seemed to be holding a white flag as he raced back and forth along the line. Confused, and still five or six hundred yards distant, Ormsby called a halt. Wise members of the expedition used the pause to tighten their saddles. One of the men possessed a rifle with a telescopic sight that revealed what he thought was an enormous battle-axe glinting in the sun whenever the chief wheeled his horse. (The chief was probably holding a spear decorated with eagle feathers.) The man took a shot at the chief.

Unharmed, the chief rode back to join his men, and as a unit, the whole force of mounted Indians advanced to the edge of the ancient floodplain. They stood for an instant, then simultaneously dismounted and fired their rifles. Their horses stayed perfectly still, a discipline that impressed those few whites disposed to carefully measure the quality of their opponents.

Ormsby suggested a charge. One of his lieutenants thought it better to make for a stand of cottonwoods, where they could anchor a flank against the river and shoot across open ground. Ormsby yelled for a charge. The whites advanced—and discovered their horses struggling through fetlock-deep sand. About thirty whites spurred ahead, racing for a wash that rose gently to the level of the plateau to the right of the Indian position. A few individuals fired their weapons. Most held their fire, hoping for closer range. (Reloading muzzle-loading rifles or revolvers with black powder and ball from horseback was no trivial undertaking.) Not liking the slant of developments, at least five whites turned tail and galloped for the bench leading out of the valley.

The whites gained the top of the rise to find the Indians vanished— into an open landscape. The Indians seemed to have ceded the ground without a fight. Lacking targets, or even a focal point of terrain worthy of capture, the vigilante force suffered a few seconds of confusion. A few even thought they'd won some kind of victory. Then rifle fire erupted on their flanks. Clumps of sagebrush resolved into dismounted Indian marksmen firing rifles and bows. Small groups of Indians on foot ducked in and out of covered positions in ravines and washes and sniped at the whites. Ormbsy had led his rabble into the heart of a perfectly sprung ambush.

Although by some minor miracle none of the whites were wounded in the initial fusillade, arrows and bullets *thwacked* into the flanks of their horses and mules. Panicked animals reared. Riders struggling to control bucking mounts couldn't return fire. Many dropped their weapons to avoid being thrown. The long charge through the deep sand and up the wash had greatly tired their mounts. The Indians seemed content to let them stay where they were. The time was by now about five o'clock. Some three hours remained until sunset. The chances of surviving a night surrounded by aggressive Indian warriors suddenly seemed dim indeed.

The whites fell back down the hill, ceding the high bench in the hopes of gaining shelter among the cottonwoods on the riverbank, two hundred yards to the rear. Indians concealed in the trees shattered their hopes. Pursued by remounted Indians astride superb, rested, recently fed animals, the white force fled, aiming for a grove of cottonwoods three-quarters of a mile to the south.

Three hundred yards short of the timber, the whites rallied a brief stand, then panicked and again fled south. Henry Meredith and a few others who had assumed battlefield leadership rallied a shaky stand in some cottonwoods near the edge of the Truckee River about 250 yards from the slope that rose out of the south end of the valley. The Indians fought their way into the cottonwoods from the north. A savage fight developed in the undergrowth. Bullets and the arrows scythed through the foliage. Indians appeared on the edge of the plateau above the battlefield and began sniping at the whites below. A number of men took wounds, including Henry Meredith. Worse, so did Meredith's mule. The terrified animal broke loose and bolted. The mule's mad flight unhinged the whites. They fled southward, toward the rise out of the valley bottom. As the whites cleared out, a man offered Meredith a spot on his mule behind him. "No, sir, it would endanger your life," Meredith replied.

Another man who'd lost his mount vaulted onto the back of sixteen-year-old Joseph Baldwin's mule and spurred the animal south without letting the teenager mount behind him. Like Meredith, Baldwin ran after his departing fellows on foot.

Wounded, Meredith lagged behind. Some fifty howling Indians charged toward him as he trailed the fleeing whites. Another projectile—either bullet or arrow—struck Meredith and he fell, clutching his shotgun. He raised himself on an elbow, and one after the other, aimed and fired both barrels at the onrushing, howling Paiutes. Meredith reached for his pistol and discovered that it had fallen from its holster during the mayhem. The front-running Paiutes cut him to pieces. Amid the chaos, several whites thought they saw a triumphant Indian hoist Meredith's blood-dripping scalp.*

Young Baldwin seemed certain to fall next, but the same brave man who'd tried to rescue Meredith swept the lad onto the back of his mule. The vanguard of the white rout confronted Indians blocking the rise to the plateau—the whites' only hope of escaping the death trap. Remarkably, only two or three whites had been killed by this point in the battle, although more had taken wounds. William Ormsby, inconspicuous in the engagement since his ill-fated order to charge, led a desperate attack up the slope. The charge broke through and opened the avenue to escape, but Ormsby was wounded in each arm and in his mouth. His mule took a hit, too. Tempted by the possibility of survival, any semblance of white discipline evaporated. They spurred and whipped their horses and galloped for their lives, driven like cattle before the thundering hooves of the Indian ponies.

The chase stretched out for miles. Whites with weak, wounded, tired, or overloaded mounts fell behind. They were dragged down and killed as their animals foundered. Others threw away their arms and begged for quarter. Indians spitted them on arrows, knives, and spears. The whites fled onto the bench above the river that contoured around the nose of the hills. One after the other, the rout stalled at each of three gulches that sliced the bench. Paiute warriors carried death and havoc to the hindmost, stabbing with spears and shooting arrows. South of the terrace, the

---

* They had not—Meredith still had his hair when his body was found three weeks later.

rout backed up against an arroyo. William Ormsby's mule gushed blood from one of its flanks. Lubricated by the slick of blood, Ormsby's saddle slipped and dumped him to the ground. Ormsby gained his feet and faced an onrushing Indian, whom he recognized. Ormsby called to the man by name and held out his palm. "Don't kill me," he implored through the bloody foam frothing from his mouth. "I'm your friend. I'll talk to the whites and make peace."

"No use now. Too late," answered the grim Indian.

He raised his bow and shot an arrow into Ormsby's stomach and another into his face.

About eight miles into the flight, the mule carrying both Joseph Baldwin and the man who'd rescued him began to tire. The teenager slipped unnoticed from the back of the animal, hid in some bushes as the Indians swept past, and fled into the hills after nightfall. The Indians chased the terror-stricken whites for fifteen miles, clear back to the Truckee River bend, killing everyone they caught. Only nightfall saved the vigilante remnants from annihilation. If the battle had started two hours earlier, there might not have been a single white survivor. Fortunately for the whites still alive, the moon didn't rise until past midnight.

Baldwin reached Virginia City on the second night after the battle, much to the relief of his parents in Sacramento. He'd been reported dead by the first of those the scathing *Sacramento Daily Union* correspondent described as "returned heroes" to reach camp, one of whom appeared atop young Baldwin's mule.

The last survivor to make it back was Greek immigrant Dr. Anton W. Tjader, a locally popular man. Impaled by three arrows before Indians killed his running horse, he tumbled to the ground and feigned death. The Indians galloped past. When sounds of the chase faded, Dr. Tjader dragged himself to a stand of willows on the riverbank, where he lay hidden for two days, terrified to move for fear of being killed by Indians in the vicinity celebrating victory. Eventually, the doctor seized an opportunity to slink off into darkness. He spent the next seventy-two hours walking back to Virginia City.

One newspaper tally documented 55 white deaths—23 known dead and 22 missing; another claimed that only 39 whites returned alive, having left 67 dead on the banks of the Truckee. Later historians counted as many as 76 white deaths. The First Battle of Pyramid Lake was the worst loss of white life in an Indian fight since the Dade Massacre in central Florida escalated the Second Seminole War in 1835. No battle would significantly exceed its toll until General Custer's disaster on the banks of the Little Bighorn sixteen years later. (A roughly similar number died in 1866 during the Fetterman Fight in Red Cloud's War in what is now north-central Wyoming.) A correspondent of the *Daily Alta California*, likely Frank Soule, offered a good summary of the debacle. He described the white force destroyed along the banks of the Truckee River as "ill-advised and hasty . . . badly chosen, ill-appointed, and . . . unfitted for the service . . . too numerous for the purposes of peace, and too few for those of war." And, it might be added, in intellect and temperament, unsuited to either. The Indians had suffered three wounded men and two slain horses.

Initial reports of the disaster reached Virginia City with the first frightened survivors who rode into camp around sunrise the next morning. The story flew over the telegraph wires to Carson City and California—along with shrill appeals for regular and militia soldiers to combat what the most agitated inhabitants of the eastern slope feared was an Indian "war of extermination against the whites."

The debacle hit the white civilization of the Pacific Coast like a dropped anvil. Residents could scarcely credit the idea that a hundred rough and ready Californians had been decimated by a band of "digger Indians." The news set San Francisco "agog." Huge crowds gathered outside the newspaper and telegraph offices and shoved against the bulletin boards to read each new posted dispatch. Rumors spoke of a white man who had precipitated the war by assassinating Paiute chief Winnemucca and of fifteen hundred Indians arriving from the Salt Lake vicinity to reinforce the fifteen thousand Paiute, Shoshone, Bannock, and Pitt River Indians "in full war paint" at Pyramid Lake determined on "clearing out Carson Valley." (The *Territorial Enterprise* estimated fewer than four hundred warriors in the entire Paiute tribe.) "Brigham Young is at the bottom of this matter," railed a writer in Marysville. With Governor John G. Downey being absent at San Quentin, Secretary of State Johnson Price assumed responsibility, ordered a company of regular U.S. Army artillery and another of infantry to deploy from Fort Alcatraz and Benicia, and set militia units from Downieville, San Juan, Placerville, Nevada City, and Sacramento marching over the Sierras.

In Virginia City, a militia captain declared martial law, posted pickets, and sent out roving patrols. At around midnight on May 14, a patrol heard noises on the outskirts of camp and sounded the alarm. Some residents barricaded "females and children" inside Pat Riley's stone hotel and prepared to fight. Others slinked out of town and spent the night secreted on the mountainside, wrapped in blankets with weapons in their laps. Morning investigation revealed a jackass caught in a stand of brush. "It is deplorable, as well as mortifying to see able-bodied men giving way so readily to childish fears," wrote one of the camp's cooler heads. A hasty meeting of the mining district passed a resolution that no claims would be voided for lack of the work required to hold them for the next sixty days. As a result, about three hundred decamped for California. Business and mining stopped. One "frightened hombre" prevailed upon a comrade to lower him to the bottom of a mineshaft for the purpose of "preserving his scalp" from the assault of the "noble red men" that he felt imminent. The man who'd done the lowering, perhaps lost in the grip of the well-polished jug, forgot the deed. His friend passed three hungry days at the bottom of the shaft before being remembered and returned to the surface.

Five days after the battle, the camp cheered the first force of California militia into town. The regular army companies and other militia units reached camp in the coming days, including the Sierra Battalion rallied from the Downieville area and commanded by Major Daniel E. Hungerford. A New Yorker who had been slightly wounded during the Mexican War, Hungerford emigrated to California in the summer of 1849 and failed as a shopkeeper, miner, butcher, auctioneer, blacksmith, merchant, and lawyer before summoning his wife and nine-year-old daughter west from Brooklyn to join him in Downieville five years later.

"The Major is now in his glory," wrote his son-in-law, Dr. Edmund G. Bryant, who served as battalion surgeon—or did serve, until, with his father-in-law's blessing, he hired another man to take his place. Both Doctor Bryant and the major felt it was in the family's best interests to have Dr. Bryant "look after some of [his] debtors and some mining claims."

Although there's no evidence John Mackay met Major Hungerford or Dr. Bryant during May or June 1860, due to their prominence in the Indian war excitement and the personal attachments all three men shared in the Downieville area, John Mackay likely knew of and recognized the two men.

Major Hungerford didn't possess the martial stature to hold the respect, confidence, and obedience of all the different officers of the disparate militia units and the two regular companies, but as luck would have it, the most renowned Indian fighter in the United States happened to be in Virginia City that May—ex–Texas Ranger John Coffee Hays. A man of astonishing personal courage, "Jack" Hays had risen through the ranks of the Texas Rangers fighting Comanches and Mexicans through the entire history of the Texas Republic, from 1836 to 1848. Honored to have such a sterling enemy, Comanche war chief Buffalo Hump sent Hays an engraved golden spoon to commemorate the birth of Hays's first son. Hays had introduced Samuel Walker and Samuel Colt and the fruit of their partnership—the Colt Walker six-shot .44 caliber revolver—resulted in a massive increase of white firepower in light cavalry fights. Hays commanded a regiment in the Mexican War, and after the war, served a brief stint as an Indian agent in the New Mexico Territory before joining the Gold Rush. In San Francisco in 1850, he became the city's first elected sheriff and served as surveyor general of the state later in the decade. Forty-three years old in 1860 and a resident of Oakland, Hays had come to Washoe to investigate business opportunities, and he was likely in Virginia City at the time of the Indians' Williams Station reprisal. If so, the veteran Indian fighter played no part in the Ormsby debacle—likely because he mistrusted the casus belli.

On May 22, the militia elected Hays colonel, which many soon regretted, because in addition to being a genius of irregular warfare, Hays was also a notorious disciplinarian. He stopped the militia practice of confiscating horses, mules, and cattle. In one egregious example, a valiant volunteer gentleman walked up to a doctor saddling his horse for a visit to an invalid patient and commandeered horse, saddle, and bridle over "the protestations of the physician and with a full understanding of the case." The prevalence of such episodes greatly eroded militia popularity among the white settlements, even as Indian raids struck four remote Pony Express stations in the deserts to the east and brought overland mail service to a standstill.

In late May, Colonel Hays led the combined "Washoe Regiment" into the lower Carson River Valley. They skirmished with a band of Indian scouts, then marched north to a bivouac on the bend of the Truckee River. Before dark, they found the naked body of one of Ormsby's men, much of his flesh eaten by beasts, birds, and insects, but still wearing a heavy gold ring. Nobody could identify the individual. Rain started about three o'clock in the afternoon and fell all night. After sunrise on June 1, the soaked command slogged four muddy miles downriver, found three more ravaged bodies of ill-fated members of the Ormsby expedition, and camped the night at "Camp Fletcher," named for a member of the regiment who accidentally blasted most of his throat out the back of his neck with his own rifle. The reconnaissance force Hays kept in front of his main force contacted Indian scouts throughout the day.

On June 2, Colonel Hays's forces fought a sharp multi-hour skirmish with a large force of Indian warriors near the site of the first battle. Hays held Major Hungerford and his Sierra Battalion as a reserve force. The Indians gradually gave ground through the long spring afternoon, almost certainly covering the evacuation of their villages near Pyramid Lake. As evening fell, the Indian force withdrew onto slopes above the battlefield, daring the whites to pursue them into a moonless evening. Colonel Hays held his force in check, and the Indians on the slopes above, safe beyond rifle range, rained defiant yells and "the most insulting gestures and abusive language, in both good and bad English" upon the heads of the astonished soldiers.

Both sides withdrew, the Indians back to Pyramid Lake and the whites to their last camp. The Washoe Regiment had suffered two killed and five men severely wounded. The whites claimed a great victory. An initial newspaper dispatch said they'd killed 160 Indians. More sober subsequent reportage claimed they'd killed 20 to 25 Indians and wounded another 20 to 30 out of a force of about 400. In truth, the Paiute losses were almost identical to those suffered by the whites—4 killed and 7 wounded.

Two days later, on June 4, Colonel Hays advanced his entire force down the Truckee River to Pyramid and Mud lakes, finding "plenty of sign, but no Injun." A Paiute rearguard killed a careless white scout, ending the Second Battle of Pyramid Lake. The tribesmen vanished into the mountainous deserts to the north.

Major Hungerford and his men had spent the campaign one step removed from the tip of Colonel Hays's spear. Other units did the bulk of the fighting. Not long after the battle, the white volunteers disbanded. Colonel Hays returned to civilian pursuits, mostly in Oakland, and never harried another Indian. The most succinct summary of the entire affair appeared in the *Marysville Daily Appeal* two weeks after the second battle. "The proportions of the whole thing have been immensely exaggerated, a single act of merited Indian vengeance having been construed into a declaration of general hostilities." Richard N. Allen, aka "Tennessee," the *San Francisco Herald*'s correspondent in Genoa and a longtime resident of the eastern slope, concurred. "I hesitate not to express my conviction that the war was commenced by outrages committed upon the Indians by mendacious whites," he wrote. John Coffee Hays's reluctance to push for a decisive engagement might well reflect his concurrence with those sentiments.

• • •

As for John Mackay, he seems to have had the good sense to stay out of the Indian war. On May 9, as excitement over the Williams Station "massacre" roiled Virginia City and the camp's volunteers trotted out toward catastrophe, John Mackay deeded twenty feet of the Union mine to his cabin mate A. E. Kennedy, business as usual.

Mackay, it would appear, had his eyes on the future, most of which was underground.

CHAPTER 5

Surrounded by Riches—
and Unable to Get Them Out

A carman of the Gould & Curry pushing a load of waste down a
wooden track to the dump below the mouth of the Lower Adit;
Mount Davidson and the core of Virginia City in the background.

———

The most wonderful operation in this mine is the timbering. . . . It sustains the superincumbent mountain as firmly
as Saint Peter's does the dome of Michael Angelo [*sic*].
—"From Nevada Territory," *Red Bluff Independent*

While snow blanketed Mount Davidson and the peaks of the Washoe
Range through the winter and spring of 1860, miners and speculators soothed one another with such platitudes as "silver veins are not soli-
tary." Where one existed, there could not fail to be others. Moneyed men,
mostly from San Francisco, awed by the product of the proven mines and
eager to get in on the ground floor, bought claims on hope. Claim holders, without coin and needing to eat and uncertain of the value of what

lay underground, sold. The speculative market had raged, but to one observer's eye, it had been mostly a "swapping of coats." Values reflected little in the way of genuine mine development.

Then came the spring thaw. Assayers' returns from the first scrapings at the exposed quartz ledges revealed that most of what had been supposed ore didn't hold profitable concentrations of royal metals. If genuine wealth existed farther underground, only significant investment of labor and capital would expose it. The market for feet took "a downward tendency" in early May. The uncertainties attendant to the Indian war hammered it again. "Washoe stock, as it now stands in the market, is a dead letter," Almarin B. Paul wrote to the *San Francisco Bulletin* on June 12.

Afterward, people made more clear-eyed evaluations of the district. They realized that many prospectors located claims without any thought of extracting gold and silver. They only wanted to sell to speculators. People also realized that ownership disputes befogged the title of every productive mine. Developing a successful mine without waging ferocious legal warfare had become impossible—a state of affairs that, although frustrating and expensive, improved on the "squally business" of "settling points of law with Colt's Code of six irresistible arguments." The fall in the value of "feet" ruined speculators who had borrowed money to purchase claims. Borrowing money on the Pacific Slope cost 3 percent interest *per month*, with loans typically running a three-month term. (With banks of the era neither as stable nor as widespread as in modern times, cash-rich individuals often chose to "let out money at interest" rather than trust coin to bank deposits—none of which carried any form of insurance.*) As the *Sacramento Daily Union* joked, many businessmen had "put their foot in it." The downturn also exposed the sharp practices of many touts.

"You became victims of your own sublime stupidity and dishonesty," a self-described "Old Resident of Washoe" gloated in the *San Francisco Bulletin*. "Fools at your end of the telegraph were deceived by knaves at our end." Scorched San Francisco investors moaned about Washoe as "a grand humbug," more "glaring and barefaced" than the Fraser River.

However, for the proven mines, the speculative discomfiture didn't

---

* The vast majority of American bank deposits wouldn't be insured until after the widespread bank failures at the beginning of the Great Depression in the early 1930s motivated Congress to pass the Banking Act of 1933 (also known as the Glass-Steagall Act)—one of its provisions created the Federal Deposit Insurance Corporation (FDIC).

represent underground reality. The narrow mines on Gold Hill continued as good as ever. The Ophir, the Mexican, and the Central, those mines working the known Comstock Lead, likewise continued productive.

With the vein going deeper underground on a forty-five-degree slant or "dip" into Mount Davidson, and an ever-greater quantity of non-paying "dead work" required to cut back the sides of the surface pits to allow them to go deeper, the Ophir Company stopped trying to work the mine through surface cuts.* Instead, the Ophir started sinking a shaft—a watershed moment in Comstock mining that would culminate twenty-five years later with miners working more than three thousand feet below the original croppings. The Ophir sank the shaft on the forty-five-degree angle of the downsloping lode, in technical parlance, making it an "incline shaft." At intervals on the way down, Ophir miners "drifted" out to the sides of the shaft to extract ore. (When mining a lode, "drifts" are tunnels that run parallel to the line of the lode or in it; "crosscuts" run perpendicular to the line of the lode or across it.) In places, the Ophir had the treasure vein of blue and black sulphurets three feet wide, cased in a twelve- to fifteen-foot width of soft, crumbly, gold- and silver-impregnated quartz, and the miners supported the "workings" with traditional post-and-cap timbering techniques.

As the miners delved deeper, water started to sweat through the walls of the ore body, then trickle. The influx collected at the shaft bottom. To raise ore and "waste" (valueless rock that had to be removed) and de-water the mine, the Ophir used a tank winched up a wooden track laid on the slope of their incline shaft with a hand-turned windlass. Mules hitched to the arms of the windlass and marching in circles arastra fashion soon replaced the men, but by the time their incline reached a depth of fifty feet—still in the richest ore any American miner had ever seen—the "horse-whim" couldn't keep pace with the water. Progress stalled. To drain the mine, the superintendent cut an adit in from farther down the slope, but the ore body dipped deeper, and the mine walls oozed a greater quantity of water with every foot of added depth. The Ophir decided to mechanize. Machines didn't protest twenty-four-hour workdays. In San Francisco, the owners ordered one of Swedish-American engine maker John Ericsson's double expansion twenty-four-inch caloric engines.†

---

* The ever-increasing volume of "dead work" required to keep enlarging an open pit to extract the ore at the bottom eventually forces a mine to either follow the ore deposit down via a shaft or shafts—if the ore is rich enough—or quit mining altogether.

† Incidentally, the next year, John Ericsson designed the Union ironclad *Monitor* with

The expansive force of heated air drove caloric engines, and although air didn't provide as much power as steam, caloric engines were much safer and less expensive for light industrial uses.* The Ophir spent $2,000 freighting the engine over the mountains. The Ericsson engine supplied the turning power of fifteen horses, which the Ophir owners expected would suffice to drive the hoists and raise the bucket until the grand new adit they'd undertaken in conjunction with the adjacent mines hit the lode 180 feet below the surface sometime in the autumn, at the end of a thousand-foot tunnel.

The productive mines still shipped most of their first-class ore to Europe, but first-class ore represented only a tiny fraction of total mine product. The precious metal locked inside the thousands of tons of lower-grade material piled up below the productive mines exceeded the quantity in the first-class ores—if only some practical man could develop a fast, efficient, low-cost, industrial-scale, on-site manner of extracting value from second- and third-class ore. Inability to do it was the single biggest obstacle preventing miners from unlocking the lode's potential. The man who figured out how to do it would make a fortune—and unleash the power of the nascent American silver mining industry.

Grounded "scientific gentlemen" put their faith in variants of expensive roasting and smelting methods. One of the few dissenting voices belonged to George Hearst's friend Almarin B. Paul, the Nevada City mill man. The previous autumn and winter, Paul had tested alternative reduction processes on Comstock ores and proved to his satisfaction that he could create a fast and profitable method of milling Washoe ores by combining elements of the traditional but slow Mexican "patio process"—developed in sixteenth-century Spanish America—with more mechanical and faster methods Gold Rush miners had invented to extract gold from California quartz veins.

Paul borrowed a large sum of money, and in late May, during the tumultuous weeks between the First and Second Battles of Pyramid Lake, began supervising construction of a mill at Silver City, a camp that had sprung up around Devil's Gate halfway down Gold Cañon. He ordered a batch of heavy machinery and engines from a San Francisco foundry

---

its novel rotating turret, which, in history's first battle between ironclad warships, fought the Confederate *Merrimack* to a draw at the Battle of Hampton Roads—a seminal event in the history of naval warfare.

* Caloric engines didn't require notoriously explosion-prone high-pressure boilers, they consumed less fuel (an important consideration in coal-less and treeless Washoe), and didn't require the oversight of trained, highly paid engineers.

customized to suit his purposes. Paul hemorrhaged money pushing the work forward. The success of the enterprise—and his solvency—hung in the balance. Only a strong revenue stream associated with the successful and profitable reduction of ore would stave off his creditors come August. Paul installed a forty-horsepower steam engine—he had no intention of trusting success to a feeble caloric engine. On August 9, less than sixty days after Paul had committed to the project, his engineer fired the boiler, got up a test head of pressure, and let out the furious screech of the steam whistle, the first ever heard on the Comstock. Four days later, the great test began.

Paul's engine drove the fast-rotating camshafts that raised and dropped the sixteen heavy iron stamps of his "California stamp mill" onto chunks of ore in quick staccato fashion. The deafening clatter of metallic blows rained on rock held in iron pans rattled over the sagebrush. The stamps crushed the ore to a fine dust, water washed the pulverized ore into wide iron pans shaped like enormous gold pans and formed a slurry, called the "pulp," stirred by heavy iron "mullers" rotating in the pans. Mill men dumped a few ounces of copper sulfate, a pint of salt, and forty pounds of mercury into each three-hundred-pound charge of crushed ore. Tiny gold particles in the pulp amalgamated with the mercury while the copper sulfate and salt reacted with the silver sulphurets to force the silver into a state from which it could also join the amalgam. After a few hours of mixing, Paul's millers opened cocks in the bottoms of the pans, drained the heavy amalgam, and retorted away the mercury, leaving behind the great prize—a heavy slug of gold and silver bullion—tangible, gorgeous evidence that Paul had developed a fast, effective, inexpensive milling process that could accomplish in four or five *hours* what the patio process did in a similar number of *weeks*, a classic example of the can-do ingenuity with which American industrialists captured the world's attention in the middle decades of the nineteenth century. Almarin Paul's method became known as the "Washoe Pan Process," or just the "Washoe Process," and it unlocked the potential of an entire industry.

Mines clamored for his services. Paul employed about one hundred men, set his mill to working around the clock, doubled his stamping capacity, and immediately started plotting to erect a second mill directly below the mines at Gold Hill, a "monster institution" to house sixty-four stamps.

Bullion belonged to the mine that supplied the ore; mills charged a fixed cost per ton reduced and guaranteed to "save" a certain portion of the ore's assayed value, usually 65 percent. (The remaining 35 percent ran off in the tailings.) With the ability to contract with different mines and fixed fees received, Paul's fortunes seemed tied to those of the entire mining region rather than to the fate of any one particular mine. That seemed to greatly lessen his risk. Eagerness to grab a slice of the milling pie sparked a frenzy of imitation. The milling boom unleashed forces that would render many mines profitable, facilitate the conduct of mining on a speed and scale never before seen anywhere else on earth, industrialize one of the most inhospitable and fragile landscapes in North America, and environmentally devastate a host of ecosystems yoked to the new industry.

As the Ophir went deeper, its ore body continued to widen. Overwhelmed with good fortune, wanting to reserve all potential profit to themselves, and desiring an above-ground monument worthy of the world's greatest mine, the Ophir trustees decided to build a massive mill on the shores of Washoe Lake, twelve miles away in the Washoe Valley between the Virginia Range and the eastern slope of the Sierras. They based the mill on the fanciest and most complicated and intricate processes available, and chose the site because of its proximity to the lake water and the many forested mountainsides the company intended to denude to fire the mill's boilers and smelters. The Ophir trustees financed construction of a road through the intervening mountains to connect the mine with the proposed mill, and spared no expense in mill construction, convinced they owned a bottomless mine.

As summer turned into autumn, Virginia City and Gold Hill rang with the sounds of hammers and saws and the shouts of workmen erecting more substantial dwellings and businesses. In Virginia City, where there had been nothing but sagebrush the year before, a midsummer census counted more than eight hundred buildings—among which were forty-two general stores and an equal number of saloons—and although a number of residents still lived in "cloth cabins," the majority resided in houses built of lumber. Construction hadn't kept pace with the needs of the population, however. The *Territorial Enterprise* reported the burning of a haystack as a public calamity that "deprived a number of people of lodgings." Gold Hill doubled in size between May and September. Like so many places in the Far West, Washoe was an overwhelmingly male place. A census counted 2,206 men and only 139 women and girls in Virginia City, and that constituted a much better ratio than that found in Gold Hill, with 605 males and just 14 females. Contrary to the myth that most early Comstock women toiled in brothels, saloons, and dance halls and the belief expressed in such mining camp song lyrics as "first came the miner to work in the mine/ then came the ladies who lived on the line," most of the 111 adult women known to be on the lode in the summer of 1860 weren't supporting themselves "in the fast life." Although some "women of the town" probably reported other occupations to the census takers, they were only a fraction of the total. Eighty-three of the 111 women were married. Forty-three had children to look after. Most who worked in the local economy did domestic work for others, mended and made clothing, cooked, ran boardinghouses, and did whatever they could to improve their fortunes. Tough-minded, hardworking, aggressive, and ambitious—just like the men around them—women went to Washoe for the same reason as the men—because it afforded them an opportunity to improve their lives.

One of them was Mrs. Eider, first name unrecorded. In Virginia City, she and her husband owned a house and a lot they rented to Thomas Devins, and by late August, Devins's rent was ten dollars in arrears. On Monday, August 27, Mr. Eider went to the house he rented to Devins and demanded payment. Devins couldn't—or wouldn't—pay, and Eider poured vitriol on his delinquent tenant, "calling him the usual variety of hard names."

After Eider wandered off, Devins collected four friends. Armed with revolvers, and irrigated with whisky, the five toughs stalked to the Eiders' home after dark. They stood in the yard and yelled for Eider to come out and account for the insults. Eider was inside with his wife and a neighbor, Mr. Hill. Through his closed door, Eider announced that he didn't want trouble. He refused to emerge.

Devins and his friends drew their revolvers and shouldered through the door.

Mrs. Eider threw herself in front of her husband and exclaimed, "Will you shoot a woman?"

She got her answer right away. A ball smacked into her thigh, just below the hip, inflicting a severe, bloody wound. Her husband took a shot through the fleshy part of his leg. Another ball hit Mr. Hill in the arm. Among the attackers was a man named Hughes. An errant shot fired by another member of the gang blew a hole in his head. Hughes fell dead. Shocked by the mayhem, Devins and his surviving cronies fled into the night.

Mr. Hill and the Eiders survived. The law, such as it was, captured none of the assailants. Two more shooting affrays rocked Virginia City the following Sunday. In the first, a drunk Mexican "raising a row" in a saloon flourished a pistol. Another patron drew a revolver and shot him in the head and the groin. Later, a man named Spitzer insulted Mr. Smith's wife. Smith shot Spitzer in the groin. An inquiry acquitted Smith of wrongdoing.

Similar "bloodshed, violence, and strife" riled the Comstock in 1860. The *Red Bluff Independent* reported that of the first thirty-six people buried in Virginia City and Gold Hill, thirty-five had died by violent means. The grave of John Jessup, the first of them, murdered by William Sides in the spring of 1859, lay right in the middle of Gold Hill's main street at the lower end of town. Freight teams dodged around it.

Given the violence and the many disputes over the ownership of mining property, the great want—besides titanic piles of gold and silver—was for properly constituted legal authority independent of the Mormon-dominated Utah territorial government five hundred miles away in Salt Lake City. Almost to a person, the inhabitants of western Utah wanted the federal government to either annex the region to the state of California or legislate it into a new territory independent of Salt Lake. Most gentiles distrusted Mormon suzerainty, the church's ecclesiastical authorities having used the bloc-voting power of their adherents to control the legislative, judicial, and executive functions of the territory. Considering the bloody pogroms Mormons had suffered at gentile hands since the founding of their religion, the distrust worked both ways. As the influx of gentiles brought to the territory by the mining discoveries threatened to undermine Mormon ballot box dominance and control of their religious destiny, the Saints grew willing to facilitate the separation of western Utah from the main body of the territory.

The Utah government dispatched the apparatus of a court to Genoa, but even though court proceedings promised criminal justice and an avenue to settle without bloodshed the many "vampire suits" filed to "befog" legitimate claims to good mining ground, most gentile inhabitants of western Utah preferred anarchy to judicial processes they perceived as being "under the shadow and shield" of the "Sodom festering" in Salt Lake City. No gentile expected a fair trial against a Mormon litigant.

In the initial claiming rush of the previous year, many claims had been located on the slopes of Mount Davidson both above and below the productive mines on Virginia City's out-sloping bench. Regardless of the good "indications" they turned up to tantalize potential investors, none had produced significant quantities of ore. Many, however, were perfectly positioned "fighting claims" from which to "float shadows" over the titles of their more prosperous neighbors.

Ignorance of the geological conditions beneath their feet contributed much to the legal chaos. Beyond the walls of the existing underground workings, miners knew very little about the ground they were working. The only obvious thing was the basic north-south orientation of the major quartz croppings. Beyond that, miners didn't know whether they were working one gigantic V-shaped fissure vein whose croppings rose to the surface in a wide mineralized zone and united in depth or if the croppings of the many independent surface veins stayed separate underground. Even though only about fourteen hundred feet separated the Central-Ophir-Mexican bonanza from a strike recently made on the Gould & Curry claim, the Gould & Curry discovery was considerably higher up the side of Mount Davidson and the character of its paying quartz differed from that of the Comstock Lead, evidence that made it seem possible—even likely—that the ore bodies belonged to different ledges. Consequently, Washoe miners held "a contrariety of opinion" about the precise nature and course of the vein. Most of the ownership disputes hinged on whether they'd struck one great ledge that ran through all the paying claims or a variety of smaller, independent ones. Only time and a great deal of work would reveal the answers. In the meantime, the question itself developed an enormous bonanza for Comstock lawyers.

As the days grew shorter, people began asking one another whether they intended to stay the winter. "You bet" came the most common answer. "If I can make the riffle." Inhabitants resolved to stay began laying in provisions. Surprising to many Washoeites, quite a number of ladies intended to stick with their menfolk through the winter, rather than return to more civilized circumstances in California. Most expected their presence to improve the camp's "tone."

Thanks to the carpentry skills he'd learned during his apprenticeship at the Webb shipyard, John Mackay made his first step that year. The Mexican mine promoted him to timberman. Mackay cut, fit, and installed the posts and lintels that supported the walls and ceilings of the shafts, crosscuts, drifts, and stopes against "caves."* Decades later, John B. Shaw, an "old Comstocker" who'd spent most of his life working for the

---

* The modern tongue wants to say that a mine "caved in," but the literature contemporary to the Comstock heyday always said that a mine "caved," or that there had been "a cave" in the such-and-such mine.

local mines, recalled working alongside Mackay in 1860. Every day, the two men ate lunch on the Mexican's dump. After completing his shift and earning his six dollars, better than the four earned by common miners, Mackay walked a few thousand feet south and did what any other man would have considered a second full day's work on the tunnel he'd contracted to build for the Buck Ledge.

Adjacent to the Mexican, the Ophir's incline shaft descended in the soft, crumbly quartz of the ore body as it angled down into Mount Davidson. The system worked reasonably well while the width of the ore body stayed under fifteen or twenty feet, the maximum width traditional post-and-cap timbering could safely support. Ophir miners "drifted" north and south through shattered quartz on the line of the lode, crosscutting the vein at intervals. Almost all of the excavations were "productive," work carried out inside the ore body, as opposed to "dead work" done in worthless country rock. However, the vein didn't behave; it continued widening. Below fifty feet, it exceeded the width that post-and-cap timbering could handle. Only "a continuous sheathing of pine logs"—one foot in diameter, sometimes twice that—lining the walls and ceiling could support the shattered, water-soaked quartz and the soft and crumbly seams of blue-black sulphurets encased within it, but even then, trouble arose whenever the Ophir tried to open a "gallery" or "stope" over a span larger than twenty feet wide or high. Beyond a certain extracted volume, no amount of reinforcement proved capable of preventing the pressure from buckling and snapping the thick timbers. Nor could miners work beyond the boundary of the timbers without causing "caves." Most refused to do it.

Mines elsewhere in the world seldom dealt with such difficulties. Most worked more solid ground that needed less reinforcement, the dimensions of their ore bodies didn't exceed the size that traditional timbering could comfortably support, and in those that did, the value of the ore outside their timbered workings didn't justify the expense and risk of extraction. The Ophir bonanza was different. The size of the ore body greatly exceeded the span that post-and-cap timbering could support, and the quality rivaled the best ever encountered. Abandoning such riches to engineering difficulties was unthinkable.

The problems came to a head in mid-October, when "the Union Tunnel"—a joint adit driven horizontally toward the lode from an entrance farther down the hillside by the Ophir, the Mexican, and the Central not to be confused with the tunnel John Mackay had built for the Union mine the previous winter—approached the vein between 180 feet and 155 feet below the surface. (In addition to being a "union" of their interests, the adit's name probably reflected the political sentiments of the mine owners—politics had become ubiquitous in the run-up to the most contentious presidential election in the history of the republic.) About thirty feet short of where they anticipated cutting the lode, miners at the working head of the tunnel encountered a wall of the tough, plastic clay whose expansive properties caused such problems in the mines above. They'd had little problem with the influx of water for the whole thousand-foot length of their adit, and they hacked at the clay wall without hesitation, failing to realize that the impermeable wall dammed an enormous reservoir of water inside the lode. They received a harsh education when the wall disintegrated in front of them, unleashing a flood.

According to a letter published in the *Sacramento Daily Union*, the torrent "discharged so rapidly as to render it prudent for them to leave without standing upon the order of their going." In short, the crew fled for their lives. The torrent tore up the planking of the wheelbarrow track on the adit floor and flushed it out the tunnel mouth. Fortunately, nobody was seriously injured. (John Mackay may have worked on the Union Tunnel; if not, he certainly knew men who did.) The flood drained off the water plaguing the three mines that shared the Union Tunnel.

Continuing explorations exposed a problem of an entirely different scale. A crosscut across the Ophir's ore body on the level of the Union Tunnel revealed a sixty-five-foot-wide span of ore. The discovery had staggering implications. Prospecting drifts and crosscuts showed that in the southern slice of the mine on that level, the ore body extended from stake to stake between its boundaries with the Mexican and the Central, the full 200 feet, and it *averaged* 55 feet in width. Above that 200-foot-by-55-foot rectangular footprint the wedge-shaped triangular prism of the ore body angled up and eastward at a forty-five-degree angle to an apex near the surface. Neither did the ore show any sign of "pinching out" below the floors.

The discovery made front-page news as far away as New Orleans, where the *Daily Crescent* described Ophir, Mexican, and Central shareholders as "much elated." If so, they hadn't pondered the scale of their problem—nothing close to that size had ever been extracted in the entire history of mining. To expand the stopes on the level of the Union Tunnel, in what they called the "Third Gallery" (the two others were in the ore body above), Ophir Superintendent W. L. Dall, formerly a ship captain for the Pacific Mail Steamship Company, directed his miners to join timbers together with iron plates, bands, and bolts in much the same manner as sailors step a topmast above a mainmast. Immense pressures within the mine mangled and snapped the joined timbers like kindling. Caves killed several miners. Others had narrow escapes, and aside from the human toll, the mine lost thousands of tons of ore in the caves, since a collapse rendered the vicinity too dangerous to work. The situation presented no small amount of irony: Surrounded by riches, the owners of the Ophir couldn't get them out.

A number of mining engineers examined the problem. None of them could figure out how to solve it. Near the end of November, one of the Ophir's trustees (and substantial owners), William F. Babcock, heard about a twenty-eight-year-old German immigrant named Philipp Deidesheimer superintending a gold mine in El Dorado County who supposedly combined the best aspects of the formal engineering education he'd acquired in the Freiberg mining school with an ability to solve real-world problems. Babcock summoned Deidesheimer to San Francisco and asked him if he'd ever seen or worked a quartz vein sixty feet in width.

Deidesheimer said he'd never heard of anything like it.

Babcock asked if he thought it was possible to work such a vein.

Deidesheimer said he had no way of knowing until he'd seen and studied the mine in question.

The German had given the only true answer. Babcock sent him to Virginia City.

Deidesheimer arrived on November 8. He studied the local geology, the Ophir's underground topography, the vein, the ore, and the method of its workings, paying particular attention to areas where underground pressures and caves had mangled the existing timbers. No obvious solution leaped to mind. The scope of the problem daunted Deidesheimer. For three more weeks, he engineered his way forward, theorizing, modeling, upsizing, testing, rethinking, tweaking, improving, testing, and retesting before he had what he hoped would be a workable solution. Time would prove it a work of simple, elegant genius.

The internal structure of beehives provided the crucial inspiration. In principle, what became known as Philipp Deidesheimer's system of "square-set timbering" involved replacing each four-foot-wide, four-foot-deep, seven-foot-tall volume of extracted ore with a strong timber frame, then replacing an adjacent extracted volume with a similar timber frame, and so on and so on as the miners stoped ore until the entire volume of the ore body was replaced by a beehive-like structure of stout rectangular cuboids.

To put it into effect, Deidesheimer ordered his miners to crosscut the

A detail of Philipp Deidesheimer's cuboids.

vein on the level of the Union adit. To serve as the sill timbers on the floor, he made his timbermen physically wrestle the longest timbers it was possible to maneuver into place up the Union adit. Deidesheimer directed them to install the sills down the *sides* of the initial crosscut, not across it, then had them mount seven-foot posts on the sills at four-foot intervals and connect them overhead with the four-foot caps. Cross-braces went across the floor and ceiling in line with the posts. Spanning the fifty-five-foot width of the ore body required several sill timbers joined end to end. Finished, a line of upright rectangular cuboids stood on the long sills. Different from traditional mine timbering, the main strength of the reinforcement ran over the sills down the sides of the crosscut, not across its course.

The importance of that distinction didn't become apparent until Deidesheimer had his workmen begin installing additional rows of "square sets" on each side of the first. The main strength of the system wasn't designed to support a single crosscut. As the systematic beehive structure of the square-set timbers grew, its main strength formed over the sill timbers, *across* the ore body, oriented to support the extraction of the entire thing. Timbermen installed a plank floor over the sills and built wooden tracks on the floor, a miniature railroad along which they ran ore cars. While one crew of miners steadily advanced four feet into the ore body on one side of the original crosscut, timbermen replacing each volume of extracted ore with a square-set until they'd completed an entire row, another crew did the same thing on the opposite side. Once they'd advanced several rows in both directions, a third gang began mining overhead, hacking ore from the ceiling into ore cars positioned beneath. When the overhead gang had removed sufficient volume, timbermen shored the void with a square-set built atop the bottom row. When the overhead miners completed a full line across the vein, they, too, turned and advanced into the ore body in both directions a few rows of square-sets behind the crews still advancing on the first floor. When the bottom two floors had "worked out" a sufficient volume, more miners began opening a third-floor overhead. Thus, the stopes advanced into the ore body on both sides of the original crosscut like the leading edges of two wedges pushing out from a central point, adding another level to the overhead work whenever sufficient space opened above. The distance between the sill timbers and the miners working overhead quickly grew to the point that falls from above presented a serious hazard—of people, of objects they might drop, and of rocks and other debris falling from the ceiling. To improve safety and aid their working, miners working overhead built plank floors. Thus, "the rats of the lower galleries" safely extracted huge volumes of ore at a velocity hitherto unknown in mining.

Few lodes orient perfectly vertical. Like the Comstock, most angle or "dip" one way or another, which gives them a high side and a low side. Miners consider the "hanging wall" to be the country rock above the lode and the "footwall" to be the country rock below, and as the square-set lattice expanded inside the ore body, it was an easy matter for timbermen to add one square-set on the footwall side of the vein and subtract one against the hanging wall to account for the lode's dip. Directly against the footwall and hanging wall on both edges of the ore body, timbermen installed "wall plates" similar to the long floor sills, then created resisting force between the wall plates with timber "angle braces" installed diagonally across the whole volume of square-sets that created solid lines of resistance between the weight of the hanging wall pressing down from above and the support of the footwall below.

Deidesheimer's square-set timbering system was pure engineering genius, plain and simple and in retrospect obvious, easy to comprehend, install, and adapt to changing underground circumstances. A man who inspected the Ophir the following year described the "strong, heavy timbers, braced and counterbraced . . . like the trestle-work of a railroad bridge." Another noted the "striking contrast" Deidesheimer's system made to "the slovenly timbering" in the neighboring Mexican mine, and an 1862 visitor from Marysville emerged from the Ophir much impressed by the "ingenious frames of massive timber of great strength" holding open stopes that climbed from several hundred feet underground to within thirty feet of the surface. And although phenomenally expensive due to the vast quantity of timber required, Philipp Deidesheimer's novel square-set timbering system made it possible to extract the Ophir's immense ore body. Along with the California stamp mill and the "Washoe Pan Process" Almarin Paul developed earlier in the year, Philipp Deidesheimer's square-set timbering system formed the third leg of the great trifecta of American contributions to the art and science of mining, worldwide. Miners today use evolutions of all three systems 150 years after the Comstock heyday.

Opening a gallery approximately one hundred feet *below* the square-set matrix revealed the final genius of Deidesheimer's system. Surveyors carefully aligned the huge sill timbers in the lower level with the ones already installed above. Since each long sill spanned several square-sets, the miners working up from below with the identical system could directly connect from the uppermost line of square-sets—albeit one at a time and *very* carefully—to the long sills above, which allowed the miners to extract every last ton of the ore body.

Not only did Deidesheimer's square-sets make practicable the extraction of the Comstock's enormous ore bodies, its employment greatly accelerated the entire mining process. Using Deidesheimer's system, a single man could mine from five to ten tons of ore per shift. The Ophir stoped out ore at a rate that would have astonished previous generations of miners.

And in mining, speed mattered. A competent, well-planned, well-executed, rapid mining operation raised a given quantity of ore with less cost. Speedy extraction minimized the total time needed to exhaust a mine, and therefore lessened the amount of fuel required to fire the engines that drove the pumps and hoists, and with mine workers paid per day, "snaking out the ore" at an efficient clip lowered total labor costs. And since even the most perfectly installed square-sets lasted only a finite time—timbers rotted, decayed, and compressed—rapid prosecution of the work extracted the ore before the expensive timbers needed replacement. Most important of all, a fast-working mine was safer. Speed minimized the total time crews spent exposed to the myriad hazards of working underground.

Deidesheimer's square-set timbering system had one drawback—its phenomenal cost. Some mines balked at the expense. Most cut corners wherever possible. One of them was the Ophir's neighbor, the Mexican. Rather than investing in square-sets, it used old Mexican mining techniques. The Mexican mined on the dip of the vein via an incline shaft, shoring its workings as needed with traditional timbering techniques, as had originally been done in the Ophir. Using steps hacked into the floor of the slope, the mine's predominantly Mexican workforce lugged enormous loads of ore to the surface in rawhide baskets held against a man's back with a tumpline around his forehead. The mine took the incline shaft down forty or fifty feet, then drifted north and south across the full hundred-foot length of the claim. At regular intervals along the drift, they sank "winzes" deeper into the ore body, still following the lode's dip. (In technical parlance, a "winze" was a mine working made driving down; one worked upward from a lower level was called an "upraise" or "raise.") Another long drift connected the bottoms of the winzes. Below the bottom drift, miners sank another series of winzes and connected their sumps with an even lower drift. And so on they descended on the dip of the lode, leaving the grid of ore pillars between the drifts and winzes in place to support the mine. The technique saved a great portion of the timbering expense required to mine with Deidesheimer's square-set system, and it had another advantage, since unlike timber, ore left in situ didn't rot and decay. Proper use of the technique in solid ground rendered mines permanently secure. The idea was to use the system to reach the bottom of the ore body, then mine out the supporting ore pillars, starting at the bottom, and allow the mine to fall in on itself one level at a time. Silver miners in Mexico and Spanish America had used the strategy to hold mines open for centuries.

John Mackay was underground through all of it, watching with his eyes and doing with his hands. Deidesheimer's new square-set timbering technique perfectly complemented Mackay's skills. For a miner at the end of 1860 and the start of 1861, there was no better place in the world to learn mining techniques both new and old than in the mine workings beginning to open below the young towns of Virginia City and Gold Hill.

Sources don't reveal much about John Mackay in 1861. We do know that he worked through the whole year on the tunnel he'd agreed to build for the Buck Ledge back in March 1860, the contract that required him to "run said tunnel five days in every week till his contract is completed." Mackay wouldn't finish that project for another twenty-three months, but when he did, mining district records noted the "full satisfaction thereof." With that job set to pay him in feet, he had to continue earning coin in the same way he had since the first day he set foot in Washoe—working for wages in the mines. Although the words of a *Daily Alta California* correspondent described "everyone" in Washoe "in a fret because he has made his fortune, or because he has not made it," *virtually* everyone would have been a more accurate assessment. Thirty-year-old John Mackay chose an entirely different course than the get-rich-quick schemes that fired the imaginations of so many men on the mining frontier. Lacking capital, he worked to earn it, saving every penny. Lacking knowledge, he worked to gain it, never overlooking a learning opportunity. He worked for wages in the Central-Ophir-Mexican bonanza, in other mines in the Gold Hill and Virginia districts, and on his own account in the tunnel he was building for the Buck Ledge on the slopes of Mount Davidson above the Chollar and the Potosi. An immensely practical man, Mackay started at the bottom and worked his way up, educating himself in every facet of Comstock mining by doing it himself, trying to peer ahead, both into the rock and into the future, to figure out how he might win his own share of the riches that surrounded him every day. Slowly, diligently, with constant endeavor, Mackay learned the characteristics of the vein, of the country rock that surrounded it, of the clay sheets that held the ore bodies—or underground floods—of the "pitch" and "dip" of the ore bodies, and of the ore itself, silver sulphurets and chlorides, pregnant with royal metals. He drove through the "horses" of worthless matter that disappointed miners where they'd otherwise expected good pay. In the dangerous, valuable labyrinth growing underneath the two camps, Mackay acquired a reputation for exacting competence. He took pride in honest toil. To him, all work was honorable, and a job was sacred. What he did, he did right, and he impressed men with his upright manner and steady judgment. His peers soon counted him among the lode's best timbermen for shoring caving ground.

Meanwhile, during the winter of 1860–61, San Francisco citizens flocked to the South Beach salesrooms of the Union Reduction Works to take a close look at what had everyone so excited—a display of $9,000 worth of Washoe bullion, a fraction of the roughly $1 million worth of gold and silver disgorged by the Comstock mines that year. Except in those few places where the casting mold had roughened the surface, the *Daily Alta California* described the huge bricks gleaming "pure silver white and bright as a new coin." Composed of two-thirds silver and one-third gold and certified by assayers as 997 fine, lacking only three parts per thousand of gold and silver, the bullion bars sat on the countertops "freely exposed to public inspection." The proprietors felt no worry about theft due to the immense weight of the ingots, each heavier than a man "could comfortably lug a hundred yards."

The successes in the new mineral territories of western Utah were welcome news in California, for the opening of new mining frontiers in the Great Basin portended well for the state's economy. News from the East provided a counterbalance. Lincoln's election had caused the gravitation that held the United States together to fail. People on the Pacific Slope awaited the arrival of the Pony Express with "breathless anxiety" and "every word on the subject of secession [was] read and discussed by all."

The first westbound Pony Express of 1861 that arrived at Fort Churchill, twenty-five miles east of Virginia City, brought the news that, depending on a person's sectional sentiments, was either anxiously awaited or long dreaded. Forwarded by telegraph to California, the story broke around the state the next morning. A South Carolina convention had "released" its state from her obligation to the "General Government" two weeks before, on December 20, 1860.

Mississippi joined South Carolina's exit from the Union on January 9, 1861, proudly proclaiming in its declaration of secession, "Our position is thoroughly identified with the institution of slavery—the greatest material interest in the world." One after the other, Florida, Alabama, Georgia, Louisiana, and Texas resolved themselves out of the Union. By February 1, the entire Deep South had seceded.

One result of the secession directly benefited the miners, businessmen, and ranchers of the western Utah Territory—the departure of the senators and representatives of the Deep South from Congress broke the logjam between free-soil and slave factions that had so long hindered the organization of new states and territories. Bills creating the Nevada and Dakota territories passed the Senate and House, and lame-duck president James Buchanan signed them into law as one of the last acts of his ineffective and unpopular administration.

Forty-eight hours later, President-elect Abraham Lincoln placed his right hand on a Bible and registered his oath as president of the United States. The crisis came to a head six weeks later. South Carolina militia forces attacked Fort Sumter, an island of federal property in Charleston Harbor garrisoned by the United States Army, and precipitated a civil war. Inflamed southern passions sparked the secession of Virginia, Arkansas, North Carolina, and Tennessee. Armies mobilized in both North and South.

While federal and rebel armies lurched toward the bloodbaths that would determine the fate of the American people, the states and territories of the Pacific Slope were a good place to be. "There never were better times all around for everybody in California than today," Podgers wrote to the *New York Times* from San Francisco a week after Fort Sumter. "Everybody is either well-to-do or absolutely getting rich." The spring weather was delightful. As the same man had written, "California is better off . . . than any State in the Union and of course better than any out of it."

And so it would remain for the duration of the war in both California and the Nevada Territory. Despite occasional rumors of secret secessionist societies aiming to pass the mineral riches of the Nevada Territory to the Confederate government and the avowedly secessionist sentiments of John L. Blackburn, the Virginia City sheriff, the most serious disloyal act in the territory seems to have been the crowd of inebriates stirred up by the saloonkeep who raised South Carolina's Palmetto flag over Newman's

Saloon on A Street in the first week of June 1861. The widely despised "rag of treason" attracted a crowd, with the well-sprung saloonkeeper threatening to shoot anyone who molested it, but before events came unmoored, other inebriates hoisted the U.S. flag alongside South Carolina's "obnoxious emblem." As the citizenry sobered up, passions calmed, and both flags came down.

But despite occasional alarms, disturbances, and frequent brawls, secessionist sentiment never took deep root in the Nevada Territory. To the Southern sympathizers who sneered that "a man is either a Secessionist or an Abolitionist," the majority always shouted back, "A man is either a Union man or a traitor!"

The non-native settlers of western Utah had almost universally rejoiced at the news that Congress had organized them into a political entity independent of what a newspaper called the "rascal prophets" in Salt Lake. With its capital in Carson City and its center of mass squarely planted in the Comstock Lode, the new territory settled down to the hard, dangerous work of extracting the gold and silver "locked up in the flinty grip of the quartz . . . waiting to reward the industry of the toiling miner."

The Gould & Curry claim had incorporated the year before, with George Hearst among the eight incorporators and trustees and four shares for every one of its theoretical 1,200 feet. (Professional surveyors could only ever find 921 feet between its boundary stakes.) The appointed treasurer was William Chapman Ralston, the same sturdy San Francisco banker who'd been serving in that capacity for the Ophir since the end of April 1860. An Ohioan who'd clerked aboard paddleboats on the Mississippi River, Ralston had worked in banking and shipping on the Isthmus of Panama after the gold discovery, immigrated to San Francisco in 1854, and risen to prominence in city financial circles. A principal of the banking firm of Fretz & Ralston in 1861, he also served as a director for diverse other companies. After the Gould & Curry's incorporation, the trustees had the mine borrow $10,000 from the owner of a San Francisco hotel on the usual Pacific Coast terms of 3 percent interest per month. They'd used the money to finance a shallow adit that crosscut two parallel veins of millable ore at one hundred feet. Developments a hundred feet deeper, at the end of their "Middle Adit," revealed that they'd struck a significant ore body. Management kept the details secret. Without extracting the ore that would have put the mine on a paying basis, the Gould & Curry trustees levied $166,000 worth of assessments on the mine's stockholders—who had to pay more than $34.50 cash on every share they owned—and developed the Middle Adit workings with a mind toward speedy extraction. The Gould & Curry started an even longer and deeper "Lower Adit," aiming to hit the lode 225 feet deeper still (on the 425-foot level), and from the ore the mine did extract, plowed all surplus earnings into construction of a massive mill at the junction of Six and Seven Mile cañons a mile and a half below Virginia City. The assessments without dividends pummeled the mine's share price and forced many small, cash-poor shareholders to sell out. Considering the magnitude of the ore body later developed through the adits, whispers—and increasingly vociferous complaints—suspected the "San Francisco moneyocratic sharps," among them George Hearst, who controlled the trustees, of running a "freezing operation" to force small shareholders to sell their stock—which was quickly scooped up by insiders with knowledge of the mine's true value. With an oblique reference to overgrooming a horse, one man quipped that the San Francisco sharps had "*curried* [the mine] so slick that there is scarcely a hair left to be rubbed against."

About twelve hundred feet south of the Gould & Curry, beyond two mines called the Savage and the Hale & Norcross, the Potosi mine drove an adit through a thick body of moderate ore. Unfortunately, the ore body dipped under the boundary of its downhill neighbor, the Chollar, and the two mines were soon bitterly litigating ownership of the ore. Dozens of other mining concerns had tunneling, shafting, and surface-mining projects under way throughout the local districts. Sixteen miles to the west, the Ophir Mill in the Washoe Valley completed its first trial runs and was soon shipping hundredweights of bullion—although the bullion was produced at great cost. Many new mining companies incorporated, including ones that would play important roles in John Mackay's future—the Hale & Norcross, the Bullion, and the Caledonia gold- and silver-mining companies.

Virginia City itself incorporated. Observant citizens built Episcopal and Methodist churches and schools. A water company laid mains to supply the town with water flumed from adits driven into the flanks of Mount Davidson above the town. Another company ordered gaslighting equipment from the eastern states with the idea of illuminating Virginia City's main streets. Work commenced to connect the overland telegraph between Fort Churchill and Salt Lake City. Shanties gave way to houses, bunks to bedsteads, and coarse blankets and straw-stuffed bedticks became mattresses fitted with clean, white sheets. Fresh butter, eggs, bread, trout, and such San Francisco luxuries as oysters and champagne became readily available. *The Daily Alta California* attributed the progress above and below ground to "the vigor, energy, perseverance, and industry of the American people."

A minor tragedy struck the Nevada Territory on June 17, 1861, at Chinatown, the Chinese settlement near the mouth of Gold Cañon. A bucking horse threw James Fenimore. Old Virginny may have been drunk. The old miner's foot tangled in a stirrup, and the animal dragged him across the landscape. Impact with a rock stove in the back of his skull before his foot finally slipped loose. Kind hands carried him to a nearby bed. Fenimore was barely conscious. Blood oozed from his mouth, ears, and nose, and he was so afflicted with violent seizures that his friends had to bind his hands and feet to prevent him from further harming himself. Thus he lingered for three days. At intervals, Old Virginny seemed to recognize the faces and voices of his old companions, but he died on June 20, around noon. Although Fenimore's name hadn't appeared in correspondence from Gold Hill and Virginia City as among those pushing Washoe's mining development since discovery of the Comstock Lode, he was well known and well liked among the territory's pioneers. The *Territorial Enterprise's* bighearted eulogy noted that although Fenimore was "at times dissipated, he bore the reputation of being an unusually kind-hearted and honest man" whose "too social disposition" had made him "the dupe of sharpers," and although he died with "but little property," the people of Washoe "universally recognized" him "as the man to whose agency the people of the United States are principally indebted for the discovery and development of the wealth of Nevada Territory." The next day, in the state that had birthed him, federal and Confederate armies fought the Battle of Bull Run near a town called Manassas Junction, an indecisive Confederate victory that disabused people of any short-war illusions. By year's end, the North and South had nearly a million men in uniform.

In the new Nevada Territory, people waited "impatiently" for the arrival of "Uncle Sam's authority"—neither of the judges assigned to the territory, nor Governor James Nye, nor his secretary had yet reached the territory despite the passage of four months. A newly elected Territorial Legislature went into session in Carson City, and it was soon debating a law to ban "foreign capitalists," meaning moneyed men from San Francisco, who aroused much local resentment, and the creation of a Sunday law designed to calm the chaos of mining camp Sundays by forcing observance of the Sabbath and annulling all contracts made on Sunday except those of marriage. Every person on the mining frontier had either witnessed or participated in bullfights, dog fights, theatrical and musical performances, gambling, dancing, alcohol consumption, and the other "noisy amusements" conducted on Sundays. Religiously inclined persons and other moralizers found such disrespect repugnant. Their representatives in the legislature made long-winded speeches advocating legal methods of calming the Sunday swivets. Theodore Winters, the only member of the original Ophir company who still owned a slice of the mine and was now a member of the new legislature, spoke for many other old pioneers when he said, "It is more annoyance to me to hear a man praying too loud than to hear him hollering when he is drunk." (A month later, Winters attacked a man with a club during a session of the legislature.) Neither the ban on California capital nor the Sunday law passed the assembly. Virginia City, Gold Hill, and the other camps carried on as always.

Men worked day and night in Washoe's tunnels, shafts, and open excavations. Rocks rattled through ore chutes at all hours. The roar of the stamp mills never ceased. More than sixty-five were in operation in the territory. Two strings of Bactrian camels carried enormous loads of salt from salt flats near Walker's Lake and along the Humboldt to the Washoe quartz mills, an oddball experiment that might have succeeded, for each camel could haul upward of eight hundred pounds and grew fat eating the sagebrush and greasewood other animals wouldn't sniff, but mules and horses panicked when they caught sight or smell of the strange beasts. Construction hands worked to improve many buildings and enhance the quality of the streets. Before the mineral discoveries of 1859, there hadn't been 800 whites in all of what had become the Nevada Territory. Two years later, there were more than 18,000, around 4,000 of whom lived in Gold Hill and Virginia City. Teams laden with quartz, machinery, merchandise, and produce arrived and departed constantly. One newspaperman guessed that the Washoe trade with California engaged as many as four thousand large wagons. Four years before, "one man on snow-shoes" had conducted the winter commerce of the entire territory. In October, the successes of Nevada inspired a party composed of California governor Leland Stanford, Collis P. Huntington, Charlie Crocker, "and others" to travel from Sacramento to Washoe "on a visit of business and pleasure." Considering that they'd recently incorporated the Central Pacific Railroad, hoping to build the western half of a transcontinental line, it's easy to surmise what business opportunity they were investigating.

Although the California observer who classified the Washoe population of late 1861 as either "dogs" or "gentlemen" would almost certainly
have counted John Mackay among the lode's canine population, those
above Mackay in the mining hierarchy began to take notice. They put
him in charge of other men. Men recalling his early years on the Comstock said that as a gang boss, shift leader, and foreman, Mackay grew
into a good leader of men, as exacting as a supervisor as he was faithful
as an employee, loyal to men above him and devoted to those beneath.
His competence went unquestioned underground, for every man knew
Mackay could do his job as well as or better than he could do it himself.
Mackay had no patience for wasted time and inefficiency and he drove
his crews hard, but never harder than he drove himself, and in the haz-
ardous environment of underground mining, he never asked a man to do
a job he wouldn't do himself. He was a stickler for detail. Underground,
he enforced rules with a direct, frank manner, and not always as a beam
of "circulating sunshine." When he was disobeyed, ignored, or thwarted,
Mackay's ruddy color rose into a burst of Irish temper. If pushed—at all—
Mackay enforced his edicts with his fists. Although he seldom said more
than a few words, men knew where they stood with John Mackay, which
they appreciated. Men liked working for him. Around John Mackay,
things got done right.

Believing that tidy conditions made for safer, more efficient operations, Mackay insisted on clean, orderly work zones. He wouldn't allow
detritus to accumulate underground, and in an environment where fire
posed the greatest hazard, thousands of feet of huge, dry, compressed
timber shored the mines, all the work was done by lantern and candlelight, and no smoking was ever allowed, Mackay insisted his men never
neglect a candle and never leave behind a "snuff"—the pooled remains
of candle—both for fear of a spark smoldering within and because any
carelessness offended his sense of the right way of doing things.

As a leader, Mackay was unpretentious, natural, unaffected. He never
"put on the dog" and lorded it over his underlings. He never made himself
out to be something he wasn't. He never pretended to know something
he didn't. John William Mackay was simply himself, always. Reflecting
on Mackay's early years on the Comstock, iron-eyed California capitalist and multimillionaire Darius Ogden Mills recalled Mackay's "truthful-
ness" and "sincerity," his "frankness of manner," and his "close application
to business," observations rendered more significant by the fact that Mills
and Mackay would spend much of the two coming decades as formidable
and often bitter rivals. "Everybody always liked Mackay," Mills remem-

bered. "He owed much of his great success to his straightforward manner of dealing with men."

The thing was, Mackay enjoyed it. To him, all work was honorable. He believed in the gospel of hard work. As he himself described, he enjoyed "the toil, privation, and hardship." He'd been happy selling newspapers in New York and learning carpentry in the Webb shipyard. He'd been happy shoveling dirt and gravel through rockers, long toms, and sluice boxes around Downieville, and he was happy wielding pick, shovel, and sledge in the Comstock mines, where, in the opinion of a man who worked alongside him, John Mackay had discovered an environment that "stimulated every fiber of his being." Mackay never talked of his own plans, but quietly, in a way he wouldn't cop to but a few times in his life, he'd begun to nurture a mighty ambition. Not even his closest intimates noticed Mackay studying Washoe's most successful men. Mackay measured himself against the superintendents, shift bosses, foremen, engineers, owners, and capitalists around him and concluded that he was every inch their equal. He worked as hard as humanly possible, he soaked up practical knowledge, and he saved his money, watching his opportunities. No one on the lode suspected the hardworking, taciturn Irish immigrant supervising the shoring of a gallery or the running of a drift had begun to nurture a burning desire "to win a name as master and manager of the greatest mines in the world."

CHAPTER 6

Revving Up the Boom

Miners loading tons of ore from the Gold Hill mines into
the freight wagons for mule teams to haul to the quartz mills
farther down Gold Cañon. (The Imperial and the Empire
were consolidations of several original small claims.)

———

**Three years ago, the huge quartz vein known as the Gold
Hill lead [that] cropped ten or fifteen feet above the surface,
with pines and cedars growing about and upon it, is now a
bewildering maze of whims, windlasses, ore bins, and sheds,
shoots and car-tracks perched high in the air on their sup-
ports of trestlework, smoke-stacks, workshops, and dwell-
ing houses. The sloping front of the hill is cut down, and
the perpendicular face walled up, while scarce a trace of the
original outline of the croppings of the lead remains.**

—"Washoe As It Is," *Daily Alta California*,
June 20, 1862, citing the *Territorial Enterprise*

Workers joined the converging strands of the transcontinental telegraph in late October 1861, fulfilling a dream held close by Pacific
Coasters since the hoary days of '49. Morse code clacking through the

131

wire almost immediately stilled the pounding hooves of the Pony Express. ("Alas! No more, a passing cheer to his memory," wrote the *San Francisco Evening Bulletin* about the demise of what most everyone on the coast called "The Pony.") The line was originally intended to terminate in St. Louis, but "rebel disturbances" in Missouri forced the rerouting of the line from Omaha across Iowa and Illinois to Chicago. News began flashing across the continent, transmitted and received within a single day, sometimes even leaping from New York to San Francisco inside a single hour. Technologically, the dots and dashes might span the continent in a single bound, but eight different companies divided the United States into separate telegraph "nations," and to get from New York to San Francisco, a message had to be repeated across the borders of four of them—at Pittsburgh, Chicago, Omaha, and Salt Lake City. The public paid "roundly" for a service that would have been completed years before had not the separate companies jockeying for advantage in the back rooms of the U.S. Congress stalled construction, much to the detriment of life and business on the Pacific Slope.

According to an early message telegraphed east by a correspondent of the *New York Times*, women were "the principal element of prosperity" lacking in the Nevada Territory. In the sagebrush country, they couldn't be had "either for marriage or to do washing and plain sewing," and the dearth of female companionship caused "the lonely miners . . . an intolerable degree of distress." Or, as another man noted a month later, with more subtext: "Ladies few; women—in demand." In Washoe, a young woman of good character was "worth her weight—several times over, in solid silver," and the miners quipped that if so inclined, such an immigrant could find a good husband "on the day of her arrival." Women, "neither young nor pretty," succeeded in bagging spouses if they were so inclined, while the "young, pretty, and virtuous" easily landed husbands with "immense feet." Indeed, a footless young beau couldn't "walk into a young lady's affections." A humorist quipped that young ladies wouldn't dream of entertaining a "proposition from any gentleman with less than a thousand feet."

Same-day transmission of news across the continent eliminated the worst of the agonizing "behind-the-times" nature of dispatches to and from the Far West, but the citizenry in Virginia City and Gold Hill suppressed their urge to "jubilate" the accomplishment, as people said at the time. Many still nursed painful memories of their premature celebration of the transatlantic telegraph. (Three *years* had passed and the failed transatlantic cable hadn't yet been replaced.) Only after the transcontinental telegraph had been in routine service for a month and seemed a "fixed fact" rather than another "cable humbug" did Washoeites allow themselves the requisite laudatory spree, ringing bells, drinking whisky, and shooting guns into the air.

They'd have nothing else to celebrate for quite some time, for winter arrived in earnest. A cavalcade of storms rolling out of the Pacific dumped colossal quantities of rain on California and the Nevada Territory in the winter of 1861–62. Noachian floods inundated the Sacramento Valley from its mouth in the San Pablo arm of San Francisco Bay to far above Marysville, a distance of more than two hundred miles. In places, the flood was fifty to sixty miles wide. Only treetops and the peaked roof of an occasional house or barn poked through the surface of the still, terrible waters. A man on a rooftop in California's "Venice"— Sacramento—noted that the summits of the coast range, thirty or forty miles to westward, were the only spots of dry land he could see from within city limits. Stockton to Sacramento, a distance of almost fifty miles, was "an unobstructed sheet of water." Steamships navigated a direct line across country between the two cities.

Over the mountains in the Nevada Territory, the precipitous creeks, cañons, and ravines of the eastern slope became western Niagaras. The Carson Valley flooded into "a vast lake" with "houses floating around loose, amidst carcasses of cattle." Below the floodwater lake, the river stampeded into Carson River cañon, bursting every dam in its course and scouring away quartz mills along the riverbank. Sheds, flumes, corrals, blacksmiths' shops, businesses, and domiciles joined the mills on "voyages of discovery" down the Carson River to its sink, which swelled into a vast inland sea.

The foul winter paralyzed transportation and prostrated business in both California and the Nevada Territory and curtailed the amount of gold and silver the Pacific Coast remitted east that served the Union cause. Podgers of the *New York Times* begged his eastern audience not to see it as "a want of patriotism," but to "make allowances" for the winter of cataclysmic inundations.*

---

* As of this writing, the winter of 1861–62 still holds the record as the wettest in San Francisco since the gold discovery. Some 49.27 inches of rain fell in San Francisco that winter. In Placerville, one Mr. Henderson measured eighty-six inches of rain. If accurate, that number more than doubles the annual average and exceeds the next closest year since 1873–74 by more than eight inches.

The previous summer, the federal government's need for money to suppress the rebellion had forced it to issue paper "demand notes" (theoretically redeemable for specie), followed by "legal tender notes" or "United States Notes," a true fiat currency unbacked by precious metal. These were nicknamed "greenbacks" on account of the green ink used to print the reverse side of the notes, but Americans in the loyal eastern states didn't fully trust Lincoln's "shinplasters," as went the common nickname for paper money. Steady infusions of precious metal from the Pacific Slope to eastern financial institutions did much to soothe anxiety, buttress confidence, and keep the wheels of the Northern economy turning. As the *New York Herald* noted that summer, "commerce rests . . . on . . . confidence." The *Herald* considered it "a matter of national importance that the silver mines in Nevada Territory be fully developed."

However, on the Pacific Coast, Californians and Nevadans universally reviled the federal greenbacks and tallied a black mark against the character of a person who tried to pass them off in normal business affairs. Greenbacks came into "brisk demand" only later in the year—people used them to pay the new federal income tax, the first ever levied from Washington, D.C.

Floods and war made for a season of gloomy uncertainty in both the eastern and far western regions of the nation. Crowds in San Francisco hung around the telegraph offices, anxious for news of the war "back in the states." Just eighteen months before, Californians had lived most of an uneasy fortnight waiting for the Pony Express to tell them who'd won the presidential election. In the spring of 1862, most residents of the Pacific Slope had word of a savage battle fought between federal and rebel armies at Pittsburg Landing in southwestern Tennessee within seventy-two hours.* Major General of Volunteers Ulysses S. Grant, a West Point graduate from Ohio who'd been working in a leather store less than a year before, commanded the U.S. forces that bore the brunt of the battle.

For Mackay, the spring of 1862 opened another season of great activity. He made his first recorded transaction in mining ground since 1860, deeding away five feet of the Union mine—presumably selling some of the equity he'd earned with sweat two years before. Hard at work among the "rats of the lower galleries," Mackay was beginning to make some-

* Now more commonly known by its southern name, the Battle of Shiloh.

thing of himself.* Over the next two years, Storey County records show him receiving or deeding away feet on more than twenty separate occasions. He almost certainly made many other stock transactions that didn't merit entry in county records. Less than three weeks after recording the Union transaction, Mackay received a modest thirty feet of interest as one of eighteen men relocating a thousand feet of ground west of the Chollar Company's Back Ledge. The mine had formerly been organized as "the Winters Company," but before that it had been known as the Buck Ledge—the mine for which Mackay had been digging a tunnel in his spare time, five days a week, for the last two years. (Mackay had deeded sixty feet of "the Winters Co." to a friend two years before, so he'd likely had a stake in the mine since the summer of 1860.)

Mackay's resolute competence, unflagging work ethic, and efforts to improve his practical, technical, and geological knowledge marked him as a man suited to greater responsibilities. The trustees of the Caledonia Gold and Silver Mining Company took advantage and made Mackay their superintendent. The Caledonia held ground a few thousand feet down Gold Cañon from Gold Hill and aimed to develop its ledge— and ten others—via a long adit. The Caledonia trustees levied a series of assessments to finance tunnel construction. Mackay threw himself into the venture with characteristic zeal, but the new job didn't stop the after-hours work on the adit he'd been digging for the Buck Ledge. By the spring of 1862, working alone or with a handful of helpmates, he'd probably driven the Buck Ledge's adit several hundred feet into the side of Mount Davidson.

The Ophir continued to produce handsomely. By early 1862, the Ophir's enormous, luxurious, and supposedly state-of-the-art quartz mill in Washoe Valley was "running full time" and known to be shipping "not less than one thousand pounds of gold and silver in bricks" per week. The mill's phenomenal cost, for both construction and operation, caused little worry to the Ophir's trustees and stockholders. They rested secure in the knowledge that they owned a bottomless mine. When the trustees declared a dividend of seventy-two dollars per foot in April, the mine's stock value price jumped on the expectation of permanent dividends. Not to be outdone, with the size of its ore body promising to rival the Ophir's, the Gould & Curry had an even more extravagant mill under

---

* The 1862 Directory of the Nevada Territory lists a "Mackey, J. miner, Mexican claim," which may or may not refer to our man.

construction at the junction of Six and Seven Mile cañons a mile and a half below Virginia City.

Washoe news continued to be good. The Mexican, the Central, the California, the Gould & Curry, the Chollar, and the Potosi all disgorged ore. In July, one of the little Gold Hill mines hacked into a neglected quartz ledge near its entrance. Neither it nor any of its neighbors had bothered to prospect the lead due to the surface hardness of the quartz. Eight feet down, they struck blue-black ore similar to that found in the Ophir, much of it "sheeted over with silver," a strong "indication" that the Gold Hill mines and the mines of the established Comstock shared the same "ledge." Ground in Gold Hill doubled in value.

Experts, such as existed, considered it "a well established fact that where there is found one large and very rich lead, others are apt to be found running in the same direction, partaking in its richness." In service of that belief, individuals and mining companies had "located" most of Washoe's "outside" or "wildcat" ledges since the Ophir/Mexican and Gold Hill discoveries of 1859. Anything that could be fobbed off as quartz got located. Too rich to work—by their own accounting—but too poor to hire, many outside owners did nothing, hoping "to procure fortunes by incubation upon their croppings." Others worked hard to open their claims via shafts and adits, lured onward in the backbreaking labor by will-o'-the-wisp concentrations of metal in the quartz, convinced they'd be rich once they "got down where it came in solid."

"It is now proven that there is gold and silver in every ledge in the Territory," a Washoe booster wrote the *Daily Alta California*. To a certain extent, that was true. Trace quantities of gold and silver did exist in most Washoe ledges. Outside mines often found pockets of profitable rock, which their touts seized upon as strong indications that their ledges shared a "spur of the Ophir" or a "dip of the Gould & Curry," and although none of them had as yet found an ore body of sufficient size to put a large-scale mining operation on a paying basis, many Washoe miners imagined vast troves of ore hiding in a network of interconnected ledges crisscrossing the innards of Mount Davidson. "There is room for all to work," crowed another *Alta* correspondent. "Elbow grease is the great expounder of the quartz question."

The plethora of lawsuits was Washoe's only negative indication. The case list ran on for pages. Lawsuits entangled every profitable mine—and every potentially profitable mine. Lawyers "raised" fortunes.

Confronted with the bustle, hum, and ferocious mechanical clatter of the stamp mills in Virginia City and Gold Hill, a wag quipped that "people do not rush about under a fierce sun if they are not making money." Virginia City had grown into "a brisk and busy place," filled with first-rate hotels and great stocks of goods. Mines, mills, shops, foundries, houses, stores, hay yards, apothecaries, assay and law offices, livery stables, saloons, hotels, and dozens of other businesses lined the lode, and new buildings were springing up "with the celerity of mushrooms." Teams of mules and oxen hauling merchandise and machinery, wood, rock, and lumber crowded the streets. Traffic jams developed. A line of freight wagons from California plodding up a grade outside Silver City came nose to nose with a train of ore haulers heading for the Carson River quartz mills. Both sides refused to give way. Tempers flared, and "a general row ensued." The teamsters fought with whips and stones. Fortunately, no one resorted to knives and pistols, and although "several were badly used up," none were seriously injured.*

Nimble stagecoach lines made the trip from Virginia City to Sacramento in less than twenty-four hours. Steamboats racing up and down the Sacramento River between Sacramento and San Francisco made it possible to make the entire trip between "above" and "below" in less than thirty-six hours. Foul-tasting tunnel water flumed to Virginia City's water works slaked the camp's thirst. Enterprising businessmen who had laid up ice the previous winter sold it to cool popular midsummer beverages—among them "mint juleps, sherry cobblers, and ice water." Flatland visitors always marveled at the precipitous slope of the town's construction. Building entrances on one street were a full flight of stairs above the exits on the next lower street, and visitors standing on the doorsteps on the uphill side of the street looked east over the peaks of the roofs of one-story cottages on the downhill side. The scribe who reported Virginia City's thronged streets as filled with "smart and fashionable people" didn't consider the men hard at work in the tunnels, drifts, and stopes beneath his feet. Wearing stiff-brimmed slouch hats, woolen shirts, and sturdy canvas pants tucked into heavy muckers' boots, the real muscle of Virginia City and Gold Hill labored by candlelight, in shifts working all the hours God made except for a few on Sundays.

Civic organization began to replace the chaos of the camp's early days. Owners and officers of the mines "in bonanza" installed their families in cozy cottages. Masons, Odd-Fellows, the Sons of Temperance, and other

---

* Things change: There probably hasn't been a traffic jam in Silver City in 130 years.

benevolent societies so crucial to the social fabric of the mining frontier established themselves. A Library Association circulated five hundred volumes of "choice works." More than a hundred ladies "draped with great taste" attended its inaugural ball, where one attendee found it "astonishing" to see "how well a calico dress can look when well made." Residents contributed to church and school construction. A newspaper boasted that of 417 children in Virginia City and Gold Hill, 109 attended school. The Methodist and Episcopal churches boasted of their many female parishioners, understanding their power to draw men to worship. Hunters sold hares, sage hens, and ducks they'd shot elsewhere in the territory. Knowing Washoeites as "not much inclined to walk when they can ride," a man carried passenger traffic between Virginia City and Gold Hill in a luxurious omnibus drawn by four fine bay horses. Carpetbagging politicians, eager for office, afflicted the territorial government. Five hundred spectators gambled on "a grand dog fight." Law and order seemed to be replacing revolvers and bowie knives. "Such men as boast of the number of men they have slain, as well as their toadies and admirers, have almost entirely disappeared," reported the *Territorial Enterprise*.

In less roseate news, a young boy died of smallpox in Carson City. A month later, the scourge killed several in Dayton, including Mary White, the schoolmistress. Unfortunately, Miss White had exposed the whole school full of children before realizing she was infected—with predictably tragic consequences.

Washoe abounded with money-making opportunities, but struggling to develop paying mines from outside claims, mucking out somebody else's ore for wages, tending a business, or working amidst the thunderous racket and mercury fumes of a quartz mill didn't appeal to everyone. Laboring men unimpressed with quartz-mining opportunities drifted north to new placer-mining regions discovered on Oregon's northeastern border with the Washington Territory.* One of them was Henry Comstock, "late of the Comstock Ledge of Washoe silver mines." He spent the summer of 1862 working a claim on the Powder River. Mercantile failures and an unsuccessful "venture in the matrimonial line" had driven him north. Less than three years before, Comstock had sold out of the Ophir, the Mexican, and his slice of Gold Hill for somewhere between $12,000 and $15,000, hoping he'd never do another day's mining in his life. In the first flush of success, he'd taken a fancy to the supernumerary wife of a Mormon man

---

* The Washington Territory's share of the area would be organized into the Idaho Territory the following year.

named Carter recently come across the desert from Salt Lake. Carter sold his wife to Comstock for $350. Comstock demanded and received a bill of sale and married the woman in Carson City. As absurd as that sounds, one occasionally reliable memory recorded the transaction fifteen years later, and two newspaper articles documented it at the time. In one of them, a letter published by the *Sacramento Daily Union* clearly identifies the purchaser as "H. P. T. Comstock [*sic*], the one that discovered and located the Comstock Ledge." Unimpressed with her new arrangements, Comstock's bride repeatedly fled the nuptial coop. Comstock retrieved her on several occasions, once from as far away as Placerville, but come springtime, she escaped to California with "a long-legged miner" and "came to anchor in a lager-beer cellar in Sacramento."

In the meantime, Comstock had invested the proceeds of his mine sales in a Carson City general store and a branch in Silver City, the Gold Cañon camp sprung up around Devil's Gate. Naturally profligate, always with an open hand, Comstock extended credit to many unworthies and soon went out of business. Alone after his short season in the sun, in the winter of 1861–62, Comstock took what remained of his "raise" and went north. Reports from Oregon described him doing well on a placer claim, but Comstock was again shoveling gravel, a terrible fall for a man who'd given his name to the most famous ledge in the world. The same week that the Comstock-in-Oregon story broke in the *Sacramento Daily Union*, the Ophir Mill shipped nine hundred *pounds* of bullion, and the feet Comstock had once owned in Virginia City and Gold Hill held an aggregate value of around $500,000. The men who possessed them in his stead aroused considerable jealousy and resentment peacocking around Virginia City and San Francisco as the most celebrated nabobs on the coast. Those can't have been easy facts to bear for a man working long, backbreaking days on a placer claim in the wilds of northeastern Oregon. Nor had Comstock given up the hope of quartz. He exhibited specimens around a camp called Auburn and pronounced a silver lead in the Burnt River Basin "as rich as anything in Washoe."

While Henry Comstock's exploits in the Powder River country made minor news during the summer of 1862, major Union setbacks commanded headlines. Swelled by success, General Robert E. Lee and his Confederate Army of Northern Virginia invaded the North. California's "Dixie-ite" newspapers crowed at such volume that to quiet their "treasonous sentiments," the military governor of California barred them from using the U.S. Mail. Later that week, confused reports of a great battle on the banks of Maryland's Antietam Creek broke in California. As the story came into clear focus, it became apparent that the U.S. Army had won a bloody victory. The feat of Union arms gave President Lincoln the political confidence to "invoke the considerate judgment of mankind, and the gracious favor of Almighty God" and issue a proclamation declaring that as of the coming New Year, slaves in locations still in rebellion against the U.S. government would be "then, thenceforth, and forever free." Although Lincoln's Emancipation Proclamation's immediate effect freed few slaves, the nation immediately foretold its consequences. As the editor of the *Washoe City Times* wrote, "The effect of it, if the Lincoln government succeed [*sic*] in crushing the rebellion, will be the eventual utter eradication of negro slavery." Lincoln's announcement committed the U.S. government and its armies not only to restoring the Union, but also to ending slavery. "The thunder in it . . . shakes the very earth," opined the *Territorial Enterprise*. "No word has ever before spoken liberty to four millions of human beings so completely manacled in soul and body."

The war and wholesale slaughter loose upon the eastern portion of the nation never stained California and the Nevada Territory, so far removed from the bloodshed that the editors of the *Sacramento Daily Union* felt compelled to remind their fellow Pacific Coasters not "to forget the fearful struggle of our patriotic brethren in the East for our glorious Union." Despite many sectional "excitements," only occasional barroom donnybrooks and small-scale street riots incited by overt displays of southern sympathy marred the peace of the Pacific Coast. Those that did occur mostly served as rallying points for the population's overwhelmingly "patriotic and union-loving" sentiments. In the Nevada Territory, gangs of loyal men quickly offered secessionists who had the audacity—usually "whisky-begotten"—to hurrah for Jeff Davis, Stonewall Jackson, or Robert Lee or heap foul abuse on President Lincoln and the Union the choice of taking the oath of allegiance or accepting the opportunity to "meditate upon Republican tyranny" from within the confines of the army's prison at Fort Churchill. Most leaped at the opportunity to make "the big swear." Quite frankly, most of those in Nevada Territory had too much money to be made and work to be done to bother with sedition.

Washoe riches did make national news that year, although generally not in leading headlines. In October, a small item at the bottom of the second page of the *Cleveland Tri-Weekly Leader* reported the Ophir Company shipping "not less" than $60,000 and sometimes $100,000 in bullion per week. The article claimed the Ophir's annual yield would probably reach "three hundred millions of dollars," and said that hundreds of Nevada mines were "equally as good." A more mathematically competent report published the same day in California estimated Washoe's annual yield at a still-impressive $18 million.

Whether or not Washoe had the world's attention in the fall of 1862, it certainly had San Francisco's, where the principal topics of conversation were the weather, the war, and the soaring values of Washoe mining stocks. A man observed that a few dozen San Francisco buildings could cover all the productive mining ground of Virginia City and Gold Hill, from which emerged "a sum equal to one-sixth" of that produced by the entire state of California. "There is not in the world so many rich mines in the same scope of territory as we have in Washoe," bragged the *Territorial Enterprise*. Pushed skyward by the "handsome dividends declared by the principal Washoe mining associations," Ophir stock soared past $2,000 per foot. Then it passed $3,000. In one year, Ophir stock had risen from $600 to $3,400 per foot, 450 percent. Gould & Curry feet did even better, rising from $350 to $2,450, a sevenfold increase. The value of many lesser mines described even more fantastic parabolas, jumping from a few dollars to hundreds of dollars per foot. The old California desire for sudden fortune gripped the city. To corral and profit from the city's "fever, not to say mania," for speculative mining investment, forty stockbrokers opened the San Francisco Stock & Exchange Board in the Montgomery Block at 600 Montgomery Street, consolidating operations previously scattered throughout the district and giving rise to a generation of joking references to Ali Baba of *The Arabian Nights*. Several other stock boards collected together to accomplish the same end. A stock-trading frenzy seized the San Francisco population. "Time sales" and "stock lending" for delivery in thirty, sixty, or ninety days made possible short sales and all manner of other speculation based on whether a person expected the price of a mine to rise or fall. "Are all [you] folks at the Bay stock mad?" the author of a "Letter from Nevada Territory" asked the *Daily Alta California*'s readership in mid-October. "Have [you] people become insane?"

Washoe stock prices fluctuated wildly, but any fool could discern the principal direction—UP! Nobody wanted to miss out on the easiest-made wealth in California history. The most successful speculators kept their noses attuned to mining developments, but not all advantage arrived from underground. Opportunity hit a ring of aggressive San Franciscans who learned the findings of a geologist hired by the Ophir trustees to expand knowledge of their holding. The "scientific cuss" spent several days investigating the Ophir and its neighbors, paying particular attention to the Virginia Ledge, the quartz ledge above the Ophir croppings located by

"Old Virginia" James Fenimore in 1858. The geologist noted the Ophir's rich Comstock Lead and the barren quartz of the long-neglected Virginia Ledge dipping toward each other. If they joined at depth, their merger would pose a "perplexing question as to who held the true vein." Miners generally considered the Virginia Ledge "forfeited for non-compliance with the mining laws," but its claim antedated the Ophir's by well over a year. Worse, the geologist gave it as his opinion that the Virginia Ledge was the "true lead," and the Ophir "but a spur." The *veta madre*, "the mother vein," couldn't belong to both companies. He advised the Ophir ownership to eliminate a weapon that could be used against them by acquiring the Virginia Ledge "at all hazards." (This was not new advice: two and a half *years* before, Adolph Sutro, the man who'd encountered the first run of the Pony Express in the Sierra snowstorm, had advised the Ophir's ownership to buy the Virginia Lead in an article he wrote for the *Daily Alta California*—for exactly the same reason.) Being "a little on the old fogie order," the Ophir directors moved slowly. While they dithered, "a few sharp ones" in San Francisco caught wind of the mine's vulnerability, raced "above" to Virginia City, and bought the old title from whomever had acquired it from Fenimore. Back in San Francisco, they laid it before the Ophir directors and demanded $500,000, "a cool half-million."

The San Francisco stock market panicked. The "filibustering arrangement" tumbled the price of Ophir stock from $3,800 to $1,800. The Gould & Curry fell along with it. Other stocks followed the leaders down. Fortunes that had been considered certain evaporated.

After several anxious days, arbitration brokered by banker and Ophir treasurer William Ralston, his wealth and influence rising in California and Washoe financial circles, settled the purchase price at $100,000—for what the Ophir trustees could have bought for $25,000 a few weeks before. The Virginia Ledge sharps "made a great row" about accepting that "trifle," but their charade didn't garner much sympathy—two-thirds of the sum represented clear profits.

Podgers of the *New York Times* felt the Ophir directors had enjoyed "a narrow escape from being stupid." If the sharps were truly on their game, they'd have shorted Ophir stock before buying the Virginia Ledge, realized short-sale profits on the market panic, and used the proceeds to buy Ophir stock on the dip. Next, with a fistful of depressed Ophir stock in hand, they could have removed fears of a clouded title by selling the Virginia Ledge to the Ophir (at massive profit to themselves) and watched the Ophir's value soar back to its former heights. "Stock job" complete, they could have settled in to enjoy a tidy sum of cash in hand, the immense rise in value of their Ophir stock, and the mine's continuing dividend of seventy-two dollars per foot, 4 percent of the mine's capital value, *per month.**

Genuine mining developments sustained the market. Gould & Curry management allowed few visitors to examine their underground workings, but everybody on the surface could see phenomenal activity manifest around the D Street entrance of their "old Tunnel," the Middle Adit. Teamsters spewing steady invective reined up eight and ten mule teams in front of the mine entrance at all hours of the day and night. Bells tied to the mule tails clanked. Roiling dust clouds rose from dozens of hooves, clogging the nostrils of men and animals with "pasty conglomerate." Gangs of men offloaded timber and other supplies and dumped tons of ore into the large freight wagons. At the mouth of the adit, the mine built a "mammoth" shop to shelter the sixteen carpenters the mine kept constantly employed shaping the one-foot-square framing timbers used to shore the underground workings. Finished shoring timbers covered the earth thereabouts, including some sill timbers sixteen feet long. Inside the mine, workers had noted the ore body changing dip to the east, opposite its previous westward dip, and "pitching" (leaning) south, toward the mine's southern boundary.

Other Comstock mines also did well. Both the Potosi and the Chollar produced significant quantities of gold and silver despite the bitter litigation raging between them, and the Yellow Jacket made a strike and started developing an ore body. On Gold Hill, the mines were again producing much valuable rock. The year before, only one or two of the Gold Hill mines employed steam-hoisting machinery and only three or four had bothered to roof over their shaft and tunnel entrances. Now, they'd all roofed their workings and more than a dozen had installed first-class steam machinery for pumping and hoisting. Smoke trailed from smokestacks rising from the boiler rooms and puffs of steam escaped from the hoisting houses that sheltered the engines. Every mill in Virginia City and Gold Hill ran at capacity, an interminable clatter. Only during a few Sunday hours did quiet settle over the lode while the mills cleaned and repaired machinery.

John Mackay played his part in the action, superintending construction of the Caledonia Tunnel, which was five feet wide and six feet high, and penetrated fifteen hundred feet into the side of Mount Davidson. In early October, Caledonia miners encountered a layer of thick, tough

---

* The corporations that compose the modern S&P 500 pay average dividends of about 2 percent *per year.*

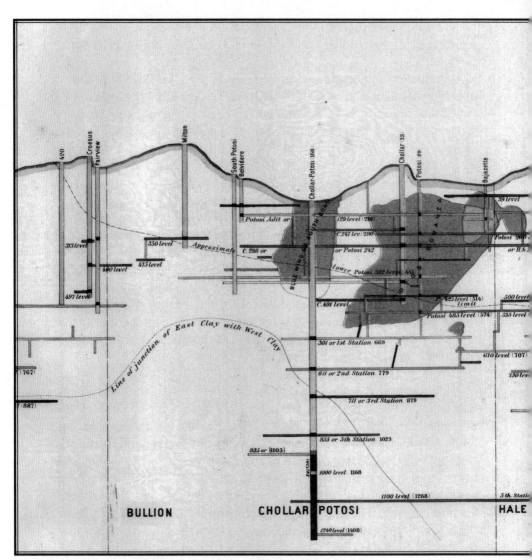

An 1870 cross-section of the Comstock through the Virginia City portion of
the lode showing the mine boundaries, the shafts, stations, and most important
adits, drifts, and winzes, and the location of the ore bodies. Although it wasn't
apparent in the frenzy of the early years, the Gould & Curry's bonanza can be
seen pitching south into the Savage and perhaps relating to the discovery made
by Mackay and his partners in the deep levels of the Hale & Norcross. Ordinary
numbers represent depths below the surface; numbers in parentheses show the
distance below the datum point (A) on the Gould & Curry croppings.

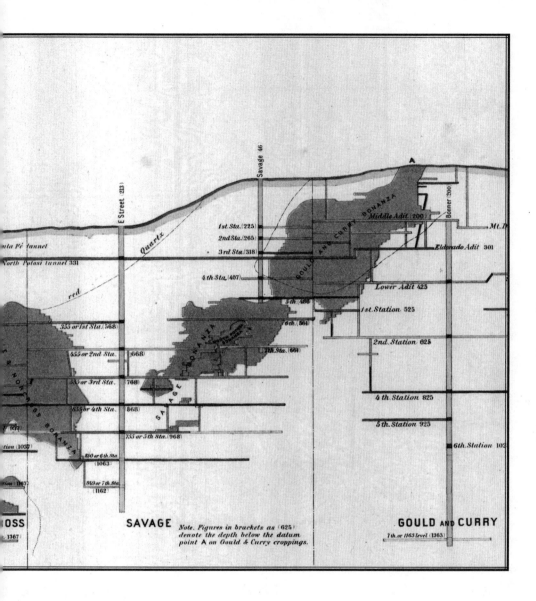

Note. Figures in brackets as (625)
denote the depth below the datum
point A on Gould & Curry croppings.

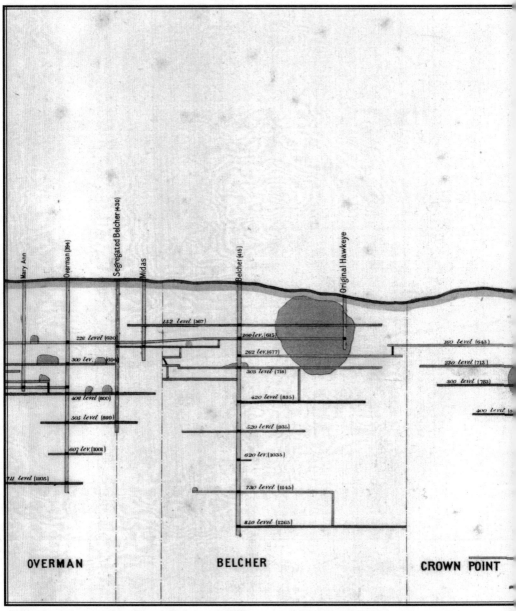

An 1870 cross-section of the Comstock through the Gold Hill portion of the lode. The workings of the Overman mine to the left with its well-organized shafts and drifts—and minuscule ore bodies—stands in stark contrast to the Gold Hill mines to the right, where the small original claims perforated their wonderful bonanza with a chaotic profusion of shafts and drifts. Mackay made his first great strike in the slice of the "C. P. West Bonanza" that belonged to the Kentuck mine.

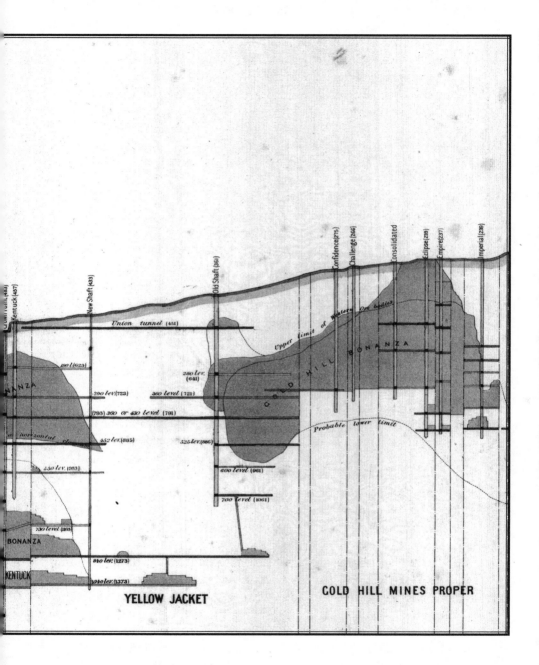

Confidence (275)
Challenge (266)
Consolidated
Eclipse (29)
Empire (237)
Imperial (228)

Kentuck (487)
New Shaft (433)
Old Shaft (36)

Union   tunnel (451)

Upper limit of Western Ore bodies

190 l.(623)

280 lev.
(641)

G O L D   H I L L   B O N A N Z A

290 lev.(723)
360 level (721)

NANZA

(793) 360 or 430 level (791)

a horizontal cross cut
452 lev.(885)
525 lev.(886)

Probable lower limit

550 lev.(933)

600 level (961)

700 level (1061)

730 level (185)

BONANZA

840 lev. (1273)

KENTUCK
940 lev. (1373)

YELLOW JACKET

GOLD HILL MINES PROPER

clay at the face of the drift. Excitement soared—Comstock miners had learned that clay walls often encased ore bodies. One of Mackay's crews cut through the wall. The clay dammed an underground reservoir. Breaking it unleashed a powerful flood. The torrent swept away wheelbarrows, tools, and five square-sets of timbers. Miners at the drift face hung on for their lives. One of the workmen washed a considerable distance among the debris. The flow subsided from 2,250 gallons per minute to about 850 over the course of the next few days. Mackay and his men forced their way back to the face of the drift, eager to examine the rock beyond the clay wall. The rock contained metal, like most Washoe quartz. Selected specimens were quite rich, but in aggregate, the rock couldn't cover milling costs. A few days later, the Caledonia levied another modest assessment, fifteen cents per share, in line with its assessments of the last year and a half. Mackay pressed forward with mine development. The water gushing from the shattered rock beyond the clay wall presented a substantial obstacle to mining progress, but did prove a boon to the mine— the Caledonia Tunnel Company profited $450 per month selling it to thirsty quartz mills farther down Gold Cañon.

Six weeks later, Mackay finally completed his extracurricular contract with the Buck Ledge, relocated and incorporated as the Milton earlier in the year. In exchange for the "full satisfaction" of the terms of the contract he'd signed in March 1860, the one that required him to work on the tunnel five days in every week, Mackay received 225 of the Milton's 1,000 feet. The mountain of hard work he'd endured running the tunnel while working in other mines beggared description, but the ground he'd earned held substantial value, even after he deeded away thirty feet of the mine (likely to men who'd helped him run the tunnel). Three months later, the Milton mine traded at $100 per foot, giving Mackay's share a paper value of $19,500, a respectable fortune by the standards of the day. Miners and speculators considered its prospects good. With the adjacent Chollar extracting large quantities of millable ore, and its owners holding their stock at $530 to $560 per foot, the *potential* value of Mackay's Milton ground was even more impressive. Mackay was making something of himself. He owned part of at least two other claims, the Caledonia and the Union. The Union was crushing rock, which "although not rich," was good enough to encourage "further prospecting, the mine apparently improving with depth." The same stock report that noted the $100 value of the Milton registered the Union at $13 per foot and the Caledonia at $10. Mackay might not have commanded much cash, but he owned mining ground with the potential to disgorge real wealth. John William Mackay would not have been alone in regarding that as a very real possibility—interested populations in Washoe and San Francisco held high hopes for all three mines, and for the Caledonia, they soared when Mackay's men struck a "formidable ledge" and "exceedingly good rock" at the face of the adit. Caledonia Tunnel items in the *Mining & Scientific Press* noted the mine being prosecuted with "industry" and "utmost vigor."

Elsewhere, Comstock miners did even better. The Ophir, the Mexican, the Central, the California, the Gould & Curry, the Chollar, the Potosi, the Yellow Jacket, and the Gold Hill mines all stoped out large volumes of profitable ore. Miners and speculators held high hopes for dozens of other Washoe mines. The *Sacramento Daily Union* estimated Washoe's bullion product at about $1 million per month, and the Gould & Curry's gargantuan mill hadn't yet gone into operation. In San Francisco, almost nightly, a huge wagon backed up to the express office of the Wells, Fargo & Company and disgorged heavy bars of Washoe bullion into the express company's vaults.

Despite outrageous expenditures, Ophir stockholders shared $470,000 in dividends in the last seven months of 1862. Adding to the euphoria, the Gould & Curry declared a $24-per-foot dividend two days before Christmas, its first. The Gould & Curry's grand mill finally began crushing ore in late December, and at the end of January 1863, the mine upped its dividend to $100 per foot, per month. Gould & Curry stock vaulted to $3,230, "an enormous advance on rates sixty days ago."

"Mining operations in and about Virginia City never presented a more favorable aspect than at the present time," opined the *Mining & Scientific Press*. A less staid commentator considered it "impossible to portray the brilliant future without being accused of 'Munchausenism'"—a winking reference to fabled Teutonic cavalry officer Baron von Münchhausen, teller of preposterous tales about his own adventures.

Less than a week after the Gould & Curry's $100 dividend announcement, an unusual pseudonym appeared for the first time in the *Territorial Enterprise* under a story that began with the line, "I feel very much as if I had just awakened out of a long sleep." The name beneath read simply, "Mark Twain."

John Mackay had already come to know the man to whom it belonged.

CHAPTER 7

The First Boom, Frenzied and Exuberant

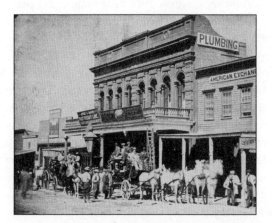

A stagecoach on C Street in flush times, when traffic was so thick that buggies and wagons sometimes had to wait half an hour for an opportunity to cross the street.

———

Our father Mammon who art in the Comstock, Bully is thy name; let thy dividends come, and stocks go up, in California as in Washoe. Give us this day our daily commissions; forgive us our swindles, as we hope to get even on those who have swindled us. "Lead" us not into temptation of promising wild cat; deliver us from lawsuits; for thine is the main Comstock, the black sulphurets and the wire-silver, from wall-rock to wall-rock, you bet!

—"Stock Broker's Prayer," *Territorial Enterprise*,
1863; possibly written by Mark Twain

Powerful gravity drew young men west during the Civil War, especially after North and South began drafting men to fill the ranks of their depleted armies. An obscure Missourian named Samuel Langhorne Clemens joined the thousands who traveled "the plains across" after spending a few weeks riding with a band of Confederate irregulars—long enough to learn that he wanted nothing to do with military service. Despite Sam's tepid secessionist sympathies, his older brother Orion Clemens was an ardent Republican who had campaigned for Abraham Lincoln. As a reward, the new president appointed Orion secretary of the Nevada Territory. Sam went west with his brother, there being, as his first great biographer would wryly observe fifty years later, "no place in the active Middle West just then for an officer of either army who had voluntarily retired from service."

The Clemens brothers traveled west on the overland stage and reached Carson City in the late summer of 1861. Orion Clemens took up his official duties while Sam dashed about the territory trying to attach himself to some of its fabulous wealth. (Writing as Mark Twain a decade later, he'd immortalize the experiences in *Roughing It*, making judicious use of "improved facts.") Sam Clemens spent the rest of the year mining near Unionville in the Humboldt region 150 miles northeast of Virginia City, and he found the labor "hard and long and dismal," not to mention dangerous and unremunerative. Passing back through Washoe in early 1862 on his way to try Aurora and the Esmeralda District on the California border some one hundred miles in the opposite direction, the loose, rangy twenty-seven-year-old marveled at an ore pile at the top of the Ophir's incline worth $2 million. Introduced to an Ophir foreman as secretary of the Nevada Territory, Sam Clemens accepted the man's offer of an against-the-rules night tour of the mine without pointing out that it was his brother Orion who held the job. One hundred and ninety feet underground, in what he described as "the bowels of the earth . . . where the ledge is 52 feet wide," Clemens pocketed specimens of first-class ore. A few days later, he included them in a letter mailed to a man whose capital he hoped to interest in sustaining his embryonic mining ventures. Clemens did a fair measure of hard work in Aurora, more than he allowed in *Roughing It*. One of his letters to his brother told of "blasting, and picking, and gadding" until blisters covered his hands. (In mining, "gadding" is breaking rock or ore from a drift face or stope with a short, chisel-like bar.) As the phrase went, Clemens "owned in" several promising ledges near Aurora, among them the Horatio and Derby, the Dashaway (likely named in honor of his partnership's poverty-induced membership in the eponymous temperance society), the Flyaway, the Annipolitan, the Live Yankee, and the Monitor. His hopes for riches ran high. Clemens described one ledge to his brother as "a dead sure thing" before adding, realistically, "but then it's the d—dest country for disappointments the world ever saw."

Fortunately for American literary destiny, none of Sam Clemens's ledges came in rich, or anything close. Attempts to levy "assessments" on his brother's purse became staples of his correspondence. A gifted yarner, Clemens amused his Aurora companions with lively storytelling, and he wrote occasional burlesque sketches, a few of which found their way into the pages of the *Territorial Enterprise* over the pseudonym "Josh," a pen name presumably intended as more verb than noun. Like so many others in the Nevada Territory, Sam Clemens was rich in feet, but poor in cash. By July 1862, he was trying to sell writing to the *Sacramento Daily Union*, the *Carson City Silver Age*, the *New Orleans Crescent*, and the *Territorial Enterprise*, among other newspapers.

Joseph T. Goodman, publisher and co-owner of the *Territorial Enterprise*, recognized a talent for clear, colorful, humorous writing in the author of the "Josh" letters and offered Clemens a job on his newspaper at twenty-five dollars per week, steady employment that promised to save Clemens from penury. Accepting it meant surrendering his dream of mining wealth. After a week of soul-searching, Clemens resigned himself to the dead sure thing. He laid aside his mining tools and went to Virginia City.

Sam Clemens arrived in mid- to late September. Joe Goodman allowed Clemens tremendous reportorial latitude, and in simple frontier language, the budding but unpolished genius quickly demonstrated a unique ability to use embellishment, hyperbole, satire, caricature, parody, mock-flattery, ribald language, and ridicule to flay bare essential truth. As his voice matured, Clemens's stories, hoaxes, and brutal sketches grew into something entirely American, encapsulating the terrible whimsy, painful irony, and outrageous hilarity of life on the mining frontier. No conceit, swelled head, or stuffed shirt in California or the Nevada Territory lived safe from the slash of his pen, and the *Enterprise* soon raised his salary. "They pay me six dollars a day," Clemens wrote his sister a few months after taking the job, "and I make 50 per cent profit by only doing three dollars worth of work."

No matter. The readership reveled in his half-day's labor. Few California editors knew what to make of his journalizing. Most smoked out his more-obvious leg-pulling, like the account of a perfectly preserved petrified man discovered "leaning against a huge mass of croppings" in the

Humboldt mountains with its crystallized "right thumb resting against the side of the nose" and the fingers of its right hand "spread apart," and ridiculed the gullible journals who printed the story "in good faith." Other Clemens hoaxes, like "A Bloody Massacre," which described eight gruesome homicides between Empire City and Dutch Nick's, proved nearly impossible for editors unfamiliar with Washoe reality to comprehend in anything except literal terms. (Among many off-kilter details, Empire City and Dutch Nick's were one and the same place.) The story of the murders—a pure fabrication—achieved its end, however, for it gulled San Francisco newspapers into reprinting the entire story, line for line, including the cause of the fictitious murderer's psychotic break—the published advice of the *San Francisco Bulletin* that had motivated him to move his life savings from mining stocks to an investment in the supposedly safer Spring Valley Water Company in San Francisco. Two *Bulletin* editors had lost significant sums investing in mine stocks spuriously inflated by "a dividend cooking system." They'd expended many column inches wailing about financial shenanigans in the Nevada Territory while simultaneously ignoring the Water Company doing the same thing right under their noses. Twain's hoax therefore tricked them into publishing a self-criticism. That many California editors didn't cotton to the hoax until after they'd printed serious commentary only increased their distrust and resentment of Mark Twain and the *Territorial Enterprise*—as well as the coarse bray of laughter echoing across the Sierras.

Sam Clemens took up residence in a B Street boardinghouse with William Wright, aka Dan de Quille, another *Enterprise* reporter, and he'd become well known about the camps—if not necessarily widely liked—by the time the pseudonym Mark Twain first appeared in the *Enterprise*. A decade later, Clemens claimed he'd appropriated his by-then-famous nom de plume from a staid Mississippi riverboat captain. However, according to more convincing Virginia City legend, Clemens had acquired the nickname before it appeared in print, derived from his habit of striding into the Old Corner Saloon and calling out to the barkeep to "Mark Twain!" a phrase Mississippi river boatmen sang out with their craft in two fathoms of water, but that in Virginia City meant bring two blasts of whisky to Sam Clemens and make two chalk marks against his account on the back wall of the saloon.

Although later in life, settled into a New England existence, Clemens claimed not to have had "a large experience in the matter of alcoholic drinks," men who knew him on the Comstock remembered substantial quantities of chalk ground down to a nub on his behalf. Regardless of how he acquired his nickname, one of the Washoeites he'd become acquainted with was the quiet, industrious, up-and-coming, and largely abstemious Irishman who superintended the Milton mine—John William Mackay.

Mackay had the Milton Company's tunnel in 450 feet at the beginning of February. His mining gangs extracted what appeared to be very rich rock, and although it hadn't yet been crushed and "proved," the mine's stock held firm at $100 per foot, especially after assays made on ore samples taken from four different parts of the mine gave returns of $47, $807, $347, and $316 per ton. If the mine had significant quantities of ore at the three latter figures, the stockholders would reap a fortune.

One day, Clemens visited Mackay in the Milton's new office, in a recently constructed frame building.* Clemens found Mackay's situation "rather sumptuous, for that day and place." Mackay hadn't been in "such very smooth circumstances" before. His office "had part of a carpet on the floor and two chairs instead of a candle-box." Perhaps sensing the opportunity for a little fun, needing fodder for one of his fancy sketches, or because he genuinely did want to try his hand at superintending a mine, Clemens proposed they switch jobs. Mackay could have his place on the *Enterprise*. Clemens would run the Milton.

Mackay considered the offer. Superintending a mine was no small undertaking. It required knowing how to bore, sink, stope, and ventilate underground workings, pump water, and hoist ore. A superintendent needed to understand the basics of static and dynamic mechanics, surveying, mineralogy, and geology, and possess the ability to lead and motivate men. Ever the practical and considerate man, Mackay asked how much Clemens's newspaper job was worth.

"Forty dollars a week," Clemens answered.

"I never swindled anybody in my life, and I don't want to begin with you," Mackay stammered. "This business of mine is not worth $40 a week. You stay where you are and I will try to get a living out of this."

In later years, when Mark Twain was the most famous American writer and raconteur in the world, he delighted in the anecdote and the light it shone on his friend, who had by then become, in Twain's description, "the first of the hundred millionaires." Most men recognized Mack-

---

* Twain's tellings described Mackay running a brokerage. There is no record of Mackay having done that, either during "the flush times of silverland" or at any other time in his life. For most of 1863, Mackay served as superintendent of the Milton Gold and Silver Mining Company.

ay's straightforward, evenhanded, fair manner of dealing with men as a cornerstone of his success. He may also have been more subtle than generally credited. It's hard to imagine him willing to trust his men and mine to Sam Clemens's supervision.

The Gould & Curry's $100 per foot dividend, announced a few days before "Mark Twain" appeared in the *Territorial Enterprise* for the first time on February 3, wasn't the only good news rippling through the mining community in early 1863. Adjacent to the Gould & Curry, the Savage mine furiously erected buildings and installed hoisting works, associated workshops, and first-class steam-powered machinery over and around the vertical shaft it was sinking, a significant technical improvement on previous works. Rectangular, stoutly framed with square-sets, and sealed top to bottom with planks to prevent rocks falling from the walls, the shaft was divided into three compartments, each four feet by four feet in the clear, two for hoisting ore and waste and the third for pumping water. Based on the prospecting drift they'd cut south from the Gould & Curry's Middle Adit, Savage management knew they were sinking on a substantial ore body, and they not only took time by the forelock, they scalped the old fellow, pushing the work with all possible speed. Before long, the Savage had a pay streak fifty feet wide, and it hoisted ore equal to the Gould & Curry's best rock. Savage stock shot through the roof.

Washoe miners had raised $6 million in 1862. A few months into 1863, current year projections expected them to raise more than twice that amount, an almost inconceivable $12 million—one-third of the production of the entire state of California from a stretch of ground just two miles long and a few hundred yards wide.* And a single 921-foot stretch of ground produced fully one-third of the Washoe total—the Gould & Curry.

The Gould & Curry reinforced the optimism at the end of February when it issued a second $100 monthly dividend and announced that it anticipated paying twice that amount by year's end. The communal euphoria skyrocketed the value of Washoe mining stocks. Newspapers crowed about the "inexhaustible" mineral wealth of Nevada Territory. Eager to share the spoils and terrified of missing out, people throughout California and the Nevada Territory clamored to invest in silver mines.

The appetite for feet waxed especially strong "below," in San Fran-

---

* The Comstock's actual 1863 production exceeded the projection, reaching $12.5 million.

cisco. Brokers' offices lined Montgomery Street, their display windows festooned with stock certificates, bullion bricks, assay certificates, and ore samples. With the Stock & Exchange Board, two other formally organized mining exchanges, and uncounted numbers of independent brokers flogging mine stock on sidewalks and street corners, Montgomery Street became the mining industry's Wall Street. People bought and sold feet by the "acre." The throngs impeded traffic. To make a fortune, it seemed only necessary for a man to "tumble over a boulder," file articles of incorporation, report that he'd discovered a lead assaying a few thousand dollars per ton, and "sell out at any price he pleased." Brokers dealt in mines from Esmeralda, Humboldt, the Reese River, the Arizona Territory, Baja California, northern Mexico, the Idaho Territory, and a host of other districts, but atop the list, towering over all other mines, rose the Washoe stocks. Of the twelve most valuable mines in the West, based on value per foot, every single one owned a slice of the Comstock Lode.* In San Francisco, everyone, positively everyone—from capitalists, bankers, and preachers to masons, hod carriers, and housewives—owned shares in Nevada silver mines. By the middle of 1863, wags joked that every San Franciscan carried a stock certificate in a pocket or tucked into a fold of a dress.

And why not? In the words of the *Daily Alta California*, the bullion raised from the Washoe mines "would have made the Count of Monte Cristo think himself a pauper." Men from every category of existence had risen to prominence through judicious investments in silver mines. Some two hundred nattily dressed men in long-tailed coats and soft hats lounged around San Francisco, propping up doorframes and lampposts and smoking immense cigars, whiling away their time with no visible means of support other than the fact that they'd bought Gould & Curry stock in the early days and drew massive monthly incomes from the mine's dividends. San Franciscans took it as a fixed fact that every man in town wearing a Shanghai coat was "a Washoe man."

If anything, the stock madness raged hotter "above," in Nevada. Comstockers had feet on the brain. They talked feet, worked feet, traded feet, jumped feet, ate and drank feet, bought and sold feet, consolidated feet, thought feet, slept feet, and dreamed feet. "Centipedes" and "millipedes" roamed the streets of Virginia City wearing black broadcloth—and the occasional satin dress. No people in history had ever had more feet,

---

* Per foot, the little mines on Gold Hill were most valuable, but they were all privately held, without stock on the market.

and although an occasional person lamented "the wearisome jargon of 'feet,'" most couldn't abide distraction, not when Gould & Curry feet had advanced 1,260 percent in the last sixteen months. The Savage, the Yellow Jacket, the Crown Point, the Hale & Norcross, the Chollar, the Potosi, and a host of other mines throughout the territory all made similar rises. "Everything—positively everything—is advancing," raved the *Territorial Enterprise*. Most Washoeites and San Franciscans believed that investment of sufficient labor and capital could make any Washoe quartz ledge profitable. As Mark Twain described the frenzy in *Roughing It*, "There was *nothing* in the shape of a mining claim that was not saleable."

John Mackay's "feet" rose with the general market. Although he'd moved his professional shingle to the Milton, he still owned a substantial portion of the Caledonia. The mine produced "considerable ore from small scattered ore bodies," and although none had proven large enough to put the mine on a paying basis, their existence created hope for better findings. In early April, Mackay's Caledonia stock took "a stride upwards." Over the course of the next three and a half months, Mackay's Caledonia holdings rose *450 percent*, and he dealt heavily in the mine, deeding and receiving interest in the Caledonia both to and from some of Washoe's most prominent capitalists, likely converting a substantial quantity of his quartz feet to solid gold cash. In addition to his holdings in the Caledonia and the Milton, Mackay also still owned a slice of the Union mine north of the Ophir. As a man who "kept his nose underground" with many friends and workmates in the mining community, he was well positioned to make intelligent speculations. Washoe's rising tide lifted Mackay into a sphere of modest financial prosperity he'd never known in his life. What he didn't have was an ore body, not in any one of the three mines that held his primary interests. He never relented in his quest to find one.

Virginia City residents held it as axiomatic that "As the Gould & Curry goes, so goes the city." The mine maintained more than five hundred men on its payroll. Indirectly, it kept more than two thousand persons in productive employment. From the retorts in its grandiose mill down Six Mile Cañon—which the company had finally gotten into operation—the Gould & Curry cast three or four enormous bricks of bullion every day, each worth about $2,500. Excitement mounted in the late spring as the Gould & Curry's Lower Adit approached the lode, having run 2,000 feet from its opening in the ravine south of Virginia City's Catholic church, a quarter-mile downslope from the mouth of the Middle Adit. The adit cut the lode in mid-June, 425 feet below the El Dorado surface croppings and around 200 feet below the deepest point from which the Gould & Curry had previously extracted ore. As if on cue, the mine upped its dividend to $150 per foot, "incontrovertible evidence of the permanence and exhaustless wealth of that mysterious depository known as the Comstock," according to the *Territorial Enterprise*. The market surged again. In the week that ended on June 27, 1863, Yellow Jacket stock rose to $1,200 per foot, the Belcher hit $1,500, the Ophir touched $2,100, the Savage topped $3,500, and the Gould & Curry reached the phenomenal sum of $6,300 per foot. "We are marching on to prosperity at railroad speed," bragged the ebullient "local" of the *Territorial Enterprise*, almost certainly Mark Twain.

The camps boomed along with the mines. Every branch of business in Virginia City and Gold Hill was "aglow with energy and activity." People eager to take advantage poured over the mountains from California in "a perfect stampede," the largest since the spring of 1860. The fever raged with "unabated fury" until "Washoe Widows" were as common in California as "California Widows" had been in the Atlantic states during the early days of the Gold Rush. The "exodus" jammed the trans-Sierran stagecoaches, forcing them to evolve from four-horse teams to six. Every day, the stages deposited about one hundred persons in Virginia City. A few backtrackers returned to California, disillusioned. Others fanned out to various mining camps throughout the Nevada Territory, but about half opted to remain on the Comstock. Virginia City's population doubled, then doubled again. By the summer of 1863, some twenty thousand people lived in the two camps, and Virginia City, terraced onto a remote desert mountainside, had grown into the second largest city on the Pacific Coast, its population double that of Sacramento and Portland, Oregon, and four times that of Stockton and Marysville. People slept in chairs. The unlucky bivouacked on curbstones and sidewalks. Entrepreneurs had three fine hotels under construction, the fanciest of which, the International, installed a mechanical elevator in its C Street entrance, the first between San Francisco and St. Louis. Newspaper articles throughout the West lauded Virginia City's wealth, growth, stability, and the "immense and astonishing" volume of business done in the camp. Teamsters freighted in fifty wagonloads of lumber each day and hauled one hundred tons of ore from the mines to the mills. Dozens of other wagons arrived with comestibles and other supplies. An immense volume of traffic jammed the main streets. Buggies on side streets sometimes had to wait half an hour for an opportunity to cross. In dry conditions, dust swirled everywhere, driven by fierce winds. When it rained, wheels and horseshoes splattered mud and offal on the sidewalks, coating anybody within the blast radius. Miners in work clothes and mucker's boots paid it no mind. Capitalists, speculators, bankers, brokers, merchants, managers, and members of "the sporting element" in their spotless black broadcloth and spit-shined shoes found it an enormous bother, as did ladies dressed for town. One busy day in the summer of 1863, a man counted sixty-eight teams on C Street, none able to move. Frustrated teamsters holding their "ribbons" (reins) blasphemed the desert air—and their mule teams—then tipped their hats and apologized if they discovered a lady within earshot. As C Street evolved into the camp's principal business thoroughfare, women of good carriage insisted the town remove the last of its higher-toned cathouses from C Street to digs further down the hillside. Most took station in the camp's budding red-light district one block below. Farther downhill stood the camp's "Chinatown" and a small neighborhood of "coloreds." Advertisements plastered the sides of stores and buildings and covered billboards erected on the neighboring hillsides. Fish taken from Lake Tahoe (ex-governor Bigler's name having been stripped from the lake due to his Southern sympathies) and transported packed in snow sold at two bits a pound. Saloons sold whisky certified to kill at forty rods for two bits a drink in cut tumblers—and for one bit if consumed from a common glass. One intrepid merchant imported a cargo of San Francisco housecats. When traffic allowed, superintendents and trustees of the important mines rolled through town driving fancy teams. The Confederate commerce raider *Alabama* delivered the only significant setback Virginia City received in the spring of 1863, when it captured and burned the California-bound merchant ship *Commonwealth* off the Brazilian coast—among its cargo were all the fixtures for Virginia City's gaslighting system.

Belowground, a series of floods plagued the Ophir. The first breach of the subterranean reservoir sent men scrambling for their lives. Miners working ahead of the rising waters raced to reinforce the timbers and backfill square-sets with waste rock in worked-out portions of the mine. The flood submerged the bottom eighty feet of the Ophir and drove miners in the neighboring Mexican from a splendid mass of ore. New, more powerful pumps drained the underground lake. Both mines resumed production, but the flood had weakened the deepest galleries of the Mexican. In early July, their ground "started." Crews worked around the clock to stave off collapse, but no matter the quantity and dimension of timbers braced across the galleries, they couldn't counteract the immense pressures and stabilize the "working" ground. Some twenty men worked inside the mine on the morning of July 15. Just as the superintendents of the Ophir and the Mexican met in the Ophir's fourth gallery at about 10:30 a.m., the gallery's huge support timbers began to crack "like firecrackers." Dirt and stones rained down from above. The two superintendents dropped into the fifth gallery and raced into the Mexican. Similar "ominous demonstrations" sent them scurrying back to the Ophir. They'd barely reached Ophir ground when a huge crash behind them collapsed the entire Mexican mine from its deepest level all the way to the surface. The blast of wind billowing out from the collapse extinguished their candles and left them in darkness. An overwhelming desire to see daylight and breathe fresh air suddenly possessed everyone underground. The superintendents groped for the base of the Ophir incline and joined the line of workmen scrambling up the narrow stairway toward the surface. Foot-thick support timbers cracking like cannon shots and clods of earth falling from the incline's ceiling sped their three-hundred-foot ascent. Men reached the surface gasping. Hurried head counts accounted for all men who'd been underground. One of the Mexican's miners had endured a closer shave than most. The first collapse entombed him in a shallow drift. A subsequent shift opened a crevasse over his head. He wormed up shouting until workmen above could get a hand to him and draw him to safety.

The ground above the mines settled all the way across the Mexican and the Ophir's south mine. Pressure threatened the Ophir's incline. To lessen it, the mine deployed workmen to cut back a high earthen bank west of the engine house. Not twenty feet west of the incline, those workmen struck a two- to three-foot-thick vein of soft, decomposed quartz shot through with "pure native silver" and large quantities of gold, which they immediately started sacking for shipment. Within a month, twenty-five Ophir miners worked the new vein. Standing from 20 to 40 feet west of the ore body the Ophir had worked since 1859, it proved to be 5 to 15 feet wide, 300 feet long, and 350 feet deep, and before it played out, it produced more than one million dollars' worth of bullion.

The first miners to reenter the Ophir found the damage concentrated in shallow areas already worked out in and above the fourth gallery. The cave hadn't harmed any of the active stopes in the deeper galleries. The situation at the Mexican wasn't so copacetic. The collapse ruined the Mexican's shaft and portions of its engine house, and although the west vein discovered behind the Ophir also ran into its ground, the cave had ruined its workings entirely, from the 225-foot level all the way to the surface. Engineers deemed the sinking of a new and expensive vertical shaft 125 feet east of the original croppings the most reasonable way of regaining access to the mine.

Sam Clemens had reported from inside the Mexican the day before the cave. Two weeks later, a fire burned him out of his B Street lodging house. Only a windless day saved the whole block. Clemens stood in the street dazed, watching the flames consume everything he owned, including what a friend later described as "an immense amount of 'wild cat,' variously estimated to be worth from ten cents to two hundred thousand dollars." Clemens lost all his possessions except the clothes on his person. Out of nowhere, a complete stranger handed him a packet of "feet." Downtown, Clemens sold the batch for $200, enough, as he told his mother and sister in a letter written ten days later, to fit himself out again "half as good as new. . . . The unknown scoundrel couldn't have done me a favor of the kind when I needed it more."

Sam Clemens never learned the man's name. Most of the lode's leading men had helped pioneer California during the Gold Rush years, and such openhanded generosity, "California-like," was expected of a successful man. Freeloading wasn't respected, but people helped each other when misfortune touched. Fierce competitiveness and good fellowship went hand in hand. People took part in local events, be they a parade, picnic, fancy ball, theatrical performance, horse race, dog or cock fight, boxing match, or funeral. Among themselves, men swore like sailors and reveled in off-color jokes, prizing laughter like rich ore; in mixed company, they guarded their tongues for fear of offending the ladies. Off-duty, men drank copious amounts of liquor and smoked cigars and pipes, scorning cigarettes as fit only for Mexicans and the "soiled doves" on D Street. "The flush times of silverland" were times of hard drinking, careless living, foolish expenditure, wild generosity, and hair-trigger violence. Most visitors never made more than cursory, guided investigations of the mine workings that underburrowed the two camps and gained little appreciation for the mighty industry of the subterranean city. Their gaze latched on to the aboveground chaos and dissipation that played out amidst the dust, noise, and traffic of the mountainside city. For the most part, the Comstock was a man's world. Women composed but a fraction of the population, and more than a few of those on the lode had come to get divorced. As the *Marysville Daily Appeal* quipped, "Do married women go there to exchange their feet?" Many blamed the boomtime mayhem on the absence of "pure, good women." The men "feed on whisky," wrote one correspondent, "and that diet causes rowdyism as naturally as turtle soup lays fat on an alderman's ribs."

Flush times and porous territorial justice drew hordes of California renegades to Washoe, and with them came a resurgence of the violence that had plagued the camps in earlier times. "Washoe cities and villages are flooded with the most desperate set of wretches that ever disgraced humanity. . . . Dishonest tradesmen, runaway wives, played out gamblers, and the votaries and disciples of every vice . . . flourish ingloriously on the Eastern Slope," whined the *Virginia Bulletin*. California editors in need of filler scoured Washoe newspapers for violent incidents. Among many such obscure items, an unidentified gunman shot and killed a murderer named Jack Williams through the open door of a gambling saloon. A butcher named George Gumpert wounded one of Williams's pistol-toting associates with a knife, and in the "brief artillery duel" that followed, finished him with a shotgun. Coin bought what passed for justice in the territorial courts. Jails couldn't hold prisoners. Police extorted from saloons, gambling hells, and brothels, and squeezed favors from prostitutes in exchange for "protection." Women in the fast life sought relief in stupefying patent medicines. Popular concoctions like Godfrey's Cordial and McMunn's Elixir all contained the same principal ingredient—opium. Another of that ilk, Mrs. Winslow's Soothing Syrup, was specifically advertised as a comfort for teething babies. Pie-eyed Charles Henry Bryan, a prominent Virginia City lawyer and former justice of the California Supreme Court, staggered into the Jenny Lind Saloon one March morning, drew a derringer from a coat pocket, and calmly informed a seated German that he intended to shoot him "for luck." Bryan pulled the trigger, but was so wretchedly inebriated that his point-blank shot merely pierced the German's shirtsleeve. Incredulous, a *Virginia Daily Union* reporter concluded that "no ill feeling existed between the parties—indeed, we believe they were strangers." Nor did the incident damage Bryan's reputation—six months later, Storey County elected him as one of its delegates to the Nevada Territory's Constitutional Convention.

Drunk Jack Butler "abused" Juana Sanchez, a "woman of the town." He drew a pistol and threatened her life. Juana disarmed Butler. When he produced a second pistol, she shot him dead with the first. A woman named Deborah Ann Phillips killed a man with a pistol for calling her "a damned whore" in public. After hearing witnesses testify about her character, an inquiry released her on $1,000 bail. Her trial returned a verdict of "justifiable homicide." Governor Nye gave her a full pardon.

At a "reception" hosted by Miss Lilly Westlake, Tom Peasley, proprietor of C Street's Sazarac Saloon, chief engineer of the Virginia City Fire
Department, and principal figure in Volunteer Fire Company No. 1,
quarreled with Joseph Jenkins, aka Sugar-foot Jack. Jenkins blackguarded
Peasley in villainous language. Peasley struck Jenkins in the face. Jenkins
retreated to Robson's saloon on the west side of North B Street and armed
himself. Peasley came in for a provocative drink, and Jenkins did nothing. Thinking the matter ended, Peasley retired to Lynch's saloon further
down B Street. Jenkins followed Peasley, however, and he was drawing
his pistol when Peasley shot him above the hip, then three times more in
quick succession.

The slaying probably increased custom at Peasley's Sazarac Saloon. As
Mark Twain wrote in *Roughing It*, "To be a saloon-keeper and kill a man
was to be illustrious." Rumors constantly circulated about town leaders
fed up with ineffective law enforcement cleaning out the ruffian element
with that time-honored frontier institution, the vigilance committee.
"Sure as there is a God in Heaven, the people will not much longer sub-
mit to the existing state of things," a man wrote to the *San Francisco Bulletin*. "There is a point in forbearance at which it ceases to be a virtue in a
people." The violence never quite reached that extremity, largely because
most of it stayed confined within the ruffian element.

The rampant gambling, drinking, whoring, and violence appalled
those moralizers trying to establish "civilization" in the mining camps.
An oldtime yon-sider who remembered 1849 California as a "vestibule
of hell," considered 1863 Virginia City "the very throne-room of Pluto
himself." Fiercely pro-Union and renowned Unitarian minister the Rev-
erend Thomas Starr King lectured in Washoe and returned to California
describing the Comstock's big mines, little mines, and whisky mills as
"Ophir holes, gopher holes, and loafer holes."

Among the thousands of people drawn to Virginia City by the boom
were Major Daniel E. Hungerford, his wife Eveline, and their six-year-
old daughter, Ada. Hungerford had gone east to serve in the U.S. Army in
1861, received promotion to lieutenant colonel, and seen "the belligerent
elephant" during General McClellan's Peninsula Campaign, after which
he "threw up his commission in disgust," resigned from the Army of the
Potomac, and returned to the Pacific Coast, possessed with the bizarre
idea of raising a volunteer force and attacking Texas through the Arizona
and New Mexico territories.

The Hungerfords' eldest daughter, eighteen or nineteen years old,

Marie Louise Antoinette, almost always called Louise; her husband, Dr. Edmund G. Bryant; and their one-year-old daughter, Eva, also succumbed to the Washoe fever and moved to Virginia City during the boom times. Louise and her mother had been on the Pacific Coast since 1854, when they came west to join then major Hungerford. Young Louise had made quite a sensation in Downieville. Gold dust was more common than children in the early California mining camps, and the few girls lived in virtual purdah. They weren't seen except at whatever passed for church services, held close to their mothers' skirts. One Saturday afternoon when they were about twelve years old, Louise and her best friend, Louise Meyer, had taken it into their heads to dress up and visit the Meyers' store at the far end of town. As the two young girls came into view, a hush swept over the wild, bewhiskered men crowding Main Street for provisions and weekend amusement. Tears filled the eyes of those from remote camps, some of whom hadn't seen a child in years, let alone a little girl in weekend finery. The two girls advanced, and the crowd parted. Men looked on in tender amazement until one of them thought to step forward and press a coin into one of the girls' hands. Others followed his lead. The girls reached Meyer's Store loaded down with gold coins and nuggets. Appalled, their parents forbade them to ever repeat the performance.

The Hungerfords had only been able to send Louise to St. Catherine's Academy in Benicia, near the mouth of the Sacramento River, for a single semester late in the decade before the press of penury forced them to return her to Downieville, but testament to the ministrations of her Europhilic mother, Louise spoke French and Spanish well and managed to exude an air of culture and refinement despite having spent most of her childhood in a mining camp.

Louise's handsome and promising husband, Dr. Edmund Gardiner Bryant, had appeared in Downieville in the late 1850s. A graduate of the College of Physicians and Surgeons at Columbia University, he probably became acquainted with then major Hungerford through service in the Sierra Guards and possibly through attending leechings and tooth extractions conducted in the major's barbershop. Dr. Bryant made a name for himself tending sick and injured in Sierra County's first hospital.

Louise's granddaughter Ellin Mackay Berlin, one of most influential writers in the early history of *The New Yorker*, who went on to marry famed composer Irving Berlin, in 1957 published a novelized account of her grandmother's life called *Silver Platter*, in which she gave a charming account of then-fifteen-year-old Louise's romance with the handsome and promising twenty-three-year-old doctor. They had married on New Year's Day, 1860, eleven days after Louise's sixteenth birthday. Louise gave birth to a daughter, Evelyn Julia Bryant, "Eva," on November 12, 1861, and around the time of their move to Virginia City, to a second daughter, Marie. Louise Bryant was still only nineteen years old.

A "winsome," pleasant young woman with "soft and round" features, "large and expressive" blue eyes, and rich brown tresses cascading past her shoulder, Louise made a home for her husband and two daughters at 10 A Street, where the doctor also kept his office. Her parents lived a few hundred yards to the north, in Cedar Ravine. Dr. Bryant's practice flourished, and several of his mining speculations showed promising "indications" as the market rode toward its June peak. An August 1863 fire that sparked a bloody brawl between two volunteer fire companies consumed the Bryants' home and the doctor's consulting office. The Bryants rebuilt, along with the rest of the street. Much worse, their eight-month-old daughter Marie contracted "the septic sore throat."

An old friend found Louise tending her sick baby. Dr. Bryant kept his office in the front room of the house. Louise begged her friend to intercede with her husband and convince him to treat their child. The friend made an effort, but the doctor "acted like an insane man" and drove her out with "curses." For reasons never explained, Dr. Bryant refused to treat his own child. Blistering fever and infection swelled little Marie's throat shut. She choked to death while her mother looked on, helpless.

Father Patrick Manogue consoled the bereaved young mother. An Irish giant, six foot three inches tall, Patrick Manogue had paid his tuition to the Saint Sulpice Seminary in Paris, France, with gold he'd raised from four years of mining at Moore's Flat, in the Sierra foothills about halfway between Nevada City and Downieville. After his 1861 ordination, the Church sent him to minister to the miners of the Nevada Territory, many of whom knew the good father from the California goldfields. His fearsome physical strength, imposing presence, and courage commanded the respect of other men. Women found his tender manner and gentle voice soothing, and he spoke straight, without unction. Even the godless admired his commitment to service. After the death of her baby, Louise Bryant leaned hard on the priest's broad shoulders. She buried her child in the gravelly soil of Virginia City's new cemetery, on the camp's northern outskirts.

Both Colonel Hungerford and Dr. Bryant dabbled substantially in mining stocks, although neither appears to have ever spent a day underground, and Dr. Bryant's returns were, if anything, more dismal than his father-in-law's. By the time of Marie's death, he'd squandered so much money in ill-fated speculations and saloons that he and his wife couldn't afford a headstone to mark their daughter's grave—a failing that only added to Louise's misery. Black depression consumed her.

No source has ever revealed why Dr. Bryant behaved so callously toward his own daughter, because professionally, he was managing to hold his medical practice together, at least for a time—in one documented instance performing a difficult and dangerous emergency surgery to repair a depressed skull fracture and save a miner's life.

Personally, Dr. Bryant wasn't doing nearly so well. Fancying himself a man of sound judgment, he continued to hemorrhage money in uninformed mining speculations, he'd developed a noticeable devotion to "the territorial destructive," whisky, and by early 1864 he'd likely begun a closet relationship with one of the only effective medicines at his disposal—opium.

The March 11, 1864, issue of the *Gold Hill News* contained a story titled "Shameless!" that chronicled the dissipation of "a well-known" Virginia City physician, "a most skillful and talented young man" arrested that morning and taken into custody "for beating his wife and smashing the furniture and in other ways conducting himself like a maniac." He'd been "over-indulging in strong drink," and his wife said he'd been "taking morphine and other drugs till almost on the verge of insanity." Nor was it the first time the physician had been "locked up under similar circumstances."

The article fingered no one by name, but it jibed with the known circumstances of the Bryants' lives. Not long after, Dr. Bryant left Virginia City for Austin, in the center of the territory, to see if he could improve his fortunes in the Reese River country. He left his wife and three-year-old daughter without funds, a fate perilously close to abandonment. Her parents also left Virginia City, Colonel Hungerford having lost confidence in the Comstock. With Louise's little sister, Ada, they removed to modest dwellings in San Francisco. Mrs. Hungerford taught Spanish and French. The colonel returned to barbering and embroiled himself in plotting another bizarre military adventure. Not wanting Louise tempted by the soul-killing but much better paid work readily available to Virginia City's threadbare young women, Father Manogue found her work sewing for the camp's well-to-do ladies. Beneath a flickering candle, Louise sewed far into the night. Only in a state of complete exhaustion could she fall asleep without the wind that moaned through the cracks in her clapboard accommodations carrying her thoughts to her baby buried in an unmarked grave in the coarse dirt of the Virginia City cemetery, comfortless soil on which grass wouldn't grow.

John Mackay worked through the boom with characteristic dedication, bent on getting ahead. He lived in a boardinghouse at 195 South C Street, an easy stroll from the Bryant household at 10 North A Street, and although Colonel Hungerford, Dr. and Louise Bryant, and John Mackay had all come to the Comstock from Downieville and all enjoyed a certain amount of local fame during the flush times, no evidence has ever suggested they associated with one another. Mackay served through 1863 as superintendent of the Milton mine. Among the twenty-four shareholders whose names appeared on the mine's deed alongside Mackay's, two became lifelong friends, A. M. Cole and Adolph ('Dolf) Hirschman. Mackay struggled with tight, crabbed penmanship and slow composition in those years, consequence of the formal education he'd missed. 'Dolf Hirschman wrote freely and easily, and he penned many letters on Mackay's behalf.

Feeling little attraction to the camp's dissipations, Mackay used his free evenings to embark on a rigorous campaign of self-improvement and professional study. He stayed up late digesting every piece of geological, scientific, and engineering literature he could lay eyes on, marrying academic knowledge to the tremendous quantity of practical mining experience he'd amassed. Nor did he confine his campaign to subjects of immediate professional relevance. He read newspapers, magazines, history, and literature, tried to improve his command of mathematics, and endeavored to smooth and loosen his handwriting.

Personally, Mackay was a hard man to know. He kept his own counsel. A man who'd known him before his star rose remembered him as "more difficult to sound" than any man he'd ever known. "Beyond a certain depth, he [was] inscrutable."

Mackay didn't talk much, and when he did, he spoke in methodical, measured tones, still fighting his embarrassing stutter, his uniquely American argot a mix of New York, California mining slang, and "rich Irish burr." In conversation, Mackay listened far more than he talked, and he said only what was absolutely necessary, a trait that often gave him the last word in professional discussions.

Taciturn John Mackay certainly was, but he was no loner. He enjoyed the company of his fellows. He particularly didn't like eating alone and made great efforts to have friends share his table. Mackay found silence comfortable and companionable, and he relished a good story. He just seldom felt the need to talk. He had a sense of humor, he teased his friends, and he made jokes, often at his own expense, with a quick, dry, and occasionally scathing Irish wit deployed in few words. He escaped his cares and responsibilities through near-religious devotion to the musical ensembles and dramatic troupes that visited Washoe, boxing workouts at a Virginia City gymnasium, and occasional games of poker. The flaw in Mackay's character was his hair-trigger temper. Many old Comstockers remembered flashes of his Irish temper. None could recall ever seeing him drunk. He was handy with his fists, and he didn't hesitate to use them, particularly when he felt his "good name" assailed.

Mackay remained devoted to Jack O'Brien and other friends from the old California diggings, one of whom, years later, remembered him as "tolerant of anything except a breach of faith." He was ever sensitive to the feelings and needs of others. He judged men fairly, and well, and when he had another man's confidence, he kept it. He had an innate scorn for pretense. His gaze looked through a suit of clothes "to the living character beneath," and he treated all men equally, whether spotless nabobs rolling down C Street in fancy carriages and fine clothes or grubby miners coming off a tough underground shift.

Mackay's leadership qualities developed at the Milton. Miners he bossed appreciated his plainspoken, unaffected manner. Peers, superiors, and subordinates took him seriously. A few friends who'd known him in old California days called him "John." A few others called him "Mackay." Most called him "Mr. Mackay." He strove hard for success and advancement, but above any lucre, he valued the "respect of men." In an industry bedeviled by dishonest dealings, he kept his good name. As he'd assured Sam Clemens, he never swindled anyone.

Mackay was happy superintending the Milton, as he had been at the Caledonia and while working as a foreman, timberman, and common miner before that. Unfortunately, the Milton had problems. Claiming the right of prior location, the Milton disputed ownership with the Chollar, its downhill neighbor, then working good ore. Battling the heavyweight legal team of a rich and powerful mine in the venal territorial courts presented a poor prospect of success. Worse, the Milton hadn't developed an ore body of its own. The promising assay results published in the February newspapers had been made on selected samples. The Milton, like most Washoe quartz leads, had gold and silver in its matrix and, in places, pockets of good ore, but just like the Caledonia, the Milton didn't have large enough volumes of ore to get itself on a paying basis.

The implications of the Comstock's eastward dip recently discovered deep in the Ophir and in the little Gold Hill mines wouldn't become widely recognized for another year, but the discovery that the lode's true dip slanted away from Mount Davidson was a profoundly adverse "indication" for the mines located above and to the west of the revealed Comstock—one of which was the Milton. As a superintendent who spent much of his working life underground, Mackay probably appreciated the consequences of that revelation long before they became generally accepted. When an opportunity to join the ownership of a mine with a clear title undeniably located on the main lead presented itself, Mackay seized it.

A local mine owner named Jonas M. Walker brought Mackay the opportunity. Looking back with the perspective of sixty years, a Comstock historian writing in the 1920s described Walker as "an agreeable man from Virginia, but not a forceful character or a man of much practical ability." That sentiment probably doesn't reflect the feelings of the Washoe mining community in 1863. In those days, Walker, like Mackay, must have seemed like someone on the way up. An imposing, handsome man with sideburns and a mustache and wavy hair combed back over his ears, Walker owned substantially in the Bullion Gold and Silver Mining Company, a consolidation of two existing claims formally organized on February 18, 1863. The Bullion held clear, undisputed title to 1,424 feet of the Comstock Lode astride the Divide between Virginia City and Gold Hill. Located between the proven mines of the Chollar and Potosi to the north and the wildly profitable claims on Gold Hill to the south, the Bullion's prospects seemed superb, especially after the *Virginia Daily Union* reported the Bullion extracting a large quantity of "good-looking quartz, blue, filled with sulphurets." Of the fifty-five local miners, businessmen, and speculators who signed the Bullion's deed (most of whom must have known John Mackay and been known to him), Jonas M. Walker's name came first.

Both men were Freemasons. When Walker suggested Mackay buy into the Bullion and merge their holdings into an equal partnership, Mackay accepted. The two men likely sealed their new relationship with a handshake. Walker was a gold rusher with a lawyerly background, and legal experience counted for much in Washoe, where it was impossible to develop a successful mine without waging ferocious courtroom warfare. Mackay had been mining on the lode without interruption since a few weeks after the first discovery. By 1863 and 1864, there can't have been but a handful of men—if any—with more practical Comstock mining ex-

perience than John Mackay. Together, Mackay and Walker made a powerful combination, greater than the sum of their individual parts.

To effect the consolidation of his and Walker's interests, Mackay likely
"realized" on most of his interest in the Milton and all the remaining feet
he held in the Union mine, likely to great advantage. A *Mining & Scientific Press* report on the Bullion's annual election in the spring of 1864
named the superintendent as J. M. Walker and mentioned the elevation
of a trustee named "J. W. Mickey," almost certainly a misprint of "Mackay."

Among the consortium's ownership, Mackay and Walker were the acknowledged leaders. As Mackay was always happy to let another man
have the official title, Walker assumed the superintendency, but as in every
other aspect of their partnership, he and Mackay operated in concert.
Determined to find ore or satisfy themselves that none existed, Bullion
management—meaning Mackay, Walker, and the other trustees—levied
a ten-dollar assessment on each of the mine's twenty-five hundred shares.
They supervised the installation of a forty-horsepower engine, the construction of "the best finished hoisting apparatus in Gold Hill," and the
sinking of a vertical shaft from which to explore the mine's most promising feature—a huge mass of soft, whitish quartz similar to ones that
had revealed valuable ore bodies in other mines. The Bullion was a dry
mine, free from the influxes of water plaguing so many other Comstock
claims, and therefore easier and less expensive to work. From stations
on the shaft, they directed crosscuts and drifts into the Bullion's quartz
mass, everywhere encountering sufficient trace quantities of metal to lure
progress forward but nowhere finding an ore body of sufficient size and
concentration to pay the costs of extraction and reduction.

Mackay and Walker had the good sense to diversify their holdings. In
mid-December 1863, Mackay acquired feet in the Cedar Hill Float Rock
and Surface Mining Company No. 1, a hydraulic mining operation that
owned gold-bearing sediments on Cedar Hill at the north end of town.
(Mackay and Walker were likely operating in partnership by this date,
but as remained true through the duration of their partnership, usually
just one of their names appeared on the deeds.) Although the wording of
the transfer doesn't make it clear, Mackay and Walker may have acquired
the entire mine. Large amounts of water in a reservoir gave the company the opportunity to wash away the south slope of Cedar Hill "regular old California style," with a jet of water shot from under a fifty-foot
head of pressure. The runoff washed gold-bearing sediments through a
long series of sluice boxes. Miners picked ore-bearing chunks of quartz

from the tailings and sold them to custom milling operations. During ten weeks of operations during the summer of 1862, the mine had sold 25,500 tons of ore washed from the hillside to custom mills for $25 per ton, and every ten days it cleaned up from $1,000 to $1,500 worth of placer gold from behind the riffle bars of the sluice boxes. Combined, revenues for each ten-week block of operations ran between $19,500 and $23,000. A newspaper article told of a four-pound block of quartz recovered from the mine "thickly encrusted with gold all over its surface" and of "fine threads and spangles of gold" filling the cracks and seams of other quartz chunks. An 1862 report said the Cedar Hill Float Rock Company owned enough ground to last several years, "in which time they should take out a dozen fortunes." By late 1863, the mine had "hydraulicked" a large gash in the south side of Cedar Hill. Although working the mine depended utterly on the available supply of inexpensive water, if the published reports were accurate, the Cedar Hill Float Rock and Surface Mining Company No. 1 had tremendous potential. John Mackay probably took control looking forward to operating the first profitable Comstock mine he'd ever owned.

Those were good times on the Comstock. As Mark Twain wrote about the flush times, "I thought they were going to last always."

CHAPTER 8

A Tiny Sliver of a Mine

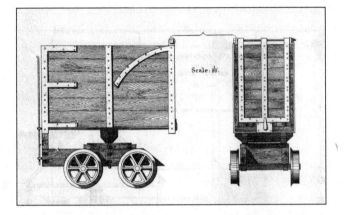

Schematic drawing of one of the many hundreds of ore
cars used in the Comstock mines, each one of which
could contain more than a thousand pounds of ore or waste.

**There are some good mines, and four thousand that are
good for nothing.**
　　　—"California Gossip," *New York Times*, April 23, 1864

The Comstock Lode touched its first high-water mark in the summer of
1863. From there, the tide ebbed, slowly. Industry observers couldn't
explain the price declines of the leading Washoe stocks. Through the rest
of 1863 and into 1864, many confident articles appeared in newspapers
repeating the sentiment expressed by a *Mining & Scientific Press* article
that stated, "The more prominent holders of both Ophir and Gould &
Curry manifest quite an indifference to their market value, having full
faith in the mine[s] as permanent dividend paying institution[s]." Such
boosterism did nothing to arrest the steady slide. Compounding problems, very little rain fell on California and the Nevada Territory during

the winter of 1863–64, extending a drought begun the previous year. Lack of water paralyzed placer mining in the Sierra foothills—and likely ruined Mackay and Walker's efforts to work the Cedar Hill Float Rock and Surface Mining Company No. 1. Crops and grass withered. Sheep and cattle starved. The economic damage forced people to sell out of their ancillary investments, increasing the downward pressure on stock prices. Many Ophir stockholders had availed themselves of its acceptability as collateral to borrow large sums for speculation in other mines. The skid forced those people to sell stock to cover their other obligations, which contributed to the downward trajectory. By the end of 1863, Gould & Curry "feet" hovered around $5,000, the Savage's around $2,700, and the Ophir's around $1,500, all high figures, but a painful pinch on those who'd bought the summer peak.

The Washoe price slip defied bullion production, which continued higher than ever. From one day's run at the end of December 1863, the Gould & Curry mill cleaned up more than 700 *pounds* of bullion—worth in the neighborhood of $20,000. The week before, Wells, Fargo & Company had transported Washoe bullion worth $473,000 to the Bay, and although Wells Fargo did the majority of "express" business, it was only one of several concerns handling bullion shipments.

In truth, although bullion production grew in the first half of 1864, Washoe had serious problems. "Adroit and profitable villainy" conducted by mine insiders to manipulate stock prices sapped public confidence. Much investment and development work had been made on the assumption that the Comstock dipped west, into Mount Davidson. The recent discovery that the lode actually dipped away from Mount Davidson put a large amount of that work to waste. Only a handful of mines paid legitimate dividends, every one of them known to own a slice of the Comstock Ledge, while dozens of mines both on and off the Comstock levied assessments. Some assessment monies financed legitimate mine development. Others paid the exorbitant salaries of mine officers. At the Gould & Curry, the president earned $10,000 per year and did very little work. Likewise, Ophir directors who knew nothing about mining drew outlandish salaries. Wanting their mine run on scientific principles, the Ophir hired Walter W. Palmer, an English mining engineer who'd supposedly become expert superintending a mine in Mexico, at $2,500 *per month*. In the "patio yard" where the Ophir mill located the arrastras for working its third-class ores, Palmer insisted that horses and mules trample through the slurry of powdered ore, water, salt, copper sulfate, and mercury, firm in his belief that only an infusion of warmth from the animals' feet and legs could properly complete the amalgamation process. Adopting "the Palmer Process" made the mine and its directors subject to "a good deal of ridicule"—and lamed many animals—without making a scrap of difference to mill yields. In an article lambasting Palmer's work pace, which ignored "the present generation altogether" and worked the mine "for posterity," Podgers of the *New York Times* thought the Ophir "wretchedly man-aged." In an age devoid of laws regulating corporate governance, small stockholders unhappy with the mine's management possessed no leverage to do anything about it. For all of Podgers's cogent criticism, there was a crucial nugget of information he did *not* have, or if he was one of the fortunate stockholders in the know, didn't share— three hundred feet beneath the surface, below the point where the vein had started its eastward dip, the Ophir's ore body narrowed and dropped in quality.

Voluminous litigation constituted another millstone around Washoe's neck. Comstock mining claims generated lawsuits like the barrels of the army's experimental hand-cranked Gatling guns spewed out bullets. The *Sacramento Daily Union* called Virginia City the lawyers' "money paradise," where lawsuits ate up "the substance of the people." Wags joked that litigation was the lode's principal industry. Since no mine wanted to invest in developing an ore body it might lose to an adverse court ruling, and perjury, violence, tampering, bribes, and other corruption tainted juries, judges, and witnesses in the territorial courts, the legal wrangling thwarted mine development. Most infamous of the "vampire suits" was the one brought by "The Grosch [*sic*] Consolidated Gold and Silver Mining Company" in the summer of 1863. Citing the provenance of Hosea and Allan Grosh, the two long-dead brothers who had prospected the Washoe Diggings for silver before the Gold Hill and Ophir discoveries, the Grosch Consolidated Company published a twenty-page pamphlet extolling their claim to 3,750 feet of the Comstock Ledge— including all the productive ground of the Gould & Curry, the Mexican, and the Ophir mines. The *Mining & Scientific Press* thundered against the lawsuit, calling it a "mammoth incubus" formed "for the simple purpose of levying blackmail." The suit named Henry Comstock a codefendant, and in March 1864, a territorial court held Comstock in default for "non-appearance" at a time when Comstock was known to be "largely interested" in quartz leads in the Idaho Territory's recently discovered South Boise mines, in a region that, at least as Comstock told it, exceeded in "extent and richness" anything he'd ever known in his life. Reports reached Virginia City of Comstock crushing Idaho quartz in a rude ara-stra driven by an overshot water wheel, and lauded the "energy" of "this famous prospector." Letters from Idaho credited him with playing "an important part in developing the wealth of Idaho," and told of him on his way back from Idaho with quartz to exhibit and claims "to dispose of." Most Washoeites thought Comstock had failed to appear for the Grosch Consolidated lawsuit because the summons hadn't reached him in time. In March 1865, the Twelfth District Court dismissed the lawsuit.

Among the many hundreds of cases that clogged Nevada's territorial courts, the most significant hinged on a single legal question: Did the Comstock Lode consist of many independent ledges parallel to and sep-arate from one another or was it one great ledge, its valuable ore bod-ies united in depth but separated near the surface by various "horses" of worthless vein matter? Popularly, Washoeites knew them as the "one ledge" and "many ledge" theories. The Ophir, the Gould & Curry, the Savage, the Yellow Jacket, and the other early locations made along the line of the Comstock expounded the one-ledge theory—its enshrine-ment would mean that all ore between the footwall and hanging wall of the lode belonged to the original locations. The many-ledge theory held that each different ore seam within the wide mineralized band of the so-called Comstock Ledge was its own unique and distinct geological entity, and therefore subject to the ownership of a separate company since it was commonly held mining law that no company could claim two separate ledges. (However, one company could *buy* another company's original location and end up owning more than one ledge.)

Many-ledge advocates considered the one-ledgers evil corporate monopolists; the one-ledge companies thought the many-ledgers were thieves. The weight of underground evidence mounting in favor of the Comstock Lode's being one single, gigantic fissure vein did little to con-tain public ire against the ruthless capitalists controlling the leading mines and the legal skulduggery they propagated to strengthen their holdings. Shrewd, forceful, politically manipulative mining attorney Wil-liam M. Stewart cleaned up a fortune representing the leading mines and the one-ledge theory. The *Virginia Daily Union* called the Ophir Com-pany "The Great Grab-All Company" and its relentless advocacy of the one-ledge theory nothing but "a moneyed effort to cripple and monopo-lize." The Yellow Jacket deployed a midnight raid that eradicated all trace of a stump that marked a boundary to strengthen one of its arguments and, according to some, "floated" its original location three hundred feet downhill. The Chollar and the Potosi brutalized each other with bitter, tit-for-tat legal warfare, as they'd done since 1861. Referencing English literary colossus Charles Dickens and his novel *Bleak House*—without realizing that a legitimate American peer was serving an apprenticeship in their midst—Washoeites nicknamed the Chollar–Potosi case "Jarndyce v. Jarndyce." Only after the Chollar and the Potosi had squandered $1.3 million in Pyrrhic legal wrangling could the two mines bring themselves to do the obvious and merge their interests.

Mines "in bonanza" spent money as if they had an endless supply. And why not? Most everybody thought Comstock mines bottomless and inexhaustible. Although many Washoe mines played loose with their fortune, none outdid the Gould & Curry. The 921-foot-wide mine led the region—and the entire mining world—in both bullion production and the size of its expense accounts. Gould & Curry superintendent Charley Strong spent the mine's money like Plutus, the veritable god of wealth himself. The mine's quartz mill towered above all other Washoe extravagance. The mill sat on a handsome plateau graded from rough and rocky slopes at the intersection of Six and Seven Mile cañons a mile below Virginia City. A massive foundation of dressed granite blocks underpinned the mill's main building and two projecting wings, which rose into a magnificent two-story edifice with splendid cruciform symmetry and "pretensions to architectural beauty."

Inside the mill, six large furnaces embedded in fireproof masonry heated three twenty-six-foot boilers that piped high-pressure steam to a 150-horsepower engine turning a drive wheel thirteen and a half feet in diameter. Leather belts passed power from the wheel to various parts of the mill, the largest of which was 160 feet long and 32 inches wide—four inches wider than any belt the Boston Belting Company had ever made. The mill opened with a forty-stamp battery capable of crushing forty tons of quartz per day, then doubled the number of its stamps and crushing capacity. To contain the choking dust clouds rising from dry-crushing ore, airtight compartments enclosed the batteries. Iron pipes fitted with powerful fans attached to the airtight rooms created a vacuum that drew off and collected the metal-rich ore dust—just one aspect of an intricately engineered system designed to keep the establishment free of airborne particulate matter, lessen wear on machinery, promote the health and cleanliness of the workforce, and preserve the dust for subsequent reduction. Elevators raised crushed ore from the batteries to sorting screens from whence too-coarse material was diverted to grinding pans for further reduction and cars carried fine-enough crushings to rows of eight-foot-diameter double-bottomed amalgamating pans designed for steam heating, mercury mixing, and other chemical enhancements supposed to aid and speed the metal recovery. The resulting amalgam, drawn from the bottom of the pans after hours of steady mixing, passed into tubs in the cleaning-up room, where large agitators connected by copper pipes completed the final, custom-modified, and highly secret steps of the "Veatch Process," supposedly a refinement of the Freiberg Process used in Europe. Ventilators atop the building encouraged the escape of steam, gas, mercury vapors, and other foul airs.

Water pumps, cisterns, and hoses gave mill workers high-pressure fire-fighting capabilities. Paint, varnish, burnish, polish, finished stonework, and other "useless ornament" completed every detail. (Rough stone and unpainted wood sufficed in other quartz mills.) Scattered around the grounds outside the main mill building were fancy offices, state-of-the-art blacksmiths and carpenters shops, stables, graded and paved roads, stone steps connecting terraces carved into the hillside, spacious boardinghouses to lodge the mill's workforce, a number of arastras for working the old Mexican patio process on low-grade ores, commodious and comfortable outhouses, and arched sewers. Before it all lay a reflecting pond, in the middle of which a statue of three water nymphs and a swan spouted a fountain of water.

By the end of 1863, mill construction had absorbed almost $900,000 of mine proceeds. With 225 employees on its payroll, the mill turned out four or five huge bricks of bullion per day, worth $8,000 to $10,000, and a lady could pass through the mill without soiling her dress. An industry observer wondered "why so much money is expended where it would appear that one-half that amount would do the same work?"

Far worse than the extravagance, the mill didn't work. Not as intended. The mill produced bullion from ore, yes, but industrial-scale ore reductions discovered that the peculiar and unique Veatch Process didn't "save" enough metal to justify its fifty- to sixty-dollar-per-ton cost—and it also rendered unprofitable the huge quantities of lesser grade Comstock ores. The Gould & Curry discarded its Veatch machinery and replaced it with the Washoe Pan Process at a cost of another half a million dollars—and even then the mill didn't work, for the mill site itself had no advantage. The mill was remote from the mine. Hauling ore to the mill was an additional cost. Distant from abundant and flowing water, the mill enjoyed no advantage of cheap water or low-cost power. East of Virginia City when timber companies cut cordwood far to the west, the

Gould & Curry mill paid more for fuel deliveries than any other mill. Unable to compete with mills situated and constructed along more practical lines, the Gould & Curry mill was a folly, nothing more.

To most Gould & Curry stockholders, the mill's failure seemed but a minor setback. A Comstock historian writing two decades later described them as convinced they were "pacing the roof of a fathomless treasure house." Men on the lode, most of whom had come of age in the wild, happy-go-lucky California gold camps, expected the owners of a successful mine to operate with panache and an open hand. A great mine ought to do things on a grand scale. Stockholders didn't expect frugality. They demanded output. "Snake it out," they insisted, almost to a man. And snake it out the mine did, expenses be damned. The Gould & Curry extracted almost fifty thousand tons of ore in 1863 and more than sixty-four thousand tons the following year. On aggregate receipts of almost $9 million, the Gould & Curry paid its stockholders dividends of nearly $3 million, the envy of the world. The mine's expense accounts attracted a whole lot less scrutiny. They'd spent $6 million for returns more prudent management could have had at much lower cost.

Costs hardly seemed to matter when a publication as respected as the *Mining & Scientific Press*, writing about the Gould & Curry, said that "the deeper they go in this mine, the richer the ore appears to be. In their lower gallery [at the level of the Lower Adit], the ore surpasses anything yet found in that famous claim, in both quality and quantity." The item didn't address a more fundamental question—what was revealed in winzes descending *below* the Lower Adit? (A "winze" is a mine workings made by excavating down.)

People who spent their lives aboveground had difficulty appreciating the scope and scale of what took place in the underground city. In the middle of 1864, most visitors entered the Gould & Curry through the Middle Adit on D Street. Seven hundred feet long, the Middle Adit's crude timbering and rough construction testified that it had been driven before discovery of the mine's full riches. Where the tunnel struck the ledge, a station opened onto an immense cavern. People approached the edge in astonishment. Left and right, up and down, the vast rectangular beehive of square-set timbers supporting the mine faded into midnight gloom. The sickly gleam of a tallow candle barely touched the opposite wall, sixty feet away. Over the edge, a yawning chasm swallowed the candlelight without revealing bottom, more than 200 feet below. The scale of the work was hard to fathom. The gigantic timber lattice filled a void 800 feet long, 300 feet tall, and varying in width between 40 and 70 feet. Contemplating the size of the extracted ore body, the immense quantity of timber replacing it, and the incomprehensible amount of labor expended in both pursuits left visitors in awe of what Comstock miners had accomplished in the last three years. There was more lumber in this one ore chamber than in the entire surface city.

A spiral staircase descended from the edge of the station at the end of the Middle Adit, but ended several levels below. From the bottom of the stairs, visitors unfamiliar with underground conditions struggled to commit themselves to a series of rickety ladders. The void tugged at their heels as they descended into the stygian darkness of the inactive galleries, guarding their candles and lanterns from drafts of air circulating through the mine, sometimes cool, at other times hot and stifling. Creepy, haunting sounds broke the melancholy silence: the splash and drip of falling water; the creaks and groans of timbers straining against the immense pressure of superincumbent earth. Occasional thunder echoed from the distance as a ton of ore clattered down a chute from an upper level to an ore car waiting on the level of the Lower Adit, hundreds of feet below. An explosion shivered the mine—a blast of black powder shattering a stubborn wall of quartz in some distant stope. The sepulchral gloom gave way as the visitors approached a working gallery in the lower levels. Voices, work sounds, and points of light reached out from under a temporary plank ceiling installed to protect the workforce from falling objects. Bright-lit life, business, and energy replaced the murk. The visitors descended into an anthill of activity illuminated by dozens of candles and lanterns. A line of miners working a stope systematically hacked out ore. In the richest concentrations, "clusters of virgin silver" glittered like "frost work" in the candlelight. Cubic pyrites and brilliant quartz flashed "a thousand merry glow-worm twinkles" before falling to the miner's pick. If this was done right, most fell directly into ore cars on wooden railroad tracks or was easily shoveled into chutes that fed cars waiting below. The well-practiced workforce allowed gravity to do as much of the work as possible. Timbermen hoisted and fixed the rectangular cuboid frames of foot-square post-and-cap timbers into place to fill voids left by removed ore. Carmen pushed trains of five or six ore cars, each one carrying half a ton of ore, down tracks laid in the floor of the two-thousand-foot-long Lower Adit to the enormous ore house built around the adit's mouth on South I Street.

Visitors unaccustomed to troglodytic existence emerged from the mouth of the Lower Adit relieved to discover themselves below cerulean Nevada skies. Inevitably, they compared the subterranean city to "Satan's sooty kingdom." Few had much desire to repeat the experience, which only exacerbated the divide between active miners and their supporting community. Underground, the Gould & Curry manager who guided one group lamented a recently struck stream of water that had flooded the winzes descending below the Lower Adit. Depending on how highly placed he was in the mine's hierarchy, he might or might not have known that the flooded winzes contained the mine's great secret. Despite the many press reports lauding the rich ore at the level of the Lower Adit, when the Gould & Curry's Lower Adit had struck the ledge in June 1863, it had traversed just fifteen feet of third-class ore veined with a few better streaks. Winzes sunk from the adit level descended on a narrowing body of ever-lower-grade ore, which pinched out entirely fifty feet below. Beneath that, there was nothing, *borrasca*, as miners termed it, the opposite of *bonanza*, just a mass of worthless porphyry (vein matter) between the footwall and hanging wall of the Comstock. The Gould & Curry's great bonanza had pitched south, into the Savage. Tens of thousands of tons of millable ore remained in the Gould & Curry above the level of the Lower Adit, and the mine would pay dividends for a few more years, but the barren winzes crushed the theory of inexhaustible silver mines paying dividends for centuries. Of course, only mine insiders had that information, and they withheld it from the public. To protect the treacherous winzes from prying eyes, Gould & Curry managers had allowed them to flood.

The mine's trustees had known since the summer of 1863. Shrewd members of the mine's inner circle, the "big fish," had been unloading their stock ever since, foot by foot, careful not to pop the stock's bubble while the public fixated on the mine's bullion production. They cleaned up substantial piles. Many members of the public, without quality information, bought at high values and held their stock for years, watching it dwindle. (George Hearst, the consummate insider, walked away from the Gould & Curry and the Comstock Lode before the bubble burst with several hundred thousand dollars, the seed of a great fortune.)

Rumors of "bad indications" in the Gould & Curry buffeted San Francisco's Montgomery Street in the spring of 1864. Stock traders heard that the mine's new superintendent had discharged 150 men from the workforce. Some said the mine was exhausted; others thought the ore quality had dropped; whispers told that the mine had borrowed money to pay its last dividend.

Podgers of the *New York Times* explained away the insiders' moves as "realizing" in order to fund a new banking concern called the Bank of California, which was forming under the leadership of Darius Ogden Mills and William C. Ralston, California's two most formidable financiers. (Many of the twenty-three leading San Francisco businessmen and capitalists who founded the Bank of California had been Gould & Curry insiders.) The conservative D. O. Mills served as president. Ralston installed himself as cashier, and although ostensibly beneath Mills, Ralston was the institution's driving force. Mills had built himself into Sacramento's leading banker in the 1850s by only loaning on gilded security. A man who knew Mills said he "transpired icicles and micturated ice water"; another thought he possessed just enough of the gambling instinct to look for a sure thing before placing a bet.

Ralston had been deeply enmeshed in San Francisco banking since the mid-1850s. He'd served as treasurer of the Ophir, the Gould & Curry, and the Savage mines since their incorporation. Since the federal government's introduction of paper currency in the early days of the Civil War, Ralston had made a fortune in greenback arbitrage. (Greenbacks held only a fraction of their face value in California, so a quantity of gold in California bought a large stack of greenbacks. Ralston shipped the greenbacks back to the eastern states, where they held more value. The greenbacks bought a stock of goods that could be sold at a profit in California, where gold transacted most business. That gold bought an even larger stack of California's heavily discounted greenbacks and thus began another profitable arbitrage cycle.)

A "rousing, reaching, staving" California booster, Ralston had grown frustrated with his conservative East Coast banking partners. For some time, Ralston had been scheming to dissolve his New York partnership and form the first California-based banking corporation (rather than partnership) under recently relaxed California laws, a bank that would focus on serving California interests unhindered by East Coast obligations. Ralston began the change in the fall of 1863 and completed it the following summer. The Bank of California formally opened its doors on July 5, 1864, with $2 million in gold coin as opening capital. With the tentacles of its ownership reached into importing, dry goods, grocery, finance, staging and express, San Francisco's nascent iron foundries, shipping and shipbuilding, the telegraph, stock brokerage, real estate, building, water delivery, and mining, the Bank of California sprang into existence as the leading financial institution on the Pacific Coast.

Washoe stocks had staged a modest rally in June 1864, but the Bank of California's opening coincided with another rout. The selling panic climaxed in late July with Gould & Curry sunk to $900 per foot. The Ophir dwindled from its April price of $1,580 to $415. The wildcats "went up the flume" entirely. They were "completely destroyed." The general public had finally realized that most Washoe claims were worthless. The steady stock market skid from the heights of 1863 ruined many men, including a small, delicate, gray-eyed Ohioan named William Sharon.

William Sharon would grow into one of the most consequential figures in the history of the Comstock Lode, a man without conscience uniquely adapted to exploit opportunities for connivery, duplicity, and market manipulation to the detriment of others—none of which was apparent when he first appeared in Virginia City in 1864. Sharon had been born on January 9, 1821, in Smithfield, in eastern Ohio, some fifty or sixty miles west of Pittsburgh, the second eldest of four brothers and three sisters. His father, a grave and determined man who ran a farm and a tannery, descended from "stern, rigid" Scotch-Irish Protestants who had emigrated to America from northern Ireland in the early eighteenth century. His mother boasted Scottish descent and cleaved to Hicksite Quaker beliefs, which emphasized the role of the inward light in guiding individual faith. William Sharon "imbibed" his mother's religion in young childhood, but "contact with the world robbed him of much of the faith." During his school years, Sharon was studious rather than athletic, with an "individuality" too pronounced to make him popular among his schoolmates.

When William Sharon was about twelve, his mother gave birth to her seventh child and died shortly thereafter. Sharon continued his common school education for the next four years. Seeing opportunity to free himself from the farming life in the commerce of the Ohio and Mississippi rivers, sixteen-year-old William Sharon invested his entire boyhood savings in an interest in a flatboat and cargo. The boat wrecked trying to pass the falls of the Ohio River at Louisville. Sharon and his associates sold what cargo they salvaged in New Orleans, but his partners stole the proceeds. William Sharon returned home at the age of seventeen having lost every penny he'd ever saved. His father didn't have the money to send Sharon to college, but his father did have a few acres of surplus land. He gifted the use of those to his son. Plowing, planting, and tending the small farm for three years—tasks he found "distasteful"—William Sharon accumulated enough agricultural profits to fund two years at Athens College. "Circumstances" prevented Sharon from completing his college course. The prospect of a lifetime spent wringing existence from the soil motivated Sharon to apprentice in a Steubenville, Ohio, law office under attorney Edwin M.

Stanton. (Stanton would rise through law and politics to become President Lincoln's secretary of war.) Sharon stayed six months with Stanton before migrating to St. Louis, Missouri, where he gained admittance to the bar. In 1844, his health failed and he withdrew from the legal profession. He went into business with his elder brother in Carrollton, Illinois, sixty miles north of St. Louis, and formed a firm friendship with John D. Fry, a Kentuckian who had been elected sheriff of Green County at age twenty-one, which earned him the frontier honorific "Colonel."

Five years later, in 1849, Fry and Sharon decided to take advantage of the gold fever. They invested in saleable merchandise and a prefabricated frame building, shipped their goods around Cape Horn to San Francisco, and crossed the plains, mountains, and deserts to California, each man riding one animal and leading another. After recovering their goods in San Francisco, they went into business, for a few months, in a tiny mining camp called "Frytown" in Placer Country, then in Sacramento. Fry and Sharon did well until January 1850, when a flood washed away their store and merchandise. The disaster dissolved their business partnership, but not their friendship. Sharon went to San Francisco and prospered in real estate. Ten years older than most gold rushers, Sharon quickly assumed a respected position in San Francisco's business community. He won election as assistant alderman in 1850, married the young daughter of a Canadian ship captain when she was still a teenager, and contributed his efforts to a property owners' association that pushed back against a plague of squatterism. Sharon helped organize the Republican Party in San Francisco and played a minor role in the 1856 Vigilance Committee. Men came to value his opinion in business affairs, particularly in relation to real estate. By the early 1860s, his wife had borne him five children, three of whom survived infancy, and he'd amassed about $150,000. Seeing fortunes made trading mine stocks inspired Sharon to obtain a seat on the San Francisco Stock & Exchange Board, and he began investing in mines—which proved his undoing, for William Sharon knew nothing about mining. Issues of the *Daily Alta California* in late 1863 and early 1864 mention his owning substantially in at least four separate mining concerns, all of them obscure, and he likely owned in others. The commonly held belief in the "permanence" of the Comstock ore bodies animated his trading, and Sharon lost "every cent of his fortune." In some of his largest transactions, Sharon thought he'd been cheated. As he would reminisce later in life, a few months into 1864, he had "the world before him and not a dollar to win it with."

Fortunately, he'd developed a relationship with William C. Ralston,

cashier of the new Bank of California. They'd known each other personally at least as early as 1857, when Ralston began courting twenty-
year-old Elizabeth "Lizzie" Fry, niece and adopted daughter of Sharon's
longtime friend. Lizzie Fry and William Ralston married in May 1858.
In July 1863, the Pacific Insurance Company opened for business with
Ralston, Sharon, and several Comstock luminaries among its directors.
Less than a year later, William Sharon was broke. Sharon's "manly action" in making good on his obligations despite the suspicion that he'd
been swindled won William Ralston's admiration. Ralston bought Sharon's real estate portfolio to help Sharon cover his stock-trading debts
and kept him afloat with a monthly $250 stipend.

Sharon's opportunity to reestablish himself came when a dodgy Virginia City banking firm failed, sticking Wells Fargo and the not-yet-
formally-opened Bank of California with substantial losses. Wells Fargo
had an agent in residence in Virginia City who took first choice of the
securities. Ralston sent Sharon to Virginia City to pick through the leftovers. Sharon culled from the shuttered bank's deeds, mortgages, and
promissory notes, and he chose well. In time, the Bank of California re-
couped most of its losses.

While in Virginia City, William Sharon examined the state of Comstock mining. Although Sharon didn't know "bird's-eye porphyry from
amalgam," as the saying went, he had a broad base of business experience, and everywhere he looked, he saw chaos, confusion, and redundant
effort. To him, it seemed obvious that the same fundamental principles
required to prosecute other forms of business ought to be applied to mining. That point of view made the Comstock's present depression into a
purifying fire that would make way for the streamlined operations, economy, prudence, hard labor, and good management that would mature the
industry. One key question remained: Could the mines expect to find
new ore bodies at greater depth? Without deeper ore bodies, no investment could be justified. Sharon conversed with the lode's leading men,
gathering information. He listened. Despite the slump, many expert miners expressed confidence in the future of the mines. Sharon must have
also seen that whether it was to Idaho, Montana, Utah, Colorado, Arizona, or other camps in Nevada, the knowledge, energy, and willpower
driving the entire new deep-mining industry radiated out from Virginia
City. San Francisco and Virginia City were the two nexuses from which
to dominate the industry. To his eye, if the Comstock were to endure and
develop newer and deeper ore bodies, it needed firm, confident management. He envisioned supplying it himself. As a first step, he became

convinced that the Bank of California should open a branch office in Virginia City. He wired the idea to William Ralston.

Ralston wired back: "Come down, and we will talk it over."

Sharon put forward his proposal to Ralston, Mills, and the other directors. A branch in Virginia City would give them clear insight into the true state of the Comstock mines, cash flows presenting more realistic information about industry affairs than the puffery of touts. Despite legends claiming that the bank directors approved Sharon's proposal only when Ralston personally guaranteed the Bank of California against losses, it seems unlikely that Sharon and Ralston's conviction would have convinced the other directors had not they agreed with the basic proposition—that opening branch offices in Virginia City and Gold Hill would prove a boon to the parent institution, facilitating capital flows between the two most important locales in the Pacific economy, diversifying the bank's asset base, and giving it a voice in Comstock affairs. Among the Bank of California's directors and original incorporators, Ralston, Mills, Joseph and William Barron, Thomas Bell, John Earl, Alpheus Bell, and Alvinza Hayward all had strong ties to the Comstock. Considering the multitude of California business interests they represented, most of them surely saw that the fortunes of the Bank of California, and to a certain extent those of the entire state, were wedded to the fate of the Comstock Lode.

Deciding who should head the Bank of California's Virginia City operation posed an important question. Sharon proposed himself. Most of the directors didn't like the idea. Sharon had just lost a fortune. Trusting him with another seemed foolish. Ralston suggested a man who had been working for him since 1856. Only after Colonel Fry and another man promised to assure Sharon's personal solvency by privately advancing him $15,000 did Ralston acquiesce to his appointment. Even then, someone cautioned Ralston against Sharon, a notorious devotee of gambling at poker.

Ralston asked if Sharon won. The man admitted that Sharon almost always did. "He sounds like the very man I want," Ralston said.

(Years later, a journalist asked a lawyer if his aggressive cross-examination had rattled William Sharon. "Rattle him?" the lawyer answered. "Do you suppose I can rattle a man who can bet a fortune on a busted flush and look as if he were going to sleep at the same time?")

In the spring, summer, and autumn of 1864, while William Ralston, D. O. Mills, and William Sharon opened the Bank of California in San

Francisco and Virginia City, the Civil War raged to its awful climax. The presidential election loomed over the battlefields. The Peace Democrats—the "Copperheads"—running against Lincoln advocated putting an immediate end to the fighting and negotiating for the reformation of the Union behind the slogan "The Union as it was, the Constitution as it is." Since the seceded states rejected anything short of Southern independence, ballot box victory of the Democrats would partition the once United States. Union forces captured Atlanta in early September and sealed Lincoln's victory. Eight days before the election, Nevada became a state. Since the start of the Civil War, several million dollars of gold and silver mined in the West had left San Francisco each month destined for eastern ports and cities, either as bullion or coin. A significant portion of that wealth had been raised from the Comstock Lode. Even though the federal greenbacks weren't backed by gold or silver, the steady infusions of western precious metals into eastern banks did much to bolster public confidence in the Northern economy and in the strength and durability of the federal government—and those repositories of confidence were cornerstones of the Union war effort. Inflation did erode the value of the federal greenbacks as the war dragged on, but economic conditions were always much worse in the South. No metal at all backed the Confederate currency, and blockaded by the U.S. Navy, the South and its economy received no substantial gold or silver infusions throughout the entire course of the war. Southern economic confidence waned. The South had no Comstock Lode, and the increasingly powerful inflationary whirlwind that battered the rebel economy sapped the Confederacy's ability to wage war.

William Sharon opened the Virginia City branch of the Bank of California in September, on the ground floor of a building at the southeast corner of C and Taylor streets in the heart of town, and took up residence on the bank's second floor. From behind tall windows, his "superlatively grand" vista stretched over the ridges and ravines falling into Six Mile Cañon and the Carson Valley lowlands beyond to touch the distant mountains. The rays of a setting sun rouging the far-off mountains made the view especially majestic. Sharon had left his wife and children in San Francisco, but he'd brought help in the person of "keen-eyed" Ah Ki, his twenty-eight-year-old Chinese valet. Ah Ki had come to California from an obscure village in South China in 1853. For three years he'd run a tenpin alley on Montgomery Street, then waited tables in the clubroom of the Bank Exchange, where he and William Sharon established a rapport.

When Sharon received the Bank of California's Virginia City appointment, he asked Ah Ki to accompany him as his valet. Ah Ki accepted at "good wages."

Sharon took care of people who served him loyally. Sharon paid good salaries, and although ruthless in business, he found any man injured or crippled in his employ a job commensurate with his reduced physical capabilities and kept him on at his accustomed earnings—as long as the accident hadn't resulted from negligence or drunkenness. Nor could Sharon abide the ill-treatment of beasts. "No offence was more certain of being followed by dismissal from his employment than ill-treatment of some dumb brute." Socially, Sharon quoted widely from Scripture, poets, and the plays of William Shakespeare, and he plowed much of his personal profits into San Francisco real estate. He became a regular player in high-stakes Comstock poker games. And he continued to win.

"Tight" money contributed to the stagnation of the Comstock mining economy in the last half of 1864. A cartel of Virginia City and Gold Hill banks fixed their loan rate at 5 percent interest *per month*—a whopping 60 percent annual rate. William Sharon and the Bank of California shoved themselves to the forefront of the financial market and shattered the cartel by opening their Virginia City doors and offering to make loans at 2 percent per month. Mine and mill owners stampeded to the Bank of California to avail themselves of the "easy" money. They hailed William Sharon and the new bank as saviors.

In what was seen as a further service to the mining community, Sharon accepted mill and mine property as loan collateral. He even went so far as to accept mine *stock* as collateral. However, whenever Sharon took stock as security, he insisted on receiving a proxy to vote the shares in the mine's stockholder elections, ostensibly because he wanted the Bank of California's voice heard in efforts to improve and streamline the management of the Comstock mines. And since many people in Virginia City and San Francisco addicted to mine speculation wanted to use their existing stock holdings as collateral to borrow money for further mining speculation, Sharon agreed to make the loans only when he was given proxies for both the collateral stock and the newly purchased shares. He quickly accumulated influence.

Whether that would prove important was an open question as one after another, the Comstock mines found the bottom of their ore bodies. The stock market kept sliding. Unemployment mounted. Thousands of people left the Comstock. Many went to a "new Comstock" at Summit

City near the spine of the Sierras. Others sought fortune in the mines of Idaho, Montana, Colorado, the Reese River, and elsewhere in Nevada. Virginia City's population shrank from about ten thousand to around four thousand. Property values plummeted. The market value of the Comstock mines shriveled, from the high they'd reached of about $40 million in the summer of 1863 to $12 million in the summer of 1864. On the positive side of the ledger, the depression drove most of the town's gun-slinging desperadoes to seek fresh pastures elsewhere in the West.

As the mining depression deepened, Sharon, Ralston, and the Bank of California continued pouring resources into the Comstock—a phenomenal risk. The Comstock would fail without further ore discoveries, and if the lode went barren, loans would default and the bank would end up owning a pile of worthless collateral property. Sharon wasn't just gambling on faith and feeling, however. He hired mining experts and geologists, and they convinced him that the Comstock was "a true fissure vein" that likely contained more ore at greater depth.

Sharon's sources held the prospects of the Yellow Jacket in particularly high regard. It was the only Comstock mine making new discoveries. Sharon launched a campaign to seize control of the mine.

At the August 4, 1864, Yellow Jacket shareholder meeting, a month before the Bank of California formerly opened its Virginia City branch, William Sharon held 14 of the mine's 742 voting shares. Three of his Bank of California associates—Thomas Bell, Alvinza Hayward, and Charles H. Wakelee (the man who had joined Fry in advancing Sharon the money that secured his appointment)—owned another 33 shares. That meeting produced no notable changes in the mine's management, but the Yellow Jacket meeting in February 1865, a few months *after* the Bank of California commenced its Virginia City operation, showed evidence of the bank's rising influence—the company treasurer resigned, and the stockholders elected William Ralston's brother James to the position. At a meeting in March, Yellow Jacket stockholders elected William Sharon as one of the mine's trustees. In May 1865, the Yellow Jacket paid a $100-per-foot dividend, making it Washoe's leading dividend producer. Sharon resigned his trusteeship at the July meeting, and although he personally owned only 8 of the mine's shares, he held proxies for 285 of the mine's 711 shares that cast ballots. Treasurer James Ralston transferred the Yellow Jacket's accounts to the Bank of California's new Gold Hill office. A year later, in July 1866, Sharon had proxies for 540 of the mine's 774 shares that voted in the election, and what would become known as "The Bank Ring" or "The Bank Crowd" held firm control of the mine. Bank Ring influence at the at-last-combined Chollar-Potosi described a similar trajectory, and the Crown Point was rapidly falling under Sharon's sway.

William Sharon never revealed how or when he conceived his far-reaching, sub-rosa plan to seize control of the Comstock Lode, quash competition, and extract monopoly profits from every aspect of the mines and their supporting industries, but in gaining control of the management of the leading mines he took the first step toward making it happen. Although at best morally dubious, in an age of outrageous corruption largely devoid of corporate oversight and governance regulation, Sharon saw no reason to resist the temptation. If the lode continued in depth, whoever had the guts and the gumption to subjugate the Comstock would become the most powerful man on the Pacific Coast.

Considering the size of the prize, William Sharon wasn't the only person scheming to rule the Comstock. Although it wasn't initially apparent, another path to dominance existed in the worsening problem of underground floods, which stalled progress in many mines in 1864. As the leading mines delved beneath the deepest adits, pumping costs increased with every foot of added depth. Mine managers found it easy to envision a day when the cost of hoisting and pumping would exceed the milling value of the ore. Hoping to head off that fateful day, companies formed to run deeper adits that would drain the lode to the 700- and 800-foot levels. Adolph Sutro gazumped their momentum with an exponentially more audacious plan. Sutro announced his intention to build a 20,498-foot-long adit from the Carson River Valley that would cut the lode at a depth of 1,800 feet, more than 1,000 feet below the deepest of the current workings. In pamphlets, book publications, newspaper articles, meetings, political circles, and into the ears of any citizen who would lend him attention, Sutro promoted his "Grand Drain Tunnel" with a gusto that many thought tipped into obsession, prepared, as he said, "to devote, if necessary, the whole balance of my life to the execution of this *one* work." Sutro insisted that his tunnel would put the Comstock mines in a position from which they could be worked profitably, economically, and extensively "for a century to come." All he asked in return was a modest two-dollar-per-ton royalty on all ore extracted, with no company to pay anything unless it took out ore.

Physically massive and imposing, pontificating in English with a thick German accent, and as persistent as a termite, Adolph Sutro wasn't a popular man. Returning to California through a snowstorm from a

Washoe fact-finding assignment in the spring of 1860, he was the corre-spondent who'd encountered the first run of the Pony Express. Sutro had been involved in Washoe affairs as a miner, miller, and industry gadfly ever since. In a "Letter from Dayton" published in the *Territorial Enter-prise*, Mark Twain pegged him as a man unable to enjoy a laugh at his own expense. Sutro constantly carped about the lack of "system" em-ployed by the Comstock mines. He intended his deep drain tunnel to provide the missing organization. The downsides of Sutro's deep drain tunnel was its $3 million projected construction cost and the many years it would take to build.

In early February 1865, the Nevada legislature granted Sutro and his associates an exclusive fifty-year franchise to construct and operate the Comstock drain tunnel. Sutro threw himself into the necessary organiza-tion, working to raise construction funds and secure contracts with the Comstock mines. For reasons that hadn't yet become widely apparent to anyone besides Adolph Sutro, the deep drain tunnel also held the power to give him control over the mines and all their attendant industries.

News of the surrender of Robert E. Lee's Rebel Army of Northern Vir-ginia broke in California and Nevada on the morning of April 10, 1865, triggering wild, spontaneous rejoicing. In Virginia City, "justly popu-lar" actress Matilda Heron sent a "trusty messenger" racing to the flag-staff on the summit of Mount Davidson with a new American flag to replace the old one tattered by the zephyrs of the past winter. The spank-ing new banner and its thirty-five stars broke forth from the liberty pole and fluttered over Washoe as the news spread.* The Comstock erupted in patriotic pandemonium. Church and fire bells clanged. The steam whistles screeched through the cañons. Blacksmiths pounded their an-vils. Rifle and pistol shots cracked into the air. Teamsters left their teams, dirt-crusted miners poured from the tunnels and shaft houses, grime-streaked mechanics and engineers abandoned their posts in the hoisting works and mills. Men embraced each other in the streets and undertook a colossal demolition of ardent fluids, toasting Lincoln, Grant, the Army of the Potomac, the flag, the United States of America, and the Union, the blessed Union, preserved at such terrible cost. Women on balconies flung confetti on the crowds below. People cheered each new flag and ban-ner strung across the streets. Two cannon boomed. Bands paraded up

---

* The thirty-six-star flag representing Nevada's statehood didn't become official until July 4, 1865—although a local seamstress might well have added Nevada's star.

and down the streets, battering out patriotic songs. After dark, bonfires blazed in the streets while skyrockets and Roman candles arced over Six Mile Cañon. With the staffs of the *Virginia Daily Union* and the *Territorial Enterprise* given over to the jubilation, both newspapers missed their Tuesday issues. San Francisco and every other town on the Pacific Coast celebrated the victorious end of the war with similar zeal.

The euphoria didn't last. Hangovers had hardly faded four days later when, at 10:00 a.m. on Saturday, April 15, the flag at the *Daily Alta California's* office at 536 Sacramento Street suddenly dropped to half-mast. Immediately after, a bulletin posted outside their office brought the street to a standstill—President Lincoln was dead, felled by an assassin's bullet fired by an actor, John Wilkes Booth. A rapid succession of dispatches clicking into the telegraph office confirmed the "fearful truth." Within twenty minutes, every business on Montgomery, Sansome, Battery, Front, and Sacramento streets had shuttered its doors and windows. The courts and the stock exchanges adjourned, and the bell on City Hall commenced a slow, mournful tolling. Bells of churches and fire companies around the city joined the dirge. Vessels in the harbor tethered their flags at half-mast, as did the fortifications at Alcatraz, Fort Point, Angel Island, and the Presidio. Minute guns boomed from Fort Point and Alcatraz. Restaurants and saloons closed. Theaters and amusement halls canceled their entertainments. Strips of black cloth banded the hats and arms of most citizens, most of whom were shocked to realize that two brothers of the assassin had formerly resided in San Francisco and played in the local theaters. By 2:00 p.m., black and white mourning sheets draped nearly every building in downtown.

News of President Lincoln's assassination struck the Comstock Lode simultaneously with its arrival in San Francisco, and as it had done "below," the tragic news paralyzed the camps. Crowds in the streets discussed Lincoln's murder in "low tones . . . expressive of mingled grief and wrath" devoid of "drunkenness or bluster." Stores, banks, saloons, whisky shops, theaters, and courts draped black cloth from their doors and windows and closed in mourning. The stamps in the quartz mills slowed to a halt. The mullers in the amalgamating pans ceased their endless rotations. Engineers running the hoisting engines over the deep shafts raised the men on shift from the mines, hissed away steam pressure, and let their engine fires cool. A silence dropped over Washoe, the first in years, broken only by the slow, mournful toll of the church bells. Lincoln's murder was the capstone tragedy of a terrible war. Lee's surrender and the president's assassination were the defining events of the generation.

For Marie Louise Hungerford, abandoned wife of Dr. Edmund G. Bryant, the war's end brought no comfort. With her husband elsewhere in Nevada and her surviving daughter Eva to support, circumstances pressed hard. She continued sewing for other Virginia City women to earn money. Father Manogue arranged additional part-time work for her teaching French and music classes at St. Mary's School for Girls. Her husband's return brought no relief. None of Dr. Bryant's Reese River schemes had borne fruit. He came back irascible, erratic, owing people money, and in no condition to rejuvenate his Virginia City practice—"very dissipated," in the words of someone who knew him. Sources don't reveal for certain whether his treatment of Louise and his three- or four-year-old daughter Eva tipped into outright abuse, but one afternoon while Louise was out working and Eva was in Dr. Bryant's care, the child "fell down a stairwell" and fractured her hip. (Six decades later, in 1929, Mrs. Louise Meyer Howland, the friend with whom Louise had paraded down Downieville's main street collecting gold nuggets when they were girls, said Dr. Bryant inflicted the injury when he kicked Eva in a drunken rage.) Either in disgrace or in an effort to pull his life together or both, Dr. Bryant went to San Francisco. Shortly thereafter, he disappeared. Louise stayed behind in Virginia City, nursing Eva. She had no idea where he'd gone, but she had more immediate problems on her hands—Eva's broken bone hadn't knit properly. The local doctors expected her to limp for the rest of her life.

Peace didn't improve Washoe's fortunes, either. The mining depression lingered. As the *Daily Alta California* said a few weeks after Appomattox, only "one thing is now certain . . . the deeper the miner sinks on the Comstock ledge, the poorer and more disappointed he gets"—the exact opposite from almost everything that had been said or written about the lode prior to the summer of 1863.

The mines hung on, working low-grade ore in the upper ore bodies. John Mackay and Jonas M. Walker had every reason to number themselves among the downhearted, for they had the shaft of the "far famed and oft struck it" Bullion down 573 feet and had drifted in every conceivable direction—to "no visible effect." They could have easily taken the proceeds of the successful speculations they'd made during the flush times and joined the many of their brethren who abandoned Washoe to seek opportunities elsewhere on the mining frontier. But Adolph Sutro and William Sharon and the Bank of California weren't the only Comstockers with the courage to move aggressively into the downturn. Mackay and Walker also did likewise, albeit backed by much less capital and government leverage.

In 1865, as the Yellow Jacket replaced the Gould & Curry as Washoe's leading mine, Mackay's and Walker's attention was caught by an obscure ninety-three-and-two-thirds-foot sliver of a mine wedged between the Yellow Jacket and the Crown Point—the long-neglected Kentuck. The stillness of Appomattox had hardly fallen over the exhausted nation when Jonas Walker crossed the entire continent in an attempt to gain control of the forgotten mine.

As recently as October 1863, the Kentuck had received no mention in an otherwise comprehensive and meticulous list of Comstock mines published by the *Sacramento Daily Union*, a north-to-south survey that catalogued every inch of Comstock ground from the Ophir's north mine to an obscure claim far south of Gold Hill. The list flowed directly from the Yellow Jacket to the Crown Point with no mention of a claim existing between. Anyone reading the article would have assumed the two mines shared a boundary. Neither did the Kentuck appear in a *Daily Alta California* story two months later that speculated on the course of the Comstock vein south of the little Gold Hill mines. The *Alta* item discoursed on the Yellow Jacket, the Crown Point, and the Belcher in detail but said not a word about the Kentuck, and despite discussing Crown Point and the Yellow Jacket developments in virtually every single one of its issues between the fall of 1862 and the spring of 1865, the *Mining & Scientific Press* included not a single blurb about the Kentuck.* Maps of the Comstock Lode published in 1864 and 1865 showed the Crown Point adjoining the Yellow Jacket. It was as if the Kentuck didn't exist.

The Yellow Jacket and the Crown Point must have desperately wanted to rid themselves of the Kentuck, but neither mine could wish or lawyer it out of existence because the Yellow Jacket's original location specifically mentioned "the Houseworth Claim" as one of its boundaries. Indisputably, Houseworth's claim antedated the Yellow Jacket.

Valentine A. Houseworth was one of the Gold Cañon miners on-site

---

*The Kentuck first appeared in the *Mining & Scientific Press* on October 7, 1865, in a small item that mentioned the mine's late-August incorporation. Thereafter, it appeared in almost every issue. The Kentuck does appear on an 1866 map.

when the Gold Hill and Ophir discoveries were made in 1859. During the first wild months before miners had much appreciation for the true value of what they'd found, Houseworth managed to buy, trade, or sweat his way into portions of the Yellow Jacket and some of the small Gold Hill claims, and he'd owned one-twenty-fourth of the Ophir. He'd sold that first season, winning $3,000 or $4,000 for mining ground that would have netted him $500,000 a few years later, and returned to his people in the East.

Somehow, the Houseworth Claim passed into the hands of John "Kentuck" Osborne, another of the original Gold Cañon miners, and the claim became known, in his honor, as "The Kentuck." Like Houseworth, he acquired interests in other claims, but parted with them for a few thousand dollars. Unfortunately, like many of his fellow Gold Cañon pioneers, sudden wealth made "Kentuck" Osborne a profligate and open-handed man. He parted with money freely and easily, and by 1864, he was living in "modest circumstances" in Silver City, near Devil's Gate. Osborne fractured a limb, the break failed to mend, and he died that year, his end "hastened," an old friend would write a dozen years later, "by grief arising from an unreciprocated attachment unwisely cherished for a young woman."*

But in the four or five years since Houseworth left Washoe, neither Osborne nor anybody else who owned the Kentuck mine did any significant development work—strange for a superb location between two proven mines. That odd situation may have had something to do with the fact that Houseworth's departure left a huge "flaw" in the mine's title. Nobody in Nevada had his quitclaim deed. That may have sapped any momentum Kentuck development might otherwise have generated. If the mine proved valuable, the owners would be legally vulnerable to anyone who appeared with Houseworth's quitclaim. The Kentuck's ownership likely kept their title's weakness as secret as possible while they tried to figure out exactly where Houseworth had gone to roost. History doesn't reveal how John Mackay and Jonas M. Walker became aware of the Kentuck's "imperfect" title, but when they did, they had an advantage—and a tremendous opportunity—for both Houseworth and Walker were Virginians, and Walker knew Houseworth's people hailed from Orange Court House, Virginia.

---

*That same friend noted that the early Washoe pioneers, having lived so long beyond the margins of civilization, proved notoriously susceptible to "the tender passions." He recalled several "despoiled" of their wealth by "the machinations of an artful woman" and others "cajoled" into "hasty and ill-advised wedlock" by women not always of "the most exemplary or deserving kind."

The small town of Orange Court House sat about two miles south of the Rapidan River, which from the spring of 1862 until May 1864 had served as the de facto northern boundary of the Confederate States of America. Federal and rebel forces had maneuvered and skirmished through the immediate vicinity on many occasions, and the bloody battles of Chancellorsville and the Wilderness had been fought nearby. (Considering the timing of his departure from the Nevada Territory, Houseworth may have gone home to support the South's bid for independence, or if he wasn't a secessionist, he may have gone home to look after his people and family property in a locale certain to suffer the ravages of war.)

To find Houseworth, Walker probably traveled either by overland stage through a flare-up of the Indian wars (the November 1864 massacre of 230 Cheyenne and Arapaho men, women, and children by Colorado cavalry volunteers at Sand Creek had set the Great Plains afire), or by steamship via the Central American isthmus. Walker succeeded in locating Houseworth, and on June 1, 1865, in Orange Court House, Virginia, Valentine Houseworth conveyed a quitclaim to Jonas M. Walker in exchange for $500 "lawful money of the United States to him in hand paid."

The transaction made John Mackay and Jonas Walker heirs to Houseworth's claim to the Kentuck ground, and it gave them tremendous leverage over anybody else who claimed ownership of the mine, since a mining court might consider the current occupants "squatters" or "jumpers." No contemporary source has ever revealed whether Mackay and Walker used that advantage to gain admittance to an existing ownership, or to induce the existing owners to sell them their interest in the mine, or if they'd gained control of the mine before Walker went East, but Walker had been a lawyer. He brought legal expertise to the partnership. The Kentuck incorporated with two thousand shares in late August 1865, but none of them hit the open market. Time has obscured the precise details of the Kentuck transactions, but whatever occurred, John Mackay and Jonas Walker emerged from the maneuverings as the Kentuck's principal owners. (Five months later, "the Kentuck Mining Company" paid Walker $20,000 in exchange for *his* quitclaim to Houseworth's quitclaim, which might have represented an exchange for the stock's nominal value.)

To fund mine development, Mackay and Walker borrowed $20,000 from San Francisco merchant and financier James Phelan* on a three-

---

* Phelan had made money in San Francisco merchandising, real estate, and money lending. In 1864–65, he owned stock in Comstock mines and served as a trustee of the

month note at 3 percent interest per month. Securing the loan required them to pledge the entirety of their little fortune, everything they'd amassed in Washoe, including all of their Kentuck stock. Walker might have handled the lawyering aspects of the partnership, but Mackay was the underground man, the miner. Mackay assembled a small workforce and put them to work sinking a shaft under a "horse whim" (a simple hoist operated by horses marching in circles, arastra fashion) and drifting for ore from shaft stations constructed at appropriate intervals. The work didn't progress as fast as hoped. The year aged, the note's due date approached, and Mackay and Walker found no ore.

In October, while Mackay and Walker pushed Kentuck development, another selling frenzy racked the mining stock market. Prices plunged. According to Podgers of the *New York Times*, many speculations hit hard reefs of reality "carrying full sail."

Most men thought the stock market had touched bottom in the aftermath of the sell-off. It hadn't. Despite a *Daily Alta California* item reporting that "recent developments in certain portions of the Comstock lode are thought to be more promising than for months past," mining stockholders pondered the larger questions and decided that go-ahead American enterprise had gutted the lode. A "fresh stampede" hit the market in the first half of December. Prices plummeted again, leaving the security Mackay and Walker had pledged to Phelan's loan worth only a fraction of its original value. In mid-December, Mackay and Walker levied an expensive $17.50 per share assessment on Kentuck stock to discharge the debt. Since they likely owned the majority of the Kentuck's shares and had no money to pay the assessment, they may have made the assessment to placate their nervous creditor—James Phelan.

Speculators who sold during the mid-December panic raised the white flag a fortnight too soon. Near the end of the month, the *Daily Alta California* noticed "reports of better ore being found in the Yellow Jacket and other mines."

The tide had turned. The Hale & Norcross struck ore on the 670-foot level. Working through a shaft sunk just a few feet south of the Kentuck, the Crown Point struck a west-dipping ore body 230 feet below the surface. On the other side of the Kentuck, the Yellow Jacket found "favorable

---

Potosi. Among the 230 San Franciscans who owned more than $50,000 in assessed property in 1865, Phelan had $130,850—ranking him three spots ahead of a San Francisco dry goods importer named Levi Strauss ("The Rich Men of San Francisco," *Daily Alta California*, October 14, 1865).

indications" running on the same level from their "New Shaft" or "South Shaft," sunk only 150 feet from the Kentuck line.

The good developments in the Crown Point and the Yellow Jacket sandwiched the Kentuck. Oddly, they actually increased Mackay and Walker's vulnerability. Phelan's note was coming due, and Mackay and Walker had burned through most of the loan sinking the Kentuck shaft and searching in vain for ore. If Phelan called the note, Mackay and Walker wouldn't have the coin to repay it. They'd lose their whole security, the entirety of their little fortune, and since they'd had to pledge their Kentuck stock to secure the loan, they'd also lose ownership of the mine. And if the ore bodies revealed in the Crown Point or the Yellow Jacket extended into the Kentuck—as seemed likely—their ninety-three-and-two-third-foot sliver of the Comstock Lode would be worth exponentially more than $20,000. If Phelan kept himself attuned to underground developments, he'd know he stood a good chance of making a fortune by calling the note, breaking Mackay and Walker, and seizing their collateral.

Mackay concocted a scheme to wrangle the loan's extension. He arranged to discuss terms with Phelan. At the meeting, Mackay protested the note's usurious interest. Three percent per month was outrageous, Mackay complained. He insisted Phelan reduce it.

Phelan slammed his fist down on the table and swore that he'd extend the note at 3 percent or not at all. Young man, he said, if you know what's good for you, you'll sign the note for six months and say nothing about the interest!

Mackay protested and argued, retaining his poker face. Inside, he could hardly restrain his joy. Eventually, Mackay relented and signed the extension. He went back to working the mine.

The stay provided the critical opportunity. Not long thereafter, on New Year's Day, 1866, working 250 feet below the surface at the bottom of the Kentuck shaft, Mackay, Walker, and their small workforce hacked into a ten-foot-wide mass of reddish, sugary, silver- and gold-infused quartz—a "very rich" body of ore.

Five weeks before, John Mackay had marked the passing of his thirty-fourth birthday. He'd been toiling in the depths of the Comstock Lode for six and a half years. The discovery shot the value of the Kentuck to the skies, saved him and Walker from bankruptcy, and set John William Mackay on the road to becoming one of the richest men in the world.

CHAPTER 9

The Rise of the Bank Ring

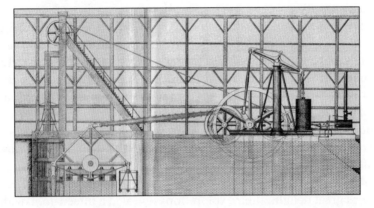

The pump engine and hoisting works in the shaft house of the Savage mine when the leading Comstock mines had become the most technologically advanced and innovative ones in the world.

———

A systemized plan of operations is carried on, in which large capital, subtle intrigue and unscrupulous misrepresentation are resorted to for the purpose . . . of draining from the many to enrich the few.

— "The Stock Jobbing Juggernaut," *San Francisco Chronicle*, May 20, 1875

For the Comstock Lode, the wheel had turned. The "Old Lead" had ridden out the hard times and "come out right," like the blessed Union itself. Fearful storms assailed Washoe in the first month of 1866. Fierce wind and furious snow blasts rendered pedestrian locomotion "precarious." People wrapped in coats laughed at unfortunates chasing their hats down C Street. Variation came in the form of a fine rain that turned the snow on the ground into a slush that froze overnight and made Washoe's steep streets "a glare of ice." Hot whiskies, "coasting" (sledding), and

199

sleigh riding constituted the only "compensating circumstances," although at ten dollars per hour, even with a pretty "duck" alongside, "well-wrapped up with rosy cheeks and bright eyes," the pleasure of sleighing came too dear for most common purses. Virginia City's industrious Chinese residents made out well. They led donkeys door to door through the blizzards, peddling firewood to households that had neglected to lay in adequate supplies.

Belowground, in the subterranean city, Comstock miners labored in more tropic climes. The December strike made on the 670-foot level of the Hale & Norcross developed into a significant ore body nearly two hundred feet deeper than any previously discovered. The stock market staged "an extraordinary advance" as a number of other mines along the line of the Comstock made "discoveries of a most encouraging character," including John Mackay's Kentuck.

Working from the New Year's Day strike in the shaft, Mackay directed a drift from the 285-foot level north to the Yellow Jacket line, and then a westward crosscut along the Yellow Jacket boundary. To Mackay and Walker's great delight, their explorations revealed a fifteen-foot-wide ore body completely spanning their ground, from the Crown Point line clear across the full ninety-three-and-two-third-foot width of the Kentuck to the Yellow Jacket boundary. All indications pointed to the Kentuck's ore being a part of the same west-dipping stratum the Crown Point was then exploiting. Of the 1,450 miners working in the Comstock mines in early February 1866, the Kentuck employed eleven—a count that might or might not have included John Mackay himself. He kept his primary focus on developing the strike for economical and efficient extraction, but he and his men still managed to raise what the *Mining & Scientific Press* reported as "a considerable quantity of excellent ore." Rising returns motivated the Kentuck trustees to do something that hadn't ever been done in the seven-year history of Comstock mining—they rescinded the mine's recent $17.50 per share assessment, and replaced it with one of $7.50 per share. A month later, they rescinded that one, too. (Although neither Mackay nor Walker sat among the Kentuck trustees, as the mine's majority stockholders, they controlled their decisions.)

Just north of the Kentuck, Yellow Jacket miners worked west from their South Shaft, crosscutting a wide "horse" of worthless rock. In March, they hit ore identical to that found in the "west stratum" of the Crown Point and the Kentuck. Mackay worked the Kentuck quietly and efficiently, and at the end of the month, supervised the installation of steam-powered hoisting machinery to replace the horse whim atop the shaft. Mackay must have learned an incredible amount engineering the extraction of the Kentuck's portion of the bonanza.

In April, the Crown Point and the Yellow Jacket sent about seven thousand tons of ore to the Gold Hill mills. Every mill in Gold Hill went "full blast" around the clock, the periodic scream of their steam whistles punctuating the unceasing clatter of their stamps. Bullion receipts for the west stratum ore extracted from the two mines ran to around $100,000 per month, per mine. In May, the Crown Point upped its dividend from fifty to eighty dollars per foot.

The Comstock's center of gravity had shifted south, to Gold Hill. By June, the ore coming up the Yellow Jacket shafts fully occupied a dozen separate reduction mills, and Gold Hill outproduced every other mining district in the United States. Indeed, the district's bullion output exceeded the combined total for the entire state of Nevada. (The Comstock's domination of Nevada showed in the young state's tax rolls: the value of the Comstock's assessed property totaled $24.2 million—the rest of the state combined assessed $5.5 million.) Mackay and Walker upped the Kentuck workforce to fifty men. Since January, they'd sunk the mineshaft at least another hundred feet, and they were raising thirty-five tons of ore per day, the best of which assayed more than $1,000 per ton. The Kentuck's bullion product proved sufficient to fund mine development, discharge the debt to James Phelan, and still leave a hefty profit. The mine started paying dividends in September. The bulk of the payouts went to Jonas Walker and John Mackay.

Not much is known about the emotions John Mackay experienced as he developed the Kentuck strike. Mackay played his cards close to his chest through his whole life, and he *never* gloated. Years later, however, the *New York World* asked him if wealth had brought him happiness. Mackay seemed incredulous at the question. He said that it hadn't. He told the reporter that he'd been happy selling newspapers in New York and working in the Webb shipyard, and that he'd been happy hefting a pick and shovel in the California gold country and swinging a pick and installing timbers as a common hand in the Comstock mines. Nevertheless, he did confess that little in life had brought him the satisfaction of watching the Kentuck strike blossom into a genuine Comstock bonanza. He'd been working toward it for twenty-four years, since he was eleven years old.

The dominoes of William Sharon's plan to control the Comstock began falling in May 1866, when Sharon and the Bank of California captured their first "custom" reduction mill, one unaffiliated with any particular mine. Sharon had come to recognize that reduction mills in constant service generated more stable cash flows than did the mines supplying them with ore. Custom mills earned money on a per-ton-reduced basis, meaning they earned money based on the *quantity* of ore they worked. With stamps pounding at full capacity, those earnings came risk free: It mattered not a whit whether they were working high- or low-grade ore. Mines earned money from bullion returns, and those varied with ore quality. Milling had seemed like a sure thing during the flush times, when the ore product of the mines exceeded the crushing capacity of their affiliated mills. Custom mills earned a fortune reducing the surplus—until the exhaustion of the Comstock's upper ore bodies in 1864 and 1865 exposed their weakness. Without ore, mills earned nothing, and as an experienced Comstocker explained, "No property deteriorates more rapidly in value than mill property when in disuse." Only constant attention kept pans, stamp shoes, dies, mullers, engines, and other heavy machinery in working order. Foundations fell out of square; untended buildings deteriorated; taxes and insurance payments sapped funds; trained employees sought other opportunities. If they weren't working ore, custom millers needed loans to keep afloat. Many distressed mill owners had gratefully accepted loans from William Sharon and the Bank of California at their lower interest rate without pausing to consider the ramifications of owing money to a man who held their loan security—usually the mill property itself—and was gathering power over the mines that supplied their mills with ore.

One of the mills in debt to the Bank of California was the Swansea Mill, located in lower Gold Cañon. In the spring of 1866, either Swansea ownership missed interest payments or William Sharon refused to extend their loan and the owners couldn't make the required balloon payment. Sharon foreclosed on the mill in May. One of his appointees took over its management.

By the summer of 1866, Sharon controlled the elections—and therefore the trustees and superintendents—of two of the Comstock's most productive mines, the Yellow Jacket and the Chollar-Potosi, and his proxy voting power was increasing at several others, including the Crown Point, the Gould & Curry, and the Savage. Combined, those mines raised the majority of the lode's millable ore. Sharon's influence with mine management gave him the power to target desirable mill property. Those mills with outstanding loans from the Bank of California were already vulnerable, but as a series of *San Francisco Chronicle* exposés published five years later described, Sharon could pressure a mill not yet indebted to the bank simply by directing the officers of "his" mines to lessen the quantity of ore the targeted mill received. The pinched mill owner soon went to mine management begging for more. He'd be told that there wasn't enough to go around. Until the mines were raising more, he'd have to make do. However, should he desire, he "could be accommodated" with a Bank of California loan to help him make the riffle. The mill owner went to the bank—which in Virginia City meant William Sharon—and Sharon insinuated that if the miller accepted a loan, Sharon would "feel an interest in his financial welfare" that would assure his future ore supply.

Many artificially distressed millers swallowed the bait, unaware that their signatures on the loan documents delivered their fates to William Sharon. Ore sufficient to cover the debt never reached the mill. Sharon foreclosed at the first opportunity and took possession. Between capturing the Swansea Mill in May 1866 and June of the following year, six additional mills fell into the Bank of California's cormorant hands, every one acquired at the sacrifice of a loan less than one-fifth of the mill's actual value.

The Crown Point's annual election on June 3, 1867, reflected another Sharon coup. The stockholders—or their proxies—voted out the serving superintendent, president, and trustees and replaced them with five new men: W. B. Johnson, Thomas Sunderland, Alvinza Hayward, Charles Bonner, and Thomas Bell—all close associates of William Sharon and members of what would soon become known as "The Bank Ring."

That same month, the Bank of California sold the seven mills it had acquired—at the bank's cost—to a recently formed private company called the Union Mill and Mining Company. The eight individuals who incorporated the new company bore a striking resemblance to the most important stockholders and officers of the Bank of California, and fully half of them were on the slate of new Crown Point trustees: Alvinza Hayward, Thomas Sunderland, Charles Bonner, Thomas Bell, William E. Barron, Darius Ogden Mills, William C. Ralston, and William Sharon. They were already among the richest and most powerful men on the Pacific Coast. The Union Mill and Mining Company racket would make them even more so.

While Sharon and the Bank of California conceptualized and consolidated their milling scheme, Adolph Sutro made great progress pushing his deep-drain tunnel project. The realization that Sutro might actually succeed in making his colossal Comstock sewer a reality bent Sharon on thwarting the endeavor, for at some point Sharon realized that Sutro's tunnel threatened to undermine his push to control the Comstock milling industry.

By the time Sharon and Sutro collided in mid-1867, Sutro had devoted well over two years to his tunnel, and although he'd never had the Bank of California's tangible financial support, for much of that time he'd enjoyed the bank's benevolent endorsement.

By February or March 1866—more than a year before Sutro clashed with the Bank of California—he had concluded contracts with nineteen leading Comstock mines that would grant his tunnel company a two-dollar-per-ton-of-extracted-ore royalty in consideration of the tunnel's ventilation and drainage. Most industry experts considered Sutro's contract generous—drainage, ventilation, and hoisting cost the mines far more. Sutro took his completed contracts, promotional materials, and a slew of expert endorsements to the East, planning to solicit government and financial support in Washington, D.C., New York, and London. Sutro carried a letter of recommendation from Bank of California luminaries William Ralston and Darius Ogden Mills—William Sharon's superiors at the bank. In Washington, Sutro lobbied his "Sutro Tunnel Bill" through Congress, which, among other benefits, granted Sutro the right to buy two square miles of land at the tunnel mouth.

A year later, in May 1867, Sutro had pledges of financial support from Comstock mining corporations and various private individuals totaling $600,000. With the financial underpinnings finally in place, Sutro was looking toward commencing construction when suddenly, in Sutro's own description, he watched support for his tunnel project "explode." Sutro blamed the Bank of California. Within the bank, William Sharon captained the opposition, using mine officers in his thrall. The Crown Point repudiated its $75,000 commitment to Sutro the day after the June 1867 election installed Sharon's slate of trustees. The Savage reneged on its $150,000 in July. One after another, the other Comstock mines withdrew their support.

In testimony delivered to the Committee on Mines and Mining in the United States House of Representatives six years later, Sutro claimed the bank tried to squash his drain tunnel because he was on the verge of obtaining a federal subsidy that would enshrine him as a Washoe powerbroker. Sutro either hadn't yet realized why he had incurred Sharon's enmity, or—*much* more likely—was masking his own ulterior motivation. Successful completion of his gigantic drainage adit would create circumstances favorable to quartz reduction mills located close to the tunnel mouth, on land owned by Sutro's tunnel company, where mills would be free of any transportation expenses and the hydraulic force of the water pouring from the tunnel or the nearby Carson River would supply low-cost motive power—a setup that would put Adolph Sutro in control of Comstock milling. All Sutro had to do to enshrine his dominance would be to refuse to sell tunnel company land to any rival concern or offer them only prohibitively expensive leases. Any mills built outside Sutro's landholding at the tunnel mouth would shoulder the crushing disadvantage of a transportation cost borne by none of the mills built close to the tunnel. Creating circumstances certain to gift Sutro domination of the Comstock milling industry may have been his plan from the beginning. In light of the timing—William Sharon had probably had his Union Mill and Mining Company project in the works for some months before it formally incorporated in June 1867—it seems likely that the deep-drain tunnel's potential to control the Comstock milling industry was what made William Sharon and the Bank of California such implacable foes of Adolph Sutro in May 1867.

Millions of dollars hinged on the outcome of the contest.

Sutro's personality didn't help his cause. In his fixed opinion, he was right and everyone else was wrong. About everything. Comstockers tired of his "insufferable egoism," and Sutro seriously blundered when he predicted in public that his tunnel would force the entire towns of Gold Hill and Virginia City to relocate to the tunnel entrance. "Owls would roost" in the current towns, he boasted. Every property or business owner on the Comstock heard Sutro promising to destroy the value of their investments. Adolph Sutro suddenly couldn't raise a cent in California or Nevada.

While Sharon and Sutro pushed their divergent schemes, the mines matured into steady, productive industry. Like most businesses in other working-class American towns, Comstock mines and mills paid their employees every thirty days, and in the words of a *Mining & Scientific Press* correspondent who described the scene, the lode throbbed with "feverish excitement" for a few days thereafter. "The toil-stained gold" of the "honest miner" churned through the "whisky shops, hurdy-houses, theaters and red-curtained palaces" of Virginia City and Gold Hill until "he got broke." The towns then calmed until "old gunny-sacks" rolled around again and paid off the "red-brawned muscle" that made "a monthly fool of itself."

John Mackay was not one of those men. Having money didn't make the camp's seedier entertainments any more attractive to him than they'd been before he made his raise. A man of few indulgences, and fewer words, Mackay's favorite meal remained the traditional Irish corned beef and cabbage of his youth. He drank sparingly and smoked the occasional cigar, just as he'd always done. Success suited John Mackay, but it didn't change him, not a whit. He comported himself exactly as he always had.

Mackay either kept a simple room in a Virginia City boardinghouse or lived in the offices of his mine. Friends who dropped by after dinner usually found him poring over a piece of literature, a mining treatise, or a grammar book, still striving for self-improvement. Chief among his pleasures remained the great delight he took in all forms of theatrical performance. He'd religiously attended the plays, concerts, and operas that toured Washoe since he was a four-dollar-a-day miner. Prosperity didn't affect the regularity of his attendance. It did improve the quality of his seats.

Mackay might not have been able to get one for Virginia City's prime cultural event of 1866—Mark Twain's glorious return—but he almost certainly sat or stood among the large and fashionable crowd of eight hundred who attended on the last day of October. Clemens had slunk away from Washoe in 1864 under disgraceful circumstances, having offended the ladies of Carson City with a boorish hoax. He'd spent the last two years loosely based in San Francisco. Clemens had struggled with debt, doubt, and depression since his Washoe absquatulation, but he'd further honed his authorial voice with extensive writings. He prospected literary ore during a sojourn in Jackass Hill and Angels Camp in the Sierra Foothills. The product of one vein, "Jim Smiley and His Jumping Frog," published the previous November in New York's *Saturday Press*, had sent Mark Twain's reputation kiting like the stock of a bonanza mine in an era in which writers dominated entertainment. Droll, unique, sublime, hilarious, the story unleashed the voice of the American frontier on the genteel prose of New England and "set all New York in a roar." American letters would never be the same. Clemens had spent four months in 1866 in the Sandwich Islands (Hawaii), commissioned to describe life in those magical isles in letters to the *Sacramento Daily Union*. On the heels of his return to California, Clemens decided to emulate the career of his friend Artemis Ward and deliver public lectures. Mark Twain gave his first in San Francisco, discoursing on his adventures among "the Kanakans" (Hawaiians) before a packed house in the city's largest venue. "Twain took his audience by storm," in the words of one critic. Best of all, he made money. Twain launched a speaking tour with appearances in Sacramento, Marysville, You Bet, and Red Dog before his eastward meandering took him across the Sierra. In Virginia City, the Comstock greeted Mark Twain with a "hurricane of applause." The prodigal had returned, his star ascendant, and in the eyewitness testimony of the *Territorial Enterprise*, Twain delivered "an entertainment of rare excellence and interest." The plainer-spoken correspondent of the *Daily Alta California* called his performance "an immense success."

Over the course of the next fortnight, Mark Twain regaled captivated, convulsing audiences in Silver City, Dayton, and even Carson City, whose ladies had apparently forgiven his churlish behavior, before returning to give one final triumphant presentation in Gold Hill. Afterward, Sam Clemens trudged back to Virginia City on foot with one companion, fighting a keen wind, on his way to join friends planning an all-night celebratory send-off. Atop the Divide separating the camps, a small, masked man burst from ambuscade and jammed a pistol in Clemens's face. "Stand and deliver!" he demanded. A half-dozen other mask-wearing "road agents" appeared from the darkness, three of whom leveled weapons at the writer. Using Confederate noms de guerre like "Beauregard" and "Stonewall Jackson," the highwaymen relieved Clemens and his companion of their valuables. Clemens lost twenty or twenty-five dollars, two jackknives, three pencils, and a gold watch he much prized. The thieves disappeared into the darkness toward Virginia City. When it seemed safe, Clemens and his friend followed after them and joined the all-night party.

The following morning, Clemens jammed aboard the Pioneer Stage, likely nursing a significant hangover. The driver was on the verge of starting the horses when someone leaned in from outside and thrust a package into Clemens's hands. Inside was his missing money, the lost knives and pencils, and the stolen watch—as well as the masks worn by the six thieves. The whole robbery had been a send-up, "a daring practical joke" played on him by his closest Comstock friends "in order, if possible, to get even on him for former practical deviltries on his part played upon them."

The ruse had worked. To Sam Clemens, the holdup had been "most uncomfortably genuine."

The stage driver cracked the ribbons, hi-yahhed the horses, and Clemens was off, leaving Washoe, never to return. Neither John Mackay nor any other Washoeite knew it then, but Clemens took with him what time would prove to be the Comstock's greatest contribution to nineteenth-century America—Mark Twain's pencils. Mark Twain would soar to greater heights than any of them imagined, but he had cut his literary teeth in Virginia City, the Queen of the Mining Camps, and for that, they would always claim him as their own.

Although Mackay seldom missed a theatrical event, he also enjoyed poker, his impassive demeanor proving difficult to read at the table, but it was an unwise—and likely poorer—player who failed to note the fierce competitiveness lurking behind his stone facade. John Mackay liked winning, make no mistake, and at his tiny sliver of a mine over in Gold Hill, he was. In early 1867, the *Daily Alta California* singled out the Kentuck as one of the most valuable properties on the Comstock "as the mine is so small and every foot of it productive." Bracing for a siege of work, Mackay again upgraded the quality of the Kentuck's hoisting apparatus and the power of its mine engine. Every day the mine raised around one hundred tons of a "superior class of ore." With an eye to controlling their mine's ore reduction, Mackay and Walker were supervising the expansion of Gold Hill's Petaluma Mill from an eight-stamp affair to one of sixteen. (They bought the mill outright a few months later, with a third partner, F. A. Tritle.) An up-and-comer on the lode in the prime of life, now thirty-five years old, John Mackay had also become one of the Comstock's most eligible bachelors.

Not every Washoeite was having such a good time of it. Some months before, Father Patrick Manogue received word that Marie Louise Hungerford Bryant's errant husband, Dr. Edmund G. Bryant, lay dying of lockjaw—tetanus—at Poverty Hill, a mining camp in the Sierra Foothills ten miles northwest of Downieville. (Medical men had been using syringes to inject opiates for more than a decade; conceivably, the opium-addicted doctor infected himself with an unsterilized needle.) Father Manogue related the bad news to Louise, and she rushed over the Sierras to her husband's side. She found him gaunt, in a squalid one-room shack, sporting an eerie, endless grin—*risus sardonicus*, lockjaw's telltale rictus grin, a sustained contraction of facial muscles that peeled Dr. Bryant's lips away from his teeth, raised his eyebrows, and held open his eyelids. Unable to speak, Dr. Bryant stared at his wife with eyes that never blinked. Tetanus's progression of horrors pushed the doctor through fever, profuse sweating, drooling, uncontrolled urination and bloody defecation, jerking, and *opisthotonus*, another of tetanus's awful signatures, massive muscle spasms that jolted the doctor's body into a rigid, back-bending arch. In the most violent episodes, the contractions could fracture bones. Louise stuck with her husband through the ordeal. Eventually, uncontrollable muscle spasms affected Dr. Bryant's ability to breathe. He suffocated to death on June 29, 1866. Louise, his widow, was just twenty-two years old.*

The doctor died in debt. Fortunately, in earlier days, he'd done good service in the gold camps of Sierra and Yuba counties. Miners passed the hat and discharged his obligations. The leftovers financed a humble funeral.

Dr. Bryant's death didn't deter Louise's father from departing from San Francisco for Mexico less than a month later. Now styling himself *General Daniel Hungerford*, he sailed south to offer his sword to the liberal republican government of Benito Juárez and prosecute "active operations" against "the usurping invaders of Mexico"—the French, whose bayonets sustained their puppet dictator, Emperor Maximilian I. Hungerford left behind his wife and Ada, their nine-year-old daughter. Mrs. Hungerford and Ada returned to Virginia City and took up residence with widowed Louise and her limping daughter, Eva. The three generations of Hungerford women sheltered together under the roof at 10 A Street.

To earn money, Louise Bryant worked in the Comstock needle trades. Victorian women considered fashionable presentation important, even in a Nevada mining camp. Fashion communicated a woman's station and cultural sophistication. Comstock women kept themselves au courant with widely circulated women's magazines and newspaper columns whose authors looked to New York and Paris society for sartorial inspiration. The steam-powered looms of the Industrial Revolution and sweatshop clothing factories had made inexpensive, ready-made men's clothing available in a variety of sizes, but although fabrics had become much less expensive over the last half century, bringing fashionable display within reach of middle-class ladies, elaborate hats and bonnets and close-fitting dresses defied mass production. They were almost exclusively custom-made.

Milliners—hat makers and trimmers of hats—stood atop the needle trades, the most well-remunerated members of the Victorian fashion industry. They used lace, feathers, flowers, ribbons, and other "fancies" to make hats and bonnets, the capstone details of style. Dressmakers ranked next below milliners. They measured, designed, and cut the bodices, sleeves, and complex layers of draped skirts Victorian dresses required.

---

* Although tetanus was one of the terrors of the nineteenth century, the United States averaged fewer than thirty cases per annum between 2001 and 2008. Most cases occurred in people who had not been properly vaccinated. Thirteen percent of the afflicted died.

Seamstresses working at "plain sewing" occupied the bottom rung of the fashion industry ladder. They did the tedious, repetitious, nitpicking drudgery of sewing up finished garments from dressmakers' instructions. The labor demanded they know hemstitching, running, whipping, tacking and backtacking, herringboning, fine drawing, darning, quilting, overcasting, buttonholing, gathering, ruching, rantering, slip stitching, picking and padding, cross-, chain- and catch-stitching, stoating, blind-stitching, and backstitching, but since the techniques of plain sewing formed an essential component of every woman's domestic education, the commonplace nature of the skillset kept their wages pinned to the industry's bottom hem. Louise Bryant was one of them. She "went out by the day" to sew for the lode's more well-to-do ladies and made extra money taking in piecework from stores and dressmakers. She worked all the hours she could tolerate, often sewing by candlelight deep into the night.

On the home front, Louise and her mother made plain, homemade calico dresses for themselves and their girls. Father Manogue catalyzed a slight improvement to their circumstances when he interceded with the Daughters of Charity—the Catholic order of religious women wearing grayish-blue habits and starched white cornets who'd founded Virginia City's St. Mary's School in 1864—and obtained Louise a place tutoring French and music. Mrs. William Mooney lived next door, and she couldn't help but notice the Hungerford women "having a hard time making ends meet."

Another woman who knew Louise at the time remembered her as "beautiful, charming, and accomplished, with a rather small rounded figure, dark blue eyes, chestnut hair, a soft voice, and a radiant engaging manner." Men still vastly outnumbered women in California and Nevada in 1866, the companionship of a respectable woman being scarcer than gold and silver, and Louise didn't lack for interested suitors. She did needlework for the Rosener Brothers' store, one of the lode's leading mercantile establishments. Camp gossips speculated that when she doffed her blacks she'd marry Harry, the younger brother.

On the opposite side of Louise Bryant's house from the Mooneys' lived an Irish couple recently moved to Virginia City, James and Theresa Fair. Although James Graham Fair stood only five feet eight inches tall, his massive physique impressed every man who met him. Years of brute labor had packed hard mining muscle onto his barrel-chested frame. He weighed well over two hundred pounds, and like Mackay, James Fair possessed a phenomenal capacity for work. The youngest son among the children of a pair of Scotch-Irish Presbyterians, Fair had been born in the Irish village of Clogher, in County Tyrone, sixty miles west of Belfast, on December 3, 1831, making him all of five days younger than John Mackay. The Fairs emigrated to the United States in 1843 and settled in Geneva, Illinois. Headstrong, cocksure, and determined, adolescent James Fair turned his nose up at opportunities to pursue the law or the printing trade, neither striking him as "the road to fortune." And as he told a biographer in his later years, a fortune he meant to have.

The California gold discovery ended Fair's adolescence. He made the long overland trek to California in 1849, when he was eighteen years old. In August of that famous year, James Fair struck a pick into the auriferous gravels of Long Bar on the Feather River, above Yuba City. He found little gold at Long Bar, but at the placers of Rich Bar, discovered the next year, he "filled his sacks" with the precious needful. In the next two years, he mined at Poor Man's Creek and Shaw's Flat and coyoted under the lava beds at Table Mountain, in Tuolumne County. Fair grew into a shrewd, practical man in the diggings, and he filled out his frame, a handsome man with a full beard, dark, deep-set eyes beneath a high forehead, and strong, stern features. Nothing about James Fair betrayed weakness. He had a gruff, manly energy and an eye for the main chance, and he "knew the exact value of a dollar."

Fair bought a farm near Petaluma in 1853. Drought wilted his first wheat crop. An overly wet season rusted his second. Mining seemed less risky. Fair leased the ranch and returned to Angels Camp in the Sierra foothills, where he found himself amidst California's first quartz-mining excitement. The more technical aspects of quartz mining and ore reduction suited Fair's mechanical inclinations, and he did well. Books, music, natural philosophy, and the arts meant nothing to him. Mining and getting ahead absorbed his entire interest. He constantly tinkered with mine machinery, seeking improvements. At Angels Camp, Fair met Theresa Rooney, an affable, enchanting, and deeply Catholic young widow who ran a boardinghouse in the nearby town of Carson Hills. Fair's Irish charm worked magic on Theresa Rooney, and they married in 1862. Four years later, James Fair sold his California holdings and moved his family to Virginia City. By that time, he and his wife had a young son. In Virginia City, they would have another son and two daughters.

Fair's competence impressed the Comstock. He was superintending the Ophir within a year of arrival. Toward the end of 1866, Fair shifted his shingle to the Hale & Norcross, at the time a much more productive mine, where he operated as an assistant to the superintendent, in charge of major constructions.

Unsentimental and untroubled by conscience, Fair labored in clear-eyed self-approval, convinced he knew more about mining than anybody else. One of the best "practical miners" in the Far West, Fair tended toward the arrogant and boastful, but he could lay on thick Irish blarney when needed, particularly around a man in a position to advance his career such as John Mackay. The two became acquainted. Fair was much more gregarious than his new friend, full of bonhomie and hail-fellow-well-met. Comparing the two men ten years later, a writer said that Mackay seemed not to trust his "conversational powers." Mackay and Fair didn't share much personal warmth, James Fair was, if anything, a harder man to get close to than John Mackay, but in light of their backgrounds, the two Irish-American miners had much in common. They got along well enough, and they respected each other's professional capabilities. Without doubt, they were two of the Comstock's best miners. Fair's wife, Theresa, was a much more genuine person, and in the last half of 1866, she and her husband often invited John Mackay to dinner at their A Street cottage.

Snows hit the lode in December, the start of a severe winter. The boys of Virginia City indulged their favorite winter amusement—"coasting" down the steep cross streets on sleds, whizzing down from the high side of the camp, shooting across the main streets, and careening down to the next level. Theresa Fair asked John Mackay to join them for Christmas dinner. Unable to resist the opportunity to play Irish matchmaker, Mrs. Fair also invited her widowed neighbor—Marie Louise Hungerford Bryant.

Christmas at the Fairs' was a great success. In John Mackay's own tongue-tied, reticent manner, he swooned for Louise Bryant. Having supported a widowed mother and sister since age eleven, he certainly understood her struggles. Unlike so many others in class-conscious nineteenth-century America, Mackay made no judgments about the menial work she'd done to survive. He admired it. All work was honorable in his eyes. And although Mackay was thirteen years older than Louise Bryant, he began courting the young widow.

Over at the Kentuck, Mackay kept operating expenses low by ensuring that his mine's deepest workings never delved below those of the adjoining Crown Point or Yellow Jacket, a trick that forced his larger neighbors to bear the cost of pumping the groundwater to drain the mines. Mackay had the mineshaft down to 485 feet, and as if the wheel of mining fortune hadn't already favored him enough, in April, Crown Point miners running a prospecting crosscut 150 feet east of their 500-foot station, away from the west stratum, broke into an entirely new quartz

In 1860–61, *Harper's New Monthly Magazine* ran a series of caricatures of silver-crazed miners and prospectors created by J. Ross Browne. At left, miners chaffering over the indications of a new location, hoping their rock contained profitable concentrations of the "precious needful."

At right, the squally business of disputing a claim, which often became violent when miners were under the influence of rotgut whisky, cut-rate wine, or stovetop brandy.

3

VIRGINI
NEVADA
PUBLISHED

Virginia City in 1861, as revealed in this panoramic illustration. The town would continue to change with both the arrival of enormous new hoisting and refining works as well as a devastating fire that swept through Virginia City's narrow streets and wooden buildings in 1875.

4

James G. Fair, known for his massive physique and expertise in running mines.

5

James Clair Flood opened the Auction Lunch Saloon in San Francisco, where he listened to speculators discussing Comstock mines over his bar top; before long he became enormously successful on San Francisco's stock exchange.

8

Marie Louise Antoinette Hungerford Mackay was living hand-to-mouth when she met her husband-to-be.

6

William O'Brien, James Flood's partner at the saloon and later on the stock exchange.

7

John William Mackay, once a paper boy on the streets of New York City, was destined to become one of the richest men in the world.

William Sharon became the leader of the Bank Ring and was ferociously opportunistic and manipulative in his efforts to monopolize the Comstock Lode.

William Ralston, perhaps the most enthusiastic booster California has ever had, not only destroyed the finances of the Bank of California but drowned the day his malfeasance became public, possibly a suicide.

With the tentacles of its ownership reaching into many of the young state's most important industries, the Bank of California sprang into existence as the most powerful financial institution on the Pacific Coast and battled John Mackay's rise to power.

Prussian immigrant and unrepentant egomaniac Adolph Sutro fought the Bank Ring for almost fifteen years to dig his gigantic drain tunnel 20,498 feet from this entrance to its intersection with the Comstock Lode.

General Ulysses S. Grant and his wife visited Virginia City for an extensive underground tour of the Consolidated Virginia and California mines in 1879. Pictured here: John Mackay on the left and James Fair on the right; General Grant holds the lantern in the middle with Fair's wife, Theresa, on his left elbow and Mrs. Grant on his right. Both Mackay and Fair kept framed copies of this photograph for the rest of their lives.

The composing room of Virginia City's paramount newspaper, the *Territorial Enterprise*. Newspapers were a crucial component of a thriving mining camp, and the *Territorial Enterprise* attained lasting national influence.

William Wright (pen name: Dan de Quille) and Sam Clemens (pen name: Mark Twain), the *Territorial Enterprise*'s two greatest "sagebrush" journalists. One would never achieve more than regional notoriety, his talents swallowed by the well-polished jug; the other would become the most famous American writer of the nineteenth century.

Comstock miners, a behatted dog, and three young lads, who may have worked in the mines as pick boys and engineers' assistants. One of the mines kept a fully stocked stable and three working mules more than a thousand feet underground.

Miners on the cages, braced for the terrifying descent underground where temperatures sometimes exceeded 135 degrees and the hazards included underground floods; collapses, or "caves," of the galleries and stopes; foul, unbreathable air; falls into winzes and mine shafts, the deepest of which exceeded two thousand feet; premature powder detonations; boiler explosions; and the one miners feared above all others—fire.

mass streaked with lenses of millable ore. Prospecting drifts quickly revealed that just as in the west stratum, the new east ore body pitched all the way through the Kentuck into the Yellow Jacket. Considering the east ore body's distance from the Kentuck shaft, the best way for Mackay and Walker to work the deposit would be to sink another shaft directly on the ore body—an expensive proposition. The obvious alternative was to work the ore through the Crown Point and the Yellow Jacket, whose shafts were much closer, but that meant negotiating complicated use agreements with Sharon-controlled mines, and Sharon, who coveted the Kentuck's slice of the east ore body, wasn't likely to make that easy. Faced with those complications, Mackay and Walker made no effort to work their new ore. They left it in situ, like money in the bank.

The Kentuck's monthly returns reached $132,334 in May and stayed well over $100,000 per month through the rest of the summer of 1867, as the neighboring Crown Point passed into William Sharon's control. Some Kentuck stock had hit the market in May, the first reported sales in over a year. The shares debuted at about $200. By July, they'd risen to $562. For the month of August, the Kentuck paid $80,000 in dividends, and the *Mining & Scientific Press* published an account of the mine's operations that included costs of extraction, hoisting, reduction (of 2,657.5 tons of ore), timber (212,623 feet installed), fuel (51.75 cords consumed), and payroll. Such detailed reporting came in direct contrast to William Sharon's regime at the adjacent Yellow Jacket. The same issue of the newspaper reported, "After diligent inquiry in various quarters, we can give no information whatever in regard to the present condition of the mine"—a lament that would frustrate Yellow Jacket stockholders for years to come.

Complicating matters for John Mackay, Jonas Walker had made a trip to the East in the autumn of 1866. When Walker returned, he told Mackay that he didn't fancy spending his whole life rooting through the bowels of barren Nevada. Success would seem sweeter if he took his wife and children East and enjoyed it. In addition, Walker had a brother in Virginia touting a spectacular railroad investment opportunity. Walker had always had it in mind that he'd be set for life if he could make a $600,000 "raise," and in four years of partnership, he and Mackay had amassed assets worth twice that amount. Jonas Walker had reached the point where he wanted to sell out.

John Mackay and Jonas Walker spent the latter half of 1867 dissolving their partnership, which they effected by selling most of their Kentuck ownership to William Sharon. Walker took his share, embarked on a long European tour, settled in Philadelphia, and made the railroad investments his brother suggested. As Mackay would say years later, "When Walker had $600,000 he thought he had all the money in the world."

Between November 1, 1865, and November 21, 1867, dates that encompassed the entirety of their management, the Kentuck had disgorged bullion worth more than $1.6 million. Of that sum, the mine had paid $592,000 to its stockholders in fourteen dividends, a 37 percent yield. Mackay and Walker pocketed a substantial chunk of those dividends and compounded their earnings by privately milling the mine's ore ($20,000 cash remained in the company treasury). No other Comstock mine had paid out such a large portion of its gross yield.

To close out the dissolution of their partnership, in late October, Jonas Walker sold his one-third interest in the Petaluma Mill to William Sharon, and John Mackay and F. A. Tritle each conveyed a one-twelfth interest to Sharon. The transaction left half of the Petaluma ownership vested with William Sharon. Mackay and Tritle equally shared the other half. Under a power of attorney, San Francisco's shrewd Irish stockbroker James Clair Flood executed the Petaluma deed on Walker's behalf—the earliest documented association between Flood and Mackay, although Flood had likely handled the stock sales associated with the dissolution of the Mackay/Walker partnership.

The Kentuck's late-October election reflected the changes. The stockholders elected a new slate of trustees—Thomas Sunderland, Alvinza Hayward, James C. Flood, James W. Bricknell, and William Sharon. The Bank Ring had drawn the Kentuck into its expanding sphere of influence. The end of his partnership with Walker left John Mackay casting about for other opportunities, for unlike his now-former partner, John Mackay wasn't ready to retire from mining. Not even close.

In 1867, while the Mackay/Walker partnership dissolved, James Fair superintended construction of the Hale & Norcross's new second line shaft.

The Hale & Norcross located its new shaft about a thousand feet downhill of the original workings and broke ground around the time that Mackay met Louise Bryant at the Fairs' house during the 1866–67 holiday season. Built under Fair's exacting eyes, what became known as "the Fair Shaft" incorporated the most important technical and technological advances Comstock miners had made since the lode's discovery.

The Fair Shaft started as a rectangular hole in the ground seventeen feet six inches long and seven feet six inches wide. A stout frame of twelve- to fourteen-inch timbers assembled along the lines of Deidesheimer's square-sets divided the shaft into three compartments, two for hoisting and one for pumping. (Several of the second line shafts included a fourth "sinking" compartment through which crews did the work of digging the shaft deeper.) Three-inch planks set outside the timber frame completely enclosed the shaft to prevent debris falling from the shaft walls. With each new six or seven feet of downward progress, carpenters added another layer of square-sets (also called "cribs") to the bottom of the shaft timbers. The cost of the work increased with depth. Enormous pressures applied by shifting, swelling ground often distorted or cracked the shaft timbers, forcing timbermen to remove and replace the disturbed sets—a dangerous job performed over an enormous drop.

Around the mouth of the shaft on the surface, mine workers built a sturdy masonry foundation to anchor the mine engines, boilers, winding reels, other machinery, and a "gallows frame" or "headframe" of massive timbers rising over the shaft mouth. They enclosed all of it in a "shaft house" with a large landing and engine room, a boiler room, smithy, carpenters' shop, repair shop, changing room, and other conveniences. Timber and wood yards outside held the mine's supplies of framing timbers and cordwood fuel, a weighing house for measuring the size of loads carried by freight wagons, and delivery landings for receiving supplies.*

Chimneys sprouting above the boiler room discharged smoke from the wood-fired boilers that generated the high-pressure steam that powered two large engines—one for hoisting and another for pumping. Gears on the drive shaft of the hoisting engine meshed with gears on two ten-foot-diameter winding reels spooled with flat ropes of braided steel wire about the width and thickness of the extended fingers of a man's hand. From the winding reels, the flat "wire ropes" passed over enormous "sheaves"—wheels of wood or iron eight to ten feet in diameter—suspended from the gallows frame above the shaft opening and positioned so the wire rope passing over the sheave dropped directly down the center of the hoisting compartment below it. In each hoisting compartment, the wire rope attached to a "cage"—the elevators that gave access to the mine.

The cages were formed from two simple seven- or eight-foot-tall triangular wrought-iron frames joined at the top by a crossbar and at the bottom by an iron grid supporting a wooden floor. Above the crossbar, a "stem" joined the cage to the hoisting cable. Attached to the iron cage frame at top and bottom on both sides were iron flanges called "ears" that

* The photo on the jacket of this book is of the shaft house of the Hale & Norcross's Fair Shaft.

embraced the "guide rods," four-by-six-inch pieces of wood that ran from surface to sump on opposite sides of the hoisting compartments. (Miners had learned the hard way that wooden guide rods were more forgiving than iron ones, less likely to stick or bind the cages, an occurrence almost always attended by serious consequences.) Both sides of the cages away from the frames and guide rods were left open for working ease.

Men underground communicated with the engine "driver," or "engineer," via a bell wire or bell rope loosely hung hundreds of feet inside a line of iron staples. (Most mines preferred hemp bell ropes to wire ones because hemp didn't rust and breaks could be quickly spliced.) Sharp tugs on the bell rope rang an iron gong or triangle in the shaft house directly in front of each hoisting compartment's driver, the number of clangs signaling whether to raise, stop, or lower the cage. (Adjacent hoisting compartments used different bells, with different clang tones.) Miners distrusted newfangled systems that relied on the closing of an electric circuit to power an electromagnet that swung a bar that struck the bell—because it was prone to short circuits that sent false signals and couldn't be relied on in a wet mine and especially because of the impossibility of sending emergency signals to the surface from points in the shaft between stations.

Early Comstock cages had been almost entirely devoid of safety features, but the newest cages incorporated many recent improvements, "safety catches" and "safety hoods" paramount among them. The safety catches worked by using the weight of the cage suspended on the cable to hold springs in tension. If the cable broke or the brake on the hoisting reel failed, the released spring pushed sharp iron teeth called "dogs" into the wooden guide rods and caught the cage in place. (In February 1867, thirteen Savage miners aboard a cage equipped with new safety catches being lowered down their shaft came to a sudden stop with so little drama they didn't realize the cable had detached from the cage. Due to the considerable weight of the cable, neither did the engine driver above in the shaft house. Only cable slack drooping past the iron "safety hood" atop the cage to protect them from falling objects alerted the miners to their close brush with death. They quickly rang for a stop.)

The best safety hoods were built in two halves that split in the middle and hinged apart, primarily so that long timbers could be sent down the shafts, but also because of what had happened to a pair of Gould & Curry miners accidentally lowered into deeper-than-expected sump water in the bottom of the shaft and trapped beneath an unhinged hood. Only the quick response of the engine driver on the surface to the clanging of the hoisting bell saved the men from drowning.

In the shaft house at the surface, the engine driver stood at his station with the throttle valve in one hand, the reversing bar in the other, and the brake underfoot. In plain view of the driver, a circular "indicator" calibrated to the winding machinery pointed to depth marks and stations marked around the circumference of the instrument that indicated the location of the cage in the shaft. Operating procedures at well-run mines strictly forbade speaking to an engineer at his station about anything not directly connected to the performance of his duties. All ingress to and egress from the mines was done via the cages and hoisting apparatus—none of the mines provided ladder access to the workings—and engineers were selected and trained as the most reliable and responsible men in the workforce. The lives of everyone underground depended on their diligent attention.

The most sophisticated shafts equipped with the most advanced hoisting apparatuses—like the one James Fair was sinking for the Hale & Norcross—could raise a loaded cage while simultaneously lowering another as counterbalance in the adjacent compartment. Twelve miners crammed aboard a cage was the normal working load of men. Of ore, the hoists easily raised a ton at a time. Drivers raised and lowered loads of men at about 300 to 400 feet per minute. They moved unaccompanied ore cars at speeds that exceeded 800 feet per minute. Many of the second line shafts increased capacity by evolving to use double-decker cages.

Sturdy iron grates covered the mouths of the hoisting compartments—a feature designed to lessen the almost always fatal occurrence of people falling into the mine shafts. The safety hoods of arriving cages simply lifted the grates from the floor. They dropped back into place when the cage lowered. Sections of track bolted to the cage floors held the loaded "ore cars" or "cars" during the hoists. "Landing attendants" in the shaft house greeted the arriving cars and disposed of their contents as appropriate. They pushed cars of milling ore down a track and dumped them into ore bins where the ore awaited transportation to the mills. They pushed cars of waste onto a track that ran out the downhill side of the shaft house onto a long, raised trestle and spilled the contents over the side onto the "dump." A large, well-run Comstock mine working a productive ore body beneath powerful hoists with a full complement of men easily raised three hundred tons per day.

The pump engine and pump machinery in the shaft's third compartment was every bit as elaborate as the mine's hoisting apparatus. In the Hale & Norcross, a "beautiful and efficient"—but desperately expensive— Corliss beam engine drove the pumps with high-pressure steam piped from the boiler room. That steam pushed a twenty-six-inch-diameter cylinder through a six-foot stroke that turned a drive shaft and rotated a massive iron "pump-wheel" or "drive wheel." To translate the rotational force of the drive wheel into a linear up-down motion that raised and lowered the pump rod, one end of a large connecting rod called a "pit-man" was attached to the outside of the drive wheel. The pitman's other end joined to the "king post" at the apex of the "pump bob," a massive wrought-iron isosceles triangle whose long, flat bottom balanced on a sturdy axle. The rotating pump wheel drove the pitman attached to the king post at the top of the triangle back and forth, rocking the pump bob on the axle like a child's teeter-totter. One end of the triangular pump bob supported the pump rod going down the pump shaft. A huge counterweight dangling from the other end of the bob rocked up and down in the "bob pit," a large hole dug in the floor of the shaft house to contain it.

The pump rod was constructed from thirty-foot sections of pine trunk, trimmed to twelve inches square by steam-powered saws in the carpenters' shop, spliced end to end and strapped on all four sides with iron plates twelve feet long, six inches wide, and half an inch thick held in place by one-inch-diameter bolts. "Catching pieces" attached to the massive pump rod at regular intervals averted calamity in the event of a fracture by catching the rod on the guide timbers that contained its rise and fall. The major Comstock mines were too deep for the pumps to raise the water to the surface in one continuous lift. Mines managed the prob-lem by engineering a series of raises between pumping stations dug into the shaft walls at two-hundred-foot intervals.

The deepest pump at the bottom of a mineshaft was always a "lift-ing pump." Lifting pumps (sometimes called "sump pumps") functioned when submerged, and because they worked on the pump rod's upstroke, they didn't need to be permanently anchored in place, a crucial feature at the bottom of an actively sinking shaft. The lifting pump drew water from the sump and up a pipe to a discharge into a cistern at the lowest pump station. From that pump station on up the shaft, firmly anchored force pumps powered on the downstroke of the pump rod did the work, pushing water up a pipe to the cistern at the next-highest pump station. The process repeated in 200- or 250-foot leaps until the water discharged either on the surface or into the mine's deepest drainage adit. The up-down strokes of the pump rod varied in the different mines, from three or four feet to about seven or eight, and a correctly balanced pump rod had enough "real" weight left over from the counterweights to do the downstroke work without help from the engine. Engine power supplied from above raised the rod back to the apex of the stroke. A slowly working pump made three or four strokes per minute, in which time every one of the pumps on the way up the shaft raised about 250 gallons of water. Combating a large influx, the pumps could accelerate to ten or twelve strokes per minute and lift 750 to 1,000 gallons—impressive capacities that still weren't always equal to floods caused by the breaching of one of the Comstock's major underground water chambers.

Washoeites considered the hoists, pumps, and machinery of the Comstock's second line shafts to be marvels of modern engineering. Compared to what would be built in the years ahead, they were but toys.

With Fair pushing the sinking, the Hale & Norcross's second line shaft progressed twenty-four hours a day, seven days a week. By early February 1867, Fair's men had completed most of the surface installations, and his miners had the shaft down 75 feet. In the first week of June 1867, the same week as the Bank Ring's takeover of the Crown Point, Fair had the shaft at 430 feet, and his miners were adding 42 feet of depth every fortnight. Fair pushed the work through the summer. Unfortunately, Hale & Norcross yields plummeted in August and September. The mine's stock price fell precipitously, from $3,500 per foot to around $900, and the mine's trustees canceled the October dividend. When the Fair Shaft reached the 930-foot level, Fair oversaw construction of a shaft station and Hale & Norcross miners began drifting back toward the ledge, hoping to cut into the lower extensions of the ore being worked farther up in the old mine.

Although mining matters and the unwinding of his partnership with Jonas Walker occupied much of Mackay's attention in 1867, there was something, or rather, *someone* who was never far from the forefront of his mind—Louise Bryant. Mackay was always making up reasons to appear at the Fair residence on A Street, hoping to have the opportunity to exchange pleasantries. Theresa Fair lent a hand, too, often including Mackay and Louise at the family table. (Mackay also found time to give some of his good fortune away. In February, he bequeathed a gallon of brandy, a case of wine, 200 pounds of flour, 115 pounds of beef, and an assortment of other items to the Catholic Daughters of Charity.)

Mackay did his awkward best to court the young widow. Very likely, he indulged Louise with trips to the theater, an entertainment that, aside from the pleasures of the performance, didn't tax his conversational powers. In the spring of 1867, the theater company of actor John McCullough, one of the great tragedians of the age, gave a month of performances in Virginia City. The company mostly did Shakespeare—*Hamlet, Othello, Julius Caesar, Macbeth,* and *Richard III* were among the company's standards—sprinkled with Edward Bulwar-Lytton's *Richelieu* ("The pen is mightier than the sword"), *Virginius* by James Sheridan Knowles ("I hear a sound so fine there's nothing lives 'twixt it and silence"), *Camille, The Fate of a Coquette* by Alexandre Dumas, and Dickens's *Cricket on the Hearth.* The *Territorial Enterprise* raved about McCullough's Othello, and claimed his departure from the Comstock would be "more generally regretted than that of any actor who ever visited Virginia, not more for the esteem in which his professional qualities are held than the regard which is entertained for him personally." William Sharon had sponsored McCullough's Comstock run, but John Mackay carted off the biggest prize—a genuine friendship with the great actor that endured for the rest of McCullough's life.

Things progressed just as well between John Mackay and the widow Bryant. After a suitable period of courtship, he proposed.

For her part, Louise was more cautious. John Mackay wasn't as handsome as James Fair, nor did he ooze affable Irish charm. In both characteristics, Mackay probably also lagged behind her departed husband. Louise had developed a warm personal affection for the unpolished, stuttering miner, but he wasn't an educated man. Louise worried about matching herself to a man who couldn't manage to break himself of such uncouth phrases as "me and Fair." However, she took his measure. Mackay exhibited none of the weakness that had unmanned the late Dr. Bryant. After much deliberation, Louise decided that, although still young, she might go farther and fare worse. She accepted Mackay's proposal.

Worried about losing his suit, at some time during his courtship, Mackay supposedly blurted, "I am a rich man and can give you everything you want."

If so, it was a promise he kept for the rest of his life.

Father Patrick Manogue married them on November 25, witnessed by James and Theresa Fair. To commemorate the event and to assure favorable press coverage, Mackay sent champagne to the local newspapers—a case of Krug to the *Territorial Enterprise*, a case of Carte d'Or to the *Daily Trespass*, and "a superabundance of sparkling wine" to the *Gold Hill News.*

Pleased with the gift, the *Gold Hill News* published "a pleasant memento of remembrance on the occasion" and added "greetings to the newly wedded" and wishes of joy and love. The *Daily Trespass* had "an old acquaintance with the couple" and knew them "worthy of each other." The *Territorial Enterprise* waxed most effusive. Likely it was local reporter Dan de Quille, who probably gushed, after loosening a cork, which he did far too often: "It is seldom that as brief an announcement affords us so much gratification, or that a case of Krug honors the chronicling of as happy an event. The union of so estimable a couple and the devotion of a thousand worthier friends make every wish of joy and prosperity which we could utter superfluous; and so we simply offer the congratulations which all who know them must extend to two so worthily mated that none can say which made the better choice."

A few days after the wedding, the Hale & Norcross fired James Fair. The way Fair always told it, having completed the hard and technical task of sinking the mine's new shaft beyond nine hundred feet, he'd been shoved aside to make way for the less competent relative of one of the mine's trustees. In the other story, he'd been fired for insubordination. Both versions probably contained elements of truth. Whatever the case, James Fair's unemployment and the dissolution of Mackay's partnership left both men at loose ends in the primes of their professional lives.

As one of her first acts after their wedding, Louise had a headstone installed over the grave of Marie Bryant, the infant daughter she'd lost to the septic sore throat four years before. She could finally afford it. Her husband bought a lot on the corner of Virginia City's Howard and Taylor streets for $5,000 and commissioned construction of a cottage with a gabled roof, a picket fence, and enough space to house his new wife, daughter, mother-in-law, and ten-year-old sister-in-law. Louise decorated it with brocade, polished oak, and a Turkish carpet. For her, the parlor—a parlor!—was the most wonderful detail. For young Marie Louise Hungerford Mackay, ashamed of the menial work she'd had to do in Virginia City, burdened by painful memories of a dead child and a failed and possibly abusive marriage, and with no love of western Nevada's awful beauty, it wouldn't prove nearly enough. She'd begun to nurse a vision of existence that leaped far beyond the alkali dust and mechanical clamor of the Comstock.

CHAPTER 10

The Irish Coup

In the deep levels, men worked dripping sweat in the
sweltering, oxygen-depleted atmosphere.

———

**Entrusted with the management of property belonging to
others, [the Bank Ring] grew rich from its plunder.**
— "Stock Swindling," *San Francisco Chronicle*,
February 21, 1872

By the end of 1867, bloc voting the shares for which the Bank of California held proxies had firmly enthroned William Sharon as the most powerful man on the Comstock. He used that muscle to fortify a vertical monopoly. Sharon elected the trustees at most of the Comstock's productive mines, among them the Crown Point, the Kentuck, the Yellow Jacket, the Alpha Consolidated (formed from several of the small original claims on Gold Hill), the Chollar-Potosi, the Savage, the Gould & Curry, and the California. Through the trustees—always well-compensated Bank Ring associates—Sharon controlled the mine superintendents, and through the superintendents, he controlled the mines' supplies and services contracts and wielded decisive influence over everybody who worked in them. William Sharon's insistence on restrained, businesslike management eliminated much of the excess and frivolity and some of the redundant effort that had plagued the Comstock's early years, and in that regard, he did the lode a service. However, his private ownership in the Union Mill and Mining Company divorced his personal interests and those of his Bank Ring co-owners from those of the shareholders in the mines they controlled. Mining dividends no longer overly concerned William Sharon. His fortune and the fortunes of the other Bank Ring insiders hinged on the nonstop pounding of the Union mills' stamps, and to make sure that happened, he wasn't above having his superintendents dilute ore with unprofitable rock.

On Sharon's instructions, "his" mine officers sent ore only to reduction mills owned by the Union Mill and Mining Company. Surviving independent mills offered to undercut the Union mills' charges for equal bullion recovery—to no avail. Over the next two years, ten more independent mills fell into Sharon's hands. He specifically targeted mills around Empire on the banks of the Carson River. Those mills had freely available hydraulic power and were close to the most practical railroad route that might one day link Virginia City and Carson City to the transcontinental railroad then cutting its way across the Sierras.

By the end of 1867, average Comstock milling charges had fallen from the $30 per ton they had been in the early years to around $20 per ton. Mills still guaranteed a return of 65 percent of an ore's assayed value—that figure hadn't changed even as mill efficiency improved a few points. The mills kept the difference. In a square transaction, from a ton of ore assayed as containing $90 worth of gold and silver, a mill extracted about $60 worth of bullion. The other $30 ran off in the tailings. (An efficient mill might keep $5 or $6 extra for itself, but even then, the quick and dirty Washoe process lost $24 or $25 worth of metal in the tailings. The tailings could be reworked at a profit, and often were, but the mines never saw a dime when it happened.) So, in that square transaction, of $60 worth of "saved" bullion, $20 paid the mill's reduction charge, and $40 returned to the mine.

The Comstock mines contained many tens of thousands of tons of low-grade quartz that held gold and silver, but not in concentrations sufficient to pay the cost of extraction and milling. Squarely run mines left that stuff underground in the hopes reduced costs would one day render it profitable. However, not all mines operated on a straight string. Mixing a ton of valuable ore with a few tons of unprofitable rock reshaped the economics. That same ton of $90 ore mixed with two tons of $9 rock and sent to a reduction mill returned bullion worth about $70. Since that bullion reduced from three tons of rock instead of one, the mill earned $60 where it should have earned $20. Of the original $70 worth of metal, only $10 ever reached the mine, just enough to show a positive mill return in the ledgers. The mine received $10 where it should have gotten $40, and the mill earned $60 instead of $20. For a mill owner, the arrangement was excellent. For mine stockholders, it was a disaster—one they didn't know was occurring. Mining had evolved into a very technical profession. Although anyone with a little experience could identify the rich black sulphurets or greenish chlorides of first-class ores, things weren't so obvious at the other end of the value spectrum. No veteran miner's casual glance into an ore bin could tell $15 rock from the $30 variety without the aid of professional-caliber assays.

In late 1867 and early 1868, Comstock mines sent in excess of five hundred tons of rock to the mills every day. In a few cases, Sharon-controlled mines diluted their ore with such large quantities of unprofitable rock that bullion returns didn't suffice to pay the milling charges. When that happened, William Sharon had his trustees impose an assessment on the shareholders to discharge the debt. Sharon held proxies. He and his Bank Ring cronies usually held very few shares in their own names, especially before they levied an assessment. Assessments therefore cost them trivial sums. They made money as long as the Union mills kept pounding. Stockholders made and lost money from assessments, dividends, and the rise and fall of their share prices. Sharon's racket was more or less a sure thing; the option left to the stockholders most definitely was not.

The Yellow Jacket provided the most egregious example of Sharon's management. In the fall of 1867, after months of lamenting the poor quality of the Yellow Jacket's official advices, the *Mining & Scientific Press* reported "a reliable source" who told them the Yellow Jacket was milling twelve-dollar ore, which would show "a deficit of at least $40,000." Stockholders who missed the brief report's implications didn't realize they were being robbed. Yellow Jacket stockholders paid an "Irish dividend"—an assessment—to make up the difference.

Under Sharon's management, the Yellow Jacket worked ore from 1866 to 1872 and every year it paid dividends. The Jacket also levied a nearly equal sum of assessments. For most of that time John D. Winters served as superintendent, at $500 per month. Winters quarreled with Sharon in the end and confessed to friends that he'd lost his self-respect feeding Sharon's mills. "I've mixed waste rock with Yellow Jacket ore until it would scarcely pay for crushing," he said.

William Sharon and the Bank Ring fleeced the stockholders of every mine they controlled in similar fashion. By directing a diluted ore product from publicly owned mines to his privately owned mills and billing the mines for the privilege, Sharon pumped money from public companies into his personal pockets.

Opportunities to work the mines for the profit of the controlling combination extended far beyond the milling racket. William Sharon ran the Bank Ring's Comstock operation from his plush office. Wearing his trademark suits of black broadcloth, Sharon seldom ventured underground, but he did have the sense to know that he possessed no meaningful mining knowledge. The top-notch mining engineer Sharon employed at a handsome salary made up his deficit. On Sharon's authority, the man roamed the mines unchecked, examining drift faces and stopes, taking rock samples wherever he thought best, and reporting the assay results privately to William Sharon. Keeping Sharon abreast of all underground developments—and their portents—was the man's sole responsibility. He laid a report describing the condition of all the Comstock mines on Sharon's desk every day at 5:00 p.m., and Sharon held the information like state secrets. In addition to his personal mining engineer, Sharon employed the best geologists, consultants, and assayers. He assured their loyalty with generous salaries—and by having other men crosscheck their work. With reams of inside information and a war chest stocked by the large accounts mines kept on deposit at the Bank of California, Sharon began "mining the Comstock from the other end"—operating in the San Francisco stock markets, a battlefield on which he held decisive advantages. Sharon knew about upcoming assessments and dividends long before the public, and aside from his early, accurate, and exclusive insider knowledge of underground conditions, many rival stockbrokers kept their accounts at the Bank of California. Sharon reviewed their ledgers whenever he needed knowledge of their operations. The large quantity of mining stock deposited at the Bank of California as loan security gave Sharon a huge temptation to run short-selling operations—sell the shares in mines with faltering ore deposits before the news became public, release unfavorable reports or levy assessments to "bear" the stock (or both), and then repurchase the same number of shares at lower prices. Sharon pocketed the difference. Falling share prices also allowed him to demand more collateral from creditors whose mining stock secured their loans. The new collateral often came in the shape of additional mining stock, which in turn strengthened his control of mine management, for as always, he insisted on receiving proxies to vote the shares.

Playing the other side of the coin, Sharon received first word of optimistic underground developments. That gave him the opportunity to close out any short positions he held in the lucky mine, buy its stock before the public caught the news, and capture profits on the inevitable rise. Sharon might not have ever worked a day underground, but he was a wizard in the equity and finance markets that backed the industry.

Sharon found many other nefarious opportunities to squeeze profit from the Comstock Lode. Virginia City and Gold Hill assayers did business with Bank Ring mines at William Sharon's pleasure. He therefore had little trouble corrupting their results. At Sharon's suggestion, assayers understamped the value of bullion bars they tested on behalf of Bank Ring mines. Thus, a bar worth $1,100 might be stamped as being worth $1,000 and was sold to the bank—the Bank of California, of course—and credited to the account of the mine that had raised it and financed its reduction at the stamped valuation. Stockholders of the mine never knew they'd had the 10 percent they lost to the Ring. Nor did any record prove its prior existence.

To sate the mines' voracious appetite for timber and cordwood fuel, Bank Ring associates acquired pine-covered mountainsides in the eastern slopes of the Sierras, incorporated timber and lumber companies and sawmills, clear-cut thousands of acres of old-growth forests, built dams that diverted water into lumber flumes, shot lumber down to the valley bottoms in the flumes, and sold the wood products to Ring-controlled mines—at substantial profit to themselves.

Water gave the Bank Ring another opportunity to extract monopoly rents. Drainage from the mouths of old adits bored into the face of Mount Davidson constituted the entirety of the local supply. The Virginia and Gold Hill Water Company bought the rights and flumed the water to small cisterns and reservoirs and then piped it to the thirsty town and mills—for a price, of course. (Legal warfare to control the water supplies mirrored that fought over the mining claims.) The vile-tasting water emerged from the tunnels saturated with minerals. Comstockers joked that only diluting a tablespoon of water in a glass of whisky rendered it safe to drink. It was, however, the only local supply. Sharon bought control of the water company and not only made profits from monopoly-priced water sales, but also assured that the mills he owned distant from the Carson River wouldn't do without in dry years.

He fought—and won—legal battles with Carson Valley ranchers to forbid them from diverting river water to irrigation. He employed "regulators" to ensure compliance.

Mines, mills, timber, fuel, water, stock market operations, government—the Bank Ring controlled them all. Pulling the levers of the extraordinarily lucrative combination made William Sharon the greatest power in Nevada. To shape legal decisions and government policy to suit his ends, William Sharon bought judges, tampered with witnesses, curried favor with—and where necessary bribed and threatened—Nevada's state legislators, governor, U.S. senators, and the state's lone congressional representative. William Sharon lost no sleep pondering the dubious morality of these endeavors. Twice in his life, sharp operators had cheated him of his life savings. People looked out for themselves. Through aggressive employment of Bank of California assets and influence, William Sharon leeched profit from the Comstock Lode like a poor man boiling sustenance from a beef shank. At the end of 1867, just half a year after the incorporation of the Union Mill and Mining Company, Sharon boasted to stockbroker George Mayre that he'd personally "made all of $250,000" in the preceding six months.

In the years ahead, he would make much, much more.

San Francisco newspapers began referring to William Sharon as "the King of the Comstock." By late 1867, the only major aspect of the local mining industry beyond his grasp was transportation, and the Hale & Norcross was the only productive mine beyond his control. William Sharon intended to have them both.

On the first trading day of 1868, Hale & Norcross shares opened on the San Francisco Stock & Exchange Board at $1,350. Comstock observers reckoned its prospects good. Three shifts of eight miners working the 930-foot level at the bottom of the Fair Shaft prospected toward the ledge, making a few feet of westward progress during the eight sweltering, gloomy hours they spent boring blast holes and hacking at the drift face by candle and lantern light.

At one of the shift changes on Thursday, January 9, Hale & Norcross officers "confined" the men finishing work to the 900-foot station. The mine wouldn't allow them to return to the surface. The eight men who came down on the cages to replace them brought "provisions and other necessaries," and when their shift ended, management "imprisoned" them, too.

News of the confinement swept the cold, snow-blown streets of Virginia City, as did rumors that the mine had made a big strike. Within minutes, the story was clicking down the telegraph wires to San Francisco. By the end of the day, the Hale & Norcross had all twenty-four miners confined at the 930-foot station.

Confining miners was an old Comstock trick. Ostensibly done to allow managers and owners to snap up shares of the mine before news of a strike broke with the general public, the ruse had also been used in reverse, to generate excitement about a strike when none existed, allowing insiders to unload their shares before prices collapsed. Which tactic the mine intended wasn't yet clear. "How much of either truth or fiction there may be in these stories is more than we can say," opined the *Territorial Enterprise*. "We hope, however, that something big has been found— the country could stand it."

In San Francisco, excitement among the Montgomery Street "stock dabblers" soared to "fever heat." The Hale & Norcross price leaped from $1,400 to $2,200 on the Stock & Exchange Board. The size of the jump surprised even the most optimistic of the Virginia City sports who'd been placing wagers on how big a bump the confinement would provoke "below"—and sparked another round of betting. The sudden climb brutally punished speculators who'd sold the mine short. A few who couldn't make the margin payments their contracts demanded were "blown up in the rise."

The next day, the Hale & Norcross management allowed its confined miners to return to the surface at the end of their shifts, but mine leadership still wouldn't let them leave the premises. An officer met the cages on the shaft landing, marched the arriving miners to the changing room, and once they'd washed the dirt from their bodies and changed clothes, directly to the company office. Superintendent C. C. Thomas confined them within. Guards prevented the miners from communicating with outsiders and permitted no one to enter the mine. The superintendent refused to answer journalists' questions. "Everything was shrouded in mystery," lamented the *Territorial Enterprise*, whose reporter failed to see the object of the proceedings, "unless for speculative purposes by parties in power."

Although Superintendent Thomas refused to allow the journalists to speak to the confined miners, he told the *Enterprise* that the confined miners were having a "jolly good time of it" in the company office. "They have all they want in terms of eatables, plenty of whisky, cigars, and cards with which to amuse themselves; and, best of all, get $12 per day," three times their usual rate. The newspaper described them kept like a jury in a mining suit—and then couldn't resist adding that they were actually making better money than "*honest* jurors usually do."

The *Enterprise's* astute reporter (almost certainly William Wright, aka Dan de Quille) sniffed around. Calculating based on reasonable rates of progress from the last known location of the drift face, he concluded that the Hale & Norcross probably wasn't "within twenty feet of the true vein." He detected other evidence. The Fair Shaft's pumps discharged the same water volume as they'd been doing in recent weeks. If the mine had broken into the vein through the eastern clay wall, it would likely have unleashed a flood that would have forced the pumps to work harder. Plus, "reliable parties" told him that the water filling the winzes sunk 50 feet below the 780-foot level of the mine's old workings showed no sign of subsiding. Reasoning that the quartz body against the Comstock's hanging wall at 780 feet would likely prove to be contained within the same clay walls as any quartz against the hanging wall 150 feet deeper, the *Enterprise's* canny "pencil" thought those winzes would have started draining if miners had struck the true vein on the 930-foot level.

His deductions proved correct. The drift hadn't reached the vein. A few days later, Hale & Norcross miners broke through the clay wall into the promising quartz and provoked the flood he expected, draining the winzes descending from the 780-foot level in the old works. News that they'd cut "very fine ore" bumped the mine's stock up another $325.

The Hale & Norcross confinement dominated the local news, but it didn't stop the lode working, business as usual. Virginia City boys too young to work in the mines enjoyed themselves sledding down Union Street, but the recent snows had brought a much more impressive "coasting course" into condition over the Divide in Gold Hill, where "lots of boys, both big and little," whizzed on sleds down Main Street from the upper end of town, past the shaft houses and dumps of the Yellow Jacket, Kentuck, Crown Point, and Belcher mines, and shot out of town away down Gold Cañon. The longest runs went for two or three *miles.*

Undampened by the foul weather, Hale & Norcross stock price continued to escalate, even though few shares changed hands. There weren't many shares *to* change hands. The mine only had eight hundred, two for every foot of the four-hundred-foot claim. Tense crowds thronged California and Montgomery streets, galvanized by the same energy and excitement that animated New York's Wall Street. The Hale & Norcross hit $3,150 at the end of January. On February 11, Hale & Norcross sold for $5,600. Only when sharps noticed that options to buy the stock thirty days later, *after* the Hale & Norcross's annual election on March 11, were available for half that price—about the value the mine achieved after news of the strike broke—did it become apparent that two factions were battling to control the mine.

What no one could understand was *why* the Hale & Norcross had become the "apple of discord" in such a bitter duel. The contest didn't make sense unless the mine had done a superb job suppressing news of an immense strike. All sensible mining industry experts thought the price completely detached from whatever intrinsic value the mine might hold. A variety of nonsense theories made the rounds. On February 13, one share of Hale & Norcross sold for $7,000 on the Stock & Exchange Board and two went for $7,100. After that, there simply weren't any available on the open market. The warring factions held tight to every share they owned. "There must be a great prize as the reward for such struggle," marveled the *Daily Alta California*.

Although the public didn't cotton to the reason, there *was* an immense prize at stake—the right to decide which mills would reduce Hale & Norcross ore. Sharon spent immense sums buying shares, but even after buying eight or nine "stray shares" at "three or four times their actual value," Sharon's voting total of owned shares and proxies still fell a few short of the number he needed to control the election. California Street rumors claimed that $10,000 had been paid for one share in a private sale and $16,000 offered for another.

Years later, a San Francisco broker who wrote a history of the San Francisco Stock & Exchange Board recalled that "a prominent banker"—by implication William Sharon or William Ralston—had three feet of the Hale & Norcross deposited at his bank that belonged to an absentee owner. The banker took possession of the shares, and "seemed happy," for they were the shares that cemented control of the mine. Then the absent owner suddenly appeared in San Francisco and demanded his missing feet. The bank settled the matter "quietly," presumably for a large sum.

The Hale & Norcross election showed the Bank Ring's victory. All six of the mine's new trustees were Bank Ring associates. The Union Mill and Mining Company soon began crushing Hale & Norcross ore.

The day after the election, a share of the mine sold for $2,900.

Although William Sharon emerged victorious, the Hale & Norcross campaign cost the Bank Ring vast sums. Sharon hoped developments on the mine's nine-hundred-foot level would justify the investment. Underground, Hale & Norcross miners had continued working from the bottom of the Fair Shaft while the Montgomery Street drama played out "below." Although the quartz they hit short of the Comstock's hanging wall had "promised, when first cut, to exceed in value anything that had ever before been found in the mine," prospecting drifts deflated those hopes. "Porphyry and waste" interrupted the quartz body. Exploring the quartz body up toward the ore being exploited at the 780-foot level of the old works revealed fair but unspectacular ore—definitely *not* the imagined bonanza that had driven the extravagant battle. In the hope of finding something better at deeper levels, Sharon's new trustees decided to sink the Fair Shaft another 137 feet.

Knowing they'd soon be levying assessments, the new trustees restructured the Hale & Norcross's stock from 800 to 8,000 shares. (A $10 per share assessment on 800 shares raised $8,000; the same assessment on 8,000 shares raised $80,000.) Sharon had hemorrhaged money, but he had control of the mine, and he expected to more than recoup his investment contracting with the Hale & Norcross for timber and cordwood and milling the mine's ore.

Only transportation stood between William Sharon and lock-tight control of Comstock industry. Cordwood fuel to fire the mine and mill engines had to be cut on the eastern slopes of the Sierras and hauled twenty or thirty miles to the Comstock, as did the framing timbers and lumber used underground. Shipping colossal mine machinery—whether manufactured in San Francisco's new foundries or abroad—over the Sierras in freight wagons was an astronomical expense, although progress of the Central Pacific Railroad's largely Chinese workforce blasting, hacking, and grading its way over Donner Summit north of Lake Tahoe and down the Truckee River into Nevada held promise of reduced transportation costs.

Since the early days, an army of independent freight wagons had served Washoe's transportation needs. They were expensive, occasionally reliable (nearly every teamster kept a whisky jug tucked within reach of the driver's seat to relieve the stupefying monotony of their work), and frequently paralyzed by foul weather. Plans to replace them with a railroad joining Virginia City to the Central Pacific in the Truckee Meadows had been footed about for years. The route would pass through Washoe Valley and Carson City, where trains could collect timber and cordwood. Although building this "Virginia & Truckee Railroad" was a staggeringly expensive proposition, a functioning railroad would lessen the cost of delivering timber and cordwood fuel to the Comstock and about halve the cost of hauling ore from the mines to the mills along the banks of the Carson River near Empire—mills that belonged to William Sharon and the Bank Ring. Such cost reductions would bring immense tonnages of low-grade ore in the upper works of the Comstock mines within range of profitable extraction, at obvious benefit to Virginia City, Gold Hill, and the Union Company mills. William Sharon had been plotting railroad construction for more than a year. In early March, simultaneously with the climax of the Hale & Norcross battle, Thomas Sunderland, A. Baldwin, W. E. Barron, Charles Bonner, Thomas Bell, J. D. Fry, F. A. Tritle, Darius Ogden Mills, William Ralston, and William Sharon—all Bank Ring associates—incorporated a new company with the intention of building the long-anticipated Virginia & Truckee Railroad. Sharon just needed to figure out how to get somebody else to pay for it.

Railroads had Nevada's attention in 1868. When the Central Pacific Railroad reached the Truckee Meadows, landowner Myron C. Lake gave land to the railroad in return for its promise to build a depot. Lake laid out a town site around the depot, named it Reno in honor of a fallen Union officer, and sold town lots at a "spirited" auction that netted him more than $30,000. The Central Pacific's first passenger train from Sacramento steamed into the new town at 8:10 p.m. on June 18, 1868.

"Hurrah for the Railroad!" applauded the *Territorial Enterprise.*

Speed mattered in the nineteenth century. In business, speed meant profit and competitive advantage. In personal matters, speed passed correspondence between friends and family in mere days where it had previously taken weeks, or even months. People paid for speed, and two rival concerns set up horse relays, Pony Express style, to bring the latest newspapers and correspondence the last twenty-seven miles from Reno to Virginia City. At the train station, the chargers and riders of the Pacific Union Company lined up against those of Wells, Fargo & Company. The express riders received their pouches tossed down from the train doors and tore off out of town. Comstockers took to wagering on the daily races. "Eager spectators" lined C Street every afternoon and cheered the winning horse into town. Dozens of drinks and hundreds of dollars changed hands. The fastest runs employed eight to ten relays of horses and two or three riders and often carried the mail from Reno to Virginia City in less than an hour and a quarter. A run made by the Wells Fargo ponies in 1869 covered the route in fifty-three and a half minutes.

The railroad race to unite the two coasts of the sprawling nation captured the attention of the entire country. Citizens of California and Nevada expected "progress" as they labored to raise a modern, "civilized" society from the wildernesses of the Pacific Slope and the Great Basin. William

Sharon used those expectations and the railroad excitement to pressure the citizens of Washoe, Lyon, Ormsby, and Storey counties into financing construction of the Virginia & Truckee Railroad. To increase the anxiety of Washoe, Lyon, and Ormsby counties, Sharon commissioned the survey of a route that bypassed them entirely, going north and northeast from Virginia City to the transcontinental line. The survey was the bluff of a consummate poker player. Sharon had no interest in a railroad that wouldn't link the Comstock mines to the Union mills on the Carson River, but the Central Pacific track building east across Nevada, away from Carson City and the Carson and Washoe valleys, provided the perfect metaphor. Sharon put it to those communities in simple terms: "Do it, and live; or refuse, and die."

In a remarkable flurry of fund-raising muscle, William Sharon pulled together $1.2 million for railroad construction in less than two months: Ormsby County bonds gave the railway $200,000; Storey County bonds contributed $300,000; Lyon County issues added $75,000; Sharon-controlled trustees of Comstock mines forked over sums that totaled another $700,000. (For credit to their transportation accounts, Yellow Jacket stockholders paid an assessment to finance their mine's $150,000 contribution.)

By December, the financial details had fallen into place. Sharon summoned surveyor Isaac E. James to his office. "Can you run a road from Virginia City to the Carson River?" Sharon asked without preamble.

"Yes," answered the surveyor.

"Do it, then. At once!" Sharon said.

Far removed from the Comstock, Adolph Sutro labored to secure financial and government support for the deep-drain tunnel scheme he refused to abandon. Sutro visited financiers in San Francisco, New York, London, and on the European continent. In Washington, D.C., he again badgered the U.S. Congress for loans and subsidies. At every turn, Sutro found himself thwarted by the tentacles of the Bank of California pulling levers thousands of miles removed from the Comstock.

Remarkably, Sutro, "the indefatigable," achieved an audience with President-elect Ulysses S. Grant in February 1869, and President Grant's Inaugural Address showed Sutro's influence. About halfway through the brief address he'd written himself, President Grant mentioned "a strong box" of precious metals "locked up in the sterile mountains of the far West [which] we are now forging the key to unlock." When, in his next breath, Grant mentioned that "it may be necessary also that the General

Government should give its aid to secure this access," mining industry people who read the address in the next day's newspapers supposed
Sutro had struck "a favorable lead." People paying closer attention might
have noted a negative indication in President Grant's emphasis on reducing the national debt. The new Congress gave Sutro's tunnel no special consideration. When Congress adjourned in the spring of 1869,
Sutro stood almost exactly where he had two years before, stymied in
every direction by William Sharon, William Ralston, and the Bank of
California.

In reality, he'd lost ground, because out in Nevada, in the sweat, grit,
and peril of the mines, technological and technical improvements revo-
lutionized capabilities. A new and more powerful explosive, ventilating
blowers, and improved hoisting and pumping machinery were making it
possible to work the Comstock Lode in depth without the aid of Sutro's
drain tunnel.

Around the time William Sharon had bragged about pocketing that first
cool quarter million in the winter of 1867–68, a letter published by the
Daily Alta California reported the lode's namesake, Henry Comstock,
"prospecting for quartz" in the Montana Territory near a remote camp
called Butte City. That was just the same as it ever was in news pertaining
to Henry Comstock. Obsessed with "finding another Comstock" in Montana quartz, he'd missed out on the phenomenally rich placers exploited at
Diamond City, Montana Bar, and Confederate Gulch, where stories told
of lucky miners washing $1,000 from single pans of dirt—just shy of four
pounds of gold. Although the letter's author portrayed the famed prospector as still having "a buoyant heart and confident faith in the future," every
miner in every camp knew he'd squandered the best chance in the West.
Around cook stoves and campfires, he must have seen it in a thousand
pairs of eyes.

More Henry Comstock information surfaced in the *Cheyenne Leader*
six months later, in June 1868. He'd braved the "scalping knife of the
crafty and vigilant Sioux" to reach another mushroom town, this time
South Pass City, principal settlement in the new Sweetwater mining region four hundred miles southeast of Butte, in the "Dacotah" Territory
(as the *Mining & Scientific Press* spelled it in 1868).

In a letter to the *Territorial Enterprise*, Comstock claimed he had personally struck the area's "principal surface diggings." A June letter from
South Pass City reprinted in the *Sacramento Daily Union* reported "Comstock, of Washoe fame" making "$100 a day" and asked, "What will the

doubting Thomases and wise men who said there were no diggings here think of that?"

They undoubtedly thought someone was lying.

The exodus soon began. By September, of the several thousand miners who'd rushed to the new diggings, "not more than 100" were left, many having rushed on to the latest, greatest discovery—White Pine, in eastern Nevada. Henry Comstock was one of the few who stayed behind. A man returning to the Boise Basin from the Sweetwater mines said that Comstock was doing backbreaking labor washing the gravels of a small claim and making about five dollars per day.

Newly married and profitably divested of a superb mine, John Mackay wasn't ready to rest on his laurels in 1868. Bullion mine stockholders made John Mackay the mine's superintendent at their April 1868 election. In that role, he continued the careful, systematic explorations that had characterized the mine since its early days. (Mackay had been involved since 1863 or 1864, and his influence had much to do with its working methods.) The Bullion had the deepest shaft in Nevada, and using "Giant Powder," the brand name of a new explosive compound produced in San Francisco under license from Swedish inventor Alfred Nobel, Mackay directed prospecting drifts from a station at twelve hundred feet. Five times more powerful than black powder and much more stable than nitroglycerine, a substance so dangerous that most miners refused to work in its vicinity, Giant Powder was also known by the name Nobel had given it—dynamite. Using dynamite in place of black powder meant miners could bore smaller-diameter holes to admit the more powerful blasting compound, which in turn moved greater quantities of rock. Dynamite speeded work, lowered costs, and improved the safety of a staggeringly dangerous profession. Using dynamite quickly became standard underground practice.

The *Mining & Scientific Press* described the bottom of the Bullion shaft as "dry as a lime-kiln and as hot as an oven." Deep in the Bullion, Mackay's men drifted through solid, close-grained veinstone that betrayed no sign of ever being broken up, cracked, or otherwise disturbed by geological agitations. It was easy and safe mining, but they found no ore. By year's end, the Bullion's shaft had encountered the Comstock's footwall. To prospect deeper, Mackay and the trustees sank an incline on the dip of the vein from twelve hundred feet to fourteen hundred feet. The mine swallowed immense sums, as it had since its incorporation, and found nothing of consequence.

To spread his risk, Mackay had maintained separate and simultaneous mining ventures since he'd first begun to acquire feet. Chaos in the Owyhee (pronounced *O-why-hee)* mining districts of southwestern Idaho, 370 miles northeast of Virginia City, attracted him to what seemed like an excellent opportunity to invest at fire-sale prices. Owyhee County was a reasonable place to look, for the region stood second only to Washoe among the silver-producing areas of the United States, albeit a distant second, producing about $1.5 million per annum.

After their discovery in the summer of 1863, the original Owyhee mines made a tremendous showing of shallow ore, but the two boss men of the Owyhee camps overextended themselves acquiring new property, went broke, and failed to pay their workforces. A flurry of forced sales, attachments, litigation, and resentment depressed prices and retarded development. George Hearst toured the Idaho mines in the spring of 1867, scouting for investment opportunities. He judged excellent the prospects of a mine called the Rising Star. In December, Hearst bought it with some San Francisco associates. Less than a week later, an entity called the Boyd Silver Mining Company incorporated in San Francisco to exploit the Rising Star's first southern extension. George Hearst and William Lent were among the Boyd's five trustees—and so was John Mackay. (Both Hearst and Lent had been among the Ophir mine's original incorporators.) By the end of the summer, either the Boyd had merged with the Rising Star (possibly in the mine's recent recapitalization), or Mackay had bought largely into the latter claim, for his name appeared as a substantial stockholder among those who hadn't yet paid the mine's most recent assessment. Among the other delinquents were Lloyd Tevis and George D. Roberts, two prominent San Franciscans with Comstock backgrounds, George Hearst, and an Irish-born San Francisco saloonkeeper-turned-stockbroker named William Shoney O'Brien (who should not be confused with Jack O'Brien, the man with whom Mackay arrived on the Comstock in 1859). Mackay's friend and neighbor James Fair had gone north to superintend the mine. When the recapitalized or consolidated company elected officers, James Clair Flood emerged as one of the trustees.

By the time they got involved with the Rising Star, James Flood and William O'Brien had been partners for at least a dozen years. Like John Mackay and James Fair, O'Brien had been born in Ireland, of humble parentage, and brought or sent to the United States at a young age. Although ethnically Irish like the others, James Flood was the only one of the four who had been born in the United States, to a pair of Irish immigrants of New York City's "hard working class." Although nothing has ever suggested that Mackay, Flood, and O'Brien knew one another before coming to California, the rough streets of New York City's Irish neighborhoods shaped their formative years. Flood learned the carriage-making trade, but caught the California fever in 1849. O'Brien came down with the same infatuation working in a store. Separately, they sailed to California. O'Brien landed in such penurious circumstances that he had to earn a few dollars helping discharge the vessel's cargo before he could afford a meal ashore. For the rest of his life, O'Brien told the story of the generous stranger who'd given him the old pair of boots that made it possible to do the job safely.

Both men worked for a year in San Francisco before going to the mines in 1850. In one set of stories, Flood raised $3,000 in the Yuba River diggings; in another, he made it working a gulch on the middle fork of the Feather River with William O'Brien and Jonas M. Walker, John Mackay's future partner (which, if true, would explain all the connections). O'Brien invested his mining proceeds in a San Francisco liquor distributorship, then sold out and opened a ship's chandlery near the waterfront. Flood took his gold back to New York and married Mary Leary, whose impoverished father had sold the family cow to fund her move to America. Flood bought a farm in southern Illinois, but didn't last in agriculture. He returned to San Francisco in 1854, accompanied by his wife, and opened a carriage livery and repair shop near O'Brien's chandlery. The two became fast friends. San Francisco's 1855 depression ruined both of their businesses. O'Brien observed that the downturn had done nothing to diminish San Francisco's thirst. The two men formed a partnership, one that only death would sunder, and opened the Auction Lunch Saloon on a corner of the Washington Market, one of San Francisco's busiest locations. Vendors of meat, game and poultry, fish, cheese, butter, fruit, and vegetables crowded the market, a spacious hall whose faux-rock-plastered arches fronted on Washington, Sansome, and Merchant streets. The Auction Lunch Saloon was a "bit house" that sold two drinks for a quarter, as opposed to the city's higher-toned "two bit houses" where twenty-five cents bought only one. Like many San Francisco watering holes, the Auction Lunch provided a spread of savory lunch snacks gratis to its patrons. The partners drew large custom from the market and the auction and commission houses that peppered the district and became famous for sartorial splendor. A kind, jolly, gregarious bachelor, William O'Brien stood out front in a broadcloth suit wearing a high silk hat, chatting with passersby and his many acquaintances and inviting them in to quench their thirst and enjoy a bite to eat. Behind the bar, James Flood mixed the drinks. A naturally fair and stocky man with a short neck, ruddy Irish features, a bushy goatee beard and mustache, and massive muscled shoulders that made him resemble "a retired gymnast," Flood always wore a high-quality gray suit in place of the barkeep's usual apron and acquired a reputation as one of the best mixers of cocktails on the Pacific Coast. Aside from their clothes, nothing distinguished Flood and O'Brien from any other pair of San Francisco's many "shrewd and thrifty vendors of drinks." Few suspected that Flood's slow, measured speech and deliberate manner hid an intense drive to succeed.

The Comstock discovery and subsequent boom in the buying and selling of feet presented Flood and O'Brien with opportunity ancillary to the sale of liquid refreshment. The foot-swapping nexus developed one block west of the Auction Lunch Saloon, on Montgomery Street, and in 1862, the San Francisco Stock & Exchange Board opened in rooms at 600 Montgomery Street, just a few hundred feet away.* The Auction Lunch became a popular watering hole for those involved. Tips and insider information flowed over Flood and O'Brien's bar top. They cultivated relationships with local brokers and speculators and with miners and touts in town from "above." Flood began making minor stock market investments on behalf of himself and his partner and discovered a latent instinct for stock market operations. They amassed a modest pile. Sometime between September 1867 and October 1868, Flood and O'Brien stepped back from active management of the Auction Lunch Saloon and opened an office devoted to stock trading three blocks away. James Flood handled the stock transactions associated with the dissolution of the Mackay/Walker partnership, and since both Flood and O'Brien on one hand and Mackay and Walker on the other operated as partners, with pooled interests, Mackay must have known both men. Considering the timing of Flood and O'Brien's shift to full-time stock market operations, handling the large-scale Mackay/Walker dissolution may have been what gave Flood and O'Brien the courage to make the change. Whatever the case, Jonas M. Walker was so pleased with Flood's friendship and services that he named a son in Flood's honor and a daughter in honor of Flood's wife—James Flood Walker, born in 1868, and Mary Flood Walker, born the following year. (The namings lend weight to the story that Walker and Flood mined together in early Gold Rush days. Not for another several years did Walker name a son in John Mackay's honor—John Mackay Walker.)

* The San Francisco Stock & Exchange Board opened on the site now occupied by the Transamerica Pyramid.

Sources don't reveal whether Mackay, Fair, Flood, and O'Brien formed a partnership before their Rising Star operations, but ownership and management of the Idaho mine involved all four men. Their go-ahead energy showed in the Rising Star's steady development. Superintendent Fair's miners found "beautiful ruby silver" spanning the entire width of a six- to ten-foot ledge, the *Mining & Scientific Press* admitted several magnificent Rising Star specimens to its prestigious display cabinet, and Rising Star stock appeared on the San Francisco Stock & Exchange Board. The public expected great things from the mine.

A problem lurked in all of that beautiful ruby silver flashing a dark, blood red color from within its crystalline structure. The scientific name of one of the principal varieties communicated the difficulty—*polybasite*, referring to the many base metals contained within.* Antimony, copper, arsenic, lead, sulfur, and silver all lurked in Rising Star ores,† making them "rebellious" or "refractory," which in mining terms meant difficult and expensive to reduce. (The Rising Star's rich deposits of "docile," easily worked near-surface ores had given way in depth to the more "rebellious" varieties—miners didn't yet understand this as the result of "supergene enrichment," an as-yet-unexplained physical process that often concentrated rich ores near the surface in western silver mines.)

European metallurgists unlocked value from rebellious ores with technical and finicky smelting and roasting techniques performed with the advantages of adjacent industry, cheap fuel, and inexpensive transportation. Taming large quantities of refractory silver ore wasn't so easily accomplished in the wilds of southwestern Idaho. Undaunted, Mackay and his Rising Star partners attacked the problem by hiring famed metallurgist Guido Kustel, the man who had smelted the very first load of ore Judge Walsh brought down from the Comstock to San Francisco in 1859. Kustel had recently taken out patents and would soon publish a book claiming to solve the very problem experienced at the Rising Star. The Rising Star invested large sums erecting a mill on the lines of Kustel's designs. When Kustel's complicated, difficult, expensive, and toxic process went into service, the ugly, base-metal-impregnated amalgam that emerged from the pans resembled nothing the Washoe miners recognized. They recovered less than half of the large quantities of the silver that "fire as-

---

* Contemporary *Mining & Scientific Press* articles mention polybasite, miargyrite, and fahlerz as being among the ore types found at the Rising Star.

† Only the silver had value in 1868. None of the base metals would bear the cost of transportation from such a remote region.

says" proved the ore contained. On the whole, Mackay, Hearst, and the other co-owners found the process "so injurious that a continuation of operations with such results [was] found quite inadmissible."

The Rising Star proved an expensive failure.* Most of the work ceased in February 1869. Long after, Mackay told a friend that the Idaho mining adventure had cost him $300,000, and that at the time, he'd really felt the pinch. Assuming the truth of that anecdote, the Rising Star probably cost Mackay half of the fortune he'd raised from the Kentuck. By the time the four Irishmen lost interest in the Rising Star in early 1869, they had without question entered into partnership, turned their attention back to the Comstock Lode, and pulled off a staggering coup.

In 1868, Virginia City and Gold Hill had high hopes for nine-hundred-foot-level explorations in the Savage, Hale & Norcross, Yellow Jacket, Crown Point, Kentuck, and Imperial-Empire (another consolidation of the small original Gold Hill claims). None met expectations. The first shares of the Hale & Norcross's new stock went on sale in May 1868 at $110 per share (a price equal to $2,200 per foot). In mid-June, unsatisfactory developments in the lower levels of the mine sparked a mini-panic that dropped the mine's value by 40 percent. Sharon sold his depressed shares, intending to repurchase them at the first hint of bonanza—notification of which he would receive before anybody else. He and his Bank Ring cohorts took an immense beating, but divested of any obligation to pony up cash to finance underground development, Sharon had his trustees levy an assessment on the stockholders. Through the summer and fall, the value of Hale & Norcross stock fluctuated as "shorts" and "holders" cited competing experts to claim the existence or absence of ore in the mine's lower levels. July and September excitements proved "considerable quartz, but no ore." Hale & Norcross bullion receipts totaled a disappointing $51,000 in July, August, and September 1868. During the same three months of the previous year, they had been $330,000. Hale & Norcross stockholders suffered another assessment in October and a third in December. "Latterly, all information concerning this mine has been kept very quiet," lamented the *Mining & Scientific Press*.

---

* Rising Star ores required smelting, a process similar to the one used in the tiny fire assays that proved its value, but smelting systems, techniques, and technology in the remote regions of the western United States hadn't evolved to the point where they could handle the ore at bearable cost. The most successful mining in the Rising Star's district was done in the first decades of the twentieth century.

Then, a few days before Christmas, the Hale & Norcross again confined its miners. They'd struck a clay seam. Investors and speculators had had enough of Hale & Norcross confinements, however. The mine's stock dropped 45 percent. The miners spent Christmas Day underground, "still shut up, far down in the bowels of the earth." To brighten their subterranean holiday, Hale & Norcross management sent one of the best meals ever cooked in Virginia City down the Fair Shaft. Eight hundred feet below the surface, at the Shaft's 1,030-foot station, the imprisoned men feasted on roast turkey bathed in the light of miners' candles. They popped corks from an army of champagne bottles and "had a high old time." The *Territorial Enterprise* ventured to claim that, "nowhere in the world was there eaten on that day so strange a Christmas dinner."

The men were still "camping underground" on New Year's Eve. The mine had sent beds and other conveniences down the shaft, and a mine official informed the *Enterprise* that the confinement would likely continue "for some days to come." The newspaper predicted "a strange sight" when the men emerged from the shaft "covered with a rank growth of fungi."

The Hale & Norcross didn't release its confined miners until the second week of January, by which time the men had spent well over a fortnight underground. Virginia City newspapers pronounced the whole business "a farce," whose results summed to "uneasy holidays" for the confined miners, "a barren vein beyond the clay," and "a loss of confidence by the public."

That loss of confidence kept downward pressure on the mine's stock price, allowing it only modest rises as moderately good news about the mine trickled out during the first six weeks of 1869. That downward pressure also made William Sharon vulnerable—it camouflaged the fact that he was under attack.

James Fair had learned enough working at the Hale & Norcross to think the mine wasn't being developed properly. Vociferous exposition of that opinion may have been what cost him his job. Considering how much milling costs had dropped in recent years, Fair felt sure that the tens of thousands of tons of low-grade ore—previously unprofitable—held in the upper levels of the Hale & Norcross could be raised at enough profit to finance the mine's deep-level explorations.

Comstock superintendents generally extended the reciprocal privilege of inspecting each other's workings. Since John Mackay superintended the Bullion, he likely availed himself of the opportunity to examine the Hale & Norcross. If so, his investigations led him to concur with Fair's assessment. No mining venture was a sure thing, but Mackay and Fair liked the mine's potential, especially with its stock price at low tide. They decided to try to sneak it from Sharon's clutches. Between them, Mackay and Fair possessed a wealth of mining knowledge and experience. They didn't know nearly as much about stock market machinations. To pull off a raid, they needed the help of experienced stock operators. If the four men hadn't already formed a partnership for their Rising Star operations, Mackay and Fair's desire to seize the Hale & Norcross led them to join forces with James Flood and William O'Brien.

Handshakes sealed the partnership. No papers and no signatures ever formalized an alliance that would eventually control tens of millions of dollars and command the lives of thousands. Mackay was the only member of the quartet able to front his full share of the capital. He bought the first three-eighths of the partnership. With their own stake and the help of a borrowed $50,000 (possibly from Mackay), O'Brien and Flood anted up to jointly fund the second three-eighths. Mackay, Flood, and O'Brien together loaned Fair enough money to allow him to finance the final quarter.

However, even with significant cash capital at their command (perhaps somewhere between $150,000 and $350,000), the Bank Ring's resources dwarfed those held by the four Irishmen. To have any chance of success, the Irish raid had to be conducted in absolute secrecy—Sharon could easily defend his position if he cottoned to their intentions.

Flood and O'Brien quietly began acquiring Hale & Norcross shares on the San Francisco Stock & Exchange Board. Large volumes of Hale & Norcross stock changed hands in early 1869, and since it was much harder to keep track of eight thousand shares than it had been to monitor eight hundred, nobody found anything untoward in the large volumes of Hale & Norcross stock flowing in and out of the hands of James Flood and William O'Brien. Nobody noticed their buying much more than they sold.

Only tiny clues that someone might be bidding for control of the Hale & Norcross surfaced in the San Francisco newspapers. In its "Financial and Commercial" column, the *Daily Alta California* mentioned one broker's "extensive" Hale & Norcross purchases on the morning of Thursday, January 7, that ran the price up from forty-six to sixty dollars per share. With the miners still confined amid rumors of a strike in the mine, the newspaper didn't think it important to mention the broker's name. The stock fell to fifty-five dollars in afternoon trading. Five hundred and fifty shares of the mine changed hands that day, almost 14 percent of the total needed for control. The *Gold Hill News* blamed the rise on the discovery of good ore on the 1,030-foot level of the mine—without crediting a source.

Rumors of that sort coincided with almost every burst of Hale & Norcross trading activity through January and February. Conceivably, up in Virginia City and Gold Hill, Mackay and Fair floated rumors from behind their whiskers, Comstock gossips latched on to them as leaks of exciting information from well-respected, well-connected, and reliable mining men, and the exciting stories provided cover for the flurries of large stock purchases Flood and O'Brien made in San Francisco.

By early February, Hale & Norcross stock had risen to around eighty-five dollars per share and around three hundred to four hundred shares changed hands most days. "The approaching election influences the stock," the *Daily Alta California* intoned on February 8. The price fell back the next week, then rose again. The *Territorial Enterprise* said that although many attributed the ascent "to the approach of the annual election of officers," several bodies of good ore recently discovered near the south line of the Savage pitching toward the Hale & Norcross actually drove the price rise.

Those quickly buried items may have been the closest William Sharon came to discovering the raid. Word of the coup didn't leak until it was already a fait accompli, on February 21, 1869, when the *Daily Alta California* printed a dispatch from "Virginia, Nevada," that said, "J. G. Fair and Wm. Mackay [*sic*], of this city, own the controlling interest in the Hale & Norcross mine." To William Sharon and the members of the Bank Ring, the announcement must have come as a terrible shock. They hadn't known they were under attack. The *Enterprise* didn't confirm the takeover for nearly a week, although it managed to get Mackay's name correct when it did. "The mine is looking exceedingly well," it added, "and the gentlemen named will doubtless shortly become millionaires."

Compounding the pain the hostile Irish takeover inflicted on the Bank Ring, in the days between the takeover announcements and the election that installed the new leadership, Hale & Norcross miners struck an eleven-foot-wide vein of "high grade ore" in the lower level of the mine. Not until the Hale & Norcross election ten days later did people realize the new combination included James Flood and William O'Brien. (Flood nearly blew the whole scheme. Only the day before the election did he learn that he couldn't vote the shares unless he reregistered their ownership in the company record books. He'd hidden them in a safe and barely made the deadline. His partners teased him about the near disaster for years.) The four Irishmen voted their shares as a bloc and deposed

Sharon's leadership. The stockholders elected Mackay a trustee, Flood president, and James Fair superintendent. Before the meeting adjourned, the new leadership rescinded the mine's most recent assessment, certain they could finance mine development with the bullion product of the low-grade quartz in the upper levels of the mine. They even refunded that portion of the assessment already paid into the company treasury. The two assessments Mackay had rescinded at the Kentuck were the only other times in Comstock history such a thing had been done. Within a fortnight, James Fair had the old hoisting works back in operation, and a dispatch writer couldn't help but notice the "energy" at the mine.

With the sting of the coup still fresh, William Sharon clashed with John Mackay in the Bank of California's Virginia City branch. The small banker stood behind the rail that divided the bank staff from the public. Mackay was a much more physically impressive man. In the description by one person who recalled the scene, Mackay stood outside the rail like a "wary tiger." Sharon fixed his frigid gray eyes on the Irish upstart and didn't invite Mackay to his office beyond the rail. Sharon suggested that since Mackay and his partners didn't have much experience, it would be best if they let the Union mills keep reducing Hale & Norcross ore.

"No. We've made other arrangements," Mackay replied.

Sharon's anger flared, an indulgence he seldom allowed. Sharon jabbed his finger toward the north flank of Mount Davidson, where the Geiger Grade passed out of town. "I'll make you pack your blankets out of this camp yet," he said.

Mackay flushed red. He mastered his temper and considered the small banker. "You will? W-well, I can do it," he stammered. "I packed 'em in."

Everybody who witnessed the scene understood the insult. Mackay had been mining in Washoe since the season of the first discovery. William Sharon was a "kid-gloved miner" of the first water who'd spent the early years buying and selling real estate in San Francisco. He'd come to the Comstock in a stagecoach.

Mackay and his partners cut the Bank Ring's mills and other associated companies from the ancillary operations of the Hale & Norcross. The Irish coup inflicted the first significant setback on William Sharon that he'd suffered since arriving on the Comstock in 1864. There would be more battles to come.

CHAPTER 11

The Lode's Worst Day

A crew of Gould & Curry miners—"the rats of the lower galleries,"
as Comstock miners styled themselves.

There is nothing so much dreaded by the miner as fire.
—Dan de Quille, *The History of the Big Bonanza*

E ven before the driving of "the last spike,"* Americans considered the
construction of the Central Pacific Railroad over the Sierras one of the
great engineering accomplishments of the age. And rightly so. No other
railroad on earth had surmounted such colossal obstacles. The successful
breaching of the mountain barrier greatly lessened the cost of transport-
ing California's industrial manufactures and agricultural produce to the
Nevada mining camps. Unfortunately, the railroad proved equally adept

---

* We moderns call it "The Golden Spike." People in 1869 referred to it as "the last
spike" or "the last rail."

at spreading disease. That was a matter of no small importance, for what a famed medical researcher described as "the most dreadful scourge of the human species"—smallpox—had broken loose in California.

Not even cholera provoked such terror. Thought to have originated in India or Egypt, smallpox had become a truly global menace by the middle of the nineteenth century. The disease's twelve- to fourteen-day incubation period and the prevalence of inter- and intracontinental travel and commerce made it almost impossible to contain. In a region served by a thriving port like San Francisco, its periodic appearance was little short of inevitable. Although California hadn't suffered a large-scale outbreak since the early 1860s, the disease provoked "considerable excitement" when it arrived in 1867, brought to San Francisco by steamship passengers who'd been exposed in Central America and the Caribbean and then carried the plague from San Francisco to other parts of the state. To the great relief of Pacific Coasters, the 1867 outbreak didn't blossom into a major epidemic. They didn't get so lucky when "the speckled monster" took hold in Petaluma and San Francisco in July 1868.

The epidemic spread: Angels Camp, Nevada City, San Juan, Napa, Sonoma, Benicia, Stockton, Oakland, Yreka, Folsom, Weaverville, Verdi, North San Juan, Marysville, and Portland, Oregon, all reported cases. From Sacramento, the pestilence spread into Nevada along the stations of the Central Pacific Railroad. In October, the *Territorial Enterprise* reported one or two cases in a Virginia City house on the east side of A Street, between Taylor and Union streets, just around the corner from the Mackay household at Howard and Taylor. Within eight weeks, Virginia City and Gold Hill had about eighty cases. Yellow plague flags dotted the streets. Two to three people died of the disease every day. The Comstock newspapers dutifully reported the number of deaths and new cases through the last months of 1868 and into 1869.

The fear Marie Louise Mackay suffered on behalf of her family can only be imagined. Children died of the disease at a greater rate than adults. She'd lost a younger brother to smallpox in the early 1850s. She'd already lost a child of her own to a much less lethal infection. She must have been terrified for her seven-year-old daughter, Eva.

Fatalistic Comstockers sought distraction playing billiards, poker, and faro, and indulging the "mania" for "velocipedes" imported from France that had swept the Pacific Coast "with almost as great rapidity as the prevailing epidemic." Mounted on a seat above and behind the front wheel of the strange, two-wheeled contraptions held together by wooden frames and holding tight to a crossbar that steered the front wheel, velocipedists propelled their contrivances forward using their feet to turn a crank that rotated the front wheel. Seven adepts racing up and down C Street amused onlookers with their "rapid and easy movement" and "grace of evolution." Someone started giving lessons at the Athletic Hall.

Not until the velocipede enthusiasm had been raging for six months did people abandon the awkward term and start referring to them as *bicycles*.

"The Firm" of Mackay, Fair, Flood, and O'Brien took charge of the Hale & Norcross in the spring of 1869. Flood and O'Brien handled the San Francisco end of business. Mackay and Fair kept their noses underground, which experience had taught them both was the only way to run a successful mine. Frugal, economical, disciplined, the mine's new Irish management insisted on a dollar's value for every dollar spent. Mackay and Fair were two of the best miners on the lode. Operating in tandem, they formed a powerful combination.

Their prime focus—and, indeed, the overarching objective of all the leading Comstock mines in early 1869—was discovering deep-level ore. The two Irishmen refurbished the Hale & Norcross's long-neglected upper levels, rebuilt the working stations, and began extracting the low-grade ore previous management had left behind. The proceeds of that efficient, systematic work coupled to lower-cost milling financed their deeper search for ore.

Making good on Mackay's promise, the Firm stopped sending Hale & Norcross ore to William Sharon's mills. They began processing Hale & Norcross ore in mills they privately owned. Although they were self-dealing in the same vein as William Sharon, no accusation of milling waste ever stuck to Mackay and Fair.

Working the Comstock was difficult, dirty, and unpleasant, but lured by the best wages in the industrial world, men had flocked from all corners of the globe to labor in the sweltering mines beneath the streets of Virginia City and Gold Hill. Irishmen, Cornishmen, and native-born Americans constituted the largest national contingents, but significant numbers of Welshmen, Germans, Frenchmen, Spaniards, Mexicans, Chinese, and Paiutes all lent their flavor to the Comstock's polyglot culture. A small community of "colored" lived in the camps, too, although, as with the Chinese, rampant racial prejudice confined their opportunities to occupations whites considered menial. Miners were the princes of the local working classes. They wore felt slouch hats to keep dirt out of their hair and eyes, and at shaft stations far below the surface, they stripped off their shirts and went to work in trousers and boots. Streaming sweat in the feeble light of candles and lanterns, they drove the work forward with picks, shovels, hand drills, sledgehammers, and the recently invented dynamite and they earned every penny of their four dollars per day, for the work was both physically hard and astonishingly dangerous.

Enterprise local Dan de Quille marveled at the "new and unheard-of ways" in which miners were "constantly being hurt and killed." Fatalities, maimings, major injuries, or hair-raising close calls occurred every day. "Hundreds upon hundreds" of accidents occurred in the Comstock mines, and they happened "in every way imaginable." Miners always thought the accidents ran in streaks, that if they'd had two or three they'd likely have a dozen, up to half of which would prove fatal. On average, the Comstock Lode suffered one death per week and one serious accident per day.

Nor were the only hazards underground. Mining made the whole district dangerous. Sampling just a tiny smattering of the accidents that had occurred on the lode in the ten years since its discovery: A boulder falling from a drift face in a Gold Hill mine broke a man's leg and collarbone; a thirsty mill worker took a swig of a clear liquid he supposed to be water and cored out his gullet with nitric acid used by prospectors and assayers to prove the presence of silver. A freight wagon ran over a child. A miner tamping a black powder charge with an iron rod struck a spark that touched off the blast—a rock put out his eye. A collapsing pile of shoring timbers crushed a teamster's skull. A popular stagecoach driver trying to control a runaway team died when the stagecoach capsized and smashed him beneath. A man trying to drive a buggy through a drove of hogs lost control of his horses, fell from his seat, and broke his thigh. A sill timber being lowered into a mine slipped from its harness and killed a man below. Two men on the surface stepped into an ore bucket attached to a horse whim without noticing that the horse had been detached from the whim. They shot 230 feet to the bottom of the shaft "at the run" and would have died except for the ten feet of water in the shaft sump and the drag of the rope spooling off the whim, which slightly slowed their descent. Coworkers fished them out unharmed. An eight-year-old boy was found dead at the bottom of an abandoned forty-foot shaft. Nine-year-old Freddie Cowles toppled into a privy and drowned. The brake of a loaded ore freighter going down Gold Cañon failed. The runaway wagon crushed and killed four of the team's six horses. A man working in a Gould & Curry ore chamber fell one hundred feet through the timber sets and died impaled on a collection of picks at the bottom. A mill worker trying to dislodge stuck amalgam poked his finger through a pan's drain hole and had it chopped off by a passing "muller," one of the rotating iron bars that stirred the pulp. A surprise jet of steam severely scalded the back of a man adjusting amalgamating pans in a mill. A miner brought home a quantity of amalgam, put it in the oven, then left to run an errand. Mercury vapors killed his child and rendered his wife and their German lodger "insensible." In the Chollar-Potosi hoisting works in the spring of 1868, a bolt connecting the brake lever to the brake shoe broke. The cage—which didn't have safety catches—plummeted down the nine-hundred-foot-deep shaft, and the braided iron wire cable spun off the twelve-and-a-half-foot-diameter hoisting reel with "fearful rapidity." Men tending the equipment scattered for their lives as the immense centrifugal force disintegrated the woodwork frame of the hoisting reel, sending heavy pieces of wood, bolts, and iron banding flying about the hoisting works. The end of the cable whipped off the reel, smashed a ten-foot trail through the ceiling, darted through the shaft house like an angry steel snake, wrapped around the crossbeam of the gallows frame and nearly wrenched it from its foundation, then slithered down the shaft after the fallen cage—which was empty, thank God.

A cage in the Kentuck crushed a fourteen-year-old pick carrier named Kennedy against the shaft timbers. He survived severe injuries. A boy named Miles working as an engineer's assistant in the hoisting works of the Yellow Jacket's South Shaft got his left thumb caught in an engine valve. The valve tore it off.

John Russell and a gang of other nightshift miners working in the Hale & Norcross shaft in the spring of 1868 dodged a mass of rock and dirt falling from above. Several of them sought safety in different compartments of the shaft. Those sheltering in the pump compartment heard Russell call out, "I'm all right! I'm all right!" But just at that moment a cage came whizzing up. A few seconds later, a man at the station one hundred feet above saw a headless figure atop the passing cage. The man recovered from his fright and rang for a stop. Miners wrestled John Russell's body to the station. The only evidence of his head was a flap of skin with an ear and some hair stuck to it. Russell's head had been torn off by the passing shaft timbers somewhere beneath. Adding to the gloomy, candlelit nightmare, searching miners couldn't find the severed head.

Twenty-eight-year-old Chauncy Griswold got tangled in the machinery of the Pacific Mill below Gold Hill. A rapidly spinning drive shaft broke his leg and wound his torn and lacerated muscles around the shaft.

A setscrew ripped a hole in his abdomen. His body spun around with the rapidly revolving shaft. His head pounding against the floor *thwack-thwack-thwack* stove in the side of his skull. Griswold was dead by the time his coworkers managed to stop the machinery.

An eight-year-old boy drowned in a flume conveying water to a mill. A Crown Point miner coming up on a cage narrowly escaped death when a negligent engineer sent the cage "up the sheaves" and crushed it against the gallows frame overhead. A carman named Michael McGuire pushed a loaded car onto the cage at the Kentuck's four-hundred-foot station. He leaned forward to secure it in place. The cage suddenly started up the shaft and jammed him between the cage floor and the station's cap timber. The engineer on the surface sensed something amiss and slacked the cable, freeing McGuire. Unconscious, McGuire slipped from the cage, bounced off the front lip of the station floor, and fell three hundred feet to his death at the bottom of the shaft. A twenty-eight-year-old Irish miner named Patrick Price was working in an inclined winze in the Chollar-Potosi when the cave of an insufficiently timbered level beneath collapsed the ground around him. A mass of dirt, rocks, and splintered timbers carried him to the bottom of the incline. The press of earth trapped his hands and feet and the whole of his body, but a group of shattered timbers somehow protected his head. His voice echoed out from inside the collapse. Price begged his companions to dig him out, but no one dared come within twenty feet. Price spoke to his friends nearby as the ground above his head creaked, cracked, and groaned. The other miners did their best to keep Price from learning the awful hopelessness of his predicament. Loose earth slowly piled up around Price's face. He bore the ordeal "manfully" for more than an hour, hoping for rescue, until a long moan escaped his lips. A moment later, "one grand crash" collapsed tons of clay, rock, and mangled timbers onto Patrick Price and stifled his voice forever.

Miners didn't like working in the vicinity of a dead man. A corpse made a mine feel like a tomb and the work like grave robbing. Repeated efforts to recover Price's body from the caving ground failed. Not until nearly two years later did two miners running a drift through the site of the collapse strike one of Pat Price's legs. Rats had flensed the flesh from his bones.

Miners took pride in their work. They did a difficult and dangerous job, they did it well, and they enjoyed their excellent pay. Old hands were blasé about the risks, all in a day's work, but there was one hazard that terrified them all, and that was fire. Working in mines shored by hundreds of thousands of feet of dry, compressed timber, they lived in fear of it, for an underground fire could suck the oxygen from the atmosphere of an entire mine, fill it with smoke and stifling gas, and inflict a horrible, suffocating death on men far from the conflagration.* Mine fires were also almost impossible to extinguish.

Before sunrise on Wednesday, April 7, 1869, the day-shift miners gathered at the mine heads along the two-mile run of the Comstock as the dawn drove the glitter of stars from the skies of Nevada. All along the lode—indeed, throughout the West and all around the country—talk was of the joining of the two railroads soon expected to take place in Utah that would link both coasts of the burgeoning nation. Bracing themselves for the nerve-racking descent on the cages into the depths of the great vein, they stood outside the shaft houses and the hoisting works sipping bitter coffee and smoking cigars and last pipefuls of tobacco. Strict edicts forbade smoking in the works below ground.

The dawn gathered no serenity. Massive mine engines belched and hissed along the lode, pumps spouted hundreds of gallons of water (all of it captured for use or sale), and smoke poured from chimney tops above the boiler rooms attached to the shaft houses and the thundering stamp mills. Among the miners slouching around the hoisting works of the Yellow Jacket and the Crown Point that morning were two sets of brothers— Edward and William Jewell, and the three Bickells, thirty-one-year-old George, Richard, aged thirty, and James, their twenty-seven-year-old kid brother.

That Wednesday, with the exception of a few carmen clearing ore and preparing the mines for the arrival of the day shift, there hadn't been any miners in any of the three mines since the night shift ended at 4:00 a.m.† Underground, drifts connected the mines on several levels, and some quirk of subterranean architecture gave them a natural "draft." The South Shaft of the Yellow Jacket was a "downcast." Air tended to flow down the Jacket's south shaft, through the tunnel workings connecting it to its two

---

* Joseph Priestley and Antoine Lavoisier had discovered oxygen nearly a hundred years earlier, and although Priestley also isolated carbon monoxide and the existence of a poisonous gas produced by the incomplete combustion of wood had been known for centuries, miners hadn't yet identified carbon monoxide as the stifling gas produced in underground fires.

† The author suspects the three mines worked two ten-hour shifts, 7:00 a.m. to 5:00 p.m., one hour off for the shift change, and 6:00 p.m. to 4:00 a.m., with three hours off between 4:00 a.m. and 7:00 a.m.—a much smaller payroll than three eight-hour shifts.

southern neighbors, and up the shafts of the Kentuck and the Crown Point, making them both "upcasts."

Forty-year-old John Percival Jones superintended the Crown Point and the Kentuck. Jones's parents had brought him to Ohio in 1831, at age two, when they emigrated from Herefordshire, on England's Welsh border. Jones developed into a dark-eyed, powerfully built youth with jutting brows. When he was twenty, he rushed to California with the '49ers. He mined in Trinity County and served as county sheriff. Elected to the California State Senate in 1863, Jones served until the California Republican Party named him its candidate for lieutenant governor in 1867. Jones stood for statewide election, but lost. In the aftermath, he went to the Comstock, signed on with the Kentuck, and settled in Gold Hill. Jones kept the tops of his cheeks clean-shaven, but beneath a line connecting the base of his nose to the point at the back of his jawbone, he cultivated a splendiferous beard that poured down to his breastbone. Jones proved himself industrious, efficient, and competent, and within a year, William Sharon elevated him to Crown Point and Kentuck superintendent. In charge of well over a hundred miners, carpenters, carmen, mechanics, engineers, blacksmiths, firemen, and other specialists, Jones discharged his duties admirably, pleasing his superiors and earning the admiration of his underlings.

In accordance with Superintendent Jones's "tight ship" expectations, the Crown Point lowered its first cageload of miners right on the stroke of 7:00 a.m. that Wednesday. The men aboard grasped the crossbar of the cage for support as they rattled down the timber-framed shaft, careful not to extend a body part beyond the edge of the open-sided cage. The cage dropped fast, and the thick timbers buttressing the shaft blurred past. They swiftly amputated the arm, leg, or head of any man fool enough to allow an appendage to protrude. While they were underground, the cages, the braided wire cables, and the hoisting machinery far above were the only threads that linked them to the surface. The Crown Point cage dropped a pair of miners at the 230-foot level and continued down, unloading men at the 600-, 800-, and 900-foot stations. When the last men were off at the deepest station, someone rang the hoisting bell, and the engineers on the surface raised the cage, leaving about twenty-five men dispersed throughout the mine, including several who worked for the neighboring Kentuck. They traveled through connecting drifts into Kentuck ground. (The Kentuck's engine and hoisting apparatus usually sat idle, an economizing measure.)

Among the first group of Crown Point miners beginning their workdays in the feeble light their candles and lanterns cast into the gloomy excavations were the two sets of brothers, Edward and William Jewell, and Richard, George, and James Bickell. A similar scene played out three hundred feet to the north, where about two dozen others rode a cage down the Yellow Jacket's South Shaft.

Ascending from the Crown Point's lowest station, the empty cage took about half a minute to reach the shaft house landing. Another few minutes passed as a foreman organized the second load, a roughly equal mix of Crown Point and Kentuck men. Counting those on the second cage, about forty-five to fifty-five men were inside the mine. A few hundred feet northward, several dozen more dropped into the Yellow Jacket.

Unbeknownst to any of them, they'd descended into a death trap.

Three hours before, at the end of the night shift, a Yellow Jacket man had violated one of mining's cardinal rules and left a candle burning unattended on the mine's 800-foot level, in a twenty- to forty-foot-wide drift 135 feet north of the Kentuck boundary. Behind the departed miner, with its wooden holder poked into a shoring timber, the forgotten candle burned to a nub. The tiny flame caught fire to its holder and spread to the mine timbers. The conflagration blazed briefly, casting hellish light into the empty drift and burning toward a closed wooden door on the Yellow Jacket/Kentuck boundary. The door slowed air circulation and contained the smoke. The fire consumed the majority of the available oxygen and burned down. For the next couple of hours, the fire smoldered in the darkness, building heat as it chewed slowly into the dry, compressed shoring timbers, producing large quantities of odorless, colorless, poisonous carbon monoxide gas as a by-product of the incomplete, oxygen-starved combustion of organic material, an incendiary time bomb ready to detonate the instant it received a fresh supply of oxygen.

That infusion probably arrived with the billows of air driven beneath the cages that lowered the first loads of day-shift miners. Charged with oxygen, the superheated timbers burst into angry flame that ate into the weakened timbers like a ravenous animal and filled the drift with smoke.

When the Crown Point cage went up for a second load, the men left underground dispersed through the tunnels toward their assigned work locations. None of them seem to have sensed anything amiss until a powerful explosion rocked the mine—probably the result of a tunnel collapse caused by the failure of fire-eroded timbers and the door burning from its hinges. Like a gigantic bellows, the cave launched a roaring shock wave of smoke and poisonous gas up the tunnels. The wind and oxygen-depleted air extinguished the miners' candles and lanterns, plunging them into darkness. Bewildered, coughing and choking in stifling smoke and in complete blackness, many men panicked, blundering wildly through the darkness, desperate to find breathable air.

A vision of the shaft station flashed through the mind of one terrified miner as he careened off the drift walls toward the eight-hundred-foot station—for working ease, the stations didn't have safety walls. Suddenly aware that he risked falling into the shaft, the man dropped to his hands and knees and groped forward, feeling for the edge. Other horror-stricken miners didn't have the same presence of mind. Three men rushed past the crawling man and pitched over the edge. Impact on a metal grating partway down dismembered one man. The other two died at the bottom of the shaft two hundred feet below.

The explosion came on several Kentuck men with a hellish roar, after they'd crossed into their mine. The blast of compressed air, smoke, and stifling gas extinguished their lights. One of them fought through blackness back to the Crown Point's eight-hundred-foot station. A second man lost his way, collapsed, and asphyxiated to death. Joseph Glasson decided his best chance lay in running for the Kentuck shaft. He made it, too, but like the three unfortunates at the Crown Point station, he misjudged the distance, ran off the edge, and plunged to his death in the sump.

John Murphy, the Crown Point's station man at eight hundred feet, heard the explosion howling toward him seconds before the gale hit the station and extinguished the lights. He sank down and wrapped his head in a coat. To no avail—he briefly passed out. When he came to, he heard a weak voice echo up the shaft from below. "Murphy . . . Send me a cage . . . I'm suffocating."

Just before the explosion, the second cageload of men was dropping into the Crown Point. Nearing the seven-hundred-foot level, they caught a strong whiff of the most feared smell in mining—smoke. Just after, the explosion jolted the cage, jumping it two feet. Several men lost their hats. Smoke billowed into the shaft. A few seconds later, the cage reached the eight-hundred-foot station, which was crowded with coughing, choking, croaking, terrified men.

Thick smoke and carbon monoxide filled their lungs. The gas bonded with the hemoglobin in their blood, drastically reducing the quantity of oxygen delivered throughout their bodies and addling their brains into a muddled, vertiginous state that resembled drunkenness. Confused, choking, gagging, in fear and agony and desperate to escape, the men fought for space on the cage.

Tragically, there were *two* cageloads of men underground, and as the first load of miners staggered out of the drifts, far more men than the cage could carry packed the eight-hundred-foot station, every one of them trying to cram aboard. Such a plethora of arms, legs, and shoulders protruded beyond the sides of the cage that Murphy, the station man, didn't dare ring for the hoist—those not wholly aboard would be torn to pieces on the way up. Several men clambered to the top of the cage. The quantity of smoke in the shaft increased. On the station and in the cage, all were suffocating. In the confusion, perhaps as many as five minutes passed, until, urged by the pleading of the fellows more securely aboard, those unlucky outermost souls abandoned their holds, one by one, knowing they'd be killed during the hoist. At the last second, one man crawled between the legs of the men already in the cage, begging to be left aboard. Finally, Murphy rang the bell. The cage whooshed up the shaft. No man aboard would ever forget the pitiful, desperate, choking, gagging sounds emanating from the men left behind slowly fading into the depths of the shaft as they rose toward deliverance.

Above, on the surface, in the Crown Point's shaft house, it seemed as if someone below had hacked into a chamber of hell. Black smoke jetting from the maw of the shaft filled the building, making it difficult to breathe and threatening to drive the engineers from their stations. The cage reached the landing. Choking, retching men stumbled off the cage and reeled around the shaft house like drunken fools. The engineers couldn't get a clear understanding of the situation. Critical seconds passed before they knew for certain that the miners had vacated the cage and that others might still be alive in the deep levels. Beginning to suffocate themselves, the engineers dropped the cage back into the hole, barely able to see the depth marks on the cable. They clung to their posts in the hopes of saving those still underground.

Eight hundred feet below, the fire raged. Blasted outward by the initial collapse and driven by the natural draft of the three mines, the fire ran south from its origin in the Yellow Jacket through timber sets and along wooden track floors to a winze connecting two mine levels at the Yellow Jacket/Kentuck boundary. There, the fire jumped a forty-foot section of tunnel through solid rock and burned through the Kentuck to the Kentuck/Crown Point line, then up a gangway to an old level. From there it took hold in the timbers of the Crown Point's main drift, burning furiously, pouring out smoke and sucking oxygen from the mine's limited atmosphere. Following the natural draft of the mines, smoke and poison gas roiled through the drifts and stations and rose up the Crown Point and Kentuck shafts. The miners who hadn't escaped on the first cage were in dire condition. Some fled the station, groping through choking darkness, the terrifying anguish of asphyxiation contorting their features as they climbed up or down ladders or ran through drifts, knowing they'd die if they didn't find breathable air. A group of miners held on at the Crown Point's eight-hundred-foot station, hoping through suffocating desperation for the return of the cage. Among them were brothers Richard and George Bickell. One by one, men sank to the floor unconscious. When the cage arrived, only the two Bickells and four other men dragged themselves aboard. One of them rang for the hoist.

Up in the shaft house, someone smashed the windows, hoping to ventilate the smoke. It seemed impossible that anyone could survive such choking conditions as must exist below, but the cage bell tolled and the engineers sprang for the controls. Thirty seconds later, the cage arrived with half a dozen bodies sprawled on its floor. Men crawled through the smoke across the shaft house floor with wet cloths clamped over their mouths and discovered unimaginable horror—of the six men on the cage, only George Bickell still drew breath, and although George was unconscious, his hands clutched the shirt of his decapitated brother, Richard, whose jawline was a ragged line of gore. The rest of Richard's head was missing, and at his left shoulder, only a scrap of flesh kept the arm attached.

Richard had made the cage alive, but he'd passed out on the way up. George grabbed at his brother, but he couldn't prevent Richard's head and shoulder lolling outside the cage and being torn off by the shaft timbers. The other four men on the cage were dead, and George himself barely clung to life, his breath rasping in and out of smoke-damaged lungs.

James, the third Bickell brother, wasn't among those on the cage. Also missing were brothers Edward and William Jewell. Chaos threatened the shaft house. Confused head counts revealed more than twenty Crown Point and Kentuck men unaccounted for. Over at the Yellow Jacket, foremen couldn't figure out how many they had missing. Anyone who whiffed the thick, stifling smoke gushing from the Crown Point and Kentuck shafts feared for their lives. The dark, ugly palls spewing from the windows and doors of the shaft houses broadcast news of disaster to every corner of Gold Hill and Virginia City. Comstockers flocked to the stricken mines.

The wives of the day-shift miners pressed through the throngs to the shaft houses and dashed back and forth trying to locate missing husbands. Nobody witnessed the dramas unaffected by the terrible contrast between the relieved reunions of wives with husbands who'd made it out alive and the rising anguish of the women who couldn't locate their menfolk. The *Territorial Enterprise* reported scenes of "heart-rending grief." The people of Gold Hill gathered on the slopes, porches, and sidewalks of the town and watched in stunned silence. No one spoke in anything but hushed tones.

The first two known widows were Mrs. Anthony Toy of the Crown Point and the Kentuck's Mrs. Patrick Quinn—their husbands' bodies had surfaced on the cage with Richard and George Bickell. The Quinns had two children. Somehow instantly on hand at the mine heads, Father Patrick Manogue—the spiritual leader of the lode's Irish, and a genuine moral force in the community—did his best to comfort the widows.

No person on the lode had experienced a mine fire of similar magnitude, and lacking an understanding of the scientific dynamics playing out below their feet, the miners nurtured hope that men might have survived below the fire, in the deepest levels. Rumors to that effect swept the crowds, and frantic wives begged to be allowed to go down to look for their husbands.

Superintendent Jones and the foremen refused to let them enter the mines. The wives waited outside the hoisting works, in mounting anxiety, and the *Territorial Enterprise* reported that "the poor women, with their weeping children, stood about with their hands clasped, rocking themselves to and fro, but uttering scarcely an audible sob—they seemed astounded and overwhelmed at the suddenness and awfulness of the calamity. . . . Their grief was such as to cause tears to flow down the cheeks of the most stout-hearted." Among them, Father Manogue and the other Catholic clergymen did what they could to ease the suffering.

To reassure anybody alive deep in the mine, Superintendent Jones wrote a message on a large piece of pasteboard and sent it down on the cage to the thousand-foot station with a lighted lantern, a bundle of miners' candles, and a supply of water. "We are fast subduing the fire," the note read. "It is death to attempt to come up from where you are. We will get to you soon. The gas in the shaft is terrible and produces sure and speedy death. Write a word to us and send it up on the cage and let us know how you are."

Some minutes later, when they raised the cage, no word was written and the lantern was extinguished.

The fire drew all of Gold Hill's fire companies to the mine heads and three from Virginia City. Nobody could survive the smoke and gas gushing up the Crown Point and Kentuck shafts, but the downcast in the Yellow Jacket's South Shaft gave firefighters an avenue to attack the blaze. Firemen laid canvas hose from a hydrant on Main Street and began rigging it down the Jacket's shaft, but even with the natural draft, some hours passed before anyone could get below the five-hundred-foot level due to stifling gas. When the worst of the gas cleared, firemen and an escort of miners extended the hose to the Jacket's eight-hundred-foot level and advanced on the fire, extinguishing burning timbers. A man involved in the firefighting effort noticed the timbers showing "no blaze of fire." Instead, "the timbers seemed to be one living and glowing coal," sending out "slight sprays of spark." Intense heat hindered their endeavors, as did the paucity of oxygen—barely enough to support a candle flame. When a cave or timber collapse seemed imminent, the firemen retreated, and miners took timbers forward to shore the drift. Soon, two or three inches of nearly boiling water steamed on the tunnel floor, further fouling the atmosphere. "It was such work as few firemen in the United States have ever undertaken and such as none but the firemen of a mining country could have done," the *Territorial Enterprise* would boast in the aftermath.

Nearly suffocating at the face of the fire, the miners brought forward ventilation pipes. Fresh air kept the men on their feet, but it also energized the fire. Every cave or tunnel collapse drove the firemen back to the shaft with a blast of hot embers, smoke, and superheated air. Only the Yellow Jacket's downcast kept the men alive. If the dynamics of the fire should cause it to reverse, they'd die, but even with the draft behind them, they made scant progress through the afternoon and evening. On the other side of the fire, in the Kentuck and the Crown Point, the situation remained unknown.

The initial firefighting efforts stabilized. Miners reported manageable conditions in the deep levels of the Yellow Jacket. Someone proposed trying to reach the base of the Crown Point shaft below the fire, through a drift that connected from the Jacket's lower levels. Volunteers rode the Yellow Jacket cage to the shaft sump. At great risk to their own lives, the men crept down the southward drift that connected to the base of the

Crown Point shaft, paying close attention to the faint flames of their candles and lanterns. Almost immediately, they found the body of a Crown Point man who'd died in throttled agony just 150 feet shy of the Yellow Jacket shaft and its promise of breathable air. They wrapped his corpse in a canvas tarp, lugged it back to the shaft, and returned to the search. Before long, they'd found four more bodies, their features contorted in the death agony of asphyxiation. Gashes and cuts on faces and arms acquired in crazed blind dashes through the black drifts further distorted their appearance.

Meanwhile, recovery crews behind the point team sent the remains of three of the four missing Yellow Jacket miners up the shaft. By 10:00 p.m., a total of thirteen corpses had been raised to the surface. Fifteen minutes later, word reached the surface that the searchers had found a clutch of bodies in a drift near the Crown Point's nine-hundred-foot station. A concentration of stifling gas aborted the recovery effort. Highlighting the hazard, one of the underground searchers collapsed unconscious in a poorly ventilated drift. His companions dragged his body back to the Yellow Jacket shaft and sent him up on the cage insensible, but alive.

Rescue efforts continued Thursday morning. With the fire still burning, John James, one of the Crown Point's foremen, and two other brave men went down the Yellow Jacket shaft to spearhead another attempt to reach the Crown Point below the level of the fire. Carefully, one by one, they inched down the connecting drift, checking each other and the mine's atmosphere, and succeeded in reaching the Crown Point shaft. They found nine grotesquely disfigured corpses tangled together in a drift and another man clinging to a ladder, his hands refusing to abandon their grip on a rung, his head lolled back in death. Other bodies floated in the shaft sump, mangled by falls.

Before descending, James and his companions had coordinated a plan with the Crown Point engineers to try to reach the eight-hundred-foot level using the cage. From the deepest station in the Crown Point shaft, they rang the bell. A thousand feet above, the engineers at the controls in the smoky shaft house dropped the empty cage to the three men below. Aboard the cage and ready to raise, the men rang the bell continuously, the prearranged signal. The engineers raised the cage slowly, poised to lower the instant the clanging stopped—indication that the rescuers had either encountered unbreathable air or lost consciousness. It didn't take long. The clamor stopped and the engineers lowered the cage to the original station. After several attempts, the men succeeded in reaching eight hundred feet. Thirty feet from the shaft, they found a dead man sitting on a log, his head resting in his hands. Shortly thereafter, foul air extinguished their lights. They groped back to the cage and descended to the trickle of fresh air coming down the drift from the Yellow Jacket. They abandoned their efforts, but by 9:45 a.m., they and other recovery crews had raised eighteen additional bodies to the surface, retching over the almost intolerable stench. The flesh of the dead seemed as much decayed as if they'd been moldering a month, perhaps due to the great heat, noxious air, and poison gas. The fingers of those handling the deceased squished completely into the dead flesh. Those who did the job swore they'd never forget the "peculiar and sickening smell."

Firefighting efforts continued simultaneously, but firefighters in the Yellow Jacket made little progress in the face of caves and tunnel collapses. The state of the fire in the Crown Point and the Kentuck remained a mystery. George Bickell, the miner who'd emerged alive on the Crown Point's second cage clutching his decapitated brother, died at noon. The lode held the first of many funerals later in the day. Hundreds of people followed the processions to the various churches and cemeteries. Every flag in Gold Hill and Virginia City flew at half-mast.

Friday, April 9, dawned hopeful, with less smoke rising from the Crown Point and Kentuck shafts than at any time since Wednesday morning, but by 8:30 a.m., soon after work had resumed, dense, black smoke, "hot and charged with cinders," spewed from the mouth of the Crown Point shaft and poured from every aperture of the hoisting works.* Until that morning, no one thought the mines themselves were in serious danger, but by 9:00 a.m., the fire appeared worse than ever. If the shafts caught fire, the entire mines would be lost. Firefighters went down the Yellow Jacket, but they couldn't stand the foul air and soon returned to the surface. Belowground, the fire had free rein.

Despite eight or ten men unaccounted for, John Percival Jones of the Crown Point and Kentuck and "Colonel" John Winters, superintendent of the Yellow Jacket, agreed that hope had vanished that any of the missing remained alive. The Gold Hill fire chief advised the superintendents to seal the shafts and inject steam down the ventilating tubes of the Crown Point and the Yellow Jacket. There seemed no reasonable alternative. Carpenters floored over the shafts, and men piled on dirt, cloth, and

---

* In retrospect, it seems likely that they charged the fire with new oxygen each time they lowered a cage.

more dirt wherever a puff of smoke appeared. Seven large boilers forced steam into the mines at as high a pressure as the tubes would bear.

The shafts stayed closed through the weekend. After they'd been sealed for seventy hours, the superintendents ordered the Crown Point and Kentuck shafts opened. No smoke or gas rose from the Kentuck, and only a trace of smoke leaked from the Crown Point. Most miners thought the fire extinguished. Fearing for their employment, all wanted to get back to work and probe the extent of the damage.

Crews sprayed water down the Crown Point shaft, hoping to absorb any remaining gas. Engineers decoupled the steam injectors and began forcing pure air down the ventilating tubes, likely an egregious mistake. Lanterns lowered to 800 feet returned extinguished. Someone proposed sending a dog to the bottom of the shaft. Miners rejected the idea as too cruel. An exploratory party descended to the Crown Point's 230-foot level, where they expected to find the bodies of John O'Brien and K. Ryan.

They found O'Brien first. He'd almost made the station. After six days in the burning mine, his body was in awful condition, the death stench overpowering. Gagging and vomiting, the recovery crew wrapped his body in canvas and raised it to the surface. The foul odor of putrefaction filled the hoisting works. The miners tipped O'Brien's corpse into a disinfectant-filled coffin.

News of the recovery of O'Brien's body had reached his wife. She met the procession carrying her husband's remains from the building with "loud and uncontrollable" manifestations of grief and an escort of other women. Mrs. O'Brien begged—then demanded—that Superintendent Jones allow her to see her husband's body. It took Jones long, painful minutes to convince Mrs. O'Brien and her supporters that it would be "folly, inhumanity, and indecency" for Mrs. O'Brien to interact with her husband's remains.

Half an hour later, foreman Hank Smith recovered K. Ryan's body from the 230-foot level. Ryan was a bachelor, so there wasn't the same scene. Much to everyone's relief.

The fire flared up, forcing the superintendents to reseal the mines.

Afraid of prematurely reopening the mines for a second time, the superintendents kept the shafts sealed all week, but they felt intense pressure to reopen—the idled mines threw five hundred men out of work, depressed trade all along the lode, and cost shareholders thousands of dollars. On the cold, blustery morning of Sunday, April 18, the superintendents relented and ordered the shafts opened.

The fire had already killed thirty-seven men, made ten women widows, and orphaned more than twenty children, but it hadn't claimed its last victim. A gang of Yellow Jacket miners descended to the mine's four-hundred-foot level. A man among them named William H. Williams felt woozy, as if he wasn't breathing good air. He asked out. On the cage up, Williams collapsed. His upper body fell outside the cage. A passing timber yanked him off. Williams plummeted five hundred feet to the bottom of the shaft, making another widow and three more fatherless children.

Not until the warm and sunny last day of April were miners finally able to hoist ore from the Yellow Jacket and the Kentuck—the first since the outbreak of the fire. Miners in the Crown Point tackled a more gruesome task: wrapping the rotten bodies of four more men in canvas shrouds and raising them to the surface. Despite hopes that the mines would be working at full capacity by the beginning of May, the fire refused to die. The Yellow Jacket collapsed its connections to the other mines, effectively ending its problem. Unable to extinguish the fires still burning, the Crown Point and the Kentuck sealed their 700- and 800-foot levels despite the paying ore still remaining in those galleries. There seemed no other way to end the debacle. The bodies of three men were never recovered.

As time gave the Comstock community perspective to reflect on the calamity, many recognized that they had much for which to be thankful. Although only some of those on the 800-foot level survived (because the cage happened to stop there after the fire announced itself) and not a soul in the Crown Point's 900-, 600-, or 230-foot levels escaped, the fire had erupted right as the day-shift miners went on duty, when the mines were mostly empty. If they'd been as full as they'd have been in the middle of a shift, many times the number of men would have been underground, most of whom would have died.

The lode tried to get back to business as usual. By the first week of May 1869, excitement over the impending connection of the Central Pacific and the Union Pacific railroads had largely displaced news of the fire from the California newspapers.

When officials of the Central Pacific and Union Pacific railroads lined up for a "last spike" ceremony at the site of their joining, Promontory Summit, Utah, on Monday, May 10, 1869, San Francisco, Sacramento, Stockton, and most of California had already celebrated the event. They'd thrown their parties two days before, on Saturday, so as not to interrupt the working week. "Above," in Nevada, Comstockers "saved their powder," preferring not to celebrate until the last rail had been laid and the last spike driven.

When it happened, a terse telegraphic message from Utah clicked into the Virginia City telegraph office: "The last rail is laid; the last spike is driven; the Pacific Railroad is completed." Of the four special spikes used at the ceremony, the Comstock had contributed one of silver, mined, reduced, refined, forged, and engraved in Virginia City. An attendant ran Old Glory up the flagstaff over the telegraph office, the awaited signal. What once seemed impossible was now an established fact. An iron highway spanned the continent.

The flag's appearance released everything capable of making a noise in Virginia City and Gold Hill. The jollification persisted through the remaining daylight and concluded after dark with a grand torchlight procession of the firemen.

Construction of "the Pacific Railroad" had taken more than six years. Completion reduced travel time between New York and San Francisco from about twenty-four days via Central America to eight days on the railroad. To the people of California and Nevada, it seemed the capstone accomplishment of a glorious decade, "the greatest industrial achievement of modern times," and "the dawn of a new era for the Pacific Coast." Old pioneers considered it the most significant event on the Pacific Slope since the discovery of the Comstock Lode almost exactly ten years before. Most people expected "the great National Highway" of iron rails would open the way to years of expanding prosperity. They could hardly have been more wrong.

One person benefited from the mine fire—Adolph Sutro, who latched on to it as a means of revitalizing his long-thwarted tunnel project. He laid blame for the thirty-seven or thirty-eight deaths squarely on the Bank of California's doorstep: If the Bank of California had allowed him to build his tunnel, the miners could have used it to escape.* (The Yellow Jacket never did figure out how many men they'd lost, exactly.)

By August, Sutro had convinced the local Miners' Unions to buy $50,000 worth of tunnel stock. That wasn't but a tiny fraction of the money needed to drive his 20,498-foot adit, but it was enough on

---

* Whether that was true was open to debate—a steady supply of fresh air might have done nothing but conjure an even more wild inferno.

which to commence work and give "foreign"—meaning East Coast and European—financiers evidence of local confidence in the endeavor. In a packed public meeting at Piper's Opera House on September 20, Sutro delivered his tunnel screed in his thick German accent and gave the first great public airing of Bank Ring malfeasance. In the aftermath, William Sharon received threats against his life.

Given that Sutro lambasted William Sharon's Virginia & Truckee Railroad project as nothing but "another gigantic scheme of pilfer," seeing the rapid progress being made on its construction must have been galling to Sutro. Twelve hundred Chinese laborers pushed the V&T toward completion, smoothing, grading, bridging, and tunneling the convoluted path that would allow steam trains to run between lumber yards around Carson City, the Bank Ring's quartz mills on the banks of the Carson River around Empire City, and the Comstock mines. Workmen constructed a spectacular bridge over Crown Point Ravine into the heart of Gold Hill. "The Crown Point Trestle" passed directly over the Kentuck mine. Excitement at the railroad's approach rode high. Nothing symbolized progress in nineteenth-century America more than a railroad.

Sutro had baked revenues for the transportation of ore and supplies to and from the mines into his tunnel company's projected earnings. The V&T would put those earnings in William Sharon's pockets instead.

Sutro held a ground-breaking celebration for his tunnel in October. In unpleasant weather, Sutro made an uncharacteristically short speech, turned around, hefted a pick, and struck the first blow. Within ten days, three shifts of three miners had the tunnel in fifty-two and a half feet. More than twenty thousand feet of hard digging lay between them and the Comstock Lode.

William Sharon derided it as "that famous tunnel . . . started the other day on a basket of champagne and four bits." With his railway nearing completion, he could afford the sarcasm.

The track reached Gold Hill in mid-November. At ten minutes to 5:00 p.m. on the blustery afternoon of November 12, 1869, the engine "Lyon" steamed around the bend south of Crown Point Ravine, Stars and Stripes streaming from both engine and tender. William Sharon rode in the engine with the driver and others prominent in the railroad. Large crowds stood watching. Conscious of all the eyes upon him, the train driver stopped his locomotive just short of the enormous trestle spanning Crown Point Ravine. After a pause, he triggered a "shrill screech" of his whistle and moved out onto the trestle. Every steam whistle in Gold Hill answered the call. Church bells rang, and "General Grant," the old thirty-two-pound cannon on Fort Homestead, boomed, joined by every other noisy thing in town. At the midpoint of the bridge, eighty-five feet above the ravine bottom, the locomotive shrieked out a succession of "unearthly howls." Sharon and the others waved their hats, and as "the iron horse" rolled the rest of the way across the bridge onto terra firma and into the crowd of men, women, and children gathered beyond, all the men afoot raised their hats and returned Sharon's salute with full-throated cheers and shouts. The train slowed to a stop.

Sharon gestured to the "champagne and other liquid refreshments" on a long table and invited all to take a drink. John Percival Jones mounted the engine tender and made a speech praising William Sharon and the railroad. Sharon came forward in response to loud cheers and made a brief speech of his own, in which he praised by name "those who had toiled with him in the planning and execution of this great and good work."

"Sharon's iron mules" went to work hauling previously unprofitable low-grade rock taken from the seven-hundred-foot level of the Yellow Jacket's north mine, where ore bins dumped directly into the freight cars. Within a week, they'd delivered nearly four hundred tons. Mule-drawn freight wagons had charged $3.50 per ton to haul ore from the Gold Hill mines to the Carson River. The V&T performed the same service for $2. Trains returned with wood, lumber, and shoring timber. The price of a cord of wood dropped from $15 to $11.50, then to $9. Transportation costs for other supplies and comestibles fell in similar proportion. The cost reductions breathed new life into many Comstock mines.

The Comstock needed the jolt. From 1867's total product of $13.7 million, the Comstock's bullion yields had slipped to $8.5 million in 1868 and then to about $7.5 million in 1869—the lowest annual total since 1862. The Bullion mine contributed nothing to those depressing results. Mackay still held the superintendent's mantle, and he'd taken the mine down to the fourteen-hundred-foot level, where his miners drifted through an immense body of low-grade quartz that filled the entire width of the vein. Not a ton of it would pay the cost of extraction. Mackay had seen the mine from close to the surface down to fourteen hundred feet without finding a single body of profitable ore. Mackay lost interest and ended the connection with the mine he'd maintained for five or six years.

Fortunately for the firm of Mackay, Fair, Flood, and O'Brien, the Hale & Norcross was one of the few Comstock mines that did well that year. The old upper levels produced bullion sufficient to finance the further sinking of the Fair Shaft. Crosscuts on a new level more than a thousand feet below the shaft landing passed through a body of "most excellent" ore filled with rich "black sulphurets and green chlorides," and varying in width from twenty-seven to forty feet. The *Mining & Scientific Press* called the ore body the most important development in the mine since 1865.

Under the Firm's able management, the Hale & Norcross paid $192,000 in dividends in the last half of 1869. Mackay, Fair, Flood, and O'Brien compounded their earnings with the profits of milling ore. John Mackay might not have known it quite yet as 1869 came to a close, but his wife was developing an even bigger bonanza. She was carrying his child.

CHAPTER 12

Jones's Sick Child

The spectacular Crown Point Trestle of the Virginia & Truckee Railroad, which passed directly over the Kentuck mine in the heart of Gold Hill.

———

Purchasers of the advanced price will probably lose their money.

—Mary Jane Simpson, "Virginia Gossip, December 1, 1870," *San Francisco Chronicle*, December 3, 1870

The Virginia & Truckee Railroad pushed William Sharon's popularity on the Comstock to the highest level it would ever attain. To raise the money needed to finish construction—and avoid spending his own coin—Sharon had mortgaged the partially completed road. Not until two and a half months after reaching Gold Hill did the railroad lay the last mile of track through to Virginia City. The first train into town kept up a "fierce tooting" as it "passed triumphantly" into a depot near the Gould & Curry hoisting works on January 29, 1870, an inspiring sound of progress to inhabitants of Virginia City long accustomed to the jingling bells of ten-mule teams and the "hi-yah mule" calls of the freight packers. Only after the railroad euphoria waned did the citizenry pause to reflect on the fact that they'd paid for the majority of the railroad's construction without receiving a share of its ownership. William Sharon kept it all for himself and his Bank Ring cohorts. The uncomfortable realization left many Comstockers feeling conned.

Regardless, the Virginia & Truckee was an impressive engineering accomplishment. The railroad traced six and a half easy miles from Carson City to the quartz mills on the Carson River at Empire City before it hit the steep, convoluted grades that took it up to the Comstock mines and made its reputation. Over the thirteen and a half winding miles beyond Empire City, the engines huffed and puffed up nearly sixteen hundred feet of elevation, bridging ravines and gullies and tunneling through spurs and ridges. Climbing toward Gold Hill from the lower end of American Flat, the course of the road swung through every point of the compass. The curves through the railroad's twenty-one-mile length summed to seventeen full 360-degree circles, although it wasn't *just* the serpentine course of the railway Dan de Quille referred to in 1876 when he called it "the crookedest road in the world."

Some years later, after the Virginia & Truckee had secured its place in railroad history as the most profitable short line in America, putting more than $2,000 *per day* of clear profit in his pockets, William Sharon boasted to a friend that he'd "built that road without its costing me a dollar."

The Virginia & Truckee built spurs to the most important mines and mills and one to Silver City, forcing hundreds of mule and ox teams that had served the mines since the early days to seek opportunities elsewhere in the West. William Sharon and the Bank Ring at last had gained monopoly control of Comstock transportation. The railroad also added a whole new class of hazard to the lode. Hopping Virginia-bound freights as the trains labored uphill through the Gold Hill Station became a popular game among local boys. The railroad superintendent published notices warning parents to keep their children away from the trains, to no avail. Perched on the freight cars, the boys rode in glory into Virginia City. In early January, a seven-year-old boy defied his elder brother's attempts to stop him and jumped for a flatcar from the end of the platform in the Gold Hill station. He lost his balance and toppled into the gap in front of the following car. The wheels of the next two or three cars nearly cut his little body in half and strung his entrails along a stretch of track. The poor child gasped for a few minutes before expiring.

Despite the reduced costs of timber and transportation, troubles dimmed the lode's long-run outlook. The railroad couldn't find new ore bodies, and although there were tens of thousands of tons of low-grade rock in the upper levels of many mines, the Hale & Norcross and the Savage shared the only ore body a thousand feet below the surface. As it had in all previous mining depressions, the Comstock's future hinged on the discovery of new, high-quality ore bodies going deeper.

California wasn't having an easy time of it, either. The economic panacea supposed to have been delivered by the new Pacific railroad never materialized. Instead, the railroad brought hard times. California manufacturers couldn't compete with cheap "foreign" products imported over the railroad from the eastern states. Many businesses failed. Unemployment soared. Real estate values tumbled. Nor had much rain fallen in the winter of 1869–70. Crop yields dwindled. Stunted grasses didn't fatten cattle and sheep. Price spikes had seen California's farmers and ranchers through previous droughts, but this time, midwestern foodstuffs rolling west on the railroad satisfied demand. Agricultural prices stayed flat. When a heavy storm finally hit California and the Comstock—too late in the season to make much difference—a depressed man in Virginia City stripped off his clothes, lay down in a puddle of rainwater, and drowned himself.

In March, a white mob attacked Chinese laborers employed at a quartz mill in Empire City and destroyed their huts and property. Lamenting the "great cost" of a trial and reasoning that one would only inflame "the feeling of prejudice already existing against the Chinese" and acquit the "parties charged," a grand jury investigation declined to pursue indictments. On March 30, Texas became the last of the former Confederate states readmitted to the Union. That same day, the secretary of state of the United States formally certified the Fifteenth Amendment to the U.S. Constitution. Eight days later, the "colored citizens" of Virginia City and Gold Hill marched through both towns to celebrate its ratification, for the amendment guaranteed them the right to vote—or at least it guaranteed that right to the men among them. The best efforts of Susan B. Anthony, Lucy Stone, Elizabeth Cady Stanton, and other women's rights activists had failed to get the franchise extended to women. The Virginia Brass Band thumped out patriotic airs at the head of the parade. Behind them, the first row of marchers carried a banner with the words "Justice is sure, but slow" around the striding figure of Liberty. Behind impassive faces, any Chinese residents of Virginia City who observed the procession, as well as any progressive-minded women, surely wished Liberty would pick up her gait.

Few Comstock mines did well in 1870. The Yellow Jacket worked ore, but the mine's assessments exceeded its dividends. In May, the Chollar-Potosi cut a rich and extensive ore body in a neglected part of the old upper mine, but the entirety of the discovery existed above the 400-foot level and did nothing to change the lode's long-run prognosis.

The only other important mine that did well that year was John Mackay's Hale & Norcross. With the richness of the mine's fourteen-hundred-foot level revealed in May and early June 1870, Mackay took his very pregnant wife and daughter Eva to San Francisco. He wanted his wife to have the best midwife in the West, and should it come to that, access to the very best doctors. Nor did Louise have any desire to spend the last two months of her confinement on the Comstock. The family checked into the Grand Hotel on June 9. Three stories tall with four hundred rooms built around a central courtyard roofed in glass, the Grand filled the block at the southeastern corner of Second and Market streets. San Francisco's newest and finest hotel, the Grand had already acquired a reputation as the preferred home of "the wealthier of the hotel-patronizing families," a place to "revel in the golden aspect of California," meet the Washoe nabobs, and join them in "drives to champagne breakfast at the Cliff House."* Early risers in the best top-floor rooms enjoyed views of the sun lifting free of the Oakland Hills while its first golden rays danced on the waters of the bay. The city around the Mackay family still suffered the hardships of the post-railroad economy, but the Hale & Norcross mine had paid $164,000 in dividends in the first six months of 1870. John Mackay's share of that probably ranged between $30,000 and $60,000. His share of the Firm's milling profits during those months probably approached the upper figure and could have been more. Louise was twenty-six years old, full with child, and fresh in the blooming of youth. Stunning fortune and a fairytale marriage had freed her from servile poverty and made her rich. She intended to enjoy it. As for her thirty-eight-year-old husband, what he most wanted was for her to be happy.

At the Grand Hotel, on August 12, Louise gave birth to a son, John William Mackay, Jr. His parents called him "Willie." Birth announce-

---

* Although it's not the same building, champagne breakfast at the Cliff House is a San Francisco experience that could still be enjoyed in 2018.

ments appeared in several California newspapers. Although fortune, intelligent speculation, and more of the hard work that had brought him so far from the squalid slums of New York and the rough diggings around Downieville would make John Mackay master of the two richest mines on earth in the years ahead, nothing in the world would ever make him prouder than his first-born son.

Willie came into the world at a harrowing time for the Comstock Lode. The Yellow Jacket discharged a large number of men in the weeks after his birth. The prices of many mine stocks sagged into the single digits, and the *Daily Alta California* considered the Comstock's prospects "not very encouraging." The last half of 1870 was the worst time on the Comstock Lode since its discovery. In that respect, the lode's fortunes mirrored those of its namesake, Henry Comstock.

Most likely, Henry Comstock worked the Sweetwater mines through 1869 and the first half of 1870. None of his endeavors in the Wyoming Territory met with enough success to hold him, however, and when the opportunity to explore new country arrived, he joined an expedition that prospected the Big Horn River basin on the west side of the Big Horn Mountains.

Nearly three months later, Henry Comstock turned up in Bozeman City in the Montana Territory, one of the thirteen members of the expedition who hadn't backtracked. They'd traversed more than four hundred miles of hostile wilderness and found nothing of value. Poking around in the dirt outside Bozeman City, Comstock must have ruminated on the eleven crucifying years that had passed since he'd sold his slice of the lode that had carried his name to all corners of the United States, to Europe, and beyond. He'd washed dirt in eastern Oregon, crushed quartz in the Idaho Territory, grubbed through gulches and ravines in the western Montana Territory, shoveled gravels and picked at quartz veins in the Sweetwater mines, and while he'd done it, for subsistence wages, through unimaginable hardships, sweltering summers and frigid winters, innumerable dangers and crushed hopes, more than $100 million worth of gold and silver had been raised from a lode he'd done much to prospect, discover, and open.* All he had to show for it was the endless humiliation of a famous name. On September 27, 1870, somewhere outside Bozeman

---

* As a share of the total national economy, $100 million in 1870 was equal to about $250 *billion* in 2018.

City in the Montana Territory, Henry Comstock clenched the barrel of a revolver between his teeth and pulled the trigger.

As if in mourning, the fortunes of the Comstock Lode sank to a low ebb in the months following Henry Comstock's suicide. Of the twenty-odd Comstock mines raising ore in late 1870, only the Chollar-Potosi, the Yellow Jacket, and the Hale & Norcross paid significant dividends, and by year's end, managers of all three companies understood the finite nature of their ore bodies. Bullion returns for the year ebbed to about half the annual return of the boom years in the early 1860s. The stock market slumped until the aggregate capital value of all the Comstock mines hovered around $4 million.

In an interview he gave ten years later, William Sharon said that at the end of 1870, the Bank of California had $3 million invested in the mines, mills, and towns "directly dependent upon the continued productiveness of the Comstock Lode." If the lode failed, Sharon said, the calamity would have endangered the bank's existence. "Only the few directly acquainted with the condition of the bank will ever realize the anxieties which beset its management at the close of the year 1870," he said.

With the lode waning, many miners wandered off to try their luck in new camps. "Virginia is dying," a visitor told the *White Pine News*.

In one of the many vain searches for ore Crown Point superintendent John Percival Jones directed in 1870, he had his miners run a crosscut east from the mine's 1,100-foot level. Jones and his foreman Hank Smith drove the crosscut completely through the Comstock vein, through the hanging wall, and out into the country rock beyond until they were 800 feet east of the shaft. They found nothing of value. The *Mining & Scientific Press* and the *Territorial Enterprise* could have described the mine in November with the same phrases they had used in February—"exhibits no change for the better," "drifting about in porphyry," and "no signs of pay ore."

Many shareholders stopped paying assessments and abandoned their shares. Unsalable and carrying the negative value of unpaid assessments, the shares returned to the company treasuries, which threw an increasing proportion of the costs of deep-level exploration on the mining companies themselves—and on the Bank Ring and the Bank of California that stood behind them. With expenses mounting and income declining, mine managers began considering halting lower-level prospecting.

At the morning session of "the Big Board" in San Francisco on November 11, 1870, twenty shares of the Belcher mine immediately south of the Crown Point sold for $2.75 per share. A trifling ten shares of the Crown Point changed hands at $2.50, making it worth $57.50 per foot, an appalling decline for a mine that had been worth more than $1,000 per foot exactly four years before. The market was as flat as one of Nevada's dry lakebeds. Management planned to run one last puffing operation to allow insiders to ditch their stock at a slightly advanced rate and then stop the pumps and abandon the mine. From a point 360 feet east of the shaft in the mine's long eastward crosscut, Superintendent Jones and Foreman Hank Smith chose to drift south at 1,100 feet, along the lode's footwall—about the only place they hadn't looked. No ore had been found on the footwall since the west stratum ore had terminated against it more than 600 feet above. However, the southern portion of the Crown Point hadn't been explored much below that level. The drift went 200 feet south in hard, gray, barren porphyry—at significant expense. Then the character of the rock changed. The color of the porphyry lightened. The vein matter became more shattered, crumbly, and streaked with reddish lines of rust. Stripes of quartz and clay began cutting the porphyry. Two hundred and thirty-nine feet south of the eastward crosscut, the drift encountered a "well-defined clay seam." Hank Smith summoned Superintendent Jones from San Francisco to view the development. Beyond the clay wall, the miners broke into a body of crumbly, creamy white quartz containing pockets of ore. Jones reassigned the miners who'd made the find to other parts of the mine and replaced them with more tight-lipped men. He stopped admitting outsiders to the mine.

In the last week of November, Crown Point shares rose from three to six dollars per share, on small volumes. Action churned hotter in other mines. On the last day of the month, volume rocketed to 1,020 shares and for some of the sales, prices pushed as high as eight dollars per share. Word leaked on December 1. Mary Jane Simpson, the *San Francisco Chronicle's* lively "Lady Correspondent" in Virginia City, reported "the discovery of ore upon the 1,100-foot level of the Crown Point, south of the shaft, and toward the Belcher." Simpson noted the unexplored nature of the ground in that section of both mines, but she'd long since lost faith in mines managed by what she called "the Sharon dynasty"—"purchasers of the advanced price will probably lose their money," she added.

Mary Jane Simpson didn't know the exact details of what had happened underground, few did, but a crosscut on the 1,100-foot level revealed a 14-foot quartz body that contained "a vein of fine ore nearly two feet wide." Small "stringers of rich ore" spiderworked the rest of the quartz mass. To Jones and Smith, the small detached veins displayed a tendency to unite as the drift went south. Crown Point stock almost doubled again on December 1, to thirteen dollars, and more than 3,000 of the mine's 12,000 shares changed hands. Traders bought and sold another 4,000 Crown Point shares over the next two days and the price climbed to sixteen dollars.

Through the next week, Crown Point prices fluctuated on contradictory rumors from "above." One said there had been "no strike in the mine to justify the excitement." Someone "supposed" to be in the know described the discovery to the *Territorial Enterprise* as "likely to prove of permanent value."

As Mary Jane Simpson explained in her next letter, written on December 8 and published three days later in the *San Francisco Chronicle* under the headline "Virginia Gossip: How the Stockholders of the Mines Are Robbed," she thought the whole thing was a put-up job by the Bank Ring designed to gull the unsuspecting public into paying the Crown Point's most recent assessment. Her next letter from Virginia City described James Fair's wife, Theresa, "a handsome brunette" wearing pink satin trimmed with pointed lace, a diamond necklace, and "other ornaments," as the belle of the annual Bachelor's Ball, before she delivered another jeremiad against the "swindlers" aiming to deceive the public into buying mine stock.

According to Mary Jane Simpson, William Sharon and his Bank Ring cronies had made "the very name of Nevada stink in the nostrils of honest men all over the world." However, in this case she'd misread the tea leaves, or been misinformed. The deep strike in the Crown Point promised so well that it had motivated Crown Point superintendent Jones to betray his Bank Ring masters and bid to seize control of the mine.

Jones had chosen not to share the immediate details of the strike with William Sharon—or, it goes without saying, with any of the Crown Point's common stockholders. (He'd likely deceived his foreman about his intentions, too; Hank Smith would remain in Sharon's employ.) Instead of telling William Sharon, Jones had bought every Crown Point share he could afford, likely in the last days of November. He wasn't a moneyed man, however. The shares he acquired barely dented the Bank Ring's control, which the ring had maintained without interruption since 1867. Jones went to San Francisco and related the mine's promising development to a cadre of carefully chosen speculators. They bought on Jones's promise to bear all losses in exchange for one-half of all profits. Jones also told his brother-in-law, Alvinza Hayward. (They'd married sisters.) A successful mine investor since the early days of the Gold Rush, Hayward was an original incorporator of the Union Mill and Mining Company. He kept large deposits at the Bank of California, and he'd served as a trustee of many Bank of California operations, among them the Crown Point, the Kentuck, the Savage, the Hale & Norcross, and the Gould & Curry mines, the California Steam Navigation Company, and the White Pine Water Company, but despite Hayward's wealth and influence and years of service, he hadn't cracked the innermost circle of the Bank Ring—that remained a Mills-Ralston-Sharon triumvirate. That may have created a wellspring of resentment. Hayward had almost certainly provided the influence that first opened Comstock opportunities to John Percival Jones. On Jones's advice, Hayward made massive purchases of Crown Point stock, likely starting in the first days of December 1870.

The Crown Point's stock price marked time through the rest of December, trading between $13 and $17.25. Aiming to accumulate as much of it as possible, Jones did everything he could to retard development of the strike. Sometime in December or early January, Jones told the speculators who'd backed him that his son, a consumptive, was "dangerously ill" in the eastern states. Since a telegram might summon him to his son's bedside at any time, he asked them to close out the shares they'd held on his account. He needed the money, he said. To prove it, Jones sold some of the Crown Point shares he held in his own name. Although Jones professed confidence in the Crown Point, his partners-of-opportunity received the story with raised eyebrows. "Jones's sick child" became a catchphrase among them. They took it as a fiction concocted to justify his stock sales and assumed the truly ailing patient was the Crown Point mine. Most sold out, turning a large profit both for themselves and, under the terms of their profit-sharing arrangement, also for Jones.

Many of Jones's now former partners took short positions against the mine. Jones plowed his gains into buying as many Crown Point shares as possible. The mine's price continued to rise, and Jones paid for his share of the mine "out of the pockets of the unhappy shorts." The only one of Jones's initial backers who maintained faith in Jones's representations of the Crown Point mine through the "sick child" affair was his brother-in-law, Alvinza Hayward.

The stock eked above $20 in early January, then leaped to $40 on rumors of $400 rock in a massive ore body. The next day, the *San Francisco Chronicle* reported that Alvinza Hayward owned four thousand Crown Point shares, and although the paper claimed to appreciate the significance of a Comstock ore body farther below the Gould & Curry croppings than any ever discovered, it also persisted in reporting, "The body of ore upon which the rise in Crown Point is based is said to be small, and although of fair grade is by no means sufficient to warrant the heavy advance in the stock." In a letter sent from Virginia City a few days later, Mary Jane Simpson offered a mock biblical parable about an Assyrian king who had foisted stock in a barren mine on an unsuspecting public before the last, final crash. To her, it was all "sharp practice to fleece the flats." Crown Point stock sank back into the mid-$20s. The acid dripping from her pen clouded her judgment. She didn't appreciate the significance of what she herself had already reported—Superintendent Jones "had bought stock for himself without notifying his superior officer of his discovery." A crack had appeared in the Bank Ring.

For reasons likely having much to do with Jones and Hayward's treachery, William Sharon was slow to cotton to Crown Point developments and to understand that two trusted associates had broken ranks to operate on their own account. Nor did Sharon occupy a strong position from which to fight back, for unknown to outsiders, the Bank of California was in serious trouble—and had been since the summer of 1869.

The bank's difficulties had much to do with the profligate habits of its cashier, William Chapman Ralston. In a land famous for boosters, California never had another one like Billy Ralston. Outgoing, positive, and gregarious, he believed in the Golden State's glorious future with all his heart and he backed that belief with cash money. Ralston was tremendously popular in California, a major celebrity. None of the vitriol that clung to William Sharon or Darius Mills ever stuck to Billy Ralston, although beneath the bonhomie he was every inch as much the monopolist and schemer as his associates. Nor did Ralston draw much distinction between his own personal finances and those of the Bank of California. In many ways, William Ralston *was* the Bank of California, and he splashed money about supporting all manner of projects.

Ralston involved himself and the bank in sugar refining, woolen mills, carriage making, a watch company, Alaska seal fisheries, a dry dock facility at Hunter's Point on the bay shore south of San Francisco, massive wineries and vineyards, a colossal hydraulic gold-mining operation at the North Broomfield mine, quicksilver mines throughout the Coast Range, tobacco cultivation south of San Jose, railroad-building ventures both small and large, the manufacture of rolling stock, advancing capital to wheat speculators and exporters, assaying and gold refining for the San Francisco Mint, sponsoring the ornate and extravagant California Theater on Bush Street, and in his pet New Montgomery Street real estate development project. Ralston spent wildly on his Belmont mansion twenty-two miles south of San Francisco and entertained with legendary opulence.

While the California economy expanded during and after the Civil War, things had gone well for the Bank of California, but a series of hammer blows beginning in the spring of 1869 seriously stressed what for years had been the coast's leading financial institution—the loss of the Hale & Norcross to Mackay and the other Irishmen; the deadly fire that stoppered the output of the Crown Point, Yellow Jacket, and Kentuck mines; gold currency gushing out of California to meet overseas and eastern demands; and most painful of all, the economic depression that had arrived with the railroad. The confluence of hardships shoved the bank toward the cliff edge. Only a dodgy overnight exchange Ralston perpetrated with two associates in which they physically carried more than two *tons* of unminted gold bullion in the vaults of the Bank of California in relays to the mint and returned with an equal gross value of coined $20 double eagles kept the bank solvent in July 1869. Less than two months later, the bank staggered through the turbulent aftermath of New York speculators Jay Gould and Jim Fisk's attempt to corner the nation's gold market—Gould and Fisk had furthered their schemes by corrupting crucial members of the Grant administration. Impacts of the "Black Friday" collapse of the gold corner reverberated through the economy for months. Eastern competition slammed Ralston's manufacturing investments. Ralston lavished enormous sums on the New Montgomery Street development while the San Francisco real estate market sank to death's door. Ralston faced personal ruin, and since the people of California so closely associated him with the Bank of California, any collapse of William Ralston had the potential to crater public confidence in the entire institution.

Sharon met Ralston at the height of the troubles. As Sharon told an associate four years later, he found Ralston "spreading out in his big way." A review of private records revealed that Ralston owed the Bank of California $3 million, a colossal sum. Ralston didn't have that kind of money. William Sharon, however, did have, as he told it, "a little matter of $4 million" socked away, and he hadn't forgotten that Ralston's aid had seen him through rough times in 1864. Sharon fronted enough money to Ralston to spare Ralston the embarrassment of making an "accounting of how much he had overdrawn." Sharon said it gave him "great pleasure" to return the favor and "get even" with Ralston, an odd manner of phrasing aid to his closest business associate.

The rescue may have soaked up the reserves with which Sharon could have defended the Crown Point. History doesn't record at what point Sharon learned that his long-time associates had turned their coats. He might not have learned until it was too late for him to stave off the raid. Whatever the case, Sharon did manage to possess himself of 4,100 of the Crown Point's 12,000 shares without provoking the sort of pitched public battle that had haunted his capture of the Hale & Norcross in 1868. That wasn't enough—Jones and Hayward had already swept up more than half of the mine's 12,000 shares. The Crown Point slipped from Sharon's clutches.

On March 1, 1871, the value of Crown Point shares jumped, taking the price to $55 and pushing the mine's per-foot value over $1,000—where it had been in 1866. From there, nothing slowed the Crown Point's ascent. Twenty days later, shares reached $160. In May, they passed $300—a staggering 120-fold increase in the seven months since its November low.

Even though he'd lost the Crown Point, William Sharon played another card. He judged it probable the new ore body would stretch south into Belcher ground. He decided to gamble on that mine rather than contest the Crown Point. So while the Crown Point held the eyes of the mining world, Sharon acquired large quantities of Belcher stock—quietly—and just as Mackay, Flood, Fair, and O'Brien had done when they spirited the Hale & Norcross out from under his nose, Sharon pulled off his Belcher coup with a perfect poker face. By the time people noticed, Sharon owned nearly the entire mine.

The Belcher gamble was a stroke of genius, one that would give a new lease on life to the Bank of California—and to William Ralston.

As for John Mackay and his partners, they missed the Crown Point and Belcher opportunities entirely. The wonderful bonanza developed in those two mines pushed them into a very distant third place. The Irishmen hoped to remain significant players in the battles to control the Comstock Lode. To push themselves back to the forefront, they'd have to make up a lot of lost ground.

CHAPTER 13

The Consolidated
Virginia Mine

A mule team hauls an enormous load of ore
to a mine's weigh station.

The ore deposits in the great Comstock Lode are distributed somewhat as are the plums in à Christmas pudding, the vein matter is the dough and the bunches of ore are the plums. As long as you keep gouging about in the dough, you are liable to come upon a plum, or a cucumber, or if you are in big luck, a great pumpkin.

—"Consolidated Virginia," *Territorial Enterprise*,
August 31, 1871

enuine warmth had sprung up between John Mackay and his daughter Eva in the four years they'd known each other. Mackay always treated Eva as one of his own, but now that he had a son in the household who occupied so much of his and her mother's attention, Mackay worried Eva would feel as if she'd lost her place in his heart and become unimportant. Thinking it might provide her a measure of permanent emotional security, John Mackay formally adopted her on Christmas Day, 1870, and gave her his name. She became Eva Bryant *Mackay*. John and Louise never tried to erase her connection to her father—they kept a likeness of Dr. Bryant in her room—but in reality John Mackay had become a much more stable and loving parental presence in her life than the late doctor ever managed to be.

The family had returned to Virginia City after Louise recovered from delivering Willie. The clanging of fire alarms jarred them from bed on the last night of January 1871. John Mackay stood outside to assess the danger. Wild, raging winds drove leaping flames through portions of D and E streets at a safe distance from their home. For a time, it looked as though the whole eastern portion of the city would be lost. Only the reckless courage of the firefighters prevented catastrophe. Firemen manned hoses on rooftops in billowing clouds of smoke, silhouetted against the flames leaping into the darkness. They sprayed down adjacent buildings while orange tongues licked up through the shingles around them. Gawkers yelled at them to save themselves, and at the last minute, they did. Before it was subdued, the blaze swept away twenty-two houses, burned two men to death, and destroyed $75,000 worth of property, much of it uninsured since it occurred in a portion of the town in which insurance agents preferred not to take risks—at least ones of the financial variety. The *Territorial Enterprise* explained: "When we say that most of the houses were occupied by women of the town, we will be understood."

A winter blessedly free from smallpox enhanced the popularity of social gatherings, and two days after the fire, three businessmen whose establishments had been saved by the valiant efforts of Knickerbocker Engine Company Number 5 sponsored a "grand blowout" at the enginehouse—a fine lunch and "all the wine, lager beer and other liquors that could be disposed of." While the firemen did themselves proud for a second time in forty-eight hours, sustaining an attack upon the beverage refreshments "of some four hours duration," a new passion for roller-skating was diverting interest from Virginia City's traditional winter pastimes of sleighing and "coasting." (The velocipede craze had faded.) A company erected roller-skating rinks at the Miners' Union and Armory halls on B Street. Washoeites took to the new sport quickly, gliding on steel wheels with great daring. Men, women, and children thronged the rinks day and night and, in the words of the *Territorial Enterprise*, soon learned to "perform feats that excite both the admiration and terror of the new beginners."

San Francisco Chronicle correspondent Mary Jane Simpson called Virginia City "skating mad," and the *Territorial Enterprise* felt secure identifying roller skating as "the most popular sport that has ever been introduced in this place." The number of men ambling about town with splinted wrists and arm slings also caught the newspaper's eye. "Skating is an amusement with which the surgeons are not likely to find fault," it noted.

If nine-year-old Eva was one of the many Comstock children experimenting with the new sport, it must have been hard for John and Louise Mackay to watch her lame hip hamper her progress. Mackay had engaged the best medical men in Virginia City and San Francisco to examine it. None offered any solution. Mackay and his wife weren't prepared to abandon hope until they'd consulted the best European doctors, however. They'd heard of a surgeon in Paris who might be able to help. To that end, thirty-nine-year-old John Mackay did something in the spring of 1871 that he might never have done before in his life—he took a vacation.

Professionally, it came at a good time. He and James Fair had opened an eighth station in the Hale & Norcross's Fair Shaft 1,251 feet below the surface, deeper than any other mine in Nevada.

The confidence Mackay had in his partners allowed him to step away from the Comstock for a season. Taking Willie's nurse, Alice O'Grady, along with them, the Mackays traversed the continent to New York City on the new railroad, through vast swaths of America none of them had ever seen. The city had changed tremendously in the twenty years since either John or Louise Mackay had seen it. Many touchstones of their youth had vanished into the city's unstoppable growth, and new landmarks had sprung up that they'd never seen before, paramount among them huge Central Park, begun in 1858 and at last nearing completion. The city's population had nearly doubled, from just over 515,000 in 1850 to just under 950,000 in 1870, a large percentage of whom lived crammed into seething immigrant tenements not much changed from the ones Mackay had endured in his youth. Newer tenements were built of brick rather than wood, but they were just as crowded and unhealthy. New York's economic muscle had grown to dominate the nation's financial and capital markets, and with three railways converging on the city in addition to the old water route through the Erie Canal to the Great Lakes, port volumes had exploded. The biggest undertaking in New York in 1871 was the construction of an enormous suspension bridge over the East River to connect Brooklyn and New York. No bridge on its scale had ever been built, anywhere in the world, and aside from the engineering particulars, which John Mackay surely found fascinating, plans for bridge construction called for the southern edge of the East River Bridge's New York' City approach to be built right through the site of the rickety tenement in which he'd grown up. John, Louise, Eva, and eight-month-old Willie departed New York for Liverpool aboard the steamship *City of Brooklyn* on April 8, 1871.

The family tarried in London. On the other side of the English Channel, France struggled to recover from the stunning defeat it had received in the recently concluded Franco-Prussian War. A conservative provisional government formed from the wreckage of France. Parisian socialists and anarchists had revolted against it in late March, formed a revolutionary government—the Paris Commune—and fortified the city. The Commune gripped Paris through April and May, and with violence seeming both imminent and inevitable, Paris seemed too dangerous to visit.

Fortunately, London was its own reward. With more than 3 million inhabitants, London dwarfed New York, the capital of an empire at its apogee sprouting modern and spectacular public spaces and architecture—Trafalgar Square; the new Houses of Parliament at Westminster; Big Ben, just twelve years old; and the Royal Albert Hall, which hosted its first concert a few weeks before the Mackays arrived. Careful tourists never saw the poverty and squalor in the East End's immigrant and working-class neighborhoods.

The Paris violence climaxed while the Mackays enjoyed London. The French regular army attacked the Commune. Thousands died in a week of bitter street fighting and summary executions that followed. Mackay took his family to Paris after the fighting subsided. The city showed the scars of the recent violence, and the surgeon they'd come so far to see wasn't to be found. He'd probably fled the city, along with many other middle- and upper-class Parisians. Instead, the Mackays enjoyed what they could of Paris, then made a grand tour of Southern France and the lakes of Northern Italy.

Sometime during their European travels in 1871, John Mackay broke away from his family and returned to Ireland, compelled to learn if there was anybody from the old days to whom he could repay a former kindness from his store of current good fortune. He hadn't seen the country in more than thirty years. The sadness of Ireland caught him unprepared. Everyone he'd known had either emigrated or vanished into the havoc of the famine and the ruinous poverty that continued to haunt the island.

Only the timeless green of the Irish countryside connected him to what had once been home. He rejoined his family shaken.

In September, John and Louise finally consulted the surgeon about Eva's hip. The doctor thought he knew an operation that could help the child, but didn't want her recovering from surgery through the gloomy Parisian fall and winter. He suggested Eva spend the winter gathering strength in Mediterranean sunshine and have the operation in the coming spring. Mackay decided that his family should stay in France while he returned to the Comstock. He'd come back to Paris the following June and see Eva through the operation.

Mackay was becoming a worldly man. He must have felt infused with confidence by his mining success and the expanding breadth of his experience. He and Louise brushed against noble European "society," but as Mackay surely saw, in his life he'd done more than all but the most exceptional European aristocrats. Much more. And as was equally apparent, he could do more, and that was how a man was measured on the mining frontier. Impeccably dressed in suits made by the finest Savile Row tailors, Mackay had fulfilled some of his life's ambitions in Europe—he'd attended some of the best symphonies, operas, and theaters with his wife, enjoying the finest seats. Together they'd seen some of the world's great art. The cultural experiences moved Mackay tremendously and whetted his appetite for more. He'd come a long way from the rag-patched newsboy jostling for a view in the galleries of the Bowery Theater.

On October 4, 1871, the *Territorial Enterprise* noted John Mackay's return to Virginia City after "a ramble of some months' duration through the Atlantic States and Europe." The newspaper thought it looked "as if the cuisine everywhere agreed with him."

Much had happened on the Comstock during Mackay's seven-month absence. The Crown Point strike had evolved from what the *Mining & Scientific Press* described in April as the best body of ore ever discovered "in that section of the Comstock" into an "absolutely immense" bonanza that dwarfed anything else ever dug out of the lode. Mining sharps regarded the discovery with "a degree of astonishment . . . not far removed from awe."

There had been other excitements during Mackay's absence, not all of them so positive. Virginia City had sprouted a Vigilance Committee, "No. 601" or "the 601" as they styled themselves, and they'd hung two men to death, one of whom deserved it without question—Arthur Perkins, a piano player and "sport" who'd shot an unarmed miner in cold blood from point-blank range in front of many witnesses. The bullet went into the victim's eye and blew blood and brains out the back of his head and all over the cigar stand at the entrance of the International Saloon. An "epidemic of crime appears to be raging, which only copious doses of hemp, liberally applied, will check!" thundered a *Chronicle* editor from the safety of his desk in San Francisco. "Virginia wants weeding out," added Mary Jane Simpson.

Weeding began that same night. At 1:00 a.m., seventy masked and armed vigilantes forced their way into the Storey County Jail, held the guards at gunpoint, and rousted Perkins. They marched him to the old Armory Hall, tried and convicted him, and hung him from a beam in an abandoned building in the old Mexican works, all within an hour. A card pinned on his body read, "Arthur Perkins, Hung by Vigilance Committee No. 601."

In the aftermath of the hanging, a number of suspicious characters received "601" notices inviting them to leave town, among them George Kirk. A Sunday school teacher George Kirk most definitely was not. He'd served time in the California penitentiary for an attempted murder in 1858, served time for burglary in Nevada, and although he'd worked in the Imperial mine after his release, the 601 judged him a "rowdy" too friendly with the man whose neck they'd recently stretched. They told him to leave town.

Kirk heeded the warning and went to Austin, but he didn't stick. He returned to Virginia City. He scurried to Carson City after receiving a second 601 missive suggesting he leave town. Kirk had a fondness for liquor, and word of the drunken threats he leveled against the Vigilance Committee filtered back to Virginia City. Kirk also nursed an affection for "Dutch Mary," who kept a bawdy house opposite City Hall on North C Street. He'd been bold enough to return to see her on at least one other occasion.

One night in mid-July, news went through Virginia City that Kirk had returned yet again. Two men lured him from Dutch Mary's house about an hour before midnight. A few dozen steps down the street, forty or fifty men converged on Kirk from the shadows and marched him away. Later that night, a group of lawmen searching with lanterns found Kirk's body dangling from the trestle work of the elevated car track of the Sierra Nevada mine beyond the northern outskirts of town. A handkerchief covered his eyes. Cords bound his hands and feet. A note pinned to his chest read, "George B. Kirk, 601 Committee."

Dutch Mary's real name was Mary Smith, or at least that was the name she used at legal proceedings. According to the testimony she gave the coroner's jury, George Kirk had dropped by to make her a gift of a dog he'd brought up from Carson City.

Upon Mackay's return, it couldn't have taken long for someone to rush up and tell him about the Comstock's latest scandal—the Belcher had been caught watering its stock. Eight more feet had been found in the mine than showed when measured by surface surveys.

Mackay might have looked puzzled, but it was true. There *were* eight new feet in the Belcher. They belonged to the pair of mules Superintendent Hank Smith had sent down to the 1,100-foot level to solve a nagging problem. John Mackay's reaction went unrecorded, but the *Territorial Enterprise* reported many persons "bit" on the joke.

While Belcher miners waited for their incline to reach the level of the ore body, all the ore they extracted from the Belcher's share of the bonanza on the 1,100-foot level had to go up the Yellow Jacket's South Shaft. One of the biggest obstacles they faced was the 100-foot difference in elevation between the track floor in the ore body at 1,100 feet and the South Shaft's 1,000-foot station. The incline gained the full elevation over the course of 500 linear feet. Pushing a 1,200-pound carload of ore up the incline required the strength of several men, and even then, most men could manage to do it only a few times in the course of a ten-hour shift. No man could sustain the labor for anything close to the entire time. Superintendent Smith decided the job called for a pair of stout American mules, one to work with each shift of miners. To that end, Smith bought a mule called "Old Pete" and his female companion.

Getting the mules into the mine presented another challenge. The dimensions of a standing adult mule didn't conform to those of a mine cage. No mule could be trusted to hold still during the descent, and Smith couldn't find anybody fool enough to share a small space over a 1,000-foot drop with a mule who might lose its temper.

Hank Smith concocted a plan to lower the mules into the mine dangling from one of the Yellow Jacket cages, and he decided to send Old Pete down first. After full darkness on September 28—a time selected to ease the animal's transition to sunless existence—miners lashed Old Pete's forelegs together and did the same with his hind legs, drew his legs against his body, and confined him in a strong canvas cover that held his legs tight.

The engineer eased the cage up close to the sheaves, drew tension into the ropes supporting Old Pete, and swung the mule out over the abyss. Trussed up in canvas and dangling from the cage, Old Pete resembled "a bed-tick stuffed with straw." When excess motion quieted, the engineer slowly lowered the cage. Much to everyone's astonishment, Old Pete stayed quiet and docile through the entire descent. One thousand feet below, miners took him by the tail and hauled him onto the station landing. They untied him with trepidation. Freed, Old Pete staggered to his feet, got his bearings, and ambled to a big pile of barley and hay laid out on the landing. He buried his snout in the feed without making the slightest fuss.

The miners soon put him to work, and Hank Smith's plan worked to perfection. Old Pete proved capable of hauling a train of four loaded ore cars up the incline. Old Pete learned the routine to such an extent that he did the work without halter or bridle, turning around of his own accord at both ends of the route. To house Old Pete in what the *Enterprise* called "the regions of darkness," Smith rigged a comfortable stable on the Belcher's "eleven hundred" complete with stalls, hay racks, and other "upper-world" accoutrements. All went smoothly, and Smith lowered the female mule a few nights later. The "jolly miners" greeted her arrival with applause and comic congratulations and christened her "Mary Jane Simpson" in cruel homage to the *San Francisco Chronicle*'s Comstock correspondent who'd expended so many column inches disparaging the ore strike the mule would work.

There had been "horses" of worthless porphyry in the Comstock mines since their original location, but mules were something entirely new, and the jokes flowed. Wags accounted for a minor downturn in Belcher stock by claiming Mary Jane Simpson "had kicked the ore so far into the east country rock" that the Belcher had to sink a new shaft in order to reach it. The *Territorial Enterprise* imagined "many long powwows" between Old Pete and Mary Jane Simpson "in regard to the nature of the place in which they find themselves," and since both mules had been lowered into the mine at night, coming "to the conclusion that it is a confounded long time until sunrise." In less frivolous news, the *Enterprise* also supposed both animals would "end their days" in the mine.

Belcher output leaped with Old Pete and Mary Jane Simpson delivering ore cars to the Yellow Jacket's South Shaft. The mine returned $310,000 in October and expected the November number to exceed $400,000. As if to repay William Sharon for John Percival Jones's treachery, Belcher ore proved "singularly rich in gold," and although the two mines shared about equally in the volume of the ore body, Belcher ore proved more valuable per ton.

The Belcher raised 5,853 tons of ore in December 1871, which was about all the rock Old Pete and Mary Jane Simpson could move. Hank Smith sent a third mule down to join them in mid-January. The Crown Point/Belcher bonanza catapulted Sharon, Jones, and Hayward into a realm of Comstock wealth and power hitherto unknown and shifted the lode's center of gravity away from the Chollar-Potosi and the Hale & Norcross, where Mackay, Fair, Flood, and O'Brien still controlled what had been one of the Comstock's leading mines since early 1869. A series of underground floods in the lower levels of the Hale & Norcross stalled work and increased costs. The ore at the bottom of the mine grew baser and less valuable. Thousands of tons of millable ore remained in the mine, but the end of the bonanza was in sight.*

Not all of the Firm's problems were subterranean, however. They also had a problem with water—or lack of it—that commanded Mackay's attention when he returned from Europe.

Water had always been a problem on the Comstock. Water flowing from the mouths of drainage adits had provided the bulk of the local water supply since the early days. As the towns grew, the local water company bought water from mining companies and drove adits into Mount Davidson over a distance of a few miles north and south of town for the express purpose of finding water. They flumed the seepage to storage tanks and piped it to the local mines, mills, businesses, and residents—all of whom paid handsomely for the service. Since the industrial demands of the mines and mills trumped the thirst of the towns, the water company could only provide the populace with about six hours of running water per day. (Private vendors also peddled water door to door.) The local water sufficed until Washoe suffered two dry winters in a row. The Comstock received less than average rainfall in 1869–70, and the winter of 1870–71 was one of the driest since 1850. That was a problem for Mackay and his partners, because they'd bought control of the Virginia and Gold Hill Water Company from William Sharon and the Bank Ring. Sharon had controlled the water company to assure the supply of water to those of his Union Company mills distant from the Carson River. (Mills consumed large quantities of water in their boilers, wet-crushing ore, and in the slurries that filled their amalgamating pans.) The Virginia & Truckee Railroad and consolidation of the Union Company's milling interests onto the banks of the Carson River around Empire City changed Sharon's

* The mine paid its last dividend in the spring of 1872.

equation. The water company became less critical to his operations. To rid himself of a headache, he sold the water company to Mackay, Flood, Fair, and O'Brien sometime in the year before July 12, 1870. Most of the Firm's mills were in Gold Cañon and Silver City, still dependent on the water company. The larger engines and boilers brought to the mines and mills in recent years consumed correspondingly larger quantities of water. The local supply had just sufficed until the drought winter of 1870–71.

In the summer of 1871, Mount Davidson ran dry above the level of the towns. Water shortages idled many Comstock mills, forcing mines to scale back ore production and leading the water company to reduce the supply of water to the town to three hours a day—at such a trickle that it took twenty minutes to fill a quart pitcher of water. Mary Jane Simpson blamed the shortage on the water company monopoly. (Holding the water company responsible for the drought seemed a trifle ungenerous, even for the *Chronicle*.) Mackay, Fair, Flood, and O'Brien pondered the situation that fall and decided to solve the problem for all time.

The nearest practicable and plentiful supply of water at higher elevation than Virginia City was in the eastern Sierras, in the peaks of the Carson Range between Lake Tahoe and Carson City. Getting that water to Virginia City meant building a pipeline in the form of a U-shaped inverted siphon that would drop the water from the Carson Range, push it across the seven-mile-wide Washoe Valley, and force it up to the crest of the Virginia Range. To do it, the pipeline would have to be capable of withstanding a 1,720-foot head of pressure. At that time, the greatest drop sustained anywhere in the world was at a hydraulic mine in California that fell 930 feet. When someone asked James Flood if such a feat were even possible, Flood shrugged. "Anything can be done nowadays," he said. "The only question is—will it pay?"

The four Irishmen decided that it would. To study and survey the problem and design a solution, they hired the best hydraulic engineer on the Pacific Slope—Hermann Schussler, who had built the Spring Valley Water Works that supplied San Francisco.

But water was small beer compared to ore. Nothing to do with water had the power to boost the four Irishmen into the sphere of Sharon, Hayward, and Jones, and they surely knew it.

John Mackay could easily have lived for the rest of his life on what he and his partners had raised from the Hale & Norcross and earned reducing ores in their mills. If they went "all in" on another mine and found no ore, they risked losing everything they'd worked so hard to gain. But the West was no place for pikers. Taking big risks was what a man did on the Pacific Coast. If risks didn't pan out, he went bankrupt. Pacific Coast culture took pride in being "game." If Mackay went broke, he'd work his way back. He was forty-one years old, in the prime of his life. The thought of giving himself over to idleness and retirement seemed repugnant, an utter waste.

No one knew for sure whether the Comstock held other deep bonanzas, but if it did, Mackay judged that he knew a likely place to find one.

He and his partners turned their attention to a neglected 1,310-foot stretch of ground at the north end of the lode between the Best & Belcher and the Ophir that hadn't yielded any ore since the early 1860s, but nor had it ever been explored more than 500 feet below the surface. Most of that ground belonged to the Consolidated Virginia Mining Corporation, or simply, the Con. Virginia.

One of the largest quartz masses on the Comstock choked the upper levels of that ground. Back in the early days, six small mines had divided that stretch of the Comstock Lode, and it had been considered one of the most promising sections. Two of the mines, the Central (No. 1) and the California, had yielded pockets of ore in the first years. After those played out, the mines honeycombed the quartz mass in their upper levels in furious, expensive, and ultimately futile searches for ore. Disappointed, the owners of those six mines slogged along for the next three years, too poor to develop their mines, loath to sell out for less than top-dollar prices, and afraid to sell stock to raise capital for fear of losing control. Murky ownership chains and poorly defined boundaries left over from the chaos of the early days further sapped development energy.

A January 1867 letter to the *Daily Alta California* lamented the lack of energy expended in that portion of the lode. "Why is it [that those mines] are today lying idle for want of energy and capital, when there is every indication of untold wealth existing in deeper levels than those thus far obtained? If those Companies . . . would all work in a comprehensive and systematic manner, and sink a large shaft [there is a good chance] that this part of the Comstock would swell the annual shipments of bullion [five] million dollars." Many Comstockers accused the owners of playing "dog in the manger" with potentially valuable assets they couldn't or wouldn't use themselves. A stirring raised expectations in June 1867, when William Sharon and the Bank Ring organized the merger and incorporation of three of those mines—the California, the White & Murphy, and the Dick Sides—into "The Consolidated Virginia Mining Company," with 1,010 feet and 1,160 shares. The dust settled, and the new corporation did nothing. "Why do [they] not sink a prospecting shaft to the eastward on a line with the new works of the other leading companies?" wondered the frustrated *Territorial Enterprise*. The mine owned more than a thousand feet "in the heart of the great lead, yet [made] not the slightest move toward its development."

The Con. Virginia bestirred itself again to recapitalize a year after its incorporation, raising the number of shares by a factor of ten, to 11,600. The new stock appeared on the market in the last days of May 1868, trading at around ten dollars per share. "Wonder when they will begin sinking a shaft?" asked the *Territorial Enterprise*.

Not for nearly another year would the Consolidated Virginia start digging. Starting from a point more than 1,000 feet east of the croppings around the time of the Irish takeover of the Hale & Norcross and the terrible mine fire, the shaft went down roughly on a line with the other second-line shafts—the Ophir's, the Bonner Shaft of the Gould & Curry, the Savage's E Street Shaft, and the Fair Shaft at the Hale & Norcross. The Con. Virginia kept sinking, and its stock price kept falling, dipping to two dollars per share in September 1869. The mine suspended work in mid-January 1870 with the shaft 500 feet deep. The owners spent a month debating whether to keep sinking or drift back to the ledge and prospect for ore. They opted to drift for the ledge.

The Con. Virginia spent the rest of 1870 and all of 1871 searching for ore above 500 feet. Like clockwork, Con. Virginia management released optimistic reports about the progress of their drifts and crosscuts. The mine's trustees levied assessments every three months, also like clockwork. Con. Virginia's stock price dipped to $1⅝ in early 1871, which valued the entire mine at $18,500. The price crept up from that low, but for much of the year, while the development of the Crown Point/Belcher bonanza vaulted the value of those mines to many millions of dollars, the Con. Virginia was worth less than $100,000. The Consolidated Virginia had expended the better part of two years and well over $150,000 gouging around in the Comstock vein above its 500-foot station without finding anything of value.

In much the same manner as that in which they'd been attracted to the Hale & Norcross in 1869, Mackay and Fair thought the Con. Virginia wasn't being properly developed. There was only one way to know for sure, as every miner recognized—dig the mine to the deep levels and find out. As Mackay once told a friend, "There is no law in mining but the point of the pick."

Such deep prospecting would swallow immense quantities of expensive and unremunerative dead work, but even though the Consolidated Virginia had never returned a penny of dividends, to John Mackay and James Fair, the mine just seemed like a good mining gamble. When James Flood quietly began scooping up Con. Virginia stock on behalf of the Firm in late 1871, likely after Mackay's return from Europe and concurrent with the inception of their great water project, the price of Con. Virginia stock fluctuated between $8 and $12.50. It stayed in that range until late December, after which it steadily climbed to $20 on January 10, 1872. The next day, at the Consolidated Mining Company's annual election, the Firm owned about 75 percent of the company's stock, and the new slate of officers and trustees reflected their control—James Flood and William O'Brien joined the trustees and James Fair became the mine's superintendent. Behind them stood John Mackay, who never felt compelled to vest his authority in a formal title. Mackay was always content to let those pass to other men. When all the pieces had fallen into place, the Firm controlled all but 250 feet of the 1,310 feet of the Comstock Lode between the Best & Belcher and the Ophir, and all told, the acquisitions probably cost them just over $100,000.

The *Territorial Enterprise* thought the Irishmen had made a good investment. The obstacles were the astronomical cost of deep-level explorations and the high probability of failure. The Firm's new trustees levied a three-dollar-per-share assessment to finance development. They paid the assessments on the shares they owned from their own pockets, which cost them about another $26,000, but rather than immediately begin mining, Mackay, Fair, Flood, and O'Brien turned their attention to acquiring "all outstanding claims to ground within the company's lines" and "quieting" the murky title of their new mine. With the help of their lawyers, the Firm worked through the list of original locators and former owners to secure signatures on a comprehensive chain of quitclaim deeds. Mackay knew all the men from the early days. "Clearing title" was an expensive process—everybody had to be paid for their ink, even if years had passed since they'd sold their interests.

While Mackay, Flood, Fair, and O'Brien attended to that legal grunt work, developments in the Crown Point/Belcher bonanza and what it might portend for the deep levels of the other mines triggered the wildest mining stock excitement since the distant summer of 1863.

Late in the afternoon of Friday, February 2, 1872, a rumor hit San Francisco's Montgomery Street that the Savage had made a strike on the fourteen-hundred-foot level—exactly the sort of deep-level development the stock market had been primed to hear. Savage stock skyrocketed from the opening bell of the Saturday morning session amidst scenes of "the wildest confusion." The booming mine pulled all the other Washoe stocks up behind it. Before Saturday's closing bell rang at 3:15 p.m., "heavy buyers" had driven the price of the Savage from around $65 to $165. On Monday, the mine touched $235. Savage had nearly quadrupled in four days. The spectacular rise whipped San Francisco into a lather. All over the city, merchants forgot their wares. Lawyers cast aside clients. Doctors abandoned patients. Women ignored their children and lovers. Everyone frantically chased mining stocks. "Everything goes up and nothing goes down," said the *San Francisco Chronicle* in an article titled "Bubble of the Day"—"The mania pervades all classes of society." Ladies in hotel elevators asked after the Savage. Attempts to console mourners returning from a funeral ended in an inquiry about the closing price of Overman. "Bubble of the Day" joked that the first wail of a newborn babe was for "Succor," a mine near Silver City, and it included the Consolidated Virginia among its list of mines that had risen dramatically despite "no developments" of note. The "perceived future prospects" of the mines had driven the entire gain. All over the city, the question on everybody's lips was, "How are stocks?"

The *Mining & Scientific Press* and the *Territorial Enterprise* urged caution. Savage management had resorted to the old dodge of confining the miners who'd made the strike, and no outsiders had been permitted to inspect the new development.

Dan de Quille of the *Territorial Enterprise* inspected the Savage discovery on February 7 and thought it looked promising, although he also took care to remind his readers, "What may be ten feet ahead in any direction no man can tell." A few days later, "The Crown Point interest"—Alvinza Hayward and John Percival Jones—bought between eight thousand and nine thousand shares of Savage, more than half of the mine. Attempting to steer the public clear of mining investments, the *San Francisco Chronicle* ran a series of exposés detailing the "hogging game" played by the Bank Ring and other mine manipulators. The warnings went unheeded. Unheard, really, amidst the classic Pacific Coast furor for easy-made wealth.

The Crown Point and the Belcher accelerated the stock frenzy when they declared fifteen-dollar-per-share dividends for March. The Belcher kept upping production despite problems with the mule that had been sent down to help Mary Jane Simpson and Old Pete. The animal became increasingly obstinate and lazy until she refused work altogether. She had "made a strike, as it were, all by herself," joked the *Gold Hill Daily News*. In early March, a foreman hauled her out and lowered a replacement, also a female. Likely reflecting his views on the contentious topic of women's suffrage, a foreman named her "Susan B. Anthony."

Further complicating the relationship between the Belcher and Crown Point interests, both William Sharon and John Percival Jones declared their intention to campaign for Nevada's senatorial seat against James Nye, the former territorial governor who'd served in the U.S. Senate for the past eight years. Since the only voters for the United States Senate were members of the Nevada State Legislature, Nye's years of honorable service couldn't compete with the deep pockets of the mining magnates. He stepped aside. The campaign became a contest between two of the three richest men in Nevada for admittance to the world's most exclusive club—and Adolph Sutro, who also declared for the seat.

Political yowlings didn't check the booming market. Virginia City reflected the excitements in both mining and stocks, with thronged streets and sidewalks, crammed hotels, and boardinghouses full to overflowing. "Even in its palmiest days Virginia never presented a more lively appearance than at the present time," crowed the *Enterprise*.

The Savage peaked on April 25 on the release of information that the ore body it shared with the Hale & Norcross was "next in magnitude" to that found in the Crown Point and the Belcher. Those two regal mines sold for around $1,500 per share that day, which valued the Crown Point at a gobsmacking $30,000 per foot. Eighteen months before, nobody had wanted anything to do with either mine.

In its "Local Mining Summary for the Week Ending April 27, 1872," the *Gold Hill Daily News* declared: "The fact is this; the leading mines are not priced at all above their merits." Hundreds of miners, laborers, boardinghouse keepers, and even servant girls who'd had the courage to wager their small earnings early in the year discovered themselves financially independent. The most savvy had "realized the hard cash." The Crown Point declared a forty-dollar-per-share dividend for May, $800 per foot, "the largest dividend ever paid by any mine in the world." Recent developments in the lower levels of the Savage and Hale & Norcross seemed to promise a Virginia City counterpart to Gold Hill's deep bonanza. The fountains of optimism boiling up from the Comstock mines gave the *Gold Hill Daily News* the confidence to assure readers of its "Local Mining Summary" for the week ending Saturday, May 4, that there was "no particular danger of any sudden crash or panic in stocks."

The *News* would soon regret that statement.

"A sort of panic" hit San Francisco's Stock & Exchange Board on Tuesday morning, May 7. Prices plummeted. The Gould & Curry, the Yellow Jacket, and the Chollar-Potosi led the declines. Wild, sensational reports that gouged right to the core of the Comstock Lode's most festering wound broke after the Tuesday close: They claimed proof that the 1869 fire in the Crown Point, Kentuck, and Yellow Jacket had been deliberately set. The most volatile rumors called the fire a stock-bearing operation orchestrated by John Percival Jones to drive down the price of the stock. Jones had been the Crown Point's superintendent at the time of the fire.

According to Jones, it was a framing operation cooked up by William Sharon and some shady associates. Sharon's version told how he'd been approached four or five months before by a man claiming to have proof that Jones had started the fire. He repudiated "all other motives" besides "a desire to sift to the bottom" of what, "if true, was a great crime and to do no more than was his duty to do in justice to the public." The *Chronicle*'s issue sold so widely the newspaper had to print a second edition of five thousand extra copies, which were also "eagerly bought up."

Roiled by the "sensational account," the Wednesday stock market again "showed an appearance of panic," which ruined hundreds of men—and not a small number of "mud hens," too, as female plungers were known. To the *San Francisco Chronicle*, "the pallid faces, quivering lips, and muttered curses" on California and Montgomery streets "told the tale more plainly than words."

Some scorched speculators believed the mine-fire accusations were "a put-up job between Sharon and Jones to bear the stock market." The *Chronicle*'s same Wednesday article that aired the scandalous accusations blamed the stock market drop on the Sharon-Jones feud and the explosive rumors, either deliberately sensationalizing or not being careful enough to notice that the precipitous drop had started at the beginning of the Tuesday session, many hours before the rumors hit the public at 5:00 p.m., and that the value of Savage, Hale & Norcross, and Chollar-Potosi stock had leaked away about 20 percent of their value since April 25, a clear indication of faltering confidence.

"Above," in Gold Hill, the panic dominated conversation. In the eyes of the *Gold Hill News*, the crash was "dead set" against "one heavy operator, who has obtained control of several of the leading mines"—implying that Alvinza Hayward was being bear-attacked by William Sharon. If Sharon did attempt such a maneuver, it was one singularly damaging to his own interests, for mines controlled by William Sharon suffered the largest percentage declines on "Bomber Tuesday" and "Black Wednesday."

Cursory investigations exposed the spurious nature of the mine fire accusations. The man who'd made them had been fired by the very foreman he accused of helping Jones set the fire. Jones scraped through without damage. William Sharon wasn't so fortunate. Every observer and commentator with the notable exception of the *Gold Hill News* believed Sharon had encouraged the aspersions against Jones in the hope of political advantage. The *Territorial Enterprise* latched on to that belief like a bulldog onto a bear. "The devilish story is a fabrication from end to end," it bellowed, predicting that it would "recoil upon the head of him who gave it shape and utterance."

Through the subsequent fortnight, a day or two of hopeful stability alternated with painful market "earthquakes," "heavy falls," "market slaughters," and "steep declines." The *Chronicle* thought stock prices had dropped to "hell" in the morning session of Wednesday, May 15, "hell-er" during the afternoon session, and "the lowermost depths of the infernal region" after yet another agonizing fall on Thursday, May 16. They hadn't. The market's Culloden, its final massacre, came after the weekend, on Monday, May 20, when it "lost bottom altogether." The fall dropped many lesser mines out of the market entirely. In the *Chronicle's* florid description, the wrecks of ruined speculators were "strewn along the strand of California and Montgomery streets," their hulks "dismasted, dismantled, shattered" by the "hurricane of low prices and vanished margins." Fortunes had been annihilated. A funereal gloom hung over San Francisco's financial district. People trudged about with pale, haggard faces. Speculators didn't know it, but stocks had finally hit bedrock. From their April highs, most Comstock mines lost between 65 and 80 percent of their value. The *Chronicle* called the decline "the heaviest ever known in the San Francisco Stock Market." John Mackay's Consolidated Virginia holdings shriveled along with the rest. The mine fell from $120 to $30. An even 75 percent of its value evaporated.

The *San Francisco Chronicle* was obsessed with uncovering the machinations, manipulations, and backstage conspiracies that had supposedly provoked the market's rise and fall and congratulated itself for "discovering hidden motives and in tracing up cause and effect." The paper credited the "wild furore" to the Savage more than any other mine and characterized Jones and Hayward as "the Great Bulls" who'd sparked the boom, and labeled William Sharon "the Great Bear" trying to tear them down. The *Chronicle* took Sharon to task for refusing to "support" the values of "his" mines, implying that Sharon had somehow done wrong by refusing to buy shares of "his" mines offered for sale at inflated prices, and for throwing blocs of stock on the market at high prices. In essence, the newspaper blamed William Sharon for being a savvy speculator.

The *Chronicle* reporter who interviewed Sharon noted his modest black suit and perfectly coifed brown hair and asked him why the market had collapsed. "Well, sir," Sharon answered, "it's all comprised in a nutshell. When you blow up a bubble beyond its capacity, it's pretty sure to burst, ain't it? . . . They accuse me of pricking the bubble. That's not so. The overstrained concern wouldn't hold any more wind; that's all."

Sharon took the blame for destroying the hoped-for fortunes of thousands of hardworking men and women he'd somehow duped into risking their savings on mining shares. The *Territorial Enterprise* took after Sharon with a hatchet. On the last day of May, Goodman described Sharon's career in Nevada as one of "merciless rapacity," and accused him of being fastened "upon the vitals of the State like a hyena," of robbing stockholders "with an unscrupulousness that would have shamed a highwayman," and of converting the Bank of California from "an institution that should have been a public aid and blessing into an instrument of tyranny."

In contrast to Sharon, the evil monopolist feasting on the lifeblood of State, the *Enterprise* hailed Jones as "the Commoner" sympathetic to the woes of Nevada's laboring men, a patently ridiculous assertion considering that Jones was the third-richest man in the state, behind only Sharon and Alvinza Hayward. Sharon didn't possess the easy charisma, bonhomie, rude good humor, or political experience of Jones, however, and the characterizations stuck. Sharon the Monopolist versus Jones the Commoner. In mid-August, Sharon withdrew from the Senate race, citing ill health. The following January, the Nevada State Legislature sent John Percival Jones to the United States Senate, where he would serve for the next thirty years and earn a reputation as the most entertaining storyteller in the Senate. Adolph Sutro didn't garner a single vote.

He had, however, managed to raise more than $1 million selling tunnel stock through the efforts of a mine promoter in London. The man's diligent and effective efforts might have had something to do with Sutro's gifting him one share of tunnel stock for every four he sold. The money rejuvenated progress on the Sutro Tunnel. By the end of 1871, Sutro had three to four hundred men at work on his "big dig." Six months later, in

June 1872, the Tunnel was in 2,933 feet from its entrance in the Carson River Valley. While great events were happening beneath Virginia City and Gold Hill, more than 17,500 feet still separated Sutro's tunnel face from the Comstock Lode.

During the great stock excitement, while James Flood and William O'Brien led the effort to clear the title and acquire the small interests near the Con. Virginia ground that remained beyond the Firm's control, Mackay and Fair considered the various options for prospecting their new mine. The Firm's fondest hope was finding enough low-grade ore in the upper levels of the Con. Virginia to finance deep-level explorations, much as they'd developed the Hale & Norcross after their 1869 takeover. That was straightforward prospecting, but it wasn't likely to reveal the sort of bonanza that had motivated their purchase of the mine. The Crown Point's deep bonanza had been struck lying against the footwall 1,100 feet below the surface. If they were to find something similar, Mackay and Fair judged it most likely they'd find it against the Con. Virginia's footwall at like depth. They considered sinking the Con. Virginia's existing shaft below one thousand feet and crosscutting back to the ledge. That was the least complicated option, because they'd control every aspect of the operation, but also the most expensive. North of the Con. Virginia, the Ophir was driving a long crosscut west from their shaft's 1,100-foot station. If the Firm bore half of the costs of operating the Ophir shaft, they could drift south into Con. Virginia ground from a point on that crosscut. They also weighed the idea of waiting until the Ophir shaft descended another 200 feet and drifting south at even greater depth. Eventually, the two veteran miners decided to attack the deep levels of the Con. Virginia from the south. From the Gould & Curry's 1,167-foot level, they'd drift across the entire 224-foot width of the Best & Belcher and then explore Con. Virginia ground. (The Best & Belcher should not be confused with the Belcher adjacent to the Crown Point on the Gold Hill end of the lode.)

William Sharon controlled both the Gould & Curry and the Best & Belcher, and he was delighted to grant Mackay and Fair use of the Gould & Curry shaft—provided they paid, of course. "I'll help those Irishmen lose some of their Hale & Norcross money," he sneered.

Besides, the Irish drift might find ore in Best & Belcher ground, which Sharon controlled.

With a satisfactory shared-use arrangement secured, Consolidated Virginia work crews started digging north from the end of the Gould &

Curry's 1,167-foot drift around May 1, 1872. They had made an excellent choice. Any of the other options Mackay and Fair mooted would have missed what was, by an immense margin, the Comstock's most valuable ore body, the one that would decide victory in the struggle to control the Comstock Lode.

CHAPTER 14

The Strike

The Consolidated Virginia hoisting works.

_____

The rise in Consolidated Virginia was the feature of the week; the reports of ore are of the very best character.
—*Mining & Scientific Press*, March 22, 1873

Either C. V. is a good mine or a big bilk—with chances favoring the later proposition.
—*San Francisco Chronicle*, March 23, 1873

Wanting to be on hand for Eva's operation, Mackay left James Fair in charge of the Consolidated Virginia in the spring of 1872 and went to Paris. Although they'd corresponded by both letter and brutally expensive telegram, Mackay enjoyed discovering firsthand that his family had thrived during the eight or nine months he was in the mines. As planned, Louise had taken everyone to winter on the French Riviera, a marvelous experience. To twenty-eight-year-old Louise, Europe seemed to possess everything coarse Nevada did not—culture, refinement, old world grandeur, and a sophisticated, luxurious existence she'd never experienced. Just five years before, she'd been a widow doing other people's sewing. Eva survived the operation in Paris and recovered quickly. Unfortunately, the procedure was only a partial success. Although perhaps slightly improved, the poor child still limped, and the doctor said she would forever. He also informed them that any further procedures would only cause needless suffering. That hit John and Louise as a substantial blow, but Mackay reiterated his promise to do everything in his power to fill Eva's life with happiness. He also warned his wife that prospecting the Consolidated Virginia could easily consume all the money he and his partners had raised from the Hale & Norcross. She asked what they'd do if it did.

"We'll go broke and start over," Mackay said.

Considering the penurious years Louise had endured before their marriage, she must have found the prospect terrifying.

While Mackay was in Europe, James Fair began exploring the Con. Virginia's 500-foot level and running the 1,167-foot level drift north, aided by Superintendent Sam Curtis, a gold rusher like Mackay and Fair and a veteran of the Comstock's early days who'd superintended a number of other mines. They pushed the work around the clock on the 1,167-foot level, drifting north in the country rock east of the Comstock's hanging wall, which experience had taught them was better ground for running a long drift. Making just over four feet of progress per day, it took them about sixty days to dig across the mine's 224-foot width. To William Sharon's chagrin, the Irish drift revealed no ore in the Best & Belcher, nor any promising indications. The drift likely crossed the Con. Virginia line in the last week of June. James Flood handled the San Francisco end of the Firm's affairs. He'd orchestrated a Con. Virginia recapitalization that increased the number of shares from 11,600 to 23,600.

Once inside Con. Virginia ground, Fair turned the drift northwest, angling to close the distance to the Comstock's hanging wall. Like Mackay, Fair believed a mine owner's place was underground. He spent much of his time supervising the slow, hard, tedious work at the sweltering, candlelit face of the 1,167-foot-level drift, among the miners pounding hammers onto handheld chisels, giving a chisel a small twist with each blow, either single-jacking, with one man handling both hammer and chisel, or using the faster but more dangerous double-jacking technique with one man holding the chisel while another swung a heavier sledge. They bored out one- to two-foot-deep holes of sufficient diameter to admit charges of Giant Powder. Through softer rock or after a blast, the men hacked at the drift face with the points of their picks or pried at loose rock with gadding bars, shoveling waste into ore cars that went back to the Bonner Shaft on wooden tracks laid on the drift floor and then up to the surface for disposal. The heat increased and the quality of the air fell. The lack of information released from the mine frustrated the local newshounds. "The management . . . are rather reticent as to actual developments," lamented the *Gold Hill Daily News*—a sentiment which it, the *San Francisco Chronicle*, and other newssheets would express repeatedly through the next year and a half.

While Con. Virginia miners "steadily prosecuted" the drift on the 1,167-foot level, 650 feet closer to the surface and a like distance to the west (farther up Mount Davidson and shallower in the east-dipping vein), other crews systematically prospected the Con. Virginia's slice of the lode above the 500-foot level, and although local mining news occasionally reported favorable indications, nothing developed into a profitable ore mass. That threw the cost of prospecting the deep levels onto the assessments levied on the stockholders, and since the Firm owned around 75 percent of the stock, the Firm had paid and would pay around three-quarters of all assessment money. Similar futility haunted the 1,167-foot drift, which developed "nothing new." No special insight was needed to see the truth of what Mackay had told his wife—exploring the Con. Virginia could swallow everything they'd raised from the Hale & Norcross. Despite tremendous quantities of the promotional puffery, no mine had made a truly significant strike since the Crown Point discovery almost two years before. William Sharon thought the four Irishmen were making the cardinal financial error of throwing good money after bad. He'd taken to calling them "the joke of the Comstock."

The Firm received another significant setback at eight-thirty in the morning on July 15, when a "dull, heavy," mortarlike explosion boomed through Gold Cañon. The two boilers of the Petaluma Mill exploded. The Firm shared ownership with Alvinza Hayward and John Percival Jones. The monstrous explosion blasted the mill to smithereens and sent metal chunks weighing hundreds of pounds flying hundreds of yards in all directions. Impacts killed three people, injured a number of others, and destroyed saloons, hotels, homes, and businesses throughout the neighborhood. The Firm had a good reputation for taking care of people who were injured or killed in its employ. Paying for the massive collateral damage, rebuilding the mill, and fairly compensating the injured and the families of the killed cost the Irishmen significant sums at a time of great financial exposure.

The 1,167-foot level drift reached a point 100 feet inside the Con. Virginia boundary in the third week of July 1872. From there, Curtis and Fair decided to make their first westward crosscut, back toward the lode, which everyone involved considered the most likely place to find ore. The Con. Virginia crews who worked the 1,167-foot level spent most of August driving the crosscut. The air quality plummeted as they turned away from the main drift. The Roots Blower in the Bonner Shaft's hoisting works that ventilated the drift struggled to push enough air through the 2,000 feet of wooden box-pipe that carried air down the shaft and along the drift to the leading edge of the workings. Candles dimmed in the oxygen-depleted air, and the work stalled in "very hard" ground. Then, the miners encountered a heavy wall of expansive clay they supposed constituted the long-hoped-for hanging wall of the Comstock vein. Observers anticipated an "important development" within the week. None came. Running through the country rock outside the vein for the last four months, Con. Virginia miners hadn't been troubled by water. However, an undrained water chamber lurked behind the heavy clay. Attempts to break through unleashed scalding torrents. Fair and Curtis had no alternative but to bulkhead the crosscut and hope they could work around the water chamber farther into Con. Virginia ground. The threatened flood was an expensive disappointment, for it meant embracing another long stretch of dead work through ground in which all experience told them there'd be no hope of making a strike. They'd run nearly 500 feet of drifts and made the one long crosscut in four and a half months of brutal, sweltering labor nearly 1,200 feet below the streets of the town, immolating the assessment money they'd raised in March and April, and they hadn't found a ton of rock worth milling.

Fair and Curtis returned their attention to running the main 1,167-foot level drift another 100 feet to the northwest, to a point from which it made sense to attempt another westward crosscut they hoped would outflank the water chamber. The stock market reflected the letdown. Con. Virginia stock gave up most of a recent rise. But on September 12, 1872, running the main drift northwestward and 178 feet inside Con. Virginia ground, one of Sam Curtis's crews hit something unusual—a 3- to 7-foot-wide cross-fissure filled with clay, porphyry, and quartz, some of which contained low-grade ore. The best portions assayed from seven to thirty-four dollars per ton, nothing close to the best ore selections of an actual Comstock bonanza, but the first genuinely positive indication they'd encountered in four and a half months. Low-grade rock sometimes presaged high-grade discoveries. Curious, they excavated the vicinity. Preliminary inspections revealed something odd, something unique— the fissure pinched off to westward, toward the Comstock. The fissure's going end trended in almost the opposite direction, to the northeast, almost exactly perpendicular to the run of the main drift. Following the fissure would mean drifting *away* from the Comstock, *away* from where they expected to have the best chance of finding ore. Fair, Curtis, and every other miner in the drift knew that no significant bonanza had been found outside the confines of the main lode in the entire thirteen-year history of the Comstock. Fair and Curtis pushed the main drift another dozen feet to the northwest, prospecting the environs of the cross-fissure, but when that effort revealed nothing of interest, they returned their attention to the cross-fissure, "ore is where you find it" being one of mining's oldest saws. They turned the main drift down the cross-fissure, away from the Comstock Lode. Fair had also likely sent a coded telegram to John Mackay at the first good indication.

"No new developments that we are advised of," said the *Gold Hill Daily News* that Saturday. "The proprietors and managers of this mine keep their own counsel. . . . They must have a good thing."

Stockbrokers bidding in "high glee" nearly doubled the value of Con. Virginia shares during the next week. The *San Francisco Chronicle* reported rumors among traders that attributed the rise to "a strike in the lower level crosscut," but added that it was "difficult to obtain decisive news." Contrarian traders thought it was "a put up job." Unremarked on by market observers were heavy purchases of Central No. 1, on rising prices. James Flood and William O'Brien almost certainly drove the advance. In the coming months, both Central No. 1 and Central No. 2 quietly came under the Firm's control, which gave them sway over every inch of ground between the Best & Belcher and the Ophir. The *Chronicle* described Con. Virginia stock "jumping up and hopping down" through the third week of September, propelled by "confidential whisperings," many of them contradictory.

In truth, on the 1,167-foot level, the Firm didn't know what they had. They'd found clay and porphyry mixed with low-grade quartz in an odd location trending in a baffling direction. They had an unusual and optimistic indication, nothing more, and certainly no guarantee of bonanza. Elsewhere on the Comstock, "ore" that hovered just below the level of profitability had proved a will-o'-the-wisp that had baited miners into pouring money into worthless mines for years—Mackay's experience with the Bullion mine providing a cardinal example. The ore in the Con. Virginia fissure averaged about twenty-two dollars per ton. Only the fact that it had to go up the shaft whether or not it contained metal justified its extraction from such an expensive location. However, James Fair took discovery of the cross-fissure as the good indication he and his partners had been awaiting. He thought it justified additional investment. Executing the strategy he and his partners must have agreed on before Mackay's departure, after months of cost-conscious development, Fair suddenly started spending money like the second coming of William Ralston. A whirlwind of activity erupted around the Con. Virginia as Fair began preparing to enlarge the hoisting works, replace and upgrade the machinery, and sink the Con. Virginia's shaft to meet the 1,167-foot-level drift coming north from the Gould & Curry.

On September 18, Con. Virginia superintendent Sam Curtis told the *Territorial Enterprise* that he was "confident of finding good ore in the mine." The next day, John Mackay landed in New York aboard the SS *California*. If Mackay had lined up the railway connections perfectly, it would have taken him another seven or eight days to reach Nevada. With Mackay probably well into his transcontinental journey, the Consolidated Virginia trustees levied another assessment on September 26. (Mackay wasn't a trustee, although his three partners were.) The Virginia & Truckee Railroad had extended from Carson City to Reno, but Mackay likely reached the Comstock a few days too early to have been aboard the V&T's first passenger train from Reno when it puffed and hissed into Virginia City at 5:45 a.m. on October 1, 1872.

The Con. Virginia assessment baffled and angered the *San Francisco Chronicle*, whose editorial policy took it as an article of faith that mine insiders manipulated stocks and information to fleece the public. "Why levy an assessment if ore is struck?" they wondered.

The question exposed their ignorance of the costs and risks of Comstock mining. The "ore" in the strike was barely profitable, there wasn't much of it, and sinking the Con. Virginia's shaft another 650 feet would cost well over $300,000, likely about doubling the Firm's financial commitment to the mine.

While large work crews swarmed over the Con. Virginia hoisting works preparing the upgrades, the Belcher connected its incline to the 1,100-foot level, improving ventilation to parts of the mine where temperatures previously reached 115 degrees. Hoisting through the incline lessened the demands on the three mules still laboring "in the subterranean." Belcher superintendent Hank Smith decided he no longer required Susan B. Anthony's services. A less humane management would have "retired" the mule in place, but William Sharon wouldn't countenance that sort of cruelty to animals. Smith had "the boys" truss up Susan B. Anthony's legs and tightly wrap her in canvas in preparation for the hoist. Honking and braying against the indignity, she bucked and kicked for every one of the thirty minutes it took to hoist her to the surface. Susan B. Anthony reached the shaft house in a "smoking lather of sweat" and couldn't stand for an hour, having strained her legs kicking against the ropes and canvas. The poor mule hadn't seen daylight in more than six months. Once she regained her feet, mine workers noted that she seemed fatter and fitter on the shaft landing than she had before being sent down. Mary Jane Simpson and Old Pete continued their long shift underground. The *Gold Hill News* reported both "in fine condition."

The great contemporary furor in the mining world blazed around "the most gigantic and barefaced swindle of the age," a bizarre fraud, started two years before by the supposed discovery of rich, hush-hush diamond fields in Arizona that climaxed that November, when the U.S. Geological Survey's explorer/scientist Clarence King exposed the hoax. (By then, the site of the strike had migrated to Colorado.) Investors eager to get in on the ground floor of the next big thing may have lost as much as $2 million. One of the bigwigs snared by the deception was the Bank of California's William Ralston, scorched to the tune of a quarter of a million dollars.

The jaw-dropping success of the Belcher mine made the loss easier for Ralston to swallow. In 1872, Nevada mines outproduced California's. Indeed, the single state of Nevada produced roughly half of the wealth mined west of the Missouri River. The Comstock Lode produced more than half of Nevada's total, and the single ore body shared between the Crown Point and the Belcher disgorged more than 75 percent of Comstock bullion. Belcher output increased fourfold in 1872. Crown Point production had more than doubled. They were the two richest mines in the world, and the opening of the Crown Point's 1,300-foot level revealed it to be chock-full of "a high and uniform grade of ore." In his annual report, Superintendent John Percival Jones described it as "by far the richest and most extensive level ever opened on the Comstock Lode." The ore body had increased in length, width, and richness as miners descended on it, which tempted Jones into inserting some hyperoptimistic puffery into his conclusion: "It is fair to presume that we have passed below the range of surface-disturbance, and that the vein will penetrate the earth in its present shape to an infinite depth."

William Ralston, William Sharon, Darius Ogden Mills, and the handful of other men who held significant blocs of Belcher stock soon knew that the Belcher's share of the 1,300-foot-level bonanza was every bit as extravagant as the Crown Point's. Booming mines also poured money into the Virginia & Truckee Railroad, which ran more than thirty trains per day into Gold Hill and Virginia City. Splendid revenues had the V&T far down the road toward eliminating its debt, which would allow it to pay dividends. The success of the V&T and the Belcher's astonishing dividends not only pulled William Ralston back from the brink of financial disaster, but re-energized his ambitions. If he learned a lesson, it was the wrong one—he behaved as if the Comstock Lode would always come to his rescue.

Ralston ran wild as underground developments revealed the extent of the Belcher ore body, and not only as the dupe of fraudulent diamond dreams. He invested in schemes all over his beloved California, and he loaned large quantities of Bank of California money to three companies he controlled himself, including the New Montgomery Real Estate Company, a stagnating property development project he'd nursed since the end of 1868.

Ralston fell ill in December 1872, possibly the consequence of stress and overwork. When he returned to work in February 1873, the bank directors assembled in his office. They'd inspected the books in his absence and discovered the three Ralston-controlled companies owed the bank in excess of $3.5 million. This time salvation came from the coffers of John D. Fry, Ralston's father-in-law and William Sharon's lifelong friend. Fry had grown wealthy serving as trustee and president of Sharon-dominated mines and trading stocks on his advice. Ralston signed the notes he'd taken from the three companies on the bank's behalf over to Fry along with all other associated collateral. He ended up owing his father-in-law $3.5 million. Ralston repaid Fry with Belcher dividends and Union mill profits, but as a consequence of Ralston's latest near-catastrophe, Darius Ogden Mills insisted on selling his last five hundred Bank of California shares and surrendering his presidency. Ralston had no choice but to acquiesce. He assumed the presidency in place of Mills. However, in Ralston's opinion, the Bank of California couldn't afford to lose the high esteem in which international and eastern banking circles held Mills. Ralston paid for Mills's stock, but didn't register the change of ownership in official records. Without Mills's permission or knowledge, Ralston had Mills elected to the Bank of California's board.

Ralston's influence extended to Washington. He was one of the thirty-odd "gentlemen" Treasury officials consulted about the reforms needed to wean the United States economy from the paper greenbacks circulating since the Civil War and return it to metallic currency. Questions about how to make that happen dominated economic policy discussions. Most Americans took it for granted that "hard" currency based on gold and silver was best for the economy, but two obstacles made it difficult to continue coining silver dollars as an official United States currency. First was political pressure brought to bear by bankers, economists, and hard-money advocates who imagined that only a gold-based currency could provide economic stability. Second was the large increase expected in the supply of silver, a significant chunk of which was being contributed by the Comstock Lode and its supposedly bottomless mines. Germany added to the anticipated increase when it announced that it would abandon silver coinage and convert to a gold standard. Unwilling to face the consequences of trying to maintain silver or bimetallic currencies in the face of German conversion, other European countries followed suit. If the United States tried to maintain its traditional sixteen-to-one fixed ratio between the two metals, traders would send European silver coins melted into bullion across the Atlantic and force the United States to sell more valuable gold for cheaper silver at the artificially fixed price, an arbitrage with the potential to bankrupt the Treasury. Ralston recognized that the United States couldn't maintain a bimetallic currency in the face of that pressure, but he also knew that eliminating silver from the currency could do great harm to the Bank of California. Such a step would lessen American demand for silver, and since the fortunes of the Bank of California were known to be tied to the Comstock Lode, a collapse in silver demand would injure the mines. If that in turn caused a loss of confidence in the bank, it could provoke a killing run. Ralston devised a scheme to prop up silver demand by having Nevada senator William M. Stewart insert a provision into the Coinage Act authorizing the San Francisco Mint to coin silver trade dollars for use in China. The clause both discouraged the import of European silver and created a demand for Comstock silver that would incur a much lower transportation cost on its way to Asia than the European article. The Coinage Act of 1873 passed both houses of Congress in January 1873 without much public notice. President Grant signed it into law in February. Most Americans didn't realize for several years that the act had demonetized silver.

Only as the nation's farmers and other debtors experienced the pain of deflation caused by the nation's return to the gold standard would "the Crime of 1873" become a political rallying cry whose ramifications lasted for decades. Ralston's creative trade dollar solution managed to find a balance between interests that seemed mutually exclusive. It wouldn't help William Ralston survive the perils ahead, but it did serve the interests of the Comstock Lode.

Mackay and Fair spent most of the autumn of 1872 and the winter of 1873 at the Con. Virginia, on site and underground, pushing their crews to finish the reconstruction and upgrade of the mine's shaft house, engines, and hoisting and pumping apparatus, sink the shaft to 1,200 feet, and run the 1,167-foot drift farther into the promising cross-fissure they'd discovered in September. Under the watchful eyes of the two veteran miners and their superintendent, all the work was done "in the strongest and most durable manner."

Mackay and Fair had their new machinery "steamed up" and tested several days before Christmas, readying the big push that would carry the shaft down to 1,200 feet. When they weren't engaged in surface decision making or supervision, Mackay and Fair would most commonly be found deep underground, on the 1,167-foot level, working alongside their miners in sweltering heat and air so foul that a man could only stand at the drift face for ten or fifteen minutes before rotating back to cooler, more oxygenated air closer to the Bonner Shaft. The breakage of an air blower stalled work. Only after repairing or replacing the blower could they resume pushing ahead. Reports obtained by the newspapers mentioned "excellent indications" on the 1,167-foot level, but also worthless mixtures of quartz, porphyry, and clay, "hard, blasting porphyry," and "no extra favorable indications in sight." Probably worried they were drifting too far from the Comstock vein and uninspired by the low-grade ore in the fissure, Mackay and Fair directed another westward crosscut from about 100 feet down the cross-fissure. They managed to make almost 200 feet of northwesterly progress before an influx of hot water stopped the work. They started a fork from about two-thirds of the way down the crosscut and made another attempt. They pushed the fork until it, too, stalled against an undrained water chamber. Having exhausted what seemed like better options, they returned their attention to the cross-fissure.

Operating on the belief that they had something deep in the Con. Virginia that might spill over into the neighboring mines—but without ever tipping the stock market to their intentions and provoking battles for control—Flood and O'Brien bought enough stock to give the Firm control of the Best & Belcher, and the Gould & Curry, which also freed them from having to pay a Sharon-controlled mine for use of its shaft. (The stupendous quantity of ore coming out of the Belcher mine and the success of the V&T railroad tipped Sharon's interests away from needing to control individual mines—all the mines paid to use the railroad.)

The stock market remained unimpressed. Con. Virginia shares opened 1873 worth about half of the peak value they'd reached after its miners had hit the cross-fissure in September. That strange feature continued to lead Mackay and Fair northeast, away from the Comstock Lode. But the fissure widened as they drifted down it, and its prospects improved, validating the decision to follow it. Two hundred eighty feet down the cross-fissure, Con. Virginia miners made a crosscut that revealed the feature had grown to forty-eight feet in width, much of it filled with profitable ore.

Below, in San Francisco, James Flood and William O'Brien started to crow. They bragged about "very rich rock" in the Consolidated Virginia and said they'd soon show the world "what the Comstock could produce." The stock market thought it was puffery. Con. Virginia shares fell almost 15 percent, despite what the *Daily Alta California* described as "growing rumors of strikes in the Virginia mines, particularly Chollar and Con. Virginia."

One of those strikes wasn't worth the ink that announced it. The other was the tip of the most valuable precious minerals discovery ever made in the United States.

On March 9, 1873, the long-dreaded epizootic, a virulent equine influenza that originated in Canada, hit Virginia City. The *New York Times* had reported its appearance in mid-October, when all the horses and mules in Toronto got sick. Within a week the epizootic was in Montreal and Buffalo. The disease raged down the line of the Erie Canal through Rochester and Utica to Albany. Two days later horses were sick in New York and Boston and the illness was spreading through the rest of New England. Coughing, wheezing animals didn't have the strength to pull empty wagons, let alone canal barges or loaded wagons, and the *New York Times* was contemplating the terrible consequences of "the withdrawal of the horse power from the nation." Everywhere it appeared, the epizootic completely paralyzed horse- and mule-dependent transportation—and the entire nation's transportation network depended on horses and mules. The disease wreaked economic havoc. Colliers couldn't move coal from storage yards to steam-powered railroads and riverboats. Farmers couldn't get their autumn harvest to market. Animal-dependent Erie Canal barges sat in slack water, heaped with produce. The horse-drawn street railways and omnibuses that handled most urban mass transportation stopped. Taxis, hackneys, jitneys, and hansom cabs normally available for private hire disappeared from the streets. Mortality stayed low, 1 to 2 percent, except among animals whipped to work—many of those beasts died—but diseased animals were totally useless for two to three weeks, and needed up to two to three months to recover their full strength. The worst cases incapacitated animals for six months. The epizootic swept through all the eastern states. In late January 1873, the disease reached the mining camps of eastern Nevada. Virginia City teamsters first noticed "the peculiar coughing of stricken animals" on March 9, and the disease spread "like a prairie fire" through the Comstock towns. By two o'clock the next afternoon, none of the livery stables in Virginia City and Gold Hill had a single healthy animal, and local transportation was paralyzed. Abandoned wagons lined the streets. Merchants and grocers couldn't get goods from the train depot to their stores, butchers couldn't get fresh meat from the slaughterhouses, milkmen couldn't distribute their product. Mail, express, and staging services stopped throughout the state. Mines like the Con. Virginia that didn't have a railroad spur extended to their premises couldn't get supplies or ship ore.*

Con. Virginia stock had behaved like a stricken horse over the last month regardless of the optimistic reports from the mine. The mine's stock finally jumped during the morning session of March 17, 1873, "under the influence of the important development in the mine."

The *San Francisco Chronicle* credited the rise to stories circulated by Flood and O'Brien—"All of which we advise our readers to receive with many grains of allowance." The *Chronicle*'s "Stock Sharp" saw it as "a first-class job" being put up in "this most promising of barren mines." Several outside "experts" gained access to the mine on March 19. When they emerged, they pronounced it "the most important development made on the Virginia end of the Comstock for years."

Con. Virginia stock plummeted the next day, a fall the *Chronicle* took as prima facie evidence of how "unscrupulous operators manage to become rich at the expense of innocent outsiders who are drawn into purchasing at high prices . . . under the influence of quasi-official reports." The *Chronicle* hounded Con. Virginia management for the rest of March.

---

* Animals in Los Angeles had "the horse disease" by March 21. By the end of April, the epizootic had swept all of California.

John Mackay fired Sam Curtis. Characteristically, Mackay never discussed the move with anybody outside his ownership group, but he never would tolerate slights to his good name. Considering the small-town nature of the West, where a man was seldom more than one person removed from anybody else, a man's reputation carried much weight. Mackay considered his of utmost importance. The *Chronicle* said Curtis had been fired for talking too much and allowing friends to inspect the mine despite express orders to the contrary. The "experts" admitted to the mine on March 18 or 19, whose reports stirred such subsequent vitriol, may have been those friends.

Ironically, as the *Chronicle*'s criticisms became increasingly savage, underground developments in the Con. Virginia made it ever more apparent to Mackay and Fair that they had a good mine. How good they didn't yet understand, but an official advice from the mine on March 23 said they'd crosscut 28.5 feet of ore in the 1,167-foot cross-fissure. By the end of March, the face of the 1,167-foot drift was well over 1,000 feet from the Gould & Curry shaft, having passed through several bends, and ventilation had become a debilitating problem. Conditions in the prospecting crosscuts became so atrocious that it was impossible to work them more than a few feet from the main drift. The mine couldn't be developed properly until the shaft connected to the 1,167-foot level drift and effected a circulation of breathable air. Mackay and Fair decided to focus efforts on making that connection without paying much attention to prospecting their strike.

To speed the process, they put four six-hour shifts to work at the shaft bottom and they sank only two of the shaft's three compartments, reasoning they could reach 1,200 feet sooner sinking just the two. They'd have crews dig out the third working up from the bottom. Doing it without bullion proceeds meant levying assessments, however, and the Con. Virginia levied one in April and another in June, both of which sent the *Chronicle* into apoplectic paroxysms against what the editorial board perceived as the greedy manipulations of the four Irishmen. The Firm had levied—and spent—$318,000 worth of assessments since taking control of the mine, most of which came from their own pockets, but they were still operating a publicly traded company, which made them vulnerable to criticism.

In addition to the massive—and massively expensive—push to prospect and develop the Con. Virginia mine in the spring and summer of 1873, the four Irishmen also pushed their even more expensive water project toward completion. They'd been aggressively advancing the project since hiring hydraulic engineer Hermann Schussler the year before. Operating through their control of the Virginia and Gold Hill Water Company, the Firm borrowed more than $1 million to finance construction of the reservoirs, flumes, pipeline, and other installations required. During the winter of 1872–73, the *Gold Hill News* prodded the Water Company to "push the work as rapidly as possible, as water is likely to be a scarce article during the coming season." The Water Company did exactly that. In accordance with Schussler's instructions, the Risdon Iron Works of San Francisco fabricated seven miles worth of high-pressure pipe from 1.15 million pounds of wrought iron and shipped it over the Sierras. Workers installed the first sections in June 1873, laid the last pipe on July 25, and joined the inverted-siphon pipeline to diversion dams, flumes, and reservoirs to make an aqueduct twenty-one miles long. Schussler had designed drain valves at the bottom of each depression in the pipeline to allow sediment to be drawn from the pipe and blow-off cocks for the top of every rise to blast out compressed air. When Schussler turned water into the pipe, Dan de Quille of the *Territorial Enterprise* witnessed the event. He described tracing the progress of the water across Washoe Valley by the explosive venting of the blow cocks, compared to which, he wrote, "the blowing of a whale was a mere whisper."

Comstockers drank glasses of pure, fresh, good-tasting Sierra water and celebrated the water's arrival with a typical jollification. Bands in the streets pounded out triumphal music. Citizens hurrahed. When that night's issue of the *Enterprise* went to the presses at 2:00 a.m., four cannon were still booming and the whole town was in a state of "unbounded hilarity." All persons connected with the Water Company were "jubilant." James Fair lit bonfires in his yard and shot up skyrockets.

The seven-mile inverted siphon withstood a drop of 1,720 feet from its high point and maximum interior pressures nearly twice as high as any other pipeline in the world. The system delivered more than 2 million gallons of water per day once it operated at full capacity—ten times the Comstock's previous supply. The fact that the desert towns of Virginia City and Gold Hill had a plentiful supply of pure mountain water became an enormous point of pride. As the preface to the Storey County directory boasted two years later, "Thus it is, that while other places, especially San Francisco, are endeavoring to solve the question of the water supply, Virginia City and vicinity has it solved for all time to come, and, in a land of barrenness and drouth [*sic*], has a full supply of better water than any of them."

The directory had it right. More than 140 years later, the system still serves Virginia City.

John Mackay wasn't on the Comstock to enjoy the triumph. With Hermann Schussler to tend to the engineering of the aqueduct and James Fair to oversee Con. Virginia development, Mackay had returned to Europe to see his family earlier in the summer. The *San Francisco Chronicle* noted his presence among other "Pacific Coasters" in Paris on Independence Day, identifying him as "one of the precious quartet who manipulate the Hale & Norcross Mine," and making a cruel joke about his uneducated French accent. A month later, the *Chronicle* reported Mackay and his family ensconced at the Hôtel Splendide.

Very little news escaped the Consolidated Virginia while Mackay was away, and most of what did was redundant: sinking and drifting, nothing new to report. Most of the mining industry was distracted by the astonishing developments emerging from the thirteen-hundred-foot levels of the Crown Point and the Belcher. No similar mass of ore had ever been revealed. Square-set timbering alone couldn't support the enormous stopes. The incredible pressures bearing down from above forced the mines to fill the square-sets with tens of thousands of feet of additional reinforcing timbers and backfill with waste. Between them, the two mines had raised $9 million in 1872. For the month of June 1873 alone, the Crown Point paid $1 million of dividends and the Belcher did even better—it paid $1,040,000. The running total of the two mines' dividends since the start of the year exceeded $8 million, and experts estimated that the two mines had between $20 and $40 *million* worth of ore "in sight," more than 50 percent of which seemed likely to end up in the pockets of the stockholders. According to the normally staid *Daily Alta California*, the deep ore body shared between the Belcher and the Crown Point made all previous mineral discoveries—anywhere in the West— seem like mere "surface lumps."

A mile and a half to the north and 1,200 feet below the streets of Virginia City, Con. Virginia miners working the long drift north from the Bonner Shaft of the Gould & Curry battled worsening conditions. The heat grew more intense. The air got harder to breathe. They fought swelling clay and an influx of hot water. Water pouring through the drift face and washing debris into the drift stopped work in late July. Con. Virginia miners mucked out the drift for three weeks without making notable progress. A mid-August attempt to detour around the sodden ground proved a perfect failure.

Not long thereafter, the *Gold Hill Daily News* reported being "reliably informed" that the 1,167-foot-level drift was "being run in the ore vein," and that the ore extracted therefrom was "equal to any rock produced for years on the Comstock." A few days later, the *News* noted a "considerable quantity of high grade ore," $150 to $200 to the ton, emerging from the Gould & Curry shaft.

John and Louise Mackay, Eva, young Willie, and a nurse arrived in New York from Liverpool aboard the SS *Adriatic* on October 4. Louise hadn't set foot on American soil in two and a half years. Two days after the Mackay family landed, the *San Francisco Chronicle* commented on the feverish activity that had ruled at the Con. Virginia for the last year, but even confronted with carloads of evidence, the newspaper still couldn't bring itself to credit the mine with an actual ore body. "Whether it is all for a purpose—to run the stock up on the strength of appearances and expectations, or whether the management really believes all that it asserts and expects dividends soon—is even more than the CHRONI-CLE stock sharp can tell." The *Chronicle* credited Flood and O'Brien with "a brilliant operation" that had sent the stock up from $100 to $250 over the last fortnight and for orchestrating a five-to-one stock split that increased the number of shares to 108,000, but still couldn't bring itself to admit that the mine was on to a good thing.

The outside world got its first look at the mine on October 28, 1873, when Mackay and Fair allowed Dan de Quille of the *Territorial Enterprise* to examine the "long-forbidden lower level" of the mine. Everything about the construction and operation of the mine impressed the lean reporter: the hoisting apparatus, the engines, and the organization of the shaft house. The smooth and speedy descent of the shaft made an impression—it happened without "the slightest jar." As James Fair boasted to the reporter, they'd built everything "as neat and handy as a duck's foot."

Two hundred and fifty feet south of the 1,200-foot station, Fair showed de Quille the miners working the ore body. Stripped to the waist in the heat, they stoped out ore on all sides and installed square-sets. They'd been at it "regular mining style" for only thirteen days, and they'd already expanded the stopes six to nine sets in all directions and had opened four levels above the main drift. The east wall was clay, but in all other directions, including the floor and ceiling, the men worked "ore of excellent quality." Prospecting drifts and crosscuts revealed the ore body angled from southwest to northeast over a distance of 200 feet, averaging 30 to 50 feet in width. The key question was, "Did it go?" Did it extend in depth? Mackay and Fair had what they called the north winze down 50 feet below the main drift, and it was in "very rich ore" the whole way. Although Dan de Quille quite reasonably reminded his readers that he couldn't see any farther into the mine than the openings already made, he did venture his impression that he was in the middle of a "very large body." In his judgment, in the Consolidated Virginia, "a first class mine [was] fast being developed."

Mackay wasn't so sure. To him, although in places rich, the rock appeared "dead," almost completely devoid of the tiny crystallization apparent elsewhere on the lode. He'd never seen anything like it in the fourteen long years of his Comstock experience. The ore looked "close" and "soggy," as if it had been dissolved in water and afterward hardened. Mackay puzzled and worried over the unfamiliar rock, having no idea what it portended.

As Mackay and Fair directed the opening of drifts, crosscuts, winzes, upraises, and galleries, rats followed the miners into the Con. Virginia's new workings. Rats had infested the Comstock mines since the early days. Healthy little fellows, they'd grown "fat and hearty" on the candle drippings, scraps of lunch, and miners' offal common underground. Rather than look upon them with revulsion or as annoyances or pests, miners looked on the rats with favor, feeling a kinship to "the rats of the lower galleries," a phrase they often used to describe themselves. Some men even went out of their way to leave them offerings, and all miners were glad of the rats and paid them attention, believing they could detect warning of an impending cave from the rats' behavior. Crown Point miners told convincing stories of narrowly escaping death by following rats out of a threatened gallery moments before it collapsed. The author of a letter about Comstock conditions that appeared in the *Mining & Scientific Press* warned his readers not to attempt to kill any rats in the mine unless they wanted "to try their skill in fighting miners." And so it was that a singular accident befell two Cornish miners at work at the bottom of the Con. Virginia's north winze three weeks after Dan de Quille's inspection. Working beneath a hand-turned windlass, they had the winze down 92 vertical feet below the 1,167-foot level, all the way in good ore, when "a frolicsome rat" attempted to jump across the top of the winze. The creature misjudged its landing and fell in. The doomed rat made a "slight humming noise" as it tumbled, which caught the attention of one of the men. He looked up, and the falling rodent hit him square in the forehead. The rat exploded blood and guts all over his face. The man reeled against the side of the winze, thinking himself mortally wounded by a falling rock. His companion leaped to his aid. The stricken man scraped "a handful of the bloody debris" from his forehead and face, stunned to discover himself mostly unharmed. Only after discovering the mangled remains of the rat at the winze bottom did they comprehend what had occurred. The story quickly made the rounds of the lower levels, provoking "much merriment."

CHAPTER 15

The Big Bonanza

Firefighters pose next to a hand-pumped engine.
The high winds that blew through Virginia City could spread flames
across the town and doom the mines in a matter of minutes.

It makes a poor man sick to look at it.
—Unidentified visitor to the Consolidated
Virginia Mine, *San Francisco Chronicle*,
December 9, 1874

While in her heart, Louise Mackay hadn't wanted to be so far from her husband, she hadn't wanted to leave Europe, either. But John missed his family. Willie was three years old, and while John was in Europe the previous summer, he and Louise had conceived another baby. She was pregnant when she returned to the United States. John knew his wife had no desire to return to Virginia City. Having her and the children in San Francisco seemed a good compromise. She'd be happier in the most civilized city on the Pacific Coast, at some remove from the Comstock's remembered horrors, and for John, having his family in San Francisco would be an immense improvement on Europe. On January 8, 1874, Mackay paid $31,000 for a three-story house in an upscale but not extravagant part of town at the corner of O'Farrell and Polk streets. Affluent tradesmen, professionals, and their families constituted the majority of the neighborhood. With business affairs likely to bring Mackay down from "above" on a regular basis, and the journey from Virginia City to San Francisco via the Virginia & Truckee and Central Pacific railroads requiring less than a day, the O'Farrell Street house was a solid, conservative purchase in which his family could enjoy the best of San Francisco. It was also by far the biggest house John or Louise Mackay had ever owned or inhabited. She decorated in the ornate French style popular with Americans pressing to expand the footprint of "civilization."

With the benefit of hindsight, many felt Mackay erred when he bought the house on O'Farrell Street—considering what the future held, Louise wouldn't find it satisfying—but when John bought it for Louise's homecoming, it suited the family of a man unsure of the extent of his fortune. Although Con. Virginia developments continued to reveal good ore and good indications, the true dimensions and contents of the ore body remained unplumbed.

Carnage in the national economy rendered the decision to buy a house well within their means even more sensible. In late 1873 and early 1874, banks and railroads were failing across the country. The Mackays had witnessed events firsthand when they passed through New York just a few months before. Trouble had been building among heavily indebted American railroads for a long time. Many lacked the revenue to cover both operating expenses and interest payments. Only new loans kept them afloat. That worked until the ocean of easy credit that had buoyed them up began to evaporate in early 1873. The Coinage Act that returned the United States to a gold standard tightened the money supply. The Bank of England raised interest rates in response to a stock market collapse in Vienna.* Worried European financiers stopped investing in the bonds of rickety American railroads and turned to safer, more stable investments closer to home. Complaints about "tight money" started appearing in the financial columns of American newspapers. Indebted

* Ironically, cheap American foodstuffs transported by the new railroads and shipped to Europe had done much to precipitate the collapse—American exports undercut the eastern European agriculture in which Austrian banks had heavily invested.

railroads unable to raise money selling bonds turned to short-term bank loans, which rendered them vulnerable to calls. The shoddy railroads also endangered the many banks that had bought their bonds or loaned them money. Among them was Jay Cooke & Company, which staggered under a grotesque load of unsalable Northern Pacific Railroad debt. Cooke & Company's New York branch failed on September 18, 1873. Panic ensued. Frantic depositors raced to withdraw money from banks all over the city. Treasury actions failed to meaningfully expand the money supply. Stock prices collapsed as pressed banks called loans they'd made to brokers, which forced brokers to toss securities into plummeting markets. On September 20, the New York Stock Exchange halted trading for the first time in its history. A list of thirty-seven failed banking and brokerage firms adorned the front page of the *New York Herald* the next morning. Markets had calmed and resumed—on much lower prices and smaller volumes—when the Mackays arrived in New York two and a half weeks later, but the *Herald* still told of "money scared too much by recent events to trust itself [to] another dark hole." Railroad construction slowed to a crawl. Coal and iron business dwindled. Demand dried up. Output plummeted. Corporate profits evaporated. Bankruptcies and failures swept the land. Real estate values fell. By year's end, twenty-five major railroads had defaulted. Seventy-one followed suit in 1874. Tens of thousands of America's new industrial laborers lost their jobs. Many of those who held their jobs had their wages reduced. The crisis dropped the economy of the eastern United States into a depression that would last more than five years and would gradually expand to encompass the Pacific Coast.

The manner in which a new invention derived from mining technology reshaped the desirability of San Francisco real estate also contributed to making the Mackays' O'Farrell Street home seem like a poor choice. Since the Gold Rush, the city's most coveted residential real estate had always been in the flat portions of town or on its modest slopes—areas readily accessible by horse-drawn conveyances that women could comfortably perambulate wearing the multilayered, long-hemmed skirts and underskirts Victorian fashion required. Women thus adorned found it almost impossible to negotiate the city's biggest and steepest hills. In consequence, those held the poor, working-class neighborhoods. Horse-drawn streetcars running on rails provided public transportation through much of the city, but it took four or five horses and copious applications of the lash to get heavy streetcars or wagons up the steep hills, particularly in wet or muddy conditions. If a horse fell, the weight of the streetcars sometimes dragged the whole team backward, including the fallen animal. Horses or mules that broke limbs usually had to be put down, often with a pistol shot administered at the scene of the accident. Watching just such a tragedy unfold on the steep hill on Jackson Street gave engineer Andrew Smith Hallidie an idea. His company made the best wire ropes available. Their use had been standard on Comstock mine hoists for years. A few years before, he'd patented an "endless-wire rope-way," a long loop of wire rope running over rollers attached to tall poles that transported ores and supplies up, down, or across otherwise inaccessible terrain. (Ski lifts are modern derivatives of the system.) Hallidie thought an adaptation could make San Francisco's hills more accessible. He tested his idea on Clay Street, which rose 307 feet from the intersection of Clay and Kearney streets to the crest of the hill more than half a mile to the west and then dropped beyond the crest to Leavenworth Street. Hallidie's workers formed a loop from a 6,600-foot length of wire rope and installed it in a slot beneath two parallel streetcar tracks, one heading west and another coming back east. A thirty-horsepower steam engine in an engine house at Clay and Leavenworth turned the "endless traveling" cable through the loop. Hallidie designed a "grip" that streetcar drivers could clamp onto the underground cable and brakes to slow the car when the driver released the grip. Hallidie tested the system in August 1873 and put his "novel railroad" into regular service in September. A long, detailed article in the *Mining & Scientific Press* that month described the "peculiar" railroad bringing "a large amount of property that was comparatively worthless on account of the difficulty of access" within an easy and comfortable five- to ten-minute ride of downtown. By mid-1874, the Clay Street Railroad was carrying an average of more than 2,250 passengers per day, and San Francisco's well-to-do were moving uphill to enjoy the fine views. Nob and Russian hills became the city's most fashionable residential locations.*

The Mackays missed the change. Nor did they really ever settle into San Francisco. To Louise, the city seemed adolescent and uncouth after Paris, and John wasn't able to spend as much time in San Francisco as he'd hoped. The demands of the Con. Virginia kept him in Virginia City, underground. That was where he was when the *Territorial Enterprise* reported "a new Superintendent" born (not appointed) to the Consolidated Virginia mine. Louise Mackay had delivered their second son in

---

*A century and a half later, seven and a half million people ride Andrew Smith Hallidie's "cable cars" every year, and they're famous the world over, the universally recognized symbol of San Francisco. Less well understood is the fact that the cable cars' roots reach back to the hoists that once served the Comstock mines.

the O'Farrell Street house on April 17, 1874. The *Enterprise* described her husband as "the happiest man on the Comstock," going about town trying to find someone "to abuse him, call him names" so that he "might not feel quite so proud of himself." Louise named the boy Clarence Hungerford Mackay. The *Enterprise* quoted Mackay as saying that his new son "must not expect to take charge of a mine at once." Mackay wanted "the young gentleman" to first "serve his time as a pick boy . . . to familiarize himself with the rudiments" before ascending to the superintendency. A month later, the newspaper described John Mackay returning from a visit to his new son, "looking as fresh and fine as though he had breakfasted, dined, and lunched upon roses."

The most intimate portrait of the Mackay family during the San Francisco years survived through the memory of Alexander O'Grady, whose mother Alice had entered the Mackay family's service in early 1871 as Willie's nurse. Alexander was the same age as Willie, but Alice had left Alexander with a friend and made the trip to Europe with Louise, Eva, and Willie, where she'd spent two and half years. Upon return, Alice took up residence with the Mackays on O'Farrell Street, and her son returned to her care. Alexander O'Grady and Willie Mackay became fast friends. Years later, Alexander recalled John Mackay often down from Virginia City, and he remembered several reciprocal visits to the Comstock he and his mother took with Louise, Eva, Willie, and Clarrie—as everyone in the family called Clarence. Alexander O'Grady remembered Louise as a small, charming, and plumpish woman with a gentle voice, dark hair, beautiful dark blue eyes, and a pleasant wit. John Mackay had drier humor and an inclination to playfully tease. During one of his visits to San Francisco, John Mackay was watching Alexander and Willie play croquet in the back garden of the O'Farrell Street house when Willie did something that miffed his father. John lifted Willie over his knee to administer a few gentle swats with the silver-tipped rattan cane he often carried (the only rich man's affectation John Mackay ever adopted). Appalled, little Alexander rushed to defend his friend. He hit Mackay square in the face with his croquet mallet, blacking the miner's eye. Mackay caught the boy's arm in his inescapable grip and dragged him to his mother. "Alice!" he stuttered—Mackay always stuttered when agitated—"If you d-don't take this d-d-damned brat out for a drive, I'll kill him!"

Alice O'Grady did as asked. Alexander remembered Mackay's temper as "quick, but quickly over," and the incident was soon forgiven. For the rest of his life, Alexander thought he'd risen in Mr. Mackay's esteem because of how he'd sprung to a friend's defense when he was four or five years old. On his own way up, John Mackay had often had to ball his fists and fight to hold his place in the world.

Aside from the joy of Clarrie's birth, John Mackay had other reasons to be happy in 1874, for the tide of Comstock events was running strongly in his favor. Midway through Louise's pregnancy, in December 1873, Mackay and James Flood had overseen the combination of the 600-foot stretch of ground between the Con. Virginia shaft and the Ophir into the "new" California mine. The reorganization divided the 1,310 feet of the Comstock Lode between the Best & Belcher and the Ophir into the 710-foot Consolidated Virginia and the 600-foot "new" California mine. Every share of the Con. Virginia received seven-twelfths of a share of the "new" mine in compensation for the 350 feet of ground they contributed to it. The Con. Virginia shaft sat just a few feet south of the boundary, and the Firm owned the lion's share of both mines.

Con. Virginia bullion returns put the mine on a paying basis. One thousand and forty feet east of the existing shaft, the Con. Virginia and the California mines began sinking a joint venture, the "Consolidated & California" shaft (invariably described as the "C&C shaft"). Mackay and Fair envisioned using it to explore the Comstock vein below 2,000 feet, deeper than anyone had ever attempted, without having to resort to the inefficiencies and complications of working through an incline, while also accessing the Con. Virginia ore body from the east, opposite the Con. Virginia's existing shaft, via connections that would improve ventilation and cool the mine. The C&C shaft was the first of the Comstock's "third-line shafts," and they outfitted it with larger, more powerful machinery and a more efficient system than any mine shaft in the country—and probably the world.

While the C&C shaft went down, Mackay and Fair continued prospecting the Con. Virginia through the existing shaft. The ore body revealed itself slowly, at the pace of excavation, about four feet per day. Mackay and Fair's miners upraising from the 1,167-foot level found the caprock of the ore body just 57 feet above where they'd encountered the cross-fissure. Any shallower than that, and they'd have missed the ore body entirely. Other miners sank the shaft and winze deeper. On the level of the strike, Mackay and Fair had prospected the pay ore as trending from southwest to northeast over a distance of nearly 200 feet and ranging in width from 30 to 50 feet. The ore body 100 feet deeper was almost twice as long and twice as wide. Con. Virginia miners opened a 1,400-foot shaft station before the end of February 1874. What few reports escaped the mine told of drifts and crosscuts at 1,400 feet as "opening out splendidly," "of a very favorable character," and looking "better and better." All the miners noted the ore improving with added depth. The character of the rock had changed, too—normal "bright" and "lively" Comstock ore began replacing the odd-looking dead stuff that had confounded Mackay's judgment of the shallower levels. By 1,400 feet, the dull, "dead" appearance of the ore vanished entirely. The Comstock's familiar crystallization ran through the ore and quartz, and occasional bright sulphurets sparkled in the matrix. The ore was also very, very rich. Three weeks into April 1874, Con. Virginia crews started building a shaft station at 1,500 feet. The Firm had all its mills crushing at capacity, and on April 23, 1874, six days after the birth of John Mackay's son Clarence, the *Gold Hill Daily News* described the prospects of the Consolidated Virginia as growing brighter every day. Bullion returns for the month of April 1874 footed up to around $400,000.

The Con. Virginia paid its first dividend in May, three dollars per share on its 108,000 shares, distributing a total of $324,000. That sum repaid every penny of the assessment money the mine had absorbed since the Firm's January 1872 takeover. The June dividend likely covered the entirety of the Firm's investment. Explorations at 1,400 feet revealed the ore body still widening and compared to 100 feet shallower, the ore body had doubled in length. Those developments made it seem as though John Mackay and his partners might have something to rival the Crown Point and the Belcher. In the last two and a half years, those mines had raised $35 million worth of gold and silver. Even though the Belcher alone was outproducing the entire states of Utah and Colorado, developments on the 1,500-foot level of the Consolidated Virginia would soon throw every other mine in the world into the deepest shade.

Miners, carpenters, and timbermen finished the Con. Virginia's 1,500-foot station. To speed and ease the work, Mackay and Fair installed one of Burleigh's new air compressors on the surface and piped compressed air down the shaft and through the drifts to power four drills and two small hoisting engines. The new pneumatic tools did double duty. Not only did they accelerate the work, but their exhaust of compressed air helped ventilate the mine. (They worked so well that within four months the Con. Virginia had five Burleigh air compressors lined up on the surface and pneumatic drills and hoists employed throughout the mine.) Mackay and Fair also supervised the fabrication and installation of the Comstock's first triple-decker safety cage in one of the shaft's hoisting compartments. The advances helped raise output to around three hundred tons per day. They could have raised more, but there was no sense in doing so until they could increase their milling capacity.

To that end, Mackay and Fair had started building a gigantic sixty-stamp steam-powered mill on F Street, just downhill from the Con. Virginia shaft house. They'd bought all the lots in the area and had two hundred men at work on the new mill. Only Virginia City's new water system made it possible, let alone economically feasible, to operate such an enormous mill within city limits. As an added benefit, the "soft" Sierra water, less impregnated with minerals than the "hard" local variety, required less than a quarter of the boiler maintenance. The Firm would still have to spend a small fortune paying William Sharon's Virginia & Truckee Railroad to bring fuel uphill to the mill, but they wouldn't have to pay the railroad the large fortune required to haul tens of thousands of tons of ore to distant mills.

Few pieces of 1,500-foot-level news escaped the mine in the summer and fall of 1874. The first report that the Con. Virginia was into something of an entirely different magnitude came when the *Gold Hill News* got an opportunity to inspect a 1,550-foot-level drift coming over from the Gould & Curry in the first week of November. Miners had pushed the 1,550-foot drift 110 feet into a mass of rich sulphuret ore beneath the deepest Con. Virginia workings. The reporter emerged shaken. "The sides and face of the drift being one glittering mass of sulphurets mixed with the richest character of chlorides," it seemed "almost useless" to attempt a fair description of the ore, he wrote. He'd watched the miners charge half a dozen bore holes in the drift face with dynamite. The show of precious metals in the drift face after each blast was enough to cause "a miser to weep with joy." The best specimens were "almost solid masses of silver."

Mackay and Fair fancied themselves miners, not stock manipulators, and in early December, they did something "hitherto unknown" in Comstock history—they threw the Con. Virginia open to inspection by anybody willing to make the terrifying descent into the mine. Among the first party John Mackay took down were Dan de Quille of the *Territorial Enterprise* and mining engineer Philipp Deidesheimer, the man who had invented the square-set timbering technique fourteen years before that had made it possible to extract the Comstock's massive ore bodies.

From the shaft station at 1,500 feet, Mackay led the party east, across the main north-south drift, and into "the California Crosscut," which went east just 14 feet from the California line. Just over 100 feet past the main drift, the crosscut entered the ore body. De Quille described the first few feet as "moderately rich." Beyond that, it grew into a pale green chloride ore shot through with streaks and nodules of black silver sulphurets upon which glittered bright points of iron and copper pyrites. The crosscut penetrated 25 feet into the ore body, and the walls, ceiling, floor, and face, all of it, was the same lively, sparkling ore. Like John Mackay, Dan de Quille had been on the Comstock for well over a decade, and the sight stopped his pencil and stilled his tongue. He'd never seen anything like it. Not a pebble in the crosscut was worth less than $600 per ton, and no small sample could be reasonably assayed for fear of grabbing a sulphuret nodule that would run the chunk into the thousands of dollars per ton. De Quille and the other visitors gazed on the ore in quiet awe until one of them broke the silence. "It makes a poor man sick to look at it," he said.

After a time, they retracted their steps to the main north-south drift. Mackay led them to Crosscut No. 2. (132 feet inside Con. Virginia ground). That crosscut had been driven east 204 feet, "nearly all the way in exceedingly rich ore," and miners pushing the face of the crosscut *still* hadn't encountered the east wall of the vein. Even if the ore in Crosscut No. 2 wasn't as spectacularly rich as the ore in the California Crosscut, the bulk of it was still worth from $150 to $200 per ton. Halfway down the crosscut, a winze sank to a connection with the 1,550-foot-level drift coming over from the Gould & Curry. The winze was in the same splendid $150 to $200 ore the whole way down. A strong air current passed through the winze, a genuine blessing in the sweltering mine. A section of ground near the winze had caved. To stop the working ground, miners had backfilled the cave with $200 ore. The sight dropped the reporter's jaw, for he knew what it meant—there wasn't *any* waste rock nearby.

Miners on the 1,550-foot level pushed to extend the drift beneath the California Crosscut. The drift ran right through the heart of the ore body, and it ran the entire distance in the same rich ore. A winze sunk from 1,550 feet had just reached 1,600 feet, and it too sank the full distance in "ore of wonderful richness." The mining men on Mackay's tour could see that between the systematic array of drifts, crosscuts, upraises, and winzes with which he and Fair had prospected the 1,500-foot level lay vast blocks of proven, untouched ore. Its value beggared imagination. Philipp Deidesheimer did quick calculations and estimated that the mine had $43 *million* of proven ore "in sight," and below 1,400 feet, Mackay and Fair's miners hadn't yet found the eastern or northern edges of the ore body. Mackay walked his guests north down the main drift across the full width of the California mine to its connection with the Ophir workings. He showed them the beginnings of the crosscuts that would prospect the California, but with Ophir miners extracting similar-in-character ore on the same level close to the California line and his men working the phenomenal ore in the California Crosscut on the California's southern boundary, it seemed a virtual certainty that the Con. Virginia's magnificent ore body spanned the entire 600-foot width of the California mine.

The flurry of reports that emerged from the mine described the 1,500-foot level of the Con. Virginia as "simply wonderful" and "surpassing belief," "extravagant," "magnificent," "vast," "wondrous," "almost incalculably rich," "apparently limitless," "of the richest possible description," "beyond computation," and, "if possible," growing richer. John Mackay hadn't seen ore that good since he'd been a common miner working the old Mexican chimney in 1860 and 1861 for four dollars a day, and back then, he hadn't seen but a tiny fraction of the staggering volume of top-quality ore he looked at in December 1874. Every pick stroke added to the "already immense wealth" of the mine.

To the *Daily Alta California*, it was "the great discovery of the age." When Dan de Quille wrote about it after emerging from the mine, he called it "the richest mineral discovery in the world's history," and he coined a beautifully alliterated moniker to describe the ore body— he named it "the Big Bonanza."

Mackay and his partners had raised more than ninety thousand tons of ore from the Con. Virginia in 1874, from which they'd reduced nearly $5 million, and they'd only just begun to scratch at its contents. In an interview conducted in his modest San Francisco office in early January 1875, James Flood assured the *Chronicle* that he and his partners had no intention of milking the Consolidated Virginia for speculative purposes. "We are running the mine to the best of our ability," Flood said, "as if we owned every dollar of the stock."

Sometime in the first half of 1875, as crosscuts on the 1,500-foot level revealed that the ore body did indeed span the entire length of the California mine, John Mackay must have realized that the Big Bonanza would make him one of the richest men in the world.

Predictably, the "stupendous mass of ore" provoked a delirium. People's lust for a chance at something similar loosed them from their senses. Hopeful miners relocated all the old Washoe mining claims neglected since the collapse of the Comstock's first boom until "every foot of land up to almost the summit of Mount Davidson and Cedar Hill" was incorporated into a mining claim and stock "sold to a people frenzied by prospective fortunes." Just as they had in the old days, prospectors located silver ledges all over California and Nevada, incorporated mining companies, and foisted stock on people clamoring for a chance at riches equal to those found in the Con. Virginia. Both rock and paper would prove worthless in almost every instance. To settle a bet, a few "sports" assayed a lump of mud "raised" from the streets of Virginia. It returned $9.86 per ton. The boom brought a huckster named Mr. Ai Peck back to the lode from North Platte, Nebraska. With his quicksilver-charged and wonderful ore-finding electromagnetic mineral rod, he'd helped Washoe miners make many worthless locations during the Comstock's early days and had "succeeded to his own satisfaction" in locating ore in the Bullion mine during an 1871 visit. In 1875, Mr. Peck promised to guide the mines to ore bodies hidden in their lower levels. Nor did he ask for any cash consideration in exchange for his services. All he sought was "a certain amount of stock" once the ore had been struck.*

Mr. Peck wasn't alone in his desire for mining stock. The market had gone crazy. The same reckless hunger for sudden fortune, which in the early years of the Gold Rush had depopulated mining camps overnight as residents dashed off in pursuit of a rumor, still animated the Pacific Coast. Stocks had been consistently rising since the spring and summer of 1874, and with most of the stock in the Con. Virginia and California mines closely held by Mackay and his partners and a few other early investors, speculative energies centered on the Ophir, which had many more shares loose in the market. As Mackay and Fair's explorations began to reveal the expanding dimensions of the ore body in the spring and summer of 1874, speculators had begun buying Ophir in the hopes that the Con. Virginia ore body would pitch through the California into the Ophir. Miners raising about fifty tons of ore per day from stopes on the 1,465-foot level of the Ophir made that a reasonable hope. No great leap of imagination was needed to see the Ophir developments as related to the marvelous reports emerging from the Con. Virginia.

Hoping to reprise the strategy he'd used to such good effect in 1871 when he'd bought the Belcher mine betting that the Crown Point discovery would stretch into Belcher ground, William Sharon had begun

* Although articles about Mr. Peck and his wonderful mineral rod appeared in the *Territorial Enterprise* in both 1871 and 1875, the author admits the possibility that Mr. Peck is a "quaint" (a story told with "improved facts") nursed through four years by the newspaper in the spirit of Mark Twain.

quietly scooping up shares of Ophir in August. By the end of September, Ophir shares had more than doubled in value, and the *Daily Alta California* reported many mining engineers expected a "continuous and united ore body at greater depths throughout the whole length of the Comstock."

Sharon also still nurtured senatorial ambitions. When Nevada senator William M. Stewart announced that he wouldn't stand for reelection in the 1874–75 elections, Sharon declared for the open seat. (Although in his autobiography Stewart said that "disastrous" mining operations prompted him to step down, knowing that Bank of California and Central Pacific Railroad support would swing to Sharon may have affected his decision.) On the Comstock, Sharon's influence remained strong in the *Gold Hill Daily News*. To neuter the enmity of the *Territorial Enterprise*, which had done so much to derail his 1872 campaign, Sharon bought the newspaper outright, paying a large premium on its actual value. With nineteenth-century elections to the United States Senate contested in state legislatures, to win, Sharon needed the support of the candidates running for those offices and the party apparatus behind them. According to persistent historical rumor wholly consistent with the nature of nineteenth-century political contests, Sharon curried favor by liberally distributing Ophir shares among Republican party operators and men standing for the state legislature. Heavily involved in industrial expansions, stock speculation, and construction of an enormous hotel in San Francisco, Sharon's wealth wasn't entirely liquid. Passing around the largesse of Ophir stock certificates while presumably retaining their proxies would have allowed Sharon to increase enthusiasm for his Senate candidacy while still accumulating power in the fight to control the Ophir. Nevada voted in the general election on November 3, 1874, and although a national wave returned the House of Representatives to Democratic control for the first time since the Civil War, the Republican Party did well in Nevada. The populace sent a Republican to the House and installed a solid Republican majority in the state legislature pledged to support the party's candidate for the United States Senate—William Sharon. The Nevada legislature wouldn't convene and formally vote for the Senate seat until early January 1875, but absent a massive scandal or major political earthquake, their pledge to Sharon wasn't easily forsaken. Alf Doten, a staunch Sharonist and the editor of the *Gold Hill Daily News*, shook Sharon's hand the night of November 3 and congratulated him on his victory. "Nevada enjoys the distinction of vast silver wealth," said the *San Francisco Chronicle*, "why should she not send some of it to the Senate."

Although Sharon had likely acquired more than 34,001 shares of the Ophir by the date Nevada voted in the general election, the mine had 108,000 shares. Sharon's slice of ownership didn't yet suffice to control the mine's upcoming election, and a succession of small-lot purchases would only further inflate the stock price in a contest he could still lose. A "cold and selfish and calculating" old San Franciscan who had operated in real estate and mining stocks since the early days named Elias J. "Lucky" Baldwin owned the only outstanding bloc of Ophir stock large enough to swing control of the mine. Sharon pried him loose from his 20,000 Ophir shares only by paying him $135 per share when the mine's open market price hovered around $80. A cool $2.7 million closed the deal, likely sometime between November 12 and November 16.

The Bank of California combination of Sharon, Ralston, and Mills moved aggressively into the boom. They were not alone. It seemed such a good time to buy. Everybody bought mining stocks, and few paid their full value in cash. Most people bought on margin, paying cash for only a fraction of a stock's total value and accepting a broker's or a bank's loan to make up the difference. They paid interest on the loan, but the risks and costs seemed trivial as stock prices soared. Expert assessments of the Comstock's glorious future appeared in all the newspapers. Picking a winning Comstock mine required no special expertise—they all rose. The *Mining & Scientific Press* described most women in Nevada as "interested in mining stocks." Many four-dollar-a-day miners bought stock during the boom, and by January, they fancied themselves millionaires. "They bought fine clothes, expensive jewelry, and talked loud" about the pleasure trips they'd take to New York and London when the weather turned.

John Mackay could scarcely move about the streets of Virginia City or San Francisco during those heady days. Everywhere he went, people buttonholed him for stock-buying advice.

He told them all the same thing: "Go and put your money in a savings bank."

Most who received the advice stared at him agog, surprised, if not outright resentful, that such an eminent miner wouldn't share his opinions.

Mackay's seemed like lousy, miserly advice in early January 1875. William Sharon's mining experts had postulated the existence of $300 million in the Big Bonanza after their December inspections. Philipp Deidesheimer made a second and then a third visit to the Con. Virginia around Christmas and the New Year and pinned the Big Bonanza's value at $1.5 *billion*, an estimate that received wide play in the press. A "free and easy talker" with a thick German accent and an odd idiom, Deidesheimer told of the many men made rich by following his advice. He advised people to buy and hold. People who owned the bonanza stocks were doing exactly that. During the first week of 1875, the price of Con. Virginia rose to $705 and the California to $780, but only 1,615 of their combined 216,000 shares changed hands, less than 1 percent of the total ownership. Ophir touched a high of $315.

Those prices valued the Con. Virginia at about $106,500 per foot and made each foot of the California worth an even more astounding $140,400. The capital value of the Con. Virginia stood at $75.6 million and the California at $84.24 million. Combined, they almost touched $160 million. The Firm's share of that paper wealth probably amounted to somewhere between $100 million and $120 million, for property they'd gained control of and developed for around $400,000. It was paper wealth, but if those figures were accurate, John Mackay's share ranged between $37.5 million and $45 million, and that sum did not include the Firm's holdings in other mines, its milling property, or the value of the massive lumber company it had incorporated to supply timber and fuel to the mines. Nor did that wealth exist only on paper: Virginia City shipped *ten tons* of bullion to San Francisco that week, valued at half a million dollars, the vast majority of which had been raised from the Consolidated Virginia mine.

The total capital value of the Comstock's leading thirty-one mines exceeded $262 million—$70 million more than the assessed value of all the real estate in the city of San Francisco.

An urge to sell hit at the end of the first week of January—"a reaction after the long rise," according to the *Daily Alta California*. Two weeks of choppy trading followed. At the end of the Saturday session on January 23, the market closed "firm."

Monday opened firm, too, but toward the end of the session someone launched two thousand shares of Ophir upon the market and started a panic. For a while, "pandemonium . . . reigned supreme." Stock plungers held the general belief and general resentment that William Sharon and "that damned pawnbroker on the corner"—meaning the Bank of California—were unloading, even though both in San Francisco and Virginia City they had advised "their friends" to buy and hold. "If the individuals composing that powerful ring did not cause the break, they certainly did nothing to stop it," squawked the *Chronicle*. The newspaper accused the Bank Ring of an "iniquitous" and "heartless" conspiracy intended to "destroy the market value" of Ophir stock and rain widespread misery, poverty, and ruin on the people of California and Nevada. The Belcher and Crown Point fell to their lowest prices in three years. In all, it was a "horribly glum day on California Street."

Tuesday was worse. At the open, one broker threw out twelve hundred shares of Ophir and recommenced the slaughter. Large declines uncovered many margins. Brokers sold out speculators who couldn't produce "mud" to cover their margins, precipitating larger declines and another round of uncovered margins, a repeating, reinforcing cycle as the failure to procure more mud precipitated the sacrifice of another round of stocks "owned" on exposed margins. Continuing declines assailed the market through the last days of January.

Nor had they yet had the worst of it. The "whole bottom" fell out of the market in the first week of February. Calls for "more mud" went unheeded, and margin holders had their stocks swept away by the steep declines "like leaves from trees in autumn."

The beautiful bubble disintegrated into mist, leaving but a few gleaming shards and a bitter wasteland of disappointment. The final slaughter came in early February. Ophir fell to $64, Con. Virginia to $385, and California to $50, which wasn't as utterly horrible as it appeared since the mine had split its stock five shares new for every one share old, but represented a still painful value of $250 old shares. Six weeks before, people who'd bet their savings on the Comstock were "rolling in imaginary wealth." By the end of the first week of February, they were "sparring for a square meal."

The market bounced on the bedrock in mid-February. The *Mining & Scientific Press* considered the worst feature of the catastrophe to be that "in the majority of instances, the losers [were] people of small means." But not all. One of William Ralston's earliest biographers claimed Ralston lost at least $2.5 million in the Ophir disaster, although considering that Ralston and Sharon operated in partnership in their stock dealings, it seems hard to credit one being harmed without the other. Six months later, a *San Francisco Chronicle* article reported the "rumor" that the bank crowd had been "badly hurt" by the tumble.

Sharon had been living in San Francisco for the last two years, nursing his gravely ill wife in a mansion he'd built near Union Square. Marie Sharon spent most of that time bedridden, fighting a painful stomach cancer. Sharon commuted to the mines—and his constituency—much less frequently than John Mackay, and he may have simply lost touch with the high-quality mining intelligence that sustained his previous success. The ore in the Ophir proved unconnected to the Big Bonanza and of lower grade, the realization of which had probably sparked the sell-off.

In the aftermath, Dan de Quille asked John Mackay to discuss the crash. "It is no affair of mine," Mackay said. "I am not speculating in stocks. My business is mining—legitimate mining. I see that my men do their work properly in the mines and that all goes on as it should in the mills. I make my money here out of the ore. Had I desired to do so, I could have gone down to San Francisco with ten thousand shares of stock in my pocket, and, by throwing it on the market at the critical moment, I could have brought about a panic and a crash, just as has been done. Suppose I had done so and had made $250,000 by the job—what is that to me? By attending to my legitimate business here at home I take out $500,000 in one week."

The stock market debacle didn't affect the Firm's mines or their splendid new mill. They'd begun testing it in early January. Like the old custom mills of the Ophir and Gould & Curry, the Consolidated Virginia mill was a colossal affair that cost the four Irishmen around $500,000. Unlike those earlier follies, Mackay and Fair ensured their mill was designed and constructed on proven, practical lines by experienced mill men and a veteran engineer. Built on sloping ground on the block below the Con. Virginia's hoisting works, the mill was the largest steam-powered silver mill in the West, with four eye-catching 90-foot-tall smokestacks rising above the boiler room. Inside the massive building, high-pressure steam powered a 600-horsepower engine that drove a main shaft 14 inches in diameter that weighed 15,000 pounds. The shaft turned a 33,000-pound, 18-foot-diameter flywheel, every bit of its angular momentum necessary to drive the mill's sixty 800-pound stamps. Below the stamp batteries and the mortars an intricate, carefully designed chain of distributing sluices, quicksilver injectors, steam-heated amalgamating pans, agitators, settlers, tail sluices, strainers, receiving tanks, a retort room, and a cooling reservoir recovered the bulk of the bullion from the crushed ore. On the hillside below the mill, settling ponds captured the mill's blue-tinted discharge and oozed it down long, blanket-lined sluices into other settling reservoirs aimed at recovering as much metal as possible before allowing the tailings to run down Six Mile Cañon. With its stamps thundering like "the roar of Niagara Falls," the mill went into service in mid-January, and it worked like a dream, able to crush and process 260 tons of ore per day. The enormous quantity of precious metal in the pulp presented the only significant operational difficulty—the metal overwhelmed the mill's retorting capacity. The Firm enlarged the retorting room by two-thirds.

An all-weather car track on a raised three-hundred-foot-long trestle joined the Con. Virginia shaft landing to the new mill. To ease the work, Mackay, Fair, and the mill's superintendent decided to use mules to haul loaded ore cars from the shaft landing to the mill's ore bins. They bought three mules, one to work with each shift of miners, and one of them was Mary Jane Simpson, the famous mule who had worked eighteen months in the Belcher mine. Her ordeal had ended when the Belcher incline reached thirteen hundred feet in the spring of 1873. She'd been raised from the mine and put out to pasture on a rich ranch in Washoe Valley with one of her underground workmates, Victoria Woodhull, a mule named for the first woman to run for president of the United States. (She'd campaigned on "the free-love ticket" in 1872, standing for women's equal rights and right to love whomever they chose.) The *San Francisco Chronicle* described Victoria Woodhull (the mule) as "a less intellectual beast" than Mary Jane Simpson, probably more of a mean-spirited dig at a woman whose presidential candidacy the newspaper had described as "a crime against womanhood" than a nod to the woman who'd been the newspaper's longtime Comstock correspondent.

Mary Jane Simpson enjoyed a year and a half of indolent bliss in the pastures of Washoe Valley, but being a strong and healthy member of that valuable and much-suffering species that did such a large share of the West's most unpleasant labor, Mary Jane Simpson was sold to the Con. Virginia and put back to work. However, perhaps in honor of her long stint of faithful underground service, she got the best shift at the mine, 3:00 to 11:00 p.m., and she didn't get hard duty. With the car track from the shaft landing to the mill's ore bins built with a slight downward slope, gravity aided Mary Jane Simpson as she hauled trains of six to ten linked ore cars to the mill. Uphill, she hauled only empty cars. She soon learned to understand the bells and whistles that regulated the mine, and she ran her own work with no man to direct her, hauling the loaded cars from mine to mill, waiting patiently for the mill workers to dump the ore, and returning to the shaft with the empties. Men supposed that she moved an average of $30,000 worth of ore per shift. When three bells struck the end of shift at 11:00 p.m., Mary Jane Simpson would return to the shaft house, step out of the track, and wait to be unharnessed, but instead of returning to her stable, she waited for the men to emerge from the mine. Nearly all of them had held back something from their dinners for her.

Apples, eggs, pie, roast beef, she ate it all without discrimination and never turned her nose away from an offering. An utterly devoted man named Ben Smith served as her groom. Smith was unmarried, and so far as is known, "had no earthly attachment" except for Mary Jane Simpson. As a team, they were a great success, as was the new mill, which nearly doubled the mine's bullion output.

In March 1875, the Con. Virginia increased its monthly dividend from the three dollars per share it had paid since the previous May to ten dollars per share. Paid on every one of the mine's 108,000 shares, the new dividend aggregated to $1,080,000. No mine had ever paid out more. The Firm's portion of that payout probably landed somewhere between $648,000 and $810,000, putting John Mackay's personal slice between $248,000 and $303,000 per month, in cash. That was, without question, the largest monthly cash income in the world. Throughout the West, people began referring to the Firm as "the Bonanza Firm" and to John Mackay as "the Bonanza King."

Mackay loathed the nickname. "It makes nothing of me but a millionaire with a swelled head," he said.

The ten-dollar dividend signified a tectonic shift on the Comstock. A new power had risen. The old power resented the upheaval, and frictions erupted between John Mackay's "Bonanza Crowd" flexing its muscles and William Sharon's Bank Ring fighting to maintain its grip. Their interests collided through the full spectrum of Comstock operations.

The first battle—a change in the tax provisions of Nevada and Storey County, which contained Virginia City and the Comstock Lode—resulted in a clear victory for the Bank Ring. In that game, William Sharon played a stacked deck against the Bonanza Firm from the start, for he was a politician, and John Mackay most definitely was not.

Sharon had politicked to hold state and county mining taxes low and drive them lower since he'd first arrived on the Comstock in 1864. Mining interests carried a light load while owners of other types of property bore the bulk of the tax burden. In Storey County, owners of other property paid $1.50 per $100 based on the assessed value of their assets. Mines only paid a tax of $0.25 per $100 worth of bullion produced and were allowed a host of ancillary deductions. Popular resentment against the unfair nature of the tax code rose in the early 1870s. In early 1875, the new state legislature—the one that made William Sharon a United States senator—revised the tax structure to make mines pay $1.50 per $100 worth of bullion, in line with what people paid on other types of property. Senator Sharon made no objection to the change. His mines were playing out. John Mackay's bonanza mines would carry the weight of the new taxes.

The tax hike wasn't the nut of what stuck in Mackay's craw, although he and his partners did complain about the midgame revision of the rules. What offended Mackay was the use to which Storey County intended to put the new tax revenue—the county planned to use the money to pay off the bonds that had financed construction of William Sharon's Virginia & Truckee Railroad. Mackay loathed the idea of his successful mines facilitating his archrival's primary business. With the Belcher and Crown Point bonanza fading and the Ophir's projected bonanza snuffed out before it had a chance to rise, the core of William Sharon's power on the Comstock had shifted to the railroad, which had paid steady dividends since retiring the last of its debt in the summer of 1874.

To leverage their monopoly control of transportation to and from Gold Hill and Virginia City, William Sharon and the Bank Ring had invested huge sums developing the Carson & Tahoe Lumber and Fluming Company to feed timber to the Comstock mines from fifty thousand acres of old-growth timber along the southern and western shores of Lake Tahoe. The company felled trees and used short-line railroads to haul logs to the lake. Steam tugboats moved them across the lake, where lakefront sawmills trimmed and shaped the logs. Another short-line railroad carried the logs to a twelve-mile-long flume that rushed them down the mountains to a spur of the Virginia & Truckee.

The Bonanza Firm gouged at the Bank Ring by incorporating its own lumber company. Sharon tried to delay or derail the project with an unsuccessful squabble over water rights, but even after the Firm got its lumber company into operation, they still had to contend with the V&T's rapacious transportation rates.

Mackay grumbled about the rates and sought to have them reduced. The V&T refused.

Mackay quietly reiterated his desire to have the rates reduced. If not, he said, "I'll build my own damn railroad."

When Sharon heard about Mackay's statement, he reduced the Virginia & Truckee's rates at once. Sharon knew his adversary. Away from the poker table, Mackay didn't bluff. His threat to build a rival road pointed a spear at the heart of what remained of Sharon's power on the Comstock. With Mackay's mine disgorging a profit in excess of $1 million per month, Sharon's railroad monopoly existed at the Irishman's mercy.

Mackay and his partners pointed another spear at William Sharon and the Bank Ring when they decided to use their avalanche of money to open a rival bank, the Nevada Bank of San Francisco. Erected over an ore body worth uncounted millions, the power and stability of the Nevada Bank would stand unquestioned. In an industry with confidence as its lynchpin, people needed no special insight to see that the Nevada Bank of San Francisco would absorb a significant portion of the city's financial business.

For the Bank of California, the competition couldn't have come at a more inopportune moment—few people knew the details, but thanks to the freewheeling financial dealings of William C. Ralston, the Bank of California's foundation was decaying into quicksand.

Ralston had always been the institution's "soul," but he'd never drawn a clear boundary between his own affairs and those of the bank. Nor had he gleaned any significant lessons from the near-disaster he'd escaped in 1870–71 when Sharon had saved him and the one in the winter of 1872–73, when Colonel Fry and the Belcher bonanza had bailed him out. Belcher dividends combined with Ralston's share of the Union mills' profits and what he could see coming from the Virginia & Truckee Railroad had embarked Ralston on a path of even more aggressive financial undertakings. (If Ralston had learned any lesson, it was the wrong one—that the Comstock would always come to his rescue.)

Emboldened, Ralston veered from one speculative scheme to another, spreading bank funds all over California. He "loaned" large sums to businesses he controlled without review by other bank officials and usually on no security but the success of the ventures themselves. Many of the projects had long-run merit. Few held the prospect of short-run returns. None of them immolated more money than the Palace Hotel, which William Ralston had started building at the corner of San Francisco's Market and New Montgomery streets in late 1873.

Ralston intended the Palace not just as the biggest and best hotel in the West, but as the largest and most spectacular hotel in the world, a landmark achievement that would stake San Francisco's claim to a place on the vanguard of progress and civilization. On the practical side of the ledger, Ralston envisioned a magnificent establishment luring upscale development and jolting life into the stagnant New Montgomery Street Real Estate Development Company, where he'd had money tied up for about five years. To that end, the project lacked originality. Ralston had already built the Grand Hotel for the same purpose—directly across the street from the Palace's proposed address. Ralston responded to that objection with scale. The Palace would be an order of magnitude bigger and better than anything ever built in California.

William Sharon took a half share in the undertaking, but the Palace was always Ralston's darling. Ralston toured the construction site daily. He knew many of the workmen by name. No detail escaped his attention. For a man like Ralston, who couldn't experience "the need . . . of a nail without desiring to establish an iron foundry," such a large-scale construction project was a singularly dangerous undertaking. The Palace had broken ground in late 1873 with a projected budget of $1.75 million. Ralston blew through that sum before construction reached the level of the sidewalk.

All sixteen brickyards around San Francisco Bay worked full time to produce the required total of 31 million bricks. The superintendent employed 225 bricklayers, and when all went well, they laid 190,000 bricks per day, incorporating iron bars into the masonry to defend the structure from earthquakes. Two hundred and forty carpenters, one hundred ironworkers, a squad of men exclusively devoted to slacking lime and another to mixing cement, dozens of hod carriers, plumbers, rope riggers, and a small army of assorted laborers pushed the total workforce over 1,200. Ralston ordered plaster and cement from kilns in New York and England, gas and water pipes from a factory in Philadelphia, marble and slate tiles from quarries in Vermont, and 340 bathtubs and 685,000 sheets of plate glass from England. He sourced yellow pine from Georgia, teak and camphor wood from India, white mahogany from Mexico, and fir, oak, and ash from Oregon. Ralston created a company to manufacture the Palace's locks and door and cabinet fittings, and another to build its furniture. He bought a huge tract of oak woodlands—and subsequently discovered that the trees didn't produce lumber adequate to the flooring.

"Where is this thing going to end?" Sharon asked. On several occasions, he advised his partner to "pull in his sails."

Ralston did no such thing.

As the Palace Hotel mushroomed toward completion in 1874 and the first months of 1875, it filled an entire city block to the height of seven stories, towering over Market and New Montgomery streets. Four-in-hand teams pulling stately carriages could drive into the interior courtyard and turn around with ease. Every one of the Palace's nearly eight hundred rooms had a flush toilet and a multifaceted exterior bay window. In aggregate, they glittered across the hotel's enormous facades. Construction costs rose to somewhere between $5 million and $6.5 million.

California boosters eager to claim the biggest and best of everything reveled in the "gigantic enterprise," as if grand ambition alone proved the world-class stature of California, but not all commentary was positive. A real estate publication in November 1874 described the Palace as "a dark menace to Montgomery Street." The *Marin Journal* called it a "vast pile" and joked about Mephistophelian bargains struck on a mythical seventeen-hundred-foot level of the basement.

In the first months of 1875, as friction between the Bank Ring and John Mackay's Bonanza Crowd intensified and the Palace Hotel built toward its autumn opening, Ralston's financial commitments mounted. The impact of the economic depression in the eastern states beginning to take a toll in California worsened Ralston's position—millions of dollars' worth of gold coin flowed from California to New York, constricting the California money supply exactly when Ralston needed "easy" money. The pace of Bank of California deposits from Mackay and the Bonanza Crowd slowed as they held back money to build a cash reserve for the opening of the Nevada Bank. Ralston's large portfolio of stagnant businesses and under- or nonperforming loans returned only a trickle of coin to the Bank of California. A steady stream of gold flowed in the opposite direction, and the money Ralston received from the Union mills, the Virginia & Truckee Railroad, and the Belcher's dwindling dividends failed to cover the outflows. Ralston's obligations began to exceed the reach of his cash flow, and since Ralston never drew a clear line between his own business and that of the bank, a crisis with Ralston automatically extended to the Bank of California.

Sharon asked Ralston what he'd do if they didn't unearth another Comstock bonanza.

"Go to the cemetery," Ralston answered.

Although Sharon would later deny it in court, he must have known that his partner was dangerously undermining the Bank of California.

Attempting to keep both himself and the bank above water, Ralston sold his half of the Palace Hotel to William Sharon for $1.75 million in May. Considering the energy and vision—not to mention the gold—Ralston had invested in the project, the deal must have pained him greatly.

The transaction made William Sharon the largest real estate owner in San Francisco, with property "worth at least seven millions." Sharon had no inclination to celebrate. His partner of a decade was in tight financial straits, and his wife of twenty-three years was at death's door. Sharon was "unrelenting" in his attentions. He was at her San Francisco bedside when she "passed quietly into a better world" on Friday, May 14, two days after the Palace sale was registered.

On Saturday, Sharon's father died in Mount Pleasant, Ohio.

Sharon hardly had time to compose himself. The coming Thursday, the *Chronicle* published "The Stock-Jobbing Juggernaut," a savage attack on Sharon, Ralston, Mills, and the Bank Ring. The article focused on Sharon's mismanagement of the Ophir mine in service of nefarious stock manipulations and said Ralston held "a large interest," but perhaps the most damaging information within had nothing to do with stock manipulations or mine management—the *Chronicle* reported the Bank of California had loaned money on Ophir stock collateral at five times its present value, another public airing of weakness within the bank.

Another article in the same issue of the paper reported a rumor that Ralston had failed. "Probably there is not another citizen of California whose failure could bring so much distress upon this community as would Mr. Ralston's."

That rumor proved false, but Flood and O'Brien definitely *did* file the Nevada Bank of San Francisco's official articles of incorporation around that time. The Nevada Bank would open in October with a paid in capital of $5 million, equal to that supposedly possessed by the Bank of California.

Ralston's hope of salvation resided in the Spring Valley Water Company, the extraordinarily profitable corporation that monopolized the supply of water to San Francisco. In 1875, the company earned just over $1 million from water deliveries and distributed a whopping $640,000 in dividends. However, Spring Valley's existing supplies couldn't meet the growing city's needs.

The year before, an engineer had recommended expanding the system into the Calaveras Creek watershed northeast of San Jose,* building a reservoir, and piping the water thirty miles to the existing system. Ralston and a partner bought the reservoir site for $100,000 and through a series of exotic financial shenanigans, gained control of the water company. (Speculation before the Water Board a few months later insinuated that Ralston's partner had corrupted the engineer's report.) In May, Ralston sold the reservoir site he owned to the water company he controlled for slightly more than $1 million, turning a quick and nifty profit. Ralston and his partner offered to sell the Spring Valley Water Company to the city of San Francisco for $15.5 million. If Ralston could get that price, he thought his share of the profits would cover his obligations and see him through to smooth water, but San Francisco news-

---

* Not to be confused with Calaveras County or the Calaveras River in the foothills of the Sierras.

papers sent up screams of protest. The *Daily Alta California* called the water company proposal "a farcical pretense of fair dealing." A "white heat of opposition" led by the *Call* and *Bulletin* welded public opinion against the "brigand plans" of the schemers. The struggle played out before the board of supervisors through May, June, and July while the *Call* and the *Bulletin* assailed Billy Ralston's business competence and speculative savvy. Worse, the newspapers questioning the solvency of the Bank of California.

The money pinch worsened. Withdrawals by agricultural interests to finance the harvest and transport of the wheat crop drained $4 million from San Francisco circulation in the midsummer months. Not enough coin circulated in the city to keep the economy in free flow, and what of it there was tended to flow away from the Bank of California. Ralston's proceeds from the sales of the Palace Hotel and the reservoir site disappeared over the Bank of California's countertops. The bank's reserves slipped below the danger point. Ralston started writing checks to the bank from his personal account and ordered his "cash tags" counted among the bank reserves.

In mid-July, on the eve of an examining committee's inspection dispatched by the board of directors, Ralston repeated the ploy he'd used years before, "borrowing" $2 million in gold coin and stashing the specie in the vaults overnight. Come morning, he watched the examiners tot up the expected sum, about $2.5 million, then trucked the money that wasn't his back to its point of origin, leaving a sheaf of his cash tags in place of the gold.

On July 30, the board of supervisors formally rejected Ralston's proposed sale of the Spring Valley Water Company. The decision likely sealed his fate.

Ralston borrowed against $300,000 worth of Southern Pacific Railroad bonds deposited at the bank by Leland Stanford. He borrowed against the stock of the Water Company he controlled, even though he didn't actually own the stock. As a last resort, Ralston sold overissued Bank of California stock and collected $1.32 million—an outright fraud.

Ralston fed the money into the maw of the Bank of California. Nothing stanched the outflow of gold. In mid-August, Ralston began sacrificing his personal assets. Sharon and Mills "relieved" Ralston of "his most valuable Virginia & Truckee Railroad property at fifty cents on the dollar of its cash valuation." People with ownership ties to the bank began transferring property to other names.

On August 20, James Flood sent a trusted runner with a sealed note to Ralston.

Ralston read it and flushed deep red. "Son, do you know what is in this note?" he asked the runner.

"No, sir," came the reply.

"Well, you go back and tell Flood that I'll send him back to selling rum over the Auction Lunch counter!"—the bar he'd once tended that still sold drinks a few blocks away.

Flood heard Ralston's message and told his runner, "You go right back and tell Ralston that *Mr.* Flood says that in a short time he will be able to sell rum over the counter of the Bank of California."

Delivery of that message turned Ralston pale. He was in Flood's office within fifteen minutes. Flood's original note had notified Ralston that the Firm intended to withdraw a substantial quantity of coin. Ralston left Flood's office with Flood's assurance that he would leave the money in place for another week.

Ralston and Sharon offered to sell two Washoe quartz mills to the Firm, knowing that lack of milling capacity forced Mackay and Fair to suppress Con. Virginia and California ore production. The "final dicker" took place between Sharon, Ralston, and Mackay at the Bank of California building in San Francisco.

Ralston and Sharon offered the mills for $300,000.

"What's the use of paying $300,000 for property worth only $100,000?" Mackay asked.

Sharon turned to Ralston and said, "You see? [These Irishmen] will never be satisfied unless they get possession of everything."

With that, Mackay got up and returned to Virginia City, refusing to waste more words on the subject.

Ralston begged aid from Sharon and D. O. Mills on August 22. Sharon claimed he'd exhausted his available resources buying Ralston's half of the Palace Hotel. Mills supposedly produced $750,000, although the report doesn't square with Mills's reputation for only loaning on gilded security. On August 23, Ralston had an associate ask the Oriental Bank of London for an extension of additional credit. The Oriental Bank didn't even bother to reply. The next day, Ralston sold sixteen thousand acres of fine agricultural land in Kern County to Colonel Fry, his de facto father-in-law.

Something "nearly akin to panic" swept the stock market on August 25, particularly among "those stocks most relied upon to raise money under pressure." Such wild turbulence hadn't roiled the market since the debacles of January and February. The declines uncovered many margins, and given the tight money market, the banks, brokers, and other operators couldn't produce "more mud" to re-cover them, precipitating forced sales and further declines. The *Daily Alta California* credited the millions of dollars of coin struck from Big Bonanza bullion and entered into circulation as the only force carrying the state's economy forward against "the existing pressure." The *San Francisco Chronicle* did exactly the opposite, describing a complex, far-reaching manipulation by Flood and O'Brien that had sucked coin from circulation. Cutting away the ridiculous complexities of the *Chronicle's* conspiracy theory revealed the nugget of truth within the story: Stocks "belonging to the bank ring came forth as if under the stimulus of a pressing necessity."

Ralston's doomsday of accountability drew nigh. The Bank of California's board of directors met at William Sharon's house that night. The bank's cashier informed them that there was only $500,000 in coin in the bank's vaults—and $1.5 million worth of Ralston's "cash tags." Those held the exact value of pieces of paper written against an overdrawn account. Tracing the bank's recent transactions revealed that Ralston had sent more than $2 million worth of bullion belonging to other people from the Assaying and Refining Company, which he controlled, to the mint, added the struck coin to the Bank of California's vaults, and debited the transactions against his empty private account. The coin had long since vanished over the countertops of the bank. (Some $1.4 million of the missing bullion belonged to the Firm.) Hasty calculations by the bank secretary and board members estimated that Ralston's personal debt to the Bank of California ranged between $4 million and $4.5 million.

Soon after the Bank of California opened on Thursday, August 26, 1875, people noticed "something like a run" in progress. Depositors, both large and small, withdrew from the bank through the morning hours. At the opening of the Stock & Exchange Board at 11:00 a.m., brokers representing William Sharon issued unlimited sell orders. Prices collapsed, amid "feverish excitement."

Behind closed doors, Sharon and Mills offered the Bank of California to Flood and O'Brien for $5 million, with a guarantee of $2.5 million of the bank's liabilities if the Bonanza Firm would assume responsibility for debts above that figure and hold the directors and stockholders harmless. The Irishmen examined the account books and refused the offer.

Around 1:00 p.m., people began to materialize around the California Street offices of the Bank of California on the rumor that the London and San Francisco Bank was refusing to cash checks drawn against the Bank of California. By one-thirty, a huge crowd pressed against the bank counters of the "beleaguered institution," pushing, shoving, reaching over the heads of those in front, jostling, yelling, desperate to get their hands on their money and avoid calamity. "Anxious men" handed in checks and retreated, "eagerly clutching the proffered gold." They exited the bank with relieved, exultant smiles that did nothing to quell the tension in those still separated from their coin.

To an inquisitive reporter, Ralston dismissed the run as due to "stringency in the money market caused by the recent heavy withdrawal of coin from circulation." The panic worsened after two o'clock.

Even then, the bank almost survived. Ralston ordered the exterior doors shut at 2:35 p.m., twenty-five minutes before normal closing time, but continued to pay people already inside. A messenger from another bank pushed forward the fateful piece of paper nine minutes later. A teller passed it to Ralston.

Ralston looked at a check for $5,485 and announced, "We will not cash any more checks today."

News that the greatest financial institution on the Pacific Coast had suspended hit the public "like a thunderclap." The Bank of California's directors went into conclave at three o'clock. They emerged at half-past five. The assembled reporters asked Darius Ogden Mills if the bank had suspended payments or failed.

The bank's affairs were in "a greatly involved condition," Mills explained. "I fear that it has failed."

The *Alta*'s reporter present noted William Ralston "striving to repress any agitation of manner, and not with perfect success." Ralston invited the reporters into his office and said that there was "no question whatsoever as to the ability of the Bank to meet all its obligations and leave considerable of a surplus beside."

A reporter asked if the bank would resume business in the morning.

"No, sir," Ralston replied. "We will not resume."

"How soon do you propose to resume business?" came another question.

Ralston hesitated. "We don't expect to resume," he said.

"Not at all?" asked an incredulous journalist.

"No, sir," Ralston said. The Bank of California's branches in Virginia City and Gold Hill and their agency in New York had all been telegraphed instructions to close.

Ralston asked the bank secretary to read a brief statement. The bank had "been compelled to suspend business." The board of trustees were examining the situation "critically." They promised a report at "the earliest possible moment." They declined to make any further comment.

Ralston moved toward the door. The journalists followed him with a press of questions.

"What caused the suspension?"

"Scarcity of coin," said Ralston. Four million dollars had gone to the interior to move the wheat crop. None was expected to return from that source before winter.

"Is the report correct that Flood and O'Brien offered to relieve this Bank?"

"We have received no such word at this office."

Someone asked if Flood and O'Brien withdrew $1,800,000 yesterday, as had been published elsewhere.

Ralston called that rumor "nonsense" and "balderdash" and said, "There is no truth in it. So far as our relations with those gentlemen are concerned, they are of a character perfectly pleasant and agreeable, nothing unpleasant in any way, shape or form; nor has there been any such words as were reported. None whatsoever.

"You see we are here with a metallic currency," Ralston continued, "and this is one disadvantage—when you get to the bottom of the tub you can't lift yourself up."

Ralston ducked into a side room and shut the door. He left the bank shortly after 9:30 p.m. That night, he told an old friend that his "great hope and desire" was to pay every dollar due to his depositors and pay a large dividend to the bank's stockholders, even if it took all of his property to do it. Ralston said that although he didn't expect to be able to leave much to his children, he did "want to leave them a good name."

On Friday, the bank directors met again at 1:00 p.m. A more detailed perusal of the books than they'd managed at Sharon's house thirty-six hours earlier revealed $14 million in liabilities against between $7 million and $8 million in assets. Subsequent reports showed Ralston's personal responsibilities at nearly $9.6 million, of which only $4.2 million was adequately secured. Of his $5.4 million in unsecured debt, he owed $4.7 million to the Bank of California. Without that money, the bank was insolvent. According to inquest and court testimony that would follow, the directors claimed that not until this meeting had they "fully understood . . . the true condition of the Bank." Behind a solid front, they would maintain, "The extent of serious abuses that had been practiced in the institution had been concealed from them up to and for some hours after the suspension." That may have had something to do with the fact that California law then held corporate directors and stockholders personally liable for a company's debt. All would suffer a gigantic assessment to pay off the balance. The directors' fury at Ralston's indiscretions—to use no harsher phrase—can only be imagined.

Ralston had been excluded from the meeting. He was in his office elsewhere in the bank. The directors appointed Darius Ogden Mills "a committee of one" to go to Ralston and request his resignation.

After Mills returned to the directors meeting with the desired document, William Sharon went to see Ralston. The *Daily Alta California* first reported that in that meeting, Ralston transferred all his real and personal property to the bank to help make good on its debts, an action "generally commented on in a tone of great respect for Mr. Ralston." Not for some time did the public understand that Ralston hadn't transferred his property to the bank. His railroad and manufacturing interests, his Belmont estate, his houses in San Francisco, and his other real estate holdings, all of it, everything he owned, down to and including his horses and carriages, had gone to William Sharon.

At the close of their meeting, Sharon asked Ralston to leave the building. Ralston walked outside, homeless and penniless, abandoned by the institution he had nurtured from infancy, unemployed and perhaps unemployable in the business he knew best, reduced to poverty by his own act, shorn of friends, and probably deeply ashamed. Ralston walked off in the direction of North Beach. A few minutes before three o'clock, three boys wandering the North Beach shoreline recognized Ralston coming down the bluff. Dressed in a neat black suit, the forlorn banker walked out an old, decaying wharf and sat down on the outermost surviving stringers. He took several letters from his pocket, tore them to shreds, and scattered the pieces in the bay. After a few moments of contemplation, Ralston heaved himself up, and passing one of the boys, asked him if he thought it was too cold for a swim. The boy said that he did not. Ralston walked west to the cove that arced out to Black Point. The boy and his friends followed, watching Ralston withdraw a few more letters from the breast pocket of his coat, shred them, and toss the scraps in the water. Ralston then did the same with the pages of two leather-bound books.

Swimming in Black Point Cove was a popular San Francisco pastime. Typically, Ralston did it two or three times a week, most recently the previous Monday. Bright-painted cabanas belonging to the Neptune Bath House lined the shore. Ralston paid the proprietor a half-dollar for towels and spoke cheerfully to one of the small children playing nearby.

After changing into his swimming costume, Ralston walked to the end of a wharf and dove in headfirst. The proprietor watched him "striking out bravely" toward the old steamship *Bullion* anchored off the Selby Lead and Silver Smelting Works. Ralston alternately dipped under the surface and swam on his back until he was some four to six hundred yards from shore. Fifteen or twenty minutes later, the bath house proprietor and his son-in-law, two men relaxing in one of the cabanas, the watchman and the assayer at the smelting works, and the *Bullion*'s engineer all noticed something wrong with Ralston in the water.

The engineer cast off the painters that secured a small boat to the *Bullion* and rowed toward Ralston. Although he told the *Daily Alta California* reporter that day that he seized Ralston by the hair and wrestled his body over the gunwales with "considerable difficulty," his inquest testimony described Ralston's flesh quivering when he first touched him, his certainty that Ralston was still alive and doing what he could to save himself, and the stricken banker's much more dignified entry into the rowboat (likely to help Ralston's widow receive his life insurance payout, because it supported the contention that he wasn't a suicide). The engineer pulled for the beach as fast as he could, calling for help. He reached the shore a few minutes before four o'clock. Helping hands hauled Ralston's stout body from the boat and laid him on the sand.

When a *Daily Alta California* reporter arrived on the scene about forty-five minutes later, he found a few boys, sailors, longshoremen, and bareheaded women gathered around Ralston. Five men "energetically manipulated the body with the purpose of winning back the almost flown spark of vital fire." Three of the men massaged Ralston's lower limbs and flexed his arms. A doctor pressed upon and released Ralston's chest at regular intervals to stimulate his heart, and a young German cradled Ralston's head in his lap and "glued his lips to those of the almost inanimate man . . . forcing his own life-giving breath into the speechless mouth."

Colonel Fry, Robert Morrow, and Lloyd Tevis—all three important figures on the Comstock—Mayor Otis, and a number of Ralston's other personal friends joined the ever-larger crowd of onlookers. To the young German giving Ralston "artificial breathing," it seemed that Ralston's cold body warmed up for the first half hour. He and the other rescuers sustained their attempt for forty-five minutes, until ten minutes to five o'clock, when "a violent gasp and shudder" shook Ralston, followed by "complete quiet."

The crowd fell silent in the strange and solemn presence of death.

The wreck of a half-sunken sloop stood in the water nearby. Only a few hushed voices and the slow, rhythmic lapping of the incoming tide broke the silence. Tears filled the eyes of many onlookers as the coroner's "dead-wagon"—"a long black box on wheels"—drawn by a single horse, hauled away the body.

Reporters on the scene noticed torn pieces of paper still floating in the water. They wet their feet recovering fragments, but couldn't make sense from the words they contained.

That night, many of Ralston's innumerable friends and associates gathered in disbelief to view his body at Colonel Fry's house and console his widow and children. Among them were William Sharon and bank secretary Stephen Franklin. Wearing dark suits of mourning, Sharon and Franklin stood together to view Ralston's body. According to Franklin, Sharon looked down at his dead partner and said, "Best thing he could have done."

Spurred to action by the Bank of California's collapse and Ralston's death, and likely by a summons from Flood and O'Brien, John Mackay reached San Francisco on Saturday morning, August 28. William Sharon met Mackay at the Ferry Building, probably wanting assurances of a truce that would allow him to execute his nascent plan to reconstitute the Bank of California. By that time, the financial panic had ended. All that remained was the ruined bank and the sadness of Ralston's death. No other commercial failures had attended the Bank of California's collapse. A hired hack took the two men up into town. Ralston had been a giant in California for much of the time Mackay had been in the West, and personally, Mackay had liked and admired him.

"Did you do everything you could to save him?" Mackay asked.

"I was afraid for a time that we would have to," Sharon answered.

"The son-of-a-bitch," Mackay added to describe Sharon when he told the story in later years.

In San Francisco, William Chapman Ralston had defined the age. Flags all over the city flew at half-mast. The *Daily Alta California* eulogized him as the city's "mainspring," lauded his energy, industry, and enterprise, and found it "sad that such a life should have closed in such awful shadow." Eyewitnesses estimated that half the population of San Francisco followed Ralston's cortege from his funeral service at Calvary Presbyterian Church in Union Square west to the Lone Mountain Cemetery.

Darius Ogden Mills, William Sharon and twenty-one other prominent San Franciscans served as pallbearers. The quiet, somber processions exceeded three miles in length and took forty-two minutes to pass.

For Ralston's death and the fall of the Bank of California, San Francisco editorialists and opinion makers blamed Darius Ogden Mills, the bank directors, the Bonanza Crowd, the *Bulletin* and *Call*, the many supposed friends who should have come to Ralston's aid, and William Sharon. *Especially* William Sharon. They blamed everyone *except* William Ralston. Rumors abroad already claimed that the institution he'd founded would be "resuscitated" based on a subscription of capital from some of the state's wealthiest men.

William Sharon fronted the scheme. Over the next several weeks of effort to revive the Bank of California, Sharon played the highest stakes poker game of his life. Nobody else among the bank's other principals had the guts to try. Darius Ogden Mills and several other directors suggested bankruptcy. Threats to their personal fortunes by Bank of California creditors changed their minds. Sharon convinced Mills to join him at the head of a syndicate of leading San Franciscans dedicated to recapitalizing and reopening the bank. Mills would assume the revived bank's presidency. Sharon and Mills each contributed $1 million. On rough tables fitted into the parlor of his San Francisco mansion, Sharon worked like a fiend, surrounded by paper, pencils, and clouds of cigar smoke, meeting with a stream of recalcitrant, reluctant, angry men with only one common interest—money. Some men Sharon convinced to join in an effort to honor Ralston's legacy. He appealed to the sense of civic duty in others. Still others he threatened. When necessary, he lied and bluffed, and in one week, Sharon collected promises totaling more than $7.5 million from sixty-three individuals and the Stock & Exchange Board.

To clear the bank's accounts, Sharon bought Ralston's debt and all of his security from the Bank of California for $1.5 million, along with the assurance that he could keep any proceeds that might result from the liquidation of Ralston's assets and the settlement of his liabilities. The purchase forced Ralston's creditors to deal with Sharon personally, in private, rather than with the institution of the bank. The paperwork detailing the precise nature of Sharon's partnership with Ralston disappeared from a safe. He located and rebought the overissued stock Ralston had sold, much of it for a fraction of the original purchase price. Sharon sponsored positive newspaper articles and kept the goodwill of Ralston alive with public meetings that honored his memory. As much as possible, he obscured the scope of Ralston's iniquities and the negligent oversight of the bank's directors. On October 2, 1875, five weeks and a day after the suspension, William Sharon reopened the bank.

He did it on the same day as the Palace Hotel's gala debut. Around 11:00 p.m., after an orchestra completed playing Franz von Suppé's *Poet and Peasant* overture in the "brilliantly illuminated" interior courtyard of his new hotel, Sharon gave a speech in which he lauded the "proud and manly spirit" of William Ralston and the "resuscitation" of the institution he'd founded. "Bursts of applause" interrupted Sharon's speech on several occasions, and "prolonged cheering" followed his conclusion. In a fit of the self-congratulatory boosterism for which San Franciscans had become famous, the *Daily Alta California* hailed the resumption as "a feat that could not have been accomplished outside of California."

That William Sharon's fancy new hotel wouldn't have sold for half of its construction cost went unmentioned in the publicity and celebration.

The four Irish Bonanza Kings opened the Nevada Bank of San Francisco two days later, with much less fanfare. Although Sharon's Bank of California reopening captured by far the larger number of column inches, the wheel of financial power had turned on the Pacific Coast. William Sharon and the Bank of California found themselves in second place. John Mackay, James Fair, James Flood, and William O'Brien had risen to dominance. A *New York Times* article that season estimated John Mackay's total net worth at $75 million, called him "the richest man on the Pacific Coast," and noted that sixteen years before, he'd been swinging a pick at the face of a drift for four dollars a day.

John Mackay, his partners, and the miners who worked for them settled down to face one of the most gargantuan mining challenges of all time—extracting the entirety of the Big Bonanza, the vast majority of which still remained underground.

Things didn't proceed in the manner they anticipated. Just three weeks later, on the morning of October 26, 1875, a gray dawn crept into leaden skies over Virginia City. The uniform layer of cloud rushing over the Sierras from California portended a storm. Fierce Washoe zephyrs thundered down the sides of Mount Davidson, one minute still, and then charging past gale force in the next to churn the dust, thrash the sagebrush, and moan around the walls of the town. One of the few persons abroad that early morning was a ten-year-old boy named Grant Smith.*

---

* Late in life, Smith would become an important Comstock historian whose book *His-*

He patrolled up B Street scouting for pigeons to shoot with his slingshot. Passing in front of Mooney's Stable, Smith heard the cry, "Fire!"

The boy looked uphill into the driving wind and saw a thin stream of smoke trailing from a small, one-story frame boardinghouse belonging to Kate Shay, otherwise known as "Crazy Kate." The *Sacramento Daily Union* called her "a woman of ill-repute;" the *San Francisco Chronicle* called hers a "lodging house [of] a low order," and reported some of the occupants up late the night before "in a drunken carousal." According to *Enterprise* reporter Dan de Quille, people in the adjoining houses heard a coal-oil lamp break during a drunken row. At a minimum, someone had left a candle burning unattended. A neighbor saw an eerie light, barged in, and found flames licking up the wallpaper and wooden walls of the room next to Kate's bedchamber. Alarm bells clanged, and within minutes, Kate's house "flamed like a torch." The house's light siding and desiccated shingles caught fire, warped, and whirled away in the angry wind. Some landed in Mooney's stable and caught fire to the hay in the hay yard, which the wind carried away like flaming chaff.

According to Grant Smith, "a garden hose could have put out the fire" when the alarm first rung, but the fire department arrived tardy. Scarcely a drop of rain had fallen for months, and the town was tinder dry. A fireman wheeled up a Babcock fire extinguisher, followed by the hand-pumped engine of Fire Company No. 4, but their efforts went for naught. The angry zephyrs whipped the fire fiend loose. Within fifteen minutes, twenty buildings were in flames. Church bells commenced ringing. Engineers at the hoisting works let loose their steam whistles. In the next five minutes, the number of burning buildings doubled. A few minutes later, an area equal to a whole city block was aflame. People nearby tumbled into the streets in their bedclothes, many just as the fire spread to their houses. Smith rushed home. The pair of two-story houses between A and B streets owned by his family caught fire. His mother salvaged a handful of valuables and hustled him and his three brothers up the hillside to the dump of the old Sides Shaft, from where they watched the calamity unfold. People below piled into the streets. Men and women shouted, screamed, and swore as greedy flames drew their lodgings and businesses into the inferno. A gigantic pyramid of fire grew over an ever-expanding base of burning buildings. Hundreds of feet overhead, the flame tips writhed into roiling clouds of smoke, showering sparks and

---

tory of the Comstock Lode and archival material held by the Bancroft Library at the University of California, Berkeley, have contributed greatly to this work.

burning fragments all over the lower city. Wind-driven cinders kindled new fires far in advance of the onrushing wall of flame.

The church bells, fire alarms, and steam whistles never ceased clanging and shrieking. Their discordant din blended with the crash and thud of falling walls, the dull report of building after building bursting into flames, the smash of iron doors falling from their mountings, the shatter of window glass burned from its frames, the howl of the wind, and the shrieks and cries of despair. Above it all moaned the bass roar of the firestorm. The "hideous and demoralizing" cacophony drove the whole town mad.

Acre after acre of buildings joined the "sea of fire." A dense, stinking cloud of gray-brown and black smoke boiled over the city, whipped north and east by the wind. Desperate to save something from the impending calamity, families three or four blocks ahead of the flames heaped belongings into the streets. Merchants vomited wares onto the sidewalks and fought to engage wagons. Teamsters jacked prices high and whipped their animals through the mayhem, cursing. Frantic citizens pressed every conceivable conveyance into service, from wheelbarrows to barouches. Without time to rig terrified animals into harness, men by the hundreds took the place of draft animals and hauled loaded wagons toward the outskirts of town. Women and children staggered beneath impossible loads. Rough hands carried a woman in labor to safety. Horsemen galloped through the crowds, heedless of the foot-bound multitudes. Behind them all, the ravening flames leaped skyward "with a rush and a loud roar." People fled as if they were trying to escape the sack of Troy.

The wind veered and lashed the fire four blocks up A and B streets. Another shift swept it down to C Street and encircled the county buildings. By 9:00 a.m., a "cyclone of fire" enveloped the county buildings, the International Hotel, the Bank of California, and the whole rest of the core of the city above C Street. Twenty-five miles away, the population of Reno could see the black cloud boiling up from behind the Virginia Range.

Telegrams from Virginia City threw San Francisco into a "ferment." A rash of panic selling cratered the stock market. Speculators pressed James Flood for information. What had he heard from his partners? Flood hadn't heard a thing. He expressed confidence that Mackay and Fair were doing their duty, fighting the fire.

Flood knew his partners well. John Mackay's house at the corner of Howard and Taylor had burnt down, along with a number of other dwellings on "millionaires row." Mackay hadn't made the slightest effort to save it. He and Fair had been on site at the Con. Virginia hoisting works since shortly after the first alarm. Both miners recognized the extreme danger—the Con. Virginia works were right in the heart of town, and wind threatened to drive the fire right over them. They ordered everyone out of the threatened mines under their control—the Con. Virginia, the California, the Best & Belcher, and the Gould & Curry. Anything on the surface could be rebuilt, the whole town if necessary, but if fire burned down the Con. Virginia shaft and got into the timber-filled stopes far below, they'd lose the richest mine in the world forever. The fire had to be kept out of the shaft at all costs. Mackay had anticipated the danger. He had a plan. With every last man hoisted from the Con. Virginia, Mackay directed the engineers to lower the cages into a flat line a few feet below the surface. Miners sprang the safety catches to fix the cages in the shaft. Men working like demons floored over the pumping compartment and piled sandbags, dirt, and ore onto the cage hoods to make a fireproof bulkhead. Others shoveled sand and dirt onto the floor of the hoisting works. Mackay was everywhere directing the work.

Outside, the fire surged across C Street toward D. If it leaped D Street and caught to the huge structure of Piper's Opera House on the east side of the street, the whole block between D and E streets would catch fire. If that happened, nothing could stop the fire leaping E Street, burning the railroad depot, and getting level with the Con. Virginia hoisting works. Then, the slightest northward twitch of wind would doom the works. The police chief gave his okay. Mackay led gangs of miners dynamiting the Opera House and a line of adjacent houses in the hopes of creating a fire break. The thudding detonations added a new touch of horror to the mayhem.

A few blocks south of the Con. Virginia hoisting works, the wood-shingled roof of the Catholic church started catching fire. A pious old Irishwoman bustled off to find John Mackay. She found him battling to save the Con. Virginia. "Oh, Mr. Mackay, the church is on fire!" she said. Perhaps he could save it?

"Damn the church!" Mackay exclaimed. "We can build another if we can keep the fire from going down these shafts!"

When the wind began scattering the church's burning shingles into the lower city, miners dynamited the entire structure. Wind-driven flames vaulted the firebreaks with hardly a pause. Inability to stop the fire at Piper's Opera House doomed the Virginia & Truckee Railroad Depot, and once the depot caught fire, the Con. Virginia hoisting works couldn't be saved. Men fell back before onrushing walls of flame.

Thousands of feet of mine timbers and hundreds of cords of firewood stored in the depot yard and outside the hoisting works caught fire and swelled to volcanic infernos. The stupendous heat pouring from the woodpiles melted the metal wheels of nearby railroad cars. By 9:30 a.m., flames began to envelop the hoisting works. Driven by wind and the hellish heat, the fire raced down the trestle work supporting the car track over which the mule Mary Jane Simpson hauled the ore from the shaft to the mill. Only when they heard her terrified braying did the men realize that no one had loosed her from her stable. By then, it was too late to save her. Getting her out was suicide, but Ben Smith, her devoted groom, secured a pistol and tried to find a vantage from which he could shoot his beloved mule. Desperate to shorten her agony, he wriggled into a crawlspace beneath the hoisting works while the building took fire over his head. Heat scorched his skin and singed his hair and whiskers. Smoke choked Smith. Mary Jane Simpson's screams drove him on. He couldn't find a position from which to administer the merciful shot. Mary Jane Simpson died in horrible agony. Ben Smith barely escaped with his life.

The fire burned along the trestle work and consumed the Con. Virginia's massive, state-of-the-art mill and the stamp batteries of the almost-complete California mill. Stopping the fire going down the Ophir shaft was just as important as keeping it out of the Con. Virginia—the mines connected underground. At the Ophir, Superintendent Sam Curtis and his men worked as furiously as Mackay and Fair and their crews at the Con. Virginia. Ophir men bulkheaded their shaft twenty feet below the surface and heaped sand and dirt atop the blockage as the building burned. At the last second, they fled for their lives.

With a solid wall of flames running through the railroad depot, the hoisting works of the Ophir and Con. Virginia and the Con. Virginia mill and all their lumber yards, the battle shifted to the C&C hoisting works a thousand feet farther down the hill. They, too, seemed doomed. With what the *Territorial Enterprise* described as "his old miner instinct and miner's knowledge," Mackay led the desperate fight to save them. Under Mackay's direction, miners dynamited a line of houses below G Street and dragged away the debris. The *San Francisco Chronicle* correspondent described the effort as "superhuman." The wind was threatening to jump the flames over the firebreak and drive the fire onto the C&C works when a southward swing of the wind gave the men the chance to complete the firebreak. The respite provided the critical opportunity. The fire never crossed H Street. The C&C hoisting works survived.

By 1:00 p.m., the worst of it was over. The flames died as they ate the fuel that sustained them, leaving ghastly wreckage. The half-mile-square heart of Virginia City had vanished. Coils and wraiths of smoke rose from charcoal and ashes. Here and there stood remnants of brick walls. The great machinery of the mines and mills stood like iron specters in the writhing smoke, every massive arm and wheel still. A gush of smoke rose from the Ophir shaft, raising fears that the mine had caught fire, but most everywhere else, the flames had burned down to smoldering embers. The majority of the burnt district had been scoured to ground level. Gale-strength wind gusts swept the desolation, carrying away sheets of tin roofing and great blasts of dust and ash.

Early estimates of the number of people rendered homeless ranged from two thousand to ten thousand. The fire swept away two hundred businesses, including the Bank of California, Piper's Opera House, most of the town's saloons, and "all the small houses on D Street," which the *Daily Alta California* described as "occupied by a class of population which will be no great loss to the city." (The *Alta*'s moralizing would have no discernible effect on the demimonde's reoccupation.)

The aftermath showed Americans of the West at their finest. The calamity obliterated social distinctions. Everybody tried to make everybody else as comfortable as possible under the circumstances. Ladies in the surviving parts of town cooked meals, then went into the streets to hunt up burnt-out families too proud to ask for assistance.

The town's population of single men burned out of lodgings and possessions soon began availing themselves of the copious stocks of whisky in the unburned portion of town. They roamed the ruined streets in packs, howling, singing, and gazing on the devastation through the distorting lenses of the liquor jugs. The overwhelming press of business in the few surviving saloons led barkeeps to refuse to mix drinks. Patrons had to content themselves with "uncompromising straights."

Storm built over the Sierras, and women and children wandered around looking for places to lay their heads. The Third Ward School housed as many as possible, but even with it and other public buildings and assembly halls packed to capacity and every surviving bed in town double- or triple-shotted with refugees, the available space didn't suffice. Burned-out men and their families sought shelter in old mine tunnels and bivouacked in the lee of boulders and behind sagebrush windbreaks. Their campfires dotted the hills around town after dark. Burning embers and a hellish orange glow emanating from the mouth of the Ophir shaft reflected onto the base of rising smoke clouds. Fire had passed the Ophir bulkhead. Bucket brigades and fire companies fought to stop its progress down the shaft. Snow began falling at 8:00 p.m. An hour later, the snowflakes turned to light rain. A series of heavy showers rode through the area on the still-blustery wind about two o'clock in the morning. The Comstock passed a miserable night.

Like so much of the city, the *Territorial Enterprise* had been burned out. Having lost its building, printing presses, boxes of type, and the entirety of its archive, the newspaper missed its next day's issue. Forty-eight hours after the fire, the *Enterprise* reappeared on just two pages instead of its usual four, thanks to the good offices of the proprietor of the *Gold Hill Daily News*, who allowed his Virginia City rivals use of his printing presses. In a brief article titled "Characteristic," the *Enterprise* described a "haggard" figure emerging from the successful battle to save the C&C hoisting works, "begrimed with dust, powder-smoke, and the smoke of the fire." The man was John Mackay, looking "like a laborer just ready to drop from exhaustion."

Mackay sat on a berm and watched the fire burn itself out. An old acquaintance approached. "Mackay, you've lost what would have bought an earldom today."

"Don't speak of it," Mackay said. "It's not any matter and isn't worth mentioning." He gathered what remained of his strength. "Let's see what we can do toward making these women and babies comfortable."

CHAPTER 16

The Bonanza King

Virginia City at the peak of the bonanza times.

To call a place dreary, desolate, homeless, uncomfortable, and wicked is a good deal, but to call it God-forsaken is a good deal more, and in a tolerably large experience of this world's wonders, we never found a place better deserving the title than Virginia City.

—Miriam Florence Leslie, *California: A Pleasure Trip from Gotham to the Golden Gate*

Of course the town rebuilt. The *San Francisco Chronicle*'s reporter on scene described Virginia as "determined to come out strong under adverse circumstances." The first burned-out man back in business was O. C. Steele. He erected a shanty and sold butchered meat from one end and whisky from the other. Not long thereafter, The Snug Saloon opened over two charred boards, dispensing bit whisky to "the Virginia sufferers" while a cold wind drove spitting clouds overhead.

Senator Sharon granted relief efforts use of the Virginia & Truckee

Railroad. The ladies of Carson City sent hot coffee, eight hundred loaves of bread, one thousand pounds of cooked ham, a comparable quantity of beef, and other "substantial vivands" up the railroad and alleviated the immediate hunger. Upward of two thousand people partook. Blankets, clothing, and shoes arrived on subsequent trains. One package of blankets came from a San Francisco clothing manufacturer named Levi Strauss whose patented rivet-reinforced denim pants had become popular among Comstock miners in the two years since their introduction.

Trudging among the devastation, John Mackay sought out Father Manogue. Knowing that if he personally opened his vaults, his good offices would attract a few grafters among many genuine sufferers, and when he found them out, he'd get angry and be liable to insult and reject subsequent worthy cases, Mackay asked the father to operate the purse strings of relief on his behalf. "Do it thoroughly," Mackay said, "and when you need help draw upon me and keep drawing." In the coming months, Mackay supported Father Manogue's efforts to the tune of $150,000. (His contributions also did much to finance reconstruction of the church he'd damned to save his mine.*)

Near the Con. Virginia's wrecked works, the *Chronicle* correspondent buttonholed James Fair as he was about to drive off in a small wagon. The reporter asked if the noxious gas rising from the shafts of the Ophir and the Con. Virginia meant that the mines were on fire.

Fair, visibly annoyed, told him that he'd just inspected both mines and that there was "no more fire [underground] than here in my buggy."

John Mackay was more accommodating. He'd been through all the mines with Fair that morning and found no gas or fire in any of them. The old Sides Shaft had burned, he explained, and gas had worked its way into the mines through the Latrobe Tunnel, which connected them all. As he'd telegrammed Flood and O'Brien in San Francisco, things looked "all right" underground. Curiously, neither Mackay nor the reporter mentioned the all-night struggle Sam Curtis and his men had waged to stop fire going down the Ophir shaft. In the coming weeks, they rebuilt it from the surface to a depth of four hundred feet.

In the immediate aftermath, the *San Francisco Call* had quoted Mackay as saying that the mines wouldn't raise ore before spring. A telegram from the president of the stock board asked for Mackay's confirmation, since "coming from you this statement has great weight."

---

* The rebuilt St. Mary's in the Mountains Catholic Church still stands, one of the most beautiful nineteenth-century buildings in Nevada.

Mackay's return telegram called the report "mistaken." He'd said no such thing. If the weather cooperated, he said, "sixty days will repair all damage to works. I think the mines are all right. . . . Things look brighter today."

Kitchens established at the Third Ward School served upward of fifteen hundred people per day. Chinese citizens shared the fare for the first day or two, which the newspapers cited as evidence of Comstock magnanimity. If so, the egalitarian mentality lasted less than forty-eight hours. Afterward, the relief committee issued Chinese refugees uncooked rations instead.

Only five days later, a *Chronicle* subheadline confidently reported "The City Rapidly Rising from Its Ashes." According to the paper's special dispatch, "Virginia comes up to the scratch smiling, with both eyes blackened, her nose swollen and red with the frost, and battered both above and below the belt." Throughout the burnt district, laborers cleaned and piled bricks for subsequent reuse. Carpenters framed houses as fast as the railroad dumped lumber in town. Not a moment went to waste in Virginia City's rush to rebuild, but in the reporter's judgment, "the palm for enterprise" went to the burnt-out saloon men. Exercising an excusable mite of artistic license, the reporter described Virginia's barkeeps standing among the flames "like salamanders," dispensing the cordial "in spite of fire, smoke and burning dust." To their everlasting credit, nobody accused them of either watering the palliative nor raising its price.

In the remains of the Con. Virginia mill, workers struggled to dislodge about $100,000 worth of bullion the fire had "retorted and deposited upon the spot" from eight thousand pounds of amalgam. The mill had thirty-seven thousand pounds of mercury in use at the time of the fire—every ounce of which had vaporized and vanished.

The same issue of the *Chronicle* described a well-dressed gentleman with business to conduct visiting the reconstruction effort already underway at the Con. Virginia hoisting works. Men worked at dismantling useless machinery. Others built derricks capable of swinging heavy metal pieces off their foundations and out of the way. The visitor asked a group of miners if they knew the whereabouts of Mr. Mackay. All their fingers swung to indicate a man standing among the ruins wearing a blue blouse and ash-stained canvas trousers beneath a slouch hat who looked every inch like any other miner on site.

"No, no," the visitor said, "I mean Mr. Mackay of the Consolidated Virginia."

"Well, that is he."

"Pshaw, you don't say," the man said. He picked his way through drooping iron, mangled cages, and general debris to John Mackay.

He found a man exactly four weeks shy of his forty-fourth birthday. Mackay's "keen, penetrating eyes" shone from a ruddy, grime-encrusted face that exhibited "decision and frankness." He appeared spare and lean, "all muscle and nerve," nothing wasted. Mackay moved with "the sure, agile tread of the leopard or the lynx," and even amidst crisis and disaster, there was a "joyous element" to the man, "which would [have been] winning were its owner only a cab-driver instead of the master of millions." Mackay spoke slowly, still fighting his stammer. Visiting "metropolitan eyes" remarked the "sense of command blended with comradeship" with which Mackay handled his miners.

They loved him for it. John Mackay's very existence proved that in America, no uncrossable chasm divided a four-dollar-a-day miner from a man worth many tens of millions of dollars.

That evening, the reporter interviewed Mackay at the Fairs' "palatial residence." Though obviously exhausted, Mackay exuded confidence. Other mills could pick up the slack while he and his partners replaced their lost mill property (which would cost them around three-quarters of a million dollars). That very afternoon, he'd spent three hours underground, inspecting the Con. Virginia, the California, the Best & Belcher, and the Ophir workings, and so far as he could see, there wasn't a single timber or wedge out of place. "Our mines are all right in every respect," he said, "and if the insurance men will pay off without delay all these poor people around us, so that they may go on and build, Virginia will soon be herself again."

The turn of the conversation away from the big bonanza to the condition of the citizenry, which the reporter considered "so characteristic of Mackay," ended the formal interview. The reporter accepted a small glass of "the purest bourbon" and "a fine Havana" and took his departure.

Ben Smith, caretaker of Mary Jane Simpson, collected the immolated mule's bones into an empty box of mine candles and buried them just outside the fence of the Virginia City Cemetery. On a board over the mule's grave he scratched the inscription: "Sacred to the Memory of Mary Jane Simpson."

The Con. Virginia's rebuilt hoisting works began raising ore seven weeks after the fire, on December 13. The Firm bought up fire-emptied lots around the shaft house and left them vacant to create storage yards and a firebreak. To improve efficiency, the Virginia & Truckee extended tracks to either side of the rebuilt works, and even with the lost time, the mine produced $16.7 million worth of bullion in 1875. Over the winter, Mackay and Fair replaced their mill property and got the C&C shaft sunk deep enough to allow them to work the bonanza from both east and west. Through that winter and over the next year, a new town sprang up to replace the old. The new International Hotel rose six stories above C Street and featured sumptuous mahogany furniture, floor-to-ceiling mirrors, magnificent chandeliers, and another mechanical elevator. About the only piece of corporate or personal property John Mackay didn't replace was his own lost house. Knowing he'd never lure his wife back to the town she so dreaded—"I know it too well," she'd say—Mackay sold the lot, took up simple rooms over the Gould & Curry office on C Street, and focused his attention on mining the Big Bonanza.

The ore body was simply colossal, 1,200 feet long, 600 feet tall at its deepest point, and although in most places "only" about 200 feet wide, at its widest on the 1,500-foot level the ore body was fully 340 feet across. Some years later, Mackay described the Big Bonanza's scale to a Gotham journalist as kidney-shaped and "about as high as the steeple of Trinity, and in an area as large as the City Hall Park." Comparing the Big Bonanza to the Crown Point–Belcher bonanza in the roughest terms, the Big Bonanza was 100 feet taller, twice as long, more than twice as wide, and filled with ore twice as rich. To get that stupendous quantity of ore out of the ground required replacing that entire volume with a carefully engineered and reinforced lattice of square-set timbers and raising the ore to the surface from between 1,100 and 1,650 feet underground.

The stress of running such a gigantic, complicated, and dangerous operation tolled on both Mackay and Fair, and Fair wasn't on the lode for a period of several months in early 1876. One report placed Fair in the East. Another said Fair "worked so long and so hard that even his abundant stamina" couldn't take the strain and that "at times," Fair sustained himself with "copious draughts of a brandy bottle." When that failed, Fair took "unwanted vacations."

Mackay went underground every day, supervising, inspecting, and directing operations, sharing the perils of his men in the greatest firetrap in the world. Underground, the heat verged on intolerable. Pools of scalding water accumulated on the drift floors and in the stopes. Air temperatures often exceeded 135 degrees, and in places the ore was too hot to touch with an ungloved hand. In a winze where a pneumatic drill couldn't be worked, a man saw Con. Virginia miners working "13 to the pick," doing two-minute rotations with the pick and then resting while the other dozen men took their turn for the course of an eight-hour shift.

The California mine joined the Con. Virginia in full production in April 1876 and paid its first dividend in May. With both mines paying a monthly dividend of $1,080,000, John Mackay's cash income—from the dividends of the two bonanza mines alone—fell somewhere between $450,000 and $607,000 *per month*. The only people in the world with a monthly cash income anywhere comparable were Mackay's three junior partners. The income and expenditures of the four-person firm exceeded those of half the states in the Union. On dividend day in San Francisco, the line of people waiting to receive their coins, stacks, or sacks of gold at the Nevada Bank extended down the whole length of the bank.

Mackay always maintained his prior relationships, and with his income risen to such dizzying heights, among a gathering of old friends, Jack O'Brien, his onetime Gold Rush mining partner, teasingly reminded him that he'd once claimed he'd have been content for his whole life with $25,000.

"W-w-well," Mackay stammered, "I've ch-ch-changed my mind."

The two bonanza mines drove the Comstock Lode to the height of its greatest boom in the summer of 1876. Of the approximately 20,000 inhabitants of Storey County, more than three-quarters lived in the booming camps of Gold Hill and Virginia City. (The 1875 census counted just over 1,300 Chinese, about 130 "colored" citizens, almost 6,000 white females, and more than 12,000 white males—about half of whom had been born in countries other than the United States.) The Con. Virginia alone used more than a million feet of lumber and more than 3,300 cords of wood fuel per month. Together, the Con. Virginia and California mines employed more than 900 men, and of the 3,000-odd miners working the Comstock, about two-thirds drew their paychecks from mines controlled and operated by the Bonanza Firm. The mines worked full blast, three shifts a day, seven days a week, those mines not "in bonanza" sinking their incline shafts and drifting and crosscutting the lower levels with all possible speed in the hope of striking a similar ore body. The principal companies banded into groups that started sinking eight third-line shafts with the intention of prospecting the lode below two thousand feet.

Men getting off shift kept Virginia City roaring at all hours of the day and night. A reporter from the *New York Tribune* described C Street crowded like Broadway. He crowed about Virginia City's fine restaurants and "drinking saloons more gorgeous in appointment than any in San Francisco, Philadelphia, and New York," and wrote, "I have never been in a place where money is so plenty, nor where it is spent with so much extravagance and recklessness." He described "inhabitants in the garb of laborers . . . with the habits of Parisians." No coin less than a quarter-dollar circulated. A bootblack returned the reporter's dime with a look of such derision that it made the New Yorker want to switch places with him "and give him the dime to boot." In the melting and assaying rooms of the Con. Virginia and California mills, bullion bars weighing ninety to one hundred pounds and worth $3,000 to $4,000 each (45 percent of their value in gold, the rest silver) were "stacked up by the hundreds in rooms and halls" and thrown into wagons for transport like "so many pigs of iron."

A *Mining & Scientific Press* article that year thought that any Comstocker could "ask no better fun" than to guide "some Massachusetts stranger" down C Street "on a Sunday evening promenade." The glaring lights, brass bands, pianos, melodeons, and wide-open doors of the saloons; the work going on in all the mines; the horse racing and dog fighting at the race track; the cigar-smoking, lounging, laughing, and swearing crowds—to say nothing of the tawdry delights available one street below—what a lovely chill of horror they would give the tight-laced New Englander. "Are we in America?" he would exclaim. "No, we are on the Comstock!" his guide would chirp. "Whether we ought to be proud of it or regretful is a question which need not be discussed," the newspaper mused, "but certainly we can send any New Englander back to the blue laws and bitter Sabbath with the valuable knowledge that although Boston may be the hub of the universe, it has one very lively spoke."

Not all descriptions of the Comstock's bonanza times waxed so ebullient. The *Pacific Tourist*, a railroad publication intended to promote western travel, said of bonanza-times Virginia City that "one expects streets of gold and silver, and instead finds them of mud and dust"— although the writer did grant the "sorrowfully beautiful" view from Virginia City. All classes of men, and occasionally women, clogged the streets and saloons. Refined personalities recoiled from the Comstock's "fearfully prevalent" profanity. Others lamented Virginia City's hot, oily smell and the smoke and steam of its machinery, the lack of level ground, the dearth of respectable women and children, the fierce cold wind, and the total absence of greenery. The *Tourist* described Comstockers worshipping heathen deities—"Mammon, Bacchus, and Venus"—with the brokers' offices, whisky shops, gambling hells, and brothels held up as temples. "There is wonderful enterprise, much intelligence, some refinement, not a little courtesy, and a sea of sin."

Anyone with "a curiosity to find the liveliest place in Virginia" in June 1876 found it by stepping into the Delta Saloon at 18 C Street.* Inside, the highfalutin' grogshop shone "resplendent" and echoed with bawdy piano music, bawls of coarse laughter, and "the ever-varying tones" of a keno dealer locally renowned for the lingering emphasis with which he announced the appearance of the number "*eeeeeeee-leven*." That same month, in the southeastern Montana Territory, the assembled power of the Lakota, Northern Cheyenne, and Northern Arapaho Indian nations killed every man in five companies of the Seventh Cavalry near the Little Big Horn River, including their flamboyant commander, General George Armstrong Custer.

Mackay wasn't in Nevada when he heard the news. Fair had returned or recovered from whatever had kept him away, allowing Mackay in turn to take a break from the mines. With John William, Jr., approaching school age, money no longer even the slightest consideration, Mackay needed at the mines for months at a stretch, and Louise never truly satisfied in San Francisco, John and Louise decided to move the family to Paris.

John and Louise probably made the decision to shift the family to Paris for three reasons: to give Willie access to what they considered the best possible international education, because Louise would rather live in Paris than anywhere else in the world, and because John Mackay thought it was an excellent idea. Mackay wanted his sons to have the top-shelf educational opportunities he'd missed, and he'd always promised Louise anything within his power to give. If John Mackay felt those things were to be had in Paris, then Paris it would be. Besides, he'd spent time in the French capital and probably fallen in love with it himself.

The Mackays escaped California in mid-May, traveling east in William Sharon's beautifully luxurious private rail carriage, toured the huge Centennial Exhibition in Philadelphia built to show off the economic muscle and talents of the rapidly expanding nation—where the Bonanza Firm won first prize for "silver ores, gold bearing"—and sailed for Liverpool aboard the SS *Adriatic* on June 10, 1876.

Marie Louise Antoinette Hungerford Mackay would never again set foot in Virginia City. As an act of gratitude to the town that she loathed

---

* The Delta Saloon still operates, although perhaps not with unbroken lineage.

and that had made her, before departure, Louise bought van Bokkelen's Beer Garden at the downhill edge of Virginia City. (Van Bokkelen had also been an explosives dealer who slept atop the boxes that held his supply—until his stash blew up one night in 1873, killing him and ten other people and injuring many others.) Louise donated the land to the Catholic Daughters of Charity, who built a hospital on the site and named it St. Mary *Louise* Hospital in honor of their benefactor.

In Paris, Mackay bought 9 Rue de Tilsitt, one of the capital's most prestigious addresses,* a "splendid" two-year-old residence on one of the roads that circled the Place de l'Étoile—at the center of which stood the Arc de Triomphe. The *New York Herald* claimed the house cost Mackay 1.5 million francs and that Louise spent another 500,000 on its furnishings. The *San Francisco Bulletin* reported Mackay back in the Comstock mines before the middle of August. In September, he sold the house in San Francisco. Louise was done with the West.

In 1876, the Con. Virginia raised $16.7 million and the California disgorged $13.4 million. That year, the three mints of the United States Treasury in San Francisco, Philadelphia, and Carson City coined a total of $70.8 million in gold and silver. The Big Bonanza contributed more than 42 percent to the total annual coinage of the United States. (Mackay's share of the $21.6 million in dividends amounted to a cash sum of between $4.6 and $6 million.)

Mackay returned to a storm of personal criticism. While he was in Europe, James Fair had publicly accused him of "gutting the mine" of its best ore. To an extent that was true—Mackay had been planning to mine $10 million in a single month to display at the Centennial Exhibition, a plan derailed by a savage bear raid on the bonanza stocks. He had indeed mined shoots of the best ore to increase production and combat the raiders' outpouring of negative publicity claiming the mines weren't worth their stock valuations. In truth, they weren't. The root problem was the mine's annual report published at the end of 1875 over Superintendent James G. Fair's signature. Fair had exaggerated the size of the ore body, gifting the mine millions of dollars it didn't possess. Fair deflected criticism with his accusation that Mackay had stripped the mine of its best ore while he was away. "Colonel Fair" promised his presence would set things right. (Although Mackay may not have seen the report before its publication, he did bear a certain amount of responsibility—he over-

---

* The Mackays' old mansion currently houses the Belgian Embassy.

saw the Firm's operations, knew the underground situation in detail, and should have insisted on the exact reporting.)

Characteristically, Mackay said nothing in public. In private, a man who placed such high value on his "good name" must have been deeply wounded. Although in the ever-racially conscious atmosphere of the nineteenth century, the *Chicago Tribune's* San Francisco correspondent described the four members of the Bonanza Firm standing together in their business dealings "like Jews," the scrutiny to which their shocking wealth subjected them brought their respective characters into sharp focus.

On display in his office, James Flood kept a painting called *Changing the Shift* showing a scene in the Con. Virginia hoisting works. He knew from whence his money came. Both he and James Fair invested heavily in San Francisco real estate and other California speculations. Flood acquired an excellent lot atop Nob Hill, but did nothing to develop it while he focused his energy on building a bizarre, forty-three-room mansion of jutting cupolas, porticos, and gables dwarfed by a 150-foot-tower on six hundred forested acres in Menlo Park, thirty miles south of San Francisco, and although his supposed stock market manipulations caused constant comment in the newspapers, stock-trading and financial circles generally credited Flood with "square dealing" and considered "his word" as "good as his bond in any business transaction."

Fair didn't attract such grudging nods. California and Nevada circles considered him "the sharpest and most unscrupulous of all the bonanza millionaires." "Colonel Fair" had taken to keeping a bodyguard of "hired fighters" on the Comstock to insulate him from the unwashed crowd, and his prodigious appetites acquired a reputation—for food, drink, flattery, and, it was increasingly whispered, for women other than his wife. Fair loved to hear himself talk, convinced that his outrageous mining success qualified him to "pass upon" any subject, and he seldom missed a chance to make himself look good at somebody else's expense. Whenever possible, he began taking those opportunities at the expense of his partners, saying, "Those lads would still be in overalls but for me" on many occasions.

For his part, "the jolly millionaire" William O'Brien—"Billy" to everyone who knew him—stayed as true to himself as possible. Asked about his success, he always said, "I caught the tail of a kite and hung on." According to the *Chicago Tribune*, O'Brien spent more time "hobnobbing with the boys" in the back room of McGovern's Saloon than he did at the offices of the Nevada Bank, playing low-stakes games of Pedro as he'd always done, careful not to drive off any old friends. He kept a pile of silver dollars nearby, to which any of his cronies were welcome to help themselves. His prized possession remained the silver trumpet he'd been given upon successful completion of a term as foreman of Volunteer Fire Company No. 4 back in the 1850s. Annually, O'Brien gave a lavish party for the gold rushers with whom he'd arrived in California aboard the ship *Farolinto* in 1849. His great service to the Firm seems to have been social—due to the high and genial regard in which he was held by men about town and his ability to keep the peace between his three strong-minded partners. The only indulgence Billy O'Brien allowed himself was a splendid trotting mare and fast buggy, which he often raced to the sand hills west of town to enjoy the dramatic view over "the Ocean Beach," the splendid strip of sand and surf running south from the Cliff House.* A committed bachelor in his personal life, O'Brien delighted in his sisters and nieces and spoiled them lavishly. Polite and chivalrous in his personal habits, he was considered by most San Franciscans the most "distinguished looking" of the bonanza millionaires, particularly when he appeared at parties escorting his sisters.

Although O'Brien presented the most decorous and mannerly appearance, most observers found Fair the most handsome, with his raven-black beard and hair, and spoke of his "indefatigable" devotion to work. Every miner acknowledged Fair's expertise, but Fair had trouble trusting subordinates, even those of long experience. He forced expert mine foremen, engineers, and superintendents to report minute details multiple times per day, and he drove himself to frequent breakdowns. The stress of managing such enormous operations likely motivated a sharp uptick in his alcohol consumption. Always the most garrulous of the bonanza quartet, Fair spoke in "suave sentences" embellished with such phrases as "my dear boy" and "old man," and when he spoke to women or girls, it was always, "my little dear," "pretty creature," and the like. But no matter how hard Fair pushed his self-aggrandizement, in comparisons of the Bonanza Firm's two leading miners, less light almost always shone on James G. Fair. The contrasts became sharper as time passed. A pair of famous anecdotes showed up their different styles.

In one story, Fair traced the smell of tobacco smoke to a group of miners deep in the workings but couldn't identify the guilty parties. (Underground miners easily discerned the differing odors of dynamite, cord-

---

* The author appreciates O'Brien's tastes. A lifelong surfer, he has spent more time at Ocean Beach than at any other place in San Francisco.

ite, black powder, blasting caps, candles, and lanterns from the one they dreaded—burning wood.) Fair told the men he wasn't feeling well but would be greatly refreshed by a pipe and a smoke. A sheepish miner produced smoking paraphernalia and tobacco from a hidden cranny. Fair took his puffs, said his thanks, and went on his way. The men thought they'd been let off easy.

They had. Back on the surface, Fair told a foreman to have the men "given their time"—meaning paid off and fired.

Discharged hands said Fair caressed with his voice while he kicked with his boot, and "the more oil in his expression the more disagreeable surprise he [has] in store."

Mackay handled similar situations in more aboveboard fashion. He followed his nose and found an otherwise hardworking man. "Pat, have you been smoking?" he asked.

Guilty, the man replied, "Mister Mackay, there's been a good deal of shooting around here this morning . . ." (meaning blasting).

Mackay looked at him for a long moment. "Don't do it again," he said.

Pat never did. "I sure thought I was fired," he later drawled.

A stocky fellow named "Shorty" Bailey worked as a top-carman—one of the men who met the cars of ore or waste at the shaft landings and dealt with them as appropriate. Walking up a trestle track after an inspection one morning, Mackay stopped a car running toward him that didn't seem to have anyone behind it. A voice piped up from behind, "What son-of-a-bitch stopped the car?"

Bailey must have blanched when he realized to whom he'd addressed the insult, but Mackay just stepped aside. "It's all right, Little One," he said, "I thought the car was running away." For the next twenty years, Mackay had a few pleasant words with Bailey whenever he encountered him about the mines.

One night during the bonanza times, local journalist and old friend Sam Davis called on Mackay in his austere rooms above the Gould & Curry office and to his astonishment, found the great miner poring over an "ordinary school book." Mackay made no effort to conceal his reading. "I never received much education and have to put in my leisure hours catching up," he said.

Davis recalled meeting Mackay at five o'clock in the morning on another occasion. Mackay was just leaving his quarters, having already had his breakfast, on his way to the Con. Virginia to begin the mine inspections with which he always started his workdays.

In the tradition of sagebrush journalism, Davis was on his way home from a night on the town. "If I had your money, John," he said, "I wouldn't get up at 5 o'clock."

"If you keep going to bed at five in the morning, you'll never have my money or anybody else's!" Mackay replied.

When he wasn't afoot, trudging between the mines, Mackay drove a shabby buggy, pulled by a single horse. Fair bought a fancy carriage and a gorgeous pair of matched bays adorned with shiny silver tack, and he employed a coachman. Boys out "coasting" down Virginia City's cross streets in the winter season would whiz down from A Street to where the hill flattened out near the Con. Virginia hoisting works. If Mackay were about, the boys waited, knowing Mackay would let them tie their sleds on behind and give them a ride uphill as he made the rounds. If they saw Fair's fancy carriage, they began the long upslope trudge, dragging their sleds.

When Mackay was on the lode, forty or fifty boys congregated outside the entrance to Piper's rebuilt Opera House before each performance, knowing Mackay would be inside, and knowing that a few moments before curtain time, Mackay would poke his head through the door, nod toward the gang, and ask the proprietor, "How much for the bunch?"

John Piper would settle on fifty cents a head, and Mackay would dig a double eagle from his pocket. "We would enjoy the show," a man reminiscing about his Virginia City childhood wrote years later, "and what is more, we would think better of all mankind because John Mackay had remembered that he was once a boy."

Journalist Wells Drury visited Mackay one day in pursuit of mine intelligence. Mackay gestured him toward a stack of official reports. Drury copied lines and figures, but couldn't help noticing Mackay looking out the window over Six Mile Cañon with a glum, lonely look. That struck Drury. He knew Mackay as a man usually "on good terms with himself and the world." Drury asked Mackay if something was wrong and if he could help.

"No, thank you," Mackay said. "Not a thing. That's the trouble." Mackay told Drury that he'd been playing poker at the Washoe Club the night before and playing well, backed by a run of luck. He opened on three aces with the man to his left "betting like a cyclone" and others behind him raising hard and fast. Mackay stayed with the flurry of heavy betting and drew his fourth ace. He had a "lock," a certain winner.

Instead of the thrill of impending victory, a chilling thought hit Mackay—"What of it?" It wouldn't make a shred of difference if he won "every cent in sight."

Mackay showed down his aces and stood up. "Leave me out, boys," he said. "I'm through." He walked away without collecting his winnings.

"I've lost the taste for poker entirely," he told another friend later, "and candidly," he added, "I miss it."

When a consortium of other mine owners suggested that the surplus of laboring men coming west to escape the eastern depression gave them an opportunity to push miners' wages down to $3.50 per day, Mackay opposed them. "I always got $4 a day when I worked in these mines," he said, "and when I can't pay that I'll go out of business."

One of the other owners complained that the men weren't worth four dollars per day.

"Worth it!" Mackay exploded. "Worth it? Why, man, it's worth $4 a day to ride up and down on that wire string!" Unsaid, but surely obvious to every man present was the fact that Mackay had taken that ride many hundreds of times more than anyone else in the room. Beyond a thousand feet, the long steel cables had developed a gentle springing action, which only added to the terrors of the descent.

Wages stayed at four dollars a day.

In the Comstock lexicon, the idea that an event, item, or person was of high quality was contained in the expression, "It's a John Mackay!"

By the end of 1876, the Firm had doubled the paid-in capital of the Nevada Bank, making it the best-capitalized bank in the country. As well as things were going, with each bonanza mine paying more than a million dollars of dividends a month, Mackay and the Firm faced constant criticism, much of it fueled by the alliance of Charles de Young, owner and editor of the *San Francisco Chronicle*, and Squire Dewey, a stockbroker and speculator who'd fronted the bear raids on the two bonanza mines in the first half of 1876. Charles de Young had bought high-priced bonanza stocks during the winter boom of 1874–75 and watched his speculation dwindle in the aftermath. De Young asked the Bonanza Firm to make his losses good. They refused, and De Young started slashing with his pen. Dewey's antagonism sprang from a similar cause. He'd made money in San Francisco real estate during the Gold Rush decade and been among the original incorporators of the Ophir in April 1860 (and had slyly used his insider knowledge to sell when he learned that the Ophir's original bonanza showed evidence of pinching out). In the middle 1870s, he was a stock speculator who felt entitled to insider information.

In the aftermath of the great fire, Dewey had inquired after the amount of money in the Con. Virginia treasury and been given the answer in cash terms—the exact answer he'd sought. Dewey decided the mine didn't have enough money to both replace the hoisting works and continue paying dividends, so he sold his stock. Dewey, however, had not asked after the amount of *bullion* in the treasury. The mint stamped that large quantity into coin, which provided a sum more than adequate to replace the works and continue the dividends. The stock price recovered quickly. Dewey lost $50,000, $52,000, or $70,000 on the speculation, depending on which of his own statements a person wanted to believe. Dewey thought Flood had intentionally deceived him, and like De Young, he wanted the Firm to make good his losses. They refused. Dewey had hounded the Firm for dishonest and incompetent management ever since. Dewey gained the ear of an English stockholder who many San Franciscans believed was also a member of the British Parliament. The two attended the Con. Virginia's annual meeting in January 1877 intent on stirring up trouble.

Dewey, noted for his "self-importance" and "pompous manner," demanded a more accurate prognostication of future events from the mine managers.

Which Mackay refused to give. "It is simply impossible . . . to tell two or three days or a week ahead what the mine may develop," he said. "Events are constantly happening to upset our calculations." Caves, bad air, rock quality, and a host of other factors were simply unknowable in advance.

Dewey and the Englishman kept up their attacks.

Mackay and Flood lost their Irish tempers.

Mackay told the Englishman that he knew nothing about running an American mine. If they could run the Con. Virginia any better than he was doing, Mackay "wished to the Lord" they would come up to Virginia City and try.

The Englishman called the mine management "outrageous and infamous" and accused management of working the mine in their own interests.

Mackay thought his honesty was being impugned.

Heated discussions continued. Dewey proposed an alternative slate of trustees. Two of the proposed men immediately asked that their names be withdrawn, saying they'd been put forward without their knowledge. One of them "did not think the interest of the stockholders could be in more competent hands than at present." The Firm's ticket won reelection in a landslide of the shares present, 483,000 to 32,500. (The mine had 540,000 shares at that time, and 515,500 of them voted.)

The Mackay-Dewey dispute continued as the meeting broke up. Mackay invited Dewey to come up and examine the mine, coupling his invitation to what the *Chronicle* described as "some insinuation that the knowledge of the Comstock at present in possession of Dewey was of a rather thin and unsubstantial character." (One would be justified in supposing Mackay used plainer and stronger language.)

Dewey countered that Mackay had worked for him when he'd been running the Ophir in 1860, and back then, Mackay hadn't been "worth a red cent."

The *Chronicle's* account gave the impression that the two men had to be physically separated, and it savaged Mackay personally, calling him a "bulldozer"—a grievous insult in the context of the middle 1870s that referred to white southern reactionaries who rigged elections by terrorizing blacks who dared to exercise their franchise with lynching, church and cross burning, flogging, rape, and murder (the piece of construction machinery familiar to moderns wouldn't be invented for decades). The paper called Mackay a "scrub . . . raised from nothing" who had attained nothing but "dirty purse pride."

The *Daily Alta California* sprang to Mackay's defense: "We believe that no other of the great millionaires of our time is so noted as Mr. Mackay for conduct so inconsistent with purse-pride."

Dewey had his revenge. He published pamphlets and filed lawsuits that haunted the Firm for the next five years. Several months later, the Englishman accepted Mackay's invitation and brought his own expert to examine the Con. Virginia. They left satisfied. "So explodes another *Chronicle* canard," said the *Stock Report*.

The *Chronicle's* abuse would worsen with the publication of many articles along the lines of the one headlined "The Bonanza Kings. Their Splendor Throned on Human Misery. Rolling in Wealth Wrung from Ruined Thousands. California and Nevada Impoverished to Enrich Four Men. Plain History of Swindling Perpetrated on a Gigantic Scale. Colossal Money Power That Menaces Pacific Coast Prosperity."

The relentless criticism wore on Mackay. He grew even more reticent. The correspondent of a St. Louis newspaper noted his "great disinclination to any notoriety, never appearing in the newspapers when he can avoid it."

In March 1877, Mackay opened the Con. Virginia's 1,650-foot level. The first crosscuts went through phenomenal ore. Comstockers and San Franciscans rejoiced. Unbeknownst to everybody, mere accident had sent those crosscuts through the richest and widest parts of the whole level. Further explorations revealed the ore body shrinking in all dimensions. They also discovered why they'd found the Big Bonanza in such a strange place—it had formed in a subfissure bubbling up vertically from the Comstock's east-dipping hanging wall. Enormous quantities of valuable ore remained in the two bonanza mines, enough to keep them producing for years, but the bottom of the great bonanza had come into view. For the Comstock Lode, the great question became: Was there another?

Mackay left Virginia City for France in May. Three months later, Mackay wrote a letter from Trouville, a fishing village on the Normandy coast, where he was relaxing with his family. He returned on October 3, after an absence of five months. In November, a strike on the nineteen-hundred-foot level of the Ophir caused a flutter. Prospecting the strike involved Mackay, but he missed out on a much greater excitement his wife generated in Paris.

Former president Grant spent most of November in Paris, having recently begun a much-publicized world tour. Louise got the general's permission to throw him a party, likely because of her husband's staunch Republican sentiments, ability to deliver a state, and because General Grant held stock in the Consolidated Virginia Mine. The dividends were financing his world tour.

Louise Mackay threw herself into a whirlwind of preparations, recognizing that desire to attend an opulent party honoring the world's most famous American would allow European aristocrats to overcome the malodor of American wealth and accept Louise's invitation. Louise spared no extravagance. She asked Parisian authorities if she could decorate and light the Arc de Triomphe for the party. They refused her request. Disappointed, Louise joked that she'd just "buy their old arch." Americans admired her panache. Frenchmen didn't find the comment so amusing.

Under Louise's direction, workmen swarmed over 9 Rue de Tilsitt making preparations. The party dominated nonpolitical conversations in the French capital, promising a spectacle the likes of which Parisian society had seldom seen. The evening began quietly, with an intimate dinner for twenty-four that included General and Mrs. Grant, the Mackay and Hungerford families, and officials of the American legation and their families. Louise presented each guest with the menu engraved on small silver *tablettes*, presumably on metal mined from the Consolidated Virginia.

The true pageant started after dinner, around 11:00 p.m., when Louise's three hundred guests began arriving for her "grand reception and ball." Louise had festooned 9 Rue de Tilsitt with national flags and set "thousands of gas jets" to brilliantly illuminate the facade, garden, and temporary dance pavilion into a "fairyland." Music played by an orchestra of thirty-six musicians wafted from the pavilion. Light from inside the house streamed out through colored curtains. Two enormous eagles stood beside the entry outlined in burning gas jets, one symbolizing France, the other the United States, with *E Pluribus Unum* written in fire across the breasts of both birds.

Crowds of idlers gathered outside, pushing and surging to catch a glimpse of the arrivals. The exclamations of swells competed with the voices of policemen diverting and directing traffic. The hooves of splendid teams pulling gorgeous carriages clip-clopped on the cobblestones of the causeway in front, as Paris coachmen not quite as profane as Comstock teamsters nosed their animals through the ranks of onlookers to the entryway, where a dozen footmen in crimson and gold livery holding halberds and rapiers waited on their arrivals. In unison, the footmen cracked the butts of their halberds on the stones as each new guest stepped down from the carriages.

Just inside, Louise Mackay, now age thirty-two, all "dark hair," charm, and "youthful appearance," wore blue satin decorated with silver flowers and introduced her guests to General and Mrs. Grant, putting everybody at ease switching between four languages, having added facility with Italian to her repertoire. Beyond the receiving line, Louise had decorated every vestibule, staircase, bedroom, bathroom, and all of her hallways with an astonishing profusion of flowers. The wines, champagnes, and liquors everywhere at hand were the best that the largest monthly income in the world could procure. In the smoking rooms, opalescent abalone shells from the California coast held top-quality cigars. Outside, in the pavilion, "an abundance of jewels" sparkled on a sea of dancers. A *New York Herald* correspondent described Louise's ornamentation of her magnificent home as "everything that money could supply and elegant taste select."

Among Louise's honored guests were the Marquis and Marquise de Lafayette, at least three dukes and duchesses, five counts and countesses, three barons and baronesses, and a pair of viscounts, along with many pillars of European political, aristocratic, and intellectual society. Dancing continued until four o'clock in the morning, although General Grant had the good sense to quietly sound his retreat many hours before. The *Herald*'s reporter remarked on the "extraordinary taste, elegance, and richness" of the costumes worn by the "beautiful women" who represented the American colony.

The transatlantic telegraph cable conveyed the story to the other side of the Atlantic, and the *Herald* published an exquisite account of the "great sensational event" the next day. The *New York World*'s reporter—also on scene—described it as "a social aurora borealis" under the headline, "Paris Astonished." The *Chicago Daily-Tribune* told of Louise Mackay "playing hostess to 'the American hero,'" and sitting "cheek by jowl with the bluest blood in France." Newspapers all over the country ran with the story of "widely ambitious and delightfully extravagant" Louise Mackay. History doesn't record the reactions of New York's upper-crust Yankee Protestant ladies outshone by the Comstock's little Catholic seamstress.

The General Grant fete gave Louise entrée into the upper echelons of European society, the first rich American woman to gain such access. Although most subsequent historians and commentators enamored of the whisky and gunsmoke glories of the Old West would "blame" Louise's social ambitions for the family's Parisian residence, the long separations from his family it forced Mackay to endure, and the long absences of John Mackay suffered by the Comstock, Mackay likely supported the arrangement entirely. It could well have been his idea, and it was certainly a decision he and his wife made together. With the exception of one five-month visit to France in the summer of 1878 around the Paris Exposition, John Mackay seems to have spent the entirety of next three years in the American West, focused on extracting the Big Bonanza and prospecting the deep levels of the Comstock. (Mackay received much acclaim for funding the Pacific Coast mineral display at the Paris Exposition out of his own pocket, the "pièce de résistance" of the presentation being the Mackay family's fifteen-hundred-piece silver service made from half a ton of Con. Virginia silver reduced from ore that Mackay had supposedly mined himself. Even more astonishing was Parisian jeweler Boucheron's debut of the necklace they'd fashioned from a flawless 159⅛-carat sapphire the size of a pigeon's egg. Mackay had bought the stone for his wife two years before. The profusion of "lesser" diamonds and sapphires encrusted into the necklace perfectly set off the center stone; it's one of the two most spectacular pieces of jewelry ever made.)

Billy O'Brien had died in May 1878, just before Mackay's departure, it being "one of the laws of our glorious climate that a man cannot have at once an immense fortune and a sound liver," according to the San Francisco correspondent of the *Chicago Tribune*. (Mackay being the exception that proved the rule, apparently.) O'Brien's money divided among his sisters, nieces, nephews, and a long-lost brother who appeared from nowhere to claim a share of the fortune.

In August, Adolph Sutro personally hacked into the 1,658-foot level of the Savage mine 20,498 feet from his tunnel entrance. He'd arrived too late. The Comstock mines were already prospecting levels hundreds of feet below his long drain tunnel. Although the tunnel allowed the mines to reduce their pumping expenses by draining water into the tunnel instead of having to raise it to the surface, not a ton of ore ever traveled out through his tunnel. Nobody ever built a mill at the tunnel entrance in the platted town of Sutro. The tunnel company earned some money from the drainage arrangements, but Sutro unloaded his stock on an unsuspecting public pumped up for profits by a dozen years of his hype. He invested his proceeds in San Francisco real estate, speculations that made him rich. The value of tunnel stock gradually sank toward zero.

In October, reports of an important strike below the two-thousand-foot level of the Sierra Nevada mine, the northernmost of the important Comstock mines, brought Mackay hustling back from Europe. The stock market went ballistic. By the time Mackay arrived from Paris, Fair had already bought control of the mine for a million of the Firm's dollars. Mackay inspected the strike and telegraphed Flood: "Fair is crazy."

The whole deal proved to be a put-up job by one of the Comstock's sharp operators. The stock market plummeted as developments revealed the small dimensions of the ore body. The collapse of "the Sierra Nevada Deal" crushed the Comstock's exuberance and put an end to "the bonanza times." Mackay and his partners pushed deep-level prospecting below two thousand feet all along the lode, but since prospecting operations didn't require the large workforces needed to extract an ore body, surplus men began drifting away, drawn to burgeoning opportunities elsewhere. New discoveries propelled Leadville, in Colorado, past the Comstock in total production. In the Black Hills of the Dakota Territory, the Homestake mine surged under the control of George Hearst and Lloyd Tevis, both longtime players in San Francisco financial and mining circles. Mines boomed at Bodie, just over the California line near the old camp at Aurora. The Comstock lost the position as the "boss camp" of the mining West it had held since 1860.

Undone by labor and relentless appetites, Fair had resigned as superintendent of the Firm's mines in the summer of 1878. Although he seemed to have been in San Francisco or Virginia City for much of the time he wasn't traveling, Fair's poor health left Mackay to direct most of the Firm's Comstock operations from late 1878 through November 1880. (A December 1879 article in the *New York Times* said Colonel Fair had been "ailing" for the last eighteen months, and that "for much of that time Mr. Mackay [had] been forced to do the Colonel's work.") If Mackay managed to visit his family during that two-year stretch, it was only a short whirlwind trip that left little trace in period newspapers.

While Mackay directed the final push to mine the Big Bonanza, the Firm parried a series of lawsuits orchestrated by Squire Dewey that sought more than $40 million in damages from the Firm for defrauding the shareholders through self-dealing. (The 1881 "Bonanza Suits" ruling cleared the Firm of fraudulent behavior and required the Firm to pay $1.72 to each of the Con. Virginia's 540,000 shares for an 1872 transaction involving twelve and a half feet of the old Kinney claim; only one stockholder ever came forward to claim his slice, and he was one of the litigants.) Mackay himself fought off a $200,000 lawsuit filed by Mr. William Smallman that accused Mackay of "wrongfully, wickedly, and unjustly" debauching Smallman's wife, and enjoying "unlawful intimacy" with her between May 15 and October 20, 1878. The Smallmans hadn't done their presuit research. Mackay had been in Europe at that time. Mr. and Mrs. Smallman were convicted of fraud on an unrelated charge in the spring of 1879 and sentenced to four years in prison.

In March 1879, Louise's sister Ada married Count Telfener, a solid man of Italian and Austrian heritage with a background in engineering. John wasn't able to escape his Comstock duties to attend. Newspapers ever after referred to Ada Hungerford from Downieville as "the Countess Telfener"—perhaps the first California-born American to achieve a European title.

Mackay got into "an old-fashioned Nevada fight" in a livery stable in August of that year with a man who insisted on his right to visit the Sierra Nevada mine. Mackay said that too many people had been going down into the mine lately, all of whom had abused him when they came out, and that "no man not working in the mine should explore it today." When "words became too feeble to express the feelings of the parties . . . the Bonanza Prince and the coal-dealer" fought until other men pulled them apart.

The climax of the Comstock's 1879 came when General Grant visited the lode in October at the end of his world tour. Gold Hill and Virginia City welcomed Grant with the typical western enthusiasms—brass bands, steam whistles, booming cannon, gunfire, cheering multitudes, a parade, and a grand mass of fluttering flags. The sixty-one-word speech the general gave to the assembled citizens couldn't have lasted longer than a minute. John Mackay, James Fair, and Senators Jones and Sharon headed the list of Comstock luminaries who hosted the Grants for dinner.

Early the next morning, Mackay and Fair rode in carriages with General Grant, Mrs. Grant, their son, the governor of Nevada, and a few other notables around to the Carson River Valley and returned to Virginia via a long underground tour of the Sutro Tunnel and the Comstock mines joined to the tunnel by the north lateral—which included the Con. Virginia and California. The colossal dripping galleries of reinforced square sets that had housed the Big Bonanza struck General Grant with awe. Grant told Mackay it was one of the most impressive things he'd seen anywhere in the world and that Mackay "might be proud to be the master and director of the greatest mining enterprise on earth."

One imagines John Mackay receiving the compliment with a nod, a stone face, and a stuttered mumble. The underground party took a group photograph in the shaft house of the Savage mine after they'd been raised to the surface. Both Mackay and Fair kept framed copies for the rest of their lives.

Grant's words made a profound impression on Mackay. Several years later, he told a friend, "That did touch me. Any man might be proud of that, coming from Grant's mouth, which never slopped over." That friend was with Mackay almost every day for two years, and he never heard him mention it again—or say another word "in glorification of his own work." General Grant, when he introduced Mackay to John Russell Young, said, "Mr. Mackay would make a great general had he been trained for the Army."

Mackay considered those two compliments from Grant to be the greatest he ever received.

By the time Colonel James Fair departed on his own around-the-world tour in 1880—without his wife—the Comstock was in steep decline. Mackay held the Firm's place on the Comstock, sinking the shafts and inclines deeper and running the drifts and crosscuts in a relentless search for ore against ever-worsening obstacles of hot, foul air, floods, and rising expenses. "Damn the heat!" Mackay said. "Give me the ore and we'll run our shafts down as far as it goes." A friend suspected that the money had become meaningless, that it was the "passion of the keenest hunt" that sustained him. "'Tis a poor man's pudding just now," he'd say, "but there may be more plums in it than we know of to-day."

Of the eight enormous third-line shafts sunk to prospect the lode below the levels of the two great ore bodies, the Belcher–Crown Point bonanza in Gold Hill and the Big Bonanza in Virginia City, Mackay and his partners led efforts in five of them. Despite the steady discovery of isolated nodules and pockets of high-grade ore and masses of low-grade quartz, nothing in the deep levels materialized into a significant ore body. An increasing number of Comstockers joined those of their compatriots who had already left, taking their knowledge to mining regions all over the West and around the world. For the rest of the nineteenth century, wherever men burrowed deep underground in attempts to wrest wealth from the bowels of the earth would be found mine hands, foremen, engineers, and superintendents who'd learned the dangerous art of hard-rock mining on the old Comstock Lode.

Considered estimates place the Comstock's total production during its twenty-year heyday at around $306 million—a sum equal in power and impact to $545 *billion* in the modern economy. More than a third of the total emerged from the Big Bonanza. By the time that stupendous ore body played out, the Con. Virginia had produced $61.13 million and the California $44.03 million, a combined total in excess of $105 million. The two mines had paid dividends totaling $74.25 million from a subterranean patch of Nevada just a little bit longer than four football fields. The return exceeded *70 percent*, a testimony to the Firm's good management. (The Gould & Curry returned less than 25 percent from the splendid ore body it had enjoyed in the early 1860s.) If the Firm's share of ownership remained the same through those years, as seems likely, the Firm earned dividends worth between $41.74 million and $55 million, of which John Mackay's share likely aggregated to between $15 million and $20 million. Mackay once remarked that with what he took out of the Bonanza, he could have rebuilt Trinity Church from basement to spire top in solid silver.

The Bonanza Firm earned another $9 million milling ore and reprocessing tailings, which added $3.8 million to Mackay's account. Profits from timber and cordwood amounted to $645,000, putting Mackay's personal take in the neighborhood of $20 million to $24 million.* Profits from the Virginia and Gold Hill Water Company, the Nevada Bank, Mackay's real estate holdings, the San Francisco Gaslight Company, a chemical works, two dynamite factories, and the Firm's other mining ventures both on the Comstock and elsewhere in the West must have added substantially to those totals. In November 1880, the tax collector assessed Mackay on a fortune worth $36 million in personal property and $250,000 in cash. Newspapers thought it should have been twice that amount. That same month, the *Santa Cruz Weekly* estimated Mackay's net worth at $50 million and made him out to be the fifth-richest person in the country, behind only W. H. Vanderbilt, W. W. Astor, Russell

---

* A $20 million fortune in 1880 would be worth about $35.6 billion today measured as an equivalent share of the total national economy.

Sage, and Jay Gould. The Irish Bonanza King was, by any measure, very wealthy, and an enormous portion of his riches existed in cold, hard cash, in gold and silver coin, unlike the fortunes of corporate paper juggled by the likes of Gould, Sage, and other Wall Street buccaneers.

Mackay hosted President Rutherford B. Hayes on the Comstock in the fall of 1880. His experience mirrored the country's—President Hayes made less of an impression than General Grant. When Fair returned from his world tour in the fall of 1880 resolved to contend for Sharon's Senate seat in the upcoming election, Mackay began planning his own escape.

Fair's campaigning as a Democrat put Mackay in a potentially awkward position, as Mackay served on the Republican National Committee. Mackay supported the Republican presidential ticket—James Garfield and Chester Arthur—and negotiated the problem of his business partner's campaigning as a Democrat with ease, since nobody in Nevada expected Mackay to stump for Republican William Sharon, who'd served Nevada with such a singular lack of distinction. Sharon hadn't actually taken his seat in Congress until January 7, 1879, four *years* after his election, and even then, "the habitual absentee" skipped the next session of Congress to focus on his western business interests. In the 1880 campaign, "venality of the grossest and most open kind" marred the campaign for what California newspapers called the "rotten borough"—Nevada—and in James G. Fair of the Bonanza Firm, Sharon faced a nemesis "more well supplied with the munitions of war" than himself. Reno lawmen arrested two of Fair's bagmen bribing voters outright on November 2. The minor news item did nothing to check Fair's momentum. The one true issue in Nevada was anti-Chinese agitation. Fair railed against "Mongolians," and Democratic candidates pledged to Fair carried the state legislature. The Candalaria *True Fissure* estimated that Colonel Fair invested $150,000 persuading the people of Nevada that he was the right man for the job. The pro-Sharon *Gold Hill Daily News* said, "Colonel Jim Fair . . . had literally sacked the state." Fair saw off an attempt by Adolph Sutro to break his caucus in the Nevada legislature, and the "saturnalia of corruption" finally ended in January 1881 when the state legislature elected Fair to the United States Senate. Nevada had replaced one lousy senator with one perhaps worse. Fair would make only one speech during his Senate tenure, in support of the Chinese Exclusion Act, one of the more onerous pieces of legislation ever passed by that august body, although one sadly popular among Nevada miners, and his personal conduct would disgrace both himself and his state.

Mackay hadn't stayed in Nevada to see Fair's election formalized. He'd left the Comstock in late November, possibly expanded his acquaintance with General Grant in New York City, and arrived in Paris on December 9. Alexander O'Grady remembered Mackay striding into the house at Rue de Tilsitt "like a sailor home from the sea," casting aside his coat, his cares, and his worries, taking the stairs two at a time and drawing the whole household to himself with unconcealed and affectionate regard. Plausibly, he hadn't seen them in two years. In O'Grady's memory, John and Louise enjoyed each other. Mackay recognized that in the manner of achievements possible for a woman of the times, his wife had come every inch as far as he had. He was proud of her accomplishments and teased her with gentle devotion. Alexander O'Grady described Louise as "openly fond" of her husband and doting on his letters during their long separation.

Mackay was the toast of Paris's American colony through the winter and spring of 1880–81. As the newspapers told it, the Count and Countess Telfener hosted a dinner for Mr. and Mrs. Mackay soon after his arrival. Louise wore her favorite color—white—appearing in a dress of white brocade and white satin trimmed with a profusion of exquisite white Brussels lace. The American vice-consul general gave the Mackays a dinner at which Louise also wore white satin and lace. At a third dinner, she appeared in a "toilet" of "extreme beauty," a train and corsage of pale blue brocade, worn over a pale blue satin skirt-front decorated with two embroidered bands from which dropped pale-blue fringes shaped like small peacock feathers, with a large pearl forming the eye of each feather. Her corsage was cut square, bordered with a narrow ruffle, and around her neck—"the whitest throat" in the American colony—hung a chain of diamonds and "an immense oval turquoise set in diamonds." Louise Mackay, with a monthly income rumored at $150,000 thanks to bonds her husband deposited on her behalf, had become the best customer in the history of Boucheron.*

The Mackays gave "a sumptuous ball" of their own, one of the remarkable luxuries at which was "a large supply of fresh strawberries." A choir of forty complemented a forty-person orchestra. The staff served dinner at midnight, the first supper at 3:00 a.m., and the second an hour later. Mr. Mackay and twenty- or twenty-one-year-old Eva had retired hours before. Louise kept at the festivities with the late-night revelers.

Mackay enjoyed his ease. He'd earned it. He got reacquainted with his

---

* Arguably, Louise Mackay still holds that distinction.

wife and his sons. He added to his collection of top-quality art, acquiring Léon Bonnat's superb canvas *The Negro Barber (of Suez)*, an arresting image of a muscular black barber bending over to shave the chin of a man seated cross-legged on a mat beneath him. The purchase, reportedly for 22,500 francs, said much about Mackay's evolved artistic sensibilities. A telegraph notice reported Mackay in Rome, buying statues and paintings. He read—Shakespeare and biographies of great men being particular literary interests—and supported his favorite actors at every opportunity.

The *Chicago Tribune* described Louise as the most charitable woman in Paris. John poked fun at the lavish scale of Louise's philanthropies and entertainments. "Louise, if you keep this up, you'll land us both in the poor house," he teased. He never constrained her expenditures, however. Alice O'Grady managed the staff and minded the normal household expenses, and Mackay never limited her outflows, either. He insisted only on accurate account books from them both. "I'm a businessman," he'd say, "and I want everything connected with my affairs, even the household, handled in a businesslike way."

Perhaps in reaction to the years of dirty mining he'd endured or to his Five Points upbringing, Mackay kept himself scrupulously clean. He bathed and changed his underwear every morning and again after exercise—more often than any other man Alexander O'Grady could remember. Strong and fit from the decades underground, Mackay dressed in simple, well-tailored clothes without adornment or affectation and carried himself like a proud old soldier who knew what it meant to be a man. Mackay summoned his son Willie and Alexander O'Grady to accompany him on his morning walks, and in Alexander's memory, he enjoyed their "prattle." He also employed them as interpreters, since both boys spoke French like natives. Perhaps with a little too much fondness, Mackay embraced his inability to learn the language. Although the household employed as many as thirty servants, Mackay refused point-blank to tolerate the attentions of one of the personal valets so commonly used by European aristocrats. A man named François, one of the household servants, looked after Mackay's luggage, clothes, errands, and other wants and made himself indispensable as what a modern executive would recognize as a personal assistant, but François was always at pains to explain that he was under no circumstances permitted to help with Mr. Mackay's bathing, dressing, or shaving.

Later in the spring of 1881, the son of Mackay's childhood hero James Gordon Bennett threw a party in the Mackays' honor in the ancient town of Pau, at the base of the Pyrenees in southwestern France. The elder

Bennett had founded the *New York Herald* in 1835 and built it into the largest and most profitable daily in the country. As a boy, John Mackay had hawked the newspaper on the New York streets, making a half-cent profit on every sale. James Gordon Bennett, Jr., assumed the *Herald*'s reins when his father retired in 1866. As the younger Bennett had a well-earned reputation as a sportsman, a rake, and a bit of a lout, New York society expected him to fail. "Society" misread the man. Bennett possessed "a curious Scotch reverence for his father's memory," according to a close friend. The *Herald* was more than a business to the younger Bennett, the newspaper was a "family pride" and a "birthright." Bennett Junior sponsored Henry Morton Stanley's famous expedition to Africa to find missing explorer David Livingstone and drove the *Herald* to even greater heights. Bennett Junior lived a grand existence in New York through most of the 1870s, but in 1877, he disgraced himself at the home of his fiancée. He arrived drunk and urinated into the family fireplace (or possibly into the grand piano). The offended lady's brother horsewhipped Bennett the next day, and the two fought a duel. Both missed. Ever since, the younger Bennett had managed the *Herald* by telegram from Paris, an expensive proposition in light of the twenty-five-cents-per-word cost of transatlantic telegraph traffic, one possible only for the owner of an astoundingly profitable newspaper. Of the great New York fortunes, Bennett's reportedly ranked only behind those of William Henry Vanderbilt and William Waldorf Astor. Two years before, Bennett and the *Herald* had financed George De Long's attempt to reach the North Pole with thirty-two men aboard the USS *Jeannette*. The expedition left San Francisco in July 1879 and hadn't been heard from since.

Although John Mackay had a decade of life experience on Bennett, the two had become friends during Mackay's previous Paris sojourns and because Louise had become such a pillar of the "American colony." Aware of the intense pleasure John Mackay took in music, Bennett hired Vienna Kapellmeister Johann Strauss (the Younger)—"the Waltz King," then considered the world's best composer, director, and performer of dance music—and his entire Vienna orchestra and brought them to perform at the party, reportedly at the cost of 140,000 francs. The younger Bennett brought the Mackays and the rest of his "brilliant company" to Pau from Paris and other cities in private express trains. A reporter at Bennett's "Diamond Ball" said that nowhere else was it possible "to behold such a wealth of diamonds"—Louise Mackay's "treasures of jewelry almost weighed her down."

Descriptions of Louise Mackay's endless social triumphs crossing

the ocean on the transatlantic telegraph cables appeared as regular fodder in the society columns of American newspapers. Digs like "Shoddy
Abroad" published in the *Sacramento Daily Union* never ceased, either—
on both sides of the Atlantic.

The Mackays arrived in England in the week before May 7 to support
Mackay's friend John McCullough's London debut as the title character in
James Sheridan Knowles's *Virginius*. "Rank, fashion, and beauty" strove
against each other in the packed house, and the audience cheered the
American tragedian with bursts of "hearty and spontaneous applause . . .
seldom heard within the walls of a London Theater." Louise attended the
Compte de Camonda's costume ball as Cleopatra in a "wondrous blend"
of a gold and turquoise satin wearing sapphires and diamonds worthy
of her namesake. John's costume went unrecorded, but anyone would be
forgiven the surmise that he attended as Mark Antony.

Mackay next surfaced in New York on June 2. His sudden appearance and dinner with Nevada senator John Percival Jones caused much
comment in mining circles. Mackay passed through Los Angeles on June
14, on his way to the Comstock, having taken the southern route from
the east, likely because of a desire to inspect mining discoveries in the
southern Arizona Territory. Apache depredations, Mexican raiding parties, and the lawless violence of the mining camps didn't deter him. He'd
lived it all before. The reason for his whirlwind trip to Nevada remained
obscure, but he'd likely been summoned by Flood to inspect a potentially
important development in the deep levels of the Comstock mines.

With the great miner on his way back to Virginia City, the *Carson
Morning Appeal* joked about the "epistletory bonanza" [*sic*] of some three
hundred letters Mackay would have to "crosscut" in the Con. Virginia
office. Mackay received hundreds of letters from gold diggers all over
the world, those from Europe often addressed to "Mackay, North America." Many letters from women sought marriage—or other less reputa-
ble arrangements. Some came from correspondents sure that $20,000 or
$30,000 in seed money would set their schemes rolling down the road to
millions, most of them "good enough to offer Mr. Mackay a half interest." One suggested a modest $1 million investment to buy up every goat
in the world and thus monopolize the kid-glove market. All found their
way into a wood stove.

Whatever Mackay found in the deep levels didn't hold his attention.
Comstock bullion production barely topped $1 million in 1881, the
worst annual showing in the twenty-two years since the lode's discovery.
Speculators made much of Mackay's giving away the sparse furnishings

that had adorned the lodgings he'd kept in the Gould & Curry office since the big fire in '75, "as if he intended to shake the dust of the Comstock from his feet forever." The whole lot wouldn't have brought $300 under the auctioneer's hammer. Mackay left New York for France aboard the steamship *St. Laurent* on July 12 and likely spent most the rest of the year touring Europe with his wife. Someone in Virginia City received a letter from him dated September 18. Mackay had penned it from Moscow and said that he hadn't seen an English-language newspaper in seven weeks. Later that autumn, a hotel keeper in The Hague, in the Netherlands, gloated about "the King and Queen of the Bonanza Mountains of California" staying at his establishment.

In San Francisco, James Flood and Senator Fair bickered. Fair withdrew from the Firm's mining operations in the autumn of 1881 and focused his money on San Francisco real estate investments and other California speculations. The Firm had sponsored development of the New Yellow Jacket shaft in the Gold Hill section of the lode. Low-grade quartz between 2,200 and 2,300 feet and small ore stringers between the 2,760-foot level and 3,000 feet kept up hopes, but 170-degree water spouting from the drill holes and foul air at such an incredible distance from the surface made progress ever-more difficult and expensive. Flood and Mackay ordered the Gold Hill pumps shut down. The Gold Hill mines flooded to the level of the Sutro Tunnel's South Lateral. Deep-level prospecting continued in the middle mines and on the north end of the lode.

Mackay arrived on the Comstock at midnight one night in July 1882. As usual, his wife, sons, and daughter had stayed in Europe. He spent the entire following afternoon examining the lower levels and emerged several hours later "looking as fresh as though he had spent the time seated in an easy chair on the surface in the shade." He hadn't been underground in a year. He spent much of the next two months in the mines.

One thing Mackay noticed during his Comstock sojourn in the summer of 1882—if conducting business across the Atlantic hadn't drawn his attention to the situation already—was that the cost of using the transatlantic telegraph to communicate with his wife had *doubled* since the last time he was in Nevada. Mackay found that painful. Not so much because of the cost—he could bear any cost to communicate with his family—but because the new rates marked a step in the wrong direction, against the march of progress. The rate rise crucified James Gordon Bennett, Jr., orchestrating the affairs of the *New York Herald* via voluminous cables between Europe and New York. The hiked rates came as a result of the new "pool" of the transatlantic cable companies organized by notorious corporate raider, secretive railroad and telegraph magnate, and "arch-trickster" Jay Gould in May 1882. Gould's "pooling agreement" had raised rates from twenty-five cents to fifty cents per word.

Mackay returned to San Francisco and probably Virginia City before heading east via the southern route, as usual likely wanting to inspect mining developments in the southern Arizona Territory, and as usual undeterred by chaotic violence of the camps that kept more "civilized" eastern businessmen at a distance. The savage Tombstone gunfight at the O.K. Corral between Virgil, Morgan, and Wyatt Earp and Doc Holliday on one side and the Cowboy gang of the Clanton and McLaury brothers and Billy Claiborne had taken place the year before, and a bloody feud between the two factions had raged ever since. Mackay arrived in Chicago on October 17. A reporter seeking an interview noted his plain suit, checked shirt, and faded, stiff brown hat. Mackay wore no diamonds, and the only ornament about his person—"if ornament it could be called"— was a gold slide on a black silk ribbon that he used as a watch guard. Mackay told the man there was "nothing new in the way of mining on the Pacific coast." That afternoon, he departed for New York and continued across the Atlantic to France.

John and Louise Mackay, their two sons, Eva, and their tutors wintered on the French Riviera and made excursions to Rome and Naples. The turn to March found them at Menton, "the Pearl of France," on the Mediterranean coast at the border with Italy, where they were joined by the Count and Countess Telfener. They returned to Paris in April, and Mackay added to the family art collection with the purchase of Flemish master Gerard Douw's canvas *The Fish Merchant*.

They were still in the French capital when salacious stories about Senator James G. Fair suddenly filled American newspapers. According to the correspondent of the *Chicago Herald* who broke the story, Fair and his family had been "at loggerheads" for the past several years, the trouble consisting of the "somewhat open way" in which "Slippery Jim of the millions" violated the Seventh Commandment. On the Comstock, it had been more or less an open secret that Fair invested in "wildcat claims" to the manifest detriment of his wife. Fair's "countless infidelities" poked through a cracked door in San Francisco and escaped the closet completely in Washington, D.C., where Fair had "soiled the senatorial toga" and sold out the marital combination "on every opportunity." Nor was Mrs. Fair, by all accounts "a most estimable lady," inclined to "suffer in silence." A portly woman with "flashing black eyes" and "a will of considerable horsepower," she filled the air about Fair's head with sulfurous remarks every time she caught him in "some new peccadillo." Rather than taking his medicine, the senator counterattacked with "abuse." He accused her of unseemly conduct, which everyone knew to be false. Fair insinuated that John Mackay had "more influence about his house than he has himself"—likely the result of Theresa Fair's holding Mackay up as an example of how a married man ought to comport himself. Not long after Colonel Fair took his seat in Washington, his wife paid him a surprise visit and found Fair enjoying a setup that "might have been the envy of [the] Khedive of Egypt." Mrs. Fair blew it up "with several pounds of moral dynamite" and treated the senator to some of the strongest—and presumably most public—"curtain lectures" that "the active tongue of a strong-willed and fearless woman ever pronounced." The colonel fell back "on his ancient privilege of abuse" and cut off his wife's money supply. She had to borrow money to fund her return to California. Back in San Francisco, Mrs. Fair and the children occupied the family mansion on a corner of Pine and Jones streets. The colonel fortified himself at the well-stocked bar inside the Occidental Hotel.

James Fair, Jr., the senator's eldest son—then twenty years of age—"a chip off the block" known to cavort with "evil companions of the female persuasion" and for liberal enjoyment of liquor, attempted to shoot his father but was prevented and tumbled aboard a train for Paso Robles, about two hundred miles south of San Francisco.

Theresa Fair went to Virginia City and filed for divorce. On May 12, the court heard the testimony of one "woman of the town" from San Francisco and read the sworn deposition of another, collected a few more details, and granted the divorce. Fair contested nothing. James Fair got custody of their eldest son, the one who had allegedly tried to shoot him. Theresa received custody of the three minor children, the family residence in San Francisco, and $4.25 million, a staggering sum by the standards of the day but far less than half of the family fortune. The trial had lasted under an hour.

Long before the scandal went public, John Mackay and James Flood had come down squarely in Theresa Fair's court. Their opprobrium may have contributed to Fair's decision to stand apart eighteen months before. As a San Francisco correspondent of the *St. Louis Globe-Democrat* wrote two years later, "Public opinion was against [Fair] at the time of the divorce suit of his wife, and nothing has since changed it." In Nevada, the *Carson Morning Appeal*'s editor considered it "a matter of regret" that

John Mackay had not been elected senator "in place of that king of duplicity and deceit, James Fair." In the editor's estimation, Mackay possessed "a thousand manly and honorable qualities." Fair had "none."

Ironically, John Mackay had accepted an official government charge that same May, but one far distant from Nevada or Washington, D.C. Just a few days after the Virginia City District Court freed Theresa Fair from the bonds of matrimony, John and Louise Mackay passed through Berlin on their way to Moscow. President Chester Arthur had asked Mackay to serve as special ambassador of the United States at the coronation of Czar Alexander III, whose father had been assassinated by bomb-throwing Nihilists two years before. Fear of the Nihilists motivated the long delay, but whisperings that "the present Emperor was only half a Czar so long as he remained uncrowned" eventually became too loud to ignore.*

Telegrams to California described "the whole European press" fawning over the magnificence of Mackay's private train carriage and the fifteen sumptuous dresses carefully hung in his wife's private baggage car. Muscovites evinced much interest in "the Big Bonanza" and his wonderful silver mines in the tumult of events leading up to the grand coronation, considering him "one of the most interesting personages attending." At the czar's reception for the diplomatic missions held a night or two before his official investment, John Mackay chatted pleasantly with the Russian empress, fielding her questions about California.

The breathtaking coronation spectacle took place inside the Kremlin's Cathedral of Michael the Archangel. The ceremony of chanting, bowing, receiving, anointing, addressing, faith-professing, cross-kissing, enrobing, and praying culminated when an attendant brought forth the imperial crown on a velvet cushion. The czar picked up the crown, held it high so all could behold its bejeweled magnificence, and put it on his own head. The *New York Times'* man in Moscow found the ceremony "fully worthy of the occasion of the assumption of autocratic power by the absolute ruler of eighty millions of people." A veteran diplomat considered the pageant the most spectacular and imposing he'd witnessed during a thirty-five-year career. Outside, in the city, mounted Cossacks patrolled every street, their steely eyes peeled for the Nihilists. At the ball held afterward, the new czar decided that Mrs. Mackay was the best-dressed

---

*In an odd twist of history, President Arthur, risen to the presidency on the assassination of James Garfield, sent Mackay to the coronation of a czar who also ascended to power as the result of an assassination.

woman present. Not even the stupendous pomp and barbaric splendor of a Russian imperial coronation could dim Louise Mackay's star.

John Mackay never recorded his thoughts on the occasion, but of all the splendid personages present, he'd possibly had the lowest birth—which wouldn't have caused him the least bit of shame. He must have been quietly proud of his wife, too, watching her enjoy the ball, fully aware that she'd covered every bit as much improbable distance as he had himself. They circulated with "the finest people in Europe." Unfortunately, John Mackay found most of them unimpressive. Mackay was chivalrous to a fault, and nobody ever heard him utter an unkind word about any woman, of any station, either in public or in private. He displayed rather a lot less charity toward male members of the European nobility. Of them, in private, he was "profanely contemptuous." He called them "bums and parasites" who "ought to go to work as I did." In high company, Mackay took malicious pleasure in telling European aristocrats that he'd once been a common miner. Yes, he'd cooked his own food, and yes, he'd washed his own clothes. "It was either that or go dirty," Mackay said. He'd been born in Ireland, he'd relate, the poorest country in the world, scion of a long line of Irish "bogtrotters." He'd gone barefoot as a child and shared a dirt floor with the family pig. Louise feigned "mortification" and embarrassment in company, but she'd known the rude press of poverty herself. They'd traveled the hard roads their European associates had not. John and Louise Mackay had come as far as—and perhaps farther than—anyone else in the world, from the slums of New York and the filthy, transient mining camps of California to serve as their country's official ambassadors at a Romanov coronation.

Except for the two brief trips to the Comstock, Mackay had enjoyed two and a half years of family time and ease after the sustained focus required to manage the extraction of the Big Bonanza. Together with his wife, he'd explored the ancient cultural capitals of Europe and soaked himself in world-class art, theater, and music, experiences so far beyond the original possibilities of an Irish street urchin that they might have existed on another planet. He'd also decided that he wasn't ready to settle into a permanent retirement. He still had the old fire. He missed the challenge of swinging great enterprise. He missed having an enemy.

The one he'd decided to make might have been the most formidable private individual on earth—Jay Gould.

CHAPTER 17

The Cable War

The Mackays' Parisian mansion at 9 Rue de Tilsitt today,
which currently houses the Belgian Embassy.

———

**Mackay's simple word is worth 100 cents on the dollar any-
where. He has resided a quarter century on this Coast, and
it would be hard to find a man who would say that he ever
broke a promise or attempted ever to mislead any one in a
business transaction.**
—"Mackay and Gould," *Carson Morning Appeal,*
October 25, 1883

A small, frail man with a thick beard and a prominent forehead long
since deserted by his hairline, Jay Gould was, without question,
the most hated man in America in the summer of 1883—and the most
feared. A former business partner, since murdered, once described

Gould as "a heap of clothes and a pair of eyes." Fairly or not, public disgust at all the distortions, dishonesty, double-dealing, and oppressions in the post–Civil War economy had come to rest in his person. Most Americans imagined Jay Gould as a demonic genius pulling the levers of the economy for his private enrichment—to the detriment of everybody else. The eyes of the times saw Gould's wealth as exactly opposite Mackay's. Gould had "extracted" his wealth "from thousands of people who have through toilsome years acquired the small investments which he has squeezed like a sponge into his own coffers." Mackay had wrested his from the earth through honest toil, paying fair wages, without taking advantage of his fellow citizens. Like almost every American newspaper beyond Gould's control, the New York Times took after him with a vengeance. The paper spoke for most Americans when it described Gould as "an unscrupulous gambler who has never yet played without cogged dice" and "a money grabber . . . universally believed to be without heart, conscience, or shame." "His touch is death," muttered ruined Wall Street operator Daniel Drew.

Gould never enjoyed Mackay's rugged good health and appetite for physical labor, but he shared Mackay's capacity for disciplined, directed, and sustained hard work. Gould had a passion for orchids, and like Mackay, he collected art. Despite decades of anti-Semitic slurs heaped on his head, Gould didn't have a drop of Jewish blood. His Puritan ancestors had pioneered the New York wilderness. Five years younger than Mackay, too young to have rushed after California gold, Gould worked as a surveyor in the middle 1850s, then ran a tannery and a leather merchandising operation—which failed. Between 1860 and 1867, while Mackay was working his way off the bottom rungs of the Comstock mining industry, Jay Gould served an apprenticeship in New York's stock and commodities trading and financial industries, ingurgitating the changing, dynamic conditions of the industrializing economy. He emerged as one of the first Wall Street operators to comprehend how to use the new tools of modern finance, law, and politics as levers with which to control large public corporations, especially railroads. Gould's masterly—and most would say devious—use of equity ownership, bonds, short-term or "floating" debt, proxy voting control, bankruptcy and receivership, contractual flaws, well-connected friends, government oversight and intervention, and litigation baffled, thwarted, and ruined competitors through the next two decades. Whereas other big wheels of business cultivated attention, Gould always sought the shadows, vesting his ambitions in secrecy. Few could fathom Gould's stratagems as he rose to control one railroad, then appeared at the helm of another before most of his rivals realized that he'd disappeared from the first. Through the 1870s, Gould consolidated railroad and newspaper interests into a powerful empire. Camouflaged behind the very public railroad dramas, the enlargement of Gould's telegraphic power went largely unremarked. In 1878, Gould sold a telegraph company called Atlantic & Pacific (A&P) to Western Union, by far the industry's dominant power.

Western Union handled between 80 and 90 percent of the nation's telegraphic traffic. The company charged high rates—especially in those large regions of the country where it had no competition at all—paid large dividends, and treated its customers as if it was doing them a favor. Western Union's stock price soared when the company went unchallenged and sank whenever effective competition materialized.

By September 1880, Gould had built another telegraph operation—American Union—into a system large enough to pain Western Union. Most businessmen thought Gould planned to make another killing selling out to Western Union. He did. As 1880 turned to 1881, Gould sold American Union stock high to Western Union. He also acquired large quantities of Western Union stock under the guise of buying shares to cover the huge short position he'd taken betting on a fall in Western Union stock price caused by effective American Union competition. (And, it went without saying, making superb profits in both transactions.) Gould shocked the nation in February 1881 when he emerged with what he'd wanted all along—control of Western Union and its near-monopoly of the domestic telegraph business of the United States.

Gould then held sway over an empire built on three interconnected pillars—railroads, newspapers, and the telegraph. The thought of Jay Gould controlling the nation's telegraphic communications filled rival businessmen with terror. A stock jobber able to tap every wire in America seemed to hold an impregnable position. Competitors grew certain that Gould read their private dispatches, employed code-breakers to unravel their ciphers, and garbled or delayed their communications. Speculators panicked, convinced Gould delayed information flows so he could read news before anyone else. Newspapers lived in particular terror of Gould's clout—their business depended on stories cabled home by far-flung correspondents. By delaying, misrouting, or losing their traffic, Gould could crush them entirely, and they had no option but to pay Western Union's exorbitant rates. Lily-livered newspapers flatly refused to publish anything inimical to Gould's interests. Broadsheets with more editorial courage spoke out in favor of telegraph reform and suddenly stopped receiving timely communications. By the summer of 1883, only a few independent telegraph companies survived, all of them hamstrung by the small size of their networks. Western Union controlled everything else, and atop Western Union lurked the dark specter of Jay Gould. Many Americans came to see Jay Gould's far-reaching influence in politics, the courts, communications, and the press as a threat to democracy itself.

Western Union's near-monopoly on American telegraph traffic also gave Gould leverage against the transatlantic cables. British and French capital controlled all three existing transatlantic cable companies, but they couldn't do business without a domestic American cable operation feeding messages into their cables and forwarding European cables to destinations within the United States. To handle message distribution within the United States, each transatlantic company had entered into a contract with a separate American telegraph entity. One sent and received traffic through Atlantic & Pacific, another worked with American Union, and the third dealt with Western Union. But Western Union and Jay Gould now owned both Atlantic & Pacific and American Union. Gould canceled A&P's and American Union's contracts, forcing all three transatlantic companies to work through Western Union. Then Gould formed a company and began laying two American cables across the Atlantic. Gould-controlled transatlantic cables put the existing ocean cable companies at his mercy—with control of the American telegraph system *and* unfettered access to transatlantic cables, Gould could freeze them out. When they'd been independent, competition between the three transatlantic companies drove rates low, but faced with Gould's power, the cable companies joined a Gould-controlled "pool"—a cartel—in the spring of 1882 that doubled rates from twenty-five cents to fifty cents per word and divided the traffic. They all earned higher profits on lower traffic volumes, making more money for less work. In the eyes of American businessmen, Gould's controlling all traffic between Europe and the United States made a bad situation worse.

Monopolies quashed competition and squeezed rich profits. They also made fat targets. John Mackay had learned both lessons battling William Sharon and the Bank Ring on the Comstock. According to a close friend, in the three years since Mackay had cleaned out the Big Bonanza, he had come to view his pharaonic wealth as a trust, one that he felt obligated him to perform "some special service" on behalf of his adopted country. During his winter on the French Riviera, he'd decided to perform that service with an assault on Gould's transatlantic telegraph monopoly—an idea surely encouraged by his friend James Gordon Bennett, Jr. (Mackay had also considered attempting to reinvigorate the New York shipbuilding industries that had given him such a boost during his youth—slow to adopt iron-hulled shipbuilding techniques, they'd been supplanted by British shipbuilders.) When he passed through New York the previous autumn, Mackay had quietly hired two telegraph experts to research the transatlantic telegraph situation on his behalf.

Their reports surely made clear the problem that had forced the other transatlantic companies into Gould's pool—no independent transatlantic company could survive, let alone compete, without access to a domestic distribution network inside the United States. Gould would simply kill it or compel it to join his pool by refusing to feed or distribute messages to or from the upstart cable company.

Western Union wasn't without troubles of its own that summer, however. Its wires went silent on July 20, 1883, stilled by a strike of the Brotherhood of Telegraphers, who sought better pay and improved working conditions. The company refused to bend, and the wires stayed quiet through the end of the month. Possibly precipitated into action by the telegraphers' strike, John Mackay landed in New York on August 2. Rumor said he'd soon head for the Pacific Coast. Instead, Mackay took control of the foundering Postal Telegraph Company, one of the few small telegraph companies independent of Western Union. "Mackey's New Venture" and "Mr. Mackey in Control" announced mid-August headlines in the *New York Times*. (The newspaper wouldn't spell Mackay's name correctly until December and wouldn't consistently get it right until the spring of 1884.)

The Postal Telegraph Company had been created to combat Western Union in June 1881, and two of its founders were men well known to John Mackay—James Keene, who had helped front the bear raids on the Con. Virginia in 1876, and George D. Roberts, an acquaintance from the old days of the Comstock, former co-owner in the Rising Star mine, Mackay's unremunerative 1868 Idaho mining venture, and a mine promoter of very dubious scruples. Mackay bought a large bloc of Postal stock (possibly Keene's share) and formed a syndicate with other large Postal stockholders that forbade members to sell stock for three years, locking up a sufficient quantity of the stock to ensure Mackay retained control. Mackay at first declined Postal Telegraph's presidency, preferring to operate without title, as was his wont in mining operations. He assumed the title a fortnight later, having been convinced that the public would gain confidence in the enterprise with his name attached to the formal title.

Although formed two years before, Postal had barely managed to get its New York to Chicago line into service in time for the Western Union strike, largely due to what the *New York Times* described as "a want of system at headquarters." Although the company had "merits" and "[desired] to furnish telegraphing cheaply," it also needed "a complete reorganization." Mackay supplied that quickly.

The *Times* interviewed Gould's new competitor in the Hoffman House, the hotel on Broadway at Madison Square, between Twenty-fourth and Twenty-fifth streets, where Mackay stayed while in New York. (Mackay had reportedly loaned money to the proprietor, Edward S. Stokes, to help him remodel the hotel. The reporter remarked on Mackay's ruddy Irish face and found him quiet in both manner and dress, but with features that "betoken a resolute will." They appeared to belong to a man who "didn't hesitate long in making a decision, and when his mind is made up, allows no obstacles to remain in the way of execution." Mackay said nothing about his plans, but the *Times* welcomed his appearance on the telegraphic battlefield, certain that the effects of "a blow struck at a monopoly" would "inure to the benefit of the public."

A few days after Mackay took formal control, the Western Union telegraphers surrendered, and the company resumed operations. Jay Gould testified before Congress in September, ironically aided in his attempts to deflect efforts to undo the Western Union monopoly and nationalize the American telegraph system by whisperings of Mackay's efforts to organize a "gigantic opposition."

A fortune built on corporate paper tied Gould's fortunes to the ups and downs of the financial markets, and Wall Street's downward trend in the latter half of 1883 limited Gould's ability to counterattack. Although the exact circumstances remained unknown outside his innermost circle, Gould was struggling to keep the fragile railroad properties of his empire afloat at a time when Mackay possessed the ultimate downturn asset—a war chest stuffed with coin. To Jay Gould, it must have seemed that Mackay was everywhere that dismal autumn: in Nevada, denying he had any interest in the state's seat in the U.S. Senate—"I am not fool enough to go into politics," Mackay told the *Nevada State Journal*; inspecting the thirty-one-hundred-foot levels of the Sierra Nevada and Union mines at the northern end of the Comstock with Senator John Paul Jones; ignoring threats of violence from Amelia Smallman, the woman who'd tried to blackmail him in 1878 and had recently been released from prison; conducting business in San Francisco; dropping hundreds of thousands of dollars on valuable mining property in Colorado; putting up money to fund two Comstock comrades' purchase of the *Salt Lake City Tribune*; "doing Texas" after spending $400,000 on the Peerless mines in the Quijotoa Mountains west of Tucson; and taking an interest in and becoming a trustee of "the National Cable Railway Company," organized in New York to install and operate San Francisco–style cable cars in other cities.

Amidst all that furious activity, Mackay put his spurs to the Postal Telegraph. Mackay knew he lacked a thorough understanding of the telegraph industry—a common cause of failure in a rich man's vanity business—so he hired competent managers, paid them well, and allowed them to run daily operations with enough rope to either hang themselves or succeed. Mackay reserved top-level strategic decisions to himself, and like Gould, he was a sphinx. Poker and mining ventures had taught him well: Mackay never gave a hint of his intentions, even to his closest associates. As he had done in mining, Mackay insisted Postal adopt the most advanced, highest-quality technology available. Postal strung new lines to add cities to its network and expanded its carrying capacity between New York and Chicago, the nation's busiest telegraph artery. As Postal grew, Mackay hired many blacklisted strike refugees desperate for opportunities beyond Western Union. Mackay reorganized the company under a more comprehensive charter to forestall the Gould-abused tactic of suing rivals out of existence for overstepping the terms of their corporate charters. The new Postal put low rates into effect, announced that the company expected to be able to do business between any of the principal American cities within two years, and swiftly morphed into a credible and expanding rival of the "Western Union anaconda." New York papers ceased "to make light of the Nevada miner."

Although news didn't leak until after the middle of October, Mackay had quietly struck a crucial blow against Gould's transatlantic monopoly before he'd left Europe: He and James Gordon Bennett, Jr., had signed contracts with Siemens Brothers of London for the construction of two new cables to lay across the Atlantic. Mackay and Bennett commissioned the building of a gigantic steel-hulled ship, *Cable Ship Mackay-Bennett*, to lay and service the cables and incorporated a new enterprise called the Commercial Cable Company, under whose auspices they hoped to have new transatlantic cables in action the following summer. (Commercial Cable was 70 percent Mackay and 25 percent Bennett, with a few other brave souls willing to defy Gould taking up the remaining 5 percent.)

While Mackay was in the West, the *Carson Morning Appeal* asked him about Jay Gould. Mackay said he didn't fear Gould as a business antagonist and expressed "mild surprise" that so many New York merchants stood "in such terror of the little Ogre of Wall Street." "This is all humbug," Mackay said. "Capital is not so powerful as people think. When a man has kept his business as a constant menace to the public and acted the bully instead of the friend of his patrons, it takes very little to knock him out, provided you give the patrons to understand that you are in the fight to stay." Mackay promised that his new lines weren't "a sell-out proposition" and that people could do business with him with confidence, without fear that he'd quit the field and give Gould the opportunity to "revenge himself" upon his former customers.

The *Daily Alta California* "thank[ed] heaven" for James Gordon Bennett and John W. Mackay and the prospect of relief from the exorbitant rates of the "monstrous monopoly." The *London Truth* "congratulated" Mackay and Bennett for their "enterprise" and "determination" and hoped for a quick end to the "obnoxious monopoly" of the Atlantic Ocean cables.

Mackay's whirlwind of 1883 activity ended when he boarded the SS *Alaska* in New York on December 11, bound for Liverpool. Aboard ship, Mackay received an ovation from the other passengers. Surrounded and congratulated, Mackay seemed "in the happiest mood," as if he relished the prospect of adversity. ("Enemies are my masseurs," he once confessed to a friend. "They keep my blood circulating.") Asked about the cable venture aboard the *Alaska*, Mackay said, "I'm as confident of success as I am that I'll have my breakfast tomorrow morning."

As if his looming fight with Jay Gould wasn't enough, Mackay had entered into another—with one of the most famous artists in the world.

Art occupied a special place in both John and Louise Mackay's hearts. They much admired artists. A friend said John Mackay would "transit a realm" to spend a few minutes with a Velásquez or a Rubens. Among the contemporary French painters he and his wife most admired were Alexandre Cabanel, Léon Bonnat, Madeleine Lemaire, and Ernest Meissonier. The Mackays owned at least one Bonnat, Cabanel had painted an excellent portrait of John in 1878, and Mrs. Mackay had commissioned three works from Mademoiselle Lemaire. All three painters had become family friends. By the early 1880s, septuagenarian Ernest Meissonier—best known for his broad and dramatic canvasses of Napoleon Bonaparte and of violent Napoleonic battlefields—had risen to assume the mantle of the "greatest" of French painters and may have considered himself above such uncultured American acquaintances. In any event, John and Louise Mackay had paid a visit to Meissonier's studio, and out of that visit came a loose arrangement for the artist to paint Louise's portrait. She'd sat for Meissonier a number of times in early 1882. Ominously, Meissonier neglected to remember at least one scheduled sitting.

Meissonier finished Louise's portrait in the summer of 1883. Louise was at her summer retreat in Villebon, southwest of Paris beyond Chartres, and she didn't see the finished painting. When Meissonier asked to exhibit it "with his works"—presumably a question posed in a letter—Louise gave her assent, under the impression that Meissonier meant to show it in a retrospective of his life's work scheduled for May 1884. Meissonier, however, referred to the upcoming National Salon, where he exhibited the canvas, which Louise still hadn't seen.

"Talk" from the salon called Meissonier's portrait "hard, and utterly wanting in distinction, grace, and female elegance." Churlish Meissonier complained that his subject's "plump and concentric roundness" realized "no type of beauty," and that he found Mrs. Mackay's face and person "wanting in distinction."

Critics focused on the extra decade Meissonier had added to Louise's features and on her coarse hands. They were the hands of a washerwoman. A "caricature" more than a likeness, the painting communicated exactly what the artist thought of Louise Mackay.

Louise asked for a "retouching." Meissonier "stood on his dignity as an artist" and refused. Adding to Louise's bitterness, Meissonier presented a bill for 70,000 francs, then worth about $14,000. Meissonier had never before charged more than $9,000 for a portrait.

Louise refused to pay. The portrait remained in Meissonier's possession.

Around that time, John arrived in Paris. He considered the whole affair an insulting swindle, and he thought Meissonier "wanting in respect for his wife."

After several rounds of increasingly warm letters, the Mackays paid Meissonier's extortionate fee through a third party, who returned with the offensive painting. "While it might be of some value as a picture," Mackay said, "it [doesn't have] the slightest value as a portrait."

In one set of stories, Louise hosted a party and burned the picture. In another, she'd destroyed it with a poker. In a third, she'd tossed it in a privy. (She hadn't destroyed the painting. Years later, after she'd aged into the portrait, Louise mischievously retrieved the Meissonier from the attic where she'd hidden it and gave the portrait prominent display.) According to the *Daily Alta California*, the portrait measured sixteen by eleven inches.

Mackay said that he'd always been an admirer of Meissonier and had "always felt well toward him," but had been disappointed by the entire episode. "I wanted a Meissonier," Mackay complained, "not Meissonier painting a slovenly imitation of a Cabanel."

Mackay's was cogent criticism. Art circles adopted the witticism.

The imbroglio divided Paris newspapers into two camps. Some were "very severe," roundly criticizing interloping Mrs. Mackay for the disrespect shown to the national treasure, Meissonier. Others supported "the amiable Yankee" who did so much to support French charities, arts, and commerce and acknowledged that much of the trouble lay in Meissonier's character, "which [was] not as gentle as that of the lamb."

When the Mackays relocated to London, newspapers supposed the "vile abuse" heaped on her by the Parisian "boulevard sheets" had caused her to "[shake] the Parisian dust from her skirts and [carry] her household gods to London." More likely, she and John made the move because one end of John's transatlantic cable ended in the English capital and because teenage John William, Jr., and his younger brother Clarence had reached an age to benefit from an English public school education before entering university. They entered Beaumont College in Old Windsor, said to be "the Catholic Eton."

To manage his ocean cable business, Mackay hired George G. Ward, a man with more than a decade of experience in transoceanic telegraphy. With George G. Ward riding herd, the Commercial Cable Company spent the rest of 1884 constructing and laying two transatlantic cables.

While that was happening, Jay Gould launched his first counterattack, dropping Western Union's domestic rates in the hopes of eliminating its budding domestic rivals, and sparking a telegraph war that would last three years. Stock market carnage in May and June prevented Gould from moving more aggressively. Many banks and brokers failed, including A. W. Dimock & Company, which held the Bankers and Merchants' Telegraph Company and a Bankers subsidiary called American Rapid, two of the companies Mackay was trying to organize into an alliance against Western Union.

The alliance of Mackay's Postal Telegraph, the Baltimore & Ohio railroad's telegraph business, and the Bankers and Merchants' telegraph systems went into effect on August 1, 1884. The *Herald* called it "the most formidable opposition to the Western Union telegraph monopoly which has ever been organized." Western Union stock fell. The weak point in the alliance was Bankers and Merchants', which was insolvent. Mackay considered advancing money to the company to keep it in the fight—until he understood the size of its debts. The coalition lasted just six weeks. The Baltimore & Ohio withdrew, citing Bankers and Merchants' failure to pull its weight in the group's expansion plans. Bankers and Merchants' fell into receivership a week later—where its subsidiary American Rapid Telegraph soon followed. The situation decayed even further when John W. Garrett, president of the Baltimore & Ohio, died on September 26. Control of the B&O devolved into the hands of his son, Robert Garrett, a much less formidable individual.

Mackay and his erstwhile allies had squandered a significant opportunity to exploit a moment of Western Union weakness. Western Union's earnings had dropped about 15 percent, forcing the company to shave its dividend, and Gould's railroad empire barely survived the chaotic summer.

In the West, Mackay and Fair had a serious falling out. The exact particulars never leaked, but Fair withdrew from the Nevada Bank, leaving Flood and Mackay to go it alone. Up on the Comstock, Mackay and Flood continued to finance deep-level explorations of the middle and north-end mines. On the north end, miners grid-worked the lode to below 3,000 feet. Miners working in hellish conditions found nodules of high-grade quartz interspersed with large quantities of mineral quartz, never in sufficient volume to constitute a bonanza. Miners reached the 3,360-foot level in the Ophir-Mexican winze. When Mackay learned that they'd found no ore, he ordered the pumps turned off. The north-end mines flooded to the level of the Sutro Tunnel, leaving only the middle mines pumping. Working beneath the gargantuan machinery of what was called the Combination Shaft, the middle mines constituted the Comstock's last great hope.

The affairs of the transatlantic Commercial Cable Company progressed much more satisfactorily in 1884. Commercial Cable had landed its first cable in July, and its second in October. Like the first, the second Mackay-Bennett cable linked London to Ireland to Nova Scotia, but from thence it went direct to Long Island. The cable came ashore at Rockaway Beach, connected to Brooklyn, crossed the East River Bridge to Manhattan, and to the great relief of New Yorkers, the company buried its line under Water and Wall streets all the way to the company offices at 21 Wall Street. The epic mess of telegraphic ganglia tangled over the New York streets had become a significant public annoyance. A *New York Times* editorial thanked the company for "declining to add to the manifold nuisances entailed by wires strung in the air."

The Gould transatlantic pool made "strenuous efforts to induce the Commercial [Cable] Company" to join their pool and raise rates to sixty cents per word. Mackay steadfastly refused. Commercial Cable went into active service at midnight on Christmas Eve—five o'clock on Christmas morning in London. Commercial Cable set rates for standard commercial traffic at forty cents per word, 20 percent less than was charged by the companies of the Gould pool. Commercial charged twenty cents per word for press traffic and ten cents per word for low-priority press dispatches that could be sent when the lines were otherwise unoccupied. Experts reckoned the Mackay-Bennett cables could carry traffic at half the cost of the Gould pool, and the *New York Times* reported "the Mackay-Bennett managers" as "highly elated at their present outlook."

The Gould pool cables dropped their regular rates to match. They also lowered their press rates, but left them a few cents per word above Commercial's in both the high- and low-priority categories, hoping to overwhelm the Mackay-Bennett cables with low-quality newspaper business.

Pool company earnings plummeted as Commercial Cable gave cheerful, timely service and proved equal to the demand. Commercial Cable began operating from inside the stock exchange in mid-January. Pleased traders discovered that Commercial Cable messages passed back and forth between the New York and London stock exchanges in just six minutes. Too long associated with a sluggish cartel, the chairman of one of the pool companies complained that the Mackay-Bennett cables had resorted to unfair means "to obtain a greater share of the traffic than the possession of two cables fairly entitled them to."

In Paris, Mackay's twenty-three-year-old daughter, Eva, married a twenty-seven-year-old Italian nobleman, Don Fernando Julien Colonna, prince of Galatro, at a religious ceremony presided over by the papal nuncio. Louise hovered on the edge of tears through much of the ceremony. Afterward, Louise gave "a grand bridal reception" at the Rue de Tilsitt that the newspapers thought "must rank with the most magnificent festivals of French history." All "the flower of European and American society" attended, and Louise somehow managed to pull off a party stamped with "quiet splendor, grace, refinement, and family intimacy." A reporter of London's *Pall Mall Gazette* was fascinated to find "The Big Bonanza . . .

perfectly at home among the princes representing the oldest houses of Italy," and he paid John Mackay what must surely be the best compliment a British newspaper gave an Irishman in the nineteenth century when he added, "Anyone who knew how to read a face would say that he was a man to whom they should all take off their hats."

Asked about her daughter's wedding, Louise raved about the quality of Italian husbands. Speaking of her sister, Louise gushed, "Ada's married life has been without a cloud." And so it had been and so it would continue. Eva wouldn't be so fortunate.

The Commercial Cable Company worked wonders from its inception. The weakness of Mackay's young telegraph network still lurked in the American distribution network he hoped to work up into a bona-fide competitor of Western Union. In that fight, his allies did as much damage as his foes. Robert Garrett slashed Baltimore & Ohio telegraph rates in early January. The cuts inflicted more damage on Postal Telegraph than they did on Western Union. Postal defaulted on its bond payments ten days before Eva's wedding. Mackay relieved Postal Telegraph's embarrassment in May by giving the company an infusion of capital.

To limit Mackay's ability to organize a system against Western Union, Jay Gould exploited the Achilles' heel that lurked in the separate receiverships of Bankers and Merchants' and American Rapid. The contract between Bankers and Merchants' and American Rapid allowed each company to string wires on the other company's poles. They'd operated together for so long that deciding who owned what had become problematic. The American Rapid receiver asked the court to rule on which company owned which lines. Not long thereafter, Jay Gould invited the American Rapid receiver aboard his yacht and convinced him to sign a secret contract granting Western Union permission to act as American Rapid's agent and operate the American Rapid telegraph lines. In a surprise move, Gould's lawyers presented that contract to the court along with an inventory of what lines belonged to which company and asked the court to hand over American Rapid's property to its new agent, Western Union. Even more surprising, the judge granted Western Union's request without taking time to investigate the inventory.

The sudden court decision caught Western Union in a curious state of readiness. Western Union goon squads marched across Wall Street into the Bankers and Merchants' operational headquarters, demanded American Rapid's property, and began cutting wires. They dragged the cut ends across the street to the Western Union building, and began operating them on behalf of the omnivore. The Bankers and Merchants' receiver rushed off to obtain an injunction, but couldn't locate the judge. By the time he did, many Bankers and Merchants' wires had "accidentally" been cut and confiscated in the mayhem. That same day, Western Union raiders attacked Bankers and Merchants' and American Rapid facilities in Baltimore, Troy, Rochester, Buffalo, and Albany. Many suspected that sub-rosa payoffs had found their way into the hands of American Rapid's receiver and the judge. Offended parties filed lawsuits that dragged on for several years, the results of which mattered little to Jay Gould, for he'd already accomplished his end—with one stroke he'd crushed one of the legs of Western Union's competition and kneecapped Mackay's efforts to organize effective opposition to Western Union.

Mackay settled into a long war of attrition, hemorrhaging money in his domestic network. Rumors in the Postal offices whispered that Mackay was trying to get out of the telegraph business. One day, during an inspection of one of his operating rooms, Mackay asked one of his telegraphers if he was married.

The man said that he wasn't, although he wished to be.

"Does the girl want to get married?" Mackay asked.

"Yes, sir," said the operator, confessing that he didn't feel financially secure enough to do so in light of the rumors that Mackay was going to leave the telegraph business.

"Go ahead and get married," Mackay said. "I am not getting out of the business."

Mackay's resolute public facade never cracked, but his private contemporary correspondence revealed his frustrations with the telegraphic ventures and his wish that he could wiggle out of his obligations.

Mackay visited the Pacific Coast in October to tend to his Western business interests. "Manhood was at its best west of the Rocky Mountains," Mackay always said. Soon after he arrived, a blood clot formed in the main artery just below William Sharon's right knee. Sharon's lower leg went cold. Terrible waves of pain washed through the afflicted region. Sharon took to bed in his suite in the Palace Hotel. His stomach rejected his attempts to eat. The following afternoon, a Thursday, gangrene attacked his right toes. The cold skin of the afflicted area turned splotchy red, then black. Sharon knew he was dying, but he bore the pain like a stoic. His doctor sustained him with injections of "morphia." On Friday, the gangrene reached his ankle. By Saturday, the rot had climbed to his calf. On Sunday, when John Mackay came down from Virginia City to pay his last respects, the gangrene had reached Sharon's knee. No report of what passed between the two old rivals escaped the sickroom.

In what his doctor described as "a marvelous exhibition of vitality," Sharon survived five more days. His weight dropped to eighty pounds and sharpened his features, making his "usually prominent forehead" appear "abnormally large." Sharon's son and son-in-law, his sister, a cousin, a niece and two nephews, his old friend Colonel J. D. Fry, and his faithful Chinese servant, forty-nine-year-old Ah Ki, surrounded Sharon's sickbed. Sharon briefly opened his eyes. Ah Ki asked to know his wants. Sharon must have seemed like a skull moving in bed when he smiled faintly and whispered, "Well, Ki . . ."

Sharon's tone unmistakably communicated to everyone present that he would want for nothing more in this world. William Sharon closed his eyes and breathed his last a few minutes thereafter. Long obituary columns and retrospectives filled the California and Nevada newspapers, not all of them flattering. All acknowledged the '49er's remarkable life. Sharon's last years had been embittered by the lawsuits of Sarah Althea Hill, a woman he'd paid $500 per month and "kept" at the Grand Hotel in 1880. In 1883, some two years after he'd cast her aside, Hill had Sharon arrested for adultery, claiming he'd secretly married her three years before. Hill sued Sharon for divorce, alimony, and a share of community property. Sharon denied everything and claimed she'd produced a forged marriage contract. William Sharon had enjoyed at least nine separate mistresses during the first three years of the 1880s and fathered one child. The lawsuits and their glorious attendant scandals eclipsed those that had attended the Fair divorce.

A few days after Sharon's death, a *Daily Alta California* reporter hunted up "keen eyed" Ah Ki in a small, dim apartment among a "wilderness of rooms" atop a stairwell leading up from a street corner in the heart of San Francisco's Chinatown. Pictures of Sharon, John Mackay, and the other bonanza kings adorned Ah Ki's walls, along with images of Washington, D.C., New York, and other places Ah Ki had accompanied ex-senator Sharon during his travels. The reporter discovered Ah Ki had a wife and twelve- and four-year-old sons, testament to the spectacular success Ah Ki had enjoyed in the United States. The family was preparing their return to China. Ah Ki dodged the question of whether he'd been left any money by the ex-senator, but the reporter noted a "merry twinkle" in Ah Ki's eyes as he said, "I guess I get along nice enough in China, yes."

Tragedy tempered Ah Ki's good fortune less than a fortnight later when his youngest son died. Ah Ki, his wife, and his surviving son sailed for China on December 9, 1885—bearing the remains of Ah Ki's relations and the $5,000 in gold coin William Sharon had left him in his will. Cared for wisely, that represented a sum large enough to support Ah Ki and his family in China for the rest of their lives. Ah Ki made off with his just reward before Sarah Althea Hill tangled Sharon's will into dizzying rounds of litigation that dragged on for years.

John Mackay never shared his feelings at the passing of his old nemesis, although the bitterness of their earlier Comstock battles seemed to have matured in the 1880s into something that passed mutual respect into a form of cordiality.

Louise Mackay rented a house in London in March 1886, Number 7 Buckingham gate, directly across the street from Buckingham Palace. The *London Truth* considered her appearance in the capital "joyful news" for the "Lord Outatelbows" and "Lady Nothing Nowheres" class of aristocrats who "sponge so assiduously upon wealthy Americans." Louise achieved the social distinction of a lifetime when she was presented among a small group of American ladies in Queen Victoria's drawing room on March 23.

John Mackay was with her in London when news of a "secret" meeting of the companies in the Gould transatlantic cable pool leaked in mid-April. The Commercial Cable Company had diverted more than $1 million worth of pool company business in 1885. (The company had done so well that Mackay gave every Commercial employee a bonus of a fortnight's salary at Christmas.) To rid themselves of the upstart or force it to join their cartel, the pool companies slashed their transatlantic rate from forty to twelve cents per word for commercial traffic and to six cents a word for press service—prices far below the actual cost of transmission. John Mackay and his general manager, George G. Ward, discussed possible responses to "this aggressive action by the united companies" in messages that clicked back and forth across the Atlantic.

"The war of cables rates is now fairly opened," the *New York Times* announced, "and will doubtless be carried on sturdily until one party or the other finds its courage or its strength too severely tried."

Meeting Gould's attack with matching price cuts struck Mackay as the path to ruination. Instead, he ordered Commercial Cable's rate cut to twenty-five cents per word and had Ward unleash a barrage of publicity from the company's executive offices at 40 Wall Street. Commercial Cable had been established "for the purpose of affording a competing and efficient service to the public at such tariff as would yield a moderate interest upon the capital actually invested," Ward's statement read. Commercial had "resisted the repeated importunity of the competing companies to join them in a largely advanced rate of sixty cents per word." The pool companies' new prices were far below actual costs, Ward explained. They intended to destroy Commercial, then regain their losses from the public through greatly increased rates. "The existence of an independent and competitive Atlantic cable service" was at stake, "and our patrons must now pronounce for or against its maintenance.

"We therefore confidently anticipate the continuance of your support," Ward concluded.

Mackay's masterstroke decisively shifted the battleground. The transatlantic cable war would not be fought on price. Instead, it would be fought on trust. In essence, Mackay bet three years of effort and millions of dollars of invested capital on the public's faith in his good name.

Support poured in. "The soundness of this argument will be generally recognized," said the *New York Times*. Commercial Cable received pledges from bankers, brokers, and merchants throughout the United States and the United Kingdom, "all declaring their intention to continue as patrons" based on "the belief that the Commercial Company is in earnest in its pledge to maintain independence."

A *New York Times* editorial considered it "perfectly plain that the purpose of the pool companies is not permanently to maintain low rates, but to break down the competition of the Commercial Company and force it into the combination in order to carry the rates higher than before." The public's interest therefore lay in "sustaining the competition and defeating the scheme."

Jay Gould might have won a fight of nickels and dimes, but in a war of trust, John Mackay's good name carried the clout of a man with mud-stained boots and callused hands. In a war of trust against such a man, thimble-rigging Jay Gould didn't stand a chance. He tried to shift the terms of the fight. When the pool companies started issuing statements expressing their satisfaction with the increased traffic generated by low rates and spoke of maintaining their "test" for a period of five years, Mackay settled in for a long war.

Mackay's weakness remained in domestic distribution. To outflank Western Union and reach the Pacific Coast, Mackay negotiated a direct connection between Commercial Cable and the wires of the Canadian Pacific Telegraph Company, the communications arm of the Canadian

Pacific Railroad, which ran across Canada from Montreal to British Columbia. In September, Western Union skipped its dividend.

By the spring of 1887, both sides were suffering. Mackay held on, sometimes making up shortfalls in both Commercial Cable and Postal Telegraph from his own coffers. Gould held on, too. Mackay left New York for Europe in July. Three weeks later he was back. The Wall Street rumor mill speculated that Mackay's surprise appearance portended an end to the cable wars. Other whisperings thought it had something to do "with the relations of the Nevada Bank to the bull deal in California wheat which collapsed last week." Newsmen watched Mackay's every move in New York, reporting the hours of his meals and his companions, looking for any hint of a meeting with Jay Gould or of messages passing between them, but couldn't penetrate his veil of secrecy.

Wall Street considered it "an auspicious omen" when, "in a democratic and conciliatory way," Mr. Mackay put five cents in Jay Gould's pocket by purchasing an elevated railroad ticket—Gould controlled the railroad. Mackay boarded in lower Manhattan and got off at Grand Central Station. At six o'clock, the Bonanza King headed west on the Chicago Express. Speculation shifted to the affairs of Nevada Bank.

They were bleak indeed. Mackay arrived in San Francisco on August 15 facing the bank's collapse. The problem originated with flaws in the judgment and character of Nevada Bank vice president George Brander. Brander's shortcomings surfaced when James Flood fell ill with the painful and debilitating kidney disorders associated with Bright's disease. With Mackay in Europe and New York and Flood sick, Brander controlled the bank. He made losses of about half a million, and in an effort to recuperate them, he started loaning Nevada Bank money to two wheat broker associates attempting to corner the California wheat market. Wheat prices rose, and Brander kept loaning to his two friends. Millions of dollars poured out of the Nevada Bank and Brander's cronies still hadn't cornered the California wheat market. Wheat prices kept rising until the bank's reserves ran out. By then Brander's only hope for escape lay in carrying the wheat corner through to a successful conclusion, but to do that he needed more money. Brander borrowed $300,000 from the Bank of California and dumped that into wheat loans. He stole $1 million of bonds Mackay kept in a safe deposit box on behalf of his wife and $600,000 in bonds owned by Flood's sister, hypothecated loans upon the stolen bonds, and loaned the money to his wheat brokers. He floated loans on other customers' property and bought still more wheat. The price of California wheat climbed until August 3, when Brander loaned the last of the money he could steal. After that, the price of wheat nosedived. Millions of dollars evaporated—none of which belonged to Brander.

When Mackay arrived in San Francisco on August 15, the Nevada Bank teetered on the cliff edge. Anticipating Gould's effort to exploit the situation and destroy the public trust on which so much depended, Mackay met Gould on the original battlefield, the one of dollars and cents. On August 17, Mackay had one of his Commercial Cable Company officers speak to the newspapers in "substantially" these words: "The war in cable rates has been going on since May last year. In that time our customers have been paying us 25 cents a word, while the pool companies have been charging only 12 cents a word. It is simply justice to our friends who stood by us steadfastly that we should adjust our rates to that of the pool companies."

Gould's attack came two days later, in a full-throated article that ran down a full column of the *New York Tribune*'s front page and continued onto page two. The article cast aspersions on Mackay's business acumen, honesty, and solvency, denigrated the size of his fortune, blamed him for "vast losses," the "certain ruin" of the Pacific Coast economy, and for bilking San Franciscans of $100 million to fund assessment mines on the Comstock. The *Tribune* described James Fair gloating over "the discomfiture of his old partners." The article was, in all its particulars, an all-out assault on Mackay's reputation.

Mackay counterattacked the *Tribune* article's crucifying weakness—many of its assertions and insinuations were provable lies—and he did what he'd always done in a crisis. He went to work. He fought back. (Only Brander's staying submissively seated when Mackay stormed into the Nevada Bank from New York saved him from receiving a thrashing from the Bonanza King's balled fists.) And in the fight to revitalize the bank, Mackay's greatest asset was what it had always been, his good name. Mackay and Flood's personal pledge secured a $1 million loan from the Bank of California. Theresa Fair stepped forward with several million dollars' worth of securities. When the holder of a $500,000 note expressed reluctance to continue carrying the loan, *James* Fair assumed the debt, a gesture from an old partner that meant much to John Mackay. The cash infusion gave the Nevada Bank time to dispose of the thousands of tons of wheat it had loaned on to best advantage. That time saved the bank.

On August 28, Mackay gave an interview in response to another *New York Tribune* attack. "Whatever may be the losses on this wheat . . . the Nevada Bank—which is equivalent to Flood and myself—will stand them." Mackay flatly denied that the bank had been involved in the wheat speculation in any capacity other than that of making bad loans, and he offered to subject the bank's accounts and his personal accounts to expert scrutiny to prove it.

"A thunderbolt out of a clear sky" hit San Francisco financial circles on September 13 when the directors of the Nevada Bank announced that James Fair had assumed the presidency, proving a partnership forged through years of mutual hardship, risk, and endeavor more durable than anyone had thought possible. The *Chronicle* lamented that the men who could tell the full story "were as reticent as oysters," but that had described the members of the Bonanza Firm with regard to business affairs since the days of their first association. Although the nearly disastrous Nevada Bank ordeal probably cost Mackay around $5.5 million and may have cost him as much as $8 million, Mackay survived with his credit and good name intact.

In the wars of the land telegraph and undersea cables, Jay Gould's next attack wasn't long in coming.

One of Mackay's prime goals in the land telegraph business had been consummating an anti–Western Union alliance with Robert Garrett and the Baltimore & Ohio Telegraph. Mackay's first effort to make that happen had failed in 1884. Mackay had tried again in 1886. After months of sluggish negotiations, Mackay and his allies thought they had an agreement with Robert Garrett. Then Garrett suddenly departed for Europe. When Garrett returned months later, he reneged on what Mackay and his lieutenants thought was a done deal. The coalition failed to materialize— for reasons Mackay and his team couldn't fathom because the strategy seemed so sound—but people were beginning to remark on Robert Garrett's increasingly erratic behavior.*

Less widely understood was that Robert Garrett had muddled the entire Baltimore & Ohio system into serious financial trouble in the three years since his father's death. When Garrett again went abroad on July 20, 1887, a few weeks before news of the Nevada Bank's "Wheat Deal" broke, a banking syndicate fronted by J. P. Morgan took control of the B&O. Although feigning a lack of interest in public, Jay Gould began sniffing around the debt-saddled B&O Telegraph. Garrett rushed back from Europe, determined to prevent the sale of a prized operation to his mortal enemy. Morgan and the men to whom Garrett had entrusted his proxy

---

* Robert Garrett really did go insane. He died in 1896, having spent the last three or four years of his life "on restraint" in an insane asylum.

voting power consummated a sale to Gould mere hours before Garrett stepped ashore in the early morning hours of October 7. Garrett embarrassed himself blustering about it in the newspapers, which elicited a shrug from Gould's son George. "There is no Baltimore and Ohio Telegraph now," he said on October 8. "Their wires are a part of our system."

Western Union swallowed Baltimore and Ohio Telegraph whole. "If Mr. Garrett had done as he promised to do the Western Union would [have never paid] another dividend," lamented one of Mackay's associates.

The collapse of Baltimore & Ohio left Mackay's Postal Telegraph and United Lines standing alone against the anaconda company, facing a battle they couldn't win. Three weeks later, Mackay accepted an arrangement that consigned Postal to permanent second-class citizenship. The agreement raised and equalized rates and ended the rate wars in land telegraphy. Postal Telegraph would become profitable, but it would never grow into anything larger than a minor competitor of Western Union.

In the aftermath of the domestic telegraph armistice, few punters were betting on John Mackay's survival in the business. Most businessmen expected him to sell out—to Jay Gould. "Mr. Gould never lets anybody escape from his hands if they have what he wants," remarked one Wall Street sage.

Mackay accepted what must have surely felt like a painful domestic defeat because it included a crucial nugget for his transoceanic interests— the pact allowed the domestic companies equal access to each other's transmission lines. That provision coupled to Postal's guaranteed survival prevented Western Union from discriminating against Commercial Cable Company messages and thus removed the primary weapon Western Union had to employ against Mackay in the transoceanic struggle.

Gould opted to tolerate Postal's survival to prove the existence of competition in the industry and deflect political pressure to either break up what would otherwise have been a Western Union monopoly or nationalize the country's telegraph lines.

Gould and his wife had sailed for Europe to join his prepositioned yacht the day before the domestic rate arrangement became public—the start of a long-cherished vacation. The Goulds cruised the Mediterranean and the West Indies for the better part of five months. The transatlantic cable war dragged on while Gould tried to outlast John Mackay.

A few months after the Goulds returned in March 1888, word of negotiations between Gould and Mackay swirled through business circles. A Gould man spoke of doubling the current rate, and of a rise to forty cents "very soon" thereafter. "You may consider this information as practically official," he said.

Mackay wouldn't agree to any such thing. Mackay said he'd raise Commercial's rate to twenty-five cents a word, but not a penny more. "I have tried twenty-five cents," Mackay said. "I am content with that rate. The public is satisfied, and I will stay where I am."

Jay Gould got the message—take it or continue the war. He took it.

As Mackay's friend John Russell Young wrote in his book *Men and Memories*, "Peace was made by the absolute surrender of the monopoly." The public had reposed its trust in the right man.

CHAPTER 18

Twilight

John William Mackay

———

There was nothing small about him.
—"An Old Friend's Tribute," *Salt Lake City Tribune,* July 21, 1902

I n his day, John Mackay's was the most beloved rags-to-riches story in America. His outlandish mining success and his victory over Gould's Atlantic cable monopoly fascinated people in the last decades of the nineteenth century and the turn of the twentieth. The strength of his character commanded their admiration. He'd risen from the infamous Five Points, the world's most notorious slum. When Mackay sailed from New York in 1851, he'd had no name, no money, and not a single influential friend on earth. He'd possessed nothing but strong arms, a clear head, and a legendary capacity for hard work. From there, he'd done it the

American way—he'd earned it. In the eyes of the times, his road to riches had made no man poorer, and few begrudged him his success.

After breaking Gould's monopoly, Mackay stayed active in the Commercial Cable Company and the Postal Telegraph, having carved out a role for himself as a major player in what people of a later age ought to recognize as the ground floor of the modern communications industry—the *digital* communications industry. The current on/current off signal of the telegraph was exactly the same as the "ones" and "zeros" processed by modern computers, the major difference being the speed at which they're processed, many billions per second as opposed to a few hundred per minute. The telegraph cables laid across the ocean floors in the second half of the nineteenth century were the direct technological and conceptual antecedents of the modern transoceanic cables that connect the continents and serve as the arterial electronic ganglia of the World Wide Web. They changed distance and perception and thus changed the world.

Mackay also stayed involved in mining. His investments in the Peerless mines west of Tucson don't seem to have panned out, but his commitments in Colorado likely did produce dividends. Mackay owned mines in California, Nevada, and Alaska, and he invested in copper mines, which complemented his telegraph interests. Although he never set foot in the place, the town of Mackay, Idaho, bears his name, thanks to the controlling interest he once held in the local copper mines. Today, some five hundred souls live in Mackay, situated about sixty miles east of Sun Valley in the Big Lost River Valley between the Lost River Range and the White Knob Mountains—one of whose summits is 10,270-foot Mackay Peak.

"[Mackay] never seemed to know the value of a dollar, but somehow could always lay his hands upon whatever millions he needed for a new enterprise," an officer of the Postal Telegraph once said. Considering the common Comstock origins of so many people who dominated the American mining industry in the 1880s and 1890s, Mackay's seemingly limitless wealth through those years, and his rigid unwillingness to discuss his own affairs, it seems at least plausible that Mackay held a silent interest in one of the era's other great mining regions.

George Hearst, Mackay's onetime co-owner of the unsuccessful Rising Star mine in Idaho, had become one of the most successful miners in the West, with successful properties in Utah's Ontario Mine, the Homestake Mine in the Black Hills, and the Anaconda Mine in Butte,

Montana. He served as one of California's U.S. senators from 1886 until his death in 1891.

In early November 1888, shortly after the Cable War armistice, a stroke paralyzed Gould's beloved wife, Helen. She died in January 1889. Gould himself had been hiding tuberculosis. He fought on, directing his empire of railroads and telegraphs until he succumbed in December 1892. Although he was decades ahead of most of his contemporaries in the wiles of finance and in understanding how to evaluate corporate values, the tenor of Gould's publicity never changed. He died as he had lived, the most hated man of the age. (In the spirit of bygones, Louise Mackay hosted an elaborate London dinner party for Jay Gould's son George and George's wife in the late spring of 1894.)

Mackay's partner James Flood survived Helen Gould by only a month. Fair reportedly described Flood as "dying by inches" when Flood went to Europe seeking relief from the kidney-failing ravages of Bright's disease. Flood died in Heidelberg, Germany, on February 21, 1889. Flood had treasured the memory of William O'Brien to his dying day. Standing with a friend in front of a portrait of O'Brien that hung in Flood's country mansion in Menlo Park, Flood once said in a voice charged with emotion, "Billy was my partner once; he is my partner now, and will be my partner forever." Reflecting on Flood's life, John Mackay said, "In all that goes toward the development of manhood, the best man I have ever known."

After Flood's death, Mackay sold a majority interest in the Nevada Bank to a syndicate led by Southern California financier Isaias W. Hellman, a man with a true calling for banking—a profession for which Mackay had no special love. Mackay retained a minority interest and stayed on the board of directors, joined by James L. Flood, son of his former partner, and, among others, San Francisco clothing manufacturer Levis Strauss. The Nevada Bank prospered under Hellman's leadership. Mackay remained on the board for the rest of his life; his son would succeed him. In April 1895, the Nevada Bank changed its name to the Nevada National Bank, and in 1905 Nevada National absorbed the Wells, Fargo & Company Bank to become the Wells Fargo Nevada National Bank of San Francisco. Led by the officers and board members of Nevada National (including Mackay's and Flood's sons), the new Wells Fargo Nevada National opened in the old Wells Fargo building at the corner of Market and Sansome streets. In 1924, Wells Fargo Nevada National merged with the Union Trust Company and became Wells Fargo Bank and Union Trust Company, unfortunately dropping the title of the original bank. Although Wells Fargo still operates from the same Market Street location, the "official" corporate website history neglects to mention the 1905 merger, let alone that in it, Wells Fargo was the subordinate entity. Anybody doing business under the stagecoach logo of Wells Fargo today makes a direct connection to the great Bonanza Firm of yore.

Mackay's son John William, Jr., "Willie" to everyone with whom he was on informal terms, graduated from Oxford and joined his father in the family businesses around the time his father ceded control of the Nevada Bank. Willie began serving as a director of the American Forcite Powder Company, an explosives manufacturer in which Mackay held a substantial investment, and took a seat on the Commercial Cable Company board. Willie grew into a man who much resembled his father, and the two Mackays made a formidable team. John Junior possessed his father's acumen, if not all of his touchy pugnacity, but also the easy social graces and casual affability his father found so difficult to master. Willie spoke French like a native, and he'd received the formal education his father had regretted not having his entire life. Willie also possessed a wide streak of fun. He knew how to enjoy himself in ways that John Mackay did not. Rather than try to quash the adventurous frolic from Willie's character, Mackay always encouraged it. John Mackay had his hopes for the future founded on his two sons.

Since the advent of John's involvement with the transatlantic cables, the Meissonier incident, and her London triumphs of 1886, Louise had been spending much of her time in England. In December 1890, Mackay bought Number 6 Carlton House Terrace and gave it to Louise on the occasion of her fiftieth birthday. Located in the heart of fashionable London, the home overlooked St. James's Park, just a short distance down the Mall in one direction from Buckingham Palace and a casual stroll in the other from Trafalgar Square and the National Gallery. Louise became every bit as much a fixture in London society as she had been in Parisian.

Three years later, Mackay was again in San Francisco. Around noon on February 24, 1893, Wesley C. Rippey, "a half-insane . . . seedy, played-out old stock gambler" who had lost "all his means" gambling on the Comstock mines, followed Mackay into Lick Alley, a narrow alley that connected Sutter and Post streets behind the Lick House. People nearby paid no attention. Lick Alley served as a popular shortcut between the two major thoroughfares. Suddenly, three shots cracked in the alley. The first eyewitnesses noticed Rippey lying on the ground with a pistol in his hand and Mackay standing a few steps beyond quizzically eying the fallen man. Someone called Mackay's attention to the smoke rising from his coat and said, "Mr. Mackay, you have been shot."

Mackay told the man he must be mistaken.

"There's a hole in your coat," the man said.

Mackay put his hand inside his coat. His fingers emerged bloody. Rippey had shot him once in the back, missed with a second shot, and turned the third into his own chest. A note in Rippey's pocket read: "FOOD FOR REFLECTION.—He paid $150,000 for one sapphire to place on the jaded person of his wife—a sum sufficient to have saved at least 500 of his paupers from a suicidal grave. Just think of it. Inscribe it on his tomb."

Mackay had a bullet wedged between his shoulder blades. The shot had missed Mackay's spine by the width of a pencil point. A bystander gave Mackay a ride to the Palace Hotel in a buggy. At the Palace, a doctor prepped Mackay for surgery. Although warned of an "exceedingly painful" operation, "the bluff old mining man" refused anesthetic. Perspiration stood out on Mackay's face while the doctor made deep incisions and pinched out the bullet, but Mackay didn't so much as utter a groan.

Newspapers all over the country reported the shooting and printed daily articles about the convalescence of a man the *New York Times* described as "one of the richest men in the world." The same *Times* article congratulated Mackay for conducting himself with "a rare degree of modesty and good sense" and excused Mackay's two points of "pardonable pride"—that he'd come so far from such humble beginnings and that his money "had never been used to the detriment of his fellow man." Mining circles all lauded Mackay as a man whose astronomical wealth "had not elevated him above his old-time associates."

A message from London reported John's cablegram to Louise: "The crank that shot me is 73 years old. I don't know him; never saw him. Doctor cut out the bullet. No reason for the least uneasiness." Louise cabled her husband every two hours for the next several days. Aside from inability to lie on his back, Mackay convalesced rapidly—until he came down with a dangerous appendix inflammation. That brought Louise and Clarence rushing over from Europe. The danger had passed without requiring surgery before they arrived in New York. Willie joined them for a more leisurely journey west.

Longtime San Francisco journalists who hadn't seen Louise in eighteen years remarked on her still-youthful features and said her hair was just as black as it had been when she'd left the city. At the Palace Hotel, Louise went into John's rooms ahead of the boys. The couple spent a few moments alone, after which their sons entered. "It was plain to be seen that a happier family had never gathered beneath the Palace roof," said Mackay's old nemesis, the *San Francisco Chronicle*. (Louise's lavish entertainments of the proprietor, Michael Henry de Young and his wife, Katherine, during their European vacations may have contributed to the improved tenor of the paper's Mackay coverage.) In the morning, Willie and Clarrie enjoyed an outing in the city. Louise shut herself up with her husband, citing her desire for "a few days' rest after her long journey." The next day, John "enjoyed a drive of several hours duration" with Louise, the first time he'd left the hotel in forty-five days.

As John gathered strength, the Mackay family reunited with many old friends, toured Chinatown, and took the train to Southern California for a carriage drive through the endless orange groves of Riverside. On their way back East in May, they spent days exploring the Chicago World's Fair. After two months of uninterrupted family time, Louise and Clarence returned to London in early June. John and Willie stayed in New York attending to business. The appendix inflammation that had bothered John in March nearly killed him in August. Emergency surgery performed in his rooms at the Belgrovia Apartments at Fifth Avenue and Forty-ninth Street saved his life.

At the end of his second 1893 convalescence, Mackay signed contracts for a third transatlantic cable, an improved design with a higher message-carrying capacity. He likely took much joy watching the fourteen-story building he'd commissioned for the Postal Telegraph's headquarters take shape on the northwest corner of Broadway and Murray Street, directly across Broadway from City Hall Park and newspaper row. Mackay owned substantially in the Sprague Elevator and Electrical Works, which would occupy suites in the building. The Sprague Company installed dynamos, electric lighting throughout the building, and the most advanced electric elevator system in the world. Four local elevators serviced floors one through ten. The two express elevators were exclusively devoted to the needs of the eleventh through the fourteenth floors, which would house the head offices of the Postal Telegraph and the Commercial Cable Company. The mahogany-furnished clubrooms and restaurant of the 360-member Hardware Club occupied the top floor.* Mackay, his sons, and many officers of his companies were members.

John Mackay and John William, Jr., hosted a grand dinner in the Hardware Club to dedicate the building on May 24, 1894, a well-chosen date—the fiftieth anniversary of Samuel F. B. Morse's first telegraph message. The building's newfangled electrical elevator system evoked much comment—they were the first in the world to use push-buttons marked "up" and "down" to automatically summon the cars, replacing the old, much despised, easily corruptible system of simply yelling the words into the shaft and hoping for the quick response of the attendant. For himself, Mackay chose a corner office directly over the junction of Broadway and Murray Street. He had his desk placed so that it afforded a view over City Hall Square and down into Frankfort Street. "From this window," he said, "I can see the site of the house in which I lived as a child, before I dreamed of going to the Coast or ever amounting to anything."

Only John Mackay knew the incredible distance between those two locations.

He'd orchestrated a much less pleasant family affair earlier that spring. His daughter Eva's marriage to the Italian prince had fallen apart. Their marriage had been at least fruitful, for they had three children, but in the Prince Don Fernando Julian Colonna, Eva had married a man remarkably like her own father, Doctor Edmund G. Bryant. Don Fernando was handsome, but also a scoundrel and a poor gambler with an unpleasant air of entitlement. Mackay had given Eva a substantial income after her wedding—reported by the *New York World* as $175,000 per annum—in addition to many extravagant presents of jewelry, coaches, and furniture. None of it sated the prince's notorious passion for gambling—and his correspondingly enormous losses. On several occasions, Eva pawned her jewels to settle his gambling debts. On other occasions, Eva received bills signed by her husband for jewelry and other "feminine adornments" that she'd never seen. Prince Colonna's treatment of Eva slipped from "neglect to brutality."

Reproached for neglecting Eva, Colonna replied that he "couldn't be

---

* The building still exists. A branch of the JP Morgan Chase bank occupies the ground floor.

expected to show [his wife] any consideration" on account of her being just "a common American."

Colonna also threatened to take all of Eva's "American independence" out of her.

"You may if you kill me," she reportedly replied.

Louise Mackay developed a particular hatred and revulsion for her son-in-law. In their final confrontation, Louise told the prince what she thought of him and his conduct. The prince supposedly "contented himself with comparing his princely origin" with the humble beginnings of Mrs. Mackay.

Eva endured all of it until October 1893, when she filed a suit for separation in Paris.

"I am glad you have taken this step," Mackay wrote to her. "People will talk, of course; but you do not live to please other people, and need not care what any one says as long as you are happy and free."

After the New Year, when Eva thought she detected her husband plotting to steal the children away to Italy, she fled with them to New York, then to California, where she sought an annulment of her marriage. Eighteen months later, Prince Colonna accepted a legal separation granting Eva custody of the children in exchange for a $12,000-per-year stipend from her stepfather. Eva's marriage to the Italian prince had done nothing to improve John Mackay's opinion of European "nobility."

James G. Fair died at the end of 1894, of Bright's disease, the same as that which had felled James Flood. When Fair died, he was one of the largest owners of real estate in San Francisco. The last major project of his life involved reclaiming marshland and developing part of what is now San Francisco's Marina District. The *San Francisco Chronicle* made the damning observation that at the time of his death, "Fair did not have an intimate friend in the world."

Fair's passing left John Mackay as the last surviving member of the Bonanza Firm. The *Santa Cruz Sentinel* commented that although all four were of an age, a race, and began their association in equal health, Mackay was the only one of four "who refused to indulge in the luxuries of the table." Or, it might be added, of the bottle. In personal habits, his life always remained as simple as when he'd been a common Comstock miner.

Mackay's other old partner, Jonas M. Walker, died a week after Fair, also in San Francisco, in a humble residence at 1715 Polk Street. He'd lost his share of the money he and Mackay had raised from the Kentuck speculating in railroads, returned to California during the bonanza times, and opened a stock brokerage. That business failed in 1879, and Walker's partner committed suicide. Walker never managed to rebuild his fortunes.

Bishop Patrick Manogue passed on to his long home in February. He'd been the founding bishop of the Sacramento diocese and built the city's cathedral, largely on contributions from Theresa Fair and John Mackay, who, although never a Catholic himself, honored the many good deeds Bishop Manogue had done for his wife during the hard years of her failed marriage to Doctor Bryant. (Ten years before, Louise had paid to have Dr. Bryant's body moved from the Sierra foothills to San Francisco's Laurel Hill Cemetery and interred alongside the remains of Marie Bryant, their baby who died on the Comstock in the early 1860s, whom Louise had also moved to more comfortable soil in San Francisco.)

The Comstock's glory had vanished. Nine years before, in 1886, Mackay and Flood had stilled the engines of the Combination Shaft, the last of the Comstock's great third-line shafts. Explorations from the Combination Shaft had found a mass of mineralized quartz on the thirty-two-hundred-foot level, but no ore. As Mackay told a reporter in 1895, they'd spent $7 million on the shaft and "it did not yield us 7 cents." The mines flooded to the level of the Sutro Tunnel, but reduced milling costs had made it feasible for the mines to survive mining low-grade quartz from the edges of the old bonanzas above the tunnel level. They'd produced $16 million in dividends mining low-grade ores in the last eleven years—solid profits, but a far cry from the bonanza times of the late 1870s, when the Con. Virginia and the California were gushing out $16 million in dividends every eight months. By 1895, miners had exhausted most of the low-grade ores, too.

John Mackay returned to the Comstock on October 10, 1895. He went straight to the Con. Virginia office and descended to the 1,650-foot and 1,750-foot levels of the mine in company with his superintendent and foreman. The trio spent many hours underground, which miners and speculators regarded as "a most encouraging sign." Superstitious to a fault, they all recalled that "mines have never failed to improve under Mr. Mackay's personal direction."

Mackay spent the next several days going over "the whole Comstock situation." As usual, his old friends said that he'd "changed but little in appearance. The hand of time and the wielding of millions leaving but little trace upon him."

Tragically, that was about to change.

• • •

Mackay was in San Francisco six days later, staying as usual at the Palace Hotel and attending to his business interests, also as usual. The first intimation of trouble came at 7:00 p.m., when Mackay's private secretary received a cable dispatch from Clarence Mackay saying his brother Willie was sick. A second arrived moments later: "Notify father to prepare for the worst."

Both telegrams reached Mackay simultaneously in his room at the Palace Hotel. Mackay rushed across the street to the office of the Postal Telegraph. The office superintendent put forth every effort to obtain more information. Silence prevailed for five agonizing hours. The receiving instrument finally ticked out a message from Clarence around midnight: "Willie was thrown from a horse to-day and never recovered consciousness. He died this evening."

Mackay sat in a chair in his superintendent's office and held his head in his hands. "His silent grief repelled any attempts at condolence, and none were attempted," said the devastating dispatch from San Francisco published in the *New York Times*. Mackay secluded himself in his room the next day, having left strict instructions that nothing was to be forwarded to his room except information pertaining to Willie's death.

The details were gruesome. Willie and several friends had been riding horses southwest of Paris on a rural estate in Mayet, in the Department of Sarthe outside Le Mans. An excellent horseman, Willie chose "a particularly restive animal"—against the advice of a friend who had ridden the horse the day before. Something spooked the horse, which bolted through a forest with Willie on its back. Willie dodged several trees before losing control completely and sprawling in the saddle. His head struck a tree trunk with such force that it stove in his forehead and crushed both of his eyes. Carried to the estate house on a mattress, Willie remained conscious for three hours. He recognized the voices of his friends and squeezed their hands while they spoke to him. Willie's favorite dog lay next to him in bed and let out an agonized whine as he died.

Louise rushed to Paris and collapsed in bed, "completely prostrated with grief." Massive curtains of black velvet drapes fringed in silver draped the facade of the Rue de Tilsitt mansion. In a coffin sealed to save his mother the sight of his mangled face, Willie's body reposed in the summer dining room, facing the Place de l'Étoile and the Arc de Triomphe.

On October 22, the members of the Mackay clan in Europe—Ada, Eva, Clarence, Mrs. Hungerford—gave Willie a funeral fit for a king. Policemen suspended street traffic in the vicinity of the Arc de Triomphe while a hearse drawn by six white horses conveyed Willie's coffin from the Rue de Tilsitt a short distance up the Avenue Carnot and the Rue d'Armaillé to the church of St. Ferdinand des Ternes. A cross bearing the inscription "Sa mere désolée" rode with the coffin. Newspapers described "the somber gorgousness [sic] of the obsequies," the black and silver draperies hung in the nave, the monumental candelabras in the church, the forest of candles burning around the catafalque, the profusion of floral devotions, and two wreaths of mauve orchids and white lilacs—one that said, "From a broken-hearted mother," and the other, "From a broken-hearted father." Louise hadn't been able to summon the strength to personally attend the service. After, the hearse took Willie's coffin to the Chapel of St. Augustin, where Louise came and prayed over the body of her dead son.

Six thousand miles away, in San Francisco, John Mackay didn't leave his room in San Francisco's Palace Hotel for six days. Two of his old Comstock friends sat with him in his room. Mackay only broke his morbid silence to say, "Oh God, what have I done to deserve this?" When Mackay finally bestirred himself to begin the long trek to New York on October 25, the friend who made the trip with him described it as "the saddest journey he ever took." Mackay hardly spoke.

John, Louise, and Clarence brought Willie's body back across the Atlantic at the end of the following January aboard the SS *La Touraine* and interred him in a temporary vault, pending completion of the $300,000 mausoleum John was having built in Brooklyn's Greenwood Cemetery.

Neither John nor Louise ever recovered. Both took huge steps back from public affairs. John Mackay bore the loss "manfully" and attended to business, because that's what a man did, but his friends remarked on how rapidly Mackay aged. Mackay's hair filled out with gray. "A serious, almost mournful expression" replaced his smile. Clarence replaced Willie at his father's side in family business affairs. Mackay kept an apartment at the Belgravia on Fifth Avenue. Willie had used part of it when he stayed in New York, and Willie's section remained untouched in the years after his death. When Mackay showed visitors around the house, he gravitated toward souvenirs of his son until "over-mastered" by emotion. In San Francisco, Mackay took long walks that often ended in the Laurel Hill Cemetery at the graves of his old friends. Nobody who knew him ever doubted that John Mackay would have exchanged every one of his millions for the life of his son.

Willie's death affected Louise as profoundly as it did John. Much to the "deep regret" of Louise's many American and British friends, she preserved her "strict mourning" through the festivities of Queen Victoria's Diamond Jubilee in June 1897, nearly two years later. Glorious pageantry commemorated the queen's sixty years on the throne, the longest reign in British history. Louise's residence at Number 6 Carlton House Terrace would have been the perfect location from which to enjoy the celebration, but she remained "secluded" throughout. Although she returned to the United States in the spring of 1898 for Clarence's wedding to Katherine Duer, described by the *Brooklyn Daily Eagle* as "one of the very best known society women of New York and Newport," Louise didn't "lighten her mourning" until January of 1899, when she finally resumed entertaining—an event considered significant enough to merit attention in the *New York Times*. (For his son and new daughter-in-law, John financed construction of an elaborate mansion designed by Stanford White on 688 acres at Harbor Hill, Long Island.)

John wore his blacks for at least another year. When an old San Francisco friend and his wife visiting New York convinced Mackay to join them at the opera in 1900, Mackay confessed that he hadn't attended a single entertainment since Willie's death five years before.

In spite of his grief, Mackay maintained his business interests. Having bought into the Southern Pacific and the Canadian Pacific railroads in the 1880s and never sold, Mackay served on the board of both roads. He was a large investor in—and vice president of—a $7 million sugar refinery in Yonkers, New York, and the largest individual stockholder in American Telephone & Telegraph, an investment presumably made to diversify his communications holdings and gain a stronghold in a new and promising technology. He owned mines in Alaska, Colorado, Idaho, California, and Nevada and likely elsewhere. In California real estate, Mackay owned about fifty-five hundred acres of ranch land in San Mateo, San Rafael, and Mendocino and about $5 million worth of property in San Francisco. In New York, Mackay owned the fourteen-story Postal Telegraph Building and the eighteen-story Commercial Cable Company Building at 20 Broad Street, adjoining the Stock Exchange, and maintained five or six free beds in New York City hospitals in memory of his son.

The goal of laying a telegraph cable across the Pacific to connect San Francisco with America's new foreign interests in Hawaii and the Philippines brought Mackay out of semi-isolation. A firm believer in the power of private enterprise, Mackay announced that he'd do it without any government "subsidy or guarantee." Even then, it took more than a year to get government approval and even longer to get the navy to part with its depth soundings of the Pacific. Long before he received formal government approval, Mackay was building 156 miles of undersea cable per day, at tremendous cost. The goal re-energized the old miner, and when Mackay met a friend in May 1902, Mackay put up his fists and sparred a round of shadow boxing, saying that he felt as if he "could handle any 70-year-old fellow in the world." Gout also slowed him, but as Mackay joked with the same friend, "as you know—well, I never earned that."

Mackay was in London in July. Cable ships loaded with the first sections of the Pacific cable would soon depart the Thames. On July 15, Mackay had lunch with George Ward, longtime manager of his transoceanic cable enterprises. As they were leaving the meal, Mackay told Ward, "I'll just lay that Pacific Cable, and then retire from business."

It was not to be. John Mackay had felt ill during his lunch with Ward. He took to bed in Number 6 Carlton House Terrace that afternoon. One of his lungs filled with fluid. He died five days later, on July 20, 1902, with Louise and a Catholic priest at his side. His son Clarence completed the transpacific job. At the time of his death, newspapers estimated Mackay's fortune at between $50 and $100 million, making him one of the world's richest men. Nobody seemed to have an exact figure. Mackay's private secretary said that Mackay didn't know how much he was worth within $20 million and probably didn't care. John Mackay was interned in the mausoleum he'd built for his son in Brooklyn's Greenwood Cemetery, where he resides among some of history's most distinguished New Yorkers. He'd been a hard, but good man. Money hadn't made him a hypocrite, and it had never stolen his good name.

In the aftermath of Mackay's death, long, laudatory obituaries filled the columns of most American newspapers—and many in England and France. Almost all of them garbled the details of Mackay's mining career, but expressed the basic sentiment that Mackay had "stormed the strongholds where nature had stored her treasures" and won them "in fair fight." (It would fall to later generations to call the mining industry to account for the colossal environmental damage it inflicted on western ecosystems and for the havoc wreaked on Native American cultures.) The *Salt Lake City Tribune* said that, "Of all the millionaires of this country, no one was more thoroughly American than Mr. Mackay, and no one among them derived his fortune more legitimately." *Goodwin's Weekly* considered Mackay's example "the highest of all rich men in America."

Ironically, therein lay the reason John Mackay would fade from the memory of his countrymen. He died a widely admired man. Although Mackay stood among the leading industrialists and mining magnates in the last decades of the nineteenth century in terms of his wealth, none of the vitriol directed at the "Robber Barons" of the age had accrued to him. Mackay never chiseled on his employees' wages. Indeed, at Postal Telegraph and Commercial, Mackay kept wages high and incentivized and aided in his employees' purchase of company stock, one of the first business leaders to take such steps. Nor did Mackay ever lose his common touch. He never lorded it over his fellow man. John Mackay was always himself, as at ease among the miners on the Con. Virginia's "fifteen hundred" as he was among the oldest families of Europe—and history records no aristocrat fool enough to have asked Mackay who he thought were the better men. Mackay's personal philanthropies through the last decades were legion and legendary, but unorganized. Unlike many of his pocketbook peers, such as Rockefeller, Carnegie, Stanford, and Huntington, Mackay felt no great compulsion to leave behind a philanthropic organization or a university that would spend the next hundred years rehabilitating the family name. He'd never lost it. When Mackay finally did set an old friend to investigating options it was too late, too little time remained to him to push the plan to completion before his death, and his will contained no specific instructions.

Like Mackay, the Comstock Lode faded from the national consciousness. Virginia City remains, still clinging to the side of Mount Davidson and surviving on nostalgic remembrance of the whisky and gunsmoke glories of the Old West while largely forgetting what it was, a working-class town of men and women who struggled to win a fortune—or even a living— from an unexploited landscape and birthed the American deep-mining industry. Huge gross quantities of gold and silver remain in the unmined portions of the great vein, just not in concentrations high enough to merit extraction. Or probably not. Once upon a time in the not too distant past, Virginia City was the biggest urban industrial concentration between Sacramento and St. Louis. In the 2010 census, Virginia City recorded 855 inhabitants, and Gold Hill had fewer than 200. They're wonderful places to visit. The feelings remain, as do the mournful glories of the desert vista.

The wealth of the Comstock best survives in the economic powerhouse of modern San Francisco. Gold and silver pouring from the veins of Nevada radically changed San Francisco, transforming the city from a seaport serving the needs of the California interior into an industrial and financial center on the cutting edge of the new industry of deep, hard-rock mining, one of the high-technology industries of its day.

If one knows how to look, San Francisco's connections to the old Comstock Lode remain strong. In 1902, James L. Flood commissioned the construction of a commercial building in his father's memory at 870 Market Street, at its corner with Powell Street. The largest building in the city when it opened, the structure survived the 1906 earthquake and fire and remained in the family. Today it houses the flagship stores for Gap, Urban Outfitters, and Anthropologie. James Clair Flood's great-great-grandson, also James Clair Flood, keeps an office inside from which he directs the business of the Flood Corporation. A display inside the business entrance on the first floor commemorates the Bonanza Kings and includes a few pieces of Comstock silver. The astonishing Nob Hill mansion James C. Flood completed in 1888 at a cost of $1.5 million also survived 1906—the only one of the millionaires' houses atop Nob Hill that was so fortunate, but also the only one built of Connecticut brownstone shipped around Cape Horn. The building and its grounds occupy an entire city block and it currently houses the Pacific-Union Club, which purchased and refurbished the structure after the fire and has been there ever since. John Mackay and James Flood were once members.

Flood's Nob Hill mansion stands directly across Mason Street from the front entrance of the Fairmont Hotel, whose construction was undertaken by James Fair's daughters Theresa and Virginia in 1902. They sold out of the project before its completion, mere days before the great earthquake. Others finished its construction, but the name remained. A gathering of the world's statesmen drafted the United Nations charter at the hotel in 1945. In 1961, Tony Bennett gave the first performance of his classic "I Left My Heart in San Francisco" in the hotel's Venetian Room.

The California Street cable car line runs alongside the Fairmont and directly in front of the Flood Mansion. Few of the people who ride the world-famous cable cars understand the Comstock Lode connection between the cable in "the slot" pulling their trolley up California Street and the two imposing structures they pass atop Nob Hill. (The Powell Street line starts at the foot of the Flood Building on Market Street.) Elsewhere in San Francisco are streets or buildings bearing the names of Sharon, Flood, Hearst, Ralston, Mills, and tiny Ophir Alley, which connects Cosmo Place and Post Street two and a half blocks west of Union Square. Unfortunately, none of the city's thoroughfares carry Mackay's name. South of the city is the town of Millbrae and Mills Field, both named for

Darius Ogden Mills—we all know Mills Field today as San Francisco International Airport. A few miles farther south, in Belmont, one can use Ralston Avenue to visit Ralston Hall, where both William Ralston and William Sharon once lived. Across San Francisco Bay from Belmont is the town of Hayward, named for Alvinza Hayward, who snuck the Crown Point mine out from under Sharon's and Ralston's noses and made a fortune at their expense. John Percival Jones founded Santa Monica, where the Los Angeles megalopolis now meets the Pacific. Many other Comstock connections lurk elsewhere in California. In the forty-five years between the end of the Gold Rush and the great San Francisco earthquake of 1906, nothing exerted a bigger influence on San Francisco's fortunes than the Comstock Lode.

Louise's daughter, Eva Bryant Mackay, the princess of Galetro and Colonna, John's daughter, raised her children to adulthood after separating from her husband, then devoted herself to charitable services. During the Great War, she worked indefatigably on behalf of the Italian Red Cross while her two sons served in the Italian army. After the armistice, Eva treated victims of the Spanish flu epidemic—which few had the courage to do—and contracted the disease herself. Louise rushed to her side. Eva died on March 28, 1919, at the age of forty-eight. Obituaries speculated that the tireless relief efforts she'd made during the war had undermined her ability to resist the virus.

Louise Mackay lived until 1928. Her long *New York Times* obituary made much of her fairytale marriage, the "enviable" position she'd enjoyed in the society whirls of Paris, London, and the French Riviera, and her many social triumphs, but failed to note the heartbreaking tragedy of her existence—she'd outlived three of her four children. In accord with Louise Mackay's specific requests, after "services of the simplest character," her body was interred in the family mausoleum alongside the bodies of her parents, son, daughter, and husband.

Clarence Hungerford Mackay successfully managed the Postal Telegraph, the Commercial Cable Company, and the other Mackay family business interests for several decades after his father's death. He and his wife, Katherine Duer Mackay, had three children and remained a significant force in society and horseracing. Effendi, a colt bred by the Mackay stables, won the Preakness Stakes in 1909. Katherine, an ardent advocate of women's rights and women's suffrage, had founded the Equal Rights Society in New York City the year before. In 1911, Katherine fell in love with Clarence's personal physician. The couple divorced in 1914. Katherine abandoned her children and station and moved to Paris with the doctor. Years later, while she was dying of cancer, the doctor left her for another woman.

Cable Ship Mackay-Bennett is best remembered for deploying from Nova Scotia and recovering the bodies of people lost in the sinking of RMS *Titanic* in 1912. The ship was retired in 1922, but served as a storage hulk in Plymouth Harbor, where she was sunk by a German air raid during the Battle of Britain. She was finally scrapped in 1963. Clarence Mackay endowed an aviation trophy still annually awarded by the United States Air Force. Among its many winners are such famous aviators as Henry H. "Hap" Arnold, who commanded the United States air forces during World War II; Jimmy Doolittle, leader of the famous "Thirty Seconds Over Tokyo" raid in early 1942; and Chuck Yeager, first person to break the sound barrier. Clarence Mackay hosted many lavish parties at his Harbor Hill estate in the 1920s. The two most widely remembered are one for the Prince of Wales, later Edward VIII, king of the United Kingdom, who abdicated the throne in 1936 in favor of American double-divorcée Wallis Simpson, and another for Charles Lindbergh on the night of Lindbergh's ticker tape parade down New York's Fifth Avenue that honored his solo flight across the Atlantic. Clarence Mackay adhered to the Roman Catholic traditions held dear by his mother, and although he'd been divorced from Katherine Duer since 1914, not until after she died in 1930 did Clarence marry soprano Anna Case, his longtime girlfriend. The Smithsonian Museum of Natural History currently displays the 167.97 carat emerald necklace Clarence gave Anna as a wedding present. Clarence had sold the majority interest in the Postal Telegraph and the Commercial Cable Company to International Telephone and Telegraph (ITT) in 1928, accepting as payment an enormous chunk of ITT stock when it was worth $201 per share. Clarence must have felt good about the deal when ITT stock rose 150 percent over the course of the next year. Then came the stock market crash and the long decline. In 1932, ITT sold for $2.87. Clarence negotiated the Great Depression selling his art and antiquities and died of cancer in 1938.

ITT operated the Postal Telegraph & Cable Corporation as a corporate shell holding the Mackay interests until merging the domestic portion of the Mackay system with Western Union in 1943. The international cable and radio portions of the Mackay system remained with ITT, which had emerged from the Great Depression as one of the great multinational conglomerate corporations of the twentieth century. ITT maintained interests on both sides of World War II and had its fingerprints on some of the nastier South American events of the 1960s and 1970s, including military coups in both Brazil and Chile. Facets of ITT survive into the twenty-first century.

In November 1925, Clarence's daughter Ellin Mackay—John Mackay's granddaughter—wrote one of the most influential articles in the early history of a then-fledgling magazine called *The New Yorker*. She enjoyed a sixty-year marriage to Irving Berlin, one of America's greatest songwriters. Clarence did not approve of the union and disowned her. Ellin Mackay Berlin wrote a novel based on her grandmother's life and inspired many of her husband's songs, including "Always," which became a postmortem anthem of legendary country singer Patsy Cline, and "Blue Skies," which equally legendary Willie Nelson took to the top of the country charts in 1978.

In remembrance of his father, Clarence endowed the Mackay School of Mines at the University of Nevada, Reno. Having his name attached to one of the world's leading mining institutions would surely fill John Mackay with satisfaction and pride. In 1908, Gutzon Borglum—the man who would sculpt Mount Rushmore—erected a statue of Mackay in front of the school, where it remains today. John William Mackay stands as a simple miner with the bottoms of his trousers tucked into a pair of mucker's boots, holding a chunk of ore in his right hand and resting his left on the handle of a pickaxe. The likeness memorializes John Mackay as he would surely want to be remembered, with his gaze turned toward Virginia City and the Comstock Lode and his sleeves rolled up, ready for work.

Acknowledgments

Having last written about China and India in the 1930s and '40s, this time around I hoped to find a story that didn't require crossing the Pacific whenever I wanted to get the feel of a location. That desire led me to ferret through the nineteenth-century history of San Francisco, one of my favorite places, both historically and geographically. Those investigations kept "striking the lead" of the Comstock Lode, for prior to the great 1906 earthquake, the Comstock Lode was one of San Francisco's strongest influences. Fond childhood memories of visiting Virginia City with my mother cemented my interest. The search for an undersung character with the heft to carry the story of the Comstock Lode led straight to John William Mackay—and one of the greatest untold rags-to-riches stories in American history.

My greatest professional debts of gratitude go to my agent, Farley Chase, and to my editor at Scribner, Colin Harrison. Farley shared my enthusiasm for John Mackay's amazing story from the moment of our first phone call, and his well-developed literary sensibilities and cogent advice have done much to shape this book from that phone call forward. Colin Harrison at Scribner had apparently long wanted to "do" a Comstock Lode story, and both Farley and I were thrilled to add his expertise and enthusiasm to *The Bonanza King*'s team. Ever since, Colin has been the best active collaborator and advocate we could have hoped to discover. Colin's carefully considered advice, insights, "nose" for story, and ability to identify compressible detail have been a tremendous aid in shaping this book. I've learned much experiencing the machinations of Colin's editorial mind, and to boot, he has been a great pleasure to work with. Also crucial in helping shape *The Bonanza King* to its final form has been the attention and expertise of Scribner assistant editor Sarah Goldberg. She did much to shepherd the project to completion and offered a critical last round of editorial advice before we took the book into final production. Between Sarah, Colin, and Farley, I feel incredibly fortunate to have marshaled such a formidable array of literary talent in service of *The Bonanza King*. Also richly deserving of thanks are Sean Devlin and

Katie Rizzo, the two copyeditors at Scribner who worked diligently on the manuscript under tight deadlines; art director Jaya Miceli; book designer Erich Hobbing; and Scribner publicist Hailey Rutledge and freelance publicist Becky Kraemer. I'm grateful to all of you for your talents and hard work. Books are among the few remaining handcrafted products of the modern world, and all of your fingerprints are on this one.

I owe great thanks to the digital collections that facilitated the research *The Bonanza King* required: the Internet Archive (archive.org); the California Digital Newspaper Collection (cdnc.ucr.edu); the *New York Times* historic archive (timesmachine.nytimes.com); the Library of Congress (chroniclingamerica.loc.gov), the David Rumsey Map Collection (davidrumsey.com), the New York Public Library (digitalcollections .nypl.org), and newspapers.com. I'm indebted to many of the Comstock writers and historians who have gone before me, most notably Henry de Groot, Dan de Quille (William Wright), Sam Clemens (Mark Twain), Eliot Lord, Ronald M. James, Michael J. Makley, and especially Grant Smith, whose collection of Comstock- and Mackay-related material assembled in the 1920s and early '30s and archived at the Bancroft Library included many interviews with people who had once known John and Louise Mackay. Of especial assistance in photo gathering were Patricia L. Keats, director of Library & Archives at the Alice Phelan Sullivan Library of the Society of California Pioneers, and Jacquelyn Sundstrand, Sean Busey, Donnelyn Curtis, and Kimberly Roberts in the Special Collections Department at the University of Nevada, Reno.

Many people offered direct assistance during the writing of *The Bonanza King*. I give thanks to medical doctors Mark and Susan Robinson for discussions of nineteenth-century medicine and diseases; San Francisco firefighter Chuck Watanabi for discussions about what the dynamics of a mine fire might have been like in 1869; George Washington University professor Tyler Anbinder, author of the excellent *Five Points*, for information about shipbuilding and Irishmen in 1840s New York City; Ro Martinoni, deputy recorder of Storey County, for tracking down information about old Comstock mining claims; Janet Whitmore, PhD, art historian, for information about Alexandre Cabanel's portrait of John Mackay; Katie Green, author of *Like a Leaf Upon the Current Cast*, for providing information about Dr. Edmund G. Bryant and Louise Bryant; Ray Brooks for consultations about minerals and Idaho mining; Katie Sauter, research librarian at the AAC Library; Professor Michael Bowers at the University of Nevada, Las Vegas; Jack Tackle for Montana advice and for visiting Henry Comstock's grave on my behalf; former

City of Rocks Ranger Kristen Bastis for sharing her knowledge of the Oregon Trail and chasing down information about supergene enrichment; Jason Todd for also tracking down information on supergene enrichment; Campbell Gardett for his local knowledge of Mackay, Idaho; John Sherman for providing information on the historical range of California condors; Benjamin Dreyer for advice on how to tame the astonishing profusion of nineteenth-century commas; Bud Sprague, Brian Coppersmith, and author Julian Stockwin for nautical advice; Tarquin Crouch for consultations about England; Tom Rapko for emails about the "feel" of placer mining and what it's like to hit a pay streak; and James Claire Flood, great-grandson of Mackay's partner James Claire Flood, for sharing family lore and a passion for the history of the Bonanza Firm. Also helpful were Nevada State Historic Preservation Officer Rebecca Lynn Palmer; Robert (Bob) Nylen, curator of history at the Nevada State Museum; and Martin Fenimore, first cousin five generations removed from James Fenimore, "Old Virginny." My thanks also go out to Bo White and Molly Rorrick; Scott Ransom and Nadia Drake; Diana McSherry and Pat Poe; Theo Emison, Melissa Fitzgerald, Dina Howard, Amy Sillars, John Blaney, Jeff Witt, and Emily Bazar; Bill McConachie and Ann Parker; Tom Lambert; Dave Saunders and economist Rod Garratt at the University of California, Santa Barbara; Charlie Downs and Professor George Wheeldon; Hans Moosmüller and Sheryl Bennett for hospitality in Reno; Steve and Patty Michiels; Sierra County Historian Virginia Lutes; and Steve Johnson.

Personally, my greatest thanks go to my son, Ryan Crouch, and my wife, Tina Rath. They've extended me limitless love and support through the years I spent in the Comstock mines and have exhibited a superhuman tolerance for both long silences and relentless bombardments of Comstock-related "fun facts." Ryan and Tina are on every page. This book could not have been written without them.

A Note on Sources

Virtually every sentence in *The Bonanza King* contains a fact, and the overwhelming majority of those facts come from some primary source. I kept careful track of all sources used while writing, and as the citations multiplied into the thousands, both my endnotes and bibliography bloated to an unmanageable size. Rather than trim them unmercifully and append them to the end of this book, I decided that the best course was to post them on my website, whole. The bibliography can be found at gregcrouch.com/the-bonanza-king-bibliography. The endnotes are at gregcrouch.com/the-bonanza-king-endnotes. Having them online also has the potential to afford some important advantages. In service of total transparency, I added live links that allow readers to jump directly to the source material from within both the endnotes and the bibliography. With that accomplished, curious readers will be able to garner as much pleasure from the source material as I did.

Much modern literature pertinent to the Comstock relies on the same few old source books. By and large, those books are accurate, if not always easy to read. However, in quite a number of places, other primary material makes the foundations of those old books worthy of scrutiny. I haven't always agreed with their conclusions, but on every occasion that I forged a different path I felt like the preponderance of contemporary evidence forced me to divergent conclusions.

The bulk of the primary material I consulted while writing *The Bonanza King* comes from two basic categories. First, the digital archives of newspapers and magazines contemporary to the Comstock heyday: archive.org; the Hathi Trust Digital Library at hathitrust.org; the California Digital Newspaper Collection at cdnc.ucr.edu; timesmachine.com, the online archive of the *New York Times*; newspapers.com; the archive of the *San Francisco Chronicle* accessible through the San Francisco Public Library at sfpl.org; and the Mark Twain Project at marktwainproject.org; among others. The ease and speed with which that was accomplished and the searchable nature of the various databases allowed me to spend much more time among the source material, meticulously track old stories as they developed through a variety of news outlets (and yes, newspapers in the nineteenth century had their own particular editorial slants, ones that historians haven't always been careful to sort through), and to refer back to the original sources as often as needed, things that previous generations of writers working in an analog world found impossible or impractical to do. Newspapers in those days regularly published letters from correspondents in distant cities. Those provided excellent material for a readership unfamiliar with local conditions, which is more or less exactly the situation we find ourselves in today as we look back on the lode from a century and a half into the future. The other bulk of the primary material came from the Grant Smith collection held by the Bancroft Library and the Ellin Berlin collection at the University of Nevada, Reno. Grant Smith grew up on the Comstock. He's the ten-year-old eyewitness who was out hunting birds with a slingshot on the morning of the 1875 fire. Later in life, Smith developed an interest in Comstock history and wrote a valuable book, *The History of the Comstock Lode*. He also began writing and collecting material for a biography of John Mackay that time never allowed him to complete. He transcribed and sourced items from interviews he conducted with a number of people who had known Mackay on the Comstock—and a few who had known him in the Gold Rush days. Those provided the best snippet views of Mackay on his way up. Mackay's granddaughter, Ellin Berlin, wrote a novelized account of Louise Mackay's life called *Silver Platter*. Although Ms. Berlin's research is historically unreliable in several important aspects, she built an impressive collection of research, which I gratefully ferreted through.

As I was researching, I used the organizational software Evernote to clip more than six thousand contemporary Comstock articles and other items into digital notes that I organized into chronological and topical folders tagged by subject matter. I suspect other Comstock historians would find those folders useful and valuable. Assuming it's technologically possible, I'll endeavor to make them available through a link on my website. In the meantime, I'm happy to give access to anyone who shares my passion for Comstock history.

Photograph Credits

Index

Numbers in italics refer to pages with images.

Adams & Company, 31
Ah Ki, 187–88, 407–8
alcohol (whisky) use
  Fenimore's death and, 126
  miners and, 32, 33, 50, 86, 87, 163, 365
  saloons and, 33, 110, 111–12, 123–24,
    154, 160, 163–64, 238, 356, 359, 361,
    365, 366
  Sunday law proposal on, 127
  violence and shootings and, 163, 164
Alexander III, Czar of Russia, 390
Allen, Richard N., 102
American Rapid, 402, 403, 405–6
American Telephone & Telegraph, 426
American Union, 395, 396
Arizona
  diamond field hoax in, 307
  mines in, 157, 185, 386, 388
Arthur, Chester, 390
Atlantic & Pacific (A&P), 395, 396
Atlantic Ocean telegraph cables, 396,
  399–400, 409, 415
Atlantic Telegraph Company, 37–38
Atwood, Melville, 63

Babcock, William F., 116
Baldwin, A., 233
Baldwin, Elias J. "Lucky," 331
Baldwin, Joseph, 97, 98
Baltimore & Ohio Telegraph, 402, 403,
  405, 412–13
Bankers and Merchants' Telegraph
  Company, 402–3, 405–6
Bank of California, 330, 410
  Belcher mine and, 280
  closure of, 342–44, 345–47, 350

Comstock Lode and, 186, 188–89,
  201–2, 274, 309, 331
economic boom and, 331
Gold Hill office of, 189
Mackay's borrowing from, 411
Mackay-Sharon clash over mines in,
  245
mine accounts at, 226
mine and mill owners' loans from, 188,
  202–3, 226–27, 274, 341
need for, 185–86
Nevada Bank as competition for, 338
Ralston's debts to, 279, 308–9, 338, 340,
  341, 342, 344
Ralston's management of, 278–79, 307,
  309, 342–43
Ralston's opening of, 182
reopening of, 349–50, 351
San Francisco fire and, 356
Sharon's assayer corruption and, 227
Sharon's control of, 298, 341, 349
Sharon's proposal on, 186
Sharon's use of assets of, 227, 228, 298
Sutro's tunnel project and, 194, 204,
  205, 235
Virginia City branch of, 186, 187–88,
  203
Bank Ring
  Comstock mines and, 223–24, 225
  Hale & Norcross mine and, 231, 232,
    243, 244
  Kentuck mine and, 214
  members of, 203
  methods of making money from
    stockholders by, 225, 226, 276
  mines controlled by, 189–90, 241
  Ophir mine stock and, 332–33
  power of, 228

Bank Ring (*cont.*)
  railroad construction and, 233, 266, 270
  timber and cordwood fuel profits of,
    227
  transportation costs and, 232
  water supply profits of, 227–28
banks. *See also* Bank of California;
    Nevada Bank of San Francisco
  Mackay's founding of, 337–38
  mine owner borrowing and, 106, 188
  mining camps with, 31, 72
  railroads' economic problems and,
    320–21
Bannock Indians, 91, 99
Barron, Joseph, 186
Barron, William E., 186, 203, 233
Belcher mine, 194
  Mackay's missing of investment in, 280
  Mackay's work in, 380
  mining operations at, 306–7, 308, 315,
    335
  mules for transportation in, 287–89,
    295, 307
  productivity of, 288–89, 307, 308, 325,
    337
  Ralston's ownership of, 308, 338
  share price and dividends of, 159, 274,
    288, 295–96, 308, 315, 332, 340
  Sharon's ownership of, 280, 289, 292,
    307, 329
  watering stock scandal at, 287
Bell, Alpheus, 186
Bell, Thomas, 186, 189, 203, 233
Bennett, James Gordon, 11, 384–85
Bennett, James Gordon, Jr., 384–85, 397,
    399, 400
Berlin, Ellin Mackay, 165–66, 432
Berlin, Irving, 432
Best & Belcher mine, 299, 302, 324, 354,
    362
Bickell brothers (George, Richard, and
    James), 253, 254, 258, 259, 262
bicycle racing, 248–49, 282
Bigler, John, 48, 160
Bishop, John, 55, 56
Blackburn, John L., 123
"Bonanza Firm," 336. *See also* Firm, the
"Bonanza King," Mackay as, 336

Bonner, Charles, 203, 233
Bowers, Alexander "Sandy," 56
Boyd Silver Mining Company, 237
Brander, George, 410–11
Brannan, Sam, 14, 70
Bricknell, James W., 214
Bryan, Charles Henry, 163
Bryant, Dr. Edmund G., 193, 282
  death of, 208–9
  marriage to Marie Louise Hungerford,
    165, 166–67
  military career of, 100
Bryant, Eva
  early life of, 165, 166, 193, 209, 248
  Mackay's adoption of, 282. *See also*
    Mackay, Eva Bryant
  as Mackay's stepdaughter, 272,
    281–82
Bryant, Marie, 166, 167, 221, 423
Bryant, Marie Louise
  first marriage to Dr. Bryant, 164–68,
    193, 208–9, 210
  second marriage to John Mackay. *See*
    Mackay, Louise
Buchanan, James, 38, 123
Buck Ledge claim, 90, 113, 121, 135, 148
Bullion mine ("the Bullion"), 125
  Mackay as superintendent of, 236–37,
    242, 267
  mining operations in, 171, 193, 236–37,
    329
  productivity of, 267
  profitability of, 171, 267, 306

cable cars, 322, 399, 429
cable companies. *See* telegraph networks
Cable Ship Mackay-Bennett, 399, 431
cages
  accidents with, 251, 252
  description of, 215–17
  Hale & Norcross mine with, 215–16
  hoisting apparatuses with, 217
  mine fires and, 256–57, 258
  safety features of, 216–17
Caledonia mine
  Mackay as superintendent of, 135
  Mackay's construction of tunnel at,
    143–48

Mackay's ownership of shares in, 125, 148, 149, 158
share price of, 148, 158
Caledonia Tunnel Company, 143–47, 149
California
Civil War and, 123–24, 139
discovery of gold at Sutter's Fort in, 13–14
economic depression and, 340
Fraser River, Canada, gold rush's impact on, 36–37
gold coins and gold dust as currency in, 26
gold fever and departure for goldfields from, 15, 22
Gold Rush in. *See* Gold Rush
lack of mining regulation in, 14–15
majestic grandeur of, 34–35
migration to Washoe Diggings from, 81–84, 159–60, 163
mine stock investment in, 156
proposed ban on mining capital from, 126, 127
railroads' impact on, 271–72
rumors of gold strike and start of gold fever in, 13
silver fever in, 77–78
smallpox in, 248
Washoe Diggings' economic impact on, 75, 77–78, 84, 122, 127, 141, 156
California mine, Comstock Lode, 73
main silver lead in, 76
mining operations in, 73, 74, 76
productivity of, 84, 136, 149
value of shares in, 88
Californian (newspaper), 14, 15
Californianos, loss of land rights to gold mining by, 35
California stamp mill mining technique, 108–10, 119
California Trail, 46–47
Canadian Pacific Telegraph Company, 409–10
Carson, Kit, 46
Carter, David, 19
Case, Anna, 431
Catholicism
Mackay family background and, 6

Mackay's wife and, 423, 431
Yankee Protestants' view of Irish immigrants and, 7, 12
Catholic Daughters of Charity, 210, 219, 366
caves (collapses in mines)
dangers to miners from, 32, 252, 255–56
inability to predict, 373
loss of work time from, 116, 161–62
in Ophir mine, 161–62
rats' movement before, 317
timber reinforcement to prevent, 113, 114, 116
use of term, 113n
Cedar Hill mine, 171–72, 173
Centennial Exhibition, Philadelphia, 366, 367
Central mine, Comstock Lode, 73
Gould & Curry claim and, 113
Mackay's work in, 90, 113–14, 121
mining operations in, 73, 74, 76
productivity of, 107, 135, 149, 291
value of shares in, 84, 88, 115, 305
Central Pacific Railroad, 264, 320, 330
construction of, 247–48, 265
disease spread by, 248
first train to Nevada from, 233
"last spike" ceremony for, 264–65
transportation costs and, 232
Virginia City business opportunities from, 127
Chicago Daily-Tribune, 377
Chicago Tribune, 368–69, 377, 384
Chinatown, Nevada Territory, 49, 126, 160
Chinese Exclusion Act, 382
Chinese immigrants, 200, 382
attacks on, 271–72
at Comstock Lode, 199, 249, 364
as miners, 22, 49, 51, 160
railroad construction and, 232, 266
Virginia City fire relief and, 361
cholera
gold miners and, 32, 248
in New York City, 17–18, 20
spread across United States of, 22
Chollar mine, 125, 136, 143, 148, 149, 158, 169, 176

Chollar-Potosi mine, 190, 202, 223, 251, 252, 272, 274, 289, 296

Civil War, 48, 127, 279
  California and Nevada Territory during, 123–24
  currency problems during, 134, 187
  Emancipation Proclamation during, 140
  Fort Sumter attack and beginning of, 123
  greenbacks in, 182, 309
  mining and economy during, 4
  move west during, 151–52
  newspaper reporting on, 139–40
  rejoicing over end of, 191–92
  secession of states before, 122–23

claims. *See* mining claims

Clemens, Orion, 152

Clemens, Sam. *See also* Twain, Mark
  leg-pulling and hoaxes by, 153–54, 206
  Mackay's offer to switch jobs with, 155–56
  meaning of nom de plume used by, 154
  as miner, 152–53
  newspaper reporting job of, 153–54, 155, 162, 207–8
  robbery practical joke pulled on, 207

Coinage Act of 1873, 309, 320

coins
  gold and silver for, 367
  gold dust for, 31

Cole, A. M., 168

Colonna, Prince Fernando Julien, 404, 405, 421–22

Colorado mines, 189, 325, 378, 399, 416, 426

Colt, Samuel, 101

Commercial Cable Company, 399, 402, 403–4, 405, 408, 409–10, 411, 413, 415, 418, 420, 426, 430, 431

Comstock, Henry, 72
  background of, 51
  decline in fortunes of, 273–74
  Gold Hill claim of, 56, 59–60, 63, 65, 67, 68
  Grosh lawsuit against, 175–76
  marriage of, 138–39
  Oregon mine claims of, 138, 139
  quartz prospecting by, 235–36
  selling of claims by, 68, 70, 138
  suicide of, 274
  Virginia City naming and, 71

Comstock & Co.
  first mention of, 42
  Gold Hill claim of, 56, 62

Comstock Lode (mines), *x–xi*, 72. *See also specific mines*
  assays proving silver vein in, 63
  Bank of California and, 186, 188–89
  Civil War end and rejoicing in, 191
  claiming frenzy over, 62–63
  classes of mine owners in, 87–88
  Comstock's bragging about, 67, 68
  Comstock's claim dispute in, 59–60
  Comstock's selling of claim in, 138
  decline of, 423, 428
  difficulty of mining at, 62, 66–67
  discovery of, 55–56
  early success at, 56–57
  eastward dip of vein in, 169
  fires in, 253–64
  floods in, 133, 190, 387
  gold and silver sent east from, 187
  gold standard and, 309, 310
  Grant's visit to, 379–80
  Hayes's visit to, 382
  Lincoln's assassination reaction in, 192
  longitudinal elevation of, *144–45*
  Mackay's later memories of, 128
  Mackay's work at, 73–74, 75, 121, 128, 129, 387–88
  map of, *64–65*
  McLaughlin and O'Reilly's discovery of gold in, 58–59
  milling charges at, 224–25
  naming of, 67
  native Indians impacted by rush to, 91
  one-ledge legal theory at, 176
  Ophir mine incorporation for, 70
  opportunity to work one's way into mine ownership in, 76–77
  ore cars in, *173*
  ownership disputes about, 113
  productivity of, 74, 107, 177, 200, 272, 281, 381
  public loss of confidence in, 174
  railroad transportation for, 234, 267

range of miners at, 249–50
rats in, 317–18
San Francisco display of ore from, 122
San Francisco's economic success and,
  428–29
selling frenzy and, 197
share price of, 157, 189, 273, 274
Sharon and, 185–86, 189, 201–3,
  223–25, 228, 330
silver for currency from, 309
speculation about locations that might
  be on main lode in, 88
speculation in mining shares in, 84–86,
  188
steady slide of value of, 173–74
Sutro's tunnel project and, 190, 191,
  194, 204–5, 235
timber needed by, 232
transportation costs and, 233, 270
Utah Territory and, 124
Walsh's push for mining development
  of, 62–65
water supply and, 227–28
Congress
  admission of new states and, 17, 123, 124
  banking legislation from, 106n
  Coinage Act in, 309
  Gould's testimony on Western Union
    before, 398
  Sutro's tunnel project and, 204, 234–35
  telegraph service and, 132
Consolidated Virginia (Con. Virginia)
    mine, 291–293, 324–28
  clearing title to, 293, 299
  hoisting works of, 301
  Mackay-Dewey dispute about
    management of, 372–74
  Mackay's visit to, 423
  mills for, 334–35, 343
  mining operations in, 292–93, 299,
    302–3, 304–6, 310–11, 312–13,
    316–17, 320, 324–25, 363–64,
    374–75
  new equipment in, 325–26
  organization of, 291–92
  productivity of, 328, 331–32, 364, 381,
    386
  rats in, 317–18

rebuilding of, after Virginia City fire,
  362–63, 372–73
reorganization of, 324
shared-use arrangement for, 299–300
share price and dividends of, 292, 297,
  305–7, 311, 312–13, 316, 325, 332,
  333, 336, 373
speculation frenzy and, 328–29
Virginia City fire and, 354–55
Cooke & Company, 321
Cradlebaugh, John, 93
Crown Point mine, 194, 254, 274–80
  Bank Ring's takeover of, 219
  fires in, 253–64, 296
  Jones's attempt to seize control of,
    276–78
  Mackay's missing of opportunity in,
    280
  mining operations at, 197, 198,
    200–201, 212–13, 241, 274–76, 299,
    315–16
  mules for transportation in, 335, 355,
    362
  productivity of, 201, 307–8
  safety issues at, 252
  share price and dividends of, 158, 201,
    275, 276, 277–78, 280, 294–95, 315,
    332, 337
  Sharon's control of, 189, 202, 203, 213,
    223, 276, 278, 280
  Sutro's tunnel project and, 204
currency
  Civil War economy and, 187
  demand note in Civil War and, 133
  gold standard for, 309–10, 320
Curry, Abram, 69
Curtis, Sam, 302, 304, 305, 306, 313, 355,
  360

Daily Alta California, 36, 38, 39, 72, 83,
  87, 92, 99, 121, 122, 125, 131, 136,
  141, 142, 157, 184, 192, 193, 194,
  197, 207, 208, 231, 235, 243, 244,
  273, 291, 311, 315, 328, 330, 332,
  342, 344, 347, 348, 349, 351, 356,
  374, 400, 402, 407
Dall, W. L., 115–16
Dashaway Association, 87n, 152

Daughters of Charity, 210, 219, 366
de Groot, Henry, 60
Deidesheimer, Philipp
Con. Virginia ore estimates from, 326, 327, 331–32
square-set timbering system of, 116–18, 119, 120, 133
demand notes, 134
de Quille, Dan, 51, 154, 221, 230, 247, 250, 270, 294, 314, 316–17, 326–28, 334, 352
Dewey, Squire, 372–74, 379
de Young, Charles, 372, 373
de Young, Michael Henry and Katherine, 420
Dick Sides mine, 292
Downey, John G., 99
Downieville mines, California, 42, 101, 129
corporate nature of, 41
declining returns at, 40, 43
Durgan's Flat claim and, 40–41
gold-rich diggings around, 27–28
Mackay and O'Brien's decision to leave, 43
Mackay's experience at, 37, 39–41
as Mackay's first mining destination, 27
Mackay's later memories of, 39
vigilante court and lynching incident in, 27
Durgan's Flat claim, California, 40–41
dynamite, 236, 250, 326, 369

Earl, John, 186
Emancipation Proclamation, 140
Epson, Warren, 83
equine influenza, 311–12
Ericsson, John, 107–8
express companies, 31

Fair, James, 210–12, 380, 387
background of, 210–11
California gold mining by, 211
Con. Virginia mine and, 292, 293, 299, 302–3, 304–6, 310–11, 313, 315, 316, 317, 324, 326, 335, 363
divorce of, 389–90, 407
Grant's visit to Comstock mine and, 379, 380

Hale & Norcross mine and, 211, 214–15, 219, 221, 242, 243, 244, 245, 267, 268, 283, 289
illness and death of, 422
Mackay's disagreement with, 367–68, 403
Mackay's relationship with, 212
mining operations in, 292–93, 299, 302–3, 304–6
Nevada Bank and, 403, 411, 412
newspaper stories about, 388–89
reputation of, 368, 369–70, 371
resignation of, 378
Rising Star mine, Idaho, and, 237, 240
senatorial campaign of, 382
Sierra Nevada mine and, 378
Virginia City fire and, 355, 360
Virginia City move of, 211–12
water supply and, 290
Fair, James, Jr., 389
Fair, Theresa, 210, 211, 212, 219, 220, 276, 389–90, 411, 422
Fair Shaft, 214–15, 219, 220, 228, 230, 231, 232, 268, 283, 292
Feather River diggings, 16, 18, 211, 238
"feet" (shares in a mine)
Clemens's ownership of, 162
Comstock and, 139
decline in value of, 106, 174
drawback to using, 77
investor appetite for, 157–58
Mackay's use of, 76–77, 89, 121, 134, 158
raising capital using, 84, 88, 156–57
trading for mine work, 76, 77, 85
Fenimore, James "Old Virginny"
background of, 48
death of, 126
Gold Cañon, Utah, settlement by, 47–48
Gold Hill claim of, 59, 60, 66, 70
naming of camp in honor of, 71
Ophir croppings located by, 141–42
reputation of, 126
search for new diggings in Washoe by, 51–52, 55–56, 58
Field, Cyrus, 37
Fifteenth Amendment, 271
fire companies and firefighters, 260, 262, 282, *319*, 352, 356–57

fires
in Crown Point, Kentuck, and Yellow Jacket mines, 253–64
Mackay's insistence on clean, orderly work zones in mines to prevent, 128
mine firefighting equipment and, 178
miners' fears of, 252–53
spurious accusations about, 296, 297
in Virginia City, 162, 282, 351–57
Firm, the (Mackay, Fair, Flood, and O'Brien)
Bank of California solvency and, 343
Fair's withdrawal from, 387
Hale & Norcross mine and, 249, 267–68, 289, 299, 302, 315
monthly income of partners in, 364
nickname of "Bonanza Firm" for, 336
Petaluma Mill explosion and, 303–4
water supply project of, 290–91, 313–15
Fisk, Jim, 279
Five Points slum, Manhattan, 5, 8–9, 384, 414
Flood, James C., 290, 344, 387, 389, 403
background and early businesses of, 237–39
Bank of California solvency and, 343, 344, 346, 349
Con. Virginia mine and, 293, 299, 312, 316, 324, 368, 373
Hale & Norcross mine and, 243, 244–45, 249, 267, 268, 289
illness and death of, 410, 417
Kentuck mine and, 214
Mackay and, 214, 417
Nevada Bank and, 341, 410
Petaluma Mill and, 214
reputation of, 368
Rising Star mine, Idaho, and, 237, 240
San Francisco residence of, 368, 429
son's building in memory of, 429
stock market investments by, 239
water supply and, 290
Flood, James L., 417, 429
Fort Sumter, South Carolina, attack on, 123
Franklin, Stephen, 349
Fraser River, Canada, gold mines, 36–37, 39, 42, 75

Freemasons, 39–40, 137, 170
Frémont, John C., 46
Fry, John D., 184, 185, 186, 189, 308, 338, 343, 348, 349, 407

gambling
gold miners and, 31, 32, 33, 34, 66, 72, 127, 138, 163, 164, 365
gold mining as, 29–30
in San Francisco, 26, 27
Sharon's reputation for, 186, 188
gambling houses and halls, 33, 72, 163
Garrett, Robert, 403, 405, 412–13
gold dust
as currency in San Francisco, 27
miners' burying of, 33
transmission of, for striking coins, 31
Gold Cañon mines. See Washoe Diggings
Gold Hill Daily News, 295–96, 304, 305, 307, 316, 325, 326, 330, 357, 382
Gold Hill mines, 131, 254
Alpha Consolidated formed from, 223
equine influenza in, 312
Houseworth's shares in, 194–95
longitudinal elevation of, 146–47
mills at, 201, 233
miner paydays in, 205
mining operations in, 72–73, 143, 171
naming of, 41, 56
Petaluma Mill at, 208, 214, 249, 303–4
productivity of, 41–42, 107, 143, 149, 201
quartz discovery and claim in, 62–63
quartz ledge in, 136
range of miners at, 259–60
resumption of mining by Comstock with new partners in, 60–62
safety issues in, 250
sell-outs and consolidations of claims in, 67–68, 69–70
square-set timbering system in, 133
transportation costs and, 233
value of shares in, 136, 138, 139, 157n
Yellow Jacket claim boundary in, 57–58
Gold Hill mining camp
bank office in, 186, 188, 189, 346
Crown Point fire and, 259, 260, 262–63
equine influenza in, 312

Gold Hill mining camp (*cont.*)
expansion of, 110, 159
Fifteenth Amendment ratification
celebration in, 271
living conditions at, 72, 75, 84, 127,
138, 205, 230
mine share price drop and, 296–97
population of, 110–11, 127, 364, 428
President Grant's visit to Comstock
and, 379
railroad construction in, 265–67, *269*,
270, 309
smallpox epidemic in, 248
transportation monopoly in, 337
violence in, 112
water supply in, 314
Gold Hill News, 167, 220–21, 244, 296,
297, 307, 314, 326
gold miners, *1*
alcohol (whisky) use by, 32, 33, 50, 86,
87, 163, 365
American imagination on, 32
anonymity of, 34
beards and physical appearance of, 32
benevolent societies and fraternal
organizations and, 39–40
California's impact on, 35–36
crimes and justice for, 32, 58, 286
death and funerals of, 40
desire for regular letters and
newspapers for, 31
diet of, 49
express companies for gold dust and,
31
Fraser River, Canada, gold rush and,
36–37
gambling by, 26, 27, 30, 32, 33, 34, 66,
72, 127, 138, 163, 164, 365
hiring out for wages by, 41
living conditions for, 33, 49
majestic grandeur of California and,
34–35
morality and religious traditions in,
33–34
native Indian populations and, 35,
78–79
opportunity to work one's way into
mine ownership by, 76–77

physical exertion and limited returns
for, 31
poor conditions and disease endured
by, 31–32
prostitution and brothels and, 33, 164,
365
gold mining
abundant water needed for, 27, 28, 49
business opportunities ancillary to,
30–31
claim rights in, 28–29
density of gold and, 28
difficulty of extracting gold from quartz
in, 53–54
Fraser River, Canada, gold rush and,
36–37, 39, 42, 75
as a gamble, 29–30
hydraulic approaches to, 35, 41, 171,
172, 278, 290
initial lack of regulation of, 14–15
lack of stigma for failures in, 31
land damage from, 35
long toms (troughs) in, 28, 29
mercury used in, 28, 55, 60–61, 109
miner's process in, 29–30
mining districts formed for, 28, 57, 62,
99
native Indian populations and, 35, 78–79
physical exertion and limited returns
in, 31–32
Pioneer Quartz Company by-laws on, 54
placer techniques in, 27, 28–29, 35, 42,
49, 50
river-turning technique in, 30, 37
rockers used in, 4, 28
sluice boxes used in, 28, 29, 35
underground mining ("drifting") in,
41, *45*
vagaries of, 30
Gold Rush
Brannan and start of, 14
California citizens' departure for, 15, 22
discovery of gold at Sutter's Fort and
beginning of, 13–14
dreams and hard reality of, 21–43
Fair and, 211
Fraser River, Canada, Gold Rush's
impact on, 36–37

impact on California of, 16
initial skepticism about, 14, 17
Mackay's awareness of early reports on, 22–23
migrants' sea and overland journeys to, 23–24
newspaper report about miners' daily earnings in, 16, 18
newspaper reports on successes and failures in, 24
New York City departures in rush to California and, 19–20
New York City newspapers on, 15–16, 18–19
poor Americans and pull of reports on, 21–22
President Polk's mention of abundance of gold in, 17
rumors and newspaper stories about, 14, 15–16
rush to goldfields at beginning of, 15
San Francisco's excitement about, 14
San Francisco's rapid expansion during, 21, 25–27
shipbuilding boom and, 23
U.S. Mint's assay of gold from, 19
worldwide pull of, 23
gold standard, 309–10, 320
Goodman, Joseph T., 36, 153, 298
Goshute Indians, 91
Gould, Alva, 69
Gould, Jay
background of, 394–95
death of, 417
gold supply and, 279
Mackay on, 400
Mackay's alliance against, 402–3, 412–13
Mackay's decision to oppose, 396–97
Mackay's negotiations with, 413–14
Mackay's ownership of competing companies and, 397–400
Mackay's transatlantic cable war against, 402, 403–4, 408–10, 411, 415
near monopoly of telegraph business by, 395
physical appearance of, 393
"pooling agreement" and, 388, 396, 397
reputation of, 393–94
wealth of, 381–82, 394, 398
Gould & Curry claim, 105, 247
description of operations at, 177–81
financing of development of, 124–25
first claim in, 69
Grosh's claim to, 175
Hearst's ownership of shares of, 77, 181
incorporation of, 124
management of, 182, 222, 277
mill connected with, 136, 149, 177–79
mining operations in, 113, 143, 156, 157, 176, 177, 178–79, 181
one-ledge legal theory at, 176
ownership changes in, 299, 311, 334, 354
ownership disputes about vein of, 113
productivity of, 85, 86, 136, 149, 156, 158–59, 174, 179, 183, 194, 202, 316
rumors about demise of, 181–82
safety issues in, 216–17, 250–51
share price of, 141, 142, 149, 155, 157, 159, 173, 174, 179, 296, 381
size of, 179–80
speculation and perceived promise of, 85, 86
Virginia City employment related to, 158
Virginia City fire's threat to, 354
Walsh's purchase of, 69
working conditions in, 315
Gracey, Robert, 39
Grant, Ulysses S., 383
Civil War and, 134, 191
Coinage Act and, 309
Comstock mine visited by, 379–80
Gould and Fisk's attempt to corner gold market and, 279
Mackay on compliments from, 380
Sutro's tunnel project and, 234–35
party thrown in Paris by Louise Mackay for, 375, 376–77
greenbacks
Civil War and, 134, 187
distrust of, 134
gold and silver supporting, 135, 187
Ralston's fortune in arbitrage of, 182
Treasury reforms needed for, 309

Grosch Consolidated Company, 175–76
Grosh, Allen and Hosea, 52, 175

Hale & Norcross mine, 125, 214–16,
   228–32, 242–45
  Bank of California's loss of, 279
  cage at, 215–16, 217
  confinement of miners at, 228–30,
    242
  factions battling for control of, 232
  Fair Shaft in, 214–15, 219, 220, 228,
    230, 231, 232, 268, 283, 292
  Fair's management of, 211, 214–15,
    219, 221, 242
  the Firm's management of, 249, 267–68,
    289, 299, 302, 315
  floods in, and loss of value, 289
  Hayward at, 277
  hopes for new exploration at, 231–32,
    241
  Mackay and, 242–43, 249, 272, 283,
    290, 302, 315
  Mackay-Sharon clash over, 245
  mills used by, 231, 245, 249, 268
  mining operations at, 215, 218, 231–32,
    271, 283
  new shaft construction at, 214–19
  partnership with Mackay to seize
    control of, 243–45
  productivity of, 158, 197, 200, 219,
    267–68, 272
  public loss of confidence in, 242,
    296
  safety issues with death at, 251
  Savage mine's sharing of ore body with,
    295
  share price of, 228, 229, 230–31, 232,
    241, 242, 244, 268, 274, 296
  Sharon and, 228, 231, 232, 241, 243,
    244, 245, 249, 280, 299
Hallidie, Andrew Smith, 322
Harrison, B. Augustus, 62–63
Hart, William, 59, 60, 61–62
Hayes, Rutherford B., 382
Hays, John Coffee "Jack," 100–102
  background of, 100–101
  militia for Williams Station reprisal
    and, 101–2

Hayward, Alvinza, 186, 189, 203, 214,
   276–78, 280, 289, 290, 294, 296, 297,
   298, 303, 430
Hearst, George, 429
  background of, 63–65
  Gould & Curry claim and, 77, 124, 125,
    181
  Homestake mine and, 378
  Idaho mines explored by, 237
  mines owned by, 69n, 416–17
  Ophir shares sold by, 77, 88, 92
  Rising Star mine, Idaho, and, 237,
    240
  Washoe Diggings and, 63, 67, 69–70
Hellman, Isaias W., 417
Hirschman, Adolph ('Dolf), 168
hoisting machinery, 171, 214, *301*, 307
  air circulation and, 304
  air compressors for, 325–26
  cage and compartments in, 215–17
  Con. Virginia mine, 325–26, 353–55,
    361
  cost of, 121, 190, 204, 254
  Ericsson caloric engine for, 107–8
  fires and, 257–58, 262, 353–56, 357
  horse, 197
  incline in, 306–7
  Mackay's knowledge of, 23
  safety issues with, 251
  smooth and speedy descent in, 316
  steam, 143, 156, 192, *199*, 200–201,
    208, 215, 219, 235
Houseworth, Valentine A., 69, 194–96
Houseworth Claim
  Kentuck mine title issues and, 195
  Mackay and Walker as heirs to, 196
  Walker's pursuit of quitclaim for, 196
Howland, Louise Meyer, 165, 193
Hughes, Thomas J., 70
Hungerford, Ada, 164, 167, 209, 379,
   405
Hungerford, Daniel E.
  background of, 100
  mining stock speculation by, 166–67
  move to Virginia City by, 164–65
  move to San Francisco by, 167
  Williams Station Indian massacre
    reprisal and, 101–2

Hungerford, Marie Louise
  early life in Virginia City of,
    164–65
  first marriage to Dr. Bryant, 164–68,
    193, 208–9, 210
  second marriage to John Mackay. *See*
    Mackay, Louise
hydraulic mining, 35, 41, 171, 172, 278,
  290

Idaho Territory mines
  Comstock's interest in, 175–76
  investor interest in, 157, 189, 237
  Mackay's investment in, 240–41, 397,
    416, 426
immigration. *See also* Irish immigrants
  cholera in New York City and, 17–18,
    22
Imperial-Empire mine, 241
Indians, ban on, as mine workers, 29
Indian tribes. *See also specific tribes*
  anti-immigrant resentment among, 91
  gold mining and culture of, 35, 78–79
  Washoe Diggings mining and, 47–48,
    50, 78–79
  Williams brothers' kidnapping of two
    Indian sisters and, 90–91
  Williams Station massacre and, 90–92,
    101, 102–3
International Telephone and Telegraph
  (ITT), 431–32
Ireland
  Mackay's birth in, 5–6
  Mackay's return to, 285–86
  potato crop failure and Great Hunger
    in, 11–12
  poverty of tenants in, 6
Irish immigrants
  cholera among, 22
  discrimination against, 7, 12
  education of children of, 10
  Fair family as, 210–11
  famine in Ireland and, 11–12
  Mackay family as, 6–7, 9–11
  New York City slum life and, 8–9
  potato famine and, 11–12
  poverty of, 6
  as unskilled workers, 6–7, 11

Jay Cooke & Company, 321
Jessup, John, 58, 112
Jewell, Edward and William, 253, 254,
  258
Johnson, W. B., 203
Jones, John Percival, 267, 297, 298
  Crown Point mine and, 274, 275–77,
    278, 280, 289, 294, 296, 307–8
  mine fires and, 254, 259, 262, 263, 297
  Nevada's senatorial seat and, 295, 298,
    379, 386, 398
  Petaluma Mill and, 303
Juárez, Benito, 209

Keene, James, 397
Kennedy, Alec E., 75, 103
Kentuck mine, 194–98, 254
  development loan for, 196–97, 198, 201
  fires in, 254–64, 296
  Houseworth Claim and flawed title to,
    195–96
  incorporation of, 196
  lack of early mentions of, 194
  Mackay and Walker's ownership of,
    194–98, 200–201, 208, 212–13, 214,
    422
  mining operations in, 197, 208
  productivity of, 200, 214
  safety issues at, 252
  share price and dividends of, 200, 213,
    214
  Sharon's ownership of, 213–14
  steam-powered hoisting machinery in,
    200–201
  vein discovery and value of, 198
Killaha, Richard, 63
King, Thomas Starr, 164
Kirby, Joe, 59, 60
Knight, William, 56
Kustel, Guido, 240

Lake, Myron C., 233
land rights. *See also* mining claims
  grazing agreements with Indians and,
    91
  Mexican Californianos' loss of, 35
  Washoe and Northern Paiute tribes in
    Utah and, 50

Larkin, Thomas O., 16
law enforcement
vigilance committees for, 164, 285–86
violence and shootings in Virginia City
and, 111–12, 138, 163
laws and legislation. *See also* mining law
California-based banking corporations
under, 182
company debt liability under, 347
company's claiming two separate ledges
under, 176
Gould's use of, to control public
corporations, 394
mine corporate governance and, 175
mining taxes and, 336
proposed ban on California capital in,
126, 127
silver coinage under, 309–10
Sunday law proposal and, 126–27
lawsuits
against Mackay for "unlawful intimacy,"
379
mine owners' use of, 106, 136, 175–76
one-ledge theory and, 176–77
against Sharon, by woman companions,
407
Lee, Robert E., 139, 191, 192–93
Lent, William, 237
lifting pumps, 218–19
Lincoln, Abraham, 184
assassination of, 192–93
Civil War and, 140, 187, 191
distrust of paper money from, 134
election of, 122, 123, 151
Emancipation Proclamation by, 140
long toms (troughs), in gold mining, 28,
29

Mackay, Anna Case, 431
Mackay, Clarence (son)
adult life of, 419, 420, 424
birth of, 322–23
business dealings of, 425, 427, 430
childhood of, 402
marriages of, 426, 430–31
memorial to father from, 432
Mackay, Ellin (granddaughter), 165–66,
432

Mackay, Eva Bryant (daughter)
children of, 421, 422, 430
early life of, 165, 166, 193, 209, 248
European trips of, 284, 285, 302, 323,
383
hip operation of, 285, 301, 302
later life and death of, 430
Mackay's adoption of, 282
as Mackay's stepdaughter, 272, 281–82
marriage of, 404, 405, 421–22
return to Virginia City by, 316, 323
brother Willie's death and, 424–25
Mackay, Idaho, 416
Mackay, John
EARLY LIFE, 2, 5–11
early years in New York City of, 9–12
education of, 10, 168
first job as newsboy, 10–11, 128, 201,
384–85
Five Points slum background of, 8–11,
384, 414
immigration to New York City by, 6,
7–8
Irish birth of, 5–6
shipyard apprenticeship of, 12, 17, 21,
23, 128, 201
MARRIAGE AND FAMILY
daughter's hip operation and, 285, 301,
302
daughter's marriage and, 421, 422
European vacations of, 284–85, 301–2,
315, 387, 388, 390, 413
Fairs' divorce and, 389–90
Mackay's death and burial and, 427
Mackay's obituaries and, 427
Paris move and residence of, 366–67,
375, 377, 382–83, *393*
San Francisco residence of, 319–20,
323–24
shooting of, 419–21
son Clarence's birth and, 323
son Willie's birth and, 272–73
son Willie's death and, 424–25, 426
as special ambassador to Russian
coronation, 390–91
MINES AND BUSINESSES
awareness of early stories about gold
discovery, 22–23, 24

Belcher mine and, 287, 380

boardinghouse and office rooms used by, 206, 363, 386–87

Buck Ledge claim work of, 90, 113, 121, 135, 148

as Bullion mine superintendent, 236–37, 242, 267

Cedar Hill mine ownership by, 171–72, 173

Comstock Lode work of, 73–74, 75

Con. Virginia mine and, 291–293, 299–300, 310–11, 316–17, 320, 324–25

decision to leave Downieville and trek to Gold Hill by, 43

decision to sail to California by, 23

Dewey's dispute with, 372–74, 379

Downieville mines and, 37, 39–41

early mining jobs of, 128

food and provisions in camp and, 77

Gold Hill mine and, 45–46

Gold Rush and, 36

Grant's visit to Comstock mine and, 379–80

Hale & Norcross mine and, 242–43, 245, 249, 272, 283, 290, 302, 315

Kentuck mine and, 194–98, 200–201, 208, 212–13, 214

learning of mining techniques by, 29, 121–22

Mackay known as "Bonanza King" in, 336

Mackay's wealth from, 364, 367, 381–82

Mackay's insistence on clean, orderly work zones in mines and, 128

Mexican mine work of, 113–14

as Milton mine superintendent, 169, 170

mining taxes and, 336, 337

multiple jobs held simultaneously by, 90, 114

Nevada Bank of San Francisco and, 338, 340, 341, 351, 410–12

Ophir mine shares of, 158, 329, 362

Ophir mine work of, 70–71, 73, 90, 113–14, 121, 374, 375, 403

opportunity to work his way into mine ownership wanted by, 76–77, 88–89, 121–22

post–Civil War depression and, 193–94

practical mining experience of, 170–71

rebuilding of mines, after Virginia City fire, 360–62, 363

Rising Star mine, Idaho, and, 237, 240–41

Sharon's illness and death and, 407, 408

son Willie's work with, 418

speculation in mining shares and, 84, 334

stock advice offered by, 331

stock market investments and, 239

transatlantic cable companies of, 402, 403–4, 408–9, 411, 416, 420

transatlantic cable war with Gould in, 399, 400, 402–3, 408, 409, 411, 415

transpacific cable project and, 426–27

Union mine ownership by, 76, 89, 103, 134–35, 148, 158, 171

Union mine work of, 76–77, 88, 90, 114–15

Virginia City fire and, 353–54, 355, 357, 360

Virginia City fire relief and, 360

Virginia City life and, 84, 86

wages paid by, 372, 408

Walker partnership with, 170–71

Williams Station Indian massacre and, 93

working for wages in mines by, 121–22

working for feet as pay by, 76–77, 89, 121, 134, 158

PERSONALITY AND TRAITS, 168–69

ambition, 90, 129, 285

art collecting, 383–84, 400–402

capacity for hard work, 39, 41, 89, 90, 129, 135, 272, 394, 415

carpentry skills, 23, 40, 113–14, 128, 201

cleanliness, 384

competence expected, 122, 128, 169

competitiveness and desire to win, 208

conversational style, 168

cooking abilities at Downieville, 39

desire to make money, 40, 88–89

devotion to and pride in wife, 383, 384, 391

efforts to improve his technical and geological knowledge, 135, 168, 206

Mackay, John; PERSONALITY AND TRAITS
(*cont.*)
fighting to hold his place, 3, 324, 411
friendships, 168, 220, 385, 400
kindness and philanthropy, 219, 371, 423
leadership qualities, 128–29, 169
mining knowledge and competence of,
128, 135
opinion of European aristocrats, 391
opinions on wealth and money, 201,
205–6, 302, 364, 371, 381, 396, 416,
427
physical appearance, 2, 40, 285, 388,
415, 432
plainspoken, unaffected manner, 156,
169, 370, 371
poker playing by, 371–72
political party affiliation, 382
pride in work, 122
rags-to-riches story, 415–16
reaction to Grant's compliments, 380
regret of lack of formal education, 10,
370
reputation, 370–72
requests from strangers for money, 386
sense of humor, 169, 323
social life with friends and, 168–69,
371–72, 385–86
stutter, 2, 10, 90, 168, 323
temper, 128, 169, 245, 323, 373
theatrical performances and music, 11,
206, 220, 371, 384, 385, 386
Mackay, John William, Jr. "Willie" (son)
birth of, 272–73
childhood of, 281–82, 283, 284, 316,
319, 323
education and career of, 366, 384, 402,
418–19, 420
sickness and death of, 424–25, 426
Mackay, Katherine Duer, 426, 430–31
Mackay, Louise (born Marie Louise; wife)
art collecting by, 400–402
childhood life of, 164–65
daughter Eva's hip operation and, 285,
302
daughter Eva's wedding and marriage
and, 404–5, 422
death and obituary of, 430

devotion to husband, 383
early sewing and teaching jobs of, 167,
193, 209–10
European vacations of, 284–85, 301–2,
387, 388, 390–91, 413
first marriage to Dr. Bryant by, 164–68,
193, 208–9, 210
granddaughter's novel about, 165–66, 432
Grant's visit to, 375, 376–77
London residences of, 402, 408, 418
Mackay's courtship of, 212, 219–20
Mackay's marriage celebration with,
220–21
Mackay's shooting and, 420–21
Meissonier's portrait of, 401–2, 418
Paris move and residence of, 366–67,
377–85, *393*
philanthropies of, 366–67, 385, 423
physical appearance of, 166, 210, 323,
376, 390–91, 420
San Francisco residence of, 319–20,
322–23, 353
social entertainments of, 383, 384, 385,
386, 390–91, 417, 420
son Clarence's birth and, 322–23
son Willie's birth and, 272–73
son Willie's death and, 425–26
Virginia fire and, 353–54
Mackay family
death of father and, 10
early years in New York City of, 9–11
immigration to New York City by, 6, 7
Irish background of, 6–7
John's first job as newsboy to support,
10–11, 128, 201, 384–85
Mackay School of Mines, University of
Nevada, Reno, 432
mail communication, 77
Pony Express and, 83, 87, 101
railroad and, 233
stagecoach lines and, 31, 38
telegraph networks and, 38
Wells Fargo and, 233
Maldonado, Gabriel, 70
Manogue, Patrick, 166, 167, 193, 208, 210,
220, 259, 360, 423
Marshall, James, 13
Mason, Richard Barnes, 18–19

Masonic Lodges and Masons, 39–40, 137, 170
Maximilian I, Emperor of Mexico, 209
McCullough, John, 220, 386
McLaughlin, Patrick, 51, 58, 59, 60, 61, 62, 66, 68, 69
Meissonier, Ernest, 400–402, 418
mercury ("quicksilver")
  dangers of using, 251
  gold mining with, 28, 55, 60–61, 109
Meredith, Henry, 77, 88, 91, 92, 96–97
Mexican-American War, 13, 17, 100, 101
Mexican Californianos, loss of land rights to gold mining by, 35
Mexican immigrant miners, at Washoe Diggings, 120, 161, 249
Mexican mine, Comstock Lode, 73
  collapse of gallery in, 160–62
  Comstock's selling of claim in, 70, 138
  Gould & Curry claim and, 113
  Grosh's claim to, 175
  Mackay's work in, 90, 113–14, 121, 329
  mining operations in, 73, 74, 76, 119, 120, 403
  naming of, 71
  productivity of, 107, 135, 149
  value of shares in, 85, 86, 88, 115
  vigilante hanging in, 286
Mexican mining techniques, 71, 120
Mexican patio process, 74, 108, 109, 178
Mexican raiding parties, in Arizona Territory, 386
Mexico
  Hungerford's fight against dictator in, 209
  silver mines of, 73, 121, 157, 174
Meyer, Louise, 165, 193
mills
  costs of, 224–25
  mechanism of, 177–78
Mills, Darius Ogden
  Bank of California and, 182, 185, 186, 344, 345, 347, 350, 351
  Belcher mine stock and, 308
  Crown Point mine and, 203
  Hayward and, 277
  on Mackay's leadership, 128–29
  Ophir mine management and, 341

Ralston's death and, 350
San Francisco streets and buildings, 429–30
Sharon's Palace Hotel project and, 343
Sutro's tunnel project and, 204
Virginia & Truckee Railroad and, 233, 342
Milton mine, 148, 155, 158, 168, 169, 170, 171
mine owners
  borrowing terms for, 106, 188, 202–3
  classes of, 87–88
  ignorance of underground geological conditions of, 113
  lawsuits commonly used by, 106, 136, 175–77
  ownership disputes between, 112–13
  personalities of, 162
  selling "feet" to raise capital by, 84, 88, 156–57
  share speculation and, 105–6, 188
  trading "feet" in a claim for work by, 76, 77, 85, 106, 174
miners. *See also* gold miners
  alcohol (whisky) use by, 32, 33, 50, 86, 87, 163, 365
  bicycle racing by, 248–49
  confining, as stock price ruse, 229
  fires feared by, 252–53
  Mackay's treatment of, 370–72
  mine accidents and, 250–52
  paydays for, 205
  pride in work by, 252
  rats and, 317–18
  socializing after shifts by, 364–65
  working conditions for, *223*
mines. *See also specific mines*
  appetite for investing in, 156–58
  cages in, 215–17
  classes of mine owners in, 87–88
  Mackay's insistence on clean, orderly work zones in, 128
  miner paydays in, 205
  multiple rich leads running in same direction in, 136
  pump engine and pump machinery in, 217–19

mines (*cont.*)
  rats in, 317–18
  rebuilding of, after Virginia City fire,
    360–62
  selling "feet" to raise capital for, 84
  speculation about locations that might
    be on main lode in, 88
  square-set timbering system in,
    115–20, *117*
  Virginia City fire and, 354–55, 360
  working conditions for, *223*
mining. *See also* gold mining; silver
    mining
  California stamp mill technique for
    processing ores in, 108–10, 119
  caves during, 32, 113, 114, 116, 317, 373
  crosscuts in, 107
  custom mills in, 201–2
  drifts in, 107
  dynamite used in, 236, 250, 326, 369
  ignorance of underground geological
    conditions in, 113
  proposed ban on California capital in,
    126, 127
  speedy extraction vital in, 120
  taxes in, 336–37
  winzes in, 120–21, 179
Mining & Scientific Press, 149, 170, 173,
    175, 179, 194, 200, 205, 213, 225,
    235, 236, 240, 241, 268, 274, 285,
    294, 301, 317, 322, 331, 333, 365
mining camps
  alcohol use in, 32, 33, 50, 86, 87, 164
  anonymity of miners in, 34
  attempts to "civilize," 164
  crimes and justice in, 32, 58, 286
  desire for regular delivery of letters and
    newspapers to, 31
  food and provisions in, 77, 86–87
  gambling in, 33
  lack of women and children in, 132,
    165, 210
  living conditions in, 33, 49
  miners' drifting between, 34
  morality and religious traditions in,
    33–34
  poor conditions and disease in, 31–32
  prostitution in, 33

  shootings and violence in, 388
  staying the winter in, 113
  Sunday law proposal and, 126–27
mining claims
  boundaries of, 57–58
  jumping of, 32
  living arrangements near, 33, 49
  marking of, 29
  one-ledge legal theory on, 176–77
  Mexican Californianos and, 35
  quartz mining and, 54, 55
  recorders for, 29, 62
  rights under, 28–29
  speculation in, 29, 41
mining districts, 28, 57, 62, 99
mining law. *See also* laws and legislation
  company's claiming two separate ledges
    under, 176
  early lack of, in California, 14–15
  first codification of quartz-mining law
    in, 54
  governance under, 175
  Mackay on, 293
  one-ledge theory in, 176–77
Montana mines, 69n, 189, 235–36, 273
morality, in mining camps, 33–34
Morrow, Robert, 348
Mormons
  California gold strike and, 13
  rumor about Williams Station Indian
    massacre and, 92
  San Francisco gold fever and, 14
  Utah mines and, 47
  Utah territorial government and, 112
mules
  equine influenza and, 312
  mine transportation using, *281*,
    287–89, 295, 307, 335–36, 362
  Virginia City fire and, 355, 362
mutual aid societies, 40

National Cable Railway Company, 399
Nevada Bank of San Francisco, 364, 368
  capitalization of, 372
  Fair and, 403, 411, 412
  founding of, 338, 340, 341
  Mackay's sale of, 417–18
  opening of, 351

problems at, 410–12
profits from, 381
Nevada legislature
Fair's election to U.S. Senate and, 382
mining tax structure and, 336–37
proposed ban on California capital and, 126, 127
Sharon's bribing of members of, 228, 330
Sharon's candidacy to U.S. Senate and, 330
Sunday law proposal and, 126–27
Sutro's tunnel project, 191
Nevada National Bank, 417
Nevada Territory
Civil War and, 123–24, 140
drought in, 173–74
Fenimore's contribution to development of, 126
migration from California to, 159
Orion Clemens as secretary of, 152
Sunday law proposal for, 126–27
Utah Territory's independence from, 124
newsboys, New York City
hard labor of, 10–11
Mackay's first job as, 10, 384–85
Mackay's later memories of work as, 128, 201
social life of, 11
newspapers. See also specific newspapers
Bank of California solvency reports in, 341, 344, 345–46, 347
California gold discovery in, 14, 17, 18
Civil War news in, 139, 140, 192
Clemens's reporting job on, 153–54, 155, 162, 207–8
Con. Virginia mine in, 303, 305, 306, 311, 312–13, 316, 325, 326–28, 332, 374
Five Points, New York City, slum in, 9
Gold Rush successes and failures reported in, 24
Gould covered in, 394, 395
Gould's ownership of, 395
Grant's visit to Louise Mackay in Paris in, 376–77
Hale & Norcross's confinement of miners in, 229–30, 242

Hale & Norcross's share prices in, 243, 244
initial Pony Express run reported by, 83
Mackay-Dewey dispute in, 374
Mackay-Gould transatlantic cable war in, 399, 400, 402–3, 408, 409, 411
Mackay's marriage and, 220–21
Mackay's wealth reported in, 351
miners' daily earnings reported in, 16, 18
miners' desire for regular shipment of, 31
newsboys and, 10–11, 384–85
Nevada Territory mineral wealth in, 156
Ophir mine mismanagement in, 341
Pyramid Lake battles in, 99, 102
Ralston's suicide in, 348, 349
Senator Fair stories in, 388–90
Sharon's coverage in, 228, 330
violence and shootings reported in, 163
Virginia City fire in, 352, 355, 356, 357, 360, 361
Virginia City life reported in, 364–66
Washoe Diggings success in, 70
New York City
cholera and unsanitary conditions in, 17–18, 20, 22
Five Points slum in, 5, 8–9, 384, 414
gold fever and departures for California from, 19–20
Irish immigrants in slums of, 5, 7, 11–12
Mackay family's arrival in, 7–8
Mackay family's early years in, 9–10
Mackay's later visits to, 283–84, 316
news of gold discovery reported in, 15–16
squalid living conditions in, 9
tenements in, 8–9, 283
New York Herald
Bennett, Jr.'s ownership of, 385
California gold strike stories in, 15–16, 21
Mackay's work as newsboy for, 11
New York Times, 89, 123, 132, 133, 142, 173, 174, 181–82, 197, 311, 351, 378, 390, 394, 397, 398, 403–4, 408, 409, 419, 424, 426, 430, 434
New York Tribune, 16, 17, 18, 22, 364, 411–12

Nobel, Alfred, 236
Northern Pacific Railroad, 321
Northern Paiute Indians, 50
Numaga (Paiute chief), 91
Nye, James, 126, 163, 295

O'Brien, Jack, 1–3
  Comstock Lode work of, 75
  decision to leave for Gold Hill by, 43
  Durgan's Flat claim, and, 40, 41
  Gold Hill mine rumors and, 41
  Mackay's friendship with, 169
  Ophir mine work of, 73
  Union mine work and, 89n
O'Brien, William "Billy," 237
  background and early businesses of,
    238, 239
  Bank of California solvency and, 343,
    344, 346, 349
  Con. Virginia mine and, 293, 299, 311,
    312, 316
  death of, 377
  Flood on, 417
  Hale & Norcross mine and, 243, 244–
    45, 249, 267, 268, 289
  Nevada Bank of and, 341, 368
  reputation of, 368–69
  Rising Star mine, Idaho, and, 237, 240
  stock market investments by, 239
  water supply and, 290
Ogden, Richard L. "Podgers," 89, 124, 133,
  142, 175, 181–82, 197
O'Grady, Alexander, 323–24, 383, 384
O'Grady, Alice, 283, 323, 384
"Old Virginny." See Fenimore, James
one-ledge legal theory, 176–77
Ophir mine, Comstock Lode, 73, 137, 429
  California Crosscut and, 327–28
  Clemens's visit to, 152
  collapse of gallery in, 161–63
  Comstock's sale of interest in, 68, 138
  Con. Virginia's shaft and, 299, 324
  Dewey's management of, 372–73, 374
  eastward dip of vein in, 115, 170, 175
  fire at, 355–57, 360
  floods in, 107, 160–61, 403
  four adjacent claims in, 73
  geologist's evaluation of, 141–42

Gould & Curry claim and, 113
Grosh's claim to, 175
Hearst's ownership of shares of, 69, 77,
  88, 92
Houseworth's work at, 194–95
Mackay's arrival at, 70–71, 73
Mackay's ownership of shares of, 158,
  329, 362
Mackay's work in, 70–71, 90, 113–14,
  121, 374, 375, 403
management issues at, 174–75, 341
mechanization of, 107–8
mill connected with, 110, 126, 139
mining operations in, 73, 74, 76, 107,
  114–17, 119, 403
naming of, 68
one-ledge legal theory at, 176–77
productivity of, 73, 107, 120, 135, 140,
  149, 291, 329
rebuilding of, after fire, 360, 372
sell-outs and consolidations of claims
  in, 69–70
share price of, 141, 142–43, 149, 159,
  172, 174, 183, 330
share sell-off and price drop of shares
  of, 332–33, 334
Sharon's ownership of, 329–31, 332,
  337, 341
square-set timbering system in, 119–20
value of ore from, 75, 84, 86, 88, 115,
  140–41, 152, 195
Virginia Ledge boundary issues and,
  141–42
opium, 163, 167
Oregon, mines in, 138, 139
O'Reilly, Peter, 51, 58, 59, 60, 61, 62, 66,
  68, 69–70
Ormsby, William, 91, 93, 94–95, 97, 98
Osborne, John "Kentuck," 62, 69, 70, 195
Ott, J. J., 63
outside claims (wildcats), 87–88
Owyhee mines, Idaho, 237

Pacific Insurance Company, 185
Pacific Ocean telegraph cable project,
  426–27
Paiute Indians, 48, 51, 71, 97, 99
  description of, 91

as mine workers, 249
mining's impact on, 78–79, 91–92
Ormsby and, 91, 93
Palmer, Walter W., 174–75
patent medicines, 163, 167
Paul, Almarin B., 63, 106, 108–10, 119
Peerless mines, Arizona, 399, 416
Penrod, Emanuel "Manny," 51, 52, 58,
  59–60, 61, 62, 66, 68, 69, 70
Penrod, Comstock & Company, 62–63,
  66
Petaluma Mill, 208, 214, 249, 303–4
Phelan, James, 196–97, 198, 201
Philadelphia Mint, 19, 31
Pine Nut claim, 86
Pioneer Quartz Company, 54–55, 57
Pitt River Indians, 99
placer, meaning of term, 28
placer gold mining, 27
  camps around, 34
  dangers encountered in, 52
  end of, 35
  on Gold Hill, 56–57
  gold in quartz mining compared with,
    53, 54
  later rewording of, 49, 50
  miners' successes in, 42
  river deposits and, 37, 50, 51, 52
  techniques in, 28–29
Placerville, California, 38, 42, 50, 72, 74,
  77, 81, 86, 133n
Placerville Route, 83n
Plato, Joseph, 56
Podgers (Richard L. Ogden), 89, 123, 133,
  142, 175, 181–82, 197
Polk, James K., 17
Pony Express
  demise of, 132
  first run over Sierra Nevada by, 83, 87,
    191
  Indian massacre news from, 90, 91
  Indian raids on stations of, 101
  Lincoln's election reported by,
    122–23
  Williams Station Indian massacre
    reported by, 90, 91
Postal Telegraph Company, 397–98, 420,
  431

Potosi mine, 125, 136, 143, 149, 158, 177,
  197n
  combined Chollar-Potosi mine, 190,
    202, 223, 251, 252, 272, 274, 289, 296
Price, Johnson, 99
Pride, Baruch, 40–41
prostitution and brothels, 33, 160, 164,
  352, 365
pump engine and pump machinery,
  217–19
Pyramid Lake, Nevada
  First Battle of, 94–99, 108
  Indian meeting about Williams Station
    massacre at, 91
  Second Battle of, 101–2, 108

quartz mining
  Comstock and, 235–36
  Pioneer Quartz Company by-laws on,
    54
  selling "feet" to raise capital in, 84

railroads. *See also* Central Pacific
    Railroad; Virginia & Truckee
    Railroad
  Gould's ownership of, 395, 403
  Mackay's investments in, 213–14
  national economic problems and,
    320–21
  Sharon's construction of, 233–34,
    266–67
  speed advantage of, 233
Ralston, James, 189
Ralston, William, 429
  Arizona diamond field hoax and, 307
  Bank of California closure and, 342–44,
    345–47, 350
  Bank of California debts of, 279, 308–9,
    338, 340, 341, 342, 344
  Bank of California management by,
    278–79, 307, 309, 342–43
  Bank of California opening by, 182
  Bank of California Virginia City branch
    and, 186–87
  Belcher mine and, 307, 308
  Comstock mine and, 189
  Crown Point mine and, 203, 278–79
  death of, 347–50

Ralston, William (*cont.*)
  federal currency issues and, 309–10
  financial problems of, 342–44, 345–47
  Gould & Curry claim and, 124
  Hale & Norcross mine and, 231
  Mackay and, 349
  Ophir mine and, 142, 331, 332, 341
  Palace Hotel and, 338–39, 340, 342, 351
  railroad construction and, 233
  Sharon's relationship with, 184–86, 279,
      331, 332, 339, 349, 350–51
  Spring Valley Water Company and,
      341–42
  Sutro's tunnel project and, 204, 235
rats, in mines, 317–18
rebellious silver ores, 66, 240–41
Red Bluff Independent, 105, 112
reduction mills, 201–2
Reese, John, 47, 48
Reese River mines, 158, 189, 193
religious traditions. *See also* Catholicism;
      Mormons
  mining camp life and, 33–34, 164
  Sunday law proposal and, 126–27
retorts, in gold mining, 28, 109, 158, 335,
      361
Rippey, Wesley C., 418–19
Rising Star mine, Idaho, 237, 240–41, 243,
      416
river-turning technique, in gold mining,
      30, 37
Roberts, George D., 237, 397
rockers, in gold mining, 28, 29
  daily amount earned using, 16, 42, 56,
      59, 60
  description of, 4
  quartz mining with, 47, 57
Rogers, James, 56, 86
roller-skating craze, 282–83
rope-ways, in San Francisco, 321–22
Roughing It (Twain), 152, 158, 164
Russia, Mackay as special ambassador to,
      390–91

Sacramento Daily Union, 42, 49, 71, 74,
      75–76, 78, 98, 106, 115, 139, 140,
      149, 153, 175, 194, 206, 235–36, 352,
      386

safety issues
  cages with, 216–17
  Mexican mine collapse and, 161
  mine accidents and, 250–52
  railroad car hopping and, 270–71
  rats' warnings about, 317
  shaft stations and, 256
Said, Kinney, 75
saloons, 33, 110, 111–12, 123–24, 154, 160,
      163–64, 238, 356, 359, 361, 365, 366
Salt Lake City Tribune, 399, 415, 427
San Francisco
  Brannan's mining-provisions store in, 14
  businesses profiting from gold in,
      26–27
  cable cars in, 322, 399, 429
  Comstock and economic success of,
      428–29
  First Battle of Pyramid Lake reported
      in, 99
  Flood's businesses in, 238–39
  Fraser River, Canada, gold rush's
      impact on, 36–37
  gold and silver sent east from, 187
  gold coins and gold dust used in, 26
  gold fever and departure for goldfields
      from, 15, 16
  Lincoln's assassination reaction in, 192
  Mackay family's later visit to, 420
  Mackay family's residence in, 319–20,
      322–23, 353
  mine stock investment in, 141–42,
      156–57
  proposed ban on mining capital from,
      126, 127
  railroad completion and, 264–65
  Ralston's suicide and, 349–50
  rapid expansion of, after beginning of
      Gold Rush, *21*, 25–26
  real estate speculation in, 26
  rope-ways used in, 321–22
  rumors of gold strike and, 14
  Sharon's political work in, 184
  smallpox in, 248
  telegraph network opening celebration
      in, 38–39
  Virginia City fire and, 353
  Washoe bullion displayed in, 122

Washoe Diggings' economic impact on, 72, 75, 77, 122, 141
water supply in, 341–42
San Francisco Bulletin, 42, 106, 154, 164, 367
San Francisco Chronicle, 199, 202, 223, 269, 275, 276, 277, 282, 284, 288, 290, 294, 296, 297–98, 301, 303, 305, 306, 312–13, 314, 315, 316, 319, 328, 330, 332–33, 335, 341, 343, 344, 351, 355, 359, 360, 361, 372, 373, 374, 412, 420, 422
San Francisco Evening Bulletin, 132
San Francisco Mint, 77, 278, 309
San Francisco Stock & Exchange Board, 141, 184, 228, 231, 243, 298
San Francisco Weekly Bulletin, 77
Savage mine, 223, 381
    mining operations in, 156, 158, 176, 181, *199*, 242, 244, 271, 294, 378
    one-ledge legal theory at, 176
    promising developments and share price of, 294–95, 296, 297
    safety issues at, 216
    share price of, 159, 174
    Sharon's control of, 182, 203, 204
Schussler, Hermann, 290, 314, 315
scurvy, 32
Segovia, Josefa, 27
Sharon, William
    assayer corruption by, 227
    background of, 183–84
    Bank of California and, 185–86, 228, 298, 340
    Bank of California reopening and, 349–50, 351
    Bank of California Virginia City branch and, 186, 187–88
    Belcher mine and, 307, 308
    bribes used by, 228, 330
    Comstock Lode and, 185–86, 189, 201–3, 223–25, 274, 330
    Con. Virginia mine and, 302, 303
    Crown Point mine and, 189, 202, 203, 213, 223, 276–77, 279
    death of, 406–7
    early business ventures of, 184
    gambling by, 186, 188

Hale & Norcross mine and, 228, 231, 232, 241, 243, 244, 245, 249, 280, 299
    Kentuck mine and, 213–14
    Mackay's shared-use arrangement with, 299
    methods of making money from stockholders by, 225, 226, 270
    mine fire accusations and, 296, 297
    mine share losses by, 241
    mining taxes and, 336
    Ophir mine and, 329–31, 332, 337, 341
    Palace Hotel and, 340, 343, 351
    personal mining engineer and other experts used by, 226, 334
    power of, 228
    railroad construction and, 233–34, 266–67, 269, 270, 337, 342
    Ralston's relationship with, 184–86, 279, 331, 332, 339, 340
    Ralston's suicide and, 347, 349, 350
    senatorial race and, 298, 330, 382
    stock market decline and, 296–97, 297–98
    stock market profits of, 226–27
    Sutro's tunnel project and, 204, 205, 235, 266
    theater company sponsored by, 220
    transportation control by, 228, 267, 270, 337
    transportation costs and, 232, 270
    Union Mill and Mining Company and, 203
    valet Ah Ki and, 187–88, 407–8
    Virginia City fire relief and, 359–60
    water supply control by, 227–28
    woman companions' lawsuits against, 407
    Yellow Jacket mine and, 189–90, 202, 213, 223, 225–26
Shaw, John B., 113–14
Sherman, William Tecumseh, 18
Shoshone Indians, 91, 99
Sides, William, 58, 112
Sierra Nevada mine, 62–63, 90, 378, 379
Sierra Nevada Mountains
    economic impact of miners' exodus from, 35

Sierra Nevada Mountains (*cont.*)
  first gold strike in, 13–14, 15–16, 17
  geological formation of gold deposits
    in, 27–28
  impact of mining in, 35
  Mackay and O'Brien journey over, 2, 44
  Mackay's camp in, 39
  Mackay's later memories of, 39
  miners' searches for gold in, 34
  Mormon settlement in, 47
  newspaper reports on mining in, 18–19
  pull of gold in, 22, 23
  quartz mining in, 44
  speed of Pony Express riders over, 83
  winter crossing problems in, 77, 78,
    82, 86
silver
  assays of Washoe Diggings quartz vein
    for, 63
  formation of quartz veins and, 52–53
Silver City mining camp, 71, 108, 137,
  139, 195, 207, 270, 290, 294
silver mining
  currency support related to, 134
  difficulty of, 66
  Grosh brothers in Great Basin and, 52
  Owyhee mines, Idaho, and, 237
  rebellious ores in, 66, 240–41
  Rising Star mine, Idaho, and, 240–41
  rush to invest in, 157
  techniques used in, 108
  winzes used in, 121
Silver Platter (Berlin), 165–66, 432
Simpson, Mary Jane, 270, 275, 276, 278,
  283, 286, 288, 290
Six Mile Cañon, 46, 51–52, 55, 58, 59, 61,
  62, 66, 71, 86, 87, 90, 158, 187, 192,
  334, 371
slavery
  admission of new states and territories
    and, 17, 123
  Emancipation Proclamation and, 140
  secession of states before Civil War
    and, 123
slaves, as mine workers, 29
sluice boxes, 28, 29, 35, 171–72
Smallman, Amelia, 379, 398–99
smallpox, 9, 32, 138, 247

Smith, Ben, 336, 355, 362
Smith, Grant, 351–52
Smith, Hank, 264, 274, 275, 276, 287–88,
  289, 307
Soule, Frank, 87, 92, 99
Sprague Elevator and Electrical Works,
  420–21
Spring Valley Water Company, 154,
  341–42
square-set timbering system
  additional reinforcing timbers needed
    in, 315
  Big Bonanza mine with, 363
  Caledonia Tunnel with, 148
  Con. Virginia with, 315, 316
  cost as drawback to using, 120, 121
  Deidesheimer's design of, 115–17, *117*
  Fair Shaft with, 214–15
  Mackay's understanding of, 121
  Gold Hill mines and, 133
  Ophir mine with, 119–20
  Savage mine with, 156
  speed of mining using, 120
  winzes used with, 120–21
stagecoach lines, 31, 38, 83, 137, *151*, 159,
  250
Stanford, Leland, 127, 342
Stanton, Edwin M., 183–84
steam-hoisting machinery, 143, 156, 192,
  199, 200–201, 208, 215, 219, 235
Stewart, William M., 176, 309, 330
Stone, J. F., 63
Strong, Charley, 177
sump pumps, 218–19
Sunday law proposal, 126–27
Sunderland, Thomas, 203, 214, 233
Sutro, Adolph
  Bank of California's conflict with, 194,
    204, 205, 234
  Comstock mine and, 83, 190, 377–78
  deep-drain tunnel project of, 190, 191,
    194, 203–5, 234–35, 265–66, 298–99
  description of, 190–91
  first Pony Express run in Sierra Nevada
    witnessed by, 83, 191
  Nevada Legislature election and, 295,
    298, 382
  Ophir mine ownership and, 142

Sutter, John, 13, 14
Sutter's Fort, California, gold discovery
    at, 13–14
Swansea Mill, 202, 203
Sweetwater mines, 235, 236, 273

Tahoe Lake, 48, 82, 160, 337
tailings
    land damage from, 35
    loss of gold and silver in, 224
    recovering metals from, 224, 334, 381
taxes
    Mackay's income and, 381
    mining and, 336–37
Taylor, Zachary, 22
telegraph networks. *See also* Western Union
    cost of, 385, 387–88
    first transatlantic, 37–39
    first transcontinental, 131–33
    Gould's "pooling agreement" and, 388
    Mackay-Gould transatlantic cable war
        and, 402, 403–4, 408–10, 413–14
    Mackay's interest in, 397, 398–99
    Mackay's transatlantic cable companies
        and, 402, 403–4, 408–9, 411, 416, 420
    Mackay's transpacific cable project and,
        426–27
    Virginia City with, 72, 85, 125
    Western Union's near monopoly of,
        395, 396
Telfener, Countess Ada Hungerford, 164,
    167, 209, 379, 405
Telfener, Count Joseph, 379, 383, 388
tenements, New York City, 8–9, 283
Territorial Enterprise, 43, 71, 100, 110, 126,
    131, 138, 140, 141, 149, 153, 154, 156,
    158, 159, 191, 192, 207, 220, 221, 229,
    233, 235–36, 242, 244, 248, 259, 260,
    274, 276, 281, 282–83, 285, 287, 288,
    292, 293, 294, 297, 298, 306, 314, 316,
    323, 326, 329n, 330, 355, 357
Tevis, Lloyd, 237, 348, 378
Thomas, C. C., 229
timber, 105
    Bank Ring's profits from, 227
    the Firm's company for, 337
    Mackay's early work felling and
        shaping, 40–41

Mackay's profits from, 381
mine fires and, 255, 260, 354–55
mines' need for supplies of, 178–79,
    213, 228, 232, 337
transportation of, 232–33, 268, 271, 332
timbering methods. *See also* square-set
    timbering system
    Dall's approach to, 115–16
    traditional post and cap, 108, 114
timberman, Mackay's work in mines as,
    113–14
Tjader, Anton W., 98
transportation
    costs of, 232, 267
    disease spread and, 248
    equine influenza's impact on, 311–12
    freight wagons used for, 232–33
    of ore to mills, 232
    Sharon's control of, 228, 267, 270, 337
    of timber, 232
    winter weather affecting amount of
        gold and silver sent using, 133
Tritle, F. A., 208, 214, 233
Twain, Mark, 45, 152. *See also* Clemens,
    Sam
    lecture tour of, 206–7
    Mackay's relationship with, 155–56
    meaning of pseudonym, 154
    mining reporting of, 149, 151, 154, 156,
        159, 173, 191, 207–8
    Roughing It novel on mining
        experiences of, 152, 158, 164

underground mining ("drifting"), 41, 45
Union Mill and Mining Company, 203,
    205, 224–25, 228, 231, 277, 398
    Hale & Norcross mine's use of, 232,
        245
    Ralston's ownership of shares of, 308,
        338, 340
    Sharon's control of, 289–90
    water supply for, 289
Union mine, 62
    Mackay's transactions in "feet" of, 76,
        89, 103, 134–35, 148, 158, 171
    Mackay's work with, 76–77, 88, 90,
        114–15
    speculation on worth of, 89

Union Pacific Railroad, 264–65
Union Reduction Works, 122
Union Trust Company, 418
Union Tunnel, 114–16
    Deidesheimer's square-set timbering
        in, 115–17
U.S. Assay Office, 26
U.S. Geological Survey, 57–58, 307
U.S. Mint, 19, 31
United States Notes, 134. *See also*
    greenbacks
U.S. Postal Office, 31
U.S. Senate
    Fair's campaign for, 382
    Hearst in, 417
    Sharon's election to, 298, 330, 382
University of Nevada, Reno, Mackay
    School of Mines, 432
Utah mines, 325
Utah Territory
    independence of, 124
    rumors of gold and silver in, 2, 41
    secession of states before Civil War
        and, 123
    territorial government in, 112

vigilance committees, 164, 285–86
Virginia and Gold Hill Water Company,
    227, 289, 314, 381
Virginia & Truckee (V&T) Railroad,
    269–71, 319
    construction of, 270
    cost of building, 232, 270
    Crown Point Trestle of, 266, *269*
    financing of, 234, 337
    Mackay's rivalry with, 337
    mine booms and use of, 308, 326,
        363
    Ralston's ownership of, 338, 340, 342
    reception for first train in, 269–70
    route decision in, 234
    safety issues with, 270–71
    Sharon and, 233, 234, 266, 269, 270,
        337
    Virginia City fire and, 354, 359–60
Virginia City, Nevada, *81, 105, 359*
    bank offices in, 72, 185–86, 187–88,
        189, 203, 346

cholera epidemic in, 248
Civil War end and rejoicing in,
    191–92
Clemens's stay in, 153–55, 207–8
Comstock mine share slides and
    economic impact on, 188–89
deep-mining industry and, 185–86
economic decline and, 188–89
equine influenza in, 311, 312
Fair family's move to, 211–12
fears of Indian massacres and martial
    law at, 99–100
Fenimore's contribution to
    development of, 126
Fifteenth Amendment ratification
    celebration in, 271
fires in, 162, 282, 351–57
focus on silver mining at, 73
gold fever migration and boom in,
    82–83, 84–85, 86, 88, 159–60
growth of, 110–11, 159–60
Hungerford family's move to, 164–66
incorporation and expansion of,
    125–26, 137
living conditions at, 71–72, 73, 75, 84,
    126–27, 137–38, 160–61, 364–66
Louise Mackay's donation to, 366–67
miner paydays and, 205
miners' socializing in, 365–66
mine stock madness in, 157–58
mining claim lawsuits in, 175–76
mining operations around, *144–45,* 149
naming of, 71
nefarious business practices in, 86
population of miners and others at,
    75–76, 364, 428
President Grant's visit to Comstock
    and, 379
railroad celebration in, 269–70
range of workers at, 259–60
rebuilding of, after fire, 359–60, 363
smallpox in, 138
snow and windstorms in, 75, 77, 78,
    93–94, 199–200, 212, 230
social life and sports in, 248–49,
    282–83
speculation in mining shares in, 84–85,
    188, 295

Sunday law proposal and, 126–27
telegraph line to, 72, 85, 132–33
theater company in, 220
traffic jams in, 137, 159–60
transportation costs and, 233
transportation monopoly in, 337
transportation options in, 137, 138
violence and shootings in, 111–12,
    123–24, 163–64, 167–68, 285–87
water supply in, 125, 290–91, 314–15,
    326
Williams Station Indian massacre and,
    90–92, 99–100, 101, 102–3
women in, 162–63
Virginia Daily Union, 163, 170, 176, 192
Virginia Ledge, 141–42

Wakelee, Charles H., 189
Walker, Jonas M., 238
    death of, 422–23
    Flood's friendship with, 239
    Mackay's partnership in Kentuck mine
        with, 170–71, 174, 208, 213, 214
    post–Civil War depression and, 193–94
Walker, Samuel, 101
Walsh, Judge James, 63, 66, 67–68, 69, 70,
    74–75, 240
Ward, George G., 402, 408–9, 427
Washington Territory, 138
Washoe Diggings, 45–80. *See also* Gold
    Hill mine; Ophir mine; *and other
    specific mines*
    Californians' journey to, 81–84,
        159–60, 163
    classes of mine owners in, 87–88
    claiming frenzy over, 62–63
    concentration of mineral wealth in,
        47
    description of topography of, 45–46
    difficulty of mining at, 53–54, 62,
        66–67
    early miners at, 41–42, 48–49
    Fenimore's contribution to
        development of, 126
    Fenimore's search for new diggings in,
        51–52, 55–56, 58
    first discovery of gold at, 46–47
    focus on silver mining at, 73

gold and silver believed to be in every
    ledge in, 136
lawsuits entangling claims in, 136,
    175–76
living conditions at, 49–50, 71–72
Mackay and O'Brien's awareness of
    rumors about, 41
Mackay and O'Brien's decision to leave
    for, 43
Mackay and O'Brien's trek to, 43
maps of, *48*, *64–65*
mining operations at, 108, 114–15,
    120
naming of, 48
native Indian settlements and, 47–48,
    50, 78–79
Pioneer Quartz Company claim in,
    54–55
post–Civil War depression in, 193
productivity of, 140–41
public loss of confidence in, 174, 183
reports of good earnings at, 42
San Francisco's economy and, 72, 75,
    77, 122, 141
search for local mother veins in, 50–51
selling panic in, 182–83
sell-outs and consolidations of claims
    in, 67–68, 69–70
speculation about locations that might
    be on main lode in, 88
speculation in shares of, 85–86
steady slide of value of, 173–74
transportation of supplies to, 232–33
Washoe Indians, 48, 50, 78–79, 91
water supply
    Bank Ring's profits from, 227–28
    gold mines' need for, 27, 28, 49, 289
    Mackay's approach to, 290–91, 313–15
    Virginia City and, 125, 289, 314, 326
Webb, William H., 12
Webb shipyard, New York City, 40, 113
    fire in, 15
    gold fever and boom in, 23, 24
    Mackay's later memories of work at,
        128, 201
    Mackay's shipyard apprenticeship at,
        12, 17, 21, 23
    Mackay's skills learned at, 23

Wells, Fargo & Company, 31, 72, 149, 174, 185, 233, 417
Wells Fargo & Company Bank, 417
Wells Fargo Bank and Union Trust Company, 418
Wells Fargo Nevada National Bank, 417–18
Western Shoshone Indians, 91
Western Union
  Baltimore and Ohio Telegraph and, 413
  coverage and dominance of, 395
  Gould's ownership of, 395, 396
  Mackay's alliance against, 402–3, 412–13
  Mackay's transatlantic cable company and, 402, 403–4, 408–9, 411
  near monopoly of, 395–96
  problems encountered by, 397
whisky use. See alcohol (whisky) use
White, James, 59, 60
White, Mary, 138
White & Murphy mine, 292
wildcats (outside claims), 87–88
Williams Station Indian massacre, 90–92, 101, 102–3
  California militia organized after, 99–100, 101–102
  Indian meeting about, 91–92
  Ormsby's force in pursuit of Indians after, 93, 94–99
  Virginia City vigilantes organized after, 93–94
  white settlers' reaction to, 91–93
  Williams brothers' kidnapping resulting in, 90–91
Winnemucca (Paiute chief), 91, 99
Winnemucca, Sarah, 91
Winters, John D., 225–26, 262
Winters, Joseph, 61–62, 66
Winters, Theodore, 127
Winters Company, 135
winzes, 120–21, 179

women
  fashion and, 209–10
  gold fever and, 17
  Irish immigrants in New York City and, 6, 7, 9, 12
  lack of, in mining camps, 132, 165, 210
  letters to Mackay from, 386
  migration to Washoe Diggings by, 46, 82, 159–60, 163
  mining camp life and, 33, 75, 93, 110–11, 113, 162–63, 195n, 209
  mining stock owned by, 298, 331
  right to vote for, 271–72
  San Francisco and, 25
  violence and shootings and, 163–64
  Virginia City and, 75, 110–11, 160, 162–63, 282, 321, 365, 428
women's rights movement, 271–72
Woodworth, Joseph, 63, 68
Wright, William, 51, 154, 230. See also de Quille, Dan

"yellow fever," 15. See also Gold Rush
Yellow Jacket mine, 195
  claim boundary issues and, 57–58, 176–77, 194
  fires in, 253–64, 265, 279, 296
  Houseworth Claim and, 194–95
  mining operations in, 200, 213, 241, 253–54, 288, 387
  naming of, 57
  one-ledge legal theory at, 176
  productivity of, 143, 149, 193, 197–98, 200, 201, 272
  railroad construction costs and, 234
  safety issues in, 251
  share price of, 158, 159, 198, 273, 274, 296
  Sharon's management of, 189–90, 202, 213, 223, 225–26
Young, Brigham, 92, 99
Young, John Russell, 380, 414
Yuba River diggings, 18, 27, 209, 238

About the Author

Gregory Crouch grew up in Goleta, California, and graduated from the United States Military Academy at West Point, with a military history field of study. He completed U.S. Army Airborne and Ranger Schools and served as an infantry officer. He is the author of the true-life World War II flying adventure *China's Wings* and the alpine memoir *Enduring Patagonia*. A regular book critic, Crouch has reviewed for the *Wall Street Journal*, the *New York Times Book Review*, and the *Washington Post*. He lives in the San Francisco Bay Area of California.